Phenomenology of Perception

PHENOMENOLOGY OF PERCEPTION

International Library of Philosophy
and Scientific Method

A Catalogue of books already published in the
International Library of Philosophy and Scientific Method
will be found at the end of this volume.

PHENOMENOLOGY
OF PERCEPTION

by

M. Merleau-Ponty

translated from the French by

Colin Smith

LONDON AND HENLEY

ROUTLEDGE & KEGAN PAUL

NEW JERSEY: THE HUMANITIES PRESS

Translated from the French
PHÉNOMÉNOLOGIE DE LA PERCEPTION
First published in England in 1962
by Routledge & Kegan Paul Ltd
39 Store Street
London WC1E 7DD and
Broadway House, Newtown Road
Henley-on-Thames, Oxon RG9 1EN
Reprinted 1965, 1966, 1967, 1970, 1974, 1976 and 1978
Printed in Great Britain by
Redwood Burn Limited
Trowbridge & Esher

Translation revisions incorporated in this
edition supplied by Forrest Williams,
Professor of Philosophy, University of Colorado

ISBN 0 7100 3613 2

CONTENTS

PREFACE

WHAT is phenomenology? It may seem strange that this question has still to be asked half a century after the first works of Husserl The fact remains that it has by no means been answered. Phenomenology is the study of essences; and according to it, all problems amount to finding definitions of essences: the essence of perception, or the essence of consciousness, for example. But phenomenology is also a philosophy which puts essences back into existence, and does not expect to arrive at an understanding of man and the world from any starting point other than that of their facticity. It is a transcendental philosophy which places in abeyance the assertions arising out of the natural attitude, the better to understand them; but it is also a philosophy for which the world is always 'already there' before reflection begins—as an inalienable presence; and all its efforts are concentrated upon re-achieving a direct and primitive contact with the world, and — endowing that contact with a philosophical status. It is the search for a philosophy which shall be a 'rigorous science', but it also offers an account of space, time and the world as we 'live' them. It tries to give a direct description of our experience as it is, without taking account of its psychological origin and the causal explanations which the scientist, the historian or the sociologist may be able to provide. Yet Husserl in his last works mentions a 'genetic phenomenology',[1] and even a 'constructive phenomenology'.[2] One may try to do away with these contradictions by making a distinction between Husserl's and Heidegger's phenomenologies; yet the whole of *Sein und Zeit* springs from an indication given by Husserl and amounts to no more than an explicit account of the 'natürlicher Weltbegriff' or the 'Lebenswelt' which Husserl, towards the end of his life, identified as the central theme of phenomenology, with the result that the contradiction reappears in Husserl's own philosophy. The reader pressed for time will be inclined to give up the idea of covering a doctrine which says everything, and will wonder whether a philosophy which cannot define its scope deserves all the discussion which has gone on around it, and whether he is not faced rather by a myth or a fashion.

[1] *Méditations cartésiennes*, pp. 120 ff
[2] See the unpublished *6th Méditation cartésienne*, edited by Eugen Fink, to which G. Berger has kindly referred us.

vii

Even if this were the case, there would still be a need to understand the prestige of the myth and the origin of the fashion, and the opinion of the responsible philosopher must be that *phenomenology can be practised and identified as a manner or style of thinking, that it existed as a movement before arriving at complete awareness of itself as a philosophy.* It has been long on the way, and its adherents have discovered it in every quarter, certainly in Hegel and Kierkegaard, but equally in Marx, Nietzsche and Freud. A purely linguistic examination of the texts in question would yield no proof; we find in texts only what we put into them, and if ever any kind of history has suggested the interpretations which should be put on it, it is the history of philosophy. We shall find in ourselves, and nowhere else, the unity and true meaning of phenomenology. It is less a question of counting up quotations than of determining and expressing in concrete form this *phenomenology for ourselves* which has given a number of present-day readers the impression, on reading Husserl or Heidegger, not so much of encountering a new philosophy as of recognizing what they had been waiting for. Phenomenology is accessible only through a phenomenological method. Let us, therefore, try systematically to bring together the celebrated phenomenological themes as they have grown spontaneously together in life. Perhaps we shall then understand why phenomenology has for so long remained at an initial stage, as a problem to be solved and a hope to be realized.

It is a matter of describing, not of explaining or analysing. Husserl's first directive to phenomenology, in its early stages, to be a 'descriptive psychology', or to return to the 'things themselves', is from the start a rejection of science. I am not the outcome or the meeting-point of numerous causal agencies which determine my bodily or psychological make-up. I cannot conceive myself as nothing but a bit of the world, a mere object of biological, psychological or sociological investigation. I cannot shut myself up within the realm of science. All my knowledge of the world, even my scientific knowledge, is gained from my own particular point of view, or from some experience of the world without which the symbols of science would be meaningless. The whole universe of science is built upon the world as directly experienced, and if we want to subject science itself to rigorous scrutiny and arrive at a precise assessment of its meaning and scope, we must begin by reawakening the basic experience of the world of which science is the second-order expression. Science has not and never will have, by its nature, the same significance *qua* form of being as the world which we perceive, for the simple reason that it is a rationale or explanation of that world. I am, not a 'living creature' nor even a 'man', nor again even 'a consciousness' endowed with all the characteristics which zoology, social anatomy or inductive psychology recognize in these various products of the natural or historical process—I am the absolute source, my existence does not stem from my antecedents, from my physical and social environment; instead it moves out towards them and sustains them, for I alone bring into being for myself (and therefore into being in the only sense that the word can have for me) the tradition which I elect to carry on, or the horizon whose distance from me would be abolished—since that distance is not one of its properties—if I were not there to scan it with my gaze. Scientific points of view, according to which my existence is a moment of the world's, are always both naïve and at the same time dishonest, because they take for granted, without explicitly mentioning it, the other point of view, namely that of consciousness, through which from the outset a world forms itself round me and begins to exist for me. To return to things themselves is to return to that world which precedes knowledge, of which knowledge always *speaks*, and in relation to which every scientific schematization is an abstract and derivative sign-language, as is geography in relation to the countryside in which we have learnt beforehand what a forest, a prairie or a river is.

This move is absolutely distinct from the idealist return to consciousness, and the demand for a pure description excludes equally the procedure of analytical reflection on the one hand, and that of scientific explanation on the other. Descartes and particularly Kant *detached* the subject, or consciousness, by showing that I could not possibly apprehend anything as existing unless I first of all experienced myself as existing in the act of apprehending it. They presented consciousness, the absolute certainty of my existence for myself, as the condition of there being anything at all; and the act of relating as the basis of relatedness. It is true that the act of relating is nothing if divorced from the spectacle of the world in which relations are found; the unity of consciousness in Kant is achieved simultaneously with that of the world. And in Descartes methodical doubt does not deprive us of anything, since the whole world, at least in so far as we experience it, is reinstated in the *Cogito*, enjoying equal certainty, and simply labelled 'thought of . . .'. But the relations between subject and world are not strictly bilateral: if they were, the certainty of the world would, in Descartes, be immediately given with that of the *Cogito*, and Kant would not have talked about his 'Copernican revolution'. Analytical reflection starts from our experience of the world and goes back to the subject as to a condition of possibility distinct from that experience, revealing the all-embracing synthesis as that without which there would be no world. To this extent it ceases to remain part of our experience and offers, in place of an account, a

ix

reconstruction It is understandable, in view of this, that Husserl, having accused Kant of adopting a 'faculty psychologism',[1] should have urged, in place of a noetic analysis which bases the world on the synthesizing activity of the subject, his own 'noematic reflection' which remains within the object and, instead of begetting it, brings to light its fundamental unity.

The world is there before any possible analysis of mine, and it would be artificial to make it the outcome of a series of syntheses which link, in the first place sensations, then aspects of the object corresponding to different perspectives, when both are nothing but products of analysis, with no sort of prior reality. Analytical reflection believes that it can trace back the course followed by a prior constituting act and arrive, in the 'inner man'—to use Saint Augustine's expression—at a constituting power which has always been identical with that inner self Thus reflection is carried away by itself and installs itself in an impregnable subjectivity, as yet untouched by being and time But this is very ingenuous, or at least it is an incomplete form of reflection which loses sight of its own beginning. When I begin to reflect my reflection bears upon an unreflective experience; moreover my reflection cannot be unaware of itself as an event, and so it appears to itself in the light of a truly creative act, of a changed structure of consciousness, and yet it has to recognize, as having priority over its own operations, the world which is given to the subject because the subject is given to himself. The real has to be described, not constructed or formed. Which means that I cannot put perception into the same category as the syntheses represented by judgements, acts or predications. My field of perception is constantly filled with a play of colours, noises and fleeting tactile sensations which I cannot relate precisely to the context of my clearly perceived world, yet which I nevertheless immediately 'place' in the world, without ever confusing them with my daydreams. Equally constantly I weave dreams round things. I imagine people and things whose presence is not incompatible with the context, yet who are not in fact involved in it: they are ahead of reality, in the realm of the imaginary. If the reality of my perception were based solely on the intrinsic coherence of 'representations', it ought to be for ever hesitant and, being wrapped up in my conjectures on probabilities, I ought to be ceaselessly taking apart misleading syntheses, and reinstating in reality stray phenomena which I had excluded in the first place. But this does not happen. The real is a closely woven fabric. It does not await our judgement before incorporating the most surprising phenomena, or before rejecting the most plausible figments of our imagination. Perception is not a science of the world, it is not even an act, a deli-

[1] *Logische Untersuchungen, Prolegomena zur reinen Logik*, p. 93

berate taking up of a position; it is the background from which all acts stand out, and is presupposed by them. The world is not an object such that I have in my possession the law of its making; it is the natural setting of, and field for, all my thoughts and all my explicit perceptions. Truth does not 'inhabit' only 'the inner man',[1] or more accurately, there is no inner man, man is in the world, and only in the world does he know himself. When I return to myself from an excursion into the realm of dogmatic common sense or of science, I find, not a source of intrinsic truth, but a subject destined to the world.

All of which reveals the true meaning of the famous phenomenological reduction There is probably no question over which Husserl spent more time—or to which he more often returned, since the 'problematic of reduction' occupies an important place in his unpublished work. For a long time, and even in recent texts, the reduction is presented as the return to a transcendental consciousness before which the world is spread out and completely transparent, quickened through and through by a series of apperceptions which it is the philosopher's task to reconstitute on the basis of their outcome Thus my sensation of redness is *perceived as* the manifestation of a certain redness experienced, this in turn as the manifestation of a red surface, which is the manifestation of a piece of red cardboard, and this finally is the manifestation or outline of a red thing, namely this book. We are to understand, then, that it is the apprehension of a certain *hylè*, as indicating a phenomenon of a higher degree, the *Sinngebung*, or active meaning-giving operation which may be said to define consciousness, so that the world is nothing but 'world-as-meaning', and the phenomenological reduction is idealistic, in the sense that there is here a transcendental idealism which treats the world as an indivisible unity of value shared by Peter and Paul, in which their perspectives blend. 'Peter's consciousness' and 'Paul's consciousness' are in communication, the perception of the world 'by Peter' is not Peter's doing any more than its perception 'by Paul' is Paul's doing; in each case it is the doing of pre-personal forms of consciousness, whose communication raises no problem, since it is demanded by the very definition of consciousness, meaning or truth. In so far as I am a consciousness, that is, in so far as something has meaning for me, I am neither here nor there, neither Peter nor Paul; I am in no way distinguishable from an 'other' consciousness, since we are immediately in touch with the world and since the world is, by definition, unique, being the system in which all truths cohere. A logically consistent transcendental idealism rids the world of its

[1] In te redi, in interiore homine habitat veritas (Saint Augustine).

opacity and its transcendence. The world is precisely that thing of
which we form a representation, not as men or as empirical subjects,
but in so far as we are all one light and participate in the One without
destroying its unity. Analytical reflection knows nothing of the problem of other minds, or of that of the world, because it insists that
with the first glimmer of consciousness there appears in me theoretically the power of reaching some universal truth, and that the other
person, being equally without thisness, location or body, the Alter
and the Ego are one and the same in the true world which is the
unifier of minds. There is no difficulty in understanding how *I* can
conceive the Other, because the I and consequently the Other are not
conceived as part of the woven stuff of phenomena; they have
validity rather than existence. There is nothing hidden behind these
faces and gestures, no domain to which I have no access, merely a
little shadow which owes its very existence to the light. For Husserl,
on the contrary, it is well known that there is a problem of other
people, and the *alter ego* is a paradox. If the other is truly for himself
alone, beyond his being for me, and if we are for each other and not
both for God, we must necessarily have some appearance for each
other. He must and I must have an outer appearance, and there must
be, besides the perspective of the For Oneself—my view of myself and
the other's of himself—a perspective of For Others—my view of
others and theirs of me Of course, these two perspectives, in each
one of us, cannot be simply juxtaposed, *for in that case it is not I*
that the other would see, nor he that I should see. I must be the
exterior that I present to others, and the body of the other must be the
other himself. This paradox and the dialectic of the Ego and the
Alter are possible only provided that the Ego and the Alter Ego are
defined by their situation and are not freed from all inherence, that is,
provided that philosophy does not culminate in a return to the self,
and that I discover by reflection not only my presence to myself, but
also the possibility of an 'outside spectator'; that is, again, provided
that at the very moment when I experience my existence—at the ultimate extremity of reflection—I fall short of the ultimate density
which would place me outside time, and that I discover within myself
a kind of internal weakness standing in the way of my being totally
individualized a weakness which exposes me to the gaze of others as
a man among men or at least as a consciousness among consciousnesses Hitherto the *Cogito* depreciated the perception of others,
teaching me as it did that the I is accessible only to itself, since it
defined *me* as the thought which I have of myself, and which clearly
I am alone in having, at least in this ultimate sense. For the 'other'
to be more than an empty word, it is necessary that my existence
should never be reduced to my bare awareness of existing, but that it

should take in also the awareness that *one* may have of it, and thus include my incarnation in some nature and the possibility, at least, of a historical situation.] The *Cogito* must reveal me in a situation, and it is on this condition alone that transcendental subjectivity can, as Husserl puts it,[1] *be* an intersubjectivity. As a meditating Ego, I can clearly distinguish from myself the world and things, since I certainly do not exist in the way in which things exist. I must even set aside from myself my body understood as a thing among things, as a collection of physico-chemical processes. But even if the *cogitatio*, which I thus discover, is without location in objective time and space, it is not without place in the phenomenological world.] The world, which I distinguished from myself as the totality of things or of processes linked by causal relationships, I rediscover 'in me' as the permanent horizon of all my *cogitationes* and as a dimension in relation to which I am constantly situating myself.] The true *Cogito* does not define the subject's existence in terms of the thought he has of existing, and furthermore does not convert the indubitability of the world into the indubitability of thought about the world, nor finally does it replace the world itself by the world as meaning.] On the contrary it recognizes my thought itself as an inalienable fact, and does away with any kind of idealism in revealing me as 'being-in-the-world'.]

It is because we are through and through compounded of relationships with the world that for us the only way to become aware of the fact is to suspend the resultant activity, to refuse it our complicity (to look at it *ohne mitzumachen*, as Husserl often says), or yet again, to put it 'out of play'. Not because we reject the certainties of common sense and a natural attitude to things—they are, on the contrary, the constant theme of philosophy—but because, being the presupposed basis of any thought, they are taken for granted, and go unnoticed, and because in order to arouse them and bring them to view, we have to suspend for a moment our recognition of them. The best formulation of the reduction is probably that given by Eugen Fink, Husserl's assistant, when he spoke of 'wonder' in the face of the world[2] Reflection does not withdraw from the world towards the unity of consciousness as the world's basis, it steps back to watch the forms of transcendence fly up like sparks from a fire; it slackens the intentional threads which attach us to the world and thus brings them to our notice; it alone is consciousness of the world because it reveals that world as strange and paradoxical. [Husserl's transcendental is not Kant's and Husserl accuses Kant's philosophy of being 'worldly',

[1] *Die Krisis der europäischen Wissenschaften und die transzendentale Phänomenologie*, III (unpublished)
[2] *Die phänomenologische Philosophie Edmund Husserls in der gegenwärtigen Kritik*, pp. 331 and ff.

because it *makes use* of our relation to the world, which is the motive force of the transcendental deduction, and makes the world immanent in the subject, instead of *being filled with wonder* at it and conceiving the subject as a process of transcendence towards the world. All the misunderstandings with his interpreters, with the existentialist 'dissidents' and finally with himself, have arisen from the fact that in order to see the world and grasp it as paradoxical, we must break with our familiar acceptance of it and, also, from the fact that from this break we can learn nothing but the unmotivated upsurge of the world. The most important lesson which the reduction teaches us is the impossibility of a complete reduction. This is why Husserl is constantly re-examining the possibility of the reduction If we were absolute mind, the reduction would present no problem But since, on the contrary, we are in the world, since indeed our reflections are carried out in the temporal flux on to which we are trying to seize (since they *sich einstromen*, as Husserl says), there is no thought which embraces all our thought. The philosopher, as the unpublished works declare, is a perpetual beginner, which means that he takes for granted nothing that men, learned or otherwise, believe they know. It means also that philosophy itself must not take itself for granted, in so far as it may have managed to say something true, that it is an ever-renewed experiment in making its own beginning, that it consists wholly in the description of this beginning, and finally, that radical reflection amounts to a consciousness of its own dependence on an unreflective life which is its initial situation, unchanging, given once and for all Far from being, as has been thought, a procedure of idealistic philosophy, phenomenological reduction
— belongs to existential philosophy Heidegger's 'being-in-the-world' appears only against the background of the phenomenological reduction

A misunderstanding of a similar kind confuses the notion of the 'essences' in Husserl. Every reduction, says Husserl, as well as being transcendental is necessarily eidetic. That means that we cannot subject our perception of the world to philosophical scrutiny without ceasing to be identified with that act of positing the world, with that interest in it which delimits us, without drawing back from our commitment which is itself thus made to appear as a spectacle, without passing from the *fact* of our existence to its *nature*, from the Dasein to the Wesen. But it is clear that the essence is here not the end, but a
— means, that our effective involvement in the world is precisely what has to be understood and made amenable to conceptualization, for it is what polarizes all our conceptual particularizations. The need to proceed by way of essences does not mean that philosophy takes them

xiv

as its object, but, on the contrary, that our existence is too tightly held in the world to be able to know itself as such at the moment of its involvement, and that it requires the field of ideality in order to become acquainted with and to prevail over its facticity. The Vienna Circle, as is well known, lays it down categorically that we can enter into relations only with meanings For example, 'consciousness' is not for the Vienna Circle identifiable with what we are. It is a complex meaning which has developed late in time, which should be handled with care, and only after the many meanings which have contributed, throughout the word's semantic development, to the formation of its present one have been made explicit Logical positivism of this kind is the antithesis of Husserl's thought Whatever the subtle changes of meaning which have ultimately brought us, as a linguistic acquisition, the word and concept of consciousness, we enjoy direct access to what it designates For we have the experience of ourselves, of that consciousness which we are, and it is on the basis of this experience that all linguistic connotations are assessed, and precisely through it that language comes to have any meaning at all for us 'It is that as yet dumb experience . . . which we are concerned to lead to the pure expression of its own meaning '[1] Husserl's essences are destined to bring back all the living relationships of experience, as the fisherman's net draws up from the depths of the ocean quivering fish and seaweed Jean Wahl is therefore wrong in saying that 'Husserl separates essences from existence'.[2] The separated essences are those of language. It is the office of language to cause essences to exist in a state of separation which is in fact merely apparent, since through language they still rest upon the ante-predicative life of consciousness. In the silence of primary consciousness can be seen appearing not only what words mean, but also what things mean: the core of primary meaning round which the acts of naming and expression take shape.

Seeking the essence of consciousness will therefore not consist in developing the *Wortbedeutung* of consciousness and escaping from existence into the universe of things said; it will consist in rediscovering my actual presence to myself, the fact of my consciousness which is in the last resort what the word and the concept of consciousness mean. Looking for the world's essence is not looking for what it is as an idea once it has been reduced to a theme of discourse, it is looking for what it is as a fact for us, before any thematization. Sensationalism 'reduces' the world by noticing that after all we never experience anything but states of ourselves. Transcendental idealism too 'reduces' the world since, in so far as it guarantees the world, it does so by regarding it as thought or consciousness of the world, and as the mere

[1] *Méditations cartésiennes*, p 33.
[2] *Réalisme, dialectique et mystère*, l'Arbalète, Autumn, 1942, unpaginated

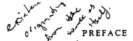

correlative of our knowledge, with the result that it becomes immanent in consciousness and the aseity of things is thereby done away
with The eidetic reduction is, on the other hand, the determination
to bring the world to light as it is before any falling back on ourselves
has occurred, it is the ambition to make reflection emulate the unreflective life of consciousness I aim at and perceive a world. If I said,
as do the sensationalists, that we have here only 'states of consciousness', and if I tried to distinguish my perceptions from my dreams
with the aid of 'criteria', I should overlook the phenomenon of the
world For if I am able to talk about 'dreams' and 'reality', to bother
my head about the distinction between imaginary and real, and cast
doubt upon the 'real', it is because this distinction is already made by
me before any analysis, it is because I have an experience of the real
as of the imaginary, and the problem then becomes one not of asking
how critical thought can provide for itself secondary equivalents of
this distinction, but of making explicit our primordial knowledge of
the 'real', of describing our perception of the world as that upon
which our idea of truth is forever based We must not, therefore,
wonder whether we really perceive a world, we must instead say: the
world is what we perceive In more general terms we must not
wonder whether our self-evident truths are real truths, or whether,
through some perversity inherent in our minds, that which is self-
evident for us might not be illusory in relation to some truth in itself.
For in so far as we talk about illusion, it is because we have identified
illusions, and done so solely in the light of some perception which at
the same time gave assurance of its own truth It follows that doubt,
or the fear of being mistaken, testifies as soon as it arises to our
power of unmasking error, and that it could never finally tear us
away from truth. We are in the realm of truth and it is 'the experience
of truth' which is self-evident.[1] To seek the essence of perception is to
declare that perception is, not presumed true, but defined as access to
truth So, if I now wanted, according to idealistic principles, to base
this *de facto* self-evident truth, this irresistible belief, on some absolute
self-evident truth, that is, on the absolute clarity which my thoughts
have for me, if I tried to find in myself a creative thought which bodied
forth the framework of the world or illumined it through and through,
I should once more prove unfaithful to my experience of the world,
and should be looking for what makes that experience possible
instead of looking for what it is The self-evidence of perception is not
adequate thought or apodeictic self-evidence [2] The world is not what

---

[1] *Das Erlebnis der Wahrheit (Logische Untersuchungen, Prolegomena zur reinen Logik)* p 190
[2] There is no apodeictic self-evidence, the *Formale und transzendentale Logik* (p 142) says in effect.

I think, but what I live through. I am open to the world, I have no
doubt that I am in communication with it, but I do not possess it,
it is inexhaustible 'There is a world', or rather 'There is the world';
I can never completely account for this ever-reiterated assertion
in my life This facticity of the world is what constitutes the
Weltlichkeit der Welt, what causes the world to be the world; just as
the facticity of the *cogito* is not an imperfection in itself, but rather
what assures me of my existence The eidetic method is the method
of a phenomenological positivism which bases the possible on the
real

   We can now consider the notion of intentionality, too often cited
as the main discovery of phenomenology, whereas it is understandable only through the reduction "All consciousness is consciousness
of something'; there is nothing new in that Kant showed, in the
Refutation of Idealism, that inner perception is impossible without
outer perception, that (the world, as a collection of connected
phenomena, is anticipated in the consciousness of my unity, and is
the means whereby I come into being as a consciousness What
distinguishes intentionality from the Kantian relation to a possible
object is that the unity of the world, before being posited by knowledge in a specific act of identification, is 'lived' as ready-made or
already there. Kant himself shows in the *Critique of Judgement* that
there exists a unity of the imagination and the understanding and a
unity of subjects *before the object*, and that, in experiencing the
beautiful, for example, I am aware of a harmony between sensation
and concept, between myself and others, which is itself without any
concept Here the subject is no longer the universal thinker of a
system of objects rigorously interrelated, the positing power who subjects the manifold to the law of the understanding, in so far as he is
to be able to put together a world—he discovers and enjoys his own
nature as spontaneously in harmony with the law of the understanding But if the subject has a nature, then the hidden art of the imagination must condition the categorial activity It is no longer merely the
aesthetic judgement, but knowledge too which rests upon this art, an
art which forms the basis of the unity of consciousness and of consciousnesses.
   Husserl takes up again the *Critique of Judgement* when he talks
about a teleology of consciousness It is not a matter of duplicating
human consciousness with some absolute thought which, from outside, is imagined as assigning to it its aims It is a question of recognizing consciousness itself as a project of the world, meant for a world
which it neither embraces nor possesses, but towards which it is perpetually directed—and the world as this pre-objective individual

whose imperious unity decrees what knowledge shall take as its goal.
This is why Husserl distinguishes between intentionality of act, which
is that of our judgements and of those occasions when we voluntarily
take up a position—the only intentionality discussed in the *Critique
of Pure Reason*—and operative intentionality (*fungierende Inten-
tionalität*), or that which produces the natural and antepredicative
unity of the world and of our life, being apparent in our desires, our
evaluations and in the landscape we see, more clearly than in objective knowledge, and furnishing the text which our knowledge tries to
translate into precise language Our relationship to the world, as it is
untiringly enunciated within us, is not a thing which can be any
further clarified by analysis, philosophy can only place it once more
before our eyes and present it for our ratification

Through this broadened notion of intentionality, phenomenological 'comprehension' is distinguished from traditional 'intellection',
which is confined to 'true and immutable natures', and so phenomenology can become a phenomenology of origins. Whether we are
concerned with a thing perceived, a historical event or a doctrine, to
'understand' is to take in the total intention—not only what these
things are for representation (the 'properties' of the thing perceived,
the mass of 'historical facts', the 'ideas' introduced by the doctrine)—
but the unique mode of existing expressed in the properties of the
pebble, the glass or the piece of wax, in all the events of a revolution,
in all the thoughts of a philosopher It is a matter, in the case of each
civilization, of finding the Idea in the Hegelian sense, that is, not a
law of the physico-mathematical type, discoverable by objective
thought, but that formula which sums up some unique manner of
behaviour towards others, towards Nature, time and death · a certain
way of patterning the world which the historian should be capable of
seizing upon and making his own. These are the *dimensions* of history.
In this context there is not a human word, not a gesture, even one
which is the outcome of habit or absent-mindedness, which has not
some meaning For example, I may have been under the impression
that I lapsed into silence through weariness, or some minister may
have thought he had uttered merely an appropriate platitude, yet my
silence or his words immediately take on a significance, because my
fatigue or his falling back upon a ready-made formula are not accidental, for they express a certain lack of interest, and hence some
degree of adoption of a definite position in relation to the situation.

When an event is considered at close quarters, at the moment
when it is lived through, everything seems subject to chance one
man's ambition, some lucky encounter, some local circumstance or
other appears to have been decisive But chance happenings offset
each other, and facts in their multiplicity coalesce and show up a

certain way of taking a stand in relation to the human situation, reveal in fact an *event* which has its definite outline and about which we can talk Should the starting-point for the understanding of history be ideology, or politics, or religion, or economics? Should we try to understand a doctrine from its overt content, or from the psychological make-up and the biography of its author? We must seek an understanding from all these angles simultaneously, everything has meaning, and we shall find this same structure of being underlying all relationships All these views are true provided that they are not isolated, that we delve deeply into history and reach the unique core of existential meaning which emerges in each perspective. It is true, as Marx says, that history does not walk on its head, but it is also true that it does not think with its feet. Or one should say rather that it is neither its 'head' not its 'feet' that we have to worry about, but its body. All economic and psychological explanations of a doctrine are true, since the thinker never thinks from any starting-point but the one constituted by what he is. Reflection even on a doctrine will be complete only if it succeeds in linking up with the doctrine's history and the extraneous explanations of it, and in putting back the causes and meaning of the doctrine in an existential structure. There is, as Husserl says, a 'genesis of meaning' (*Sinngenesis*),[1] which alone, in the last resort, teaches us what the doctrine 'means.' Like understanding, criticism must be pursued at all levels, and naturally, it will be insufficient, for the refutation of a doctrine, to relate it to some accidental event in the author's life its significance goes beyond, and there is no pure accident in existence or in co-existence, since both absorb random events and transmute them into the rational.

Finally, as it is indivisible in the present, history is equally so in its sequences. Considered in the light of its fundamental dimensions, all periods of history appear as manifestations of a single existence, or as episodes in a single drama—without our knowing whether it has an ending. Because we are in the world, we are *condemned to meaning*, and we cannot do or say anything without its acquiring a name in history.

Probably the chief gain from phenomenology is to have united extreme subjectivism and extreme objectivism in its notion of the world or of rationality. Rationality is precisely measured by the experiences in which it is disclosed. To say that there exists rationality is to say that perspectives blend, perceptions confirm each other, a meaning emerges. But it should not be set in a realm apart, transposed

---

[1] The usual term in the unpublished writings The idea is already to be found in the *Formale und transzendentale Logik*, pp. 184 and ff

into absolute Spirit, or into a world in the realist sense. The phenomenological world is not pure being, but the sense which is revealed
where the paths of my various experiences intersect, and also where
my own and other people's intersect and engage each other like gears.
It is thus inseparable from subjectivity and intersubjectivity, which
find their unity when I either take up my past experiences in those of
the present, or other people's in my own. For the first time the
philosopher's thinking is sufficiently conscious not to anticipate itself
and endow its own results with reified form in the world. The
philosopher tries to conceive the world, others and himself and their
interrelations But the meditating Ego, the 'impartial spectator'
(*uninteressierter Zuschauer*)[1] do not rediscover an already given
rationality, they 'establish themselves',[2] and establish it, by an act of
initiative which has no guarantee in being, its justification resting
entirely on the effective power which it confers on us of taking our
own history upon ourselves.

The phenomenological world is not the bringing to explicit expression of a pre-existing being, but the laying down of being.
Philosophy is not the reflection of a pre-existing truth, but, like art,
the act of bringing truth into being. One may well ask how this
creation is *possible*, and if it does not recapture in things a pre-existing
Reason The answer is that the only pre-existent Logos is the world
itself, and that the philosophy which brings it into visible existence
does not begin by being *possible*, it is actual or real like the world of
which it is a part, and no explanatory hypothesis is clearer than the
act whereby we take up this unfinished world in an effort to complete
and conceive it. Rationality is not a *problem*. There is behind it no
unknown quantity which has to be determined by deduction, or,
beginning with it, demonstrated inductively. We witness every minute
the miracle of related experiences, and yet nobody knows better than
we do how this miracle is worked, for we are ourselves this network
of relationships. The world and reason are not problematical We
may say, if we wish, that they are mysterious, but their mystery defines them there can be no question of dispelling it by some 'solution',
it is on the hither side of all solutions True philosophy consists in re-
learning to look at the world, and in this sense a historical account
can give meaning to the world quite as 'deeply' as a philosophical
treatise We take our fate in our hands, we become responsible for
our history through reflection, but equally by a decision on which we
stake our life, and in both cases what is involved is a violent act which
is validated by being performed.

Phenomenology, as a disclosure of the world, rests on itself, or

---

[1] *6th Méditation cartésienne* (unpublished)
[2] Ibid.

rather provides its own foundation [1] All knowledge is sustained by a 'ground' of postulates and finally by our communication with the world as primary embodiment of rationality Philosophy, as radical reflection, dispenses in principle with this resource As, however, it too is in history, it too exploits the world and constituted reason It must therefore put to itself the question which it puts to all branches of knowledge, and so duplicate itself infinitely, being, as Husserl says, a dialogue or infinite meditation, and, in so far as it remains faithful to its intention, never knowing where it is going The unfinished nature of phenomenology and the inchoative atmosphere which has surrounded it are not to be taken as a sign of failure, they were inevitable because phenomenology's task was to reveal the mystery of the world and of reason.[2] If phenomenology was a movement before becoming a doctrine or a philosophical system, this was attributable neither to accident, nor to fraudulent intent. It is as painstaking as the works of Balzac, Proust, Valéry or Cézanne—by reason of the same kind of attentiveness and wonder, the same demand for awareness, the same will to seize the meaning of the world or of history as that meaning comes into being In this way it merges into the general effort of modern thought.

[1] 'Rückbeziehung der Phanomenologie auf sich selbst,' say the unpublished writings
[2] We are indebted for this last expression to G Gusdorf, who may well have used it in another sense

INTRODUCTION

Traditional Prejudices and the Return to Phenomena

THE 'SENSATION' AS A UNIT OF EXPERIENCE

AT the outset of the study of perception, we find in language the notion of sensation, which seems immediate and obvious· I have a sensation of redness, of blueness, of hot or cold It will, however, be seen that nothing could in fact be more confused, and that because they accepted it readily, traditional analyses missed the phenomenon of perception

I might in the first place understand by sensation the way in which I am affected and the experiencing of a state of myself. The greyness which, when I close my eyes, surrounds me, leaving no distance between me and it, the sounds that encroach on my drowsiness and hum 'in my head' perhaps give some indication of what pure sensation might be. I might be said to have sense-experience (*sentir*) precisely to the extent that I coincide with the sensed, that the latter ceases to have any place in the objective world, and that it signifies nothing for me. This entails recognizing that sensation should be sought on the hither side of any qualified content, since red and blue, in order to be distinguishable as two colours, must already form some picture before me, even though no precise place be assigned to them, and thus cease to be part of myself Pure sensation will be the experience of an undifferentiated, instantaneous, dotlike impact It is unnecessary to show, since authors are agreed on it, that this notion corresponds to nothing in our experience, and that the most rudimentary *factual perceptions* that we are acquainted with, in creatures such as the ape or the hen, have a bearing on relationships and not on any absolute terms [1] But this does not dispose of the question as to why we feel justified *in theory* in distinguishing within experience a layer of 'impressions' Let us imagine a white patch on a homogeneous background All the points in the patch have a

[1] See *La Structure du Comportement*, pp 142 and ff

certain 'function' in common, that of forming themselves into a 'shape'. The colour of the shape is more intense, and as it were more resistent than that of the background; the edges of the white patch 'belong' to it, and are not part of the background although they adjoin it. the patch appears to be placed on the background and does not break it up Each part arouses the expectation of more than it contains, and this elementary perception is therefore already charged with a *meaning*. But if the shape and the background, as a whole, are not sensed, they must be sensed, one may object, in each of their points To say this is to forget that each point in its turn can be perceived only as a figure on a background When Gestalt theory informs us that a figure on a background is the simplest sense-given available to us, we reply that this is not a contingent characteristic of factual perception, which leaves us free, in an ideal analysis, to bring in the notion of impressions. It is the very definition of the phenomenon of perception, that without which a phenomenon cannot be said to be perception at all. The perceptual 'something' is always in the middle of something else, it always forms part of a 'field'. A really homogeneous area offering *nothing to be* cannot be given to *any perception* The structure of actual perception alone can teach us what perception is. The pure impression is, therefore, not only undiscoverable. but also imperceptible and so inconceivable as an instant of perception If it is introduced, it is because instead of attending to the experience of perception, we overlook it in favour of the object perceived. A visual field is not made up of limited views But an object seen is made up of bits of matter, and spatial points are external to each other. An isolated datum of perception is inconceivable, at least if we do the mental experiment of attempting to perceive such a thing. But in the world there are either isolated objects or a physical void

I shall therefore give up any attempt to define sensation as pure impression Rather, to see is to have colours or lights, to hear is to have sounds, to sense (*sentir*) is to have qualities To know what sense-experience is, then, is it not enough to have seen a red or to have heard an A? But red and green are not sensations, they are the sensed (*sensibles*), and quality is not an element of consciousness, but a property of the object Instead of providing a simple means of delimiting sensations, if we consider it in the experience itself which evinces it, the quality is as rich and mysterious as the object, or indeed the whole spectacle, perceived This red patch which I see on the carpet is red only in virtue of a shadow which lies across it, its quality is apparent only in relation to the play of light upon it, and hence as an element in a spatial configuration. Moreover the colour can be said to be there only if it occupies an area of a certain size, too small an area not being describable in these terms Finally this

4

red would literally not be the same if it were not the 'woolly red' of a carpet.[1] Analysis, then, discovers in each quality meanings which reside in it. It may be objected that this is true only of the qualities which form part of our actual experience, which are overlaid with a body of knowledge, and that we are still justified in conceiving a 'pure quality' which would set limits to a pure sensation. But as we have just seen, this pure sensation would amount to no sensation, and thus to not feeling at all. The alleged self-evidence of sensation is not based on any testimony of consciousness, but on widely held prejudice We think we know perfectly well what 'seeing', 'hearing', 'feeling' are, because perception has long provided us with objects which are coloured or which emit sounds. When we try to analyse it, we transpose these objects into consciousness We commit what psychologists call 'the experience error', which means that what we know to be in things themselves we immediately take as being in our consciousness of them. We make perception out of things perceived And since perceived things themselves are obviously accessible only through perception, we end by understanding neither We are caught up in the world and we do not succeed in extricating ourselves from it in order to achieve consciousness of the world If we did we should see that the quality is never experienced immediately, and that all consciousness is consciousness of something. Nor is this 'something' necessarily an identifiable object There are two ways of being mistaken about quality: one is to make it into an element of consciousness, when in fact it is an object *for* consciousness, to treat it as an incommunicable impression, whereas it always has a meaning, the other is to think that this meaning and this object, at the level of quality, are fully developed and determinate. The second error, like the first, springs from our prejudice about the world. Suppose we construct, by the use of optics and geometry, that bit of the world which can at any moment throw its image on our retina Everything outside its perimeter, since it does not reflect upon any sensitive area no more affects our vision than does light falling on our closed eyes. We ought, then, to perceive a segment of the world precisely delimited, surrounded by a zone of blackness, packed full of qualities with no interval between them, held together by definite relationships of size similar to those lying on the retina. The fact is that experience offers nothing like this, and we shall never, using the world as our starting-point, understand what a *field of vision* is. Even if it is possible to trace out a perimeter of vision by gradually approaching the centre of the lateral stimuli, the results of such measurement vary from one moment to another, and one never manages to determine the instant when a stimulus

[1] J. P Sartre, *L'Imaginaire*, p. 241

5

once seen is seen no longer. The region surrounding the visual field is not easy to describe, but what is certain is that it is neither black nor grey. There occurs here an *indeterminate vision*, a *vision of something or other*, and, to take the extreme case, what is behind my back is not without some element of visual presence. The two straight lines in Müller-Lyer's optical illusion (Fig 1) are neither of equal nor unequal length; it is only in the objective world that this question arises [1] The visual field is that strange zone in which contradictory notions jostle each other because the objects—the straight lines of Muller-Lyer—are not, in that field, assigned to the realm of being, in which a comparison would be possible, but each is taken in its private

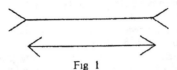

Fig 1

context as if it did not belong to the same universe as the other. Psychologists have for a long time taken great care to overlook these phenomena. In the world taken in itself everything is determined. There are many unclear sights, as for example a landscape on a misty day, but then we always say that no real landscape is in itself unclear. It is so only for us The object, psychologists would assert, is never ambiguous, but becomes so only through our inattention. The bounds of the visual field are not themselves variable, and there is a moment when the approaching object begins absolutely to be seen, but we do not 'notice' it. But the notion of attention, as we shall show more fully, is supported by no evidence provided by consciousness It is no more than an auxiliary hypothesis, evolved to save the prejudice in favour of an objective world. We must recognize the indeterminate as a positive phenomenon It is in this atmosphere that quality arises Its meaning is an equivocal meaning, we are concerned with an expressive value rather than with logical signification. The determinate quality by which empiricism tried to define sensation is an object, not an element, of consciousness, indeed it is the very lately developed object of scientific consciousness For these two reasons, it conceals rather than reveals subjectivity.

The two definitions of sensation which we have just tried out were only apparently direct We have seen that they were based on the object perceived In this they were in agreement with common sense, which also identifies the sensible by the objective conditions which govern it. The visible is what is seized upon *with* the eyes, the sensible

[1] Koffka, *Psychologie*, p 530

6

is what is seized on *by* the senses Let us follow up the idea of sensation on this basis,[1] and see what becomes of this 'by' and this 'with', and the notion of sense-organ, in the first-order thinking constituted by science. Having shown that there is no experience of sensation, do we at least find, in its causes and objective origins, any reasons for retaining it as an explanatory concept? Physiology, to which the psychologist turns as to a higher court of appeal, is in the same predicament as psychology. It too first situates its object in the world and treats it as a bit of extension. *Behaviour* is thus hidden by the reflex, the elaboration and patterning of stimuli, by a longitudinal theory of nervous functioning, which establishes a theoretical correspondence between each element of the situation and an element of the reaction.[2] As in the case of the reflex arc theory, physiology of perception begins by recognizing an anatomical path leading from a *receiver* through a definite *transmitter* to a recording station,[3] equally specialized. The objective world being given, it is assumed that it passes on to the sense-organs messages which must be registered, then deciphered in such a way as to reproduce in us the original text. Hence we have in principle a point-by-point correspondence and constant connection between the stimulus and the elementary perception But this 'constancy hypothesis'[4] conflicts with the data of consciousness, and the very psychologists who accept it recognize its purely theoretical character[5] For example, the intensity of a sound under certain circumstances lowers its pitch, the

[1] There is no justification for dodging the issue, as does Jaspers, for example (*Zur Analyse der Trugwahrnehmungen*) by setting up in opposition, on the one hand a descriptive psychology which 'understands' phenomena, and on the other an explanatory psychology, which concerns itself with their origin The psychologist always sees consciousness as placed in the body in the midst of the world, and for him the series stimulus-impression-perception is a sequence of events at the end of which perception begins. Each consciousness is born in the world and each perception is a new birth of consciousness. In this perspective the 'immediate' data of perception can always be challenged as mere appearances and as complex products of an origin The descriptive method can acquire a genuine claim only from the transcendental point of view But, even from this point of view, the problem remains as to how consciousness perceives itself or appears to itself as inserted in a nature For the philosopher, as for the psychologist, there is therefore always a problem of origins, and the only method possible is to follow, in its scientific development, the causal explanation in order to make its meaning quite clear, and assign to it its proper place in the body of truth. That is why there will be found no *refutation*, but only an effort to understand the difficulties peculiar to causal thinking

[2] See *La Structure du Comportement*, Chap. I.

[3] We are translating roughly the series 'Empfänger-Übermittler-Empfinder spoken of by J. Stein, *Über die Veränderung der Sinnesleistungen und die Entstehung von Trugwahrnehmungen*, p 351

[4] Koehler, *Über unbemerkte Empfindungen und Urteilstauschungen*

[5] Stumpf does so explicitly Cf Koehler, ibid , p. 54

addition of auxiliary lines makes two figures unequal which are objectively equal,[1] a coloured area appears to be the same colour over the whole of its surface, whereas the chromatic thresholds of the different parts of the retina ought to make it red in one place, orange somewhere else, and in certain cases colourless.[2] Should these cases in which the phenomenon does not correspond to the stimulus be retained within the framework of the law of constancy, and explained by additional factors—attention and judgement—or must the law itself be jettisoned? When red and green, presented together, give the result grey, it is conceded that the central combination of stimuli can immediately give rise to a different sensation from what the objective stimuli would lead us to expect When the apparent size of an object varies with its apparent distance, or its apparent colour with our recollections of the object, it is recognized that 'the sensory processes are not immune to central influences'[3] In this case, therefore, the 'sensible' cannot be defined as the immediate effect of an external stimulus. Cannot the same conclusion be drawn from the first three examples we have mentioned? If attention, more precise instructions, rest or prolonged practice finally bring perception into line with the law of constancy, this does not prove the law's universal validity, for, in the examples quoted, the first appearance possessed a sensory character just as incontestable as the final results obtained. So the question is whether attentive perception, the subject's concentration on one point of the visual field—for example, the 'analytic perception' of the two main lines in Muller-Lyer's optical illusion—do not, instead of revealing the 'normal sensation', substitute a special set-up for the original phenomenon.[4] The law of constancy cannot avail itself, against the testimony of consciousness, of any crucial experience in which it is not already implied, and wherever we believe that we are establishing it, it is already presupposed[5] If we turn back to the phenomena, they show us that the apprehension of a quality, just as that of size, is bound up with a whole perceptual context, and that the stimuli no longer furnish us with the indirect means we were seeking of isolating a layer of immediate impressions But when we look for an 'objective' definition of sensation, it is not only the physical stimulus

---

[1] Koehler, ibid , pp 57–8, cf pp 58-66

[2] R Dejean, *Les Conditions objectives de la Perception visuelle*, pp 60 and 83.

[3] Stumpf, quoted by Koehler, ibid , p 58

[4] Koehler, ibid , pp 58-63

[5] It is only fair to add that this is true of all theories, and that nowhere is there a crucial experience For the same reason the constancy hypothesis cannot be completely refuted on the basis of induction It is discredited because it overlooks phenomena and does not permit any understanding of them. To discern them and to pass judgement on the hypothesis, indeed one must 'suspend' it

which slips through our fingers The sensory apparatus, as conceived by modern physiology, is no longer fitted for the rôle of 'transmitter' cast for it by traditional science Non-cortical lesions of the apparatus of touch no doubt lessen the concentration of points sensitive to heat and cold, or pressure, and diminish the sensitivity of those that remain. But if, to the injured system, a sufficiently extensive stimulus be applied, the specific sensations reappear The raising of the thresholds is compensated by a more vigorous movement of the hand [1]

One can discern, at the rudimentary stage of sensibility, a working together on the part of partial stimuli and a collaboration of the sensory with the motor system which, in a variable physiological constellation, keeps sensation constant, and rules out any definition of the nervous process as the simple transmission of a given message The destruction of sight, wherever the injuries be sustained, follows the same law all colours are affected in the first place,[2] and lose their saturation Then the spectrum is simplified, being reduced to four and soon to two colours; finally a grey monochrome stage is reached, although the pathological colour is never identifiable with any normal one. Thus in central as in peripheral lesions 'the loss of nervous substance results not only in a deficiency of certain qualities, but in the change to a less differentiated and more primitive structure'.[3] Conversely, normal functioning must be understood as a process of integration in which the text of the external world is not so much copied, as composed And if we try to seize 'sensation' within the perspective of the bodily phenomena which pave the way to it, we find not a psychic individual, a function of certain known variables, but a formation already bound up with a larger whole, already endowed with a meaning, distinguishable only in degree from the more complex perceptions, and which therefore gets us no further in our attempt to delimit pure sensation There is no physiological definition of sensation, and more generally there is no physiological psychology which is autonomous, because the physiological event itself obeys biological and psychological laws. For a long time it was thought that peripheral conditioning was the surest method of identifying 'elementary' psychic functions, and of distinguishing them from 'superior' functions less strictly bound up with the bodily substructure A closer analysis, however, reveals that the two kinds of function overlap. The elementary is no longer that which by addition will cumulatively constitute the whole, nor is it a mere

---

[1] Stein, op cit , pp 357–9

[2] Even daltonism does not prove that certain systems are, and are alone in being, entrusted with 'seeing' red and green, since a colour-blind person manages to distinguish red if a large area in that colour is put before him, or if the presentation of the colour is made to last a long time Id ibid , p 365

[3] Weizsacker, quoted by Stein, ibid , p 364

occasion for the whole to constitute itself. The elementary event is already invested with meaning, and the higher function will bring into being only a more integrated mode of existence or a more valid adaptation, by using and sublimating the subordinate operations. Conversely, 'the experience of feeling is a vital process, no less than procreation, breathing or growth'.[1] Psychology and physiology are no longer, then, two parallel sciences, but two accounts of behaviour, the first concrete, the second abstract.[2] We said that when the psychologist asks the physiologist for a definition of sensation 'in causal terms', he encounters once more on this new ground his familiar difficulties, and now we can see why. The physiologist for his part has to rid himself of the realistic prejudice which all the sciences borrow from common sense, and which hampers them in their development. The changed meaning of the terms 'elementary' and 'more advanced' in modern physiology proclaims a changed philosophy.[3] The scientist too must learn to criticize the idea of an external world in itself, since the facts themselves prompt him to abandon that of the body as a transmitter of messages. The sensible is what is apprehended *with* the senses, but now we know that this 'with' is not merely instrumental, that the sensory apparatus is not a conductor, that even on the periphery the physiological impression is involved in relations formerly considered central.

Once more, reflection—even the second-order reflection of science— obscures what we thought was clear. We believed we knew what feeling, seeing and hearing were, and now these words raise problems. We are invited to go back to the experiences to which they refer in order to redefine them. The traditional notion of sensation was not a concept born of reflection, but a late product of thought directed towards objects, the last element in the representation of the world, the furthest removed from its original source, and therefore the most unclear. Inevitably science, in its general effort towards objectification, evolved a picture of the human organism as a physical system undergoing stimuli which were themselves identified by their physico-chemical properties, and tried to reconstitute actual perception[4] on this basis, and to close the circle of scientific knowledge

[1] Weizsacker, quoted by Stein, ibid, p 354

[2] On all these points see *La Structure du Comportement*, in particular pp 52 and ff, 65 and ff

[3] Gelb, *Die Farbenkonstanz der Sehdinge*, p 595

[4] 'The sensations are certainly artificial products, but not arbitrary ones, they are the last component wholes into which the natural structures can be decomposed by the "analytical attitude". Seen from this point of view, they contribute to the knowledge of structures, and consequently the results of the study of sensations, correctly interpreted, are an important element in the psychology of perception' Koffka, *Psychologie*, p 548

by discovering the laws governing the production of knowledge itself, by establishing an objective science of subjectivity.[1] But it is also inevitable that this attempt should fail. If we return to the objective investigations themselves, we first of all discover that the conditions external to the sensory field do not govern it part for part, and that they exert an effect only to the extent of making possible a basic pattern—which is what Gestalt theory makes clear. Then we see that within the organism the structure depends on variables such as the biological meaning of the situation, which are no longer physical variables, with the result that the whole eludes the well-known instruments of physico-mathematical analysis, and opens the way to another type of intelligibility.[2] If we now turn back, as is done here, towards perceptual experience, we notice that science succeeds in constructing only a semblance of subjectivity it introduces sensations which are things, just where experience shows that there are meaningful patterns; it forces the phenomenal universe into categories which make sense only in the universe of science. It requires that two perceived lines, like two real lines, should be equal or unequal, that a perceived crystal should have a definite number of sides,[3] without realizing that the perceived, by its nature, admits of the ambiguous, the shifting, and is shaped by its context. In Müller-Lyer's illusion, one of the lines ceases to be equal to the other without becoming 'unequal': it becomes 'different'. That is to say, an isolated, objective line, and the same line taken in a figure, cease to be, for perception, 'the same'. It is identifiable in these two functions only by analytic perception, which is not natural. In the same way the perceived contains gaps which are not mere 'failures to perceive'. I may, through sight or touch, recognize a crystal as having a 'regular' shape without having, even tacitly, counted its sides I may be familiar with a face without ever having perceived the colour of the eyes in themselves The theory of sensation, which builds up all knowledge out of determinate qualities, offers us objects purged of all ambiguity, pure and absolute, the ideal rather than the real themes of knowledge in short, it is compatible only with the lately developed superstructure of consciousness. That is where 'the idea of sensation is approximately realized'[4]

The images which instinct projects before it, those which tradition recreates in each generation, or simply dreams, are in the first place presented on an equal footing with genuine perceptions, and gradually, by critical labour, the true, present and explicit perception is

[1] Cf Guillaume, *L'Objectivité en Psychologie.*
[2] Cf. *La Structure du Comportement*, Chap III
[3] Koffka, *Psychologie*, pp 530 and 549
[4] M Scheler, *Die Wissenformen und die Gesellschaft*, p 412

11

distinguished from phantasms The word perception indicates a *direction* rather than a primitive function [1] It is known that the uniformity of apparent size of objects at different distances, or of their colour in different lights, is more perfect in children than in adults [2] It follows that perception is more strictly bound up with the local stimulus in its developed than in its undeveloped state, and more in conformity with the theory of sensation in the adult than in the child It is like a net with its knots showing up more and more clearly [3] 'Primitive thought' has been pictured in a way which can be understood only if the responses of primitive people, their pronouncements and the sociologists' interpretations are related to the fund of perceptual experience which they are all trying to translate [4] It is sometimes the adherence of the perceived object to its context, and, as it were, its viscosity, sometimes the presence in it of a positive indeterminate which prevents the spatial, temporal and numerical wholes from becoming articulated into manageable, distinct and identifiable terms. And it is this pre-objective realm that we have to explore in ourselves if we wish to understand sense experience

[1] M Scheler, *Die Wissenformen und die Gesellschaft*, p 397 'Man approaches ideal and exact images better than the animal, the adult better than the child, men better than women, the individual better than the member of a group, the man who thinks historically and systematically better than the man impelled by tradition, "imprisoned" in it and incapable of objectivizing, by building up recollection, the environment in which he is involved, of localizing it in time and possessing it by setting it away from himself in a past context '

[2] Hering, Jaensch

[3] Scheler, *Die Wissenformen und die Gesellschaft*, p 412

[4] Cf Wertheimer, *Uber das Denken der Naturvölker*, in *Drei Abhandlungen zur Gestalttheorie*

'ASSOCIATION' AND THE 'PROJECTION OF MEMORIES'

ONCE introduced, the notion of sensation distorts any analysis of perception. Already a 'figure' on a 'background' contains, as we have seen, much more than the qualities presented at a given time. It has an 'outline', which does not 'belong' to the background and which 'stands out' from it, it is 'stable' and offers a 'compact' area of colour, the background on the other hand having no bounds, being of indefinite colouring and 'running on' under the figure. The different parts of the whole—for example, the portions of the figure nearest to the background—possess, then, besides a colour and qualities, a particular *significance* The question is, what makes up this significance, what do the words 'edge' and 'outline' mean, what happens when a collection of qualities is *apprehended* as a figure on a background? But once sensation is introduced as an element of knowledge, we are left no leeway in our reply. A being capable of sense-experience (*sentir*)—in the sense of coinciding absolutely with an impression or a quality—could have no other mode of knowing. That a quality, an area of red should signify something, that it should be, for example, seen as a patch on a background, means that the red is not this warm colour which I feel and live in and lose myself in, but that it announces something else which it does not include, that it exercises a cognitive function, and that its parts together make up a whole to which each is related without leaving its place. Henceforth the red is no longer merely there, it represents something for me, and what it represents is not possessed as a 'real part' of my perception, but only aimed at as an 'intentional part' [1] My gaze does not merge with the outline or the patch as it does with the redness considered concretely: it ranges over and dominates them In order

[1] The expression is Husserl's The idea is taken up with insight by M Pradines, *Philosophie de la Sensation*, I, particularly on pp 152 and ff.

to receive in itself a meaning which really transfuses it, in order to become integrated into an 'outline' which is bound up with the 'figure' and independent of 'background', the atomic sensation ought to cease to be an absolute coincidence, which means ceasing to exist as a sensation If we admit 'sensation' in the classical sense, the meaning of that which is sensed can be found only in further sensations, actual or virtual Seeing a figure can be only simultaneously experiencing all the atomic sensations which go to form it Each one remains for ever what it is, a blind contact, an impression, while the whole collection of these becomes 'vision', and forms a picture before

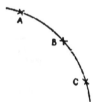

us because we learn to pass quickly from one impression to another A shape is nothing but a sum of limited views, and the consciousness of a shape is a collective entity The sensible elements of which it is made up cannot lose the opacity which defines them as sensory given, and open themselves to some intrinsic connection, to some law of conformation governing them all.

Let three points A, B and C be taken on the outline of a figure. their spatial order is both their way of co-existing before our eyes and that co-existence itself, however near together be the points chosen the sum of their separate existences, *the position of A, plus the position of B, plus the position of C*. It may well happen that empiricism abandons this atomistic manner of expression, and begins to talk about pieces of space or pieces of duration, thus adding an experience of relationships to that of qualities But that does not affect the empiricist position in the slightest degree. Either the piece of space is traversed and inspected by a mind, in which case empiricism is abandoned, since consciousness is no longer defined in terms of the impression, or else it is itself given in the manner of an impression, when it becomes just as exclusive of any more extensive co-ordination as the atomic impression first discussed.

The fact is that a shape is not only the sum of present data, for these latter call up other complementary ones. When I say that I have before me a red patch, the meaning of the word patch is provided by previous experiences which have taught me the use of the word. The distribution in space of the three points A, B and C recalls other comparable distributions, and I say that I see a circle Nor does the appeal to experience gained affect the empiricist thesis The 'association of ideas' which brings past experience into play can restore only extrinsic connections, and can be no more than one itself, because the original experience involved no others. Once consciousness has been defined as sensation, every mode of conscious-

14

nees will have to derive its clarity from sensation. The word *circle*, or the word *order*, could only signify, in the earlier experiences to which I refer, the concrete manner in which our sensations distributed themselves before us, a certain *de facto* arrangement, a way of sensing (*sentir*) If the three points, A, B and C are on a circle, the path AB 'resembles' the path BC, but this resemblance means no more than that one path makes one think of the other. The path ABC resembles other circular paths over which my eye has travelled, but that merely means that it recalls them and brings the image of them to mind. It is never possible for two terms to be *identified*, perceived or understood as *the same*, for that would presuppose that their this-ness is overcome. They can only be indissolubly associated and everywhere substituted for each other. Knowledge thus appears as a system of substitutions in which one impression announces others without ever justifying the announcement, in which words lead one to expect sensations as evening leads one to expect night. The significance of the percept is nothing but a cluster of images which begin to reappear without reason The simplest images or sensations are, in the last analysis, all that there is to understand in words, concepts being a complicated way of designating them, and as they are themselves inexpressible impressions, understanding is a fraud or an illusion. Knowledge never has any hold on objects, which bring each other about, while the mind acts as a calculating machine,[1] which has no idea why its results are true. Sensation admits of no philosophy other than that of nominalism, that is, the reduction of meaning to the misinterpretation of vague resemblance or to the meaninglessness of association by contiguity

Now the sensations and images which should be the beginning and end of all knowledge never make their appearance anywhere other than within a horizon of meaning, and the significance of the percept, far from resulting from an association, is in fact presupposed in all association, whether it concerns the conspectus of a figure before one, or the recollection of former experiences Our perceptual field is made up of 'things' and 'spaces between things'[2] The parts of a thing are not bound together by a merely external association arising from their interrelatedness observed while the object is in movement For in the first place I see, as things, groupings which I have never seen in movement: houses, the sun, mountains, for example Whether or not it is insisted that I extend to static objects a notion acquired through the experience of objects in motion, the fact remains that

[1] Husserl, *Logische Untersuchungen*, Chap I, *Prolegomena zur reinen Logik*, p 68

[2] See, for example, Koehler, *Gestalt Psychology*, pp 164–5

15

the mountain must present in its actual appearance some character-istic which gives ground for recognizing it as a thing, and justifies this transference In which case the characteristic is sufficient, without any such transference, to explain the segregation of the perceptual field. Even the unity of ordinary things, which a child may handle and move about, does not amount to establishing their substantiality If we set ourselves to see as things the intervals between them, the appearance of the world would be just as strikingly altered as is that of the puzzle at the moment when I pick out 'the rabbit' or 'the hunter'. There would not be simply the same elements differently related, the same sensations differently associated, the same text charged with a different sense, the same matter in another form, but in truth another world

There are not arbitrary data which set about combining into a thing because de facto proximities or likenesses cause them to associate, it is, on the contrary, because we perceive a grouping as a thing that the analytical attitude can then discern likenesses or proximities This does not mean simply that without any perception of the whole we would not think of noticing the resemblance or the contiguity of its elements, but literally that they would not be part of the same world and would not exist at all The psychologist, who always conceives consciousness as in the world, includes resemblance and contiguity of stimuli among the objective conditions which bring about the grouping together of a whole. The stimuli nearest to each other or most similar, he says,[1] or those which together endow the spectacle with the best balance, tend, for perception, to unite into the same configuration But this way of talking is misleading, because it confronts objective stimuli which belong to the perceived world—and even to the second-order world elaborated by scientific consciousness—with perceptual consciousness, which it is the duty of psychology to describe according to direct experience. The psychologist's hybrid thinking always runs the risk of reintro-ducing into the description relationships belonging to the objective world Thus it was possible to think of Wertheimer's law of con-tiguity and law of resemblance as bringing back the associationist's objective contiguity and resemblance in the rôle of constitutive prin-ciples of perception In reality, for pure description—and Gestalt theory claims to be a description—the contiguity and resemblance of stimuli do not precede the constitution of the whole 'Good form' is not brought about because it would be good in itself in some meta-physical heaven; it is good form because it comes into being in our experience The alleged conditions of perception precede perception

[1] Wertheimer, for example (the laws of proximity, of resemblance and the law of 'good form')

itself only when, instead of describing the perceptual phenomenon as the first way of access to the object, we suppose round about it a setting in which all disclosure of the implicit and all cross-checking performed by analytic perception are included, and all the norms of actual perception vindicated—in short, a realm of truth, a *world*. In doing so we relieve perception of its essential function, which is to lay the foundations of, or inaugurate, knowledge, and we see it through its results If we confine ourselves to phenomena, the unity of the thing in perception is not arrived at by association, but is a condition of association, and as such precedes the delimitations which establish and verify it, and indeed precedes itself.

If I walk along a shore towards a ship which has run aground, and the funnel or masts merge into the forest bordering on the sand dune, there will be a moment when these details suddenly become part of the ship, and indissolubly fused with it. As I approached, I did not perceive resemblances or proximities which finally came together to form a continuous picture of the upper part of the ship. I merely felt that the look of the object was on the point of altering, that something was imminent in this tension, as a storm is imminent in storm clouds. Suddenly the sight before me was recast in a manner satisfying to my vague expectation. Only afterwards did I recognize, as justifications for the change, the resemblance and contiguity of what I call 'stimuli'—namely the most determinate phenomena, seen at close quarters and with which I compose the 'true' world. 'How could I have failed to see that these pieces of wood were an integral part of the ship? For they were of the same colour as the ship, and fitted well enough into its superstructure.' But these reasons for correct perception were not given as reasons beforehand The unity of the object is based on the foreshadowing of an imminent order which is about to spring upon us a reply to questions merely latent in the landscape. It solves a problem set only in the form of a vague feeling of uneasiness, it organizes elements which up to that moment did not belong to the same universe and which, for that reason, as Kant said with profound insight, could not be associated. By placing them on the same footing, that of the unique object, synopsis makes continuity and resemblance between them possible. An impression can never by itself be associated with another impression

Nor has it the power to arouse others It does so only provided that it is already *understood* in the light of the past experience in which it co-existed with those which we are concerned to arouse Imagine a set of double syllables[1] in which the second is a 'softened' rhyme of the first (*tak-dak*), and another set in which the second syllable has

---

[1] K Lewin, *Vorbemerkungen uber die psychischen Krafte und Energien und uber die Struktur der Seele*

the letters of the first in reverse order (*ged-deg*), if the two sets have been learnt by heart and if, in a critical experiment, the subject is given the uniform task of 'finding a softened rhyme', it is noticeable that he has more difficulty in finding such a rhyme for *ged* than for a neutral syllable. But if the task is to change the vowel in the syllables given, no delay occurs. It could not, then, be powers of association which operated in the first experiment, for if they existed they ought to operate equally in the second. The truth is that, faced with syllables often associated with softened rhymes, the subject, instead of rhyming in reality, takes advantage of what he knows, and sets in motion a 'reproduction intention',[1] so that when he arrives at the second set of syllables, in which the task is no longer related to the patterns with which he has been trained to deal, the reproduction intention can lead only to mistakes. When, in the second critical experiment, the subject is told to change the vowel in the prompting syllable, as the task has never figured in the preparatory drill, he cannot use the by-pass of reproduction, and under these circumstances the preparatory drill has no effect. Association therefore never comes into play as an autonomous force, it is never the word suggested which 'induces' the reply in the manner of an efficient cause, it acts only by making probable or attractive a reproduction intention; it operates only in virtue of the meaning it has acquired in the context of the former experience and in suggesting recourse to that experience; it is efficacious to the extent to which the subject recognizes it, and grasps it in the light or appearance of the past If finally it were desired to bring into operation, instead of simple continuity, association by resemblance, it would still be seen that in order to recall a former image which present perception resembles, the latter must be *patterned* in such a way that it can sustain this resemblance Whether a subject[2] has seen Figure 1 five or five hundred times he will recognize it almost equally easily in Figure 2 where it appears 'camouflaged'; moreover he will never see it there constantly On the other hand a subject who is looking, in Figure 2, for another disguised figure (without knowing which one), rediscovers it there more quickly and more frequently than a passive subject who is equally familiar with the figures. Resemblance is, therefore, like co-existence in not being a force so to speak in the third person, which directs a traffic of images or 'states of consciousness' Figure 1 is not recalled *by* Figure 2, or rather it is so recalled only if one has first seen in Figure 2 'a possible Figure 1', which amounts to saying that the actual resemblance does not relieve us of

[1] 'Set to reproduce', Koffka, *Principles of Gestalt Psychology*, p 581
[2] Gottschaldt, *Über den Einfluss der Erfahrung auf die Wahrnehmungen von Figuren.*

the necessity of asking how it is first made possible by the present organization of Figure 2. The 'prompting' figure must take on the same meaning as the induced figure before it can recall it, and finally the *de facto* past is not imported into present perception by a mechanism of association, but arrayed in present consciousness itself.

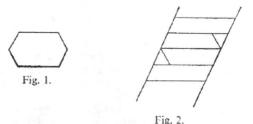

Fig. 1.

Fig. 2.

From this can be judged the worth of accepted formulas about 'the rôle of memories in perception'. Even outside empiricism there is talk of 'the contributions of memory'.[1] People go on saying that 'to perceive is to remember'. It is shown that in the reading of a book the speed of the eye leaves gaps in the retinal impressions, *therefore* the sense-data must be filled out by a projection of memories.[2] A landscape or newspaper seen upside down are said to represent our original view of them, our normal view of them being now natural by reason of what is added to it by memory. 'Because of the unaccustomed arrangement of impressions the influence of psychic causes can no longer be felt.[3] It is not asked why differently arranged impressions make the newspaper unreadable or the landscape unrecognizable. The answer is: because in order to fill out perception, memories need to have been made possible by the physiognomic character of the data. Before any contribution by memory, what is seen must at the present moment so organize itself as to present a picture to me in which I can recognize my former experiences. Thus the appeal to memory presupposes what it is supposed to explain: the patterning of data, the imposition of meaning on a chaos of sense-data. No sooner is the recollection of memories made possible than it becomes superfluous, since the work it is being asked to do is already done. The same may be said of this 'colouring of memory' (*Gedächtnisfarbe*) which, in the opinion of other psychologists, eventually takes the place of the present colour of objects, so that we

---

[1] Brunschvicg, *L'Expérience humaine et la Causalité physique*, p. 466.
[2] Bergson, *L'Energie spirituelle*, 'L'effort intellectuel', e.g., p. 184.
[3] Cf. for example Ebbinghaus, *Abriss der Psychologie*, pp. 104–5.

see them 'through the spectacles' of memory.[1] The question is, what at this moment awakens the 'colouring of memory'. It is recalled, says Hering, every time we see an object we already know, *'or believe we see it'* But on what basis have we this belief? What is it, in present perception, which teaches us that we are dealing with an already familiar object, since *ex hypothesi* its properties are altered? If it is argued that recognition of shape or size is bound up with that of colour, the argument is circular, since apparent size and shape are also altered, and since recognition here too cannot result from the recollection of memories, but must precede it. Nowhere then does it work from past to present, and the 'projection of memories' is nothing but a bad metaphor hiding a deeper, ready-made recognition

In the same way, the illusion of correction cannot be understood as the fusion of a few elements truthfully read off with memories merging indistinguishably with them How could the evocation of memories come about unless guided by the look of the strictly visible data, and if it is thus guided, what use is it then, since the word already has its structure or its features before taking anything from the storehouse of memory? Obviously it is the analysis of illusions which has lent credence to the 'projection of memories', and which follows roughly this sketchy reasoning illusory perception cannot rest upon 'present data', since I read 'deduction' when the word printed is 'destruction' The letter *d*, which has taken the place of the group *str*, not being presented to the eye, must come from somewhere else It is then said to come from memory In the same way in a flat picture a few patches of light and shade are enough to provide relief, a few branches of a tree in a puzzle suggest a cat, several blurred lines in the clouds a horse. But past experience can appear only afterwards as the cause of the illusion, and the present experience has, in the first place, to assume form and meaning in order to recall precisely this memory and not others It is, then, before my eyes and at this moment that the horse, the cat, the wrong word and the relief come into being The light and shade of the picture convey relief by imitating 'the original phenomenon of relief',[2] where they were invested with a basic spatial meaning To enable me to find a cat in the puzzle, it is necessary that 'the meaning-unit "cat" should in some way prescribe those elements of the picture which the co-ordinating activity is to retain and those which it is to overlook'.[3] Illusion deceives us, and passes itself off as genuine perception precisely in those cases where the meaning originates in the source of sensation and nowhere else It imitates that privileged experience in

---

[1] Hering, *Grundzuge der Lehre vom Lichtsinn*, p 8
[2] Scheler, *Idole der Selbsterkenntnis*, p. 72.
[3] Id ibid

which the meaning exactly fits the sensation, clearly cohering, or being evinced, in it. It implies this norm of perception, and therefore cannot spring from any *contact* between sensation and memory, and this is even more true of perception The 'projection of memories' makes nonsense of both For if a thing perceived were made up of sensations and memories, it would depend for its precise identification on the contribution of memories, and would have in itself nothing capable of stemming the flood of the latter, with the result that, being deprived even of that outer fringe of vagueness which it always in fact has, it would be, as we have said, intangible, elusive, and always bordering on illusion. Illusion would, *a fortiori*, never present the firm and well-defined appearance which a thing eventually assumes, since perception itself would not have it, and so illusion would not mislead us. If finally it is conceded that memories do not by themselves project themselves upon sensations, but that consciousness compares them with the present data, retaining only those which accord with them, then one is admitting an original text which carries its meaning within itself, and setting it over against that of memories· this original text is perception itself. In snort, it is a mistake to think that with the 'projection of memories' we are bringing into perception some mental activity, and that we have taken up a position opposed to that of empiricism The theory is no more than a consequence, a tardy and ineffective correction of empiricism, accepting its postulates, sharing the same difficulties and, like empiricism, concealing phenomena instead of elucidating them.

The postulate, as always, consists in *deducing* the given from what happens to be furnished by the sense organs For example, in the illusion of correction, the elements actually seen are reconstituted according to the eye movements, the speed of reading and the time needed for the retinal impression. Then, by subtracting these theoretical data from total perception, the 'recollected elements' are obtained which, in turn, are treated as mental entities. Perception is built up with states of consciousness as a house is built with bricks, and a mental chemistry is invoked which fuses these materials into a compact whole Like all empiricist theories, this one describes only blind processes which could never be the equivalent of knowledge, because there is, in this mass of sensations and memories, *nobody who sees*, nobody who can appreciate the falling into line of datum and recollection, and, on the other hand, no solid object protected by a meaning against the teeming horde of memories We must then discard this postulate which obscures the whole question The cleavage between given and remembered, arrived at by way of objective causes, is arbitrary. When we come back to phenomena we find, as a basic layer of experience, a whole already pregnant with an irreducible

21

meaning not sensations with gaps between them, into which memories may be supposed to slip, but the features, the layout of a landscape or a word, in spontaneous accord with the intentions of the moment, as with earlier experience

It is at this stage that the real problem of memory in perception arises, in association with the general problem of perceptual consciousness We want to know how, by its own vitality, and without carrying complementary material into a mythical unconscious, consciousness can, in course of time, modify the structure of its surroundings; how, at every moment, its former experience is present to it in the form of a horizon which it can reopen—'if it chooses to take that horizon as a theme of knowledge'—in an act of recollection, but which it can equally leave on the fringe of experience, and which then immediately provides the perceived with a present atmosphere and significance. A field which is always at the disposal of consciousness and one which, for that very reason, surrounds and envelops its perceptions, an atmosphere, a horizon or, if you will, given 'sets' which provide it with a temporal situation, such is the way in which the past is present, making distinct acts of perception and recollection possible. To perceive is not to experience a host of impressions accompanied by memories capable of clinching them; it is to see, standing forth from a cluster of data, an immanent significance without which no appeal to memory is possible. To remember is not to bring into the focus of consciousness a self-subsistent picture of the past, it is to thrust deeply into the horizon of the past and take apart step by step the interlocked perspectives until the experiences which it epitomizes are as if relived in their temporal setting. To perceive is not to remember

The relationships 'figure' and 'background', 'thing' and 'nothing', and the horizon of the past appear, then, to be structures of consciousness irreducible to the qualities which appear in them. Empiricism will always retain the expedient of treating this *a priori* as if it were the product of some mental chemistry. The empiricist will concede that every object is presented against a background which is not an object, the present lying between two horizons of absence, past and future But, he will go on, these significations are derivative The 'figure' and the 'background', the 'thing' and its 'surrounding', the 'present' and the 'past', are words which summarize the experience of a spatio-temporal perspective, which in the end comes down to the elimination either of memory or of the marginal impressions Even though, once formed in actual perception, structures have more meaning than can be supplied by a quality, I am not entitled to regard this evidence of consciousness as adequate, I must reconstruct theoretically these structures with the aid

22

of the impressions whose actual relationships they express. On this ⌐
footing empiricism cannot be refuted Since it rejects the evidence of
reflection and produces, by associating external impressions, the
structures which we are conscious of understanding by proceeding
from the whole to its parts, there is no phenomenon which can be
adduced as a crucial proof against it. Generally speaking, the
description of phenomena does not enable one to refute thought
which is not alive to its own existence, and which resides in things.
The physicist's atoms will always appear more real than the historical
and qualitative face of the world, the physico-chemical processes
more real than the organic forms, the psychological atoms of
empiricism more real than perceived phenomena, the intellectual
atoms represented by the 'significations' of the Vienna Circle more
real than consciousness, as long as the attempt is made to build up
the shape of the world (life, perception, mind) instead of recognizing,
as the source which stares us in the face and as the ultimate court of
appeal in our knowledge of these things, our *experience* of them The
adoption of this new way of looking at things, which reverses the
relative positions of the clear and the obscure, must be undertaken by
each one for himself, whereupon it will be seen to be justified by the
abundance of phenomena which it elucidates Before its discovery,
these phenomena were inaccessible, yet to the description given of
them empiricism can always retort that it *does not understand.* In this
sense, reflection is a system of thought no less closed than insanity,
with this difference that it understands itself and the madman too,
whereas the madman does not understand *it* But though the phenomenal field may indeed be a new world, it is never totally overlooked
by natural thought, being present as its horizon, and the empiricist
doctrine itself is an attempt to analyse consciousness By way of
guarding against myths it is, then, desirable to point out everything
that is made incomprehensible by empiricist constructions and all the
basic phenomena which they conceal. They hide from us in the first
place 'the cultural world' or 'human world' in which nevertheless
almost our whole life is led For most of us, Nature is no more than a
vague and remote entity, overlaid by cities, roads, houses and above
all by the presence of other people Now, for empiricism, 'cultural'
objects and faces owe their distinctive form, their magic power, to
transference and projection of memory, so that only by accident has
the human world any meaning There is nothing in the appearance of
a landscape, an object or a body whereby it is predestined to look 'gay'
or 'sad', 'lively' or 'dreary', 'elegant' or 'coarse' Once more seeking
a definition of what we perceive through the physical and chemical
properties of the stimuli which may act upon our sensory apparatus,
empiricism excludes from perception the anger or the pain which I

nevertheless read in a face, the religion whose essence I seize in some hesitation or reticence, the city whose temper I recognize in the attitude of a policeman or the style of a public building There can no longer be any *objective spirit*: mental life withdraws into isolated consciousnesses devoted solely to introspection, instead of extending, as it apparently does in fact, over human space which is made up by those with whom I argue or live, filling my place of work or the abode of my happiness. Joy and sadness, vivacity and obtuseness are data of introspection, and when we invest landscapes or other people with these states, it is because we have observed in ourselves the coincidence between these internal perceptions and the external signs associated with them by the accidents of our constitution Perception thus impoverished becomes purely a matter of knowledge, a progressive noting down of qualities and of their most habitual distribution, and the perceiving subject approaches the world as the scientist approaches his experiments If on the other hand we admit that all these 'projections', all these 'associations', all these 'transferences' are based on some intrinsic characteristic of the object, the 'human world' ceases to be a metaphor and becomes once more what it really is, the seat and as it were the *homeland* of our thoughts The perceiving subject ceases to be an 'acosmic' thinking subject, and action, feeling and will remain to be explored as original ways of positing an object, since 'an object looks attractive or repulsive before it looks black or blue, circular or square'.[1]

But not only does empiricism distort experience by making the cultural world an illusion, when in fact it is in it that our existence finds its sustenance. The natural world is also falsified, and for the same reasons What we object to in empiricism is not its having taken this as its primary theme of analysis. For it is quite true that every cultural object refers back to a natural background against which it appears and which may, moreover, be confused and remote Our perception senses how near is the canvas underneath the picture, or the crumbling cement under the building, or the tiring actor under the character But the nature about which empiricism talks is a collection of stimuli and qualities, and it is ridiculous to pretend that nature thus conceived is, even in intention merely, the primary object of our perception· it does in fact follow the experience of cultural objects, or rather it is one of them We shall, therefore, have to rediscover the natural world too, and its mode of existence, which is not to be confused with that of the scientific object. The phenomenon of the background's continuing under the figure, and being *seen* under the figure—when in fact it is covered by the figure—a phenomenon which embraces the whole problem of the *presence* of

[1] Koffka, *The Growth of the Mind*, p 320

24

the object, is equally obscured by empiricist philosophy, which treats this covered part of the background as invisible (in virtue of a physiological definition of vision) and brings it down to the status of a mere sensible quality by supposing that it is provided by an image, that is, by a watered-down sensation. In more general terms, the real objects which are not part of our visual field can be present to us only as images, and that is why they are no more than 'permanent possibilities of sensations' If we abandon the empiricist postulate of the priority of contents, we are free to recognize the strange mode of existence enjoyed by the object behind our back. The hysterical child who turns round 'to see if the world behind him is still there',[1] suffers from no deficiency of images, but the perceived world has lost for him that original structure which ensures that for the normal person its hidden aspects are as indubitable as are its visible ones Once again the empiricist can always build up, with psychic atoms, near equivalents of all these structures But the inventory of the perceived world given in the following chapters will increasingly show it up as a kind of mental blindness, and as the system least able to give an inclusive account of experience as it is revealed to us, while on the other hand reflection embraces empiricism's subordinate truth and assigns to it its proper place.

[1] Scheler, *Idole der Selbsterkenntnis*, p 85

3

'ATTENTION'
AND 'JUDGEMENT'

THE discussion of traditional prejudices has so far been directed
against empiricism, but in fact it was not empiricism alone that we
were attacking We must now show that its intellectualist antithesis
is on the same level as empiricism itself. Both take the objective
world as the object of their analysis, when this comes first neither in
time nor in virtue of its meaning; and both are incapable of expressing the peculiar way in which perceptual consciousness constitutes its object Both keep their distance in relation to perception,
instead of sticking closely to it.

This may be shown by studying the history of the concept of
attention It is deduced, in empiricist thinking, from the 'constancy
hypothesis', or, as we have explained, from the priority of the
objective world. Even if what we perceive does not correspond to
the objective properties of the source of the stimulus, the constancy
hypothesis forces us to admit that the 'normal sensations' are
already there They must then be unperceived, and the function
which reveals them, as a searchlight shows up objects pre-existing in
the darkness, is called attention Attention, then, creates nothing,
and it is a natural miracle, as Malebranche to all intents and purposes said, which strikes up like sparks just those perceptions or
ideas capable of providing an answer to the questions which I was
asking Since 'bemerken' or taking notice is not an efficient cause of
the ideas which this act arouses, it is the same in all acts of attention,
just as the searchlight's beam is the same whatever landscape be
illuminated. Attention is therefore a general and unconditioned
power in the sense that at any moment it can be applied indifferently
to any content of consciousness Being everywhere barren, nowhere
can it have its own purposes to fulfil In order to relate it to the life of
consciousness, one would have to show how a perception awakens

attention, then how attention develops and enriches it Some internal connection would have to be described, and empiricism has at its disposal only external ones, and can do no more than juxtapose states of consciousness The empiricist's subject, once he has been allowed some initiative—which is the justification for a theory of attention— can receive only absolute freedom Intellectualism, on the other hand, starts with the fruitfulness of attention since I am conscious that through attention I shall come by the truth of the object, the succession of pictures called up by attention is not a haphazard one The new appearance of the object assigns to the previous one a subordinate place, and expresses all that its predecessor was trying to communicate. The wax is from the start a fragment of extension both pliable and alterable, I simply realize this clearly or confusedly 'according as my attention is applied more or less to the things which are in it and of which it is composed' [1] Since in attention I experience an elucidation *of* the object, the perceived object must already contain the intelligible structure which it reveals If consciousness finds a geometrical circle in the circular form of a plate, it is because it had already put the circle there. For it to gain possession of the knowledge brought by attention, it is enough for it to come to itself again, in the sense in which a man is said to come to himself again after fainting. On the other hand, inattentive or delirious perception is a semi-torpor, describable only in terms of negations, its object has no consistency, the only objects about which one can speak being those of waking consciousness. It is true that we carry with us, in the shape of our body, an ever-present principle of absent-mindedness and bewilderment But our body has not the power to make us see what is not there, it can only make us believe that we see it. The moon on the horizon is not, and is not seen to be, bigger than at its zenith: if we look at it attentively, for example through a cardboard tube or a telescope, we see that its apparent diameter remains constant.[2] Inattentive perception contains nothing more and indeed nothing other than the attentive kind. So philosophy need attach no importance to any credit which appearance may be thought to enjoy. Clear consciousness, freed from the obstacles which it was prepared to create, the real world purged of any admixture of daydreams, are there for everyone. We are not called upon to analyse the act of attention as a passage from indistinctness to clarity, because the indistinctness is not there. Consciousness does not begin to exist until it sets limits to an object, and even the phantoms of 'internal experience' are possible only as things borrowed from external experience Therefore consciousness has no private life, and the only obstacle it

[1] *2nd Meditation*, AT, IX, p 25.
[2] Alain, *Système des Beaux-Arts*, p 343

encounters is chaos, which is nothing But, in a consciousness which constitutes everything, or rather which eternally possesses the intelligible structure of all its objects, just as in empiricist consciousness which constitutes nothing at all, attention remains an abstract and ineffective power, because it has no work to perform. Consciousness is no less intimately linked with objects of which it is unheeding than with those which interest it, and the additional clearness brought by the act of attention does not herald any new relationship. It therefore becomes once more a light which does not change its character with the various objects which it shines upon, and once more empty acts of attention are brought in, in place of 'the modes and specific directions of intention'.[1] Finally, the act of attention is unconditioned, for it has all objects at its disposal, as was the 'bemerken' of the empiricists, because in relation to that all objects were transcendent How could an object, distinguished by its presence, call forth an act of attention, since consciousness includes all objects? Where empiricism was deficient was in any internal connection between the object and the act which it triggers off What intellectualism lacks is contingency in the occasions of thought In the first case consciousness is too poor, in the second too rich for any phenomenon to appeal compellingly to it Empiricism cannot see that we need to know what we are looking for, otherwise we would not be looking for it, and intellectualism fails to see that we need to be ignorant of what we are looking for, or equally again we should not be searching. They are in agreement in that neither can grasp consciousness *in the act of, learning*, and that neither attaches due importance to that circumscribed ignorance, that still 'empty' but already determinate intention which *is* attention itself. Whether attention gets what it wants by ever-renewed miracles or whether it possesses it in advance, in both cases silence is maintained over the production of the object Whether it be a collection of qualities or a system of relationships, no sooner does it exist than it must be pure, transparent, impersonal—not imperfect—a truth for one moment of my life and of my knowledge as it emerges into consciousness Perceptual consciousness is confused with the exact forms of scientific consciousness and the indeterminate does not enter into the definition of the mind In spite of the intentions of intellectualism, the two doctrines, then, have this idea in common that attention creates nothing, since a world of impressions in itself or a universe of determining thought are equally independent of the action of mind

Against this conception of an inactive subject, the analysis of

[1] Cassirer *Philosophie der symbolischen Formen*, t III, *Phänomenologie der Erkenntnis*, p 200

attention by the psychologists acquires the value of self-discovery, and the criticism of the 'constancy hypothesis' develops into a criticism of the dogmatic belief in the 'world' seen as a reality in itself by empiricists, and as the immanent end of knowledge by intellectualists. Attention first of all presupposes a transformation of the mental field, a new way for consciousness to be present to its objects. Take the act of attention whereby I locate a point on my body which is being touched. The analysis of certain disorders having their origin in the central nervous system, and which make such an identification impossible, reveals the profound workings of consciousness. Head has spoken summarily of 'a local weakening of attention'. It is in reality neither a question of one or more 'local signals', nor of the collapse of a secondary power of apprehension The primary condition of the disorder is a disintegration of the sensory field which no longer remains stable while the subject perceives, but moves in response to the exploratory movements and shrinks while it is being probed.[1] A *vaguely located spot*, contradictory phenomenon that reveals a pre-objective space where there is indeed extension, since several points on the body touched together are not confused by the subject, but as yet no univocal position, because no spatial framework persists from one perception to another. The first operation of attention is, then, to create for itself a *field*, either perceptual or mental, which can be 'surveyed' (*uberschauen*), in which movements of the exploratory organ or elaborations of thought are possible, but in which consciousness does not correspondingly lose what it has gained and, moreover, lose itself in the changes it brings about. The precise position of the point touched will be the invariable factor among the various feelings that I experience according to the dispositions of my limbs and body. The act of attention can localize or objectify this invariable factor because it has stepped back from the changes of appearance Attention, therefore, as a general and formal activity, does not exist [2] There is in each case a certain liberty to be acquired, and a certain mental space to make the most of. It remains to bring to light the object of attention itself. There it is literally a question of creation For example, it has long been known that during the first nine months of life, infants distinguish only globally the coloured from the colourless; thereafter coloured areas form into 'warm' and 'cold' shades, and finally the detailed colours are arrived at. But psychologists[3] would concede here no more than that ignorance or the confusion of names

---

[1] J Stein, *Über die Veranderungen der Sinnesleistungen und die Entstehung von Trugwahrnehmungen*, pp. 362 and 383
[2] E Rubin, *Die Nichtexistenz der Aufmerksamkeit*
[3] Cf Peters, *Zur Entwickelung der Farbenwahrnehmung*, pp 152-3

prevents the child from distinguishing colours The child must, it was alleged, see green *where it is*, all he was failing to do was to pay attention and apprehend his own phenomena The reason for these assertions was that psychologists were not yet able to conceive a world in which colours were indeterminate, or a colour which was not a precise quality. The criticism of these prejudices, on the other hand, allows the world of colours to be perceived as a secondary formation, based on a series of 'physiognomic' distinctions: that between the 'warm' and 'cold' shades, that between the 'coloured' and the 'non-coloured'. We cannot compare these phenomena, which take the place of colour in children, to any determinate quality, and in the same way the 'strange' colours seen by a diseased person cannot be identified with any colour of the spectrum.[1] The first perception of colours properly speaking, then, is a change of the structure of consciousness,[2] the establishment of a new dimension of experience, the setting forth of an *a priori*.

Now attention has to be conceived on the model of these originating acts, since secondary attention, which would be limited to recalling knowledge already gained, would once more identify it with acquisition. To pay attention is not merely further to elucidate pre-existing data, it is to bring about a new articulation of them by taking them as *figures*.[3] They are preformed only as *horizons*, they constitute in reality new regions in the total world. It is precisely the original structure which they introduce that brings out the identity of the object before and after the act of attention Once the colour-quality is acquired, and only by means of it, do the previous data appear as preparations of this quality. Once the idea of an equation has been acquired, equal arithmetical quantities appear as varieties of the same equation It is precisely by overthrowing data that the act of attention is related to previous acts, and the unity of consciousness is thus built up step by step through a 'synthesis of transition'. The miracle of consciousness consists in its bringing to light, through attention, phenomena which re-establish the unity of the object in a new dimension at the very moment when they destroy it Thus attention is neither an association of images, nor the return to itself of thought already in control of its objects, but the active constitution of a new object which makes explicit and articulate what was until then presented as no more than an indeterminate horizon At the same time as it sets attention in motion, the object is at every moment recaptured and placed once more in a state of dependence on it It gives rise to the 'knowledge-bringing event', which is to

[1] Cf supra, p 9
[2] Koehler, *Über unbemerkte Empfindungen*, p 52
[3] Koffka, *Perception*, pp 561 and ff

transform it, only by means of the still ambiguous meaning which it requires that event to clarify; it is therefore the motive[1] and not the cause of the event But at least the act of attention is rooted in the life of consciousness, and one can finally understand how it emerges from its liberty of indifference and gives itself a present object. This passage from the indeterminate to the determinate, this recasting at every moment of its own history in the unity of a new meaning, is thought itself 'The work of the mind exists only in act '[2] The result of the act of attention is not to be found in its beginning If the moon on the horizon appears to me no bigger than at the zenith, when I look at it through a telescope or a cardboard tube, the conclusion[3] cannot be drawn that in free vision equally its appearance is invariable. This is what empiricism believes, because it is not concerned with what we see, but with what we ought to see, according to the retinal image It is also what intellectualism believes because *it* describes *de facto* perception according to the data of 'analytic' and attentive perception, in which the moon in fact resumes its *true* apparent diameter. The precise and entirely determinate world is still posited in the first place, no longer perhaps as the cause of our perceptions, but as their immanent end. If the world is to be possible, it must be implied in the first adumbration of consciousness, as the transcendental deduction so forcibly brings out [4] And that is why the moon on the horizon should never appear bigger than it is. Psychological reflection, on the contrary, makes us put the world of the exact back into its cradle of consciousness, and ask how the very idea of the world or of exact truth is possible, and look for its first appearance in consciousness When I look quite freely and naturally, the various parts of the field interact and *motivate* this enormous moon on the horizon, this measureless size which nevertheless is a size Consciousness must be faced with its own unreflective life in things and awakened to its own history which it was forgetting such is the true part that philosophical reflection has to play, and thus do we arrive at a true theory of attention.

Intellectualism set out, it is true, to discover by reflection the structure of perception, instead of explaining it in terms of a combination of associative forces and attention, but its gaze upon

[1] E. Stein, *Beitrage zur philosophischen Begrundung der Psychologie und der Geisteswissenschaften*, pp 35 and ff.
[2] Valery, *Introduction à la poétique*, p. 40.
[3] As Alain does, *Systeme des Beaux-Arts*, p 343.
[4] The following pages will make clearer in what respects Kantian philosophy is, in Husserl's language, a 'worldly' and dogmatic philosophy Cf. Fink, *Die phanomenologische Philosophie Husserls in der gegenwartigen Kritik*, pp. 531 and ff.

perception is not yet direct This will be seen better by examining the rôle played in its analysis by the notion of *judgement* Judgement is often introduced as *what sensation lacks to make perception possible* Sensation is no longer presupposed as a real element of consciousness But when it is desired to delineate the structure of perception, it is done by joining up the points of sensation. Analysis is then dominated by this empiricist notion which, however, is accepted only as the boundary of consciousness and serves merely to throw into relief a power of co-ordination of which it is itself the antithesis. Intellectualism thrives on the refutation of empiricism, and here judgement often has the job of offsetting the possible dispersal of sensations [1] Analytical reflection makes its position firm by carrying to their logical conclusions the realist and empiricist theses, and validating their opposite by showing their absurdity But in the *reductio ad absurdum* no contact is necessarily made with the actual workings of consciousness It remains possible that the theory of perception, ideally starting from a blind intuition, may end compensatorily with some empty concept, and that judgement, the counterpart of pure sensation, may degenerate into a general function of indiscriminate union with its objects, or even become once more a psychic force detectable in its effects The famous analysis of the piece of wax jumps from qualities such a smell, colour and taste, to the power of assuming an infinity of forms and positions, a power which lies beyond the perceived object and defines only the wax of the physicist For perception there is no wax left when all its sensible properties have vanished, and only science supposes that there is some matter which is preserved The 'perceived' wax itself, with its original manner of existing, its permanence which is not yet the exact identity of science, its 'interior horizon'[2] of possible variation of shape and size its dull colour suggestive of softness, which in turn suggests the dull sound I shall get when I pat it, in short, the perceptual structure of the object, are lost sight of, because specifications of a predicative kind are needed to link up objective and hermetically sealed qualities The men I see from a window are hidden by their hats and coats, and their image cannot be imprinted on my retina I therefore do not see them, I judge them to be there [3] Once vision is defined in the empiricist way as the possession of a quality impressed upon the body by the

---

[1] 'Hume's nature needed Kantian reason and Hobbes' man needed Kant's practical reason if both were to approximate to the actual, natural experience we have of them ' Scheler, *Der Formalismus in der Ethik*, p 62

[2] Cf Husserl, *Erfahrung und Urteil*, e g , p 172

[3] Descartes, *2nd Meditation*, 'I do not fail to say that I see men, just as I say I see wax, yet what do I see from the window, except hats and coats which may cover ghosts or dummies worked by springs? Yet I judge them to be real men ' AT IX p 25

stimulus,[1] the least illusion, endowing the object as it does with properties which it does not possess on my retina, is sufficient to establish that perception is a judgement[2] As I have two eyes, I ought to see the object double, and if I see only one of it, that is because I construct by means of two images the idea of one object a distance away[3] Perception becomes an 'interpretation' of the signs that our senses provide in accordance with the bodily *stimuli*,[4] a 'hypothesis' that the mind evolves to 'explain its impressions to itself'.[5] But judgement also, brought in to explain the excess of perception over the retinal impressions, instead of being the act of perception itself grasped from within by authentic reflection, becomes once more a mere 'factor' of perception, responsible for providing what the body does not provide—instead of being a transcendental activity, it becomes simply a logical activity of drawing a conclusion.[6] In this way we are drawn away from reflection,

[1] 'Here too relief seems obvious, yet it is concluded from an appearance which bears no resemblance to a relief, namely from a difference between the appearances presented to our two eyes by the same things' Alain, *Quatre-vingt-un chapitres sur l'esprit et les passions*, p. 19. Moreover Alain (ibid., p. 17) refers to the *Physiological Optics* of Helmholz in which the constancy hypothesis is always assumed, and where judgement intervenes only to fill the gaps in physiological explanation Cf again ibid, p 23, 'It is fairly obvious that in the case of this forest horizon, sight presents it to us not as remote but as bluish, by reason of the intervening layers of air.' This is logically entailed if we define sight by its bodily stimulus or by the possession of a quality, for then it can give us blueness but not distance, which is a relationship But it is not strictly speaking *obvious*, that is, attested by consciousness Consciousness is in fact astonished to discover in the perception of distance relations which precede all assessment, calculation or conclusion.

[2] 'What proves here that I judge is that painters know perfectly how to provide me with the perception of a distant mountain by imitating its appearance on a canvas' Alain, ibid, p 14

[3] 'We see objects double because we have two eyes, but we pay no attention to these double images except in order to gain from them knowledge about the distance or relief of the unique object which they afford our perception' Lagneau, *Celebres Leçons*, p 105 And generally 'we must first of all look for the elementary sensations which belong to the nature of the human mind, the human body represents this nature' Ibid, p 75 'I have met a person', says Alain, 'who was not prepared to admit that our eyes present us with two images of each thing, it is, however, sufficient to fix our eyes on a fairly close object such as a pencil to see that the images of distant objects are immediately doubled' (*Quatre-vingt-un chapitres*, pp. 23–4) That does not prove that they were double beforehand Here can be seen the prejudice in favour of the law of constancy which demands that phenomena corresponding to bodily impressions be given in places where they are not observed

[4] 'Perception is an interpretation of the primitive intuition, an interpretation apparently immediate, but in reality gained from habit corrected by reasoning.', Lagneau, *Célèbres Leçons*, p 158.   [5] Id ibid, p 160

[6] Cf for example Alain, *Quatre-vingt-un chapitres*, p 15 Relief is 'thought, concluded, judged, or however you like to put it'

33

and we construct perception instead of revealing its distinctive working, we miss once more the basic operation which infuses significance into the sensible, and which is taken for granted by any logical mediation or any psychological causality. The result is that intellectualist analysis eventually makes nonsense of the perceptual phenomena which it is designed to elucidate While judgement loses its constitutive function and becomes an explanatory principle, the words 'see', 'hear', 'feel' lose all their meaning, since the least significant vision outruns the pure impression and thus comes under the general heading of 'judgement' Ordinary experience draws a clear distinction between sense experience and judgement It sees judgement as the taking of a stand, as an effort to know something which shall be valid for myself every moment of my life, and equally for other actual or potential minds; sense experience, on the contrary, is taking appearance at its face value, without trying to possess it and learn its truth. This distinction disappears in intellectualism, because judgement is everywhere where pure sensation is not—that is, absolutely everywhere The evidence of phenomena will therefore everywhere be challenged

A large cardboard box seems heavier to me than a small one made of the same cardboard, and if I confined myself to phenomena I should say that in advance. I *feel* it heavier in my hand. But intellectualism limits sense experience to the action of a real stimulus on my body Since here there is none, we have to say that the box is not felt but judged to be heavier, and this example which seemed ready-made to show the sensory aspect of illusion serves on the contrary to prove that there is no sensory knowledge, and that we feel as we judge [1] A cube drawn on paper changes its appearance according as it is seen from one side and from above or from the other and from below. Even if I *know* that it can be seen in two ways, the figure in fact refuses to change its structure and my knowledge must await its intuitive realization. Here again one ought to conclude that judging is not perceiving. But the alternatives of sensation and judgement force us to say that the change in the figure, since it does not depend on the 'sensible elements' which, like the stimuli, remain constant, can only depend on a change of interpretation, and that 'the mind's conception modifies perception itself',[2] 'appearance assumes form and meaning to order' [3] Now if we see what we judge, how can we distinguish between true and false perception? How will it then be possible to say that the sufferer from hallucinations or the madman 'think they see what they do not see'?[4] Where will be the

---

[1] Alain, *Quatre-vingt-un chapitres*, p 18
[2] Lagneau, *Celebres Leçons*, pp 132 and 128   [3] Alain, ibid , p 32
[4] Montaigne, quoted by Alain, *Système des Beaux-Arts*, p. 15

difference between 'seeing' and 'thinking one sees'? If the reply is
made that the sane man judges only by adequate signs and completely
coherent material, it is, then, because there is a difference between
the motivated judgement of veridical perception and the empty
judgement of false perception And as the difference is not in the
form of the judgement but in the sensible text to which it gives form,
to perceive in the full sense of the word (as the antithesis of imagining) is not to judge, it is to apprehend an immanent sense in the
sensible before judgement begins. The phenomenon of true perception offers, therefore, a meaning inherent in the signs, and of which
judgement is merely the optional expression. Intellectualism can
make comprehensible neither this phenomenon nor the imitation
which illusion gives of it. More generally it is blind to the mode of
existence and co-existence of perceived objects, to the life which
steals across the visual field and secretly binds its parts together In
Zöllner's optical illusion, I 'see' the main lines converging Intellectualism simply reduces the phenomenon to a mistake, saying that
it all comes of my bringing in the auxiliary lines and their relation to
the main ones, instead of comparing their main lines themselves.
Basically I mistake the task given to me, and I compare the two
wholes instead of comparing the principal elements [1] My mistake
apparently remains unexplained. The question ought to arise: How
does it come about that it is so difficult in Zöllner's illusion to compare in isolation the very lines that have to be compared according
to the task set? Why do they thus refuse to be separated from the
auxiliary lines?[2] It should be recognized that acquiring auxiliary
lines, the main lines have ceased to be parallel, that they have
lost that meaning and acquired another, that the auxiliary lines
introduce into the figure a new meaning which henceforth clings to it
and cannot be shifted [3] It is this meaning inseparable from the figure,
this transformation of the phenomenon, which motivates the false
judgement and which is so to speak *behind* it. It is at the same time
this meaning which gives a sense to the word 'see' on the hither side
of judgement and on the far side of the quality or impression, and
causes the problem of perception to reappear. If we agree to call
any perception of a relationship a judgement and to keep the term
visual impression for the atomic impression, then certainly illusion
is a judgement But this analysis presupposes at least in theory a

[1] Cf for example Lagneau, *Cèlèbres Leçons*, p 134
[2] Koehler, *Über unbemerkte Empfindungen und Urteilstauschungen*, p 69.
[3] Koffka, *Psychologie*, p. 533 'One is tempted to say: the side of a rectangle is
after all just a line But an isolated line, both as a phenomenon and as a functional element, is something other than the side of a rectangle To limit ourselves
to one property, the side of a rectangle has an inner and an outer face, the
isolated line on the other hand has two faces absolutely equivalent '

layer of impressions in which the main lines are parallel, as they are in the world, that is, in the physical environment which we measure —and a second-order operation which changes the impressions by bringing in auxiliary lines, thus distorting the relationships of the principal lines. Now the first of these phases is purely conjectural, and with it the judgement which produces the second We construct the illusion, but we do not understand it Judgement in this very general and quite formal sense explains perception, true or false, only when it is guided by the spontaneous organization and the special mode of arrangement of the phenomena. It is true that the illusion consists in involving the principal elements in the figure in auxiliary relationships which break up the parallelism. But why do they break it up? Why is it that two straight lines so far parallel cease to make a pair and begin to converge by reason of the immediate surroundings provided? It is as if they no longer belonged to the same world Two genuinely oblique lines are situated in the same space which is objective space. But these do not actually converge upon each other, and it is impossible to *see* them in this way if our eyes are fixed on them. It is when we look away from them that they move insidiously towards this new relationship. There is here, preceding objective relationships, a perceptual syntax constructed according to its own rules. the breaking of old relationships and the establishment of new ones—judgement—express merely the result of this complex operation and place it on record True or false, in this way must perception first be constituted for predication to be possible It is quite true that the distance from us of an object, or its relief, are not properties of the object as are its colour or its weight. It is true that they are relations introduced into a total grouping which, moreover, includes weight and colour. But it is untrue that this grouping is effected through an 'inspection of the mind'. It would follow from this that the mind runs over isolated impressions and gradually discovers the meaning of the whole as the scientist discovers the unknown factors in virtue of the data of the problem. Now here the data of the problem are not prior to its solution, and perception is just that act which creates at a stroke, along with the cluster of data, the meaning which unites them—indeed which not only discovers the meaning *which they have*, but moreover sees to it *that they have a meaning*

It is true that these criticisms are valid only against the first stages of analytical reflection, and intellectualism might reply that one is forced at the beginning to talk the language of common sense. The conception of judgement as a psychic force or a logical mediator, and the theory of perception as 'interpretation'—the intellectualism of the psychologists—is indeed simply a counterpart of empiricism,

36

but it paves the way to true self-discovery One can begin only with a natural attitude, complete with its postulates, until the internal dialectic of these postulates destroys them Once perception is understood as interpretation, sensation, which has provided a starting-point, is finally superseded, for all perceptual consciousness is already beyond it. The sensation is not experienced,[1] and consciousness is always consciousness of an object. We arrive at sensation when we think about perceptions and try to make it clear that they are not completely our work Pure sensation, defined as the action of *stimuli* on our body, is the 'last effect' of knowledge, particularly of scientific knowledge, and it is an illusion (a not unnatural one, moreover) that causes us to put it at the beginning and to believe that it precedes knowledge. It is the necessary, and necessarily misleading way in which a mind sees its own history [2] It belongs to the domain of the constituted and not to the constituting mind. To the world or opinion, perception can appear as an interpretation. For consciousness itself, how could it be a process of reasoning since there are no sensations to provide it with premises, or an interpretation, because there is nothing prior to it to interpret? At the same time as we thus discard, along with the idea of sensation, that of a purely logical activity, our foregoing objections disappear. We asked what seeing or feeling are, what makes this knowledge still enmeshed in its object, and inherent in one point of time and space, distinct from the concept. But reflection shows that there is nothing here to understand. It is a fact that I believe myself to be first of all surrounded by my body, involved in the world, situated here and now. But each of these words, when I come to think about them, is devoid of meaning, and therefore raises no problem: would I perceive myself as 'surrounded by my body' if I were not in it as well as being in myself, if I did not myself conceive this spatial relationship and thus escape inherence at the very instant at which I conceive it? Would I know that I am caught up and situated in the world, if I were truly caught up and situated in it? I should then merely *be* where I was, as a thing, and since I know where I am and see myself among things, it is because I am a consciousness, a strange creature which resides nowhere and can be everywhere present in intention. Everything that exists exists as a thing or as a consciousness, and there is no half-way house The thing is in a

[1] 'In fact the pure impression is conceived and not felt ' Lagneau, *Celebres Leçons*, p. 119
[2] 'When we have evolved this notion by scientific knowledge and reflection, we think that what is in fact the last effect of the process of knowing, namely the expression of the relationship between one being and others, is the beginning, but this is an illusion. The idea of time which leads us to think of sensation as anterior to knowledge, is a construction of the mind.' Id. ibid.

place, but perception is nowhere, for if it were situated in a place it could not make other things *exist for itself*, since it would repose in itself as things do Perception is thus thought about perceiving Its incarnation furnishes no positive characteristic which has to be accounted for, and its thisness (ecceity) is simply its own ignorance of itself Analytical reflection becomes a purely regressive doctrine, according to which every perception is a muddled form of intellection, and every setting of bounds a negation. It thus does away with all problems except one: that of its own beginning The finitude of a perception which gives me, as Spinoza expressed it, 'consequences without premises', the inherence of consciousness in a point of view, these things amount to my ignorance of myself, to my negative power of not reflecting But how is this ignorance possible? we want to ask To reply that it never *is*, would be to abolish me as an inquiring philosopher. No philosophy can afford to be ignorant of the problem of finitude under pain of failing to understand itself as philosophy; no analysis of perception can afford not to conceive perception as a totally original phenomenon under pain of misconceiving itself as analysis, and the infinite thought discovered as immanent in perception would not be the culminating point of consciousness, but on the contrary a form of unconsciousness The impetus of reflection would overshoot its goal it would transport us from a fixed and determinate world to a consciousness without a rift in it, whereas the perceived object is infused with secret life, and perception as a unity disintegrates and reforms ceaselessly We shall have only an abstract essence of consciousness as long as we refrain from following the actual movement by which it resumes its own operations at every instant, focusing and concentrating them on an identifiable object, gradually passing from 'seeing' to 'knowing' and achieving the unity of its own life. We shall not reach this constitutive dimension if we replace the plenary unity of consciousness by a completely transparent subject, and the 'hidden art' which calls up meaning from 'the depths of nature', by some eternal thought. The intellectualist process of self-discovery does not penetrate as far as this living nucleus of perception because it is looking for the conditions which make it *possible* or without which it would not exist, instead of uncovering the operation which brings it *into reality*, or whereby it is constituted In actual perception taken at its origin, before any word is uttered, the sign offered to sense and the signification are not even theoretically separable An object is an organism of colours, smells, sounds and tactile appearances which symbolize, modify and accord with each other according to the laws of a real logic which it is the task of science to make explicit, and which it is far from having analysed completely Intellectualism is unequal to dealing with this perceptual life, either falling short of it or overshooting it: it calls up as limitations the manifold qualities which are merely the outer casing of the object, and from there it passes on to a consciousness of the object which claims to hold within itself the law or secret of that object, and which for this reason deprives the development of the experience of its contingency and the object of its distinctive perceptual style This move from thesis to antithesis, this flying from one extreme to the other which is the regular procedure of intellectualism leaves the starting-point of analysis unaffected We started off from a world in itself which acted upon our eyes so as to cause us to see it, and we now have conscious-ness of or thought about the world, but the nature of this world re-mains unchanged it is still defined by the absolute mutual exteriority of its parts, and is merely duplicated throughout its extent by a thought which sustains it. We pass from absolute objectivity to absolute subjectivity, but this second idea is no better than the first and is upheld only against it, which means by it. The affinity between intellectualism and empiricism is thus much less obvious and much more deeply rooted than is commonly thought It arises not only from the anthropological definition of sensation used equally by both, but from the fact that both persist in the natural or dogmatic attitude, and the survival of sensation in intellectualism is merely a sign of this dogmatism Intellectualism accepts as completely valid the idea of truth and the idea of being in which the formative work of consciousness culminates and is embodied, and its alleged reflection consists in positing as powers of the subject all that is required to arrive at these ideas. The natural attitude, by throwing me into the world of things, gives me the assurance of apprehending a 'real' beyond appearance, the 'true' beyond illusion. The value of these notions is not questioned by intellectualism it is merely a matter of conferring upon a universal creative force the power of recognizing this same absolute truth that realism ingenuously places in a given creation Intellectualism no doubt normally sets itself up as a doctrine of science and not of perception, purporting to base its analysis on the test of mathematical truth and not on the naive acceptance of the self-evidence of the world: *habemus ideam veram*. But in reality I would not know that I possess a true idea if my memory did not enable me to relate what is now evident with what was evident a moment ago, and, through the medium of words, correlate my evidence with that of others, so that Spinozist self-evidence presup-poses that of memory and perception. If, on the other hand, we insist on basing our constitution of the past and of other people on our power of recognizing the intrinsic truth of the idea, we do away with the problem of others and that of the world, but

39

then only because we persist in the natural attitude which takes them for granted, and because we put into action the force of naive certainty For never, as Descartes and Pascal realized, can I at one stroke coincide with the pure thought which constitutes even a simple idea My clear and distinct thought always uses thoughts already formulated by myself or others, and relies on my memory, that is, on the *nature of my mind*, or else on the memory of the community of thinkers, that is, upon the *objective mind* To take for granted that we *have* a true idea is to believe in uncritical perception. Empiricism retained an absolute belief in the world as the totality of spatio-temporal events, and treated consciousness as a province of this world Analytical reflection, it is true, breaks with the world in itself, since it constitutes it through the working of consciousness, but this constituting consciousness, instead of being directly apprehended, is built up in such a way as to make possible the idea of an absolute determinate being It is the correlative of a universe, the subject possessing in absolutely completed form all the knowledge which is adumbrated by our actual knowledge. What happens is that what exists for us only in intention is presumed to be fully realized *somewhere*: there is thought to be a system of absolutely true thoughts, capable of co-ordinating all phenomena, a flat projection which clarifies all perspectives, a pure object upon which all subjective views open. Nothing less than this absolute object and this divine subject are needed to ward off the threat of the malicious demon and to ensure that we possess the true idea. Now there is indeed one human act which at one stroke cuts through all possible doubts to stand in the full light of truth this act is perception, in the wide sense of knowledge of existences. When I begin to perceive this table, I resolutely contract the thickness of duration* which has elapsed while I have been looking at it, I emerge from my individual life by apprehending the object as an object for everybody. I therefore bring together in one operation concordant but discrete experiences which occupy several points of time and several temporalities We do not blame intellectualism for making use of this decisive act which, within time, does the work of the Spinozist eternity, this 'original doxa';[1] what we do complain of, is that it is here used tacitly There is here a *de facto* power, as Descartes put it, a quite irresistibly self-evident truth, which, by invoking an absolute truth, brings together the separate phenomena of my present and my past, of my duration* and that of others, which, however, must not be severed from its perceptual origins and detached from its 'facticity' Philosophy's task is to reinstate it in the private field of experience

* *durée* in the Bergsonian sense (Translator's note).
[1] Husserl, *Erfahrung und Urteil*, e g , p 331

40

from which it arises and elucidate its origin If, however, this *de facto*
power is used without being explicitly posited, we become incapable
of *seeing* past the rending of separate experiences the phenomenon
of perception, and the world born in perception, we dissolve the
perceived *world* into a *universe* which is nothing but this very world
cut off from its constitutive origins, and made manifest because they
are forgotten

Thus intellectualism leaves consciousness on a footing of familiarity with absolute being, while the idea of a world in itself persists
as a horizon or as the clue to analytical reflection. Doubt has certainly interrupted the explicit assertions concerning the world, but
leaves untouched its insidious presence, even though it be sublimated into the ideal realm of absolute truth. Reflection, then,
furnishes an essence of consciousness, which is accepted dogmatic-
ally, and no one wonders what an essence is, or whether the essence
of thought adequately covers the fact of thought It loses the character of observation and henceforth there can be no question of
describing phenomena the perceptual appearance of illusions is
challenged as the illusion of illusions, now only what is can be seen,
the view itself and experience being no longer distinct from conception. Hence a philosophy with two guises, and observable in any
doctrine of the understanding a leap is undertaken from a naturalistic view, which expresses our *de facto* condition, to a transcendental
sphere in which all bondage is theoretically removed, and we never
have to wonder how the same subject comes to be a part of the world
·and at the same time its principle because the thing constituted exists
only for the constituting agent. In fact, the image of a constituted
world where, with my body, I should be only one object among
others, and the idea of an absolute constituting consciousness are
only apparently antithetical, they are a dual expression of a universe
perfectly explicit in itself Authentic reflection, instead of turning
from one to the other as both true, in the manner of a philosophy of
the understanding, rejects them as both false.

It is true that we are perhaps once more distorting intellectualism
When we say that analytical reflection anticipates all possible knowledge over and above what we at present know, that it includes
reflection in its results and abolishes the phenomenon of finitude,
perhaps we are caricaturing intellectualism, and offering in its name
a world-centred reflection, a truth as seen by the prisoner in the cave
who prefers the shadows to which he is accustomed and who does
not understand that they owe their existence to the light. Perhaps we
have not yet understood the real function of judgement in perception.
The analysis of the piece of wax means, one may say, not that there
is a reason hidden behind nature, but that reason is rooted in nature,

the 'inspection of the mind' would then be, not the concept gravitating towards nature, but nature rising to the concept. Perception would be a judgement, which, however, is unaware of the reasons underlying its own formation,[1] which amounts to saying that the perceived object presents itself as a totality and a unity before we have apprehended the intelligible law governing it, and that the wax is not originally a pliable and alterable bit of extension. When he says that natural judgement has not 'time to weigh and consider any reasons', Descartes lets us know that by the word 'judgement' he is thinking of the constitution of a meaning for the thing perceived which is not prior to the perception itself and which seems to emanate from it [2] The vital knowledge or 'natural inclination' which shows us the union of body and soul, once the light of nature has taught us to distinguish them, is a thing which it seems contradictory to guarantee by divine truthfulness; for this is after all nothing but the intrinsic clarity of the idea, and can in any case validate only self-evident thoughts. But perhaps Descartes' philosophy consists in embracing this contradiction [3] When Descartes says that the understanding knows itself incapable of knowing the union of soul and body and leaves this knowledge for life to achieve,[4] this means that the act of understanding presents itself as reflection on an unreflective experience which it does not absorb either in fact or in theory When I discover the intelligible structure of the piece of wax, I do not identify myself with some absolute thought in relation to which the wax is a mere result, I do not constitute it, I re-constitute it 'Natural judgement' is nothing but the phenomenon of passivity It will always be the task of perception to know perception Reflection never lifts itself out of any situation, nor does the analysis of perception do away with the fact of perception, the thisness of the percept or the inherence of perceptual consciousness in some temporality and some locality Reflection is not absolutely transparent for itself, it is always given to itself in an *experience*, in the Kantian sense of the word, it always springs up without itself know-

---

[1] '. I noticed that the judgements which I was accustomed to make about these objects were formed within me before I had time to weigh and consider any reasons which might have forced me to make them.' *6th Meditation*, AT, IX, p 60

[2] ' it seemed to me that I had learnt from nature all the other things that I judged concerning the objects of my senses ' ibid

[3] ' since it did not seem to me that the human mind was capable of conceiving distinctly and simultaneously the distinction between soul and body and their union, for in that case it would be necessary to conceive them as a single thing and at the same time as two things, which is contradictory ' To Elizabeth, 28th June, 1643, AT, III, p 690 and ff

[4] Ibid

ing whence it springs and offers itself to me as a gift of nature. But if the description of the unreflective experience remains valid after reflection and the *Sixth Meditation* after the *Second*, conversely this unreflective experience is known to us only through reflection and cannot be posited outside itself as an unknowable final stage Between the self which analyses perception and the self which perceives, there is always a distance. But in the concrete act of reflection, I abolish this distance, I prove by that very token that I am capable of *knowing* what I was perceiving, I control in practice the discontinuity of the two selves, and it would seem that, in the last resort, the significance of the *cogito* lies not in revealing a universal constituting force or in reducing perception to intellection, but in establishing the *fact* of reflection which both pierces and sustains the opacity of perception. It would be quite consistent with the Cartesian intention to have thus identified reason and the human condition, and it might be held that the ultimate significance of Cartesianism is to be found here The 'natural judgement' of intellectualism in this case anticipates the Kantian judgement which sees the birth of the individual objects meaning in the object itself, and does not see it as imposed ready-made.[1] Cartesianism, like Kantianism, would seem to have seen quite clearly that the problem of perception resides in its being an *originating* knowledge There is an empirical or second-order perception, the one which we exercise at every moment, and which conceals from us the former basic phenomenon, because it is loaded with earlier acquisitions and plays, so to speak, on the surface of being

When I glance rapidly about at the objects surrounding me in order to find my bearings and locate myself among them, I scarcely can be said to grasp the world in some instantaneous aspect. I identify here the door, there the window, over there my table, all of which are the props and guides of a practical intention directed elsewhere, and which are therefore given to me simply as meanings. But when I contemplate an object with the sole intention of watching it exist and unfold its riches before my eyes, then it ceases to be an allusion to a general type, and I become aware that each perception, and not merely that of sights which I am discovering for the first time, re-enacts on its own account the birth of intelligence and has some element of creative genius about it: in order that I may recognize the tree as a tree, it is necessary that, beneath this familiar meaning,

---

[1] The faculty of judging 'must, then, itself provide a concept, which in reality does not bring knowledge of any thing, and which serves as a rule only for itself, not an objective rule to which its judgement is to be adapted, for then would be needed another faculty of judging in order to be able to discern whether this is or is not a case to which the rule applies ' (*Critique of Judgement*, Preface)

the momentary arrangement of the visible scene should begin all over again, as on the very first day of the vegetable kingdom, to outline the individual idea of this tree. Such would be natural judgement, which cannot yet know its reasons since it is in process of creating them But even if we grant that existence, individuality, 'facticity' are on the horizon of Cartesian thought, there remains the question whether it has posited them Now we must recognize that it could have done so only by transforming itself radically To make perception into an original knowledge, we should have had to endow finitude with a positive significance and take seriously the strange phrase in the *4th Meditation* which makes me 'a middle term between God and nothingness' But if nothingness is without properties, as the *5th Meditation* leads one to understand, and as Malebranche asserts, if it is *nothing*, this definition of the human subject is merely a manner of speaking and the finite has nothing positive about it. In order to see in reflection a creative deed, a reconstituting of past thought not prefigured in that past thought, yet specifying it perfectly validly—because only thus have we any idea of it, because the past in itself is for us as if it had never been—it would have been necessary to develop an intuition of time to which the *Meditations* contain only a brief allusion. 'Let who will deceive me, the fact remains that he cannot cause me to be nothing when I think I am something; *or cause it to be true one day that I have never existed, since it is true that I now exist.*'[1] The experience of the present is that of a being assured of his existence once and for all, whom nothing could ever prevent from having been In the certitude of the present, there is an intention which outruns the presentness of the present, which posits it in advance as an indubitable 'former present' in the series of recollections, and perception as knowledge of the present is the central phenomenon which makes possible the unity of the ego and with it the ideas of objectivity and truth But in the text it is given merely as one of those self-evidences which are irresistible *only de facto*, and which remain in doubt [2] The Cartesian solution is therefore not to accept as a guarantee of itself human thought in its factual reality, but to base it on a thought which possesses itself absolutely The connection between essence and existence is not found in experience, but in the idea of the infinite It is, then, true in the last resort that analytical reflection entirely rests on a dogmatic idea of being, and that in this sense it does not amount to an act of self-discovery [3]

---

[1] *3rd Meditation*, AT, IX, p 28
[2] On the same footing as 2 and 3 make 5 Ibid
[3] Following its own line, analytical reflection does not bring us back to authentic subjectivity, it conceals from us the vital node of perceptual consciousness

When intellectualism took over the naturalistic notion of sensation, a whole philosophy was implied in the step Conversely, now that psychology finally discards this notion, we can look forward, in consequence, to the beginning of a new type of reflection. On the

---

because it looks for the conditions in which absolutely determinate being is possible, and is dazzled by the theological view, falsely regarded as self-evident, that nothingness is nothing. The philosophers who practised this method, however, have always felt that it was necessary to search *beneath* absolute consciousness We have just seen that this is so in the case of Descartes One could show it equally with Lagneau and Alain

Analytical reflection carried to its limit should leave on the subject's side only a universal creative force for which the system of experience exists, including my body and my empirical self, linked to the world by the laws of physics and psychophysiology The sensation which we construct as the 'psychic' extension of the sensory stimuli obviously does not belong to the universal force and all idea of a genesis of mind is a hybrid idea, because it puts back into time the mind for which time exists, and confuses the two selves Nevertheless, if we are this absolute mind, without a history, and if nothing stands between us and the true world, if the empirical self is constituted by the transcendental ego and set out before it, we ought to pierce its opacity, and it is not possible to see how error is possible, still less illusion—the 'abnormal perception' which no knowledge can conjure away. . (Lagneau, *Celebres Leçons*, pp 161–2) It *can* be said (ibid) that illusion and perception in its entirety are on this side of both truth and error This does not help us to solve the problem, since it then becomes one of knowing how a mind can be 'on this side of' truth and error When we feel (*sentir*), we do not perceive our sensation as object in a network of psycho-physiological relationships We do not possess the truth of sensation We are not confronted by the true world 'It amounts to the same thing to say either that we are individuals or to say that in these individuals there is a sentient nature in which something happens which is not a result of the action of the environment If everything in our sentient nature were subject to necessity, if there were for us a manner of feeling which was the true one, if at every moment our manner of feeling were produced by the external world, we should not feel at all ' (*Célebres Leçons*, p 164) Thus feeling does not belong to the order of the constituted, nor does the ego find this order set out before it, it escapes from its gaze, it is as it were piled up behind it and produces a kind of thickness or opacity which makes error possible, it marks out an area of subjectivity or solitude, it represents for us what is 'anterior to' the mind, evokes the latter's birth and calls for a more searching analysis capable of elucidating 'the genealogy of logic' The mind is conscious of itself as 'based' on this nature. There is therefore a dialectic of the *naturata* and of the *naturans*, of perception and judgement, in the course of which their relationship is reversed.

The same tendency is to be found in Alain in the analysis of perception One realizes that a tree always looks bigger than a man, even if it is at a distance and the man near I am tempted to say that 'Here again a judgement enlarges the object. But let us look more closely. The object is unchanged because an object in itself has no size; size is always relative, and so the size of these objects and of all objects forms an indivisible whole and one truly without parts Sizes must be judged together From which it is seen that one must not confuse material things, always separate and made up of mutually external parts, and the thought of these things, in which no division can be admitted However obscure this distinction may be now, and however difficult it must always remain to conceive it, let us keep

psychological level, the criticism of the 'constancy hypothesis' means merely that the judgement is abandoned as an explanatory factor in the theory of perception How can we pretend that the perception of distance is a conclusion reached from the apparent size of objects, from the disparity between retinal images, from the adjustment of the crystalline lens, from the varying convergence of the eyes, or that the perception of relief is a conclusion drawn from the difference between the images furnished respectively by the left and right eyes, since, if we stick to pehnomena, none of these 'signs' is clearly given to consciousness, and since there could be no reasoning where the premises are lacking? But this criticism of intellectualism only affects its popularization by psychologists And, like intellectualism itself, it has to be transferred to the level of reflection, where the philosopher is no longer trying to explain perception, but to coincide with and understand the perceptual process Here the criticism of the constancy hypothesis reveals that perception is not an act of understanding I have only to look at a landscape upside down to recognize nothing in it. Now 'top' and 'bottom' have only a relative meaning for the understanding, which can hardly regard the orientation of the landscape as an absolute obstacle For the understanding a square is always a square, whether it stands on a side or an angle For perception it is in the second case hardly recognizable The *Paradox of symmetrical objects* contrasted the originality of perceptual experience with logicism This idea has to be taken up and generalized there is a significance of the percept which has no

it in mind In a sense, considered materially, things are divided into parts of which one is not another, but in another sense, considered as thoughts, perceptions of things are indivisible and without parts ' (*Quatre-vingt-un chapitres sur l'Esprit et les Passions*, p 18) But then an inspection of the mind which surveyed them and established one in virtue of the other would not be true subjectivity and would borrow too much from things considered as in themselves Perception does not draw conclusions about the size of the tree from that of the man, or about the man's size from the tree's, nor either from the meaning of the two objects, it does all these things at once the size of the tree, that of the man, and their significance as tree and man, with the result that each element agrees with all the others and composes with them a landscape in which all *co-exist* Thus do we broach the analysis of what makes size possible, and more generally the relations or properties of the predicative order, and we broach that subjectivity 'prior to all geometry' which Alain nevertheless declared unknowable (Ibid , p 29) Analytical reflection becomes more strictly conscious of itself as analysis It becomes aware that it had left behind its object, perception It recognizes behind the judgement which it had brought into evidence, a deeper function than judgement which makes judgement possible, it rediscovers, before arriving at things, phenomena This is the function envisaged by psychologists when they talk about a *Gestaltung* of the landscape It is to the description of phenomena that they redirect the philosopher, by separating them rigidly from the constituted objective world, and they do it in terms which are almost identical with Alain's equivalent in the universe of the understanding, a perceptual domain which is not yet the objective world, a perceptual being which is not yet determinate being However, the psychologists who practise the description of phenomena are not normally aware of the philosophical implications of their method They do not see that the return to perceptual experience, in so far as it is a consequential and radical reform, puts out of court all forms of realism, that is to say, all philosophies which leave consciousness and take as given one of its results—that the real sin of intellectualism lies precisely in having taken as given the determinate universe of science, that this reproach applies *a fortiori* to psychological thinking, since it places perceptual consciousness in the midst of a ready-made world, and that the attack on the constancy hypothesis carried to its logical conclusion assumes the value of a genuine 'phenomenological reduction' [1] Gestalt theory has clearly shown that the alleged signs of distance—the apparent size of the object, the number of objects interposed between it and us, the disparity of retinal images, the degree of adjustment and convergence—are expressly known only in an analytic or reflective perception which turns away from the object to its mode of presentation, and that we do not go through these stages in knowing distances Nevertheless, it goes on to conclude that, not being *signs* or *reasons* in our perception of distance, bodily impressions or the interposed objects in the field can only be *causes* of this perception. [2] So we are back in an explanatory psychology, the ideal of which has never been abandoned by Gestalt psychology, [3] because, as psychology, it has never broken with naturalism But by this very fact it betrays its own descriptions A subject whose oculo-motor muscles are paralysed sees objects moving to his left while he believes that he is himself turning his eyes towards the left. This, classical psychology maintains, is because perception reasons the eye is supposed to swing to the left, and since nevertheless the retinal images have not moved, the view must have slipped leftwards to have kept them in place in the eye Gestalt theory informs us that the perception of the position of objects does not pass through the detour of an express body-consciousness at no moment do I know that the images remain stationary on the retina, I see directly the landscape move to the left. But consciousness is not confined to receiving ready-made an illusory phenomenon produced outside itself by physiological causes For the illusion to be produced, the

[1] See A Gurwitsh, Review of *Nachwort zu meiner Ideen* of Husserl, pp 401 and ff

[2] Cf for example P. Guillaume, *Traité de Psychologie*, Coap IX, *La Perception de l'Espace*, p 151

[3] Cf *La Structure du Comportement*, p 178

subject must have intended to look to the left and must have thought he moved his eye The illusion regarding the subjects' body entails the appearance of movement in the object. The movements of his body are naturally invested with a certain perceptual significance, and form, with the external phenomena, such a well articulated system that external perception 'takes account' of the movement of the organs of perception, finding in them if not the *express explanation*, at least the *motive* for the changes brought about in the spectacle, and can thus understand them instantly When I intend to look left, this movement of the eye carries within it as its natural translation an oscillation of the visual field the objects remain in place, but after a moment's fluctuation This consequence is not learnt but is one of the natural formations of the psychosomatic subject. It is, as we shall see, an annex of our 'bodily schema', the immanent meaning of a shift of 'gaze' When it stops short of such a change, when we are conscious of moving our eyes without the view's being affected, the phenomenon is translated, without any express deduction, by an apparent shift of the object leftwards The gaze and the landscape remain as it were glued together, no quiver dissociates them, and the gaze, in its illusory movement, carries with it the landscape, and the latter's sideslip *is* fundamentally nothing but its fixity in a gaze which we think is moving Thus the immobility of images on the retina and the paralysis of the oculo-motor muscles are not objective causes which produce the illusion and carry it ready-made into consciousness Nor are the intention to move the eye and the landscape's passivity in relation to this impulse premises or reasons for the illusion. But they are the *motives* (*motifs*) In the same way, the objects interposed between me and the thing upon which I fix my eyes are not perceived for themselves; they are nevertheless perceived, and we have no reason for refusing to recognize that this marginal perception plays a part in seeing distance, since, when the intervening objects are hidden by a screen, the distance appears to shrink The objects filling up the field do not act on the apparent distance in the relation of cause to effect. When the screen is removed, we see remoteness born of the intervening objects This is the silent language whereby perception communicates with us. interposed objects, in the natural context, 'mean' a greater distance. It is not, however, a question of a connection recognized by objective logic, the logic of constituted truth for there is *no reason* why a steeple should appear to me to be smaller and farther away when I am better able to see in detail the slopes and fields between me and it. There is no reason, but there is a motive It is precisely Gestalt psychology which has brought home to us the tensions which run like lines of force across the visual field and the

system: own body-world, and which breathe into it a secret and
magic life by exerting here and there forces of distortion, contraction and expansion. The disparity between retinal images,
and the number of intermediate objects do not act either as mere
objective causes producing from outside my perception of distance,
or as demonstrative reasons for it. They are tacitly known to perception in an obscure form, and they validate it by a wordless
logic. But what Gestalt psychology lacks for the adequate expression of these perceptual relationships is a set of new categories:
it has admitted the principle, and applied it to a few individual
cases, but without realizing that a complete reform of understanding is called for if we are to translate phenomena accurately,
and that to this end the objective thinking of classical logic and
philosophy will have to be questioned, the categories of the
world laid aside, the alleged self-evidence of realism placed in
doubt, in the Cartesian sense, and a true 'phenomenological reduction' undertaken. Objective thought, as applied to the universe and
not to phenomena, knows only alternative notions; starting from
actual experience, it defines pure concepts which are mutually
exclusive: the notion of *extension*, which is that of an absolute
externality of one part to another, and the notion of *thought* which
is that of a being wrapped up in himself; the notion of the vocal *sign*
as a physical phenomenon arbitrarily linked to certain thoughts, and
that of *meaning* as a thought entirely clear to itself; the notion of
cause as a determining factor external to its effect, and that of *reason*
as a law of intrinsic constitution of the phenomenon Now, as we
have seen, the perception of our own body and the perception of
external things provide an example of *non-positing* consciousness,
that is, of consciousness not in possession of fully determinate
objects, that of a *logic lived through* which cannot account for itself,
and that of an *immanent meaning* which is not clear to itself and becomes fully aware of itself only through experiencing certain natural
signs. These phenomena cannot be assimilated by objective thought,
and that is why Gestalt psychology which, like all psychology, is
imprisoned within the 'self-evident truths' of science and of the
world, can choose only between reason and cause, and that is why
any criticism of intellectualism which it undertakes ends with the
rehabilitation of realism and causal thinking On the other hand,
the phenomenological notion of *motivation* is one of those 'fluid'[1]

[1] 'flieszende', Husserl, *Erfahrung und Urteil*, p 428 It was not until his last
period that Husserl himself became fully aware of what the return to phenomena
meant, and tacitly broke with the philosophy of essences He was in this way
merely explicitly laying down analytic procedures which he had long been apply-
ing, as is precisely shown by the notion of motivation to be found already in the
Ideen

concepts which have to be formed if we want to get back to phenomena One phenomenon releases another, not by means of some
objective efficient cause, like those which link together natural events,
but by the meaning which it holds out—there is a *raison d'être* for a
thing which guides the flow of phenomena without being explicitly
laid down in any one of them, a sort of operative reason Thus
the intention to look to the left and the fact that the landscape
remains stubbornly fixed in one's gaze bring about the illusion of
movement in the object To the degree that the motivated phenomenon comes into being, an internal relation to the motivating
phenomenon appears, hence, instead of the one merely succeeding
the other, the motivated phenomenon makes the motivating phenomenon explicit and comprehensible, and thus seems to have pre-
existed its own motive Thus the object at a distance and its physical
projection on the retinas explain the disparity of images, and,
through a retrospective illusion, we speak with Malebranche about
a natural geometry of perception We place beforehand within
perception a science constructed upon it, and we lose sight of the
original relationship of motivation, in which distance springs into
existence ahead of any science, not from a judgement of 'the two
images', for these are not numerically distinct, but from the phenomenon of the 'fog', from the forces which reside in this rough outline, which are trying to come to rest and which lead it to the most
determinate form possible To a Cartesian doctrine, these descriptions will never have any philosophic importance they will be
treated as allusions to unreflective states of mind, which, by their
nature, can never become articulate and which, like any form of
psychology, are without truth in the eyes of the understanding. In
order to admit them completely, it would be necessary to show that
in no case can consciousness entirely cease to be what it is in perception, that is, a fact, and that it cannot take full possession of its
operations. The recognition of phenomena, then, implies a theory
of reflection and a new *cogito* [1]

---

[1] See below, Part III Gestalt psychology has adopted a kind of reflection the
theory of which is furnished by Husserl's phenomenology Are we wrong to discern à whole philosophy implicit in the criticism of the 'constancy hypothesis'?
Although we are not here concerned with history, it may be pointed out that the
affinity of Gestalt psychology and phenomenology is equally attested by external
similarities It is no chance occurrence that Kohler should propose, as the task of
psychology, 'phenomenological description' (*Über unbemerkte Empfindungen und
Urteilstäuschungen*, p 70) Or that Koffka, a former disciple of Husserl, should
trace the leading ideas of his psychology back to this influence, and try to show
that the attack on psychologism leaves Gestalt psychology untouched (*Principles
of Gestalt Psychology*, pp 614-83), the Gestalt being, not a mental event of the
type of an impression, but a whole which develops a law of internal coherence.

Or that finally Husserl, in his last period, still further away from logicism, which he had moreover attacked along with psychologism, should have taken up the notion of 'configuration' and even of Gestalt (cf *Die Krisis der europaischen Wissenschaften und die transzendentale Phanomenologie*, I, pp 106, 109) What is true is that the reaction against naturalism and against causal thinking is, in Gestalt psychology, neither consequential, nor radical, as can be seen from the naïve realism of its theory of knowledge (cf *La Structure du Comportement*, p 180) Gestalt psychology cannot see that psychological atomism is only one particular case of a more general prejudice, the prejudice of determinate being or of the world, and that is why it forgets its most valid descriptions when it tries to provide itself with a theoretical framework It is unexceptionable only in the middle regions of reflection When it tries to reflect on its own analysis, it treats consciousness, despite its principles, as a collection of 'forms' This is enough to justify Husserl's criticisms expressly directed against formalism, but applicable to all psychology (*Nachwort zu meiner Ideen*, pp 564 and ff) at a time when he was still distinguishing fact and essence, when he had not yet arrived at the idea of historical constitution, and when, consequently, he was stressing the break, rather than the parallelism, between psychology and phenomenology We have quoted elsewhere (*La Structure du Comportement*, p 280) a text of E Fink restoring the balance. As for the fundamental question, which is that of the transcendental attitude in relation to the natural attitude, it will not be possible to settle it until we reach the last part of this work, where we shall examine the transcendental meaning of time.

4

THE PHENOMENAL FIELD

IT will now be seen in what direction the following chapters will carry their inquiry 'Sense experience'* has become once more a question for us Empiricism had emptied it of all mystery by bringing it down to the possession of a quality. This had been possible only at the price of moving far from the ordinary acceptation of the word. Between sense experience and knowing, common experience establishes a difference which is not that between the quality and the concept This rich notion of sense experience is still to be found in Romantic usage, for example in Herder. It points to an experience in which we are given not 'dead' qualities, but active ones. A wooden wheel placed on the ground is not, *for sight*, the same thing as a wheel bearing a load. A body at rest because no force is being exerted upon it is again for sight not the same thing as a body in which opposing forces are in equilibrium [1] The light of a candle changes its appearance for a child when, after a burn, it stops attracting the child's hand and becomes literally repulsive.[2] The vision is already inhabited by a significance which gives it a function in the spectacle of the world and in our existence. The pure *quale* would be given to us only if the world were a spectacle and one's own body a mechanism with which some impartial mind made itself acquainted [3] Sense experience, on the other hand, invests the quality with vital value, grasping it first in its meaning for us, for that heavy mass which is our body, whence it comes about that it always involves a reference to the body The problem is to understand these strange relationships which are woven between the parts of the landscape, or between it and me as incarnate subject, and through which an object perceived can concentrate in itself a whole scene or become the *imago* of a whole segment of life Sense experience is that vital communication with the world which makes it present as a

* The original French word is 'le sentir' (Translator's note).

[1] Koffka *Perception, an Introduction to the Gestalt Theory*, pp 558-9
[2] Id , *Mental Development*, p 138
[3] Scheler, *Die Wissenformen und die Gesellschaft*, p. 408.

familiar setting of our life It is to it that the perceived object and the perceiving subject owe their thickness It is the intentional tissue which the effort to know will try to take apart With the problem of sense experience, we rediscover that of association and passivity They have ceased to be problematical because the classical philosophies put themselves either below or above them, giving them everything or nothing sometimes association was understood as a mere *de facto* co-existence, sometimes derived from an intellectual construction; sometimes passivity was imported from things into the mind, and sometimes analytical reflection would find in it an activity of understanding. Whereas these notions take on their full meaning if sense experience is distinguished from quality· then association, or rather 'affinity', in the Kantian sense, is the central phenomenon of perceptual life, since it is the constitution, without any ideal model, of a significant grouping The distinction between the perceptual life and the concept, between passivity and spontaneity is no longer abolished by analytical reflection, since we are no longer forced by the atomism of sensation to look to some connecting activity for our principle of all co-ordination Finally, after sense experience, understanding also needs to be redefined, since the general connective function ultimately attributed to it by Kantianism is now spread over the whole intentional life and no longer suffices to distinguish it. We shall try to bring out in relation to perception, both the instinctive substructure and the superstructures erected upon it by the exercise of intelligence As Cassirer puts it, by mutilating perception from above, empiricism mutilated it from below too.[1] the impression is as devoid of instinctive and affective meaning as of ideal significance. One might add that mutilating perception from below, treating it immediately as knowledge and forgetting its existential content, amounts to mutilating it from above, since it involves taking for granted and passing over in silence the decisive moment in perception the upsurge of a *true* and *accurate* world Reflection will be sure of having precisely located the centre of the phenomenon if it is equally capable of bringing to light its vital inherence and its rational intention.

So, 'sensation' and 'judgement' have together lost their apparent clearness we have observed that they were clear only as long as the prejudice in favour of the world was maintained. As soon as one tried by means of them, to picture consciousness in the process of perceiving, to revive the forgotten perceptual experience, and to relate them to it, they were found to be inconceivable By dint of making these difficulties more explicit, we were drawn implicitly into a new kind of analysis, into a new dimension in which they were

[1] Cassirer, *Philosophie der symbolischen Formen*, T III, *Phänomenologie der Erkenntnis*, pp 77-8

destined to disappear. The criticism of the constancy hypothesis and more generally the reduction of the idea of 'the world' opened up a *phenomenal field* which now has to be more accurately circumscribed, and suggested the rediscovery of a direct experience which must be, at least provisionally, assigned its place in relation to scientific knowledge, psychological and philosophical reflection.

Science and philosophy have for centuries been sustained by unquestioning faith in perception Perception opens a window on to things This means that it is directed, quasi-teleologically, towards a *truth in itself* in which the reason underlying all appearances is to be found. The tacit thesis of perception is that at every instant experience can be co-ordinated with that of the previous instant and that of the following, and my perspective with that of other consciousnesses—that all contradictions can be removed, that monadic and intersubjective experience is one unbroken text—that what is now indeterminate for me could become determinate for a more complete knowledge, which is as it were realized in advance in the thing, or rather which is the thing itself. Science has first been merely the sequel or amplification of the process which constitutes perceived things Just as the thing is the invariant of all sensory fields and of all individual perceptual fields, so the scientific concept is the means of fixing and objectifying phenomena Science defined a theoretical state of bodies not subject to the action of any force, and *ipso facto* defined force, reconstituting with the aid of these ideal components the processes actually observed. It established statistically the chemical properties of pure bodies, deducing from these those of empirical bodies, and seeming thus to hold the plan of creation or in any case to have found a reason immanent in the world The notion of geometrical space, indifferent to its contents, that of pure movement which does not by itself affect the properties of the object, provided phenomena with a setting of inert existence in which each event could be related to physical conditions responsible for the changes occurring, and therefore contributed to this freezing of being which appeared to be the task of physics. In thus developing the concept of the thing, scientific knowledge was not aware that it was working on a presupposition Precisely because perception, in its vital implications and prior to any theoretical thought, is presented as perception of a being, it was not considered necessary for reflection to undertake a genealogy of being, and it was therefore confined to seeking the conditions which make being possible Even if one took account of the transformations of determinant consciousness,[1] even if it were conceded that the constitution of the object is never completed, there was nothing to add to what

[1] As L Brunschvicg does

science said of it, the natural object remained an ideal unity for us and, in the famous words of Lachelier, a network of general properties It was no use denying any ontological value to the principles of science and leaving them with only a methodical value,[1] for this reservation made no essential change as far as philosophy was concerned, since the sole conceivable being remained defined by scientific method The living body, under these circumstances, could not escape the determinations which alone made the object into an object and without which it would have had no place in the system of experience. The value predicates which the reflecting judgement confers upon it had to be sustained, in being, by a foundation of physico-chemical properties In ordinary experience we find a fittingness and a meaningful relationship between the gesture, the smile and the tone of a speaker But this reciprocal relationship of expression which presents the human body as the outward manifestation of a certain manner of being-in-the-world, had, for mechanistic physiology, to be resolved into a series of causal relations.

It was necessary to link to centripetal conditions the centrifugal phenomenon of expression, reduce to third person processes that particular way of dealing with the world which we know as behaviour, bring experience down to the level of physical nature and convert the living body into an interiorless thing The emotional and practical attitudes of the living subject in relation to the world were, then, incorporated into a psycho-physiological mechanism. Every evaluation had to be the outcome of a transfer whereby complex situations became capable of awakening elementary impressions of pleasure and pain, impressions bound up, in turn, with nervous processes The impelling intentions of the living creature were converted into objective movements to the will only an instantaneous fiat was allowed, the execution of the act being entirely given over to a nervous mechanism. Sense experience, thus detached from the affective and motor functions, became the mere reception of a quality, and physiologists thought they could follow, from the point of reception to the nervous centres, the projection of the external world in the living body The latter, thus transformed, ceased to be my body, the visible expression of a concrete Ego, and became one object among all others. Conversely, the body of another person could not appear to me as encasing another Ego It was merely a machine, and the perception of the other could not really be *of the other*, since it resulted from an inference and therefore placed behind the automaton no more than a consciousness in general, a transcendent cause and not an inhabitant of his movements So we no longer had a grouping of factors constituting the self co-existing

[1] Cf for example, *L'Expérience humaine et la Causalité physique*, p 536.

55

in a world. The whole concrete content of 'psychic states' resulting, according to the laws of psychophysiology and psychology, from a universal determinism, was integrated into the *in-itself* There was no longer any real *for-itself* other than the thought of the scientist which perceives the system and which alone ceases to occupy any place in it. Thus, while the living body became an exterior without interior, subjectivity became an interior without exterior, an impartial spectator. The naturalism of science and the spiritualism of the universal constituting subject, to which reflection on science led, had this in common, that they levelled out experience in face of the constituting I, the empirical selves are objects. The empirical Self is a hybrid notion, a mixture of in-itself and for-itself, to which reflective philosophy could give no status In so far as it has a concrete content it is inserted in the system of experience and is therefore not a subject; in so far as it *is* a subject, it is empty and resolves itself into the transcendental subject The ideality of the object, the objectification of the living body, the placing of spirit in an axiological dimension having no common measure with nature, such is the transparent philosophy arrived at by pushing further along the route of knowledge opened up by perception. It could be held that perception is an incipient science, science a methodical and complete perception,[1] since science was merely following uncritically the ideal of knowledge set up by the perceived thing.

Now this philosophy is collapsing before our eyes. The natural object was the first to disappear and physics has itself recognized the limits of its categories by demanding a recasting and blending of the pure concepts which it had adopted. For its part the organism presents physico-chemical analysis not with the practical difficulties of a complex object, but with the theoretical difficulty of a meaningful being [2] In more general terms the idea of a universe of thought or a universe of values, in which all thinking lives come into contact and are reconciled, is called into question. Nature is *not* in itself geometrical, and it appears so only to a careful observer who contents himself with macrocosmic data. Human society is *not* a community of reasonable minds, and only in fortunate countries where a biological and economic balance has locally and temporarily been truck has such a conception of it been possible. The experience of haos, both on the speculative and the other level, prompts us to see itionalism in a historical perspective which it set itself on principle) avoid, to seek a philosophy which explains the upsurge of reason i a world not of its making and to prepare the substructure of

[1] Cf. for example Alain, *Quatre-vingt-un chapitres sur l'Esprit et les Passions,*) 19, and Brunschvicg, *L'Expérience humaine et la causalité physique,* p 468
[2] Cf *La Structure du Comportement,* and below, First Part

living experience without which reason and liberty are emptied of their content and wither away We shall no longer hold that perception is incipient science, but conversely that classical science is a form of perception which loses sight of its origins and believes itself complete. The first philosophical act would appear to be to return to the world of actual experience which is prior to the objective world, since it is in it that we shall be able to grasp the theoretical basis no less than the limits of that objective world, restore to things their concrete physiognomy, to organisms their individual ways of dealing with the world, and to subjectivity its inherence in history. Our task will be, moreover, to rediscover phenomena, the layer of living experience through which other people and things are first given to us, the system 'Self-others-things' as it comes into being, to re-awaken perception and foil its trick of allowing us to forget it as a fact and as perception in the interest of the object which it presents to us and of the rational tradition to which it gives rise

This phenomenal field is not an 'inner world', the 'phenomenon' is not a 'state of consciousness', or a 'mental fact', and the experience of phenomena is not an act of introspection or an intuition in Bergson's sense It has long been the practice to define the object of psychology by saying that it was 'without extension' and 'accessible to one person only', with the result that this peculiar object could be grasped only by means of a special kind of act, 'internal perception' or introspection, in which subject and object were mingled and knowledge achieved by an act of coinciding The return to the 'immediate data of consciousness' became therefore a hopeless enterprise since the philosophical scrutiny was trying to *be* what it could not, in principle, *see* The difficulty was not only to destroy the prejudice of the exterior, as all philosophies urge the beginner to do, or to describe the mind in a language made for representing things It was much more fundamental, since interiority, defined by the impression, by its nature evaded every attempt to express it It was not only the imparting of philosophical intuitions to others which became difficult—or rather reduced itself to a sort of incantation designed to induce in them experiences comparable to the philosopher's—but the philosopher himself could not be clearly aware of *what* he saw in the instant, since he would have had to think it, that is fix and distort it. The immediate was therefore a lonely, blind and mute life. The return to the phenomenal presents none of these peculiarities The sensible configuration of an object or a gesture, which the criticism of the constancy hypothesis brings before our eyes, is not grasped in some inexpressible coincidence, it 'is understood' through a sort of act of appropriation which we all experience when we say that we have 'found' the rabbit in the foliage

57

of a puzzle, or that we have 'caught' a slight gesture. Once the prejudice of sensation has been banished, a face, a signature, a form of behaviour cease to be mere 'visual data' whose psychological meaning is to be sought in our inner experience, and the mental life of others becomes an immediate object, a whole charged with immanent meaning More generally it is the very notion of the immediate which is transformed: henceforth the immediate is no longer the impression, the object which is one with the subject, but the meaning, the structure, the spontaneous arrangement of parts My own 'mental life' is given to me in precisely the same way, since the criticism of the constancy hypothesis teaches me to recognize the articulation and melodic unity of my behaviour as original data of inner experience, and since introspection, when brought down to its positive content, consists equally in making the immanent meaning of any behaviour explicit.[1] Thus what we discover by going beyond the prejudice of the objective world is not an occult inner world. Nor is this world of living experience completely closed to naive consciousness, as is Bergson's interiority In criticizing the constancy hypothesis and in laying bare phenomena, the psychologist, it is true, runs counter to the natural direction of the process of knowing, which goes blindly through the operations of perception straight on to their teleological results. Nothing is more difficult than to know precisely *what we see* 'There is in natural intuition a sort of "crypto-mechanism" which we have to break in order to reach phenomenal being'[2] or again a dialectic whereby perception hides itself from itself. But although it is of the essence of consciousness to forget its own phenomena thus enabling 'things' to be constituted, this forgetfulness is not mere absence, it is the absence of something which consciousness could bring into its presence in other words consciousness can forget phenomena only because it can recall them, it neglects them in favour of things only because they are the cradle of things For example they are never completely unknown to scientific consciousness, which borrows all its models from the structures of living experience, it simply does not 'thematize' them, or make explicit the horizons of perceptual consciousness surrounding it to whose concrete relationships it tries to give objective expression. Experience of phenomena is not, then, like Bergsonian intuition, that of a reality of which we are ignorant and leading to which there is no methodical bridge—it is the making explicit or bringing to light of the prescientific life of consciousness which alone

---

[1] We shall, consequently, in the following chapters, resort indifferently to the internal experience of our perception and to the 'external' experience of perceiving subjects

[2] Scheler, *Idole der Selbsterkenntnis*, p 106

endows scientific operations with meaning and to which these latter always refer back It is not an irrational conversion, but an intentional analysis.

If, as we see, phenomenological psychology is distinguished in all its characteristics from introspective psychology, it is because it is different in basic principle Introspective psychology detected, on the perimeter of the physical world, a zone of consciousness in which physical concepts are no longer valid, but the psychologist still believed consciousness to be no more than a sector of being, and he decided to explore this sector as the physicist explores his. He tried to describe the givens of consciousness but without putting into question the absolute existence of the world surrounding it In company with the scientist and common sense, he presupposed the objective world as the logical framework of all his descriptions, and as the setting of his thought He was unaware that this presupposition dominated the meaning given to the word 'being', forcing it to bring consciousness into existence under the name of 'psychic fact', and thus diverting it from a true grasp of consciousness or from truly immediate experience, and stultifying the many precautions taken to avoid distorting the 'interior' This is what happened to empiricism when it replaced the physical world by a world of inner events. It is again what happens to Bergson precisely when he contrasts 'multiplicity of fusion' and 'multiplicity of juxtaposition'. For it is here still a question of two modes of being. All that has happened is that mechanical energy has been replaced by spiritual, the discontinuous being of empiricism by being of a fluid kind, but of which we can say that *it* flows, describing it in the third person. By taking the *Gestalt* as the theme of his reflection, the psychologist breaks with psychologism, since the meaning, connection and 'truth' of the percept no longer arise from the fortuitous coming together of our sensations as they are given to us by our psycho-physiological nature, but determine the spatial and qualitative values of these sensations, and *are* their irreducible configuration.[1] It follows that the transcendental attitude is already implied in the descriptions of the psychologist, in so far as they are faithful ones Consciousness as an object of study presents the peculiarity of not being analysable, even naively, without carrying us beyond common sense postulates If, for example. we set out to create a positive psychology of perception, while still allowing consciousness to be enclosed in the body, and through it suffer the action of a world in itself, we are led to describe the object and the world as they appear to consciousness, and in this way to inquire whether this immediately present world, the only one we know, may not also be the only one of which there is reason to

[1] Cf *La Structure du Comportement*, pp 106–19 and 261

speak A psychology is always brought face to face with the problem of the constitution of the world

Psychological reflection, once begun, then, outruns itself through its own momentum Having recognized the originality of phenomena in relation to the objective world, since it is through them that the objective world is known to us, it is led to integrate with them every possible object and to try to find out how that object is constituted through them At the same time the phenomenal field becomes a transcendental field. Since it is now the universal focus of knowledge, consciousness definitely ceases to be a particular region of being, a certain collection of 'mental' contents, it no longer resides or is no longer confined within the domain of 'forms' which psychological reflection had first recognized, but the forms, like all things, exist for it It can no longer be a question of describing the world of living experience which it carries within itself like some opaque datum, it has to be constituted. The process of making explicit, which had laid bare the 'lived-through' world which is prior to the objective one, is put into operation upon the 'lived-through' world itself, thus revealing, prior to the phenomenal field, the transcendental field. The system 'self-others-world' is in its turn taken as an object of analysis and it is now a matter of awakening the thoughts which constitute other people, myself as individual subject and the world as a pole of my perception. This new 'reduction' would then recognize only one true subject, the thinking Ego This move from *naturata* to *naturans*, from constituted to constituting, would complete the thematizing begun by psychology and would leave nothing implicit or tacitly accepted in my knowledge. It would enable me to take complete possession of my experience, thus equating thinking and thought Such is the ordinary perspective of a transcendental philosophy, and also, to all appearances at least, the programme of a transcendental phenomenology.[1] Now the phenomenal field as we have revealed it in this chapter, places a fundamental difficulty in the way of any attempt to make experience directly and totally explicit It is true that psychologism has been left behind, that the meaning and structure of the percept are for us no longer the mere outcome of psycho-physiological events, that rationality is no longer a fortunate accident bringing together dispersed sensations, and that the Gestalt is recognized as primary But although the Gestalt may be expressible in terms of some internal law, this law must not be considered as a model on which the phenomena of structure are built up Their appearance is not the external unfolding of a pre-existing reason It is not *because* the

[1] It is set forth in these terms in most of Husserl's works, even in those published during his last period

'form' produces a certain state of equilibrium, solving a problem of maximum coherence and, in the Kantian sense, making a world possible, that it enjoys a privileged place in our perception; it is the very appearance of the world and not the condition of its possibility, it is the birth of a norm and is not realized according to a norm, it is the identity of the external and the internal and not the projection of the internal in the external. Although, then, it is not the outcome of some circulation of mental states in themselves, neither is it an idea. The Gestalt of a circle is not its mathematical law but its physiognomy. The recognition of phenomena as an original order is a condemnation of empiricism as an *explanation* of order and reason in terms of a coming together of facts and of natural accidents, but it leaves reason and order themselves with the character of facticity. If a universal constituting consciousness were possible, the opacity of the fact would disappear. If then we want reflection to maintain, in the object on which it bears, its descriptive characteristics, and thoroughly to understand that object, we must not consider it as a mere return to a universal reason and see it as anticipated in unreflective experience, we must regard it as a creative operation which itself participates in the facticity of that experience. That is why phenomenology, alone of all philosophies, talks about a transcendental *field*. This word indicates that reflection never holds, arrayed and objectified before its gaze, the whole world and the plurality of monads, and that its view is never other than partial and of limited power. It is also why phenomenology is phenomenology, that is, a study of the *advent* of being to consciousness, instead of presuming its possibility as given in advance. It is striking how transcendental philosophies of the classical type never question the possibility of effecting the complete disclosure which they always assume *done somewhere* It is enough for them that it should be necessary, and in this way they judge what is by what ought to be, by what the idea of knowledge requires. In fact, the thinking Ego can never abolish its inherence in an individual subject, which knows all things in a particular perspective Reflection can never make me stop seeing the sun two hundred yards away on a misty day, or seeing it 'rise' and 'set', or thinking with the cultural apparatus with which my education, my previous efforts, my personal history, have provided me. I never actually collect together, or call up simultaneously. all the primary thoughts which contribute to my perception or to my present conviction A critical philosophy attaches in the last analysis no importance to this resistance offered by passivity, as if it were not necessary to become the transcendental subject in order to have the right to affirm it. It tacitly assumes, consequently, that the philosopher's thinking is not conditioned by any situation.

Staiting from the spectacle of the world, which is that of a nature open to a plurality of thinking subjects, it looks for the conditions which make possible this unique world presented to a number of empirical selves, and finds it in a transcendental ego in which they participate without dividing it up, because it is not a Being, but a Unity or a Value This is why the problem of the knowledge of other people is never posed in Kantian philosophy: the transcendental ego which it discusses is just as much other people's as mine, analysis is from the start located outside me, and has nothing to do but to determine the general conditions which make possible a world for an ego—myself or others equally—and so it never comes up against the question· *who is thinking?* If on the other hand contemporary philosophy takes this as its main theme, and if other people become a problem for it, it is because it is trying to achieve a more radical self-discovery Reflection cannot be thorough-going, or bring a complete elucidation of its object, if it does not arrive at awareness of itself as well as of its results We must not only adopt a reflective attitude, in an impregnable *Cogito*, but furthermore reflect on this reflection, understand the natural situation which it is conscious of succeeding and which is therefore part of its definition, not merely practise philosophy, but realize the transformation which it brings with it in the spectacle of the world and in our existence Only on this condition can philosophical knowledge become absolute knowledge, and cease to be a speciality or a technique. So there will be no assertion of an absolute Unity, all the less doubtful for not having to come into Being The core of philosophy is no longer an autonomous transcendental subjectivity, to be found everywheie and nowhere it lies in the perpetual beginning of reflection, at the point where an individual life begins to reflect on itself Reflection is truly reflection only if it is not carried outside itself, only if it knows itself as reflection-on-an-unreflective-expeiience, and consequently as a change in structure of our existence. We earlier attacked Bergsonian intuitionism and introspection for seeking to know by coinciding. But at the opposite extremity of philosophy, in the notion of a universal constituting consciousness, we encounter an exactly corresponding mistake Bergson's mistake consists in believing that the thinking subject can become fused with the object thought about, and that knowledge can swell and be incorporated into being The mistake of reflective philosophies is to believe that the thinking subject can absorb into its thinking or appropriate without remainder the object of its thought, that our being can be brought down to our knowledge As thinking subject we are never the unreflective subject that we seek to know, but neither can we become wholly consciousness, or make ourselves into the transcendental consciousness If we were consciousness, we would have to have before us the world, our history and perceived objects in their uniqueness as systems of transparent relationships Now even when we are not dealing with psychology, when we try to comprehend, in direct reflection and without the help of the varied associations of inductive thought, what a perceived movement, or a circle, are, we can elucidate this singular fact only by varying it somewhat through the agency of imagination, and then fastening our thought upon the invariable element of this mental experience We can get through to the individual only by the hybrid procedure of finding an *example*, that is, by stripping it of its facticity. Thus it is questionable whether thought can ever quite cease to be inductive, and whether it can assimilate any experience to the point of taking up and appropriating its whole texture. A philosophy becomes transcendental, or radical, not by taking its place in absolute consciousness without mentioning the ways by which this is reached, but by considering itself as a problem, not by postulating a knowledge rendered totally explicit, but by recognizing as the fundamental philosophic problem this *presumption* on reason's part.

That is why we had to begin our examination of perception with psychological considerations If we had not done so, we would not have understood the whole meaning of the transcendental problem, since we would not, starting from the natural attitude, have methodically followed the procedures which lead to it We had to frequent the phenomenal field and become acquainted, through psychological descriptions, with the subject of phenomena, if we were to avoid placing ourselves from the start, as does reflexive philosophy, in a transcendental dimension assumed to be eternally given, thus by-passing the whole problem of constitution. We could not begin, however, our psychological description without suggesting that once purged of all psychologism it can become a philosophical method. In order to revive perceptual experience buried under its own results, it would not have been enough to present descriptions of them which might possibly not have been understood, we had to establish by philosophical references and anticipations the point of view from which they might appear true Thus we could begin neither without psychology nor with psychology alone. Experience anticipates a philosophy and philosophy is merely an elucidated experience But now that the phenomenal field has been sufficiently circumscribed, let us enter this ambiguous domain and let us make sure of our first steps as far as the psychologist is concerned, until the psychologist's self-scrutiny leads us, by way of a second-order reflection, to the phenomenon of the phenomenon, and decisively transforms the phenomenal field into a transcendental one

PART ONE

The Body

Experience and objective thought The problem of the body

Our perception ends in objects, and the object once constituted, appears as the reason for all the experiences of it which we have had or could have For example, I see the next-door house from a certain angle, but it would be seen differently from the right bank of the Seine, or from the inside, or again from an aeroplane· the house *itself* is none of these appearances, it is, as Leibnitz said, the flat projection of these perspectives and of all possible perspectives, that is, the perspectiveless position from which all can be derived, the house seen from nowhere But what do these words mean? Is not to see always to see from somewhere? To say that the house itself is seen from nowhere is surely to say that it is invisible' Yet when I say that I see the house with my own eyes, I am saying something that cannot be challenged: I do not mean that my retina and crystalline lens, my eyes as material organs, go into action and cause me to see it with only myself to consult, I can know nothing about this I am trying to express in this way a certain manner of approaching the object, the 'gaze' in short, which is as indubitable as my own thought, as directly known by me. We must try to understand how vision can be brought into being from somewhere without being enclosed in its perspective.

To see an object is either to have it on the fringe of the visual field and be able to concentrate on it, or else respond to this summons by actually concentrating upon it When I do concentrate my eyes on it, I become anchored in it, but this coming to rest of the gaze is merely a modality of its movement: I continue inside one object the exploration which earlier hovered over them all, and in one movement I close up the landscape and open the object The two operations do not fortuitously coincide it is not the contingent aspects of my bodily make-up, for example the retinal structure, which force me to see my surroundings vaguely if I want to see the object clearly Even if I knew nothing of rods and cones, I should realize that it is necessary to put the surroundings in abeyance the better to see the object, and to lose in background what one gains in focal figure, because to look at the object is to plunge oneself into it, and because objects form a system in which one cannot show itself without concealing others More precisely, the inner horizon of an object cannot become an object without the surrounding objects' becoming a horizon, and so vision is an act with two facets For I do not identify the detailed object which I now have with that over which my gaze ran a few minutes ago, by expressly comparing these details with a memory of my first general view When, in a film, the camera is trained on an object and moves nearer to it to give a close-up view, we can *remember* that we are being shown the ash tray or an actor's hand, we do not actually identify it This is because the screen has no horizons. In normal vision, on the other hand, I direct my gaze upon a sector of the landscape, which comes to life and is disclosed, while the other objects recede into the periphery and become dormant, while, however, not ceasing to be there. Now, with them, I have at my disposal their horizons, in which there is implied, as a marginal view, the object on which my eyes at present fall. The horizon, then, is what guarantees the identity of the object throughout the exploration; it is the correlative of the impending power which my gaze retains over the objects which it has just surveyed, and which it already has over the fresh details which it is about to discover No distinct memory and no explicit conjecture could fill this rôle· they would give only a probable synthesis, whereas my perception presents itself as actual The object-horizon structure, or the perspective, is no obstacle to me when I want to see the object: for just as it is the means whereby objects are distinguished from each other, it is also the means whereby they are disclosed To see is to enter a universe of beings which *display themselves*, and they would not do this if they could not be hidden behind each other or behind me In other words· to look at an object is to inhabit it, and from this habitation to grasp all things in terms of the aspect which they present to it. But in so far as I see those things too, they remain abodes open to my gaze, and, being potentially lodged in them, I already perceive from various angles the central object of my present vision Thus every object is the mirror of all others When I look at the lamp on my table, I attribute to it not only the qualities visible from where I am, but also those which the chimney, the walls, the table can 'see', but back of my lamp is nothing but the face which it 'shows' to the chimney I can therefore see an object in so far as objects form a system or a world, and in so far as each one treats the others round it as spectators of its hidden aspects and as guarantee of the permanence of those aspects Any seeing of an object by me is instantaneously reiterated among all those objects in the world which are apprehended as co-existent, because each of them is all that the others 'see' of it. Our previous formula must therefore be modified; the house itself is not the house seen from nowhere, but the house seen from everywhere. The completed object is translucent, being shot through from all sides by an infinite number of present scrutinies which intersect in its depths leaving nothing hidden.

What we have just said about the spatial perspective could equally be said about the temporal. If I contemplate the house attentively and with no thought in my mind, it has something eternal about it, and an atmosphere of torpor seems to be generated by it. It is true that I see it from a certain point in my 'duration', but it is the same house that I saw yesterday when it was a day younger, it is the same house that either an old man or a child might behold. It is true, moreover, that age and change affect it, but even if it should collapse tomorrow, it will remain for ever true that it existed today: each moment of time calls all the others to witness, it shows by its advent 'how things were meant to turn out' and 'how it will all finish', each present permanently underpins a point of time which calls for recognition from all the others, so that the object is seen at all times as it is seen from all directions and by the same means, namely the structure imposed by a horizon. The present still holds on to the immediate past without positing it as an object, and since the immediate past similarly holds its immediate predecessor, past time is wholly collected up and grasped in the present. The same is true of the imminent future which will also have its horizon of imminence. But with my immediate past I have also the horizon of futurity which surrounded it, and thus I have my actual present seen as the future of that past. With the imminent future, I have the horizon of past which will surround it, and therefore my actual present as the past of that future. Thus, through the double horizon of retention and protention, my present may cease to be a factual present quickly carried away and abolished by the flow of duration, and become a fixed and identifiable point in objective time.

But, once more, my human gaze never *posits* more than one facet of the object, even though by means of horizons it is directed towards all the others. It can never come up against previous appearances or those presented to other people otherwise than through the intermediary of time and language. If I conceive in the image of my own gaze those others which, converging from all directions, explore every corner of the house and define it, I have still only a harmonious and indefinite set of views of the object, but not the object in its plenitude. In the same way, although my present draws into itself time past and time to come, it possesses them only in intention, and even if, for example, the consciousness of my past which I now have seems to me to cover exactly the past as it was, the past which I claim

69

to recapture is not the real past, but my past as I now see it, perhaps
after altering it. Similarly in the future I may have a mistaken idea
about the present which I now experience. Thus the synthesis of
horizons is no more than a presumptive synthesis, operating with
certainty and precision only in the immediate vicinity of the object.
The remoter surrounding is no longer within my grasp, it is no
longer composed of still discernible objects or memories, it is an
anonymous horizon now incapable of bringing any precise testimony, and leaving the object as incomplete and open as it is indeed,
in perceptual experience. Through this opening, indeed, the sub-
- stantiality of the object slips away. If it is to reach perfect density, in
other words if there is to be an absolute object, it will have to consist of an infinite number of different perspectives compressed into a
strict co-existence, and to be presented as it were to a host of eyes all
engaged in one concerted act of seeing. The house *has its* water
pipes, *its* floor, perhaps its cracks which are insidiously spreading in
the thickness of its ceilings. We never see them, but it *has them*
along with its chimneys and windows which we can see. We shall
forget our present perception of the house: every time we are able to
compare our memories with the objects to which they refer, we are
surprised, even allowing for other sources of error, at the changes
which they owe to their own duration. But we still believe that there
is a truth about the past; we base our memory on the world's vast
Memory, in which the house has its place as it really was on that day,
and which guarantees its *being* at this moment. Taken in itself—and
as an object it demands to be taken thus—the object has nothing
cryptic about it, it is completely displayed and its parts co-exist while
our gaze runs from one to another, its present does not cancel its
past, nor will its future cancel its present. The positing of the object,
therefore makes us go beyond the limits of our actual experience
which is brought up against and halted by an alien being, with the
result that finally experience believes that it extracts all its own
teaching from the object. It is this *ek-stase**** of experience which
causes all perception to be perception of something.

Obsessed with being, and forgetful of the perspectivism of my
experience, I henceforth treat it as an object and deduce it from a
relationship between objects. I regard my body, which is my point of
view upon the world, as one of the objects of that world. My recent
awareness of my gaze as a means of knowledge I now repress, and
treat my eyes as bits of matter. They then take their place in the same
objective space in which I am trying to situate the external object and

* Active transcendence of the subject in relation to the world. The author uses
either the French word *extase*, or Heidegger's form *ek-stase*. The latter is the one
used throughout this translation (Translator's note)

I believe that I am producing the perceived perspective by the projection of the objects on my retina In the same way I treat my own perceptual history as a result of my relationships with the objective world, my present, which is my point of view on time, becomes one moment of time among all the others, my duration a reflection or abstract aspect of universal time, as my body is a mode of objective space. In the same way, finally, if the objects which surround the house or which are found in it remained what they are in perceptual experience, that is, acts of seeing conditioned by a certain perspective, the house would not be posited as an autonomous being Thus the positing of one single object, in the full sense, demands the compositive bringing into being of all these experiences in one act of manifold creation Therein it exceeds perceptual experience and the synthesis of horizons—as the notion of a *universe*, that is to say, a completed and explicit totality, in which the relationships are those of reciprocal determination, exceeds that of a *world*, or an open and indefinite multiplicity of relationships which are of reciprocal implication [1] I detach myself from my experience and pass to the *idea* Like the object, the idea purports to be the same for everybody, valid in all times and places, and the individuation of an object in an objective point of time and space finally appears as the expression of a universal positing power.[2] I am no longer concerned with my body, nor with time, nor with the world, as I experience them in antepredicative knowledge, in the inner communion that I have with them I now refer to my body only as an idea, to the universe as idea, to the idea of space and the idea of time. Thus 'objective' thought (in Kierkegaard's sense) is formed—being that of common sense and of science—which finally causes us to lose contact with perceptual experience, of which it is nevertheless the outcome and the natural sequel The whole life of consciousness is characterized by the tendency to posit objects, since it is consciousness, that is to say self-knowledge, only in so far as it takes hold of itself and draws itself together in an identifiable object And yet the absolute positing of a single object is the death of consciousness, since it congeals the whole of existence, as a crystal placed in a solution suddenly crystallizes it

We cannot remain in this dilemma of having to fail to understand either the subject or the object We must discover the origin of the object at the very centre of our experience, we must describe the emergence of being and we must understand how, paradoxically, there is *for us* an *in-itself* In order not to prejudge the issue, we shall

[1] Husserl, *Umsturz der kopernikanischen Lehre die Erde als Ur-Arche bewegt sich nicht* (unpublished)
[2] 'I understand by the sole power of judging, which resides in my mind, what I thought I saw with my eyes.' *2nd Meditation*, AT, IX, p 25

take objective thought on its own terms and not ask it any questions which it does not ask itself If we are led to rediscover experience behind it, this shift of ground will be attributable only to the difficulties which objective thought itself raises. Let us consider it then at work in the constitution of our body as object, since this is a crucial moment in the genesis of the objective world. It will be seen that one's own body evades, even within science itself, the treatment to which it is intended to subject it And since the genesis of the objective body is only a moment in the constitution of the object, the body, by withdrawing from the objective world, will carry with it the intentional threads linking it to its surrounding and finally reveal to us the perceiving subject as the perceived world.

I

THE BODY AS OBJECT AND MECHANISTIC PHYSIOLOGY

THE definition of the object is, as we have seen, that it exists *partes extra partes*, and that consequently it acknowledges between its parts, or between itself and other objects only external and mechanical relationships, whether in the narrow sense of motion received and transmitted, or in the wider sense of the relation of function to variable. Where it was desired to insert the organism in the universe of objects and thereby close off that universe, it was necessary to translate the functioning of the body into the language of the *in-itself* and discover, beneath behaviour, the linear dependence of stimulus and receptor, receptor and *Empfinder*.[1] It was of course realized that in the circuit of behaviour new particular forms emerge, and the theory of specific nervous energy, for example, certainly endowed the organism with the power of transforming the physical world. But in fact it attributed to the nervous systems the occult power of creating the different structures of our experience, and whereas sight, touch and hearing are so many ways of gaining access to the object, these structures found themselves transformed into compact qualities derived from the local distinction between the organs used. Thus the relationship between stimulus and perception could remain clear and objective, and the psycho-physical event was of the same kind as the causal relations obtaining 'in the world' Modern physiology no longer has recourse to these pretences It no longer links the different qualities of one and the same sense, and the data of different senses, to distinct material instruments In reality injuries to centres and even to conductors are not translated into the loss of certain qualities of sensation or of certain sensory data, but into loss of differentiation in the function We have already discussed this: wherever the seat of the injury in the sensory routes

[1] Cf *La Structure du Comportement*, Chap. I and II.

73

and whatever its origin, one observes, for example, a decay of sensitivity to colour, at the beginning, all colours are affected, their basic shade remaining the same, but their saturation decreasing, then the spectrum is simplified and reduced to four colours yellow, green, blue, crimson, and indeed all short-wave colours tend towards a kind of blue, all long-wave colours towards a kind of yellow, vision being liable, moreover, to vary from moment to moment, according to degree of fatigue. Finally a monochrome stage in grey is reached, although favourable conditions (contrast, long exposure) may momentarily bring back dichromic sight.[1] The progress of the lesion in the nervous tissue does not, therefore, destroy, one after another, ready-made sensory contents, but makes the active differentiation of stimuli, which appears to be the essential function of the nervous system, increasingly unreliable In the same way, in the case of non-cortical injury to the sense of touch, if certain contents (temperatures) are more easily destroyed and are the first to disappear, this is not because a determinate region, lost to the patient, enables us to feel heat and cold, since the specific sensation will be restored if a sufficiently extensive stimulus is applied;[2] it is rather that the sensation succeeds in taking its typical form only under a more energetic stimulus. Central lesions seem to leave qualities intact, on the other hand they modify the spatial organization of data and the perception of objects This is what had led to the belief in specialized gnosic centres for the localization and interpretation of qualities In fact, modern research shows that central lesions have the effect in most cases of raising the chronaxies, which are increased to two or three times their normal strength in the patient. The excitation produces its effects more slowly, these survive longer, and the tactile perception of roughness, for example, is jeopardized in so far as it presupposes a succession of circumscribed impressions or a precise consciousness of the different positions of the hand [3] The vague localization of the stimulus is not explained by the destruction of a localizing centre, but by the reduction to a uniform level of sensations, which are no longer capable of organizing themselves into a stable grouping in which each of them receives a univocal value and is translated into consciousness only by a limited change [4] Thus the excitations of one and the same sense differ less by reason of the material instrument which they use than in the way in which the elementary stimuli are spontaneously organized among themselves, and this organization is the crucial factor both at the level of sensible 'qualities' and at that of perception It is this, and not the specific energy of the nervous apparatus examined, which causes an

[1] J Stein, *Pathologie der Wahrnehmung*, p 365.
[2] Ibid , p 358   [3] Ibid , pp 360-1.   [4] Ibid., p. 362.

excitant to give rise to a tactile or thermic sensation If a given area of skin is several times stimulated with a hair, the first perceptions are clearly distinguished and localized each time at the same point As the stimulus is repeated, the localization becomes less precise, perception widens in space, while at the same time the sensation ceases to be specific· it is no longer a contact, but a feeling of burning, at one moment cold and at the next hot Later still the patient thinks the stimulus is moving and describing a circle on his skin Finally nothing more is felt [1] It follows that the 'sensible quality', the spatial limits set to the percept, and even the presence or absence of a perception, are not *de facto* effects of the situation outside the organism, but represent the way in which it meets stimulation and is related to it. An excitation is not perceived when it strikes a sensory organ which is not 'attuned' to it.[2] The function of the organism in receiving stimuli is, so to speak, to 'conceive' a certain form of excitation [3] The 'psychophysical event' is therefore no longer of the type of 'worldly' causality, the brain becomes the seat of a process of 'patterning' which intervenes even before the cortical stage, and which, from the moment the nervous system comes into play, confuses the relations of stimulus to organism The excitation is seized and reorganized by transversal functions which make it *resemble* the perception which it is *about to* arouse I cannot envisage this form which is traced out in the nervous system, this exhibiting of a structure, as a set of processes in the third person, as the transmission of movement or as the determination of one variable by another I cannot gain a removed knowledge of it In so far as I guess what it may be, it is by abandoning the body as an object, *partes extra partes*, and by going back to the body which I experience at this moment, in the manner, for example, in which my hand moves round the object it touches, anticipating the stimuli and itself tracing out the form which I am about to perceive I cannot understand the function of the living body except by enacting it myself, and except in so far as I am a body which rises towards the world.

Thus exteroceptivity demands that stimuli be given a shape; the consciousness of the body invades the body, the soul spreads over all its parts, and behaviour overspills its central sector But one might reply that this 'bodily experience' is itself a 'representation', a 'psychic fact', and that as such it is at the end of a chain of physical

---

[1] J Stein, *Pathologie der Wahrnehmung*, p 364.

[2] Die Reizvorgange treffen ein ungestimmtes Reaktionsorgan Stein, *Pathologie der Wahrnehmung*, p 361

[3] 'Die Sinne   die Form eben durch ursprungliches Formbegreifen zu erkennen geben ' Ibid . p 353.

and physiological events which alone can be ascribed to the 'real body'. Is not my body, exactly as are external bodies, an object which acts on receptors and finally gives rise to the consciousness of the body? Is there not an 'interoceptivity' just as there is an 'exteroceptivity'? Cannot I find in the body message-wires sent by the internal organs to the brain, which are installed by nature to provide the soul with the opportunity of feeling its body? Consciousness of the body, and the soul, are thus repressed. The body becomes the highly polished machine which the ambiguous notion of behaviour nearly made us forget. For example, if, in the case of a man who has lost a leg, a stimulus is applied, instead of to the leg, to the path from the stump to the brain, the subject will feel a phantom leg, because the soul is immediately linked to the brain and to it alone.

What has modern physiology to say about this? Anaesthesia with cocaine does not do away with the phantom limb, and there are cases of phantom limbs without amputation as a result of brain injury.[1] Finally the imaginary limb is often found to retain the position in which the real arm was at the moment of injury a man wounded in battle can still feel in his phantom arm the shell splinters that lacerated his real one.[2] Is it then necessary to abandon the 'peripheral theory' in favour of a 'central theory'? But a central theory would get us no further if it added no more to the peripheral conditions of the imaginary limb than cerebral symptoms. For a collection of cerebral symptoms could not represent the relationships in consciousness which enter into the phenomenon. It depends indeed on 'psychic' determinants An emotion, circumstance which recalls those in which the wound was received, creates a phantom limb in subjects who had none.[3] It happens that the imaginary arm is enormous after the operation, but that it subsequently shrinks and is absorbed into the stump 'as the patient consents to accept his mutilation'.[4] The phenomenon of the phantom limb is here elucidated by that of anosognosia,* which clearly demands a psychological explanation. Subjects who systematically ignore their paralysed right hand, and hold out their left hand when asked for their right, refer to their paralysed arm as 'a long, cold snake', which rules out any hypothesis of real anaesthesia and sug-

[1] Lhermitte, L'Image de notre Corps, p 47.

[2] Ibid, pp. 129 and ff.

[3] Ibid, p. 57

[4] Ibid, p 73 J Lhermitte points out that the illusion of the limbless bears a relationship to the patient's psychological make-up it is more frequent among educated people

* Failure or refusal on the patient's part to recognize the existence of a disease or disability (Translator's note)

gests one in terms of the refusal to recognize their deficiency [1] Must we then conclude that the phantom limb is a memory, a volition or a belief, and, failing any physiological explanation, must we provide a psychological explanation for it? But no psychological explanation can overlook the fact that the severance of the nerves to the brain abolishes the phantom limb [2]

What has to be understood, then, is how the psychic determining factors and the physiological conditions gear into each other: it is not clear how the imaginary limb, if dependent on physiological conditions and therefore the result of a third person causality, can *in another context* arise out of the personal history of the patient, his memories, emotions and volitions. For in order that the two sets of conditions might together bring about the phenomenon, as two components bring about a resultant, they would need an identical point of application or a common ground, and it is difficult to see what ground could be common to 'physiological facts' which are in space and 'psychic facts' which are nowhere: or even to objective processes like nervous influxes which belong to the realm of the *in-itself*, and *cogitationes* such as acceptance and refusal, awareness of the past, and emotion, which are of the order of the *for-itself*. A hybrid theory of the phantom limb which found a place for both sets of conditions [3] may, then, be valid as a statement of the known facts; but it is fundamentally obscure The phantom limb is not the mere outcome of objective causality; no more is it a *cogitatio* It could be a mixture of the two only if we could find a means of linking the 'psychic' and the 'physiological', the 'for-itself' and the 'in-itself', to each other to form an articulate whole, and to contrive some meeting-point for them· if the third person processes and the personal acts could be integrated into a common middle term

In order to describe the belief in the phantom limb and the unwillingness to accept mutilation, writers speak of a 'driving into the unconscious' or 'an organic repression'.[4] These un-Cartesian terms force us to form the idea of an organic thought through which the relation of the 'psychic' to the 'physiological' becomes conceivable We have already met elsewhere, in the case of substitutions, phenomena which lie outside the alternatives of psychic and physiological, of final and mechanistic causes [5] When the insect, in the performance

---

[1] Lhermitte, *L'Image de notre Corps*, pp 129 and ff.

[2] Ibid , pp 129 and ff

[3] The phantom limb lends itself neither to a purely physiological explanation, nor to a purely psychological one Such is the conclusion of J Lhermitte, *L'Image de notre Corps*, p. 126

[4] Schilder, *Das Korperschema*, Menninger-Lerchenthal, *Das Truggebilde der eigenen Gestalt*, p 174, Lhermitte, *L'Image de notre Corps*, p 143

[5] Cf. *La Structure du Comportement*, pp 47 and ff

of an instinctive act, substitutes a sound leg for one cut off, it is not, as we saw, that a stand-by device, set up in advance, is automatically put into operation and substituted for the circuit which is out of action. But neither is it the case that the creature is aware of an aim to be achieved, using its limbs as various means, for in that case the substitution ought to occur every time the act is prevented, and we know that it does not occur if the leg is merely tied The insect simply continues to belong to the same world and moves in it with all its powers. The tied limb is not replaced by the free one, because it continues to count in the insect's scheme of things, and because the current of activity which flows towards the world still passes through it There is in this instance no more choice than in the case of a drop of oil which uses all its strength to solve in practical terms the maximum and minimum problem which confronts it. The difference is simply that the drop of oil adapts itself to given external forces, while the insect itself projects the norms of its environment and itself lays down the terms of its vital problem,[1] but here it is a question of an *a priori* of the species and not a personal choice. Thus what is found behind the phenomenon of substitution is the impulse of being-in-the-world, and it is now time to put this notion into more precise terms. When we say that an animal *exists*, that it *has* a world, or that it *belongs* to a world, we do not mean that it has a perception or objective consciousness of that world The situation which unleashes instinctive operations is not entirely articulate and determinate, its total meaning is not possessed, as is adequately shown by the mistakes and the blindness of instinct. It presents only a practical significance; it asks for only bodily recognition; it is experienced as an 'open' situation, and 'requires' the animal's movements, just as the first notes of a melody require a certain kind of resolution, without its being known in itself, and it is precisely what allows the limbs to be substituted for each other, and to be of equal value before the self-evident demands of the task In so far as it anchors the subject to a certain 'environment', is 'being-in-the-world' something like 'attention to life' in Bergson or 'the function of the real' in P. Janet? Attention to life is the awareness we experience of 'nascent movements' in our bodies Now reflex movements, whether adumbrated or executed, are still only objective processes whose course and results consciousness can observe, but in which it is not involved [2]

[1] Cf. *La Structure du Comportement*, pp 196 and ff
[2] When Bergson stresses the unity of perception and action and invents, for its expression, the term 'sensory-motor process', he is clearly seeking to involve consciousness in the world But if feeling is representing a quality to oneself, and if movement is changing one's position in the objective world, then between sensation and movement, even taken in their nascent state, no *compromise* is possible, and they are distinct from each other as are the *for-itself* and the *in-itself* Gener-

In fact the reflexes themselves are never blind processes they adjust themselves to a 'direction' of the situation, and express our orientation towards a 'behavioural setting' just as much as the action of the 'geographical setting' upon us They trace out from a distance the structure of the object without waiting for its point by point stimulation It is this global presence of the situation which gives a meaning to the partial stimuli and causes them to acquire importance, value or existence for the organism The reflex does not arise from objective stimuli, but moves back towards them, and invests them with a meaning which they do not possess taken singly as psychological agents, but only when taken as a situation It causes them to exist as a situation, it stands in a 'cognitive' relation to them, which means that it shows them up as that which it is destined to confront The reflex, in so far as it opens itself to the meaning of a situation, and perception, in so far as it does not first of all posit an object of knowledge and is an intention of our whole being, are modalities of a *pre-objective view* which is what we call being-in-the-world Prior to stimuli and sensory contents, we must recognize a kind of inner diaphragm which determines, infinitely more than they do, what our reflexes and perceptions will be able to aim at in the world, the area of our possible operations, the scope of our life. Some subjects can

---

ally speaking, Bergson saw that the body and the mind communicate with each other through the medium of time, that to be a mind is to stand above time's flow and that to have a body is to have a present The body, he says, is an instantaneous section made in the becoming of consciousness (*Matière et Memoire*, p 150). But the body remains for him what we have called the objective body; consciousness remains knowledge, time remains a successive 'now', whether it 'snowballs upon itself' or is spread in spatialized time Bergson can therefore only compress or expand the series of 'present moments', he never reaches the unique movement whereby the three dimensions of time are constituted, and one cannot see why duration is squeezed into a present, or why consciousness becomes involved in a body and a world.

As for the 'function of the real', P Janet *uses* it as an existential notion This is what enables him to sketch out a profound theory of emotion as the collapse of our customary being, and a flight from our world. (Cf. for example the interpretation of the fit of hysterics, *De l'Angoisse à l'Extase*, T II, p 450 and ff) But this theory of emotion is not followed out and, as J P. Sartre shows, it conflicts, in the writings of P Janet, with a mechanistic conception rather close to that of James· the collapse of our existence into emotion is treated as a mere *derivation* from psychological forces, and the emotion itself as the consciousness of this process expressed in the third person, so that there is no longer reason to look for a meaning in the emotional behaviour which is the result of the blind momentum of the tendencies, and we return to dualism (Cf J P Sartre, *Esquisse d'une théorie de l'Emotion*) P Janet, moreover, treats psychological tension—that is, the movement whereby we spread our 'world' before us—expressly as a representative hypothesis, so he is far from considering it in general terms as the concrete essence of man, though he does so implicitly in particular analyses.

come near to blindness without changing their 'world' they can be seen colliding with objects everywhere, but they are not aware of no longer being open to visual qualities, and the structure of their conduct remains unmodified. Other patients, on the other hand, lose their world as soon as its contents are removed; they abandon their habitual way of life even before it has become impossible, making themselves into premature invalids and breaking their vital contact with the world before losing sensory contact with it There is, then, a certain consistency in our 'world', relatively independent of stimuli, which refuses to allow us to treat being-in-the-world as a collection of reflexes—a certain energy in the pulsation of existence, relatively independent of our voluntary thoughts, which prevents us from treating it as an *act* of consciousness It is because it is a preobjective view that being-in-the-world can be distinguished from every third person process, from every modality of the *res extensa*, as from every *cogitatio*, from every first person form of knowledge—and that it can effect the union of the 'psychic' and the 'physiological'.

Let us return now to the problem with which we began. Anosognosia and the phantom limb lend themselves neither to a physiological nor to a psychological explanation, nor yet to a mixture of the two, though they can be related to the two sets of conditions. A physiological explanation would account for anosognosia and the phantom limb as the straightforward suppression or equally straightforward persistence of 'interoceptive' stimulations According to this hypothesis, anosognosia is the absence of a fragment of representation which ought to be given, since the corresponding limb is there; the phantom limb is the presence of part of the representation of the body which should not be given, since the corresponding limb is not there. If one now gives a psychological account of the phenomena, the phantom limb becomes a memory, a positive judgement or a perception, while anosognosia becomes a bit of forgetfulness, a negative judgement or a failure to perceive. In the first case the phantom limb is the actual presence of a representation, anosognosia the actual absence of a representation In the second case the phantom limb is the representation of an actual presence, whereas anosognosia is the representation of an actual absence. In both cases we are imprisoned in the categories of the objective world, in which there is no middle term between presence and absence In reality the anosognosic is not simply ignorant of the existence of his paralysed limb: he can evade his deficiency only because he knows where he risks encountering it, just as the subject, in psychoanalysis, knows what he does not want to face, otherwise he would not be able to avoid it so successfully. We do not understand the absence or death of a friend until the time comes when we expect a reply from him and when we realize that we shall never again receive one, so at first we avoid asking in order not to have to notice this silence; we turn aside from those areas of our life in which we might meet this nothingness, but this very fact necessitates that we intuit them In the same way the anosognosic leaves his paralysed arm out of account in order not to have to feel his handicap, but this means that he has a preconscious knowledge of it It is true that in the case of the phantom limb the subject appears to be unaware of the mutilation and relies on his imaginary limb as he would on a real one, since he tries to walk with his phantom leg and is not discouraged even by a fall. But he can describe quite well, in spite of this, the peculiarities of the phantom leg, for example its curious motility, and if he treats it in practice as a real limb, this is because, like the normal subject, he has no need, when he wants to set off walking, of a clear and articulate perception of his body· it is enough for him to have it 'at his disposal' as an undivided power, and to sense the phantom limb as vaguely involved in it The consciousness of the phantom limb remains, then, itself unclear. The man with one leg feels the missing limb in the same way as I feel keenly the existence of a friend who is, nevertheless, not before my eyes; he has not lost it because he continues to allow for it, just as Proust can recognize the death of his grandmother, yet without losing her, as long as he can keep her on the horizon of his life. The phantom arm is not a representation of the arm, but the ambivalent presence of an arm The refusal of mutilation in the case of the phantom limb, or the refusal of disablement in anosognosia are not deliberate decisions, and do not take place at the level of positing consciousness which takes up its position explicitly after considering various possibilities The will to have a sound body or the rejection of an infirm one are not formulated for themselves; and the awareness of the amputated arm as present or of the disabled arm as absent is not of the kind· 'I think that . . .'

This phenomenon, distorted equally by physiological and psychological explanations, is, however, understood in the perspective of being-in-the-world. What it is in us which refuses mutilation and disablement is an *I* committed to a certain physical and inter-human world, who continues to tend towards his world despite handicaps and amputations and who, to this extent, does not recognize them *de jure*. The refusal of the deficiency is only the obverse of our inherence in a world, the implicit negation of what runs counter to the natural momentum which throws us into our tasks, our cares, our situation, our familiar horizons. To have a phantom arm is to remain open to all the actions of which the arm alone is capable, it is to retain the practical field which one enjoyed before mutilation The body is the vehicle of being in the world, and having a body is, for a living creature, to be intervolved in a definite environment, to identify oneself with certain projects and be continually committed to them. In the self-evidence of this complete world in which manipulatable objects still figure, in the force of their movement which still flows towards him, and in which is still present the project of writing or playing the piano, the cripple still finds the guarantee of his wholeness But in concealing his deficiency from him, the world cannot fail simultaneously to reveal it to him· for if it is true that I am conscious of my body *via* the world, that it is the unperceived term in the centre of the world towards which all objects turn their face, it is true for the same reason that my body is the pivot of the world: I know that objects have several facets because I could make a tour of inspection of them, and in that sense I am conscious of the world through the medium of my body It is precisely when my customary world arouses in me habitual intentions that I can no longer, if I have lost a limb, be effectively drawn into it, and the utilizable objects, precisely in so far as they present themselves as utilizable, appeal to a hand which I no longer have. Thus are delimited, in the totality of my body, regions of silence The patient therefore realizes his disability precisely in so far as he is ignorant of it, and is ignorant of it precisely to the extent that he knows of it. This paradox is that of all being in the world when I move towards a world I bury my perceptual and practical intentions in objects which ultimately appear prior to and external to those intentions, and which nevertheless exist for me only in so far as they arouse in me thoughts or volitions In the case under consideration, the ambiguity of knowledge amounts to this: our body comprises as it were two distinct layers, that of the habit-body and that of the body at this moment. In the first appear manipulatory movements which have disappeared from the second, and the problem how I can have the sensation of still possessing a limb which I no longer have amounts to finding out how the habitual body can act as guarantee for the body at this moment. How can I perceive objects as manipulatable when I can no longer manipulate them? The manipulatable must have ceased to be what I am now manipulating, and become what *one* can manipulate, it must have ceased to be a thing *manipulatable for me* and become a thing *manipulatable in itself* Correspondingly, my body must be apprehended not only in an experience which is instantaneous, peculiar to itself and complete in itself, but also in some general aspect and in the light of an impersonal being.

In that way the phenomenon of the phantom limb is absorbed into that of repression, which we shall find throwing some light on it For repression, to which psycho-analysis refers, consists in the subject's entering upon a certain course of action—a love affair, a career, a piece of work—in his encountering on this course some barrier, and, since he has the strength neither to surmount the obstacle nor to abandon the enterprise, he remains imprisoned in the attempt and uses up his strength indefinitely renewing it in spirit Time in its passage does not carry away with it these impossible projects; it does not close up on traumatic experience, the subject remains open to the same impossible future, if not in his explicit thoughts, at any rate in his actual being One present among all presents thus acquires an exceptional value; it displaces the others and deprives them of their value as authentic presents We continue to be the person who once entered on this adolescent affair, or the one who once lived in this parental universe. New perceptions, new emotions even, replace the old ones, but this process of renewal touches only the content of our experience and not its structure Impersonal time continues its course, but personal time is arrested Of course this fixation does not merge into memory; it even excludes memory in so far as the latter spreads out in front of us, like a picture, a former experience, whereas this past which remains our true present does not leave us but remains constantly hidden behind our gaze instead of being displayed before it The traumatic experience does not survive as a representation in the mode of objective consciousness and as a 'dated' moment; it is of its essence to survive only as a manner of being and with a certain degree of generality I forgo my constant power of providing myself with 'worlds' in the interest of one of them, and for that very reason this privileged world loses its substance and eventually becomes no more than *a certain dread* All repression is, then, the transition from first person existence to a sort of abstraction of that existence, which lives on a former experience, or rather on the memory of having had the memory, and so on, until finally only the essential form remains. Now as an advent of the impersonal, repression is a universal phenomenon, revealing our condition as incarnate beings by relating it to the temporal structure of being in the world To the extent that I have 'sense organs', a 'body', and 'psychic functions' comparable with other men's, each of the moments of my experience ceases to be an integrated and strictly unique totality, in which details exist only in virtue of the whole, I become the meeting point of a host of 'causalities' In so far as I inhabit a 'physical world', in which consistent 'stimuli' and typical situations recur—and not merely the historical world in which situations are never exactly comparable— my life is made up of rhythms which have not their *reason* in what I

83

have chosen to be, but their *condition* in the humdrum setting which is mine Thus there appears round our personal existence a margin of *almost* impersonal existence, which can be practically taken for granted, and which I rely on to keep me alive; round the human world which each of us has made for himself is a world in general terms to which one must first of all belong in order to be able to enclose oneself in the particular context of a love or an ambition Just as we speak of repression in the limited sense when I retain through time one of the momentary worlds through which I have lived, and make it the formative element of my whole life—so it can be said that my organism, as a prepersonal cleaving to the general form of the world, as an anonymous and general existence, plays, beneath my personal life, the part of an *inborn complex*. It is not some kind of inert thing, it too has something of the momentum of existence. It may even happen when I am in danger that my human situation abolishes my biological one, that my body lends itself without reserve to action.[1] But these moments can be no more than moments,[2] and for most of the time personal existence represses the organism without being able either to go beyond it or to renounce itself, without, in other words, being able either to reduce the organism to its existential self, or itself to the organism While I am overcome by some grief and wholly given over to my distress, my eyes already stray in front of me, and are drawn, despite everything, to some shining object, and thereupon resume their autonomous existence Following upon that minute into which we wanted to compress our whole life, time, or at least, prepersonal time, begins once more to flow, carrying away, if not our resolution, at least the heartfelt emotions which sustained it. Personal existence is intermittent and when this tide turns and recedes, decision can henceforth endow my life with only an artificially induced significance. The fusion of soul and body in the act, the sublimation of biological into personal existence, and of the natural into the cultural world is made both possible and precarious by the temporal structure of our experience. Every present grasps, by stages, through its horizon of immediate past and near future, the totality of possible time; thus does it overcome the dispersal of instants, and manage to endow our past itself with its definitive mean-

[1] Thus Saint-Exupery, above Arras, with shells bursting all round him, can no longer feel as a thing distinct from him his body which shortly before seemed to escape him 'It is as if my life were given to me every second, as if my life became every moment more keenly felt I live. I am alive I am still alive. I am always alive I am now nothing but a source of life ' *Pilote de Guerre*, p 174

[2] 'But it is true that, in the course of my life, when not in the grip of urgency, when my meaning is not at stake, I can see no more serious problems than those raised by my body.' A. de Saint-Exupéry, *Pilote de Guerre*, p. 169

ing, re-integrating into personal existence even that past of all pasts which the stereotyped patterns of our organic behaviour seem to suggest as being at the origin of our volitional being. In this context even reflexes have a meaning, and each individual's style is still visible in them, just as the beating of the heart is felt as far away as the body's periphery. But this power naturally belongs to all presents, the old no less than the new. Even if we claim to have a better understanding of our past than it had of itself, it can always reject our present judgement and shut itself up in its own autonomous self-evidence. It necessarily does so in so far as I conceive it as a former present. Each present may claim to solidify our life, and indeed that is what distinguishes it as the present. In so far as it presents itself as the totality of being and fills an instant of consciousness, we never extricate ourselves completely from it, time never completely closes over it and it remains like a wound through which our strength ebbs away. It can now be said that, *a fortiori*, the specific past, which our body is, can be recaptured and taken up by an individual life only because that life has never transcended it, but secretly nourishes it, devoting thereto part of its strength, because its present is still that past. This can be seen in cases of illness in which bodily events become the events of the day. What enables us to centre our existence is also what prevents us from centring it completely, and the anonymity of our body is inseparably both freedom and servitude. Thus, to sum up, the ambiguity of being-in-the-world is translated by that of the body, and this is understood through that of time.

We shall return later to the question of time Let it merely be noted for the moment that starting with this central phenomenon the relationships between the 'psychic' and the 'physiological' become conceivable Why can the memories recalled to the one-armed man cause the phantom arm to appear? The phantom arm is not a recollection, it is a quasi-present and the patient feels it now, folded over his chest, with no hint of its belonging to the past. Nor can we suppose that the image of an arm, wandering through consciousness, has joined itself to the stump. for then it would not be a 'phantom', but a renascent perception. The phantom arm must be that same arm, lacerated by shell splinters, its visible substance burned or rotted somewhere, which appears to haunt the present body without being absorbed into it. The imaginary arm is, then, like repressed experience, a former present which cannot decide to recede into the past. The memories called up before the patient induce in him a phantom limb, not as an image in associationism summons up another image, but because any memory reopens time lost to us and invites us to recapture the situation evoked. Intellectual memory, in Proust's sense, limits itself to a description of the

85

past, a past as idea, from which it extracts 'characteristics' or communicable meaning rather than discovering a structure. But it would not be memory if the object which it constructs were not still held by a few intentional threads to the horizon of the lived-through past, and to that past itself as we should rediscover it if we were to delve beyond these horizons and reopen time. In the same way, if we put back emotion into being-in-the-world, we can understand how it can be the origin of the phantom limb. To feel emotion is to be involved in a situation which one is not managing to face and from which, nevertheless, one does not want to escape. Rather than admit failure or retrace one's steps, the subject, caught in this existential dilemma, breaks in pieces the objective world which stands in his way and seeks symbolical satisfaction in magic acts.[1] The ruin of the objective world, abandonment of true action, flight into a self-contained realm are conditions favouring the illusion of those who have lost a limb in that it too presupposes the erasure of reality. In so far as memory and emotion can call up the phantom limb, this is not comparable to the action of one *cogitatio* which necessitates another *cogitatio*, or that of one condition bringing about its consequence. It is not that an ideal causality here superimposes itself on a physiological one, it is that an existential attitude motivates another and that memory, emotion and phantom limb are equivalents in the context of being in the world.

Now why does the severing of the afferent nerves banish the phantom limb? In the perspective of being in the world this fact means that the impulses arriving from the stump keep the amputated limb in the circuit of existence. They establish and maintain its place, prevent it from being abolished, and cause it still to count in the organism. They keep empty an area which the subject's history fills, they enable the latter to build up the phantom, as structural disturbances allow the content of psychosis to form into delirium. From our point of view, a sensori-motor circuit is, within our comprehensive being in the world, a relatively autonomous current of existence. Not that it always brings to our total being a separable contribution, but because under certain circumstances it is possible to bring to light constant responses to stimuli which are themselves constant. The question is, therefore, how the refusal of the deficiency, which is a total attitude of our existence, needs for its expression such a highly specialized modality as a sensori-motor circuit, and why our being-in-the-world, which provides all our reflexes with their meaning, and which is thus their basis, nevertheless delivers itself over to them and is finally based upon them. Indeed, as we have shown elsewhere, sensori-motor circuits are all the more

[1] Cf J P Sartre, *Esquisse d'une théorie de l'émotion*

clearly marked as one is concerned with more integrated existences, and the reflex in its pure state is to be found only in man, who has not only a setting (*Umwelt*), but also a world (*Welt*) [1]

From the existential point of view, these two facts, which scientific induction contents itself with setting side by side, are linked internally and are understood in the light of one and the same idea. If man is not to be embedded in the matrix of that syncretic setting in which animals lead their lives in a sort of *ek-stase*, if he is to be aware of a world as the common reason for all settings and the theatre of all patterns of behaviour, then between himself and what elicits his action a distance must be set, and, as Malebranche put it, forms of stimulation from outside must henceforth impinge on him 'respectfully'; each momentary situation must cease to be, for him, the totality of being, each particular response must no longer fill his whole field of action. Furthermore, the elaboration of these responses, instead of occurring at the centre of his existence, must take place on the periphery and finally the responses themselves must no longer demand that on each occasion some special position be taken up, but they must be outlined once and for all in their generality. Thus it is by giving up part of his spontaneity, by becoming involved in the world through stable organs and pre-established circuits that man can acquire the mental and practical space which will theoretically free him from his environment and allow him to *see* it. And provided that even the realization of an objective world is set in the realm of existence, we shall no longer find any contradiction between it and bodily conditioning it is an inner necessity for the most integrated existence to provide itself with an habitual body What allows us to link to each other the 'physiological' and the 'psychic', is the fact that, when reintegrated into existence, they are no longer distinguishable respectively as the order of the *in-itself*, and that of the *for-itself*, and that they are both directed towards an intentional pole or towards a world Probably the two histories never quite coincide one is commonplace and cyclic, the other may be open and unusual, and it would be necessary to keep the term 'history' for the second order of phenomena if history were a succession of events which not only have a meaning, but furnish themselves with it. However, failing a true revolution which breaks up historical categories so far valid, the figure in history does not create his part completely: faced with typical situations he takes typical decisions and Nicholas II, repeating the very words of Louis XVI, plays the already written part of established power in face of a new power. His decisions translate the *a priori* of a threatened prince as our reflexes translate a specific *a priori*. These stereotypes, moreover, are

[1] *La Structure du Comportement*, p 55

not a destiny, and just as clothing, jewellery and love transfigure the biological needs from which they arise, in the same way within the cultural world the historical *a priori* is constant only for a given phase and provided that the balance of *forces* allows the same *forms* to remain. So history is neither a perpetual novelty, nor a perpetual repetition, but the *unique* movement which creates stable forms and breaks them up The organism and its monotonous dialectical processes are therefore not alien to history and as it were inassimilable to it. Man taken as a concrete being is not a psyche joined to an organism, but the movement to and fro of existence which at one time allows itself to take corporeal form and at others moves towards personal acts. Psychological motives and bodily occasions may overlap because there is not a single impulse in a living body which is entirely fortuitous in relation to psychic intentions, not a single mental act which has not found at least its germ or its general outline in physiological tendencies. It is never a question of the incomprehensible meeting of two causalities, nor of a collision between the order of causes and that of ends But by an imperceptible twist an organic process issues into human behaviour, an instinctive act changes direction and becomes a sentiment, or conversely a human act becomes torpid and is continued absent-mindedly in the form of a reflex. Between the psychic and the physiological there may take place exchanges which almost always stand in the way of defining a mental disturbance as psychic *or* somatic The disturbance described as somatic produces, on the theme of the organic accident, tentative psychic commentaries, and the 'psychic' trouble confines itself to elaborating the human significance of the bodily event. A patient feels a second person implanted in his body. He is a man in half his body, a woman in the other half How are we to distinguish in this symptom the physiological causes and psychological motives? How are we to associate the two explanations and how imagine any point at which the two determinants meet? 'In symptoms of this kind, the psychic and the physical are so intimately linked that it is unthinkable to try to complete one of these functional domains by the other, and that both must be subsumed under a third . (We must) . . move on from knowledge of psychological and physiological facts to a recognition of the animic event as a vital process inherent in our existence' [1] Thus, to the question which we were asking, modern physiology gives a very clear reply: the psycho-physical event can no longer be conceived after the model of Cartesian physiology and as the juxtaposition of a process in itself and a *cogitatio* The union of soul and body is not an amalgamation between two mutually external

[1] E. Menninger-Lerchenthal, *Das Truggebilde der eigenen Gestalt,* pp

terms, subject and object, brought about by arbitrary decree. It is enacted at every instant in the movement of existence. We found existence in the body when we approached it by the first way of access, namely through physiology. We may therefore at this stage examine this first result and make it more explicit, by questioning existence this time on its own nature, which means, by having recourse to psychology.

THE EXPERIENCE OF THE BODY AND CLASSICAL PSYCHOLOGY

IN its descriptions of the body from the point of view of the self, classical psychology was already wont to attribute to it 'characteristics' incompatible with the status of an object In the first place it was stated that my body is distinguishable from the table or the lamp in that I can turn away from the latter whereas my body is constantly perceived. It is therefore an object which does not leave me But in that case is it still an object? If the object is an invariable structure, it is not one *in spite of* the changes of perspective, but *in* that change or *through* it. It is not the case that ever-renewed perspectives simply provide it with opportunities of displaying its permanence, and with contingent ways of presenting itself to us. It is an object, which means that it is standing in front of us, only because it is observable situated, that is to say, directly under our hand or gaze, indivisibly overthrown and re-integrated with every movement they make. Otherwise it would be true like an idea and not present like a thing It is particularly true that an object is an object only in so far as it can be moved away from me, and ultimately disappear from my field of vision. Its presence is such that it entails a possible absence. Now the permanence of my own body is entirely different in kind: it is not at the extremity of some indefinite exploration, it defies exploration and is always presented to me from the same angle. Its permanence is not a permanence in the world, but a permanence from my point of view To say that it is always near me, always there for me, is to say that it is never really in front of me, that I cannot array it before my eyes, that it remains marginal to all my perceptions, that it is *with* me. It is true that external objects too never turn one of their sides to me without hiding the rest, but I can at least freely choose the side which they

90

are to present to me. They could not appear otherwise than in perspective, but the particular perspective which I acquire at each moment is the outcome of no more than physical necessity, that is to say, of a necessity which I can use and which is not a prison for me. from my window only the tower of the church is visible, but this limitation simultaneously holds out the promise that from elsewhere the whole church could be seen. It is true, moreover, that if I am a prisoner the church will be restricted, for me, to a truncated steeple If I did not take off my clothes I could never see the inside of them, and it will in fact be seen that my clothes may become appendages of my body. But this fact does not prove that the presence of my body is to be compared to the *de facto* permanence of certain objects, or the organ compared to a tool which is always available. It shows that conversely those actions in which I habitually engage incorporate their instruments into themselves and make them play a part in the original structure of my own body. As for the latter, it is my basic habit, the one which conditions all the others, and by means of which they are mutually comprehensible Its permanence near to me, its unvarying perspective are not a *de facto* necessity, since such necessity presupposes them: in order that my window may impose upon me a point of view of the church, it is necessary in the first place that my body should impose upon me one of the world; and the first necessity can be merely physical only in virtue of the fact that the second is metaphysical, in short, I am accessible to factual situations only if my nature is such that there are factual situations for me. In other words, I observe external objects with my body, I handle them, examine them, walk round them, but my body itself is a thing which I do not observe: in order to be able to do so, I should need the use of a second body which itself would be unobservable When I say that my body is always perceived by me, these words are not to be taken in a purely statistical sense, for there must be, in the way my own body presents itself, something which makes its absence or its variation inconceivable. What can it be? My head is presented to my sight only to the extent of my nose end and the boundaries of my eye-sockets. I can see my eyes in three mirrors, but they are the eyes of someone observing, and I have the utmost difficulty in catching my living glance when a mirror in the street unexpectedly reflects my image back at me. My body in the mirror never stops following my intentions like their shadow, and if observation consists in varying the point of view while keeping the object fixed, then it escapes observation and is given to me as a simulacrum of my tactile body since it imitates the body's actions instead of responding to them by a free unfolding of perspectives. My visual body is certainly an object as far as its parts far removed from my head are concerned, but as we come nearer to the

91

eyes, it becomes divorced from objects, and reserves among them a quasi-space to which they have no access, and when I try to fill this void by recourse to the image in the mirror, it refers me back to an original of the body which is not out there among things, but in my own province, on this side of all things seen. It is no different, in spite of what may appear to be the case, with my tactile body, for if I can, with my left hand, feel my right hand as it touches an object, the right hand as an object is not the right hand as it touches: the first is a system of bones, muscles and flesh brought down at a point of space, the second shoots through space like a rocket to reveal the external object in its place. In so far as it sees or touches the world, my body can therefore be neither seen nor touched. What prevents its ever being an object, ever being 'completely constituted'[1] is that it is that by which there are objects. It is neither tangible nor visible in so far as it is that which sees and touches The body therefore is not one more among external object, with the peculiarity of always being there If it is permanent, the permanence is absolute and is the ground for the relative permanence of disappearing objects, real objects The presence and absence of external objects are only variations within a field of primordial presence, a perceptual domain over which my body exercises power. Not only is the permanence of my body not a particular case of the permanence of external objects in the world, but the second cannot be understood except through the first: not only is the perspective of my body not a particular case of that of objects, but furthermore the presentation of objects in perspective cannot be understood except through the resistance of my body to all variation of perspective If objects may never show me more than one of their facets, this is because I am myself in a certain place from which I see them and which I cannot see If nevertheless I believe in the existence of their hidden sides and equally in a world which embraces them all and co-exists with them, I do so in so far as my body, always present for me, and yet involved with them in so many objective relationships, sustains their co-existence with it and communicates to them all the pulse of its duration. Thus the permanence of one's own body, if only classical psychology had analysed it, might have led it to the body no longer conceived as an object of the world, but as our means of communication with it, to the world no longer conceived as a collection of determinate objects, but as the horizon latent in all our experience and itself ever-present and anterior to every determining thought

[1] Husserl, *Ideen* T. II (unpublished) We are indebted to Mgr Noel and the Institut Supérieur de Philosophie of Louvain, trustees of the collected *Nachlass*, and particularly to the kindness of the Reverend Father Van Bréda, for having been able to consult a certain amount of unpublished material.

The other 'characteristics' whereby one's own body was defined were no less interesting, and for the same reasons. My body, it was said, is recognized by its power to give me 'double sensations'. when I touch my right hand with my left, my right hand, as an object, has the strange property of being able to feel too. We have just seen that the two hands are never simultaneously in the relationship of touched and touching to each other. When I press my two hands together, it is not a matter of two sensations felt together as one perceives two objects placed side by side, but of an ambiguous set-up in which both hands can alternate the rôles of 'touching' and being 'touched'. What was meant by talking about 'double sensations' is that, in passing from one rôle to the other, I can identify the hand touched as the same one which will in a moment be touching. In other words, in this bundle of bones and muscles which my right hand presents to my left, I can anticipate for an instant the integument or incarnation of that other right hand, alive and mobile, which I thrust towards things in order to explore them. The body catches itself from the outside engaged in a cognitive process; it tries to touch itself while being touched, and initiates 'a kind of reflection'[1] which is sufficient to distinguish it from objects, of which I can indeed say that they 'touch' my body, but only when it is inert, and therefore without ever catching it unawares in its exploratory function.

It was also said that the body is an affective object, whereas external things are from my point of view merely represented. This amounted to stating a third time the problem of the status of my own body. For if I say that my foot hurts, I do not simply mean that it is a cause of pain in the same way as the nail which is cutting into it, differing only in being nearer to me; I do not mean that it is the last of the objects in the external world, after which a more intimate kind of pain should begin, an unlocalized awareness of pain in itself, related to the foot only by some causal connection and within the closed system of experience. I mean that the pain reveals itself as localized, that it is constitutive of a 'pain-infested space'. 'My foot hurts' means not: 'I think that my foot is the cause of this pain', but: 'the pain comes from my foot' or again 'my foot has a pain'. This is shown clearly by the 'primitive voluminousness of pain' formerly spoken of by psychologists It was therefore recognized that my body does not present itself as the objects of external impressions do, and that perhaps even these latter objects do no more than stand out against the affective background which in the first place throws consciousness outside itself.

Finally when the psychologists tried to confine 'kinaesthetic

---

[1] Husserl, *Méditations cartésiennes*, p 81.

sensations' to one's own body, arguing that these sensations present the body's movements to us globally, while attributing the movements of external objects to a mediating perception and to a comparison between successive positions, it could have been objected that movement, expressing a relationship, cannot be felt, but demands a mental operation. This objection, however, would merely have been an indictment of their language. What they were expressing, badly it is true, by 'kinaesthetic sensation', was the originality of the movements which I perform with my body: they directly anticipate the final situation, for my intention initiates a movement through space merely to attain the objective initially given at the starting point; there is as it were a germ of movement which only secondarily develops into an objective movement. I move external objects with the aid of my body, which takes hold of them in one place and shifts them to another. But my body itself I move directly, I do not find it at one point of objective space and transfer it to another, I have no need to look for it, it is already with me—I do not need to lead it towards the movement's completion, it is in contact with it from the start and propels itself towards that end The relationships between my decision and my body are, in movement, magic ones.

If the description of my own body given by classical psychology already offered all that is necessary to distinguish it from objects, how does it come about that psychologists have not made this distinction or that they have in any case seen no philosophical consequence flowing from it? The reason is that, taking a step natural to them, they chose the position of impersonal thought to which science has been committed as long as it believed in the possibility of separating, in observation, on the one hand what belongs to the situation of the observer and on the other the properties of the absolute object. For the living subject his own body might well be different from all external objects; the fact remains that for the unsituated thought of the psychologist the experience of the living subject became itself an object and, far from requiring a fresh definition of being, took its place in universal being. It was the life of the 'psyche' which stood in opposition to the real, but which was treated as a second reality, as an object of scientific investigation to be brought under a set of laws. It was postulated that our experience, already besieged by physics and biology, was destined to be completely absorbed into objective knowledge, with the consummation of the system of the sciences Thenceforth the experience of the body degenerated into a 'representation' of the body, it was not a phenomenon but a fact of the psyche. In the matter of living appearance, my visual body includes a large gap at the level of the head, but biology was there ready to fill that gap, to explain it through the structure of the eyes, to instruct me in what the body really is, showing that I have a retina and a brain like other men and like the corpses which I dissect, and that, in short, the surgeon's instrument could infallibly bring to light in this indeterminate zone of my head the exact replica of plates illustrating the human anatomy. I apprehend my body as a subject-object, as capable of 'seeing' and 'suffering', but these confused representations were so many psychological oddities, samples of a magical variety of thought the laws of which are studied by psychology and sociology and which has its place assigned to it by them, in the system of the real world, as an object of scientific investigation This imperfect picture of my body, its marginal presentation, and its equivocal status as touching and touched, could not therefore be *structural* characteristics of the body itself'; they did not affect the idea of it; they became 'distinctive characteristics' of those *contents* of consciousness which make up our representation of the body· these contents are consistent, affective and strangely duplicated in 'double sensations', but apart from this the representation of the body is a representation like any other and correspondingly the body is an object like any other. Psychologists did not realize that in treating the experience of the body in this way they were simply, in accordance with the scientific approach, shelving a problem which ultimately could not be burked. The inadequacy of my perception was taken as a *de facto* inadequacy resulting from the organization of my sensory apparatus, the presence of my body was taken as a *de facto presence* springing from its constant action on my receptive nervous system, finally the union of soul and body, which was presupposed by these two explanations, was understood, in Cartesian fashion, as a *de facto union* whose *de jure* possibility need not be established, because the fact, as the starting point of knowledge, was eliminated from the final result Now the psychologist could imitate the scientist and, for a moment at least, see his body as others saw it, and conversely see the bodies of others as mechanical things with no inner life. The contribution made from the experiences of others had the effect of dimming the structure of his own, and conversely, having lost contact with himself he became blind to the behaviour of others He thus saw everything from the point of view of universal thought which abolished equally his experience of others and his experience of himself But as a psychologist he was engaged in a task which by nature pulled him back into himself, and he could not allow himself to remain unaware to this extent. For whereas neither the physicist nor the chemist are the objects of their own investigation, the psychologist *was himself*, in the nature of the case, the fact which exercised him This representation of the body, this magical experience, which he approached in a detached frame of mind, was himself; he lived it while he thought about it It is true that, as has been shown,[1] it was not enough for him to be a psyche in order to know this, for this knowledge, like other knowledge, is acquired only through our relations with other people. It does not emerge from any recourse to an ideal of introspective psychology, and between himself and others no less than between himself and himself, the psychologist was able and obliged to rediscover a pre-objective relationship. But as a psyche speaking of the psyche, he *was* all that he was *talking* about. This history of the psyche which he was elaborating in adopting the objective attitude was one whose outcome he already possessed within himself, or rather he was, in his existence, its contracted outcome and latent memory. The union of soul and body had not been brought about once and for all in a remote realm, it came into being afresh at every moment beneath the psychologist's thinking, not as a repetitive event which each time takes the psyche by surprise, but as a necessity that the psychologist knew to be in the depths of his being as he became aware of it as a piece of knowledge. The birth of perception from 'sense-data' to 'world' had to be renewed with each act of perception, otherwise the sense-data would have lost the meaning they owed to this development Hence the 'psyche' was not an object like others: it had done everything that one was about to say of it before it could be said, the psychologist's being knew more about itself than he did, nothing that had happened or was happening according to science was completely alien to it. Applied to the psyche, the notion of fact, therefore, underwent a transformation. The *de facto* psyche, with its 'peculiarities', was no longer an event in objective time and in the external world, but an event with which we were in internal contact, of which we were ourselves the ceaseless accomplishment or upsurge, and which continually gathered within itself its past, its body and its world. Before being an objective fact, the union of soul and body had to be, then, a possibility of consciousness itself and the question arose as to what the perceiving subject is and whether he must be able to experience a body as his own. There was no longer a fact passively submitted to, but one assumed. To be a consciousness or rather *to be an experience* is to hold inner communication with the world, the body and other people, to be with them instead of being beside them. To concern oneself with psychology is necessarily to encounter, beneath objective thought which moves among ready-made things, a first opening upon things without which there would be no objective knowledge The psychologist could not fail to rediscover himself as experience, which means as an immediate presence to the past, to the world, to the body

[1] P Guillaume, *L'Objectivité en Psychologie.*

and to others at the very moment when he was trying to see himself as an object among objects. Let us then return to the 'characteristics' of one's own body and resume the study of it where we left off. By doing so we shall trace the progress of modern psychology and thereby effect along with it the return to experience

3

THE SPATIALITY OF ONE'S OWN BODY AND MOTILITY

LET us first of all describe the spatiality of my own body If my arm is resting on the table I should never fhink of saying that it is *beside* the ash-tray in the way in which the ash-tray is beside the telephone. The outline of my body is a frontier which ordinary spatial relations do not cross This is because its parts are inter-related in a peculiar way they are not spread out side by side, but enveloped in each other For example, my hand is not a collection of points In cases of allocheiria,* in which the subject feels in his right hand stimuli applied to his left hand, it is impossible to suppose that each of the stimulations changes its spatial value on its own account [1] The various points on the left hand are transferred to the right as relevant to a total organ, a hand without parts which has been suddenly displaced Hence they form a system and the space of my hand is not a mosaic of spatial values. Similarly my whole body for me is not an assemblage of organs juxtaposed in space I am in undivided possession of it and I know where each of my limbs is through a *body image* in which all are included But the notion of body image is ambiguous, as are all notions which make their appearance at turning points in scientific advance They can be fully developed only through a reform of methods. At first, therefore, they are used only in a sense which falls short of their full sense, and it is their immanent development which bursts the bounds of methods hitherto used. 'Body image' was at first understood to mean a *compendium* of our bodily experience, capable of giving a commentary and meaning to the internal impres-

* A disorder of sensation in which sensations are referred to the wrong part of the body (Translator's note) Cf for example Head, *On disturbances of sensation with especial reference to the pain of visceral disease*

[1] Ibid We have discussed the notion of the local signal in *La Structure du Comportement*, pp. 102 and ff

sions and the impression of possessing a body at any moment. It was supposed to register for me the positional changes of the parts of my body for each movement of one of them, the position of each local stimulus in the body as a whole, an account of the movements performed at every instant during a complex gesture, in short a continual translation into visual language of the kinaesthetic and articular impressions of the moment When the term body image was first used, it was thought that nothing more was being introduced than a convenient name for a great many associations of images, and it was intended merely to convey the fact that these associations were firmly established and constantly ready to come into play The body image was supposed gradually to show itself through childhood in proportion as the tactile, kinaesthetic and articular contents were associated among themselves or with visual contents, and more easily evoked them [1] Its physiological representation could then be no more than a focus of images in the classical sense Yet in the use made of it by psychologists, it is clear that the body image does not fit into this associationist definition For example, in order that the body image may elucidate allocheiria, it is not enough that each sensation of the left hand should take its place among generic images of all parts of the body acting in association to form around the left hand, as it were, a superimposed *sketch* of the body, these associations must be constantly subject to a unique law, the spatiality of the body must work downwards from the whole to the parts, the left hand and its position must be implied in a comprehensive bodily *purpose* and must originate in that purpose, so that it may at one stroke not only be superimposed on or cleave to the right hand, but actually become the right hand. When we try[2] to elucidate the phenomenon of the phantom limb by relating it to the body image of the subject, we add to the accepted explanations, in terms of cerebral tracks and recurrent sensations, only if the body image, instead of being the residue of habitual cenesthesis, becomes the law of its constitution If a need was felt to introduce this new word, it was in order to make it clear that the spatial and temporal unity, the inter-sensory or the sensori-motor unity of the body is, so to speak, *de jure*, that it is not confined to contents actually and fortuitously associated in the course of our experience, that it is in some way anterior to them and makes their association possible We are therefore feeling our way towards a second definition of the body image· it is no longer seen as the

[1] Cf for example Head, *Sensory disturbances from cerebral lesion*, p 189, Pick, *Störungen der Orientierung am eigenen Körper*, and even Schilder, *Das Körperschema*, although Schilder admits that 'such a complex is not the sum of its parts but a new whole in relation 'to them'

[2] As for example Lhermitte, *L'Image de notre Corps*

straightforward result of associations established during experience, but a total awareness of my posture in the intersensory world, a 'form' in the sense used by Gestalt psychology.[1] But already this second definition too is superseded by the analyses of the psychologists It is inadequate to say that my body is a form, that is to say a phenomenon in which the totality takes precedence over the parts. How is such a phenomenon possible? Because a form, compared to the mosaic of a physico-chemical body or to that of 'cenesthesis', is a new type of existence The fact that the paralysed limb of the anosognosic no longer counts in the subject's body image, is accounted for by the body image's being neither the mere copy nor even the global awareness of the existing parts of the body, and by its active integration of these latter only in proportion to their value to the organism's projects. Psychologists often say that the body image is *dynamic*.[2] Brought down to a precise sense, this term means that my body appears to me as an attitude directed towards a certain existing or possible task. And indeed its spatiality is not, like that of external objects or like that of 'spatial sensations', a *spatiality of position*, but a *spatiality of situation* If I stand in front of my desk and lean on it with both hands, only my hands are stressed and the whole of my body trails behind them like the tail of a comet. It is not that I am unaware of the whereabouts of my shoulders or back, but these are simply swallowed up in the position of my hands, and my whole posture can be read so to speak in the pressure they exert on the table If I stand holding my pipe in my closed hand, the position of my hand is not determined discursively by the angle which it makes with my forearm, and my forearm with my upper arm, and my upper arm with my trunk, and my trunk with the ground. I know indubitably where my pipe is, and thereby I know where my hand and my body are, as primitive man in the desert is always able to take his bearings immediately without having to cast his mind back, and add up distances covered and deviations made since setting off. The word 'here' applied to my body does not refer to a determinate position in relation to other positions or to external co-ordinates, but the laying down of the first co-ordinates, the anchoring of the active body in an object, the situation of the body in face of its tasks Bodily space can be distinguished from external space and envelop its parts instead of spreading them out, because it is the darkness needed in the theatre to show up the performance, the background of somnolence or re-

[1] Konrad, *Das Korperschema, eine kritische Studie und der Versuch einer Revision*, pp 365 and 367 Burger-Prinz and Kaila define the body image as 'knowledge of one's own body as the collective expression both of the mutual relations of its limbs and of its parts' Ibid , p 365.
[2] Cf for example Konrad, op cit

serve of vague power against which the gesture and its aim[1] stand out, the zone of not being *in front of which* precise beings, figures and points can come to light In the last analysis, if my body can be a 'form' and if there can be, in front of it, important figures against indifferent backgrounds, this occurs in virtue of its being polarized by its tasks, of its *existence towards* them, of its collecting together of itself in its pursuit of its aims: the body image is finally a way of stating that my body is in-the-world [2] As far as spatiality is concerned, and this alone interests us at the moment, one's own body is the third term, always tacitly understood, in the figure-background structure, and every figure stands out against the double horizon of external and bodily space One must therefore reject as an abstraction any analysis of bodily space which takes account only of figures and points, since these can neither be conceived nor be without horizons.

It will perhaps be replied that the figure-background structure or the point-horizon structure themselves presuppose the notion of objective space, that in order to experience a display of dexterity as a figure *against* the massive background of the body, the hand and the rest of the body must be linked by this relationship of objective spatiality, so that the figure-background structure becomes once again one of the contingent contents of the universal form of space. But what meaning could the word 'against' have for a subject not placed by his body face to face with the world? It implies the distinction of a top and a bottom, or an 'orientated space'.[3] When I say that an object is *on* a table, I always mentally put myself either in the table or in the object, and I apply to them a category which theoretically fits the relationship of my body to external objects. Stripped of this anthropological association, the word *on* is indistinguishable from the word 'under' or the word 'beside'. Even if the universal form of space is that without which there would be for us no bodily space, it is not that by which there is one. Even if the form is not the *setting in which*, but the *means whereby* the content is posited, it is not the sufficient means of this act of positing as far as bodily space is concerned, and to this extent the bodily content remains, in relation to it, something opaque, fortuitous and unintelligible. The only solution along this road would be to acknowledge that the body's spatiality has no meaning of its own to distinguish it from objective spatiality, which would do away with the content as a phenomenon and hence with the problem of its relation to form. But can we pretend to discover

[1] Grunbaum, *Asphasie und Motorik*, p 395.

[2] We have already seen (cf supra pp 81-2) that the phantom limb, which is a modality of the body image, is understood in terms of the general movement of being-in-the-world

[3] Cf Becker, *Beitrage zur phanomenologischen Begrundung der Geometrie und ihren physikalischen Anwendungen*

no distinctive meaning in the words 'on', 'under', 'beside', or in the dimensions of orientated space? Even if analysis discovers in all these relationships the universal relation of externality, the self-evidentness of top and bottom, right and left, for the person who has his being in space, prevents us from treating all these distinctions as nonsense, and suggests to us that we should look beneath the explicit meaning of definitions for the latent meaning of experiences. The relationships between the two spaces would therefore be as follows as soon as I try to posit bodily space or bring out its meaning I find nothing in it but intelligible space. But at the same time this intelligible space is not extracted from orientated space, it is merely its explicit expression, and, when separated from that root has no meaning whatsoever The truth is that homogeneous space can convey the meaning of orient-ated space only because it is from the latter that it has received that meaning In so far as the content can be really subsumed under the form and can appear as the content *of* that form, it is because the form is accessible only through the content Bodily space can really become a fragment of objective space only if within its individuality as bodily space it contains the dialectical ferment to transform it into universal space. This is what we have tried to express by saying that the point-horizon structure is the foundation of space. The horizon or background would not extend beyond the figure or round about it, unless they partook of the same kind of being as the figure, and un-less they could be converted into points by a transference of the gaze. But the point-horizon structure can teach me what a point is only in virtue of the maintenance of a hither zone of corporeality from which to be seen, and round about it indeterminate horizons which are the counterpart of this seeing The multiplicity of points or 'heres' can in the nature of things be constituted only by a chain of experiences in which on each occasion one and no more of them is presented as an object, and which is itself built up in the heart of this space. And finally, far from my body's being for me no more than a fragment of space, there would be no space at all for me if I had no body.

If bodily space and external space form a practical system, the first being the background against which the object as the goal of our action may stand out or the void in front of which it may *come to light*, it is clearly in action that the spatiality of our body is brought into being, and an analysis of one's own movement should enable us to arrive at a better understanding of it. By considering the body in movement, we can see better how it inhabits space (and, moreover, time) because movement is not limited to submitting passively to space and time, it actively assumes them, it takes them up in their basic significance which is obscured in the commonplaceness of established situations We should like to analyse closely an example of morbid motility which clearly shows the fundamental relations between the body and space.

A patient[1] whom traditional psychiatry would class among cases of psychic blindness is unable to perform 'abstract' movements with his eyes shut; movements, that is, which are not relevant to any actual situation, such as moving arms and legs to order, or bending and straightening a finger Nor can he describe the position of his body or even his head, or the passive movements of his limbs. Finally, when his head, arm or leg is touched, he cannot identify the point on his body, he cannot distinguish two points of contact on his skin even as much as three inches apart, and he cannot recognize the size or shape of objects placed against his body. He manages the abstract movements only if he is allowed to watch the limb required to perform them, or to go through preparatory movements involving the whole body. The localization of stimuli, and recognition of objects by touch also become possible with the aid of the preparatory movements. Even when his eyes are closed, the patient performs with extraordinary speed and precision the movements needed in living his life, provided that he is in the habit of performing them· he takes his handkerchief from his pocket and blows his nose, takes a match out of a box and lights a lamp. He is employed in the manufacture of wallets and his production rate is equal to three quarters of that of a normal workman. He can even[2] without any preparatory movement, perform these 'concrete' movements to order In the same patient, and also in cerebellar cases, one notices[3] a dissociation of the act of pointing from reactions of taking or grasping: the same subject who is unable to point to order to a part of his body, quickly moves his hand to the point where a mosquito is stinging him Concrete movements and acts of grasping therefore enjoy a privileged position for which we need to find some explanation.

Let us examine the question more closely. A patient, asked to point to some part of his body, his nose for example, can only manage to do so if he is allowed to take hold of it. If the patient is set the task of interrupting the movement before its completion, or if he is allowed to touch his nose only with a wooden ruler, the action becomes impossible[4] It must therefore be concluded that 'grasping' or 'touching', even for the body, is different from 'pointing'. From the

[1] Gelb and Goldstein, *Über den Einfluss des vollstandigen Verlustes des optischen Vorstellungsvermogens auf das taktile Erkennen —Psychologische Analysen hirnpathologischer Falle*, Chap II, pp 157-250

[2] Goldstein, *Über die Abhangigkeit der Bewegungen von optischen Vorgangen* This second work makes use of observations made on the same patient, Schneider, two years after those collected in the work just referred to

[3] Goldstein, *Zeigen und Greifen*, pp 453-66

[4] Ibid This is a cerebellar case

outset the grasping movement is magically at its completion, it can begin only by anticipating its end, since to disallow taking hold is sufficient to inhibit the action. And it has to be admitted that a point on my body can be present to me as one to be taken hold of without being given in this anticipated grasp as a point to be indicated. But how is this possible? If I know where my nose is when it is a question of holding it, how can I not know where it is when it is a matter of pointing to it? It is probably because knowledge of where something is can be understood in a number of ways. Traditional psychology has no concept to cover these varieties of consciousness of place because consciousness of place is always, for such psychology, a positional consciousness, a representation, *Vor-stellung*, because as such it gives us the place as a determination of the objective world and because such a representation either is or is not, but, if it is, yields the object to us quite unambiguously and as an end identifiable through all its appearances. Now here, on the other hand, we have to create the concepts necessary to convey the fact that bodily space may be given to me in an intention to take hold without being given in an intention to know The patient is conscious of his bodily space as the matrix of his habitual action, but not as an objective setting; his body is at his disposal as a means of ingress into a familiar surrounding, but not as the means of expression of a gratuitous and free spatial thought. When ordered to perform a concrete movement, he first of all repeats the order in a questioning tone of voice, then his body assumes the general position required for the task; finally he goes through the movement It is noticeable that the whole body is involved in it, and that the patient never cuts it down, as a normal subject would, to the strict minimum. To the military salute are added the other external marks of respect. To the right hand pantomime of combing the hair is added, with the left, that of holding a mirror; when the right hand pretends to knock in a nail, the left pretends to hold the nail. The explanation is that the order is taken quite seriously and that the patient manages to perform these concrete movements to order only provided that he places himself mentally in the actual situation to which they correspond. The normal subject, on giving, to order, a military salute, sees in it no more than an experimental situation, and therefore restricts the movement to its most important elements and does not throw himself into it.[1] He is using his body as a means to play acting; he finds it entertaining to pretend to be a soldier, he escapes from reality in the rôle of the soldier[2] just as the actor slips his real body into the 'great phantom'[3] of the

[1] Goldstein, *Über die Abhangigkeit*, p 175
[2] J P Sartre, *L'Imaginaie*, p 243
[3] Diderot, *Paradoxe sur le Comédien*

character to be played. The normal man and the actor do not mistake imaginary situations for reality, but extricate their real bodies from the living situation to make them breathe, speak and, if need be, weep in the realm of imagination This is what our patient is no longer able to do. In the course of living, he says 'I experience the movements as being a result of the situation, of the sequence of events themselves, myself and my movements are, so to speak, merely a link in the whole process and I am scarcely aware of any voluntary initiative . . It all happens independently of me.' In the same way, in order to make a movement to order he places himself 'in the affective situation as a whole, and it is from this that the movement flows, as in real life' [1] If his performance is interrupted and he has the experimental situation recalled to him, all his dexterity disappears. Once more kinetic initiative becomes impossible, the patient must first of all 'find' his arm, 'find', by the preparatory movements, the gesture called for, and the gesture itself loses the melodic character which it presents in ordinary life, and becomes manifestly a collection of partial movements strung laboriously together I can therefore take my place, through the medium of my body as the potential source of a certain number of familiar actions, in my environment conceived as a set of *manipulanda* and without, moreover, envisaging my body or my surrounding as objects in the Kantian sense, that is, as systems of qualities linked by some intelligible law, as transparent entities, free from any attachment to a specific place or time, and ready to be named or at least pointed out There is my arm seen as sustaining familiar acts, my body as giving rise to determinate action having a field or scope known to me in advance, there are my surroundings as a collection of possible points upon which this bodily action may operate,—and there is, furthermore, my arm as a mechanism of muscles and bones, as a contrivance for bending and stretching, as an articulated object, the world as a pure spectacle into which I am not absorbed, but which I contemplate and point out. As far as bodily space is concerned, it is clear that there is a knowledge of place which is reducible to a sort of co-existence with that place, and which is not simply nothing, even though it cannot be conveyed by a description or even by the mute reference of a gesture. A patient of the kind discussed above, when stung by a mosquito, does not need to look for the place where he has been stung He finds it straight away, because for him there is no question of locating it in relation to axes of co-ordinates in objective space, but of reaching with his phenomenal hand a certain painful spot on his phenomenal body, and because between the hand as a scratching potentiality and the place stung as a spot to be scratched a directly experienced relationship

[1] Goldstein, *Über die Abhängigkeit*, pp 175-6.

105

is presented in the natural system of one's own body The whole operation takes place in the domain of the phenomenal, it does not run through the objective world, and only the spectator, who lends his objective representation of the living body to the acting subject, can believe that the sting is perceived, that the hand moves in objective space, and consequently find it odd that the same subject should fail in experiments requiring him to point things out Similarly the subject, when put in front of his scissors, needle and familiar tasks, does not need to look for his hands or his fingers, because they are not objects to be discovered in objective space. bones, muscles and nerves, but potentialities already mobilized by the perception of scissors or needle, the central end of those 'intentional threads' which link him to the objects given It is never our objective body that we move, but our phenomenal body, and there is no mystery in that, since our body, as the potentiality of this or that part of the world, surges towards objects to be grasped and perceives them.[1] In the same way the patient has no need to look for a theatre of action and a space in which to deploy these concrete movements: the space is given to him in the form of the world at this moment; it is the piece of leather 'to be cut up'; it is the lining 'to be sewn'. The bench, scissors, pieces of leather offer themselves to the subject as poles of action; through their combined values they delimit a certain situation, an open situation moreover, which calls for a certain mode of resolution, a certain kind of work. The body is no more than an element in the system of the subject and his world, and the task to be performed elicits the necessary movements from him by a sort of remote attraction, as the phenomenal forces at work in my visual field elicit from me, without any calculation on my part, the motor reactions which establish the most effective balance between them, or as the conventions of our social group, or our set of listeners, immediately elicit from us the words, attitudes and tone which are fitting Not that we are trying to conceal our thoughts or to please others, but because we are literally what others think of us and what our world is. In the concrete movement the patient has a positing awareness neither of the stimulus nor of his reaction quite simply he is his body and his body is the potentiality of a certain world.

---

[1] It is not a question of how the soul acts on the objective body, since it is not on the latter that it acts, but on the phenomenal body So the question has to be reframed, and we must ask why there are two views of me and of my body my body for me and my body for others, and how these two systems can exist together It is indeed not enough to say that the objective body belongs to the realm of 'for others', and my phenomenal body to that of 'for me', and we cannot refuse to pose the problem of their relations, since the 'for me' and the 'for others' coexist in one and the same world, as is proved by my perception of an other who immediately brings me back to the condition of an object for him

What, on the other hand, happens in experiments in which the patient fails? If a part of his body is touched and he is asked to locate the point of contact, he first of all sets his whole body in motion and thus narrows down the problem of location, then he comes still nearer by moving the limb in question, and the process is completed in the form of quiverings of the skin in the neighbourhood of the point touched [1] If the subject's arm is extended horizontally, he cannot describe its position until he has performed a set of pendular movements which convey to him the arm position in relation to the trunk, that of the forearm to the rest of the arm, and that of the trunk in relation to the vertical In the case of passive movement, the subject feels that there is movement but cannot say of what kind and in what direction. Here again he resorts to active movements The patient concludes that he is lying down from the pressure of the mattress on his back, or that he is standing from the pressure of the ground on his feet [2] If the two points of a compass are placed on his hand, he can distinguish them only if he is allowed to rotate his hand, and bring first one and then the other point into contact with his skin If letters or figures are traced out on his hand, he identifies them only provided that he can himself move his hand, and it is not the movement of the point on his hand which he perceives, but conversely the movement of his hand in relation to the point. This is proved by tracing on his left hand normal letters, which are never recognized, then the mirrored image of the same letters, which is immediately understood. The mere touching of a paper rectangle or oval gives rise to no recognition, whereas the subject recognizes the figures if he is allowed to make exploratory movements to 'spell out' the shapes, to spot their 'characteristics' and to identify the object on this basis [3] How are we to co-ordinate this set of facts and how are we to discover by means of it what function, found in the normal person, is absent in the patient? There can be no question of simply transferring to the normal person what the deficient one lacks and is trying to recover. Illness, like childhood and 'primitive' mentality, is a complete form of existence and the procedures which it employs to replace normal functions which have been destroyed are equally pathological phenomena. It is impossible to deduce the normal from the pathological, deficiencies from the substitute functions, by a mere change of the sign We must take substitutions as substitutions, as allusions to some

[1] Goldstein, *Uber den Einfluss*, pp 167–206

[2] Ibid , pp 206–13

[3] For example, the subject runs his fingers over an angle several times 'My fingers,' he says, 'move straight along, then stop, and then move off again in another direction, it is an angle, it must be a right angle '—'Two, three, four angles, the sides are each two centimetres long, so they are equal, all the angles are right angles It's a dice ' Ibid , p 195 Cf pp 187–206

fundamental function that they are striving to make good, and the direct image of which they fail to furnish. The genuine inductive method is not a 'differential method', it consists in correctly reading phenomena, in grasping their meaning, that is, in treating them as modalities and variations of the subject's total being. We observe that when the patient is questioned about the position of his limbs or of a tactile stimulus, he tries, by means of preparatory movements, to make his body into an object of present perception Asked about the shape of an object in contact with his body, he tries to trace it out himself by following the outline of the object Nothing would be more misleading than to suppose the normal person adopting similar procedures, differing merely in being shortened by constant use. The kind of patient under consideration sets out in search of these explicit perceptions only in order to provide a substitute for a certain mutual presence of body and object which is a datum of normal experience and which we still have to reconstitute It is true that even in the normal person the perception of the body and of objects in contact with the body is vague when there is no movement [1] The fact remains that the normal person can, in the absence of any movements, always distinguish a stimulus applied to his head from one applied to his body Are we to suppose that [2] excitations felt as coming either from outside or from one's own body have brought into play, in that person, 'kinaesthetic residua' which take the place of actual movements? But then how could data supplied by the sense of touch arouse 'kinaesthetic residua' of a determinate kind unless they carried within themselves some characteristic which enables them to do so, unless they themselves, in other words, had some well defined or obscure spatial significance? [3] At least we can say that the normal subject can immediately 'come to grips' with his body [4] He enjoys the use of his body not only in so far as it is involved in a concrete setting, he is in a situation not only in relation to the tasks imposed by a particular job, he is not open merely to real situations; for, over and above all this, his body is correlated with pure stimuli devoid of any practical bearing, he is open to those verbal and imaginary situations which he can choose for himself or which may be suggested to him in the course of an experiment His body, when touched, is not presented to him as a geometrical outline in which each stimulus occupies an explicit position, and Schneider's disease lies precisely in his need, in order to find out where he is being touched, to convert the bodily area touched into a shape But each stimulus applied to

---

[1] Goldstein, *Über den Einfluss* , pp 206–13
[2] As Goldstein does, ibid , pp 167–206
[3] Cf supra the general discussion of the 'association of ideas', pp 17 and ff
[4] A patient named Schneider says he needs *Anhaltspunkte*

the body of the normal person arouses a kind of 'potential move-ment', rather than an actual one; the part of the body in question sheds its anonymity, is revealed, by the presence of a particular tension, as a certain power of action within the framework of the anatomical apparatus. In the case of the normal subject, the body is available not only in real situations into which it is drawn. It can turn aside from the world, apply its activity to stimuli which affect its sensory surfaces, lend itself to experimentation, and generally speaking take its place in the realm of the potential. It is because of its confinement within the actual that an unsound sense of touch calls for special movements designed to localize stimuli, and for the same reason the patient substitutes, for tactile recognition and perception, a laborious decoding of stimuli and deduction of objects. For a key, for instance, to appear as such in my tactile experience, a kind of fulness of touch is required, a tactile field in which local impressions may be co-ordinated into a shape just as notes are mere stepping-stones in a melody; and that very viscosity of tactile data which makes the body dependent upon actual situations reduces the object to a collection of successive 'characteristics', perception to an abstract account, recognition to a rational synthesis or a plausible conjecture, and strips the object of its carnal presence and facticity Whereas in the normal person every event related to movement or sense of touch causes consciousness to put up a host of intentions which run from the body as the centre of potential action either towards the body itself or towards the object, in the case of the patient, on the other hand, the tactile impression remains opaque and sealed up. It may well draw the grasping hand towards itself, but does not stand in front of the hand in the manner of a thing which can be pointed out. The normal person *reckons with* the possible, which thus, without shifting from its position as a possibility, acquires a sort of actuality. In the patient's case, however, the field of actuality is limited to what is met with in the shape of a real contact or is related to these data by some explicit process of deduction.

The analysis of 'abstract movement' in patients throws into relief this possession of space, this spatial existence which is the primary condition of all living perception If the patient is ordered to shut his eyes and then perform an abstract movement, a set of preparatory operations is called for in order to enable him to 'find' the operative limb, the direction or pace of the movement, and finally the plane in which it is to be executed If, for instance, he is ordered to move his arm, with no detail as to how, he is first of all perplexed. Then he moves his whole body and after a time his movements are confined to his arm, which the subject eventually 'finds'. It it is a question of 'raising his arm' the patient must also 'find' his head (which symbolizes 'up' for him) by means of a set of pendulum movements which are continued throughout the action and which serve to establish the objective If the subject is asked to trace a square or a circle in the air, he first 'finds' his arm, then lifts it in front of him as a normal subject would do to find a wall in the dark and finally he makes a few rough movements in a straight line or describing various curves, and if one of these happens to be circular he promptly completes the circle. Moreover he can find the requisite movement only in a certain plane, which is not quite perpendicular to the ground, and apart from this special plane he cannot begin to trace the figures.[1] Clearly the patient finds in his body only an amorphous mass into which actual movement alone introduces divisions and links In looking to his body to perform the movement for him he is like a speaker who cannot utter a word without following a text written beforehand The patient himself neither seeks nor finds his movement, but moves his body about until the movement comes. The order given is not meaningless to him, since he recognizes the inadequacy of his first attempts, and also since, if a fortuitous gesture produces the required movement, he is aware of it and can immediately turn his piece of good fortune to account But if the order has an *intellectual significance* for him and not a *motor* one, it does not communicate anything to him as a mobile subject; he may well find in the shape of a movement performed an illustration of the order given, but he can never convert the thought of a movement into actual movement. What he lacks is neither motility nor thought, and we are brought to the recognition of something between movement as a third person process and thought as a representation of movement—something which is an anticipation of, or arrival at, the objective and is ensured by the body itself as a motor power, a 'motor project' (*Bewegungsentwurf*), a 'motor intentionality' in the absence of which the order remains a dead letter The patient either conceives the ideal formula for the movement, or else he launches his body into blind attempts to perform it, whereas for the normal person every movement is, indissolubly, movement and consciousness of movement This can be expressed by saying that for the normal person every movement has a *background*, and that the movement and its background are 'moments of a unique totality'.[2] The background to the movement is not a representation associated or linked externally with the movement itself, but is immanent in the movement inspiring and sustaining it at every moment. The plunge into action is, from the subject's point of view,

---

[1] Goldstein, *Über den Einfluss*, pp 213–22
[2] Goldstein, *Über die Abhangigkeit*, p 161, Bewegung und Hintergrund bestimmen sich wechselseitig, sind eigentlich nur zwei herausgegriffene Momente eines einheitlichen Ganzes

an original way of relating himself to the object, and is on the same
footing as perception. Light is thus thrown upon the distinction between abstract and concrete movement the background to concrete
movement is the world as given, whereas the background to abstract
movement is built up When I motion my friend to come nearer, my
intention is not a thought prepared within me and I do not perceive
the signal in my body. I beckon across the world, I beckon over there,
where my friend is, the distance between us, his consent or refusal are
immediately read in my gesture, there is not a perception followed by
a movement, for both form a system which varies as a whole If,
for example, realizing that I am not going to be obeyed, I vary my
gesture, we have here, not two distinct acts of consciousness What
happens is that I see my partner's unwillingness, and my gesture of —
impatience emerges from this situation without any intervening
thought [1] If I then execute 'the same' movement, but without having
any present or even imaginary partner in mind, and treat it as 'a set
of movements in themselves', [2] if, that is, I perform a 'flexion' of the
forearm in relation to the upper arm, with 'supination' of the arm and
'flexion' of the fingers, my body, which a moment ago was the vehicle
of the movement, now becomes its end, its motor project is no longer
directed towards someone in the world, but towards my fore and
upper arm, and my fingers, and it is directed towards them, furthermore, in so far as they are capable of breaking with their involvement
in the given world and giving shape round about me to an imaginary
situation, or even in so far as, independently of any fictitious partner,
I look with curiosity upon this strange signifying contrivance and set
it to work for my amusement [3] The abstract movement carves out
within that plenum of the world in which concrete movement took
place a zone of reflection and subjectivity; it superimposes upon
physical space a potential or human space Concrete movement is
therefore centripetal whereas abstract movement is centrifugal. The
former occurs in the realm of being or of the actual, the latter on the
other hand in that of the possible or the non-existent, the first adheres
to a given background, the second throws out its own background
The normal function which makes abstract movement possible is one
of 'projection' whereby the subject of movement keeps in front of
him an area of free space in which what does not naturally exist may
take on a semblance of existence One knows of patients with powers

[1] Goldstein, *Über die Abhangigkeit*,   , p 161
[2] Ibid
[3] Goldstein (*Über die Abhangigkeit* . ., pp 160 and ff) merely says that the
background of abstract movement is the body, and this is true in that the body
during abstract movement is no longer merely the vehicle, but becomes the aim
of the movement Nevertheless, by changing function, it also changes its existential modality and passes from the actual to the possible

less seriously affected than Schneider's who perceive forms, distances
and objects in themselves, but who are unable either to trace in objects
the directions which are useful from the point of view of action, or
to arrange them according to some given principle, or generally to
assign to the spatial scene delimitations in human terms which make
it the field of our action. For instance, patients faced with a dead end
in a labyrinth have difficulty in finding 'the opposite direction' If a
ruler is laid between them and the doctor they cannot, to order, distribute the objects between 'their side' and 'the doctor's side'. They
are very inaccurate in pointing out, on another person's arm, the
point corresponding to the one stimulated on their own. Knowing
that the month is March and the day a Monday, they will have difficulty in saying what the previous month and day were, though they
may well know by heart the days and months in their correct order.
They are incapable of comparing the number of units contained in
two sets of sticks placed in front of them they may count the same
stick twice over, or else include in one set of sticks some which belong
to the other [1] The reason is that all these operations require the same
ability to mark out boundaries and directions in the given world, to
establish lines of force, to keep perspectives in view, in a word, to
organize the given world in accordance with the projects of the present moment, to build into the geographical setting a behavioural
one, a system of meanings outwardly expressive of the subject's internal activity For these patients the world exists only as one ready-
made or congealed, whereas for the normal person his projects
polarize the world, bringing magically to view a host of signs which
guide action, as notices in a museum guide the visitor This function
of 'projection' or 'summoning' (in the sense in which the medium
summons an absent person and causes him to appear) is also what
makes abstract movement possible: for, in order to be in possession
of my body independently of any urgent task to be performed; in
order to enjoy the use of it as the mood takes me, in order to describe
in the air a movement formulated only verbally or in terms of moral
requirements, I must reverse the natural relationship in which the
body stands to its environment, and a human productive power must
reveal itself through the density of being

It is in these terms that the disorder discernible in the movements
in question may be described. But it may be thought that this description (and this criticism has often been made of psychoanalysis) [2]

[1] Van Woerkom, *Sur la notion de l'espace (le sens géométrique)*, pp 113-19
[2] Cf for example, H Le Savoureux, 'Un philosophe en face de la Psychanalyse',
Nouvelle Revue Française, February 1939 'For Freud the mere fact of having
related symptoms to each other through plausible logical links is a sufficient confirmation that a psychoanalytical interpretation, which means a psychological
one, is soundly based The adoption of logical coherency as the criterion for

presents to us only the significance or essence of the disease and not its cause. Science, it may be objected, waits upon explanation, which means looking beneath phenomena for the circumstances upon which they depend, in accordance with the tried methods of induction Here, for example, we know that the motor disorders of Schneider are related to far-reaching disorders of sight, which in turn arise from the occipital injury which lies at the root of his condition Schneider does not recognize any object by merely looking at it [1] His visual data are almost-amorphous patches.[2] As for objects not in sight, he is unable to form any visual image of them.[3] It is known, on the other hand, that 'abstract' movements become possible for the subject provided that he keeps his eyes fixed on the limb which is to perform them.[4] Thus the remnant of volitional motility is aided by what remains of visual knowledge The famous methods of Mill might allow us to conclude here that abstract movements and *Zeigen* are dependent on the power of visual representation, whereas concrete movements, which are preserved by the patient as are those imitative movements, whereby he compensates for his paucity of visual data, arise from the kinaesthetic or tactile sense, which incidentally was remarkably exploited by Schneider. It would appear, then, that the distinction between concrete and abstract movement, like that between *Greifen* and *Zeigen*, is reducible to the traditional distinction between tactile and visual, and the function of projection or evocation, which we brought to light above, to perception and visual representation.[5]

---

accepting an interpretation beings Freudian proof much nearer to metaphysical deduction than to scientific explanation . . In medical treatment of mental disease, psychological plausibility is regarded as practically worthless in the investigation of causes' (p 318)

[1] He succeeds only by being allowed 'imitative movements' (*nachfahrende Bewegungen*) of the head, hands or fingers which sketch in the imperfect outline of the object Gelb and Goldstein, *Zur Psychologie des optischen Wahrnehmungs-und Erkennungsvorganges, Psychologische Analysen hirnpathologischer Falle*, Chap I.

[2] 'The patient's visual data lack any specific and characteristic structure His impressions, unlike those of a normal person's, have no firm configuration, they have not, for instance, the typical look of a "square", a "triangle", a "straight line" or a "curve" Before him he sees only patches in which his sight allows him to pick out only salient characteristics, such as height and breadth and their relation to each other'. (Ibid , p '77) A gardener sweeping a path fifty yards away is 'a long streak with something moving backwards and forwards towards the top of it' (p 108) In the street the patient distinguishes men from vehicles by the fact that 'men are all the same, long and thin—vehicles are wide, unmistakeably so, and much thicker' (ibid)

[3] Ibid , p 116

[4] Gelb and Goldstein, *Über den Einfluss* . , pp. 213–22.

[5] It was in this sense that Gelb and Goldstein interpreted Schneider's case in the first works which they devoted to him (*Zur Psychologie* and *Über den*

In reality, an inductive analysis carried out according to Mill's methods is fruitless For the disturbances of abstract movement and *Zeigen* are encountered not only in cases of psychological blindness, but also in cerebellar patients and in many other disorders [1] There is no justification for picking out as crucial just one of these concordances and using it to 'explain' the act of pointing out. In face of the ambiguity of facts one must abandon the mere statistical noting-down of coincidences, and try to 'understand' the relation which they reveal In cerebellar cases it is observed that visual as distinct from auditory stimuli produce only imperfect motor reactions, and yet there is with them no reason to presume any primary disturbance of the visual function. It is not because the latter is deficient that designatory movements become impossible, but, on the contrary, because the attitude of *Zeigen* is impossible that the visual stimuli arouse only partial reactions. We must admit that the sound, of itself, prompts rather a grasping movement, and visual perception the act of pointing 'The sound always leads us towards its content, its significance for us, in visual presentation, on the other hand, we can much more easily "disregard" the content and we are drawn much more definitely towards the part of space where the object is to be found '[2] A meaning then is definable less in terms of the indescribable quality of its 'mental contents' than in terms of a certain manner of presenting its object, of its epistemological structure having its quality as concrete realization and, in the language of Kant, exhibition The doctor who brings to bear upon the patient 'visual' or 'auditory stimuli' believes that he is testing 'visual' or 'auditory sensibility' and drawing up an inventory of sensible qualities which make up consciousness (in empiricist language) or of the material at the disposal of cognition (in intellectualist language) The doctor and the psychologist borrow the concepts of 'sight' and 'hearing' from common sense which considers them univocal, because our body includes as a matter of fact sets of visual and auditory apparatus which are anatomically distinct and to which isolatable contents of consciousness are supposed to correspond according to a general postulate of 'constancy'[3] which expresses our natural ignorance of ourselves But, when taken up and systematically applied by science these confused concepts hinder research and finally necessitate a general revision of these naive cate-

---

Einfluss) It will be seen how subsequently (*Über die Abhangigkeit* and particularly *Zeigen und Greifen* and the works published under their editorship by Benary, Hocheimer and Steinfeld) they broadened their diagnosis The progress of their analysis is a particularly clear example of the progress of psychology.

[1] *Zeigen und Greifen*, p. 456

[2] Ibid , pp 458-9

[3] Cf above, Introduction, p 7

gories. In fact, the measuring of thresholds tests functions prior to any specific identification of sensible qualities and to the elaboration of knowledge, the way in which the subject makes his surroundings exist for him, either as a pole of activity and the terminus of an act of seizure or expulsion, or else as a spectacle and theme of knowledge. The motor disturbances of cerebellar cases and those of psychological blindness can be co-ordinated only if we identify the basis of movement and vision not as a collection of sensible qualities but as a certain way of giving form or structure to our environment We are led back by the very use of this inductive method to 'metaphysical' questions which positivism would wish to avoid Induction succeeds only provided that it is not restricted to noting things as present or absent, with concomitant variations, and that it conceives and comprehends facts as subsumed under ideas not contained in them. It is not a matter of choosing between a description of the disorder which furnishes the meaning and an explanation which provides the cause There are, moreover, no explanations without comprehension

But let us make our objection more explicit On examination it is seen to be twofold.

1 The 'cause' of a 'psychic fact' is never another 'psychic fact' capable of being disclosed to straightforward observation. For example, visual representation does not explain abstract movement, for it is itself endowed with the same power of throwing out a spectacle which is revealed in abstract movement and the act of pointing. Now this power does not come under the senses, not even under any inner sense Let it be said provisionally that it is disclosed only to a certain kind of reflection, the nature of which we shall examine closely later It follows that psychological induction is not a mere inventory of facts. Psychology does not provide its explanations by identifying, among a collection of facts, the invariable and unconditioned antecedent It conceives or comprehends facts in exactly the same way as induction in physical science, not content to note empirical sequences, creates notions capable of co-ordinating facts. That is why, in psychology as in physics, no induction can avail itself of any crucial experiment. Since explanation is not discovered but created, it is never given with the fact, but is always simply a probable interpretation. So far we have merely applied to psychology what has been fully demonstrated with regard to physical induction,[1] and our first complaint is against the empiricist manner of conceiving induction and against Mill's methods.

2 Now we shall see that this first objection covers a second one. In psychology it is not only empiricism that has to be challenged It is

[1] Cf. Brunschvicg, *L'Expérience humaine et la Causalité physique*, Part I

115

the inductive method and causal thinking generally. The object of psychology is such that it cannot possibly be expressed as the relations of function to variable. Let us make these two points clear in some detail.

(1) We notice that Schneider's motor disturbances are associated with large-scale deficiency of knowledge gained by visual means. We are therefore tempted to regard psychological blindness as a distinctive variety of pure tactile behaviour, and, since consciousness of bodily space and abstract movement, which has potential space in view, are almost totally absent, we are inclined to conclude that the sense of touch alone gives us no experience of objective space.[1] We shall then say that touch by itself is not of a kind to provide a background to movement, that is to say, to set out in front of the moving subject his departure and arrival points in strict simultaneity. The patient tries to provide for himself a 'kinaesthetic background' by means of preparatory movements, and is successful in thus 'marking' the position of his body at the outset and in launching into the movement, yet this kinaesthetic background is precarious, and could not possibly equal the visual background in constantly relating motion to its points of departure and arrival throughout the movement's duration. It is thrown out of gear by the movement itself and needs to be restored after each phase of the movement. That is why, as we propose to put it, Schneider's abstract movements have lost their melodic flow, why they are made up of fragments placed end to end, and why they often 'run off the rails' on the way. The practical field which Schneider lacks is none other than the visual field.[2] But in order to be justified in relating, in psychological blindness, the motor to the visual disturbance, and, in the normal subject, the projective function to vision as its invariable and unconditioned antecedent, then we must be sure that only the visual data have been affected by the disease and that all other pre-conditions of behaviour, particularly tactile experience, have been left exactly as they were in the normal person. Can we confidently maintain this? At this stage it becomes clear that the facts are ambiguous, that no experience is decisive and no explanation final. When we observe that a normal subject is capable of making abstract movements with his eyes shut, and that the tactile experience of the normal person is sufficient to govern motility, it can always be retorted that the tactile data of the normal person have received their objective structure from visual data according to the old conception of the education of the senses. When we observe that a blind person is able to localize *stimuli* on the surface of his body and perform abstract movements—apart from

[1] Gelb and Goldstein, *Über den Einfluss* , pp. 227 50
[2] Goldstein, *Über die Abhängigkeit*, pp. 163 and ff

the fact that there are examples of preparatory movements among the blind, the reply can always be made that frequent associations have imparted the qualitative colouring of kinaesthetic impressions to tactile ones and welded the former into a quasi-simultaneous occurrence [1] Indeed, many factors in the behaviour of patients[2] lead one to suspect some primary modification of tactile experience For example, a subject may know how to knock at a door, but he can no longer do so if the door is hidden or merely out of reach In the latter case, the patient cannot perform the action of knocking or opening in a void, *even if his eyes are open and fixed on the door.*[3] How can we invoke visual failure here, when the patient enjoys a visual perception of the objective which is ordinarily sufficient to govern his movements more or less satisfactorily? Have we not brought to light a primary disturbance of touch? Clearly, for an object to be able to produce a movement it must be included in the patient's field of movement, and the disturbance consists of a shrinkage in this field, which is henceforth limited to objects actually touchable, and exclusive of that horizon of possible touch which surrounds them for the normal person. The deficiency would appear, in the last resort, to affect a function much deeper than vision, deeper too than touch conceived as a collection of given qualities. It appears to concern the subject's vital area that opening upon the world which has the effect of making objects at present out of reach count notwithstanding for the normal person; they exist for him as touchable things and are part of his world of movement According to this hypothesis, when patients observe their hand and the goal of their action throughout a movement,[4] we must understand this not as a mere amplification of a normal procedure, for the recourse to vision is to be seen as necessitated merely by the collapse of the sense of potential touch. But, on the strictly inductive plane this interpretation, in which touch is primarily involved, remains optional, and we may always prefer, with Goldstein, a different one: according to this the patient, wishing to strike, needs a goal within physical reach, precisely because his sight, in which he is deficient, is no longer adequate to provide a substantial background to the movement. There is, then, no fact capable of decisively bearing out that the tactile experience of patients is or is not identical with that of normal people, and Goldstein's conception, like the physical theory, can always be reconciled with the facts, given some auxiliary hypothesis. No rigorously exclusive interpretation is possible in psychology as in physics.

[1] Goldstein, *Über den Einfluss* . , pp 244 and ff

[2] We are here concerned with the case of S which Goldstein himself puts alongside the Schneider case, in his book *Über die Abhangigkeit*

[3] *Über die Abhangigkeit* .   , pp 178–84   [4] Ibid , p 150

However, if we look more closely, we shall see that the impossibility of a decisive experiment, in psychology, is attributable to special reasons It arises from the very nature of the object under investigation, namely behaviour, and leads to important consequences Between theories, neither of which is either ruled out or completely vindicated by the facts, physics can nevertheless choose according to the degree of probability, that is, according to the number of facts which each succeeds in co-ordinating without loading itself with auxiliary hypotheses elaborated to meet the needs of the case. In psychology this criterion is lacking no auxiliary hypothesis is necessary, as we have seen, to explain in terms of visual disturbance the impossibility of the action of 'knocking' in front of a door. Not only do we never arrive at an exclusive interpretation (deficiency of sense of potential touch *or* deficiency of visual world), but, what is more, we necessarily have to do with *equally probable* interpretations because 'visual representations', 'abstract movement' and 'sense of potential touch' are only different names for one and the same central phenomenon Hence psychology is not in the same position as physics, that is to say, confined within the probability of inductions, it is unable to choose, even on the basis of plausibility, between hypotheses which from a strictly inductive point of view remain incompatible. For an induction, even when it is merely probable, to remain a possibility, the 'visual representation' or the 'tactile perception' must be the cause of the abstract movement, or alternatively both must be effects of another cause. The three or four terms must be able to be considered from the outside and we must be able to pick out the correlative variations But if they should prove incapable of being isolated, if each of them presupposed the rest, the failure involved would not be a failure of empiricism or of attempts to find a decisive experiment, it would be the failure of the inductive method or of causal thinking in the realm of psychology. We thus arrive at the second point that we were trying to make.

(ii) If, as Goldstein recognizes, the co-existence of the tactile with the visual data, in the case of the normal person, modifies the former sufficiently to enable them to provide a background for abstract movement, the tactile data of the patient, which are cut off from the visual contribution, cannot be forthwith identified with those of the normal person. Tactile and visual data, says Goldstein, are not juxtaposed in the normal person; the former derive from the proximity of the latter a 'qualitative colouring' which they have lost for Schneider It follows, he adds, that the study of the purely tactile is impossible as far as the normal person is concerned, and that derangement alone provides a picture of what tactile experience reduced to itself would comprise [1] The conclusion is sound, but it amounts to maintaining that the word 'touch' has not the same meaning applied to the normal as to the abnormal subject, that the 'purely tactile' is a pathological phenomenon which does not enter as a component into normal experience It is further implied that illness, by disturbing the visual function, has not disclosed the pure essence of touch, that it has indeed changed the whole of the subject's experience, or, if one prefers it put in this way, that there is not in the normal subject a tactile experience and also a visual one, but an integrated experience to which it is impossible to gauge the contribution of each sense. The experiences mediated by touch in psychological blindness have nothing in common with those which touch mediates in the normal subject, and neither set really deserves to be called 'tactile' data. Tactile experience is not a condition apart which might be kept constant while the 'visual' experience was varied with a view to pinning on to each its own causality, nor is behaviour a function of these variables. It is on the contrary presupposed in defining them just as each is presupposed in defining the other [2] Psychological blindness, deficiency of sense of touch and motor disturbances are three *expressions* of a more fundamental disturbance through which they can be understood and not three component factors of morbid behaviour Visual representations, tactile data and motility are three phenomena which

---

[1] *Über den Einfluss* , pp 227 and ff

[2] On the conditioning of sensory data by motility, cf *Structure du Comportement*, p 41, and the experiments which show that a dog when chained up does not perceive as does a dog free in its movements The procedures of traditional psychology are strangely mixed, in the writings of Gelb and Goldstein, with the concrete emphasis derived from Gestalt psychology They recognize clearly enough that the perceiving subject reacts as a whole, but the totality is conceived as a mixture and touch receives from its co-existence with sight only a 'qualitative colouring', whereas according to the spirit of Gestalt psychology, two sensory realms can communicate only by becoming absorbed as inseparable constituents into an intersensory system Now if tactile data, along with visual ones, make up a composite formation, it is clearly on condition that they themselves, on their own ground, bring into being a spatial organization, for otherwise the connection between touch and sight would be an external association, and the tactile data would remain, in the total configuration, what they are taken each in isolation—two consequences equally ruled out by Gestalt theory. It is fair to add that, in another work (Bericht uber den IX Kongress für experimentelle Psychologie in Munchen, *Die psychologische Bedeutung pathologischer Storungen der Raumwahrnehmung*), Gelb himself points out the inadequacy of the work which we have just analysed We may not even speak, he says, of a coalescence of touch and sight in the normal subject, or even make any distinction between these two components in reactions to space. Both pure tactile and pure visual experience, with its space of juxtaposition and its represented spaces, are products of analysis There is a concrete manipulation of space in which all senses collaborate in an 'undifferentiated unity' (p 76) and the sense of touch is ill-adapted only to the theoretical knowledge of space.

119

stand out sharply within the unity of behaviour. When, by reason of the fact that they show correlated variations, we try to explain one in terms of the other, we forget, for example, that the act of visual representation, as is proved in cerebellar cases, already presupposes the same power of projection as is seen in abstract movement and in the act of pointing out, and thus we beg the question. Inductive and causal thought, by vesting in vision or touch or any one *de facto* datum the power of projection which is found in them all, conceals that power from us and blinds us to that dimension of behaviour which is precisely the one with which psychology is concerned. In physics, the establishment of a law requires the scientist to conceive the idea under which the facts are to be co-ordinated, and this idea, which is not found in the facts, will never be verified by any conclusive experiment, and will never be more than probable But it is still the idea of a causal link, in the sense of a relationship of function to variable. Atmospheric pressure had to be invented but, after all, it was still a third person process, the function of a certain number of variables. In so far as behaviour is a form, in which 'visual' and 'tactile contents', sensibility and motility appear only as inseparable moments, it remains inaccessible to causal thought and is capable of being apprehended only by another kind of thought, that which grasps its object as it comes into being and as it appears to the person experiencing it, with the atmosphere of meaning then surrounding it, and which tries to infiltrate into that atmosphere in order to discover, behind scattered facts and symptoms, the subject's whole being, when he is normal, or the basic disturbance, when he is a patient.

We cannot explain disturbances in the power of abstract movement in terms of loss of visual contents, nor, consequently, the function of projection in terms of the actual presence of these contents. So one method alone still seems possible: it consists in reconstituting the basic disturbance by going back from the symptoms not to a *cause* which is itself observable, but to a *reason* or intelligible condition of possibility for the state of affairs It involves treating the human subject as an irresolvable consciousness which is wholly present in every one of its manifestations If the disturbance is not to be related to the contents, it must be linked to the form of knowledge, if psychology is not empiricist and explicative, it ought to be rationalistic and reflective In exactly the same way as the act of naming,[1] the act of pointing out presupposes that the object, instead of being approached, grasped and absorbed by the body. is kept at a distance and stands as a picture in front of the patient Plato still allowed the empiricist the power of pointing a finger at things, but the truth is that even this silent gesture is impossible if *what* is pointed out is not

[1] Cf Gelb and Goldstein, *Über Farbennamenamnesie*

120

already torn from instantaneous existence and monadic existence, and treated as representative of its previous appearances in me, and of its simultaneous appearances in others, in other words, subsumed under some category and promoted to the status of a concept If the patient is no longer able to point to some part of his body which is touched, it is because he is no longer a subject face to face with an objective world, and can no longer take up a 'categorial attitude'.[1] In the same way, abstract movement is endangered in so far as it pre-supposes awareness of an objective, is borne on by that awareness, and is movement for itself Indeed it is not triggered off by any existing object, but is clearly centrifugal, outlining in space a gratui-tous intention which has reference to one's own body, making an object of it instead of going through it to link up with things by means of it It is, then, diffused with a power of objectification, a 'symbolical function',[2] a 'representative function',[3] a power of 'projection'[4] which is, moreover, already at work in forming 'things'. It consists in treating sense-data as mutually representative, and also collectively representative of an 'eidos', in giving a meaning to these data, in breathing a spirit into them, in systematizing them, in centring a plurality of experiences round one intelligible core, in bringing to light in them an identifiable unity when seen in different perspectives To sum up, it consists in placing beneath the flow of impressions an explanatory invariant, and in giving a form to the stuff of experience Now it is not possible to maintain that consciousness *has* this power, it *is* this power itself As soon as there is consciousness, and in order that there may be consciousness, there must be something to be con-scious of, an intentional object, and consciousness can move towards this object only to the extent that it 'derealizes' itself and throws itself into it, only if it is wholly in this reference to .   something, only if it is a pure meaning-giving act. If a being is consciousness, he must be nothing but a network of intentions. If he ceases to be definable in terms of the act of sense-giving, he relapses into the condition of a thing, the thing being precisely what does not know, what slumbers in absolute ignorance of itself and the world, what consequently is not a true 'self', i e a 'for-itself', and has only a spatio-temporal form of individuation, existence in itself [5] Consciousness, therefore, does

[1] Gelb and Goldstein, *Zeigen und Greifen*, pp 456-7.
[2] Head
[3] Bouman and Grunbaum
[4] Van Woerkom
[5] Husserl has often been credited with this distinction In fact, it is found in Descartes and Kant In our opinion Husserl's originality lies beyond the notion of intentionality it is to be found in the elaboration of this notion and in the discovery, beneath the intentionality of representations, of a deeper intentionality, which others have called existence

not admit of degree. If the patient no longer exists as a consciousness, he must then exist as a thing Either movement is movement for itself, in which case the 'stimulus' is not its cause but its intentional object—or else it disintegrates and is dispersed in existence in itself, and becomes an objective process in the body, whose phases are successive but unknown to each other The special status of concrete movements in illness is explained by seeing them as reflexes in the traditional sense. The patient's hand meets the point on his body where the mosquito has settled because pre-established nerve circuits, not the excitation, control the reaction Actions performed in the course of his work are preserved because they are dependent upon firmly rooted conditioned reflexes. They persist in spite of psychic deficiencies because they are movements in themselves. The distinction between concrete and abstract movement, between *Greifen* and *Zeigen* comes down to that between the physiological and the psychic, existence in itself and existence for itself [1]

But we shall see that in reality the first distinction, far from covering also the second, is incompatible with it. Every 'physiological explanation' tends to become generalized. If the grasping action or the concrete movement is guaranteed by some factual connection between each point on the skin and the motor muscles which guide the

---

[1] Gelb and Goldstein sometimes tend to interpret phenomena in this sense They have done more than anyone to go beyond the traditional dualism of automatism and consciousness. But they have never named this third term *between* the psychic and the physiological, between the for itself and the in itself to which their analyses always led them and which we call existence. Hence their earliest works often fall back on the traditional dichotomy of body and consciousness 'The act of seizing is, much more than that of pointing, determined by relationships existing between the organism and its surrounding field . . ., it is less a question of relations consciously formed than of immediate reactions , we are here concerned with a much more vital process, one describable in biological language as primitive ' (*Zeigen und Greifen*, p 459) 'The act of seizing remains completely insensitive to modifications affecting the conscious part of this performance, to any deficiency of simultaneous apprehension (in psychological blindness), to the instability of perceived space (in cerebellar cases), to disturbances of sensitivity (in certain cortical lesions), because it is not carried out in this objective domain It is preserved as long as the peripheral excitations are still sufficient to govern it accurately ' (*Zeigen und Greifen*, p 460) Gelb and Goldstein question the existence of localizing reflex movements (Henri), but only in so far as there might be a tendency to regard them as innate They retain the idea of an 'automatic localization not inclusive of any awareness of space, since it operates even during sleep' (thus conceived as total unconsciousness) It is certainly 'learnt' from the time of comprehensive reactions of the whole body to tactile stimuli in babyhood—but this apprenticeship is conceived as the accumulation of 'kinaesthetic residues' which are 'awakened' in the normal adult by external excitations, and which direct him towards the appropriate outlets (*Über den Einfluss* , pp 167–206). In correctly performing the actions required by his trade, Schneider shows that they are habitual totalities which demand no consciousness of space (ibid , pp 221–2)

hand, it is difficult to see why the same nerve circuit communicating a scarcely different movement to the same muscles should not guarantee the gesture of *Zeigen* as it does the movement of *Greifen* Between the mosquito which pricks the skin and the ruler which the doctor presses on the same spot, the physical difference is not great enough to explain why the grasping movement is possible, but the act of pointing impossible. The two 'stimuli' are really distinguishable only if we take into account their affective value or biological meaning, and the two responses cease to merge into one another only if we consider the *Zeigen* and the *Greifen* as two ways of relating to the object and two types of being in the world. But this is precisely what cannot be done once we have reduced the living body to the condition of an object If it is once conceded that it may be the seat of third person processes, nothing in behaviour can be reserved for consciousness Both gestures and movements, employing as they do the same organ-objects, the same nerve-objects, must be given their place on the map of interiorless processes, and inserted in the compactly woven stuff of 'physiological conditions'. Does not the patient who, in doing his job, moves his hand towards a tool lying on the table, displace the segments of his arm exactly as he would have to do to perform the abstract movement of extending it? Does not an everyday gesture involve a series of muscular contractions and innervations? It is therefore impossible to set limits to physiological explanation In another way it is impossible also to set limits to consciousness If we relate the act of pointing to consciousness, if once the stimulus can cease to be the cause of the reaction and become its intentional object, it becomes inconceivable that it should ever function as a pure cause or that the movement should ever be blind. For if 'abstract' movements are possible, in which consciousness of the starting and finishing points is present, we must at every moment in our life know where our body is without having to look for it as we look for an object moved from its place during our absence Even 'automatic' movements must therefore announce themselves to our consciousness, which means that there never occur, in our bodies, movements in themselves. And if all objective space is for intellectual consciousness only, we must recognize the categorial attitude even in the movement of grasping itself [1] Like physiological causality, arrival

[1] Goldstein himself, who tended (as we have seen in the preceding note) to relate *Greifen* to the body and *Zeigen* to the categorial attitude, is forced to go back on this 'explanation' The act of grasping, he says, may 'be performed to order, and the patient *tries* to grasp In order to do so he does not need to be aware of the point in space towards which he thrusts forward his hand, but he nevertheless has a feeling of orientation in space ' (*Zeigen und Greifen*, p 461) The act of grasping, as found in normal subjects, 'still demands a categorial and conscious attitude' (ibid , p 465)

at self-awareness has nowhere to start We must either reject physiological explanation or admit that it is all-inclusive—either deny consciousness or accept it as comprehensive We cannot relate certain movements to bodily mechanism and others to consciousness. The body and consciousness are not mutually limiting, they can be only parallel Any physiological explanation becomes generalized into mechanistic physiology, any achievement of self-awareness into intellectualist psychology, and mechanistic physiology or intellectualist psychology bring behaviour down to the same uniform level and wipe out the distinction between abstract and concrete movement, between *Zeigen* and *Greifen* This distinction can survive only if there are *several ways for the body to be a body, several ways for consciousness to be consciousness* As long as the body is defined in terms of existence in-itself, it functions uniformly like a mechanism, and as long as the mind is defined in terms of pure existence for-itself, it knows only objects arrayed before it The distinction between abstract and concrete movement is therefore not to be confused with that between body and consciousness, it does not belong to the same reflective dimension, but finds its place only in the behavioural dimension. Pathological phenomena introduce variations before our eyes in something which is not the pure awareness of an object. Any diagnosis, like that of intellectualist psychology, which sees here a collapse of consciousness and the freeing of automatism, or again that of an empiricist psychology of contents, would leave the fundamental disturbance untouched

The intellectualist analysis, here as everywhere, is less false than abstract It is true that the 'symbolic function' or the 'representative function' underlies our movements, but it is not a final term for analysis. It too rests on a certain groundwork. The mistake of intellectualism is to make it self-subsistent, to remove it from the stuff in which it is realized, and to recognize in us, as a non-derivative entity, an undistanced presence in the world. For, using this consciousness, an entirely transparent consciousness, this intentionality which admits of no degrees of more or less, as a starting point, everything that separates us from the real world—error, sickness, madness, in short incarnation—is reduced to the status of mere appearance Admittedly intellectualism does not bring consciousness into being independently of its material. For example it takes great care not to introduce behind the word, the action and the perception, any 'symbolic consciousness' as the common and numerically sole form of linguistic, perceptual and motor material. There is no 'general symbolic faculty', says Cassirer,[1] and analytical reflection does not seek

[1] Symbolvermogen schlechthin, Cassirer, *Philosophie der symbolischen Formen*, III, p 320

to establish between pathological phenomena relating to perception, language and action a 'community in being', but a 'community in meaning'.[1] Just because it has finally gone beyond causal thought and realism, intellectualist psychology would be able to see the meaning or essence of illness, and recognize a unity of consciousness which is not evident on the plane of being, and which is vouched for, in its own eyes, on the plane of truth But the distinction between community in being and community in sense, the conscious passage from the existential order to the order of value and the transvaluation which allows meaning and value to be declared autonomous are, for practical purposes, equivalent to an abstraction, since, from the point of view finally adopted, the variety of phenomena becomes insignificant and incomprehensible. If consciousness is placed outside being, the latter cannot breach it, the empirical variety of consciousnesses—morbid, primitive, childlike consciousness, the consciousness of others—cannot be taken seriously, there is nothing to be known or understood, one thing alone makes sense the pure essence of consciousness. None of these consciousnesses could fail to effect the *Cogito.* The lunatic, *behind* his ravings, his obsessions and lies, *knows that he* is raving, that he is allowing himself to be haunted by an obsession, that he is lying, in short he *is* not mad, *he thinks he is.* All is then for the best and insanity is only perversion of the will. The analysis of the meaning of illness, once it ends with the symbolic function, identifies all disorders as the same, uniting aphasia, apraxia and agnosia[2] and perhaps even has no way of distinguishing them from schizophrenia[3] It then becomes understandable that doctors and psychologists should decline the invitation to intellectualism and fall back, for want of anything better, on the attempts at causal explanation which at least have the merit of taking into account what is peculiar to illness, and to each form of it, and which by this means give at any rate the illusion of possessing actual knowledge. Modern pathology shows that there is no strictly elective disturbance, but it shows equally that each one is coloured by the sector of behaviour which it principally attacks.[4] Even if all aphasia, when closely observed, is seen to involve disturbances of both gnosic* and praxic

---

[1] Gemeinsamkeit im Sein, Gemeinsamkeit im Sinn, ibid
[2] Cf for example Cassirer, *Philosophie der Symbolischen Formen*, III, Chap VI, *Pathologie des Symbolbewusstseins*
[3] One can indeed imagine an intellectualist interpretation of schizophrenia which would equate the atomistic conception of time and the loss of the future with a collapse of the categorial attitude
[4] *Structure du Comportement*, pp 91 and ff

* *Gnosia* The perceptive faculty, enabling one to recognize the form and nature of persons and things (Translator's note).

kinds, if all apraxia* involves linguistic and perceptual disturbances, and all agnosia† disturbances of language and action, the fact remains that the core of these disorders is here to be found in the domain of language, there in that of perception, and elsewhere in that of action When we invoke in all these cases the symbolic function, we are, it is true, characterizing the structure common to the different derangements, but this structure should not be separated from the stuff through which on each occasion it is realized, if not electively, at least in great measure. After all Schneider's trouble was not initially metaphysical, for it was a shell splinter which wounded him at the back of the head. The damage to his sight was serious, but it would be ridiculous, as we have said, to explain all the other deficiencies in terms of the visual one as their cause; but no less ridiculous to think that the shell splinter directly struck symbolic consciousness. – It was through his sight that Mind in him was impaired.

Until some means has been discovered whereby we can link the origin and the essence or meaning of the disturbance, until some definition is found for a *concrete essence*, a *structure* of illness which shall express both its generality and its particularity, until phenomenology becomes genetic phenomenology, unhelpful reversions to causal thought and naturalism will remain justified. Our problem therefore becomes clearer. The task for us is to conceive, between the linguistic, perceptual and motor contents and the form given to them or the symbolic function which breathes life into them, a relationship which shall be neither the reduction of form to content, nor the subsuming of content under an autonomous form. We need to understand both how Schneider's complaint everywhere overshoots particular contents—visual, tactile and motor—of his experience, and how it nevertheless attacks the symbolic function only through the specially chosen material provided by sight The senses and one's own body generally present the mystery of a collective entity which, without abandoning its thisness and its individuality, puts forth beyond itself meanings capable of providing a framework for a whole series of thoughts and experiences Although Schneider's trouble affects motility and thought as well as perception, the fact remains that what it damages, particularly in the domain of thought, is his power of apprehending simultaneous wholes, and in the matter of motility, that,

* *Apraxia* (i) A disorder of voluntary movement, consisting in a more or less complete incapacity to execute purposeful movements, notwithstanding the preservation of muscular power, sensibility, and co-ordination in general (ii) A psychomotor defect in which one is unable to apply to its proper use an object which one is nevertheless able to name and the uses of which one can describe (Translator's note)

† *Agnosia* Absence of ability to recognize the form and nature of persons and things, or the perceptive faculty (Translator's note)

so to speak, of taking a bird's-eye view of movement and projecting it outside himself. It is then in some sense mental space and practical space which are destroyed or impaired, and the words themselves are a sufficient indication of the visual origin of the disturbance. Visual trouble is not the cause of the other disturbances, particularly that directly affecting thought But neither is it a mere consequence of them. Visual contents, moreover, are not the cause of the function of projection, but neither is sight a mere opportunity given to Mind to bring into play a power in itself unconditioned. Visual contents are taken up, utilized and sublimated to the level of thought by a symbolical power which transcends them, but it is on the basis of sight that this power can be constituted. The relationship between matter and form is called in phenomenological terminology a relationship of *Fundierung* the symbolic function rests on the visual as on a ground, not that vision is its cause, but because it is that gift of nature which Mind was called upon to make use of beyond all hope, to which it was to give a fundamentally new meaning, yet which was needed, not only to be incarnate, but in order to be at all Form integrates within itself the content until the latter finally appears as a mere mode of form itself, and the historical stages leading up to thought as a ruse of Reason disguised as Nature But conversely, even in its intellectual sublimation, content remains in the nature of a radical contingency, the initial establishment or foundation[1] of knowledge and action, the first laying hold of being or value, whose concrete richness will never be finally exhausted by knowledge and action, and whose spontaneous method they will ceaselessly reapply. This dialectic of form and content is what we have to restore, or rather, since 'reciprocal action' is as yet only a compromise with causal thought, and a contradictory principle, we have to describe the circumstances under which this contradiction is conceivable, which means existence, the perpetual re-ordering of fact and hazard by a reason non-existent before and without those circumstances.[2]

[1] We are translating Husserl's favourite word *Stiftung*

[2] See below third part E Cassirer clearly has the same aim when he takes Kant to task for having most of the time analysed only an 'intellectual sublimation of experience' (*Philosophie der Symbolischen Formen*, T III, p 14), when he tries to express, through the notion of symbolic pregnancy, the absolute simultaneity of matter and form, or when he adopts for his own purposes Hegel's declaration that the mind carries and preserves its past in the depths of its present But the relationships between the various symbolic forms remain ambiguous One always wonders whether the function of *Darstellung* is a stage in the return to itself of an eternal consciousness, the shadow of the function of *Bedeutung*—or whether, on the contrary, the function of Bedeutung is an unforeseeable amplification of the first constitutive 'wave' When Cassirer takes up the Kantian formula according to which consciousness can analyse only what it has synthesized, he is manifestly returning to intellectualism despite the phenomenological and even existentail analyses which his book contains and which we shall have occasion to use.

127

If we want to observe what underlies the 'symbolic function' itself, we must first of all realize that even intelligence is not reconcilable with intellectualism. What impairs thought in Schneider's case is not that he is incapable of perceiving concrete data as specimens of a unique *eidos*, or of subsuming them under some category, but on the contrary, that he can relate them only by a quite explicit subsumption It is noticeable, for example, that the patient does not understand even such simple analogies as 'fur is to cat as plumage is to bird', or 'light is to lamp as heat is to stove', or 'eye is to light and colour as ear is to sounds' In the same way he cannot understand, in their metaphorical sense, such common expressions as 'the chair leg' or 'the head of a nail', although he knows what part of the object is indicated by these words. It may happen that normal subjects of equal educational standard are no more able to *explain* the analogy, but this is for diametrically opposed reasons It is easier for the normal subject to understand the analogy than to analyse it, whereas the patient manages to understand only when he has made it explicit by recourse to conceptual analysis 'He looks for . . a common material characteristic from which he can infer, as from a middle term, the identity of the two relationships' [1] For example, he thinks about the analogy between eye and ear and clearly does not understand it until he can say 'The eye and the ear are both sense organs, therefore they must give rise to something similar.' If we described analogy as the apperception of two given terms under a co-ordinating concept, we should be giving as normal a procedure which is exclusively pathological, and which represents the roundabout way in which the patient makes good the normal understanding of analogy. 'This freedom in choosing a *tertium comparationis* on the patient's part is the opposite of the intuitive formation of the image in the normal subject the latter seizes a specific identity in conceptual structures, for him the living processes of thought are symmetrical and mutually complementary Thus does he 'catch' the essential feature of the analogy, and one may always wonder whether a subject does not remain able to understand, even when this understanding is not adequately expressed through the formulation and clarification which he provides '[2] Living thought, then, does not consist in subsuming under some category The category imposes on the terms brought together a meaning external to them. It is by drawing upon already constituted language and upon the sense-relationships which it holds in store that Schneider succeeds in relating eye to ear as 'sense-organs' In normal thought eye and ear are immediately ap-

[1] Benary, *Studien zur Untersuchung der Intelligenz bei einem Fall von Seelenblindheit,* p 262
[2] Ibid , p 263

prehended in accordance with the analogy of their function, and their relationship can be fixed in a 'common characteristic' and recorded in language only because it has first been perceived in its origin in the singularity of sight and hearing

It will perhaps be objected that our criticism is valid only against a summary intellectualism which absorbs thought into a purely logical activity, whereas analytical reflection goes back to the origin of predication, finding behind the judgement of inherence that of relation, behind subsumption, seen as a mechanical and formal operation, the categorial act whereby thought bestows upon the subject the meaning expressed in the predicate Thus our criticism of the categorial function, it might be said, does nothing but reveal, behind the empirical use of the category, a transcendental use without which indeed the first is incomprehensible The distinction, however, between the empirical and transcendental use conceals the problem rather than solves it Critical philosophy duplicates the empirical operations of thought with a transcendental activity which has the task of bringing about all those syntheses for which empirical thought provides the elements But when I think something at the present moment, the guarantee of a non-temporal synthesis is insufficient and even unnecessary as a basis of my thought It is now, in the living present that the synthesis has to be effected, otherwise thought would be cut off from its transcendental premises. It cannot therefore be asserted that when I think I take my place once more in the eternal subject which I have never ceased to be For the true subject of thought is the person who achieves the conversion and resumption of action at this very moment, and it is he who breathes his own life into the non-temporal ghost We need therefore to understand how temporal thought links up with itself and brings about its own synthesis. The fact that the normal subject immediately grasps that the eye is to sight as the ear is to hearing shows that the eye and ear are immediately given to him as means of access to one and the same *world*, and furthermore that one world is for him antepredicatively self-evident, so that the equivalence of the 'sense-organs' and their analogy is to be read off from things and can be lived before being conceived. The Kantian subject posits a world, but, in order to be able to assert a truth, the actual subject must in the first place have a world or be in the world, that is, sustain round about it a system of meanings whose reciprocities, relationships and involvements do not require to be made explicit in order to be exploited When I move about my house, I know without thinking about it that walking towards the bathroom means passing near the bedroom, that looking at the window means having the fireplace on my left, and in this small world each gesture, each perception is immediately located in relation to a great number of possible co-ordinates When I chat with a friend whom I know well, each of his remarks and each of mine contains, in addition to the meaning it carries for everybody else, a host of references to the main dimensions of his character and mine, without our needing to recall previous conversations with each other These acquired worlds, which confer upon my experience its secondary meaning, are themselves carved out of a primary world which is the basis of the primary meaning. In the same way there is a 'world of thoughts', or a sediment left by our mental processes, which enables us to rely on our concepts and acquired judgements as we might on things there in front of us, presented globally, without there being any need for us to resynthesize them

In this way there can be for us a sort of mental panorama, with its clear-cut and its vague areas, a physiognomic disposition of questions and intellectual situations, such as research, discovery and certainty But the word 'sediment' should not lead us astray this acquired knowledge is not an inert mass in the depths of our consciousness My flat is, for me, not a set of closely associated images It remains a familiar domain round about me only as long as I still have 'in my hands' or 'in my legs' the main distances and directions involved, and as long as from my body intentional threads run out towards it Similarly my acquired thoughts are not a final gain, they continually draw their sustenance from my present thought, they offer me a meaning, but I give it back to them. Indeed our available store expresses for ever afresh the energy of our present consciousness Sometimes it weakens, as in moments of weariness, and then my 'world' of thought is impoverished and reduced to one or two obsessive ideas; sometimes, on the other hand, I am at the disposal of all my thoughts and every word spoken in front of me then stimulates questions and ideas, recasting and reorganizing the mental panorama, and presenting itself with a precise physiognomy. Thus what is acquired is truly acquired only if it is taken up again in a fresh momentum of thought, and a thought is assigned to its place only if it takes up its place itself The essence of consciousness is to provide itself with one or several worlds, to bring into being its own thoughts *before* itself, as if they were things, and it demonstrates its vitality indivisibly by outlining these landscapes for itself and then by abandoning them The world-structure, with its two stages of sedimentation and spontaneity, is at the core of consciousness, and it is in the light of a levelling-down of the 'world' that we shall succeed in understanding Schneider's intellectual, perceptual and motor disturbances, without assimilating them to each other

The traditional analysis of perception [1] distinguishes within it sense-

---

[1] We are holding over until the second part a closer study of perception, and we here confine our remarks to what is essential for the elucidation of the basic

givens and the meaning which they receive from an act of understanding Perceptual disturbances, from this point of view, could be only sensory deficiencies or gnosic disturbances Schneider's case, on the other hand, shows deficiencies affecting the junction of sensitivity and significance, deficiencies which disclose the existential conditioning of both If a fountain pen is shown to the patient, in such a way that the clip is not seen, the phases of recognition are as follows. 'It 's black, blue and shiny,' says the patient 'There is a white patch on it, and it is rather long, it has the shape of a stick It may be some sort of instrument. It shines and reflects light. It could also be a coloured glass ' The pen is then brought closer and the clip is turned towards the patient He goes on 'It must be a pencil or a fountain pen.' (He touches his breast pocket). 'It is put there, to make notes with '[1] It is clear that language intervenes at every stage of recognition by providing possible meanings for what is in fact seen, and that recognition advances *pari passu* with linguistic connections· from 'long' to 'shaped like a stick', from 'stick' to 'instrument', and from there to 'instrument for noting things down', and finally to 'fountain pen' The sense-data are limited to suggesting these meanings as a fact suggests a hypothesis to the physicist The patient, like the scientist, verifies mediately and clarifies his hypothesis by cross-checking facts, and makes his way blindly towards the one which co-ordinates them all.

This procedure contrasts with, and by so doing throws into relief, the spontaneous method of normal perception, that kind of living system of meanings which makes the concrete essence of the object immediately recognizable, and allows its 'sensible properties' to appear only through that essence. It is this familiarity and communication with the object which is here interrupted. In the normal subject the object 'speaks' and is significant, the arrangement of colours straight away 'means' something, whereas in the patient the meaning has to be brought in from elsewhere by a veritable act of interpretation Conversely in the normal person the subject's intentions are immediately reflected in the perceptual field, polarizing it, or placing their seal upon it, or setting up in it, effortlessly, a wave of significance In the patient the perceptual field has lost this plasticity If he is asked to make a square with four triangles identical with a given one, he replies that it is impossible and that with four triangles only two squares can be built. The experimenter insists, showing him that a square has two diagonals and can always be divided into four

---

and also the motor disturbance in Schneider's case. These anticipations and repetitions are unavoidable if, as we shall try to show, perception and experience of one's own body are mutually implied

[1] Hochheimer, *Analyse eines Seelenblinden von der Sprache*, p 49

131

triangles. The patient's reply is 'Yes, but that is because the parts necessarily fit each other When a square is divided into four, if the parts are brought together in the correct way, they must make a square '[1] He knows therefore what a square and a triangle are, even the relationship between these two meanings does not escape him, at least after the doctor's explanations, and he understands that any square can be split into triangles But he does not go on to conclude that any right-angled isosceles triangle can be used to construct a square, because the construction of this square requires that the given triangles be arranged differently and that the sensory-givens must become the means of illustration of an imaginary meaning. The world in its entirety no longer suggests any meaning to him and conversely the meanings which occur to him are not embodied any longer in the given world We shall say, in a word, that the world no longer has any *physiognomy* for him [2] This is what reveals the nature of the peculiarities seen in his drawings. Schneider never draws *from* the model (*nachzeichnen*); perception is not carried directly into movement With his left hand he feels the object, recognizes certain characteristics (a corner, a right angle), formulates his discovery and finally draws without any model a figure corresponding to the verbal formula.[3]

The translation of percept into movement is effected via the express meanings of language, whereas the normal subject penetrates into the object by perception, assimilating its structure into his substance, and through this body the object directly regulates his movements [4] This subject-object dialogue, this drawing together, by the subject, of the meaning diffused through the object, and, by the object, of the subject's intentions—a process which is physiognomic perception—arranges round the subject a world which speaks to him of himself, and gives his own thoughts their place in the world Since this function is impaired in Schneider's case, it is foreseeable that, *a fortiori*, perception of human events and other people will show deficiencies, for these presuppose the same taking up of external by internal and of internal by external. And indeed if a story is told to the patient, it is observed that instead of grasping it as a melodic whole with down and up beats, with its characteristic rhythm or

[1] Benary, op cit , p 255

[2] Schneider can hear read, or himself read, without recognizing it, a letter which he has written He even states that without signature one cannot know whose a letter is (Hochheimer, op cit , p 12)

[3] Benary, op cit , p 256

[4] It is this appropriation of the 'motive' in its full sense that Cezanne achieved after hours of meditation 'We are germinating,' he would say After which suddenly 'Everything would fall into place ' J Gasquet, *Cézanne*, II* Partie, *Le Motif*, pp 81-3

flow, he remembers it only as a succession of facts to be noted one by one. That is why he can understand it only if pauses are made in the narrative and used to sum up briefly the gist of what he has so far been told. When he tells back the story, he never does so *according to* the account given to him (*nacherzahlen*). he finds nothing to emphasize; he can understand the course of the story only as he tells it, and it is, as it were, reconstituted part by part.[1] There is, then, in the normal subject an essence of the story which emerges as it is told, without any express analysis, and this subsequently guides along any reproduction of the narrative. The story for him is a certain human event, recognizable by its style, and here the subject 'understands' because he has the power to live, beyond his immediate experience, through the events described. Generally speaking, nothing but what is immediately given is present to the speaker. The thought of others will never be present to him, since he has no immediate experience of it.[2] The words of others are for him signs which have to be severally deciphered, instead of being, as with the normal subject, the transparent envelope of a meaning *within* which he might live. Like events, words are for the patient not the theme of an act of drawing together or projecting, but merely the occasion for a methodical interpretation Like the object, other people 'tell' him nothing, and the phantoms which present themselves to him are devoid, not, it is true, of that intellectual meaning arrived at through analysis, but that primary meaning reached through co-existence.

Specifically intellectual disturbances, those of judgement and meaning—cannot be considered ultimate deficiencies, and must also be placed in the same existential context. Take, for example, 'number blindness'.[3] It has been possible to demonstrate that the patient, though able to count, add, subtract, multiply or divide in relation to the things placed in front of him, cannot conceive number, and that all his results are obtained by ritual procedures, which have no significant bearing on it. He knows by heart the sequence of numbers and recites it mentally, while checking off on his fingers the objects to be counted, added, subtracted, multiplied or divided. 'a number for him merely belongs to a sequence of numbers, and has no meaning as a fixed quantity, as a group or a determinate measure '[4] Of two numbers

[1] Benary, op cit , p 279
[2] Of a conversation of importance to him, he recalls only the general theme and the decision taken at the end of it, but not his interlocutor's words. 'I know what I said in a conversation from the reasons I had for saying it, what the other said is more difficult because I have nothing to hold on to (*Anhaltspunkt*) in order to remember' (Benary, op cit , p 214) It can be seen, furthermore, that the patient reconstitutes and infers his own attitude at the time of the conversation, and that he is incapable of directly 'taking hold' even of his own thoughts
[3] Benary, op cit , p 224   [4] Ibid , p 223

the greater for him is the one which comes 'after' in the numerical series. When he is given $5 + 4 - 4$ to work out, he does the sum in two stages without 'noticing anything in particular'. He merely agrees, if it is pointed out to him, that the number 5 'remains' He fails to understand that 'twice half' a given number is the number itself.[1] Are we then to say that he has lost number as a category or schema? Yet when he runs his eyes over the objects to be counted, checking each of them on his fingers, even though it often happens that he confuses objects already counted with those still to come, even though the synthesis may be vague, he obviously has the notion of a synthetic operation which is nothing other than numeration And conversely, with the normal subject the sequence of numbers as a kinetic melody practically devoid of genuinely numerical meaning is most often substituted for the concept of number. Number is never a pure concept, the absence of which would allow us to define Schneider's mental state, it is a structure of consciousness involving degrees of more or less. The true act of counting requires of the subject that his operations as they develop and cease to occupy the centre of his consciousness, shall not cease to be there for him and shall constitute, for subsequent operations, a *ground* on which they may be established. Consciousness holds in reserve, behind itself, completed syntheses; these are still available and might be brought back into action, and it is on this basis that they are taken up and transcended in the total act of numeration What is called pure number or authentic number is only a development or extension, through repetition, of the process which constitutes any perception. Schneider's conception of number is affected only in so far as it implies, to a great extent, the power of laying out a past in order to move towards a future. It is this existential basis of intelligence which is affected, much more than intelligence itself, for, as we have shown,[2] Schneider's general intelligence is intact his replies are slow, never meaningless, but those of a mature, thinking man who takes an interest in the doctor's experiments. Beneath the intelligence as an anonymous function or as a categorial process, a personal core has to be recognized, which is the patient's being, his power of existing It is here that the illness has its seat Schneider would still like to arrive at political or religious opinions, but knows that it is useless to try. 'He must now be content with large-scale beliefs, without the power to express them.'[3] He never sings or whistles of his own accord [4] We shall see later that he never takes any initiative sexually He never goes out for a walk, but always on an errand, and he never recognizes Professor Goldstein's house as he passes it 'because he did not go out with the intention of

---

[1] Benary, op cit , p 240.   [2] Ibid p 284
[3] Ibid , op cit , p 213   [4] Hochheimer, op cit , p 37

going there'.[1] Just as he needs, by means of preparatory movements, to be able to 'take a grip' on his own body before performing movements when they are not mapped out ahead in a familiar situation,—so, a conversation with another person does not constitute for him a situation significant in itself, and requiring extempore replies. He can speak only in accordance with a plan drawn up in advance: 'He cannot fall back on the inspiration of the moment in order to find the ideas required in response to a complex stage of the conversation, and this is true whether it is a question of new or old points of view'[2] There is in his whole conduct something meticulous and serious which derives from the fact that he is incapable of play-acting. To act is to place oneself for a moment in an imaginary situation, to find satisfaction in changing one's 'setting' The patient, on the other hand, cannot enter into a fictitious situation without converting it into a real one. he cannot tell the difference between a riddle and a problem [3] In his case, the possible situation at every moment is so narrow that two sectors of the environment not having anything in common for him cannot simultaneously form a situation.[4] If one talks to him he cannot hear the sound of another conversation in the next room; if a dish is brought and placed on the table, he does not stop to wonder where the dish comes from. He states that one can see only in the direction in which one is looking, and only objects at which one is looking [5] Future and past are for him only 'shrunken' extensions of the present. He has lost 'our power of looking according to the temporal vector'.[6] He cannot take a bird's eye view of his past and unhesitatingly rediscover it by going from the whole to the parts: he rebuilds it, starting with a fragment which has kept its meaning and which provides him with a 'supporting-point' [7] Since he complains of the weather, he is asked if he feels better in winter. He replies: 'I can't say now, I can't say anything at the moment' [8] Thus all Schneider's troubles are reducible to a unity, but not the abstract unity of the 'representative function'. he is 'tied' to actuality, he 'lacks liberty',[9] that concrete liberty which comprises the general power of putting oneself into a situation. Beneath intelligence as beneath perception, we discover a more fundamental function, 'a vector mobile in all directions like a searchlight, one through which we can direct ourselves towards anything, in or outside ourselves, and display a form

[1] Hochheimer, op cit., p. 56

[2] Benary, op. cit , p 213

[3] In the same way there are for him no double meanings or puns because words have only one meaning at a time, and because the actual is entirely without any horizon of possibilities Benary, op. cit , p 283.

[4] Hochheimer, op. cit , p 32   [5] Ibid., pp. 32–33

[6] 'Useres Hineinsehen in den Zeitvektor', ibid   [7] Benary, op cit , p 213

[8] Hochheimer, op cit , p 33   [9] Ibid , p 32

135

of behaviour in relation to that object'.[1] Yet the analogy of the search-light is inadequate, since it presupposes given objects on to which the beam plays, whereas the nuclear function to which we refer, before bringing objects to our sight or knowledge, makes them exist in a more intimate sense, for us Let us therefore say rather, borrowing a term from other works,[2] that the life of consciousness—cognitive life, the life of desire or perceptual life—is subtended by an 'intentional arc' which projects round about us our past, our future, our human setting, our physical, ideological and moral situation, or rather which results in our being situated in all these respects. It is this intentional arc which brings about the unity of the senses, of intelligence, of sensibility and motility And it is this which 'goes limp' in illness

The study of a pathological case, then, has enabled us to glimpse a new mode of analysis—existential analysis—which goes beyond the traditional alternatives of empiricism and rationalism, of explanation and introspection. If consciousness were a collection of mental facts each disturbance should be elective. If it were a 'representative function', a pure power of signification, it could be or not be (and with it everything else), but it could not cease to be having once been, or become sick, that is, deteriorate. If, in short, it is a projective activity, which leaves objects all round it, like traces of its own acts, but which nevertheless uses them as springboards from which to leap towards other spontaneous acts, then it becomes understandable that any 'content' deficiency should have its repercussions on the main body of experience and open the door to its disintegration, that any pathological degeneration should affect the whole of consciousness—and that nevertheless the derangement should on each occasion attack a certain 'side' of consciousness, that in each case certain symptoms should dominate the clinical picture of the disease, and, in short, that consciousness should be vulnerable and able to receive the illness into itself. In attacking the 'visual sphere', illness is not limited to destroying certain contents of consciousness, 'visual representations' or sight literally speaking; it affects sight in the figurative sense, of which the former is no more than the model or symbol—the power of 'looking down upon' (*uberschauen*) simultaneous multiplicities,[3] a certain way of positing the object or being aware. However, as this type of consciousness is only the sublimation of sensory vision, as it is schematized constantly within the dimensions of the visual field albeit endowing them with a new meaning, it will be realized that this general function has its psychological roots Consciousness freely develops

[1] Hochheimer, op cit , p 69

[2] Cf Fischer, *Raum-Zeitstruktur und Denkstorung in der Schizophrenie*, p. 250

[3] Cf. *La Structure du Comportement*, pp 91 and ff

its visual data beyond their own specific significance; it uses them for the expression of its spontaneous acts, as semantic evolution clearly shows in loading the terms intuition, self-evidence and natural light with increasingly rich meaning But conversely, not one of these terms, in the final sense which history has given them, is understandable without reference to the structures of visual perception. Hence one cannot say that man sees because he is Mind, nor indeed that he - is Mind because he sees to see as a man sees and to be Mind are synonymous In so far as consciousness is consciousness of something only by allowing its furrow to trail behind it, and in so far as, in order to conceive an object one must rely on a previously constructed 'world of thought', there is always some degree of depersonalization at the heart of consciousness Hence the principle of an intervention from outside. consciousness may be ailing, the world of its thoughts may collapse into fragments,—or rather, as the 'contents' dissociated by the illness did not appear in the rôle of parts in normal consciousness and served only as stepping-stones to significances which outstrip them, consciousness can be seen trying to hold up its superstructures when their foundations have given way, aping its everyday processes, but without being able to come by any intuitive realization, and without being able to conceal the particular deficiency which robs them of their complete significance It is in the same way theoretically understandable that mental illness may, in its turn, be linked with some bodily accident, consciousness projects itself into a physical world and has a body, as it projects itself into a cultural world and has its habits because it cannot be consciousness without playing upon significances given either in the absolute past of nature or in its own personal past, and because any form of lived experience tends towards a certain generality whether that of our habits or that of our 'bodily functions'.

These elucidations enable us clearly to understand motility as basic intentionality Consciousness is in the first place not a matter of 'I think that' but of 'I can' [1] Schneider's motor trouble cannot, any more than his visual deficiency, be reduced to any failure of the general function of representation. Sight and movement are specific ways of entering into relationship with objects and if, through all these experiences, some unique function finds its expression, it is the momentum of existence, which does not cancel out the radical diversity of contents, because it links them to each other, not by placing them all under the control of an 'I think', but by guiding them towards the intersensory unity of a 'world' Movement is not thought about movement, and bodily space is not space thought of or represented. 'Each voluntary movement takes place in a setting, against a

---

[1] This term is the usual one in Husserl's unpublished writings

background which is determined by the movement itself. We perform our movements in a space which is not "empty" or unrelated to them, but which on the contrary, bears a highly determinate relation to them movement and background are, in fact, only artificially separated stages of a unique totality.'[1] In the action of the hand which is raised towards an object is contained a reference to the object, not as an object represented, but as that highly specific thing towards which we project ourselves, near which we are, in anticipation, and which we haunt.[2] Consciousness is being towards the thing

[1] Goldstein, *Uber die Abhangigkeit*, p 163

[2] It is not easy to reveal pure motor intentionality it is concealed behind the objective world which it helps to build up. The history of apraxia would show how the description of Praxis is almost always contaminated and finally made impossible by the notion of representation Liepmann (*Uber Storungen des Handelns bei Gehirnkranken*) draws a clear distinction between apraxia and agnosic disturbances of conduct, in which the object is not recognized, but in which, however, conduct is in harmony with the representation of the object, and generally between apraxia and disturbances affecting the 'ideational preparation of action' (forgetting the aim, confusing two aims, premature performance, transfer of the aim through some intrusive perception) (op cit , pp 20–31) With Liepmann's subject (the 'counsellor of state'), the ideational process is normal, since the subject can perform with his left hand everything that he is prevented from performing with his right Moreover, the hand is not paralysed 'The case of the counsellor of state shows that between the so-called higher mental processes and motor nerve-impulses there is room for another deficiency which prevents any application of the project (*Entwurf*) for action to the motility of one particular limb The whole sensory-motor apparatus of a limb is so to speak dislocated (*exarticuleit*) in relation to the whole physiological process (ibid , pp. 40–1) Normally, then, every formula of movement, while offering us a representation, presents itself to our body as a specific practical possibility The patient has retained the formula of movement as a representation, but it no longer conveys anything to his right hand, or at any rate his right hand has no longer any sphere of action ' 'He has retained everything communicable in an action, everything objective and perceptible in it for others What he lacks, namely his capacity to move his right hand according to a plan already mapped out, is something incommunicable and incapable of being an object for an outside consciousness, it is a power, not a thing known (*ein Konnen, kein Kennen*)' (ibid , p 47) But when Liepmann tries to make his analysis more explicit, he returns to traditional views and dissects movement into a *representation* (the 'formula of movement' which, along with the main goal provides me with intermediate aims) and a system of *automatisms* (which, for each intermediate aim, brings appropriate nerve impulses into play) (ibid , p 59) The 'power' earlier mentioned becomes a 'property of the nervous substance' (ibid , p 47) This brings us back to the dualism of consciousness and body which we thought we had left behind when we introduced the notion of *Bewegungsentwurf* or motor project If it is a question of a simple action, the representation of the goal and of the intermediate aims is transformed into movement because it releases involuntary actions acquired once and for all (p. 55) If it is a matter of complex action, it calls up the 'kinaesthetic memory of the component movements· as movement is composed of partial acts, the project of movement is composed of the representation of its parts or of the intermediate aims: it is this representation that we have called the formula of movement' (p

through the intermediary of the body. A movement is learned when the body has understood it, that is, when it has incorporated it into its 'world', and to move one's body is to aim at things through it, it - is to allow oneself to respond to their call, which is made upon it independently of any representation. Motility, then, is not, as it were, a handmaid of consciousness, transporting the body to that point in space of which we have formed a representation beforehand. In order that we may be able to move our body towards an object, the object must first exist for it, our body must not belong to the realm of the 'in-itself' Objects no longer exist for the arm of the apraxic, and this is what causes it to remain immobile. Cases of pure apraxia in which the perception of space remains unaffected, in which even the 'intellectual notion of the gesture to be made' does not appear to be obscured, and yet in which the patient cannot copy a triangle,[1] cases of constructive apraxia, in which the subject shows no gnosic disturbance except as regards the localization of stimuli on his body, and yet is incapable of copying a cross, a v or an o,[2] all prove that the body has its world and that objects or space may be present to our knowledge but not to our body

We must therefore avoid saying that our body is *in* space, or *in* — time It *inhabits* space and time If my hand traces a complicated path

---

57) Praxis is torn asunder by representations and automatic actions The case of the counsellor of state becomes unintelligible, since it becomes necessary to relate his troubles either to the ideational preliminaries to movement, or else to some deficiency of the automatic actions, which Liepmann ruled out from the start So motor apraxia comes down either to ideational apraxia, which is a form of agnosia, or else to paralysis We shall make sense of apraxia and do justice to Liepmann's observations only if the movement to be performed can be anticipated, though not by a representation This is possible only provided that consciousness is understood not as the explicit positing of its objects, but more generally as reference to a practical as well as a theoretical object, as being in the world, and if the body for its part is understood not as one object among all objects, but as the vehicle of being in the world As long as consciousness is understood as representation, the only possible operation for it is to form representations Consciousness will be motor as long as it furnishes itself with a 'representation of movement'. The body then executes the movement by copying it from the representation which consciousness presents to itself, and in accordance with a formula of movement which it receives from that representation (Cf O Sittig, *Über Apraxie*, p. 98) We still need to understand by what magical process the representation of a movement causes precisely that movement to be made by the body. The problem can be solved only provided that we cease to draw a distinction between the body as a mechanism in itself and consciousness as being for itself

[1] Lhermitte, G. Lévy and Kyriako, *Les Perturbations de la representation spatiale chez les apraxiques*, p 597

[2] Lhermitte and Trelles, *Sur l'apraxie constructive, les troubles de la pensée spatiale et de la somatognosie dans l'apraxie*, p 428 Cf Lhermitte, de Massary and Kyriako, *Le Rôle de la pensée spatiale dans l'apraxie*

through the air, I do not need, in order to know its final position, to add together all movements made in the same direction and subtract those made in the opposite direction 'Every identifiable change reaches consciousness already loaded with its relations to what has preceded it, as on a taximeter the distance is given already converted into shillings and pence [1] At every moment, previous attitudes and movements provide an ever ready standard of measurement. It is not a question of a visual or motor 'memory' of the starting position of the hand: cerebral lesions may leave visual memory intact while destroying awareness of movement. As for the 'motor memory', it is clear that it could hardly establish the present position of the hand, unless the perception which gave rise to it had not, stored up in it, an absolute awareness of 'here', for without this we should be thrown back from memory to memory and never have a present perception Just as it is necessarily 'here', the body necessarily exists 'now', it can never become 'past', and if we cannot retain in health the living memory of sickness, or, in adult life that of our body as a child, these 'gaps in memory' merely express the temporal structure of our body. At each successive instant of a movement, the preceding instant is not lost sight of. It is, as it were, dovetailed into the present, and present perception generally speaking consists in drawing together, on the basis of one's present position, the succession of previous positions, which envelop each other. But the impending position is also covered by the present, and through it all those which will occur throughout the movement Each instant of the movement embraces its whole span, and particularly the first which, being the active initiative, institutes the link between a here and a yonder, a now and a future which the remainder of the instants will merely develop. In so far as I have a body through which I act in the world, space and time are not, for me, a collection of adjacent points nor are they a limitless number of relations synthesized by my consciousness, and into which it draws my body. I am not in space and time, nor do I conceive space and time; I belong to them, my body combines with them and includes them. The scope of this inclusion is the measure of that of my existence, but in any case it can never be all-embracing. The space and time which I inhabit are always in their different ways indeterminate horizons which contain other points of view. The synthesis of both time and space is a task that always has to be performed afresh. Our bodily experience of movement is not a particular case of knowledge; it provides us with a way of access to the world and the object, with a 'praktognosia',[2] which has to be recognized as original and perhaps as primary My body has its world, or understands its world, without

[1] Head and Holmes, *Sensory disturbances from cerebral lesions*, p 187
[2] Grunbaum, *Aphasie und Motorik*

140

having to make use of my 'symbolic' or 'objectifying function'. Certain patients can imitate the doctor's movements and move their right hand to their right ear and their left to their nose, so long as they stand beside the doctor and follow his movements through a mirror, but not if they face him Head explained the patient's failure in terms of the inadequacy of his 'formulation'. according to him the imitation of the action is dependent upon a verbal translation. In fact, the formulation may be correct although the imitation is unsuccessful, or again the imitation may be successful without any formulation Writers on the subject[1] then introduce, if not exactly verbal symbolism, at least a general symbolic function, an ability to 'transpose', in which imitation, like perception or objective thought, is merely a particular case. But it is obvious that this general function does not explain adapted action. For patients are capable, not only of formulating the action to be performed, but of picturing it to themselves They are quite aware of what they have to do, and yet, instead of moving the right hand to the right ear and the left hand to the nose, they touch one ear with both hands, or else their nose and one eye, or one ear and one eye [2] What has become impossible is the application and adaptation to their own body of the objective particularity of the action. In other words, the right and left hand, the eye and ear are still presented to them as absolute locations, and not inserted into any system of correlations which links them up with the corresponding parts of the doctor's body, and which makes them usable for imitation, even when the doctor is face to face with the patient In order to imitate the actions of someone facing me, it is not necessary that I should know expressly that 'the hand which appears on the right side of my visual field is for my partner the left one'. Now it is precisely the victim of disturbances who has recourse to these explanations. In normal imitation, the subject's left hand is immediately identified with his partner's, his action immediately models itself on the other's, and the subject projects himself or loses his separate reality in the other, becomes identified with him, and the change of co-ordinates is pre-eminently embodied in this existential process. This is because the normal subject has his body not only as a system of present positions, but besides, and thereby, as an open system of an infinite number of equivalent positions directed to other ends. What we have called the body image is precisely this system of equivalents, this immediately given invariant whereby the different motor tasks are instantaneously transferable It follows that it is not only an experience of my body, but an experience of my body in the world, and that this is what gives a motor meaning to verbal orders The

[1] Goldstein, Van Woerkom, Bouman and Grunbaum.
[2] Grunbaum, op, cit , pp 386–92

function destroyed in apraxic disturbances is therefore a motor one 'It is not the symbolic or sense-giving function in general which is affected in cases of this kind: it is a much more primary function, in its nature motor, in other words, the capacity for motor differentiation within the dynamic body image'[1] The space in which normal imitation operates is not, as opposed to concrete space with its absolute locations, an 'objective space' or a 'representative space' based on an act of thought It is already built into my bodily structure, and is its inseparable correlative. 'Already motility, in its pure state, possesses the basic power of giving a meaning (Sinngebung)'[2] Even if subsequently, thought and the perception of space are freed from motility and spatial being, for us to be able to conceive space, it is in the first place necessary that we should have been thrust into it by our body, and that it should have provided us with the first model of those transpositions, equivalents and identifications which make space into an objective system and allow our experience to be one of objects, opening out on an 'in itself' 'Motility is the primary sphere in which initially the meaning of all significances (der Sinn aller Signifikationen) is engendered in the domain of represented space.'[3]

The cultivation of habit as a rearrangement and renewal of the body image presents great difficulties to traditional philosophies, which are always inclined to conceive synthesis as intellectual synthesis. It is quite true that what brings together, in habit, component actions, reactions and 'stimuli' is not some external process of association[4] Any mechanistic theory runs up against the fact that the learning process is systematic the subject does not weld together individual movements and individual stimuli but acquires the power to respond with a certain type of solution to situations of a certain general form. The situations may differ widely from case to case, and the response movements may be entrusted sometimes to one operative organ, sometimes to another, both situations and responses in the various cases having in common not so much a partial identity of elements as a shared significance. Must we then see the origin of habit in an act of understanding which organizes the elements only to withdraw subsequently?[5] For example, is it not the case that forming the habit of dancing is discovering, by analysis, the formula of the movement in question, and then reconstructing it on the basis of the ideal outline by the use of previously acquired movements, those of walking and running? But before the formula of the new dance can incorporate certain elements of general motility, it must

---

[1] Grunbaum, op cit , pp. 397-98   [2] Ibid , p 394   [3] Ibid , p 396
[4] See, on this point, La Structure du Comportement, pp 125 and ff.
[5] As Bergson, for example, thinks when he defines habit as 'the fossilized residue of a spiritual activity'

first have had, as it were, the stamp of movement set upon it. As has often been said, it is the body which 'catches' (*kapiert*) and 'comprehends' movement. The cultivation of habit is indeed the grasping of a significance, but it is the motor grasping of a motor significance Now what precisely does this mean ? A woman may, without any calculation, keep a safe distance between the feather in her hat and things which might break it off. She feels where the feather is just as we feel where our hand is [1] If I am in the habit of driving a car, I enter a narrow opening and see that I can 'get through' without comparing the width of the opening with that of the wings, just as I go through a doorway without checking the width of the doorway against that of my body.[2] The hat and the car have ceased to be objects with a size and volume which is established by comparison with other objects. They have become potentialities of volume, the demand for a certain amount of free space. In the same way the iron gate to the Underground platform, and the road, have become restrictive potentialities and immediately appear passable or impassable for my body with its adjuncts The blind man's stick has ceased to be an object for him, and is no longer perceived for itself, its point has become an area of sensitivity, extending the scope and active radius of touch, and providing a parallel to sight In the exploration of things, the length of the stick does not enter expressly as a middle term the blind man is rather aware of it through the position of objects than of the position of objects through it The position of things is immediately given through the extent of the reach which carries him to it, which comprises besides the arm's own reach the stick's range of action If I want to get used to a stick, I try it by touching a few things with it, and eventually I have it 'well in hand', I can see what things are 'within reach' or out of reach of my stick. There is no question here of any quick estimate or any comparison between the objective length of the stick and the objective distance away of the goal to be reached. The points in space do not stand out as objective positions in relation to the objective position occupied by our body; they mark, in our vicinity, the varying range of our aims and our gestures. To get used to a hat, a car or a stick is to be transplanted into them, or conversely, to incorporate them into the bulk of our own body. Habit expresses our power of dilating our being in the world, or changing our existence by appropriating fresh instruments [3] It is

[1] Head, *Sensory disturbances from cerebral lesion*, p 188

[2] Grunbaum, *Aphasie und Motorik*, p 395.

[3] It thus elucidates the nature of the body image When we say that it presents us immediately with our bodily position, we do not mean, after the manner of empiricists, that it consists of a mosaic of 'extensive sensations' It is a system which is open on to the world, and correlative with it

possible to know how to type without being able to say where the letters which make the words are to be found on the banks of keys. To know how to type is not, then, to know the place of each letter among the keys, nor even to have acquired a conditioned reflex for each one, which is set in motion by the letter as it comes before our eye. If habit is neither a form of knowledge nor an involuntary action, what then is it? It is knowledge in the hands, which is forthcoming only when bodily effort is made, and cannot be formulated in detachment from that effort. The subject knows where the letters are on the typewriter as we know where one of our limbs is, through a knowledge bred of familiarity which does not give us a position in objective space The movement of her fingers is not presented to the typist as a path through space which can be described, but merely as a certain adjustment of motility, physiognomically distinguishable from any other. The question is often framed as if the perception of a letter written on paper aroused the representation of the same letter which in turn aroused the representation of the movement needed to strike it on the machine. But this is mythological language. When I run my eyes over the text set before me, there do not occur perceptions which stir up representations, but patterns are formed as I look, and these are endowed with a typical or familiar physiognomy. When I sit at my typewriter, a motor space opens up beneath my hands, in which I am about to 'play' what I have read The reading of the word is a modulation of visible space, the performance of the movement is a modulation of manual space, and the whole question is how a certin physiognomy of 'visual' patterns can evoke a certain type of motor response, how each 'visual' structure eventually provides itself with its mobile essence without there being any need to spell the word or specify the movement in detail in order to translate one into the other. But this power of habit is no different from the general one which we exercise over our body if I am ordered to touch my ear or my knee, I move my hand to my ear or my knee by the shortest route, without having to think of the initial position of my hand, or that of my ear, or the path between them We said earlier that it is the body which 'understands' in the cultivation of habit. This way of putting it will appear absurd, if understanding is subsuming a sense-datum under an idea, and if the body is an object. But the phenomenon of habit is just what prompts us to revise our notion of 'understand' and our notion of the body. To understand is'to experience the harmony between what we aim at and what is given, between the intention and the performance—and the body is our anchorage in a world. When I put my hand to my knee, I experience at every stage of the movement the fulfilment of an intention which was not directed at my knee as an idea or even as an object, but as a present and real part of my living

144

body, that is, finally, as a stage in my perpetual movement towards a world. When the typist performs the necessary movements on the typewriter, these movements are governed by an intention, but the intention does not posit the keys as objective locations It is literally true that the subject who learns to type incorporates the key-bank space into his bodily space.

The example of instrumentalists shows even better how habit has its abode neither in thought nor in the objective body, but in the body as mediator of a world. It is known[1] that an experienced organist is capable of playing an organ which he does not know, which has more or fewer manuals, and stops differently arranged, compared with those on the instrument he is used to playing He needs only an hour's practice to be ready to perform his programme. Such a short pre-paration rules out the supposition that new conditioned reflexes have here been substituted for the existing sets, except where both form a system and the change is all-embracing, which takes us away from the mechanistic theory, since in that case the reactions are mediated by a comprehensive grasp of the instrument Are we to maintain that the organist analyses the organ, that he conjures up and retains a representation of the stops, pedals and manuals and their relation to each other in space? But during the short rehearsal preceding the concert, he does not act like a person about to draw up a plan He sits on the seat, works the pedals, pulls out the stops, gets the measure of the instrument with his body, incorporates within himself the rele-vant directions and dimensions, settles into the organ as one settles into a house He does not learn objective spatial positions for each stop and pedal, nor does he commit them to 'memory'. During the rehearsal, as during the performance, the stops, pedals and manuals are given to him as nothing more than possibilities of achieving cer-tain emotional or musical values, and their positions are simply the places through which this value appears in the world. Between the musical essence of the piece as it is shown in the score and the notes which actually sound round the organ, so direct a relation is estab-lished that the organist's body and his instrument are merely the medium of this relationship. Henceforth the music exists by itself and through it all the rest exists [2] There is here no place for any 'memory' of the position of the stops, and it is not in objective space that the organist in fact is playing. In reality his movements during rehearsal

---

[1] Cf Chevalier, *L'Habitude*, pp 202 and ff

[2] 'As though the musicians were not nearly so much playing the little phrase as performing the rites on which it insisted before it would consent to appear ' (Proust, *Swann's Way*, II, trans C K Scott Moncrieff, Chatto & Windus, p 180)
'Its cries were so sudden that the violinist must snatch up his bow and race to catch them as they came ' (Ibid , p 186)

are consecratory gestures they draw affective vectors, discover emotional sources, and create a space of expressiveness as the movements of the augur delimit the *templum*

The whole problem of habit here is one of knowing how the musical significance of an action can be concentrated in a certain place to the extent that, in giving himself entirely to the music, the organist reaches for precisely those stops and pedals which are to bring it into being. Now the body is essentially an expressive space. If I want to take hold of an object, already, at a point of space about which I have been quite unmindful, this power of grasping constituted by my hand moves upwards towards the thing I move my legs not as things in space two and a half feet from my head, but as a power of locomotion which extends my motor intention downwards. The main areas of my body are devoted to actions, and participate in their value, and asking why common sense makes the head the seat of thought raises the same problem as asking how the organist distributes, through 'organ space', musical significances But our body is not merely one expressive space among the rest, for that is simply the constituted body It is the origin of the rest, expressive movement itself, that which causes them to begin to exist as things, under our hands and eyes Although our body does not impose definite instincts upon us from birth, as it does upon animals, it does at least give to our life the form of generality, and develops our personal acts into stable dispositional tendencies In this sense our nature is not long-established custom, since custom presupposes the form of passivity derived from nature The body is our general medium for having a world Sometimes it is restricted to the actions necessary for the conservation of life, and accordingly it posits around us a biological world, at other times, elaborating upon these primary actions and moving from their literal to a figurative meaning, it manifests through them a core of new significance. this is true of motor habits such as dancing Sometimes, finally, the meaning aimed at cannot be achieved by the body's natural means, it must then build itself an instrument, and it projects thereby around itself a cultural world At all levels it performs the same function which is to endow the instantaneous expressions of spontaneity with 'a little renewable action and independent existence'.[1] Habit is merely a form of this fundamental power We say that the body has understood and habit has been cultivated when it has absorbed a new meaning, and assimilated a fresh core of significance.

To sum up, what we have discovered through the study of motility, is a new meaning of the word 'meaning'. The great strength of intellectualist psychology and idealist philosophy comes from their having

[1] Valéry, *Introduction a la Méthode de Léonard de Vinci, Variété*, p 177

146

no difficulty in showing that perception and thought have an intrinsic significance and cannot be explained in terms of the external association of fortuitously agglomerated contents. The *Cogito* was the coming to self-awareness of this inner core. But all meaning was *ipso facto* conceived as an act of thought, as the work of a pure *I*, and although rationalism easily refuted empiricism, it was itself unable to account for the variety of experience, for the element of senselessness in it, for the contingency of contents. Bodily experience forces us to acknowledge an imposition of meaning which is not the work of a universal constituting consciousness, a meaning which clings to certain contents. My body is that meaningful core which behaves like a general function, and which nevertheless exists, and is susceptible to disease. In it we learn to know that union of essence and existence which we shall find again in perception generally, and which we shall then have to describe more fully.

4

THE SYNTHESIS OF ONE'S OWN BODY

THE analysis of bodily space has led us to results which may be generalized We notice for the first time, with regard to our own body, what is true of all perceived things: that the perception of space and the perception of the thing, the spatiality of the thing and its being as a thing are not two distinct problems The Cartesian and Kantian tradition already teaches us this, it makes the object's spatial limits its essence, it shows in existence *partes extra partes*, and in spatial distribution, the only possible significance of existence in itself But it elucidates the perception of the object through the perception of space, whereas the experience of our own body teaches us to realize space as rooted in existence. Intellectualism clearly sees that the 'motif of the thing' and the 'motif of space'[1] are interwoven, but reduces the former to the latter Experience discloses beneath objective space, in which the body eventually finds its place, a primitive spatiality of which experience is merely the outer covering and which merges with the body's very being To be a body, is to be tied to a certain world, as we have seen; our body is not primarily *in* space it is *of* it. Anosognosics who describe their arm as 'like a snake', long and cold,[2] do not, strictly speaking, fail to recognize its objective outline and, even when the patient looks unsuccessfully for his arm or fastens it in order not to lose it,[3] he *knows* well enough where his arm is, since that is where he looks for it and fastens it If, however, patients experience their arm's space as something alien, if generally speaking I can feel my body's space as vast or minute despite the evidence of my senses, this is because there exists an affective presence and enlargement for which objective spatiality is not a suffi-

[1] Cassirer, *Philosophie der symbolischen Formen*, III, Second Part, Chap II
[2] Lhermitte, *L'Image de notre corps*, p 130
[3] Van Bogaert, *Sur la Pathologie de l'Image de soi*, p 541

cient condition, as anosognosia shows, and indeed not even a necessary condition, as is shown by the phantom arm. Bodily spatiality is the deployment of one's bodily being, the way in which the body comes into being as a body. In trying to analyse it, we were therefore simply anticipating what we have to say about bodily synthesis in general.

We find in the unity of the body the same implicatory structure as we have already described in discussing space. The various parts of my body, its visual, tactile and motor aspects are not simply co-ordinated If I am sitting at my table and I want to reach the telephone, the movement of my hand towards it, the straightening of the upper part of the body, the tautening of the leg muscles are superimposed on each other. I desire a certain result and the relevant tasks are spontaneously distributed amongst the appropriate segments, the possible combinations being presented in advance as equivalent I can continue leaning back in my chair provided that I stretch my arm further, or lean forward, or even partly stand up. All these movements are available to us in virtue of their common meaning That is why, in their first attempts at grasping, children look, not at their hand, but at the object: the various parts of the body are known to us through their functional value only, and their co-ordination is not learnt. Similarly, when I am sitting at my table, I can instantly visualize the parts of my body which are hidden from me As I contract my foot in my shoe, I can see it. This power belongs to me even with respect to parts of the body which I have never seen Thus certain patients have the hallucination of their own face *seen from inside* [1] It has been possible to show that we do not recognize our own hand in a photograph, and that many subjects are even uncertain about identifying their own handwriting among others, and yet that everyone recognizes his own silhouette or his own walk when it is filmed Thus we do not recognize the appearance of what we have often seen, and on the other hand we immediately recognize the visual representation of what is invisible to us in our own body [2] In heautoscopy the double which the subject sees in front of him is not always recognized by certain visible details, yet he feels convinced that it is himself, and consequently declares that he sees his double.[3] Each of us sees himself as it were through an inner eye which from a few yards away is looking at us from the head to the knees.[4] Thus the connecting link between the parts of our body and that between our

[1] Lhermitte, *L'Image de notre corps*, p 238
[2] Wolff, *Selbstbeurteilung und Fremdbeurteilung in wissentlichen und unwissentlichen Versuch*
[3] Menninger-Lerchental, *Das Truggebilde der eigenen Gestalt*, p 4
[4] Lhermitte, *L'Image de notre corps*, p. 238.

visual and tactile experience are not forged gradually and cumulatively I do not translate the 'data of touch' 'into the language of seeing' or *vice versa*—I do not bring together one by one the parts of my
body; this translation and this unification are performed once and
for all within me they are my body itself Are we then to say that we
perceive our body in virtue of its law of construction, as we know in
advance all the possible facets of a cube in virtue of its geometrical
structure? But—to say nothing at this stage about external objects—
our own body acquaints us with a species of unity which is not a
matter of subsumption under a law In so far as it stands before me
and presents its systematic variations to the observer, the external
object lends itself to a cursory mental examination of its elements and
it may, at least by way of preliminary approximation, be defined in
terms of the law of their variation. But I am not in front of my body,
I am in it, or rather I am it. Neither its variations nor their constant
can, therefore, be expressly posited. We do not merely behold as
spectators the relations between the parts of our body, and the correlations between the visual and tactile body we are ourselves the
unifier of these arms and legs, the person who both sees and touches
them. The body is, to use Leibnitz's term, the 'effective law' of its
changes. If we can still speak of interpretation in relation to the perception of one's own body, we shall have to say that it interprets itself
Here the 'visual data' make their appearance only through the sense
of touch, tactile data through sight, each localized movement against
a background of some inclusive position, each bodily event, whatever
the 'analyser' which reveals it, against a background of significance
in which its remotest repercussions are at least foreshadowed and the
possibility of an intersensory parity immediately furnished What
unites 'tactile sensations' in the hand and links them to visual perceptions of the same hand, and to perceptions of other bodily areas,
is a certain style informing my manual gestures and implying in turn
a certain style of finger movements, and contributing, in the last
resort, to a certain bodily bearing [1] The body is to be compared, not
to a physical object, but rather to a work of art. In a picture or a
piece of music the idea is incommunicable by means other than the
display of colours and sounds Any analysis of Cézanne's work, if I
have not seen his pictures, leaves me with a choice between several
possible Cézannes, and it is the sight of the pictures which provides
me with the only existing Cézanne, and therein the analyses find their
full meaning. The same is true of a poem or a novel, although they
are made up of words It is well known that a poem, though it has a

---

[1] The mechanics of the skeleton cannot, even at the scientific level, account for
the distinctive positions and movements of my body Cf *La Structure du Comportement*, p 196

superficial meaning translatable into prose, leads, in the reader's mind, a further existence which makes it a poem. Just as the spoken word is significant not only through the medium of individual words, but also through that of accent, intonation, gesture and facial expression, and as these additional meanings no longer reveal the speaker's thoughts but the source of his thoughts and his fundamental manner of being, so poetry, which is perhaps accidentally narrative and in that way informative, is essentially a variety of existence. It is distinguishable from the cry, because the cry makes use of the body as nature gave it to us. poor in expressive means; whereas the poem uses language, and even a particular language, in such a way that the existential modulation, instead of being dissipated at the very instant of its expression, finds in poetic art a means of making itself eternal. But although it is independent of the gesture which is inseparable from living expression, the poem is not independent of every material aid, and it would be irrecoverably lost if its text were not preserved down to the last detail. Its meaning is not arbitrary and does not dwell in the firmament of ideas: it is locked in the words printed on some perishable page. In that sense, like every work of art, the poem exists as a thing and does not eternally survive as does a truth. As for the novel, although its plot can be summarized and the 'thought' of the writer lends itself to abstract expression, this conceptual significance is extracted from a wider one, as the description of a person is extracted from the actual appearance of his face. The novelist's task is not to expound ideas or even analyse characters, but to depict an inter-human event, ripening and bursting it upon us with no ideological commentary, to such an extent that any change in the order of the narrative or in choice of viewpoint would alter the *literary* meaning of the event. A novel, poem, picture or musical work are individuals, that is, beings in which the expression is indistinguishable from the thing expressed, their meaning, accessible only through direct contact, being radiated with no change of their temporal and spatial situation. It is in this sense that our body is comparable to a work of art. It is a nexus of living meanings, not the function of a certain number of mutually variable terms. A certain experience tactile felt in the upper arm signifies a certain tactile experience in the forearm and shoulder, along with a certain visual aspect of the same arm, not because the various tactile perceptions among themselves, or the tactile and visual ones, are all involved in one intelligible arm, as the different facets of a cube are related to the idea of a cube, but because the arm seen and the arm touched, like the different segments of the arm, together *perform* one and the same action.

Just as we saw earlier that motor habit threw light on the particular nature of bodily space, so here habit in general enables us to understand the general synthesis of one's own body And, just as the analysis of bodily spatiality foreshadowed that of the unity of one's own body, so we may extend to all habits what we have said about motor ones. In fact every habit is both motor and perceptual, because it lies, as we have said, between explicit perception and actual movement, in the basic function which sets boundaries to our field of vision and our field of action. Learning to find one's way among things with a stick, which we gave a little earlier as an example of motor habit, is equally an example of perceptual habit Once the stick has become a familiar instrument, the world of feelable things recedes and now begins, not at the outer skin of the hand, but at the end of the stick. One is tempted to say that through the sensations produced by the pressure of the stick on the hand, the blind man builds up the stick along with its various positions, and that the latter then mediate a second order object, the external thing. It would appear in this case that perception is always a reading off from the same sensory data, but constantly accelerated, and operating with ever more attenuated signals But habit does not *consist* in interpreting the pressures of the stick on the hand as indications of certain positions of the stick, and these as signs of an external object, since it *relieves us of the necessity* of doing so The pressures on the hand and the stick are no longer given; the stick is no longer an object perceived by the blind man, but an instrument *with* which he perceives. It is a bodily auxiliary, an extension of the bodily synthesis. Correspondingly, the external object is not the flat projection or invariant of a set of perspectives, but something towards which the stick leads us, and the perspectives of which, according to perceptual evidence, are not signs, but aspects. Intellectualism cannot conceive any passage from the perspective to the thing itself, or from sign to significance otherwise than as an interpretation, an apperception, a cognitive intention. According to this view sensory data and perspectives are at each level contents grasped as (*aufgefasst als*) manifestations of one and the same intelligible core [1] But this analysis distorts both the sign and the meaning; it separates out, by a process of objectification of both, the sense-content, which is already 'pregnant' with a meaning, and the invariant core, which is not a law but a thing it conceals the organic relationship between subject and world, the active transcendence of consciousness, the momentum

---

[1] Husserl, for example, for a long time defined consciousness or the imposition of a significance in terms of the *Auffassung-Inhalt* framework, and as a *beseelende Auffassung* He takes a decisive step forward in recognizing, from the time of his *Lectures on Time*, that this operation presupposes another deeper one whereby the content is itself made ready for this apprehension 'Not every constitution is brought about through the *Auffassungsinhalt-Auffassung*.' *Vorlesungen zur Phänomenologie des inneren Zeitbewusstseins*, p 5, note 1

which carries it into a thing and into a world by means of its organs and instruments The analysis of motor habit as an extension of existence leads on, then, to an analysis of perceptual habit as the coming into possession of a world. Conversely, every perceptual habit is still a motor habit and here equally the process of grasping a meaning is performed by the body. When a child grows accustomed to distinguishing blue from red, it is observed that the habit cultivated in relation to these two colours helps with the rest [1] Is it, then, the case that through the pair blue-red the child has perceived the meaning 'colour'? Is the crucial moment of habit-formation in that coming to awareness, that arrival at a 'point of view of colour', that intellectual analysis which subsumes the data under one category? But for the child to be able to perceive blue and red under the category of colour, the category must be rooted in the data, otherwise no subsumption could recognize it in them It is necessary that, on the 'blue' and 'red' panels presented to him, the particular kind of vibration and impression on the eye known as blue and red should be represented. In the gaze we have at our disposal a natural instrument analogous to the blind man's stick. The gaze gets more or less from things according to the way in which it questions them, ranges over or dwells on them. To learn to see colours is to acquire a certain style of seeing, a new use of one's own body, it is to enrich and recast the body image Whether a system of motor or perceptual powers, our body is not an object for an 'I think', it is a grouping of lived-through meanings which moves towards its equilibrium Sometimes a new cluster of meanings is formed our former movements are integrated into a fresh motor entity, the first visual data into a fresh sensory entity, our natural powers suddenly come together in a richer meaning, which hitherto has been merely foreshadowed in our perceptual or practical field, and which has made itself felt in our experience by no more than a certain lack, and which by its coming suddenly reshuffles the elements of our equilibrium and fulfils our blind expectation

[1] Koffka, *Growth of the Mind*, pp 174 and ff

5

THE BODY IN ITS SEXUAL BEING

OUR constant aim is to elucidate the primary function whereby we bring into existence, for ourselves, or take a hold upon, space, the object or the instrument, and to describe the body as the place where this appropriation occurs. Now so long as we considered space or the things perceived, it was not easy to rediscover the relationship between the embodied subject and its world, because it is transformed by its own activity into the intercourse between the epistemological subject and the object. Indeed the natural world presents itself as existing in itself over and above its existence for me; the act of transcendence whereby the subject is thrown open to the world runs away with itself and we find ourselves in the presence of a nature which has no need to be perceived in order to exist. If then we want to bring to light the birth of being for us, we must finally look at that area of our experience which clearly has significance and reality only for us, and that is our affective life Let us try to see how a thing or a being begins to exist for us through desire or love and we shall thereby come to understand better how things and beings can exist in general

Ordinarily affectivity is conceived as a mosaic of emotional states, of pleasures and pains each sealed within itself, mutually incomprehensible, and explicable only in terms of the bodily system If it is conceded that in man the emotional life is 'shot through with intelligence' we mean that simple representations can take the place of the natural stimuli of pleasure and pain, according to the laws governing the association of ideas or governing the conditioned reflex, that these substitutions superimpose pleasure and pain on circumstances which are, naturally speaking, matters of indifference to us and that, through one displacement after another, second or third order values are created which bear no obvious relation to our natural pleasures and pains The objective world plays less and less directly on the

154

keyboard of 'elementary' emotional states, but their value remains nevertheless as a possibility of pleasure and pain Apart from experience of pleasure and pain, of which there is nothing to be said, the subject stands out by his power of representation, and affectivity is not recognized as a distinctive form of consciousness If this conception were correct, any sexual incapacity ought to amount either to the loss of certain representations or else to a weakening of the capacity for satisfaction We shall see that this is not the case. One patient [1] no longer seeks sexual intercourse of his own accord Obscene pictures, conversations on sexual topics, the sight of a body do not arouse desire in him The patient hardly ever kisses, and the kiss for him has no value as sexual stimulation Reactions are strictly local and do not begin to occur without contact If the prelude is interrupted at this stage, there is no attempt to pursue the sexual cycle. In the sexual act intromission is never spontaneous If orgasm occurs first in the partner and she moves away, the half-fulfilled desire vanishes. At every stage it is as if the subject did not know what is to be done There are no active movements, save a few seconds before the orgasm which is extremely brief. Nocturnal emissions are rare and never accompanied by dreams Are we to try to explain this sexual inertia—as earlier we explained the loss of initiative in general movements—in terms of the disappearance of visual representations? The difficulty here is in maintaining that there is no tactile representation of sexual activity, and one is thus still left wondering why in Schneider's case touch stimulation, and not only visual perception, has lost much of its sexual significance If now we work on the supposition of some general failure of representation, both of touch and vision, the problem still remains of describing the concrete aspect assumed by this wholly formal deficiency in the realm of sexuality. For indeed the infrequency of nocturnal emissions, for example, is not explained by the weakness of representations, which are its effect rather than its cause, and which would seem to point to some change in the character of the sexual life itself. If we presuppose some decline of normal sexual reflexes or of pleasurable states, we are then faced with a case tending rather to show that there are no sexual reflexes and no pure state of pleasure For, it will be recalled, all Schneider's troubles spring from a wound of limited extent in the occipital region If sexuality in man were an autonomous reflex apparatus, if the object of sexual desire affected some organ of pleasurable sensation anatomically defined, then the effect of the cerebral injury would be to free these automatic responses and take the form of accentuated

---

[1] Schneider once more, the patient whose motor and intellectual deficiencies we have studied above, and whose emotional and sexual behaviour has been analysed by Steinfeld, *Ein Beitrag zur Analyse der Sexualfunktion*, pp. 175–80

sexual behaviour. Pathology brings to light, somewhere between automatic response and representation, a vital zone in which the sexual possibilities of the patient are elaborated, in the same way, as we saw above, as are his motor, perceptual and even intellectual possibilities. There must be, immanent in sexual life, some function which ensures its emergence, and the normal extension of sexuality must rest on internal powers of the organic subject. There must be an Eros or a Libido which breathes life into an original world, gives sexual value or meaning to external stimuli and outlines for each subject the use he shall make of his objective body. It is the very structure of perception or erotic experience which has undergone change in Schneider. In the case of the normal subject, a body is not perceived merely as any object; this objective perception has within it a more intimate perception the visible body is subtended by a sexual schema, which is strictly individual, emphasizing the erogenous areas, outlining a sexual physiognomy, and eliciting the gestures of the masculine body which is itself integrated into this emotional totality. But for Schneider a woman's body has no particular essence it is, he says, pre-eminently character which makes a woman attractive, for physically they are all the same Close physical contact causes only a 'vague feeling', the knowledge of 'an indeterminate something' which is never enough to 'spark off' sexual behaviour and create a situation which requires a definite mode of resolution. Perception has lost its erotic structure, both spatially and temporally What has disappeared from the patient is his power of projecting before himself a sexual world, of putting himself in an erotic situation, or, once such a situation is stumbled upon, of maintaining it or following it through to complete satisfaction. The very word satisfaction has no longer any meaning for him, since there is no intention or initiative of a sexual kind which calls up a cycle of movements and states, which 'patterns' them and finds its satisfaction in them In so far as the tactile stimuli themselves, which the patient turns to excellent account under different circumstances, have lost their sexual significance, it is because they have so to speak ceased to speak to his body, to locate it in a sexual context, or, in other words, because the patient no longer asks, of his environment, this mute and permanent question which constitutes normal sexuality Schneider, and the majority of impotent subjects, 'do not throw themselves into what they are doing' But absent-mindedness and inappropriate representations are not causes but effects, and in so far as the subject coolly perceives the situation, it is in the first place because he does not live it and is not caught up in it At this stage one begins to suspect a mode of perception distinct from objective perception, a kind of significance distinct from intellectual significance, an intentionality which is not pure 'awareness of

156

something'. Erotic perception is not a *cogitatio* which aims at a *cogitatum*; through one body it aims at another body, and takes place in the world, not in a consciousness. A sight has a sexual significance for me, not when I consider, even confusedly, its possible relationship to the sexual organs or to pleasurable states, but when it exists for my body, for that power always available for bringing together into an erotic situation the stimuli applied, and adapting sexual conduct to it. There is an erotic 'comprehension' not of the order of understanding, since understanding subsumes an experience, once perceived, under some idea, while desire comprehends blindly by linking body to body. Even in the case of sexuality, which has nevertheless long been regarded as pre-eminently the type of bodily function, we are concerned, not with a peripheral involuntary action, but with an intentionality which follows the general flow of existence and yields to its movements. Schneider can no longer put himself into a sexual situation any more than generally he occupies an affective or an ideological one. Faces are for him neither attractive nor repulsive, and people appear to him in one light or another only in so far as he has direct dealings with them, and according to the attitude they adopt towards him, and the attention and solicitude which they bestow upon him. Sun and rain are neither gay nor sad; his humour is determined by elementary organic functions only, and the world is emotionally neutral. Schneider hardly extends his sphere of human relationships at all, and when he makes new friendships they sometimes come to an unfortunate end: this is because they never result, as can be seen on analysis, from a spontaneous impulse, but from a decision made in the abstract. He would like to be able to think about politics and religion, but he does not even try, knowing that these realms are closed to him, and we have seen that generally speaking he never performs an act of authentic thought and substitutes for the intuitive understanding of number or the grasp of meanings the manipulation of signs and a technique depending on 'points of support'.[1] We discover both that sexual life is one more form of original intentionality, and also bring to view the vital origins of perception, motility and representation by basing all these 'processes' on an 'intentional arc' which gives way in the patient, and which, in the normal subject, endows experience with its degree of vitality and fruitfulness.

Thus sexuality is not an autonomous cycle. It has internal links with the whole active and cognitive being, these three sectors of behaviour displaying one typical structure, and standing in a relationship to each other of reciprocal expression. Here we concur with the most lasting discoveries of psychoanalysis. Whatever the theoretical

[1] Cf supra, p 133

declarations of Freud may have been, psychoanalytical research is in fact led to an explanation of man, not in terms of his sexual substructure, but to a discovery in sexuality of relations and attitudes which had previously been held to reside *in consciousness* Thus the significance of psychoanalysis is less to make psychology biological than to discover a dialectical process in functions thought of as 'purely' bodily', and to reintegrate sexuality into the human being. A break-away disciple of Freud[1] shows, for example, that frigidity is scarcely ever bound up with anatomical or physiological conditions, but that it expresses in most cases a refusal of orgasm, of femininity or of sexuality, and this in turn expresses the rejection of the sexual partner and of the destiny which he represents. It would be a mistake to imagine that even with Freud psychoanalysis rules out the description of psychological motives, and is opposed to the phenomenological method psychoanalysis has, on the contrary, albeit unwittingly, helped to develop it by declaring, as Freud puts it, that every human action 'has a meaning',[2] and by making every effort to understand the event, short of relating it to mechanical circumstances.

For Freud himself the sexual is not the genital, sexual life is not a mere effect of the processes having their seat in the genital organs, the libido is not an instinct, that is, an activity naturally directed towards definite ends, it is the general power, which the psychosomatic subject enjoys, of taking root in different settings, of establishing himself through different experiences, of gaining structures of conduct It is what causes a man to have a history. In so far as a man's sexual history provides a key to his life, it is because in his sexuality is projected his manner of being towards the world, that is, towards time and other men. There are sexual symptoms at the root of all neuroses, but these symptoms, correctly interpreted, symbolize a whole attitude, whether, for example, one of conquest or of flight. Into the sexual history, conceived as the elaboration of a general form of life, all psychological constituents can enter, because there is no longer an interaction of two causalities and because the genital life is geared to the whole life of the subject So the question is not so much whether human life does or does not rest on sexuality, as of knowing what is to be understood by sexuality. Psychoanalysis represents a double

---

[1] W Stekel, *La Femme frigide*

[2] Freud, *Introductory Lectures*, p 31 Freud himself, in his concrete analyses, abandons causal thought, when he demonstrates that symptoms always have several meanings, or, as he puts it, are 'overdetermined' For this amounts to admitting that a symptom, at the time of its onset, always finds *raisons d'être* in the subject, so that no event in a life is, strictly speaking, externally determined Freud compares the accident occurring from outside to the foreign body which, for the oyster, is merely the occasion for secreting a pearl See for example *Cinq psychanalyses*, Chap. I, p. 91, note 1.

trend of thought on the one hand it stresses the sexual substructure of life, on the other it 'expands' the notion of sexuality to the extent of absorbing into it the whole of existence. But precisely for that reason, its conclusions, like those of our last paragraph but one, remain ambiguous. When we generalize the notion of sexuality, making it a manner of being in the physical and inter-human world, do we mean, in the last analysis, that all existence has a sexual significance or that every sexual phenomenon has an existential significance? In the first hypothesis, existence would be an abstraction, another name for the sexual life But since sexual life can no longer be circumscribed, since it is no longer a separate function definable in terms of the causality proper to a set of organs, there is now no sense in saying that all existence is understood through the sexual life, or rather this statement becomes a tautology. Must we then say, conversely, that the sexual phenomenon is merely an expression of our general manner of projecting our setting? But the sexual life is not a mere reflection of existence an effective life, in the political and ideological field, for example, can be associated with impaired sexuality, and may even benefit from such impairment. On the other hand, the sexual life may, as in Casanova's case for example, possess a kind of technical perfection corresponding to no particularly vigorous version of being in the world Even though the sexual apparatus has, running through it, the general current of life, it may monopolize it to its own advantage Life is particularized into separate currents If words are to have any meaning, the sexual life is a sector of our life bearing a special relation to the existence of sex. There can be no question of allowing sexuality to become lost in existence, as if it were no more then an epiphenomenon For if we admit that the sexual troubles of neurotics are an expression of their basic drama in magnified form, it still remains to be seen why the sexual expression of the drama is more immature, more frequent and more striking than the rest; and why sexuality is not only a symptom, but a highly important one. Here we meet once more a problem which we have already encountered several times. We showed with Gestalt theory that no layer of sensory data can be identified as immediately dependent on sense-organs: the smallest sensory datum is never presented in any other way than integrated into a configuration and already 'patterned' This, as we have said, does not prevent the words 'see' and 'hear' from having a meaning We have drawn attention elsewhere[1] to the fact that the specialized regions of the brain, the 'optical zone', for example, never function in isolation The fact remains, as we pointed out, that the visual or auditory side predominates in the picture of the illness, according to the region in which the lesions are situated. Finally, as

[1] *La Structure du Comportement*, pp 80 and ff

159

we have indicated above, biological existence is synchronized with human existence and is never indifferent to its distinctive rhythm. Nevertheless, we shall now add, 'living' (*leben*) is a primary process from which, as a starting point, it becomes possible to 'live' (*erleben*) this or that world, and we must eat and breathe before perceiving and awakening to relational living, belonging to colours and lights through sight, to sounds through hearing, to the body of another through sexuality, before arriving at the life of human relations Thus sight, hearing, sexuality, the body are not only the routes, instruments or manifestations of personal existence: the latter takes up and absorbs into itself their existence as it is anonymously given When we say that the life of the body, or the flesh, and the life of the psyche are involved in a relationship of reciprocal *expression*, or that the bodily event always has a psychic *meaning*, these formulations need to be explained. Valid as they are for excluding causal thought, they do not mean that the body is the transparent integument of Spirit. The return to existence, as to the setting in which the communication between body and mind can be understood, is not a return to Consciousness or Spirit, and existential psychoanalysis must not serve as a pretext for a revival of mentalistic philosophy (*spiritualisme*). This will be better understood if we clarify the notions of 'expression' and 'meaning' which belong to the world of language and thought as already constituted, which we have just applied uncritically to the body-mind relationship, and which bodily experience must in fact lead us to correct.

A girl[1] whose mother has forbidden her to see again the young man with whom she is in love, cannot sleep, loses her appetite and finally the use of speech An initial manifestation of this loss of speech is found to have occurred during her childhood, after an earthquake, and subsequently again following a severe fright. A strictly Freudian interpretation of this would introduce a reference to the oral phase of sexual development. But what is 'fixated' on the mouth is not merely sexual existence, but, more generally, those relations with others having the spoken word as their vehicle. In so far as the emotion elects to find its expression in loss of speech, this is because of all bodily functions speech is the most intimately linked with communal existence, or, as we shall put it, with co-existence. Loss of speech, then, stands for the refusal of co-existence, just as, in other subjects, a fit of hysterics is the means of escaping from the situation The patient breaks with relational life within the family circle. More generally, she tends to break with life itself. her inability to swallow food arises from the fact that swallowing symbolizes the movement of existence which carries events and assimilates them; the patient is unable, literally, to 'swallow' the prohibition which has been imposed

[1] Binswanger, *Über Psychotherapie*, pp 113 and ff

upon her.[1] In the subject's childhood, fear was translated by loss of speech because the imminence of death violently interrupted co-existence, and threw her back upon her own personal fate. The symptom of aphonia reappears because the mother's prohibition restores the situation metaphorically, and because, moreover, by shutting off the future from the subject, it leads her back to her favourite forms of behaviour. These motivations may be supposed to take advantage of a particular sensitivity of the throat and the mouth in the case of our subject, a sensitivity which may be related to the history of her libido and to the oral phase of sexuality Thus through the sexual significance of symptoms can be discerned, in faint outline, their more general significance in relation to past and future, to the self and others, that is to say, to the fundamental dimensions of existence But as we shall see, the body does not constantly express the modalities of existence in the way that stripes indicate rank, or a house-number a house: the sign here does not only convey its significance, it is filled with it; it is, in a way, what it signifies, as a portrait is the quasi-presence of the absent Peter,[2] or as wax figures in magic are what they stand for. The sick girl does not mime with her body a drama played out 'in her consciousness'. By losing her voice she does not present a public version of an 'inner state', she does not make a 'gesture' like that of the head of a state shaking hands with the engine driver and embracing a peasant, or that of a friend who takes offence and stops speaking to me. To have lost one's voice is not to keep silence one keeps silence only when one can speak. It is true that loss of voice is not paralysis, and this is proved by the fact that, treated by psychological means and left free by her family to see the man she loves, the girl recovers her power of speech. Yet neither is aphonia a deliberate or voluntary silence. It is generally known how, by the notion of pithiatism,* the theory of hysteria has been carried beyond the dilemma of paralysis (or of anasthesia) and simulation. If the hysterical patient is a deceiver, it is first and foremost himself that he deceives, so that it is impossible to separate what he *really* feels or thinks and what he overtly expresses· pithiatism is a disease of the *Cogito*, consciousness which has become ambivalent and not a deliberate refusal to declare what one knows. Here, in the same way, the girl does not *cease* to speak, she 'loses' her voice as one loses a memory. It is true again that, as psychoanalysis shows, the lost memory is not accidentally lost, it is lost rather in so far as it belongs to an area of

[1] Binswanger (*Über Psychotherapie*, p 188), points out that one patient, as he recollects a traumatic memory, and tells it to the doctor, relaxes the sphincter
[2] J P Sartre, *L'Imaginaire*, p 38

* *Pithiatism*. the class of hysterical symptoms which can be made to disappear or be reproduced by means of suggestion (Translator's note).

my life which I reject, in so far as it has a certain significance and, like all significances this one exists only for someone Forgetfulness is therefore an act I keep the memory at arm's length, as I look past a person whom I do not wish to see Yet, as psychoanalysis too shows to perfection though the resistance certainly presupposes an intentional relationship with the memory resisted, it does not set it before us as an object, it does not specifically reject the memory It is directed against a region of our experience, a certain category, a certain class of memories The subject who has left a book, which was a present from his wife, in a drawer, and forgotten all about it, and who rediscovers it when they have become reconciled once more,[1] had not really lost the book, but neither did he *know* where it was Everything connected with his wife had ceased to exist for him, he had shut it out from his life, and at one stroke, broken the circuit of all actions relating to her, and thus placed himself on the hither side of all knowledge and ignorance, assertion and negation, in so far as these were voluntary Thus, in hysteria and repression, we may well overlook something although we know of it, because our memories and our body, instead of presenting themselves to us in singular and determinate conscious acts, are enveloped in generality Through this generality we still 'have them', but just enough to hold them at a distance from us We discover in this way that sensory messages or memories are expressly grasped and recognized by us only in so far as they adhere generally to that area of our body and our life to which they are relevant Such adherence or rejection places the subject in a definite situation and sets bounds, as far as he is concerned, to the immediately available mental field, as the acquisition or loss of a sense organ presents to or removes from his direct grasp an object in the physical field It cannot be said that the factual situation thus created is the mere consciousness of a situation, for that would amount to saying that the 'forgotten' memory, arm or leg are arrayed before my consciousness, present and near to me in the same sense as are the 'preserved' regions of my past or of my body. No more can it be said that the loss of voice is voluntary. Will presupposes a field of possibilities among which I choose here is Peter, I can speak to him or not But if I lose my power of speech, Peter no longer exists for me as an interlocutor, sought after or rejected, what collapses is the whole field of possibilities I cut myself off even from that mode of communication and significance which silence provides Of course we may go on to speak of hypocrisy or bad faith But then it will be necessary to draw a distinction between psychological and metaphysical hypocrisy The former deceives others by concealing from them thoughts expressly in the mind of the subject It is fortuitous and easily avoided The

[1] Freud, *Introductory Lectures*, p 43.

latter is self-deceiving through the medium of generality, thus leading finally to a state or a situation which is not an inevitability, but which is not posited or voluntary. It is even to be found in the 'sincere' or 'authentic' man whenever he undertakes to be something or other unqualifiedly It is part of the human lot When the hysterical fit has reached its climax, even if the subject has sought it as the means of escaping from an intolerable situation and plunges into it as into a place of refuge, he *scarcely* hears anything more, he can *scarcely* see, he has *almost* become the spasmodic and panting existence which struggles on the bed The intensity of resentment is such that it becomes resentment against X, against life, an absolute resentment With every minute that passes, freedom is depreciated and becomes less probable. Even if freedom is never impossible and even if it may always derail the dialectics of bad faith, the fact remains that a night's sleep has the same power what can be surmounted by this anonymous force must indeed be of the same nature as it, and so it must at least be admitted that resentment or loss of voice, as they persist, become consistent like things, that they assume a structure, and that any decision that interrupted them would come from a *lower* level than that of 'will' The patient cuts himself off from his voice as certain insects sever one of their own legs. He is literally without a voice In treating this condition, psychological medicine does not act on the patient by making him *know* the origin of his illness sometimes a touch of the hand puts a stop to the spasms and restores to the patient his speech[1] and the same procedure, having acquired a ritual significance, will subsequently be enough to deal with fresh attacks. In any case, in psychological treatment of any kind, the coming to awareness would remain purely cognitive, the patient would not accept the meaning of his disturbances as revealed to him without the personal relationship formed with the doctor, or without the confidence and friendship felt towards him, and the change of existence resulting from this friendship. Neither symptom nor cure is worked out at the level of objective or positing consciousness, but below that level. Loss of voice as a situation may be compared to sleep· I lie down in bed, on my left side, with my knees drawn up, I close my eyes and breathe slowly, putting my plans out of my mind. But the power of my will or consciousness stops there. As the faithful, in the Dionysian mysteries, invoke the god by miming scenes from his life, I call up the visitation of sleep by imitating the breathing and posture of the sleeper The god is actually there when the faithful can no longer distinguish themselves from the part they are playing, when their body and their consciousness cease to bring in, as an obstacle, their particular opacity, and when they are totally fused in the myth There is a

[1] Binswanger, *Über Psychotherapie*, pp 113 and ff

moment when sleep 'comes', settling on this imitation of itself which I have been offering to it, and I succeed in becoming what I was trying to be an unseeing and almost unthinking mass, riveted to a point in space and in the world henceforth only through the anonymous alertness of the senses It is true that this last link makes waking up a possibility through these half-open doors things will return or the sleeper will come back into the world In the same way the patient who has broken with co-existence can still perceive the sensible integument of other people, and abstractly conceive the future by means, for instance, of a calendar In this sense the sleeper is never completely isolated within himself, never totally a sleeper, and the patient is never totally cut off from the intersubjective world, never totally ill. But what, in the sleeper and the patient, makes possible a return to the real world, are still only impersonal functions, sense organs and language We remain free in relation to sleep and sickness to the exact extent to which we remain always involved in the waking and healthy state, our freedom rests on our being in a situation, and is itself a situation Sleep and waking, illness and health are not modalities of consciousness or will, but presuppose an 'existential step' [1] Loss of voice does not merely represent a refusal of speech, or anorexia * a refusal of life, they are that refusal of others or refusal of the future, torn from the transitive nature of 'inner phenomena', generalized, consummated, transformed into *de facto* situations

The body's rôle is to ensure this metamorphosis It transforms ideas into things, and my mimicry of sleep into real sleep. The body can symbolize existence because it brings it into being and actualizes it It sustains its dual existential action of systole and diastole. On the one hand, indeed, it is the possibility enjoyed by my existence of discarding itself, of making itself anonymous and passive, and of bogging itself down in a scholastic In the case of the girl just discussed, the move towards the future, towards the living present or towards the past, the power of learning, of maturing, of entering into communication with others, have become, as it were, arrested in a bodily symptom, existence is tied up and the body has become 'the place where life hides away' [2] For the patient, nothing further happens, nothing assumes meaning and form in life, or more precisely there occurs only a recurrent and always identical 'now', life flows back on itself and history is dissolved in natural time Even when normal and even when involved in situations with other people, the subject, in so far as he has a body, retains every moment the power to withdraw from it. At the very moment when I live in the world, when I am given

[1] Binswanger, *Über Psychotherapie*, p 188
[2] Ibid , p 182

* *Anorexia* loss of appetite (Translator s note)

over to my plans, my occupations, my friends, my memories, I can
close my eyes, lie down, listen to the blood pulsating in my ears, lose
myself in some pleasure or pain, and shut myself up in this anonymous life which subtends my personal one But precisely because my
body can shut itself off from the world, it is also what opens me out
upon the world and places me in a situation there The momentum of
existence towards others, towards the future, towards the world can
be restored as a river unfreezes The girl will recover her voice, not by
an intellectual effort or by an abstract decree of the will, but through
a conversion in which the whole of her body makes a concentrated
effort in the form of a genuine gesture, as we seek and recover a name
forgotten not 'in our mind', but 'in our head' or 'on the tip of our
tongue'. The memory or the voice is recovered when the body once
more opens itself to others or to the past, when it opens the way to
co-existence and once more (in the active sense) acquires significance
beyond itself. Moreover, even when cut off from the circuit of existence, the body never quite falls back on to itself. Even if I become
absorbed in the experience of my body and in the solitude of sensations, I do not succeed in abolishing all reference of my life to a world.
At every moment some intention springs afresh from me, if it is only
towards the things round about me which catch my eye, or towards
the instants, which are thrown up, and which thrust back into the
past what I have just lived through. I never become quite a thing in
the world; the density of existence as a thing always evades me, my
own substance slips away from me internally, and some intention is
always foreshadowed. In so far as it carries within it 'sense organs',
bodily existence is never self-sufficient, it is always a prey to an active
nothingness, it continually sets the prospect of living before me, and
natural time at every successive moment adumbrates the empty form
of the true event This prospect may indeed fail to elicit any response.
The instant of natural time does not establish anything, it has to be
immediately renewed, and indeed is renewed in another instant, and
the sensory functions by themselves do not cause me to be in the
world· when I become absorbed in my body, my eyes present me with
no more than the perceptible outer covering of things and of other
people, things themselves take on unreality, behaviour degenerates
into the absurd, and the present itself, as in cases of false recognition,
loses its consistency and takes on an air of eternity. Bodily existence
which runs through me, yet does so independently of me, is only the
barest raw material of a genuine presence in the world. Yet at least
it provides the possibility of such presence, and establishes our first
consonance with the world I may very well take myself away from
the human world and set aside personal existence, but only to rediscover in my body the same power, this time unnamed, by which I am

condemned to being. It may be said that the body is 'the hidden form of being ourself',[1] or on the other hand, that personal existence is the taking up and manifestation of a being in a given situation. If we therefore say that the body expresses existence at every moment, this is in the sense in which a word expresses thought Anterior to conventional means of expression, which reveal my thoughts to others only because already, for both myself and them, meanings are provided for each sign, and which in this sense do not give rise to genuine communication at all, we must, as we shall see, recognize a primary process of signification in which the thing expressed does not exist apart from the expression, and in which the signs themselves induce their significance externally In this way the body expresses total existence, not because it is an external accompaniment to that existence, but because existence comes into its own in the body. This incarnate significance is the central phenomenon of which body and mind, sign and significance are abstract moments.

Understood in this way, the relation of expression to thing expressed, or of sign to meaning is not a one-way relationship like that between original text and translation Neither body *nor existence* can be regarded as the original of the human being, since they presuppose each other, and because the body is solidified or generalized existence, and existence a perpetual incarnation What is particularly important, is that when we say that sexuality has an existential significance or that it expresses existence, this is not to be understood as meaning that the sexual drama[2] is in the last analysis *only* a manifestation or a symptom of an existential drama. The same reason that prevents us from 'reducing' existence to the body or to sexuality, prevents us also from 'reducing' sexuality to existence the fact is that existence is not a set of facts (like 'psychic facts') capable of being reduced to others or to which they can reduce themselves, but the ambiguous setting of their inter-communication, the point at which their boundaries run into each other, or again their woven fabric. There is no question of making human existence walk 'on its head' There is no doubt at all that we must recognize in modesty, desire and love in general a metaphysical significance, which means that they are incomprehensible if man is treated as a machine governed by natural laws, or even as 'a bundle of instincts', and that they are relevant to man as a consciousness and as a freedom. Usually man does not show his body, and, when he does, it is either nervously or with an intention to fascinate. He has the impression that the alien gaze which runs over his body is

[1] Binswanger, *Über Psychotherapie*, 'eine verdeckte Form unseres Selbstseins' p 188

[2] We here take the word in its etymological sense (and without any Romantic overtone) as did Politzer, *Critique des fondements de la psychologie*, p 23

166

stealing it from him, or else, on the other hand, that the display of his body will deliver the other person up to him, defenceless, and that in this case the other will be reduced to servitude Shame and immodesty, then, take their place in a dialectic of the self and the other which is that of master and slave in so far as I have a body, I may be reduced to the status of an object beneath the gaze of another person, and no longer count as a person for him, or else I may become his master and, in my turn, look at *him* But this mastery is self-defeating, since, precisely when my value is recognized through the other's desire, he is no longer the person by whom I wished to be recognized, but a being fascinated, deprived of his freedom, and who therefore no longer counts in my eyes

Saying that I have a body is thus a way of saying that I can be seen as an object and that I try to be seen as a subject, that another can be my master or my slave, so that shame and shamelessness express the dialectic of the plurality of consciousnesses, and have a metaphysical significance. The same might be said of sexual desire if it cannot accept the presence of a third party as witness, if it feels that too natural an attitude or over-casual remarks, on the part of the desired person, are signs of hostility, this is because it seeks to fascinate, and because the observing third party or the person desired, if he is too free in manner, escapes this fascination What we try to possess, then, is not just a body, but a body brought to life by consciousness. As Alain says, one does not love a madwoman, except in so far as one has loved her before the onset of madness. The importance we attach to the body and the contradictions of love are, therefore, related to a more general drama which arises from the metaphysical structure of my body, which is both an object for others and a subject for myself. The intensity of sexual pleasure would not be sufficient to explain the place occupied by sexuality in human life or, for example, the phenomenon of eroticism, if sexual experience were not, as it were, an opportunity, vouchsafed to all and always available, of acquainting oneself with the human lot in its most general aspects of autonomy and dependence The embarrassments and fears involved in human behaviour are not explainable in terms of the sexual concern, since it contains them already On the other hand we do not reduce sexuality to something other than itself by relating it to the ambiguity of the body For, to thought, the body as an object is not ambiguous, it becomes so only in the experience which we have of it, and pre-eminently in sexual experience, and through the fact of sexuality. To treat sexuality as a dialectic is not to make a process of knowledge out of it, nor to identify a man's history with the history of his consciousness. The dialectic is not a relationship between contradictory and inseparable thoughts, it is

167

the tending of an existence towards another existence which denies
it, and yet without which it is not sustained Metaphysics—the coming to light of something beyond nature—is not localized at the level
of knowledge it begins with the opening out upon 'another', and is
to be found everywhere, and already, in the specific development of
sexuality It is true that, with Freud, we have generalized the notion
of sexuality How can we then talk about a distinctive development
of sexuality? How can we identify a content of consciousness as
sexual? Indeed we cannot Sexuality conceals itself from itself beneath a mask of generality, and continually tries to escape from the
tension and drama which it sets up. But again, how are we justified
in saying that it hides itself from itself, as if it were our life's subject?
Should we not simply say that it is transcended and submerged in
the more general drama of existence? Here two mistakes are to be
avoided one is to fail to recognize in existence any content other than
its obvious one, which is arranged in the form of distinct representations, as do philosophies of consciousness; the other is to duplicate
this obvious content with a latent content, also consisting of representations, as do psychologies of the unconscious. Sexuality is
neither transcended in human life nor shown up at its centre by
unconscious representations It is at all times present there like an
atmosphere The dreamer does not first visualize the latent content
of his dream, the one, that is, which is to be revealed with the help of
suitable images by the 'second account'; he does not first openly
perceive the stimuli of genital origin as being genital, only subsequently translating the text into figurative language. For the dreamer,
indeed, who is far removed from the language of the waking state,
this or that genital excitation or sexual drive *is* without more ado this
image of a wall being climbed or cliff-face being scaled, which are seen
as the obvious content. Sexuality becomes diffused in images which
derive from it only certain typical relationships, only a certain general
emotional physiognomy The dreamer's penis *becomes* the serpent
which appears in the manifest content.[1] What we have just said about
the dreamer applies equally to that ever slumbering part of ourselves
which we feel to be anterior to our representations, to that individual
haze through which we perceive the world. There are here blurred
outlines, distinctive relationships which are in no way 'unconscious'
and which, we are well aware, are ambiguous, having reference to
sexuality without specifically calling it to mind From the part of the
body which it especially occupies, sexuality spreads forth like an
odour or like a sound. Here we encounter once more that general
function of unspoken transposition which we have already recognized
in the body during our investigation of the body image When I move

[1] Laforgue, *L'Echec de Baudelaire*, p 126

my hand towards a thing, I know implicitly that my arm unbends.
When I move my eyes, I take account of their movement, without
being expressly conscious of the fact, and am thereby aware that the
upheaval caused in my field of vision is only apparent Similarly
sexuality, without being the object of any intended act of conscious
ness, can underlie and guide specified forms of my experience Taken
in this way, as an ambiguous atmosphere, sexuality is co-extensive
with life In other words, ambiguity is of the essence of human existence, and everything we live or think has always several meanings A
way of life—an attitude of escapism and need of solitude—is perhaps
a generalized expression of a certain state of sexuality. In thus becoming transformed into existence, sexuality has taken upon itself so
general a significance, the sexual theme has contrived to be for the
subject the occasion for so many accurate and true observations in
themselves, of so many rationally based decisions, and it has become
so loaded with the passage of time that it is an impossible undertaking
to seek, within the framework of sexuality, the explanation of the
framework of existence. The fact remains that this existence is the
act of taking up and making explicit a sexual situation, and that in
this way it has always at least a double sense There is interfusion
between sexuality and existence, which means that existence permeates sexuality and *vice versa*, so that it is impossible to determine,
in a given decision or action, the proportion of sexual to other
motivations, impossible to label a decision or act 'sexual' or 'non-
sexual'. Thus there is in human existence a principle of indeterminacy, and this indeterminacy is not only for us, it does not stem
from some imperfection of our knowledge, and we must not imagine
that any God could sound our hearts and minds and determine what
we owe to nature and what to freedom. Existence is indeterminate in
itself, by reason of its fundamental structure, and in so far as it is the
very process whereby the hitherto meaningless takes on meaning,
whereby what had merely a sexual significance assumes a more
general one, chance is transformed into reason, in so far as it is the
act of taking up a *de facto* situation. We shall give the name transcendence to this act in which existence takes up, for its own purposes,
and transforms such a situation Precisely because it is transcendence,
existence never utterly outruns anything, for in that case the tension
which is essential to it would disappear It never abandons itself
What it is never remains external and accidental to it, since this is
always taken up and integrated into it. Sexuality therefore ought not,
any more than the body in general, to be regarded as a fortuitous
content of our experience. Existence has no fortuitous attributes, no
content which does not contribute towards giving it its form, it does
not give admittance to any pure fact because it is the process by

which facts are drawn up It will perhaps be objected that the organization of our body is contingent, that we can 'conceive a man without hands, feet, head'[1] and, *a fortiori* a sexless man, self-propagating by cutting or layering. But this is the case only if we take an abstract view of hands, feet, head or sexual apparatus, regarding them, that is, as fragments of matter, and ignoring their living function Only, indeed, if we form an abstract notion of man in general, into which only the *Cogitatio* is allowed to enter If, on the other hand, we conceive man in terms of his experience, that is to say, of his distinctive way of patterning the world, and if we reintegrate the 'organs' into the functional totality in which they play their part, a handless or sexless man is as inconceivable as one without the power of thought It will be further objected that our contention ceases to be paradoxical only at the price of becoming a tautology we are saying in effect that a man would be different from what he is, and would therefore no longer be a man, if he were without any of the relational systems which in fact he possesses But, it will be added, this arises from our conception of man as empirical man, as he in fact exists, and from our relating, as through an essential necessity and within the context of a human *a priori*, characteristics of this given totality which have been brought together simply by the interplay of multiple causes and the caprice of nature In fact, we do not imagine, through any backward-looking illusion, any essential necessity, we point out an existential connection Since, as we have shown above in the examination of Schneider's case, all human 'functions', from sexuality to motility and intelligence, are rigorously unified in one synthesis, it is impossible to distinguish in the total being of man a bodily organization to be treated as a contingent fact, and other attributes necessarily entering into his make-up. Everything in man is a necessity For example, it is no mere coincidence that the rational being is also the one who holds himself upright or has a thumb which can be brought opposite to the fingers; the same manner of existing is evident in both aspects.[2] On the other hand everything in man is contingency in the sense that this human manner of existence is not guaranteed to every human child through some essence acquired at birth, and in the sense that it must be constantly reforged in him through the hazards encountered by the objective body. Man is a historical idea and not a natural species In other words, there is in human existence no unconditioned possession, and yet no fortuitous attribute Human existence will force us to revise our usual notion of necessity and contingency, because it is the transformation of contingency into necessity by the act of taking in hand. All that we

[1] Pascal, *Pensées et Opuscules* (ed Brunschvicg), Section VI, No 339, p 486.
[2] Cf *La Structure du Comportement*, pp 160–1

are, we are on the basis of a *de facto* situation which we appropriate to ourselves and which we ceaselessly transform by a sort of *escape* which is never an unconditioned freedom. There is no explanation of sexuality which reduces it to anything other than itself, for it is already something other than itself, and indeed, if we like, our whole being. Sexuality, it is said, is dramatic *because* we commit our whole personal life to it. But just why do we do this? Why is our body, for us, the mirror of our being, unless because it is a *natural self*, a current of given existence, with the result that we never know whether the forces which bear us on are its or ours—or with the result rather that they are never entirely either its or ours. There is no outstripping of sexuality any more than there is any sexuality enclosed within itself. No one is saved and no one is totally lost.[1]

[1] One can no more get rid of historical materialism than of psychoanalysis by impugning 'reductionist' conceptions and causal thought in the name of a descriptive and phenomenological method, for historical materialism is no more linked to such 'causal' formulations as may have been given than is psychoanalysis, and like the latter it could be expressed in another language It consists just as much in making economics historical as in making history economic The economics on which it bases history is not, as in classical economics, a closed cycle of objective phenomena, but a correlation of productive forces and forms of production, which is completed only when the former emerge from their anonymity, become aware of themselves and are thus capable of imposing a form on the future Now, the coming to awareness is clearly a cultural phenomenon, and through it all psychological motivations may find their way into the web of history A 'materialist' history of the 1917 Revolution does not consist of explaining each revolutionary thrust in terms of the retail price index at the moment in question, but of putting it back in the class dynamism and interplay of psychological forces, which fluctuated between February and October, between the new proletarian power and the old conservative power. Economics is reintegrated into history rather than history's being reduced to economics 'Historical materialism', in the works inspired by it, is often nothing but a concrete conception of history which brings under consideration, besides its obvious content (the official relations between 'citizens' in a democracy, for instance) its latent content, or the relations between human persons as they are actually established in concrete living When 'materialist' history identifies democracy as a 'formal' regime, and describes the conflicts with which such a regime is torn, the real subject of history, which it is trying to extract from beneath the juridical abstraction called the citizen, is not only the economic subject, man as a factor in production, but in more general terms the living subject, man as creativity, as a person trying to endow his life with form, loving, hating, creating or not creating works of art, having or not having children Historical materialism is not a causality exclusive to economics. One is tempted to say that it does not base history and ways of thinking on production and ways of working, but more generally on ways of existing and co-existing, on human relationships It does not bring the history of ideas down to economic history, but replaces these ideas in the one history which they both express, and which is that of social existence Solipsism as a philosophical doctrine is not the result of a system of private property, nevertheless into economic institutions as into conceptions of the world is projected the same existential prejudice in favour of isolation and mistrust

171

Yet this interpretation of historical materialism may appear ambiguous. We are 'expanding' the notion of economics as Freud expands that of sexuality, we are bringing into it, besides the process of production and the struggle of economic forces against economic forms, the constellation of psychological and moral motives which combine to determine this struggle. But does not the word 'economics' thus lose all definite meaning? If it is not that economic relations are expressed in the mode of *Mitsein*, is it not the mode of *Mitsein* that is expressed in economic relations? When we relate both private property and solipsism to a certain structure of *Mitsein*, are we not once more turning history upside down? And must we not choose between the following two theses: either the drama of co-existence has a purely economic significance, or else the economic drama is absorbed into a wider drama and has only an existential meaning, which brings back mentalistic philosophy (*spiritualisme*)

It is precisely this dilemma, which the notion of existence, properly understood, enables us to leave behind, and what we have said above about the existential conception of 'expression' and 'significance' must be reapplied here An existential theory of history is ambiguous, but this ambiguity cannot be made a matter of reproach, for it is inherent in things. Only at the approach of revolution does history follow the lines dictated by economics, and, as in the case of the individual life, sickness subjects a man to the vital rhythm of his body, so in a revolutionary situation such as a general strike, factors governing production come clearly to light, and are specifically seen as decisive Even so we have seen just now that the outcome depends on how the opposing forces think of each other. It is all the more true, then, that during periods of depression, economic factors are effective only to the extent that they are lived and taken up by a human subject, wrapped up, that is, in ideological shreds by a process amounting to self-deception, or rather permanent equivocation, which is yet part of history and has a weight of its own. Neither the conservative nor the proletarian is conscious of being engaged in merely an economic struggle, and they always bring a human significance to their action In this sense there is never any pure economic causality, because economics is not a closed system but is a part of the total and concrete existence of society But an existential conception of history does not deprive economic situations of their power of *motivation* If existence is the permanent act by which man takes up, for his own purposes, and makes his own a certain *de facto* situation, none of his thoughts will be able to be quite detached from the historical context in which he lives, and particularly from his economic situation Precisely because economics is not a closed world, and because all motivations intermingle at the core of history, the external becomes internal, and the internal external, and no constituent of our existence can ever be outrun It would be ridiculous to regard Paul Valéry's poetry as a mere episode of economic disturbance pure poetry can have an eternal meaning But it is not ridiculous to seek, in the social and economic drama, in the world of our *Mitsein*, the motive for this coming to awareness Just as all our life, as we have said, breathes a sexual atmosphere, without its being possible to identify a single content of consciousness which is 'purely sexual' or which is not sexual at all, so the economic and social drama provides each consciousness with a certain background or even a certain *imago* which it sets about deciphering in its own way and, in this sense, it is co-extensive with history The act of the artist or philosopher is free, but not motiveless Their freedom resides in the power of equivocation of which we spoke above, or in the process of escape discussed earlier, it consists in appropriating a *de facto* situation by endowing it with a figurative meaning beyond its real one Thus Marx, not content to *be* the son of a lawyer and student of philosophy, *conceives* his own situation as that of a 'lower middle class intellectual' in the new perspective of the class struggle. Thus does Valéry transmute into pure poetry a disquiet and solitude

of which others would have made nothing Thought is the life of human relationships as it understands and interprets itself. In this voluntary act of carrying forward, this passing from objective to subjective, it is impossible to say just where
historical forces end and ours begin, and strictly speaking the question is meaningless, since there is history only for a subject who lives through it, and a subject
only in so far as he is historically situated. There is no one meaning of history;
what we do has always several meanings, and this is where an existential conception of history is distinguishable from materialism and from spiritualism But
every cultural phenomenon has, among others, an economic significance, and
history by its nature never transcends, any more than it is reducible to, economics. Conceptions of law, morality, religion and economic structure are involved
in a network of meanings within the Unity of the social event, as the parts of the
body are mutually implicatory within the Unity of the gesture, or as 'physiological', 'psychological' and 'moral' motives are linked in the Unity of an action
It is impossible to reduce the life which involves human relationships either to
economic relations, or to juridical and moral ones thought up by men, just as it
is impossible to reduce individual life either to bodily functions or to our knowledge of life as it involves them. But in each case, one of the orders of significance
can be regarded as dominant. one gesture as 'sexual', another as 'amorous', another as 'warlike', and even in the sphere of co-existence, one period of history
can be seen as characterized by intellectual culture, another as primarily political
or economic The question whether the history of our time is pre-eminently significant in an economic sense, and whether our ideologies give us only a derivative
or secondary meaning of it is one which no longer belongs to philosophy, but to
politics, and one which will be solved only by seeking to know whether the economic or ideological scenario fits the facts more completely. Philosophy can only
show that it is *possible*, starting from the human condition.

6

THE BODY AS EXPRESSION,
AND SPEECH

WE have seen in the body a unity distinct from that of the scientific
object We have just discovered, even in its 'sexual function', intentionality and sense-giving powers. In trying to describe the phenomenon of speech and the specific act of meaning, we shall have the
opportunity to leave behind us, once and for all, the traditional
subject–object dichotomy

The realization that speech is an originating realm naturally comes
late. Here as everywhere, the relation of *having*, which can be seen in
the very etymology of the word habit, is at first concealed by relations
belonging to the domain of *being*, or, as we may equally say, by ontic
relations obtaining within the world [1] The possession of language is
in the first place understood as no more than the actual existence of
'verbal images', or traces left in us by words spoken or heard.
Whether these traces are physical, or whether they are imprinted on
an 'unconscious psychic life', is of little importance, and in both cases
the conception of language is the same in that there is no 'speaking
subject' Whether the stimuli, in accordance with the laws of neurological mechanics, touch off excitations capable of bringing about the
articulation of the word, or whether the states of consciousness cause,
by virtue of acquired associations, the appearance of the appropriate

---

[1] This distinction of having and being does not coincide with M. G. Marcel's
(*Lire et Avoir*), although not incompatible with it M Marcel takes having in the
weak sense which the word has when it designates a proprietary relationship (I
have a house, I have a hat) and immediately takes being in the existential sense of
belonging to . , or taking up (I am my body, I am my life) We prefer to take
account of the usage which gives to the term 'being' the weak sense of existence
as a thing, or that of predication (the table is, or is big), and which reserves 'having'
for the relation which the subject bears to the term into which it projects itself (I
have an idea, I have a desire, I have fears) Hence our 'having' corresponds
roughly to M Marcel's being, and our being to his 'having'

verbal image, in both cases speech occurs in a circuit of third person phenomena There is no speaker, there is a flow of words set in motion independently of any intention to speak The meaning of words is considered to be given with the stimuli or with the states of consciousness which it is simply a matter of naming, the shape of the word, as heard or phonetically formed, is given with the cerebral or mental tracks; speech is not an action and does not show up the internal possibilities of the subject · man can speak as the electric lamp can become incandescent. Since there are elective disturbances which attack the spoken language to the exclusion of the written one, or *vice versa*, and since language can disintegrate into fragments, we have to conclude that it is built up by a set of independent contributions, and that speech in the general sense is an entity of rational origin.

The theory of aphasia and of language seemed to be undergoing complete transformation when it became necessary to distinguish, over and above anarthria,* which affects the articulation of the word, true aphasia which is inseparable from disturbances affecting intelligence—and over and above automatic language, which is in effect a third person motor phenomenon, an intentional language which is alone involved in the majority of cases of aphasia The individuality of the 'verbal image' was, indeed, dissociated: what the patient has lost, and what the normal person possesses, is not a certain stock of words, but a certain way of using them. The same word which remains at the disposal of the patient in the context of automatic languages escapes him in that of language unrelated to a purpose—the patient who has no difficulty in finding the word 'no' in answer to the doctor's questions, that is when he intends to furnish a denial arising from his present experience, cannot do so when it is a question of an exercise having no emotional and vital bearing There is thus revealed, underlying the word, an attitude, a function of speech which condition it The word could be identified as an instrument of action and as a means of disinterested designation. Though 'concrete' language remained a third person process, gratuitous language, or authentic denomination, became a phenomenon of thought, and it is in some disturbance of thinking that the origin of certain forms of aphasia must be sought. For example, amnesia concerning names of colours, when related to the general behaviour of the patient, appeared as a special manifestation of a more general trouble The same patients who cannot name colours set before them, are equally incapable of classifying them in the performance of a set task. If, for example, they are asked to sort out samples according to basic colour, it is immediately noticed that they do it more slowly and painstakingly than a normal subject:

* *Anarthria* loss of power of articulate speech (Translator's note)

175

they slowly place together the samples to be compared and fail to see at a glance which ones 'go together'. Moreover, having correctly assembled several blue ribbons, they make unaccountable mistakes: if for example the last blue ribbon was of a pale shade, they carry on by adding to the collection of 'blues' a pale green or pale pink—as if it were beyond them to stick to the proposed principle of classification, and to consider the samples from the point of view of basic colour from start to finish of the operation They have thus become unable to subsume the sensory givens under a category, to see immediately the samples as representatives of the *eidos* blue. Even when, at the beginning of the test, they proceed correctly, it is not the conformity of the samples to an idea which guides them, but the experience of an immediate resemblance, and hence it comes about that they can classify the samples only when they have placed them side by side. The sorting test brings to light in these subjects a fundamental disorder, of which forgetting names of colours is simply another manifestation. For to name a thing is to tear oneself away from its individual and unique characteristics to see it as representative of an essence or a category, and the fact that the patient cannot identify the samples is a sign, not that he has lost the verbal image of the words red or blue, but that he has lost the general ability to subsume a sensory given under a category, that he has lapsed back from the categorial to the concrete attitude [1] These analyses and other similar ones lead us, it would seem, to the antithesis of the theory of the verbal image, since language now appears as conditioned by thought

In fact we shall once again see that there is a kinship between the empiricist or mechanistic psychologies and the intellectualist ones, and the problem of language is not solved by going from one extreme to the other. A short time ago the reproduction of the word, the revival of the verbal image, was the essential thing Now it is no more than what envelops true denomination and authentic speech, which is an inner process And yet these two conceptions are at one in holding that the word *has* no significance. In the first case this is obvious since the word is not summoned up through the medium of any concept, and since the given stimuli or 'states of mind' call it up in accordance with the laws of neurological mechanics or those of association, and that thus the word is not the bearer of its own meaning, has no inner power, and is merely a psychic, physiological or even physical phenomenon set alongside others, and thrown up by the working of an objective causality. It is just the same when we duplicate denomination with a categorial operation. The word is still bereft of any effectiveness of its own, this time because it is only the external sign of an internal recognition, which could take place

[1] Gelb and Goldstein, *Über Farbennamenamnesie*

without it, and to which it makes no contribution. It is not without meaning, since behind it there is a categorial operation, but this meaning is something which it does not *have*, does not possess, since it is thought which has a meaning, the word remaining an empty container. It is merely a phenomenon of articulation, of sound, or the consciousness of such a phenomenon, but in any case language is but an external accompaniment of thought. In the first case, we are on this side of the word as meaningful, in the second we are beyond it In the first there is nobody to speak; in the second, there is certainly a subject, but a thinking one, not a speaking one As far as speech itself is concerned, intellectualism is hardly any different from empiricism, and is no better able than the latter to dispense with an explanation in terms of involuntary action Once the categorial operation is performed, the appearance of the word which completes the process still has to be explained, and this will still be done by recourse to a physiological or psychic mechanism, since the word is a passive shell Thus we refute both intellectualism and empiricism by simply saying that *the word has a meaning*.

If speech presupposed thought, if talking were primarily a matter of meeting the object through a cognitive intention or through a representation, we could not understand why thought tends towards expression as towards its completion, why the most familiar thing appears indeterminate as long as we have not recalled its name, why the thinking subject himself is in a kind of ignorance of his thoughts so long as he has not formulated them for himself, or even spoken and written them, as is shown by the example of so many writers who begin a book without knowing exactly what they are going to put into it A thought limited to existing for itself, independently of the constraints of speech and communication, would no sooner appear than it would sink into the unconscious, which means that it would not exist even for itself. To Kant's celebrated question, we can reply that it is indeed part of the experience of thinking, in the sense that we present our thought to ourselves through internal or external speech It does indeed move forward with the instant and, as it were, in flashes, but we are then left to lay hands on it, and it is through expression that we make it our own The denomination of objects does not follow upon recognition, it is itself recognition. When I fix my eyes on an object in the half-light, and say: 'It is a brush', there is not in my mind the concept of a brush, under which I subsume the object, and which moreover is linked by frequent association with the word 'brush', but the word bears the meaning, and, by imposing it on the object, I am conscious of reaching that object As has often been said,[1] for the child the thing is not known until it is named, the name

[1] E g Piaget, *La Représentation du Monde chez l'Enfant*, pp 60 and ff

177

is the essence of the thing and resides in it on the same footing as its colour and its form. For pre-scientific thinking, naming an object is causing it to exist or changing it. God creates beings by naming them and magic operates upon them by speaking of them. These 'mistakes' would be unexplainable if speech rested on the concept, for the latter ought always to know itself as distinct from the former, and to know the former as an external accompaniment. If it is pointed out in reply that the child learns to know objects through the designations of language, that thus, given in the first place as linguistic entities, objects receive only secondarily their natural existence, and that finally the actual existence of a linguistic community accounts for childish beliefs, this explanation leaves the problem untouched, since, if the child can know himself as a member of a linguistic community before knowing himself as thinking about some Nature, it is conditional upon the subject's being able to overlook himself as universal thought and apprehend himself as speech, and on the fact that the word, far from being the mere sign of objects and meanings, inhabits things and is the vehicle of meanings. Thus speech, in the speaker, does not translate ready-made thought, but accomplishes it.[1] A fortiori must it be recognized that the listener receives thought from speech itself. At first sight, it might appear that speech heard can bring him nothing: it is he who gives to words and sentences their meaning, and the very combination of words and sentences is not an alien import, since it would not be understood if it did not encounter in the listener the ability spontaneously to effect it. Here, as everywhere, it seems at first sight true that consciousness can find in its experience only what it has itself put there. Thus the experience of communication would appear to be an illusion. A consciousness constructs—for x—that linguistic mechanism which will provide another consciousness with the chance of having the same thoughts, but nothing really passes between them. Yet, the problem being how, to all appearances, consciousness learns something, the solution cannot consist in saying that it knows everything in advance. The fact is that we have the power to understand over and above what we may have spontaneously thought. People can speak to us only a language which we already understand, each word of a difficult text awakens in us thoughts which were ours beforehand, but these meanings sometimes combine to form new thought which recasts them all, and we are transported to the heart of the matter, we find the source. Here there is nothing comparable to the solution of a problem, where we dis-

[1] There is, of course, every reason to distinguish between an authentic speech, which formulates for the first time, and second-order expression, speech about speech, which makes up the general run of empirical language. Only the first is identical with thought.

cover an unknown quantity through its relationship with known ones. For the problem can be solved only if it is determinate, that is, if the cross-checking of the data provides the unknown quantity with one or more definite values. In understanding others, the problem is always indeterminate[1] because only the solution will bring the data retrospectively to light as convergent, only the central theme of a philosophy, once understood, endows the philosopher's writings with the value of adequate signs There is, then, a taking up of others' thought through speech, a reflection in others, an ability to think *according to others*[2] which enriches our own thoughts Here the meaning of words must be finally induced by the words themselves, or more exactly, their conceptual meaning must be formed by a kind of deduction from a *gestural meaning*, which is immanent in speech. And as, in a foreign country, I begin to understand the meaning of words through their place in a context of action, and by taking part in a communal life—in the same way an as yet imperfectly understood piece of philosophical writing discloses to me at least a certain 'style'—either a Spinozist, criticist or phenomenological one—which is the first draft of its meaning. I begin to understand a philosophy by feeling my way into its existential manner, by reproducing the tone and accent of the philosopher. In fact, every language conveys its own teaching and carries its meaning into the listener's mind. A school of music or painting which is at first not understood, eventually, by its own action, creates its own public, if it really *says* something, that is, it does so by secreting its own meaning. In the case of prose or poetry, the power of the spoken word is less obvious, because we have the illusion of already possessing within ourselves, in the shape of the common property meaning of words, what is required for the understanding of any text whatsoever. The obvious fact is, however, that the colours of the palette or the crude sounds of instruments, as presented to us in natural perception, are insufficient to provide the musical sense of music, or the pictorial sense of a painting. But, in fact, it is less the case that the sense of a literary work is provided by the common property meaning of words, than that it contributes to changing that accepted meaning. There is thus, either in the man who listens or reads, or in the one who speaks or writes, a *thought in speech* the existence of which is unsuspected by intellectualism

To realize this, we must turn back to the phenomenon of speech

[1] Again, what we say here applies only to first-hand speech—that of the child uttering its first word, of the lover revealing his feelings, of the 'first man who spoke', or of the writer and philosopher who reawaken primordial experience anterior to all traditions.

[2] *Nachdenken, nachvollziehen* of Husserl, *Ursprung der Geometrie*, pp 212 and ff

and reconsider ordinary descriptions which immobilize thought and speech, and make anything other than external relations between them inconceivable We must recognize first of all that thought, in the speaking subject, is not a representation, that is, that it does not expressly posit objects or relations. The orator does not think before speaking, nor even while speaking, his speech is his thought. In the same way the listener does not form concepts on the basis of signs. The orator's 'thought' is empty while he is speaking and, when a text is read to us, provided that it is read with expression, we have no thought marginal to the text itself, for the words fully occupy our mind and exactly fulfil our expectations, and we feel the necessity of the speech Although we are unable to predict its course, we are possessed by it. The end of the speech or text will be the lifting of a spell. It is at this stage that thoughts on the speech or text will be able to arise Previously the speech was improvised and the text understood without the intervention of a single thought; the sense was everywhere present, and nowhere posited for its own sake The speaking subject does not think of the sense of what he is saying, nor does he visualize the words which he is using To know a word or a language is, as we have said, not to be able to bring into play any pre-established nervous network But neither is it to retain some 'pure recollection' of the word, some faded perception. The Bergsonian dualism of habit-memory and pure recollection does not account for the near-presence of the words I know: they are behind me, like things behind my back, or like the city's horizon round my house, I reckon with them or rely on them, but without having any 'verbal image'. In so far as they persist within me, it is rather as does the Freudian Imago which is much less the representation of a former perception than a highly specific emotional essence, which is yet generalized, and detached from its empirical origins. What remains to me of the word once learnt is its style as constituted by its formation and sound What we have said earlier about the 'representation of movement' must be repeated concerning the verbal image· I do not need to visualize external space and my own body in order to move one within the other. It is enough that they exist for me, and that they form a certain field of action spread around me. In the same way I do not need to visualize the word in order to know and pronounce it It is enough that I possess its articulatory and acoustic style as one of the modulations, one of the possible uses of my body. I reach back for the word as my hand reaches towards the part of my body which is being pricked, the word has a certain location in my linguistic world, and is part of my equipment I have only one means of representing it, which is uttering it, just as the artist has only one means of representing the work on which he is engaged by doing it When I imagine

Peter absent, I am not aware of contemplating an image of Peter numerically distinct from Peter himself. However far away he is, I visualize him in the world, and my power of imagining is nothing but the persistence of my world around me [1] To say that I imagine Peter is to say that I bring about the pseudo-presence of Peter by putting into operation the 'Peter-behaviour-pattern' Just as Peter in imagination is only one of the modalities of my being in the world, so the verbal image is only one of the modalities of my phonetic gesticulation, presented with many others in the all-embracing consciousness of my body. This is obviously what Bergson means when he talks about a 'motor framework' of recollection, but if pure representations of the past take their place in this framework, it is not clear why they should need it to become actual once more. The part played by the body in memory is comprehensible only if memory is, not only the constituting consciousness of the past, but an effort to reopen time on the basis of the implications contained in the present, and if the body, as our permanent means of 'taking up attitudes' and thus constructing pseudo-presents, is the medium of our communication with time as well as with space.[2] The body's function in remembering is that same function of projection which we have already met in starting to move: the body converts a certain motor essence into vocal form, spreads out the articulatory style of a word into audible phenomena, and arrays the former attitude, which is resumed, into the panorama of the past, projecting an intention to move into actual movement, because the body is a power of natural expression.

These considerations enable us to restore to the act of speaking its true physiognomy. In the first place speech is not the 'sign' of thought, if by this we understand a phenomenon which heralds another as

---

[1] Sartre, *L'Imagination*, p. 148.

[2] ' . when I awoke like this, and my mind struggled in an unsuccessful attempt to discover where I was, everything would be moving round me through the darkness, things, places, years My body, still too heavy with sleep to move, would make an effort to construe the form which its tiredness took as an orientation of its various members, so as to induce from that where the wall lay and the furniture stood, to piece together and to give a name to the house in which it must be living. Its memory, the composite memory of its ribs, knees, and shoulder-blades offered it a whole series of rooms in which it had at one time or another slept, while the unseen walls kept changing, adapting themselves to the shape of each successive room that it remembered, whirling madly through the darkness . . My body, the side upon which I was lying, loyally preserving from the past an impression which my mind should never have forgotten, brought back before my eyes the glimmering flame of the night-light in its bowl of Bohemian glass, shaped like an urn and hung by chains from the ceiling, and the chimney-piece of Sienna marble in my bedroom at Combray, in my great-aunt's house, in those far-distant days which, at the moment of waking, seemed present without being clearly defined ' (Proust, *Swann's Way*, I, trans C K Scott Moncrieff, Chatto and Windus, pp 5–6)

smoke betrays fire. Speech and thought would admit of this external
relation only if they were both thematically given, whereas in fact they
are intervolved, the sense being held within the word, and the word
being the external existence of the sense Nor can we concede, as is
commonly done, that speech is a mere means of fixation, nor yet
that it is the envelope and clothing of thought. Why should it be
easier to recall words or phrases than thoughts, if the alleged verbal
images need to be reconstructed on every occasion? And why should
thought seek to duplicate itself or clothe itself in a succession of utterances, if the latter do not carry and contain within themselves their
own meaning? Words cannot be 'strongholds of thought', nor can
thought seek expression, unless words are in themselves a comprehensible text, and unless speech possesses a power of significance
entirely its own. The word and speech must somehow cease to be a
way of designating things or thoughts, and become the presence of
that thought in the phenomenal world, and, moreover, not its clothing but its token or its body There must be, as psychologists say, a
'linguistic concept' (*Sprachbegriff*)[1] or a word concept (*Wortbegriff*),
a 'central inner experience, specifically verbal, thanks to which the
sound, heard, uttered, read or written, becomes a linguistic fact'.[2]
Certain patients can read a text, 'putting expression into it', without,
however, understanding it This is because the spoken or written
words carry a top coating of meaning which sticks to them and which
presents the thought as a style, an affective value, a piece of existential mimicry, rather than as a conceptual statement. We find here,
beneath the conceptual meaning of the words, an existential meaning
which is not only rendered by them, but which inhabits them, and is
inseparable from them. The greatest service done by expression is
not to commit to writing ideas which might be lost A writer hardly
ever re-reads his own works, and great works leave in us at a first
reading all that we shall ever subsequently get out of them. The process of expression, when it is successful, does not merely leave for the
reader and the writer himself a kind of reminder, it brings the meaning into existence as a thing at the very heart of the text, it brings it to
life in an organism of words, establishing it in the writer or the reader
as a new sense organ, opening a new field or a new dimension to our
experience This power of expression is well known in the arts, for
example in music. The musical meaning of a sonata is inseparable
from the sounds which are its vehicle: before we have heard it no
analysis enables us to anticipate it; once the performance is over, we
shall, in our intellectual analyses of the music, be unable to do anything but carry ourselves back to the moment of experiencing it

[1] Cassirer, *Philosophie der symbolischen Formen*, III, p 383.
[2] Goldstein, *L'Analyse de l'aphasie et l'essence du langage*, p 459

During the performance, the notes are not only the 'signs' of the sonata, but it is there through them, it enters into them.[1] In the same way the actress becomes invisible, and it is Phaedra who appears. The meaning swallows up the signs, and Phaedra has so completely taken possession of Berma that her passion as Phaedra appears the apotheosis of ease and naturalness.[2] Aesthetic expression confers on what it expresses an existence in itself, installs it in nature as a thing perceived and accessible to all, or conversely plucks the signs themselves—the person of the actor, or the colours and canvas of the painter—from their empirical existence and bears them off into another world. No one will deny that here the process of expression brings the meaning into being or makes it effective, and does not merely translate it. It is no different, despite what may appear to be the case, with the expression of thoughts in speech. Thought is no 'internal' thing, and does not exist independently of the world and of words. What misleads us in this connection, and causes us to believe in a thought which exists for itself prior to expression, is thought already constituted and expressed, which we can silently recall to ourselves, and through which we acquire the illusion of an inner life But in reality this supposed silence is alive with words, this inner life is an inner language 'Pure' thought reduces itself to a certain void of consciousness, to a momentary desire The new sense-giving intention knows itself only by donning already available meanings, the outcome of previous acts of expression, The available meanings suddenly link up in accordance with an unknown law, and once and for all a fresh cultural entity has taken on an existence. Thought and expression, then, are simultaneously constituted, when our cultural store is put at the service of this unknown law, as our body suddenly lends itself to some new gesture in the formation of habit The spoken word is a genuine gesture, and it contains its meaning in the same way as the gesture contains its. This is what makes communication possible. In order that I may understand the words of another person, it is clear that his vocabulary and syntax must be 'already known' to me But that does not mean that words do their work by arousing in me 'representations' associated with them, and which in aggregate eventually reproduce in me the original 'representation' of the speaker. What I communicate with primarily is not 'representations' or thought, but a speaking subject, with a certain style of being and with the 'world' at which he directs his aim. Just as the sense-giving intention which has set in motion the other person's speech is not an explicit thought, but a certain lack which is asking to be made good, so my taking up of this intention is not a process of thinking on my

[1] Proust, *Swann's Way*, II, trans C K Scott Moncrieff, p 185.
[2] Proust, *The Guermantes Way*, I, pp 55 and ff.

part, but a synchronizing change of my own existence, a transformation of my being. We live in a world where speech is an *institution*. For all these many commonplace utterances, we possess within ourselves ready-made meanings. They arouse in us only second order thoughts; these in turn are translated into other words which demand from us no real effort of expression and will demand from our hearers no effort of comprehension. Thus language and the understanding of language apparently raise no problems. The linguistic and intersubjective world no longer surprises us, we no longer distinguish it from the world itself, and it is within a world already spoken and speaking that we think. We become unaware of the contingent element in expression and communication, whether it be in the child learning to speak, or in the writer saying and thinking something for the first time, in short, in all who transform a certain kind of silence into speech. It is, however, quite clear that constituted speech, as it operates in daily life, assumes that the decisive step of expression has been taken Our view of man will remain superficial so long as we fail to go back to that origin, so long as we fail to find, beneath the chatter of words, the primordial silence, and as long as we do not describe the action which breaks this silence. The spoken word is a gesture, and its meaning, a world.

Modern psychology[1] has demonstrated that the spectator does not look about within himself among his closest experiences for the meaning of the gestures which he is witnessing. Faced with an angry or threatening gesture, I have no need, in order to understand it, to recall the feelings which I myself experienced when I used these gestures on my own account I know very little, from inside, of the mime of anger so that a decisive factor is missing for any association by resemblance or reasoning by analogy, and what is more, I do not see anger or a threatening attitude as a psychic fact hidden behind the gesture, I read anger in it. The gesture *does not make me think* of anger, it is anger itself However, the meaning of the gesture is not perceived as the colour of the carpet, for example, is perceived. If it were given to me as a thing, it is not clear why my understanding of gestures should for the most part be confined to human ones. I do not 'understand' the sexual pantomime of the dog, still less of the cockchafer or the praying mantis. I do not even understand the expression of the emotions in primitive people or in circles too unlike the ones in which I move. If a child happens to witness sexual intercourse, it may understand it although it has no experience of desire and of the bodily attitudes which translate it. The sexual scene will be merely an unfamiliar and disturbing spectacle, without meaning unless the child has reached the stage of sexual maturity at

[1] For example, M. Scheler, *Nature et Formes de la Sympathie*, pp. 347 and ff.

which this behaviour becomes possible for it. It is true that often knowledge of other people lights up the way to self-knowledge the spectacle outside him reveals to the child the meaning of its own impulses, by providing them with an aim. The example would pass unnoticed if it did not coincide with the inner possibilities of the child. The sense of the gestures is not given, but understood, that is, recaptured upon by an act on the spectator's part The whole difficulty is to conceive this act clearly without confusing it with a cognitive operation The communication or comprehension of gestures comes about through the reciprocity of my intentions and the gestures of others, of my gestures and intentions discernible in the conduct of other people It is as if the other person's intention inhabited my body and mine his. The gesture which I witness outlines an intentional object. This object is genuinely present and fully comprehended when the powers of my body adjust themselves to it and overlap it. The gesture presents itself to me as a question, bringing certain perceptible bits of the world to my notice, and inviting my concurrence in them Communication is achieved when my conduct identifies this path with its own. There is mutual confirmation between myself and others. Here we must rehabilitate the experience of others which has been distorted by intellectualist analyses, as we shall have to rehabilitate the perceptual experience of the thing. When I perceive a thing, a fireplace for example, it is not the concordance of its various aspects which leads me to believe in the existence of the fireplace as the flat projection and collective significance of all these perspectives. On the contrary I perceive the thing in its own self-evident completeness and this is what gives me the assurance that, in the course of perceptual experience, I shall be presented with an indefinite set of concordant views. The identity of the thing through perceptual experience is only another aspect of the identity of one's own body throughout exploratory movements, thus they are the same in kind as each other. Like the body image, the fireplace is a system of equivalents not founded on the recognition of some law, but on the experience of a bodily presence. I become involved in things with my body, they co-exist with me as an incarnate subject, and this life among things has nothing in common with the elaboration of scientifically conceived objects. In the same way, I do not understand the gestures of others by some act of intellectual interpretation: communication between consciousnesses is not based on the common meaning of their respective experiences, for it is equally the basis of that meaning. The act by which I lend myself to the spectacle must be recognized as irreducible to anything else. I join it in a kind of blind recognition which precedes the intellectual working out and clarification of the meaning. Successive generations 'understand' and perform sexual

185

gestures, such as the caress, before the philosopher[1] makes its intellectual significance clear, which is that we lock within itself a passive body, enwrap it in a pleasurable lethargy, thus imposing a temporary respite upon the continual drive which projects it into things and towards others It is through my body that I understand other people, just as it is through my body that I perceive 'things'. The meaning of a gesture thus 'understood' is not behind it, it is intermingled with the structure of the world outlined by the gesture, and which I take up on my own account. It is arrayed all over the gesture itself—as, in perceptual experience, the significance of the fireplace does not lie beyond the perceptible spectacle, namely the fireplace itself as my eyes and movements discover it in the world.

The linguistic gesture, like all the rest, delineates its own meaning This idea seems surprising at first, yet one is forced to accept it if one wishes to understand the origin of language, always an insistent problem, although psychologists and linguistics both question its validity in the name of positive knowledge It seems in the first place impossible to concede to either words or gestures an immanent meaning, because the gesture is limited to showing a certain relationship between man and the perceptible world, because this world is presented to the spectator by natural perception, and because in this way the intentional object is offered to the spectator at the same time as the gesture itself. Verbal 'gesticulation', on the other hand, aims at a mental setting which is not given to everybody, and which it is its task to communicate. But here what nature does not provide, cultural background does Available meanings, in other words former acts of expression, establish between speaking subjects a common world, to which the words being actually uttered in their novelty refer as does the gesture to the perceptible world And the meaning of speech is nothing other than the way in which it handles this linguistic world or in which it plays modulations on the keyboard of acquired meanings I seize it in an undivided act which is as short as a cry It is true that the problem has been merely shifted one stage further back· how did the available meanings themselves come to be constituted? Once language is formed, it is conceivable that speech may have meaning, like the gesture, against the mental background held in common. But do syntactical forms and vocabulary, which are here presupposed, carry their meaning within themselves? One can see what there is in common between the gesture and its meaning, for example in the case of emotional expression and the emotions themselves the smile, the relaxed face, gaiety of gesture really have in them the rhythm of action, the mode of being in the world which are joy itself. On the other hand, is not the link between the verbal sign and its meaning

[1] Here J P Sartre, *L'Être et le Néant*, pp. 453 and ff.

186

quite accidental, a fact demonstrated by the existence of a number of languages? And was not the communication of the elements of language between the 'first man to speak' and the second necessarily of an entirely different kind from communication through gesture? This is what is commonly expressed by saying that gesture or emotional pantomime are 'natural signs', and the word a 'natural convention' But conventions are a late form of relationship between men, they presuppose an earlier means of communication, and language must be put back into this current of intercourse If we consider only the conceptual and delimiting meaning of words, it is true that the verbal form—with the exception of endings—appears arbitrary But it would no longer appear so if we took into account the emotional content of the word, which we have called above its 'gestural' sense, which is all-important in poetry, for example. It would then be found that the words, vowels and phonemes are so many ways of 'singing' the world, and that their function is to represent things not, as the naive onomatopoeic theory had it, by reason of an objective resemblance, but because they extract, and literally express, their emotional essence. If it were possible, in any vocabulary, to disregard what is attributable to the mechanical laws of phonetics, to the influences of other languages, the rationalization of grammarians, and assimilatory processes, we should probably discover in the original form of each language a somewhat restricted system of expression, but such as would make it not entirely arbitrary, if we designate night by the word 'nuit', to use 'lumiere' for light. The predominance of vowels in one language, or of consonants in another, and constructional and syntactical systems, do not represent so many arbitrary conventions for the expression of one and the same idea, but several ways for the human body to sing the world's praises and in the last resort to live it. Hence the *full* meaning of a language is never translatable into another. We may speak several languages, but one of them always remains the one in which we live In order completely to assimilate a language, it would be necessary to make the world which it expresses one's own, and one never does belong to two worlds at once[1] If

[1] 'In my case, the effort for these years to live in the dress of Arabs, and to imitate their mental foundation, quitted me of my English self, and let me look at the West and its conventions with new eyes they destroyed it all for me At the same time I could not sincerely take on the Arab skin it was an affectation only Easily was a man made an infidel, but hardly might he be converted to another faith I had dropped one form and not taken on the other, and was become like Mohammed's coffin in our legend.   Such detachment came at times to a man exhausted by prolonged physical effort and isolation. His body plodded on mechanically, while his reasonable mind left him, and from without looked down critically on him, wondering what that futile lumber did and why Sometimes these selves would converse in the void, and then madness was very near, as I

there is such a thing as universal thought, it is achieved by taking up the effort towards expression and communication in *one* single language, and accepting all its ambiguities, all the suggestions and overtones of meaning of which a linguistic tradition is made up, and which are the exact measure of its power of expression A conventional algorithm—which moreover is meaningful only in relation to language—will never express anything but nature without man Strictly speaking, therefore, there are no conventional signs, standing as the simple notation of a thought pure and clear in itself, there are only words into which the history of a whole language is compressed, and which effect communication with no absolute guarantee, dogged as they are by incredible linguistic hazards We think that language is more transparent than music because most of the time we remain within the bounds of constituted language, we provide ourselves with available meanings, and in our definitions we are content, like the dictionary, to explain meanings in terms of each other The meaning of a sentence appears intelligible throughout, detachable from the sentence and finitely self-subsistent in an intelligible world, because we presuppose as given all those exchanges, owed to the history of the language, which contribute to determining its sense In music, on the other hand, no vocabulary is presupposed, the meaning appears as linked to the empirical presence of the sounds, and that is why music strikes us as dumb But in fact, as we have said, the clearness of language stands out from an obscure background, and if we carry our research far enough we shall eventually find that language is equally uncommunicative of anything other than itself, that its meaning is inseparable from it. We need, then, to seek the first attempts at language in the emotional gesticulation whereby man superimposes on the given world the world according to man. There is here nothing resembling the famous naturalistic conceptions which equate the artificial sign with the natural one, and try to reduce language to emotional expression. The artificial sign is not reducible to the natural one, because in man there is no natural sign, and in assimilating language to emotional expressions, we leave untouched its specific quality, if it is true that emotion, viewed as a variation of our being in the world, is contingent in relation to the mechanical resources contained in our body, and shows the same power of giving shape to stimuli and situations which is at its most striking at the level of language It would be legitimate to speak of 'natural signs' only if the anatomical organization of our body produced a correspondence

---

believe it would be near the man who could see things through the veils at once of two customs, two educations, two environments ' T E Lawrence, *The Seven Pillars of Wisdom*, Jonathan Cape, pp 31-2.

between specific gestures and given 'states of mind'. The fact is that the behaviour associated with anger or love is not the same in a Japanese and an Occidental Or, to be more precise, the difference of behaviour corresponds to a difference in the emotions themselves It is not only the gesture which is contingent in relation to the body's organization, it is the manner itself in which we meet the situation and live it The angry Japanese smiles, the westerner goes red and stamps his foot or else goes pale and hisses his words It is not enough for two conscious subjects to have the same organs and nervous system for the same emotions to produce in both the same signs. What is important is how they use their bodies, the simultaneous patterning of body and world in emotion The psychophysiological equipment leaves a great variety of possibilities open, and there is no more here than in the realm of instinct a human nature finally and immutably given The use a man is to make of his body is transcendent in relation to that body as a mere biological entity It is no more natural, and no less conventional, to shout in anger or to kiss in love[1] than to call a table 'a table'. Feelings and passional conduct are invented like words. Even those which, like paternity, seem to be part and parcel of the human make-up are in reality institutions.[2] It is impossible to superimpose on man a lower layer of behaviour which one chooses to call 'natural', followed by a manufactured cultural or spiritual world. Everything is both manufactured and natural in man, as it were, in the sense that there is not a word, not a form of behaviour which does not owe something to purely biological being—and which at the same time does not elude the simplicity of animal life, and cause forms of vital behaviour to deviate from their pre-ordained direction, through a sort of leakage and through a genius for ambiguity which might serve to define man. Already the mere presence of a living being transforms the physical world, bringing to view here 'food', there a 'hiding place', and giving to 'stimuli' a sense which they have not hitherto possessed A fortiori does this apply to the presence of a man in the animal world Behaviour creates meanings which are transcendent in relation to the anatomical apparatus, and yet immanent to the behaviour as such, since it communicates itself and is understood. It is impossible to draw up an inventory of this irrational power which creates meanings and conveys them Speech is merely one particular case of it.

[1] It is well known that the kiss is not one of the traditional customs of Japan.

[2] Paternity is unknown to the Trobriand Islanders Children are brought up under the authority of the maternal uncle A husband, on his return from a long journey, is delighted to find new children in his home He looks after them, watches over them and cherishes them as if they were his own children. Malinowski, *The Father in Primitive Psychology*, quoted by Bertrand Russell, *Marriage and Morals*, Allen and Unwin, pp 20 and ff

What is true, however—and justifies the view that we ordinarily take of language, as being in a peculiar category—is that, alone of all expressive processes, speech is able to settle into a sediment and constitute an acquisition for use in human relationships. This fact cannot be explained by pointing out that speech can be recorded on paper, whereas gestures or forms of behaviour are transmitted only by direct imitation. For music too can be written down, and, although there is in music something in the nature of an initiation into the tradition, although, that is, it would probably be impossible to graduate to atonal music without passing through classical music, yet every composer starts his task at the beginning, having a new world to deliver, whereas in the realm of speech, each writer is conscious of taking as his objective the same world as has already been dealt with by other writers. The worlds of Balzac and Stendhal are not like planets without communication with each other, for speech implants the idea of truth in us as the presumptive limit of its effort. It loses sight of itself as a contingent fact, and takes to resting upon itself; this is, as we have seen, what provides us with the ideal of thought without words, whereas the idea of music without sounds is ridiculous. Even if this is pushing the principle beyond its limits and reducing things to the absurd, even if a linguistic meaning can never be delivered of its inherence in some word or other, the fact remains that the expressive process in the case of speech can be indefinitely reiterated, that it is possible to speak about speech whereas it is impossible to paint about painting, and finally that every philosopher has dreamed of a form of discourse which would supersede all others, whereas the painter or the musician does not hope to exhaust all possible painting or music. Thus there is a privileged position accorded to Reason. But if we want to understand it clearly, we must begin by putting thought back among the phenomena of expression.

This conception of language carries further the best and most recent analysis of aphasia, of which we have so far made use of only a part. We have seen, to start with, that after an empiricist phase, the theory of aphasia, since Pierre Marie, seemed to move over to intellectualism, and that, in linguistic disturbances, it invoked the 'representative function' (*Darstellungsfunktion*) or 'categorial' activity[1] and that it based speech on thought. In reality, it is not towards a new intellectualism that the theory moves. Whether its authors are aware of it or not, they are trying to formulate what we shall call an existential theory of aphasia, that is, a theory which treats thought and objective language as two manifestations of that fundamental activity

[1] Notions of this kind appear in the works of Head, van Woerkom, Bouman and Grunbaum, and Goldstein

whereby man projects himself towards a 'world'.[1] Take, for example, amnesia relating to names of colours. It is demonstrated, by sorting tests, that the sufferer from amnesia has lost the general ability to subsume colours under a category, and to this same cause is attributed the verbal deficiency But if we go back to concrete descriptions we notice that the categorial activity, before being a thought or a form of knowledge, is a certain manner of relating oneself to the world, and, correspondingly, a style or shape of experience. In a normal subject, the perception of a heap of samples is organized in virtue of the task set. 'The colours belonging to the same category as the model sample stand out against the background of the rest',[2] all the reds, for example, forming a group, and the subject has now only to split up this group in order to bring together all the samples which belong to it For the patient, on the other hand, each of the samples is confined within its individual existence Against the formation of any group according to a given principle, they bring a sort of viscosity or inertia When two objectively similar colours are presented to the patient, they do not necessarily appear similar· it may happen that in one the basic shade is dominant, in the other the degree of lightness or warmth.[3] We can ourselves experience something similar by taking up, before a pile of samples, an attitude of passive perception· the identical colours group themselves before our eyes, but those colours which are merely rather alike establish only vague mutual relations, 'the heap seems unstable, shifting, and we observe an incessant alteration in it, a kind of contest between several possible groupings of colours according to different points of view'.[4] We are reduced to the immediate experience of relationships (*Koharenzerlebnis, Erlebnis des Passens*) and such is probably the experience of the patient. We were wrong to say that he cannot abide by a given principle of classification, but goes from one to the other in reality he never adopts any [5] The disturbance touches 'the way in which the colours group themselves for the observer, the way in which the visual field is put together from the point of view of colours'.[6] It is not only the thought or knowledge, but the very experience of colours which is in question. We might say with another author that normal experience involves 'circles' or 'vortices' within which each element is representative of all others and carries, as it were, 'vectors' which

---

[1] Grunbaum, for example (*Aphasie und Motorik*) shows both that aphasic disturbances are *general* and that they are *motor*, in other words he makes motility into an original mode of intentionality or meaning (cf. above, pp. 227–8), which amounts to conceiving man, no longer in terms of consciousness, but in terms of existence.

[2] Gelb and Goldstein, *Über Farbennamenamnesie*, p 151.

[3] Ibid , p 149

[4] Ibid., pp. 151–2.

[5] Ibid , p 150.

[6] Ibid , p 162

link it to them. In the patient, 'this life is enclosed in narrower limits, and, compared to the normal subject's perceived world, it moves in smaller and more restricted circles A movement which has its origin on the periphery of the vortex no longer spreads immediately as far as its centre, but remains, so to speak, within the stimulated area or may be transmitted to its immediate surrounding, but no further. More comprehensive units of meaning can no longer be built up within the perceived world . Here again, each sense impression is provided with a "meaning-vector", but these vectors have no common direction, for, being no longer directed towards main determinate centres, they diverge much more than in the normal person '[1] Such is the disturbance of 'thought' discoverable at the root of amnesia; it can be seen that it concerns not so much the judgement as the setting of experience in which the judgement has its source, not so much spontaneity as the footing which spontaneity has in the perceptible world, and our ability to discern in it any intention whatsoever In Kantian terms it affects not so much the understanding as the productive imagination. The categorial act is therefore not an ultimate fact, it builds itself up into a certain 'attitude' (Einstellung). It is on this attitude, moreover, that speech is based, so that there can be no question of making language rest upon pure thought 'Categorial behaviour and the possession of meaningful language express one and the same fundamental form of behaviour. Neither can be a cause or effect of the other.'[2] In the first place, thought is not an effect of language. It is true that certain patients,[3] being unable to group colours by comparing them to a given sample, succeed through the intermediary of language: they name the colour of the exemplar and subsequently collect together all the samples which that name fits without looking back at the exemplar. It is true also that abnormal children[4] classify even different colours together if they have been taught to call them by the same name But these are precisely abnormal procedures; they do not express the essential relationship between language and thought, but the pathological or accidental relaship of language and thought both cut off from their living significance. Indeed, many patients are able to repeat the names of the colours without being any more capable of classifying them. In cases of amnesic aphasia, 'it cannot, therefore, be the lack of the word taken in itself which makes categorial behaviour difficult or impossible. Words must have lost something which normally belongs to them and which fits them for use in relation to categorial behaviour '[5]

---

[1] E Cassirer, *Philosophie der symbolischen Formen*, T III, p 258.
[2] Gelb and Goldstein, *Über Farbennamenamnesie*, p 158
[3] Ibid.   [4] Ibid.
[5] Ibid.

What have they lost? Their notional significance? Must we say that the concept has been withdrawn from them, thus making thought the cause of language? But clearly, when the word loses its meaning, it is modified down to its sensible aspect, *it is emptied* [1] The patient suffering from amnesia, to whom a colour name is given, and who is asked to choose a corresponding sample, repeats the name as if he expected something to come of it. But the name is now useless to him, it *tells* him nothing more, it is alien and absurd, as are for us names which we go on repeating for too long a time.[2] Patients for whom words have lost their meaning sometimes retain in the highest degree the ability to associate ideas.[3] The name, therefore, has not become separated from former 'associations', it has suffered deterioriation, like some inanimate body. The link between the word and its living meaning is not an external link of association, the meaning inhabits the word, and language 'is not an external accompaniment to intellectual processes' [4] We are therefore led to recognize a gestural or existential significance in speech, as we have already said. Language certainly has an inner content, but this is not self-subsistent and self-conscious thought. What then does language express, if it does not express thoughts? It presents or rather it *is* the subject's taking up of a position in the world of his meanings The term 'world' here is not a manner of speaking it means that the 'mental' or cultural life borrows its structures from natural life and that the thinking subject must have its basis in the subject incarnate The phonetic 'gesture' brings about, both for the speaking subject and for his hearers, a certain structural co-ordination of experience, a certain modulation of existence, exactly as a pattern of my bodily behaviour endows the objects around me with a certain significance both for me and for others The meaning of the gesture is not contained in it like some physical or physiological phenomenon The meaning of the word is not contained in the word as a sound But the human body is defined in terms of its property of appropriating, in an indefinite series of discontinuous acts, significant cores which transcend and transfigure its natural powers. This act of transcendence is first encountered in the acquisition of a pattern of behaviour, then in the mute communication of gesture: it is through the same power that the body opens itself to some new kind of conduct and makes it understood to external witnesses. Here and there a system of definite powers is suddenly

---

[1] Gelb and Goldstein, *Über Farbennamenamnesie*, p 158.
[2] Ibid
[3] One sees them faced with a given sample (red), recalling some object of the same colour (strawberry), and from there rediscovering the name of the colour (red strawberry, red) Ibid , p 177.
[4] Ibid , p. 158.

decentralized, broken up and reorganized under a fresh law unknown to the subject or to the external witness, and one which reveals itself to them at the very moment at which the process occurs For example, the knitting of the brows intended, according to Darwin, to protect the eye from the sun, or the narrowing of the eyes to enable one to see sharply, become component parts of the human act of meditation, and convey this to an observer. Language, in its turn, presents no different a problem a contraction of the throat, a sibilant emission of air between the tongue and teeth, a certain way of bringing the body into play suddenly allows itself to be invested with a *figurative significance* which is conveyed outside us. This is neither more nor less miraculous than the emergence of love from desire, or that of gesture from the unco-ordinated movements of infancy. For the miracle to come about, phonetic 'gesticulation' must use an alphabet of already acquired meanings, the word-gesture must be performed in a certain setting common to the speakers, just as the comprehension of other gestures presupposes a perceived world common to all, in which each one develops and spreads out its meaning. But this condition is not sufficient speech puts up a new sense, if it is authentic speech, just as gesture endows the object for the first time with human significance, if it is an initiating gesture Moreover significances now acquired must necessarily have been new once We must therefore recognize as an ultimate fact this open and indefinite power of giving significance—that is, both of apprehending and conveying a meaning—by which man transcends himself towards a new form of behaviour, or towards other people, or towards his own thought, through his body and his speech

When authors try to bring the analysis of aphasia to its conclusion in some general conception of language[1] they can more clearly be seen forsaking the intellectualist language which they adopted after Pierre Marie and in reaction against the conceptions of Broca It cannot be said of speech either that it is an 'operation of intelligence', or that it is a 'motor phenomenon'· it is wholly motility and wholly intelligence What establishes its inherence in the body is the fact that linguistic deficiencies cannot be reduced to a unity, and that the primary disturbances affect sometimes the body of the word, the material instrument of verbal expression—sometimes the word's physiognomy, the verbal intention, the kind of group image on the basis of which we succeed in saying or writing down a word exactly—sometimes the immediate meaning of the word, what German writers call the verbal concept—and sometimes the structure of the whole experience, not merely the linguistic experience, as in the case of amnesic aphasia examined above Speech, then, rests upon a strati-

[1] Cf Goldstein, *L'Analyse de l'aphasie et l'essence du langage*

fication of powers relatively capable of being isolated. But at the same time it is impossible to find anywhere a linguistic disturbance which is 'purely motor' and which does not to some extent impinge upon the significance of language In pure alexia,* if the subject can no longer recognize the letters of a word, it is through inability to pattern the visual data, or constitute the word's structure, or apprehend its visual significance. In motor aphasia, the list of words lost and preserved does not correspond to their objective characteristics (length or complexity), but to their value from the subject's point of view: the patient is unable to pronounce, in isolation, a letter or word within a familiar motor series, through being incapable of differentiating between the 'figure' and 'background' and freely conferring upon a certain word or letter the value of a figure. Articulatory and syntactical accuracy always stand in inverse ratio to each other, which shows that the articulation of a word is not a merely motor phenomenon, but that it draws upon the same energies which organize the syntactical order. When disturbances of verbal intention are present, as in the case of literal paraphasia † in which letters are omitted, displaced, or added, and in which the rhythm of the word is changed, it is, *a fortiori*, clearly not a question of a destruction of engrams,‡ but of the reduction to a common level of figure and background, of a powerlessness to structurize the word and grasp its articulatory physiognomy [1]

If we are to summarize these two sets of observations, we shall have to say that any linguistic operation presupposes the apprehension of a significance, but that the significance in both cases is, as it were, specialized· there are different layers of significance, from the visual to the conceptual by way of the verbal concept. These two ideas will never be simultaneously understood unless we cease to vacillate between the notions of 'motility' and 'intelligence', and unless we discover a third notion which enables us to integrate them, a

* *Alexia* Loss of power to grasp meaning of written or printed words and sentences: word-blindness (Translator's note)

† *Paraphrasia* jargon, form of aphasia in which patient has lost power of speaking correctly, though words are heard and comprehended he substitutes one word for another, and jumbles his words and sentences in such a way as to make his speech unintelligible (Translator's note)

‡ *Engram* traces left by stimuli on protoplasm of animal or plant (Translator's note).

[1] Goldstein, *L'Analyse de l'aphasie et l'essence du langage*, p 460 Goldstein here agrees with Grunbaum (*Aphasie und Motorik*) in going beyond the situation in which one is faced with the choice between the traditional conception (Broca) and the modern works (Head) Grunbaum's complaint against the moderns is that they do not 'give absolute priority to motor exteriorization, and the psychophysical structures on which it rests, as a fundamental field which dominates the picture of aphasia' (p 386)

function which shall be the same at all levels, which shall be equally at work in the hidden preliminaries to speech and in articulatory phenomena, which shall support the whole edifice of language, and which nevertheless shall be stabilized in relatively autonomous processes. We shall have the opportunity of seeing this power, essential to speech, in cases in which neither thought nor 'motility' is noticeably affected, and yet in which the 'life' of language is impaired. It does happen that vocabulary, syntax and the body of language appear intact, the only peculiarity being that main clauses predominate. But the patient does not make the same use as the normal subject of these materials. He speaks practically only when he is questioned, or, if he himself takes the initiative in asking a question, it is never other than of a stereotyped kind, such as he asks daily of his children when they come home from school. He never uses language to convey a merely possible situation, and false statements (e.g. the sky is black) are meaningless to him. He can speak only if he has prepared his sentences.[1] It cannot be held that language in his case has become automatic; there is no sign of a decline of general intelligence, and it is still the case that words are organized through their meaning. But the meaning is, as it were, ossified. Schneider never feels the need to speak; his experience never tends towards speech, it never suggests a question to him, it never ceases to have that kind of self-evidence and self-sufficiency of reality which stifles any interrogation, any reference to the possible, any wonder, any improvisation. We can perceive, in contrast with this, the essence of normal language: the intention to speak can reside only in an open experience. It makes its appearance like the boiling point of a liquid, when, in the density of being, volumes of empty space are built up and move outwards. 'As soon as man uses language to establish a living relation with himself or with his fellows, language is no longer an instrument, *no longer a means; it is a manifestation, a revelation of intimate being and of the psychic link which unites us to the world and our fellow men.* The patient's language may display great knowledge, it may be capable of being turned to account for specific activities, but it is totally lacking in that productivity which is man's deepest essence and which is perhaps revealed nowhere so clearly, among civilisation's creations, as in the creation of language itself.'[2] It might be said, restating a celebrated distinction, that *languages* or constituted systems of vocabulary and syntax, empirically existing 'means of expression', are both the repository and residue of acts of *speech*, in which unformulated significance not only finds the means of being conveyed

[1] Benary, *Analyse eines Seelenbildes von der Sprache aus.* This is again Schneider's case, which we have analysed in connection with motility and sexuality

[2] Goldstein, *L'Analyse de l'aphasie et l'essence du langage*, p 496 Our italics

outwardly, but moreover acquires existence for itself, and is genuinely created as significance Or again one might draw a distinction between the *word in the speaking* and the *spoken word* The former is the one in which the significant intention is at the stage of coming into being. Here existence is polarized into a certain 'significance'[1] which cannot be defined in terms of any natural object. It is somewhere at a point beyond being that it aims to catch up with itself again, and that is why it creates speech as an empirical support for its own not-being. Speech is the surplus of our existence over natural being. But the act of expression constitutes a linguistic world and a cultural world, and allows that to fall back into being which was striving to outstrip it Hence the spoken word, which enjoys available significances as one might enjoy an acquired fortune. From these gains other acts of authentic expression—the writer's, artist's or philosopher's—are made possible. This ever-recreated opening in the plenitude of being is what conditions the child's first use of speech and the language of the writer, as it does the construction of the word and that of concepts. Such is the function which we intuit through language, which reiterates itself, which is its own foundation, or which, like a wave, gathers and poises itself to hurtle beyond its own limits.

The analysis of speech and expression brings home to us the enigmatic nature of our own body even more effectively than did our remarks on bodily space and unity. It is not a collection of particles, each one remaining in itself, nor yet a network of processes defined once and for all—it is not where it is, nor what it is—since we see it secreting in itself a 'significance' which comes to it from nowhere, projecting that significance upon its material surrounding, and communicating it to other embodied subjects. It has always been observed that speech or gesture transfigure the body, but no more was said on the subject than that they develop or disclose another power, that of thought or soul. The fact was overlooked that, in order to express it, the body must in the last analysis become the thought or intention that it signifies for us It is the body which points out, and which speaks; so much we have learnt in this chapter Cézanne used to say of a portrait: 'If I paint in all the little blue and brown touches, I make him gaze as he does gaze ... Never mind if they suspect how, by bringing together a green of various shades and a red, we sadden a mouth or bring a smile to a cheek '[2] This disclosure of an immanent or incipient significance in the living body extends, as we shall see, to the whole sensible world, and our gaze, prompted by the experience of our own body, will discover in all other 'objects' the miracle of expression. In his *Peau de Chagrin* Balzac describes a

[1] 'sens' in French means 'direction' and 'significance' (Translator's note)
[2] J Gasquet, *Cézanne*, p. 117

'white tablecloth, like a covering of snow newly fallen, from which rose symmetrically the plates and napkins crowned with light-coloured rolls'. 'Throughout my youth,' Cézanne said, 'I wanted to paint that table-cloth like freshly fallen snow. . . . I know now that one must try to paint only: "the plates and napkins rose symmetrically", and "the light-coloured rolls". If I paint "crowned", I'm finished, you see. And if I really balance and shade my napkins and rolls as they really are, you may be sure that the crowning, the snow and all the rest of it will be there.'[1] The problem of the world, and, to begin with, that of one's own body, consists in the fact that *it is all there.*

We have become accustomed, through the influence of the Cartesian tradition, to jettison the subject· the reflective attitude simultaneously purifies the common notions of body and soul by defining the body as the sum of its parts with no interior, and the soul as a being wholly present to itself without distance. These definitions make matters perfectly clear both within and outside ourselves: we have the transparency of an object with no secret recesses, the transparency of a subject which is nothing but what it thinks it is. The object is an object through and through, and consciousness a consciousness through and through. There are two senses, and two only, of the word 'exist' one exists as a thing or else one exists as a consciousness. The experience of our own body, on the other hand, reveals to us an ambiguous mode of existing If I try to think of it as a cluster of third person processes—'sight', 'motility', 'sexuality'—I observe that these 'functions' cannot be interrelated, and related to the external world, by causal connections, they are all obscurely drawn together and mutually implied in a unique drama Therefore the body is not an object For the same reason, my awareness of it is not a thought, that is to say, I cannot take it to pieces and reform it to make a clear idea Its unity is always implicit and vague It is always something other than what it is, always sexuality and at the same time freedom, rooted in nature at the very moment when it is transformed by cultural influences, never hermetically sealed and never left behind Whether it is a question of another's body or my own, I have no means of knowing the human body other than that of living it, which means taking up on my own account the drama which is being played out in it, and losing myself in it. I am my body, at least wholly to the extent that I possess experience, and yet at the same time my body is as it were a 'natural' subject, a provisional sketch of my total being Thus experience of one's own body runs counter to the reflective procedure which detaches subject and object from each other,

[1] J Gasquet, *Cézanne*, pp 123 and ff.

and which gives us only the thought about the body, or the body as
an idea, and not the experience of the body or the body in reality
Descartes was well aware of this, since a famous letter of his to Elizabeth draws the distinction between the body as it is conceived through
use in living and the body as it is conceived by the understanding.[1]
But in Descartes this peculiar knowledge of our body, which we enjoy
from the mere fact that we are a body, remains subordinated to our
knowledge of it through the medium of ideas, because, behind man
as he in fact is, stands God as the rational author of our *de facto*
situation. On the basis of this transcendent guarantee, Descartes can
blandly accept our irrational condition it is not we who are required
to bear the responsibility for reason and, once we have recognized it
at the basis of things, it remains for us only to act and think in the
world.[2] But if our union with the body is substantial, how is it possible for us to experience in ourselves a pure soul from which to
accede to an absolute Spirit? Before asking this question, let us look
closely at what is implied in the rediscovery of our own body. It is
not merely one object among the rest which has the peculiarity of
resisting reflection and remaining, so to speak, stuck to the subject.
Obscurity spreads to the perceived world in its entirety

[1] To Elizabeth, 28th June 1643, AT, T III, p 690

[2] 'Finally, as I consider that it is very necessary to have understood, once in
one's lifetime, the principles of metaphysics, since they are what provide us with
knowledge of God and our soul, I think too, however, that it would be extremely
harmful to occupy our mind often in meditating upon them, since it could not
then attend so effectively to the work of imagination and the senses, but that the
best course is merely to retain in memory and belief conclusions once arrived at,
and thenceforth to employ the rest of the time one can devote to study to thoughts
in which the understanding acts along with the imagination and the senses ' Ibid

PART TWO

The World as Perceived

The theory of the body is already a theory of perception

Our own body is in the world as the heart is in the organism it keeps the visible spectacle constantly alive, it breathes life into it and sustains it inwardly, and with it forms a system. When I walk round my flat, the various aspects in which it presents itself to me could not possibly appear as views of one and the same thing if I did not know that each of them represents the flat seen from one spot or another, and if I were unaware of my own movements, and of my body as retaining its identity through the stages of those movements I can of course take a mental bird's eye view of the flat, visualize it or draw a plan of it on paper, but in that case too I could not grasp the unity of the object without the mediation of bodily experience, for what I call a plan is only a more comprehensive perspective: it is the flat 'seen from above', and the fact that I am able to draw together in it all habitual perspectives is dependent on my knowing that one and the same embodied subject can view successively *from* various positions It will perhaps be objected that by restoring the object to bodily experience as one of the poles of that experience, we deprive it of precisely that which constitutes its objectivity. From the point of view of my body I never see as equal the six sides of the cube, even if it is made of glass, and yet the word 'cube' has a meaning; the cube itself, the cube in reality, beyond its sensible appearances, has *its* six equal sides As I move round it, I see the front face, hitherto a square, change its shape, then disappear, while the other sides come into view and one by one become squares But the successive stages of this experience are for me merely the opportunity of conceiving the whole cube with its six equal and simultaneous faces, the intelligible structure which provides the explanation of it. And it is even necessary, for my tour of inspection of the cube to warrant the judgement: 'here is a cube', that my movements themselves be located in objective space and, far from its being the case that the experience of my own movement conditions the position of an object, it is, on the contrary, by conceiving my body itself as a mobile object that I am able to interpret perceptual appearance and construct the cube as it truly is. The experience of my own movement would therefore appear to be no more than a psychological circumstance of perception and to

203

make no contribution to determining the significance of the object The object and my body would certainly form a system, but we would then have a nexus of objective correlations and not, as we were saying earlier, a collection of lived-through correspondences. The unity of the object is thus conceived, and not experienced as the correlate of our body's unity.

But can the object be thus detached from the actual conditions under which it is presented to us? One can bring together discursively the notion of the number six, the notion of 'side' and that of equality, and link them together in a formula which is the definition of the cube But this definition rather puts a question to us than offers us something to conceive. One emerges from blind, symbolic thought only by perceiving the particular spatial entity which bears these predicates all together. It is a question of tracing in thought that particular form which encloses a fragment of space between six equal faces. Now, if the words 'enclose' and 'between' have a meaning for us, it is because they derive it from our experience as embodied subjects. In space *itself* independently of the presence of a psycho-physical subject, there is no direction, no inside and no outside. A space is 'enclosed' between the sides of a cube as we are enclosed between the walls of our room In order to be able to conceive the cube, we take up a position in space, now on its surface, now in it, now outside it, and from that moment we see it in perspective. The cube with six equal sides is not only invisible, but inconceivable, it is the cube as it would be for itself; but the cube is not for itself, since it is an object There is a first order dogmatism, of which analytical reflection rids us, and which consists in asserting that the object is in itself, or absolutely, without wondering what it is. But there is another, which consists in affirming the ostensible significance of the object, without wondering how it' enters into our experience. Analytical reflection puts forward, instead of the absolute existence of the object, the thought of an absolute object, and, through trying to dominate the object and think of it from no point of view, it destroys the object's internal structure If there is, for me, a cube with six equal sides, and if I can link up with the object, this is not because I constitute it from the inside: it is because I delve into the thickness of the world by perceptual experience. The cube with six equal sides is the limiting idea whereby I express the material presence of the cube which is there before my eyes, under my hands, in its perceptual self-evidence. The sides of the cube are not projections of it, but precisely sides. When I perceive them successively, with the appearance they present in different perspectives, I do not construct the idea of the flat projection which accounts for these perspectives; the cube is already there in front of me and reveals itself through them. I do not need to take an objective

view of my own movement, or take it into account, in order to reconstitute the true form of the object behind its appearance; the account
is already taken, and already the new appearance has compounded
itself with the lived-through movement and presented itself as an
appearance of a cube. The thing, and the world, are given to me
along with the parts of my body, not by any 'natural geometry', but
in a living connection comparable, or rather identical, with that
existing between the parts of my body itself.

External perception and the perception of one's own body vary
in conjunction because they are the two facets of one and the same
act. The attempt has long been made to explain Aristotle's celebrated
illusion by allowing that the unaccustomed position of the fingers
makes the synthesis of their perceptions impossible: the right side of
the middle finger and the left side of the index do not ordinarily
'work' together, and if both are touched at once, then there must be
two marbles. In reality, the perceptions of the two fingers are not
only disjoined, they are inverted the subject attributes to the index
what is touched by the middle finger and *vice versa*, as can be shown
by applying two distinct stimuli to the fingers, a point and a ball, for
example.[1] Aristotle's illusion is primarily a disturbance of the body
image. What makes the synthesis of the two tactile perceptions in one
single object impossible, is not so much that the position of the
fingers is unaccustomed or statistically rare, it is that the right face
of the middle finger and the left face of the index cannot combine in
a joint exploration of the object, that the crossing of the fingers, being
a movement which has to be imposed on them, lies outside the motor
possibilities of the fingers themselves and cannot be aimed at in a
project towards movement. The synthesis of the object is here
effected, then, through the synthesis of one's own body, it is the reply
or correlative to it, and it is literally the same thing to perceive one
single marble, and to use two fingers as one single organ. The disturbance of the body image may even be directly translated into the
external world without the intervention of any stimulus. In heautoscopy, before seeing himself, the subject always passes through a state
akin to dreaming, musing or disquiet, and the image of himself which
appears outside him is merely the counterpart of this depersonalization.[2] The patient has the feeling of being in the double outside

[1] Tastevin, Czermak, Schilder, quoted by Lhermitte, *L'Image de notre Corps*,
pp 36 and ff.

[2] Lhermitte, *L'Image de notre Corps*, pp 136–88, cf p 191 · 'During the period
of autoscopy the subject is overcome by a feeling of profound sadness which
spreads outwards and into the very image of the double, which seems to be filled
with effective vibrations identical with those experienced by the original person',
'his consciousness seems to have moved wholly outside himself' And Menninger-
Lerchenthal, *Das Truggebilde der eigenen Gestalt*, p. 180. 'I suddenly had the
impression of being outside my body.'

himself, just as, in a lift which goes upwards and suddenly stops, I feel
the substance of my body escaping from me through my head and
overrunning the boundaries of my objective body. It is in his own
body that the patient feels the approach of this Other whom he has
never seen with his eyes, as the normal person is aware, through a
certain burning feeling in the nape of the neck, that someone is
watching him from behind.[1] Conversely, a certain form of external
experience implies and produces a certain consciousness of one's own
body Many patients speak of a 'sixth sense' which seems to produce
their hallucinations. Stratton's subject, whose visual field has been
objectively inverted, at first sees everything upside down; on the
third day of the experiment, when things are beginning to regain
their upright position, he is filled with 'the strange impression of
looking at the fire out of the back of his head'[2] This is because there
is an immediate equivalence between the orientation of the visual
field and the awareness of one's own body as the potentiality of that
field, so that any upheaval experimentally brought about can appear
indifferently either as the inversion of phenomenal objects or as a
redistribution of sensory functions in the body If a subject focuses
for long-distance vision, he has a double image of his own finger as
indeed of all objects near to him If he is touched or pricked, he is
aware of being touched or pricked in two places.[3] Diplopia is thus
extended into a bodily duplication Every external perception is
immediately synonymous with a certain perception of my body,
just as every perception of my body is made explicit in the language
of external perception If, then, as we have seen to be the case,
the body is not a transparent object, and is not presented to us in
virtue of the law of its constitution, as the circle is to the geometer,
if it is an expressive unity which we can learn to know only by
actively taking it up, this structure will be passed on to the
sensible world The theory of the body image is, implicitly, a theory
of perception We have relearned to feel our body; we have found
underneath the objective and detached knowledge of the body
that other knowledge which we have of it in virtue of its always being
with us and of the fact that we are our body. In the same way we shall
need to reawaken our experience of the world as it appears to us in so
far as we are in the world through our body, and in so far as we perceive the world with our body But by thus remaking contact with
the body and with the world, we shall also rediscover ourself, since,
perceiving as we do with our body, the body is a natural self and, as
it were, the subject of perception

[1] Jaspers, quoted by Menninger-Lerchenthal, op cit , p 76
[2] Stratton, *Vision without Inversion of the Retinal Image*, p 350
[3] Lhermitte, *L'Image de notre Corps*, p 39

SENSE EXPERIENCE

OBJECTIVE thought is unaware of the subject of perception. This is because it presents itself with the world ready made, as the setting of every possible event, and treats perception as one of these events For example, the empiricist philosopher considers a subject *x* in the act of perceiving and tries to describe what happens· *there are* sensations which are the subject's states or manners of being and, in virtue of this, genuine mental things. The perceiving subject is the place where these things occur, and the philosopher describes sensations and their substratum as one might describe the fauna of a distant land—without being aware that he himself perceives, that he is the perceiving subject and that perception as he lives it belies everything that he says of perception in general For, seen from the inside, perception owes nothing to what we know in other ways about the world, about *stimuli* as physics describes them and about the sense organs as described by biology. It does not present itself in the first place as an event in the world to which the category of causality, for example, can be applied, but as a re-creation or re-constitution of the world at every moment. In so far as we believe in the world's past, in the physical world, in 'stimuli', in the organism as our books depict it, it is first of all because we have present at this moment to us a perceptual field, a surface in contact with the world, a permanent rootedness in it, and because the world ceaselessly assails and beleaguers subjectivity as waves wash round a wreck on the shore All knowledge takes its place within the horizons opened up by perception There can be no question of describing perception itself as one of the facts thrown up in the world, since we can never fill up, in the picture of the world, that gap which we ourselves are, and by which it comes into existence for someone, since perception is the 'flaw' in this 'great diamond'.* Intellectualism certainly represents a step

* Cf   Mes repentirs, mes doutes, mes contraintes
           Sont le defaut de ton grand diamant.

Translator's note)   Paul Valéry, *Le Cimetière marin.*

forward in coming to self-consciousness: that place outside the world at which the empiricist philosopher hints, and in which he tacitly takes up his position in order to describe the event of perception, now receives a name, and appears in the description. It is the transcendental Ego. Through it every empiricist thesis is reversed: the state of consciousness becomes the consciousness of a state, passivity the positing of passivity, the world becomes the correlative of thought about the world and henceforth exists only for a constituting agent. And yet it remains true to say that intellectualism too provides itself with a ready-made world. For the constitution of the world, as conceived by it, is a mere requirement that to each term of the empiricist description be added the indication 'consciousness of . . ' The whole system of experience—world, own body and empirical self—are subordinated to a universal thinker charged with sustaining the relationships between the three terms But, since he is not actually involved, these relationships remain what they were in empiricism: causal relations spread out in the context of cosmic events Now, if one's own body and the empirical self are no more than elements of the system of experience, objects among other objects in the eyes of the true *I*, how can we ever be confused with our body? How can we ever have believed that we saw with our eyes what we in fact grasp through an inspection of the mind; how is it that the world does not present itself to us as perfectly explicit; why is it displayed only gradually and never 'in its entirety'? In short, how does it come about that we perceive? We shall understand this only if the empirical self and the body are not immediately objects, in fact only if they never quite become objects, if there is a certain significance in saying that I can see the piece of wax with my eyes, and if correlatively the possibility of absence, the dimension of escape and freedom which reflection opens in the depths of our being, and which is called the transcendental Ego, are not initially given and are never absolutely acquired, if I can never say 'I' absolutely, and if every act of reflection, every voluntary taking up of a position is based on the ground and the proposition of a life of pre-personal consciousness The subject of perception will remain overlooked as long as we cannot avoid the dilemma of *natura naturata* and *natura naturans*, of sensation as a state of consciousness and as the consciousness of a state, of existence in itself and existence for itself Let us then return to sensation and scrutinize it closely enough to learn from it the living relation of the perceiver to his body and to his world

Inductive psychology will help us in our search for a new status for sensation, by showing that it is neither a state or a quality, nor the consciousness of a state or of a quality. In fact, each of the alleged qualities—red, blue, colour, sound—is inserted into a certain form of

208

behaviour. In the normal subject a sensory excitation, particularly of the experimental kind which has practically no living significance for him, scarcely has any effect on general motility. But diseases of the cerebellum or the frontal cortex clearly show what effect sensory excitations would have on muscular tonicity, if they were not integrated into a comprehensive situation, and if tonicity were not, in the normal person, adjusted to certain special tasks. The gesture of raising the arm, which can be taken as an indicator of motor disturbance, is differently modified in its sweep and its direction according as the visual field is red, yellow, blue or green. Red and yellow are particularly productive of smooth movements, blue and green of jerky ones; red applied to the right eye, for example, favours a corresponding stretching of the arm outwards, green the bending of the arm back towards the body.[1] The privileged position of the arm—the one in which the arm is felt to be balanced and at rest—which is farther away from the body in the patient than in the normal subject, is modified by the presentation of colours: green brings it back nearer to the body.[2] The colour of the visual field affects the accuracy of the subject's reactions, whether it is a question of performing a movement of a given extent or measuring with the finger a definite length. With a green visual field the assessment is accurate, with a red one the subject errs on the side of excess. Movements outwards are accelerated by green and slowed down by red. Localization of stimuli on the skin is modified by red in the direction of abduction. Yellow and red emphasize errors in judging weight and time, though in the case of cerebellar patients blue and particularly green have a compensating effect. In these various experiments each colour always acts with the same tendency, with the result that a definite motor value can be assigned to it Generally speaking, red and yellow favour abduction, blue and green adduction. Now, on the whole, the significance of adduction is that the organism turns towards the stimulus and is attracted by the world—of abduction that it turns away from the stimulus and withdraws towards its centre.[3] Sensations, 'sensible qualities' are then far from being reducible to a certain indescribable state or *quale*; they present themselves with a motor physiognomy, and are enveloped in a living significance. It has long been known that sensations have a 'motor accompaniment', that stimuli set in motion 'incipient movements' which are associated with the sensation of the quality and create a halo round it, and that the 'perceptual side' and the 'motor side' of behaviour are in communication with

[1] Goldstein and Rosenthal, *Zum Problem der Wirkung der Farben auf den Organismus*, pp. 3–9.
[2] Ibid.
[3] *La Structure du Comportement*, p. 201

each other But it is usual to proceed as if this relation left unaffected the terms between which it stands. For there is no question, in the examples given above, of an external, causal relationship leaving the sensation itself unchanged Motor reactions produced by blue, 'blue-occasioned conduct', are not the effects of colour on the objective body, defined in terms of specific wavelength and intensity: for a blue produced by contrast, and therefore having no physical phenomenon corresponding to it, has around it the same motor halo [1] Where the motor physiognomy of colour is constituted is not in the physicist's world, as a result of some occult process Is it then 'in consciousness', and must we say that the experience of blue as a sensible quality produces a certain change in the phenomenal body? But it is not obvious why the clear awareness of a certain *quale* should affect my judgement of sizes, and moreover the *felt* effect of colour does not always exactly correspond to the influence exerted by it on behaviour red may accentuate my reactions without my being aware of it [2] The motor significance of colours is comprehensible only if they cease to be closed states or indescribable qualities presented to an observing and thinking subject, and if they impinge within me upon a certain general setting through which I come to terms with the world; if, moreover, they suggest to me a new manner of evaluating, and yet if motility ceases to be the mere consciousness of my movements from place to place in the present or immediate future, and becomes the function which constantly lays down my standards of size and the varying scope of my being in the world. Blue is that which prompts me to look in a certain way, that which allows my gaze to run over it in a specific manner. It is a certain field or atmosphere presented to the power of my eyes and of my whole body. Here the experience of colours confirms and elucidates the correlations established by inductive psychology. Green is commonly regarded as a 'restful' colour. 'It encloses me within myself and brings a peaceful state,' says one patient.[3] It 'makes no demands on us and does not enjoin us to do anything,' says Kandinsky. Blue seems to 'yield to our gaze,' says Goethe On the other hand, he adds, red 'invades the eye '[4] Red has a 'rending', and yellow a 'stinging' effect, says one of Goldstein's patients. Generally speaking we have on the one hand, with red and yellow, 'an experience of being torn away, of a movement away from the centre', on the other hand, with blue and green, that of 'repose and concentration' [5] We can reveal the soporific and motor basis of

[1] Goldstein and Rosenthal, art cit , p. 23.

[2] Ibid

[3] Ibid

[4] Kandinsky, *Form und Farbe in der Malerei*, Goethe, *Farbenlehre*, in particular Abs 293, quoted by Goldstein and Rosenthal. Ibid

[5] Goldstein and Rosenthal, pp. 23-5

qualities, or their vital significance, by employing stimuli which are either weak or of short duration. In this case the colour, before being seen, gives itself away through the experience of a certain bodily attitude appropriate only to that colour and precisely indicative of it· 'there is in my body a sensation of slipping downwards, so that it cannot be green, and can be only blue but in fact I see no blue',[1] says one subject Another says: 'I clenched my teeth, and so I know that it is yellow '[2] If a light stimulus is gradually increased from a sub-liminal intensity, there is first of all the experience of a certain bodily disposition and suddenly the sensation runs into and 'spreads through the visual domain' [3] Just as, when I look closely at snow, I break its apparent 'whiteness' up into a world of reflections and transpar-encies, so within a musical note a 'micromelody' can be picked out and the interval heard is merely the final patterning of a certain tension felt throughout the body [4]

The representation of a colour in subjects who have lost it is made possible by displaying before them any real colours whatsoever The real colour produces in the subject a 'concentration of colour experi-ence' which enables him to 'draw together the colours in his eye'.[5] Thus, before becoming an objective spectacle, quality is revealed by a type of behaviour which is directed towards it in its essence, and this is why my body has no sooner adopted the attitude of blue than I am vouchsafed a quasi-presence of blue. We must therefore stop wonder-ing how and why red signifies effort or violence, green restfulness and peace, we must rediscover how to live these colours as our body does, that is, as peace or violence in concrete form. When we say that red increases the compass of our reactions, we are not to be understood as having in mind two distinct facts, a sensation of redness and motor reactions—we must be understood as meaning that red, by its texture as followed and adhered to by our gaze, is already the amplification of our motor being. The subject of sensation is neither a thinker who takes note of a quality, nor an inert setting which is affected or changed by it, it is a power which is born into, and simultaneously with, a certain existential environment, or is synchronized with it. The relations of sentient to sensible are comparable with those of the sleeper to his slumber: sleep comes when a certain voluntary attitude suddenly receives from outside the confirmation for which it was waiting I am breathing deeply and slowly in order to summon sleep, and suddenly it is as if my mouth were connected to some great lung outside myself which alternately calls forth and forces back my

[1] Werner, *Untersuchungen uber Empfindung und Empfinden*, I, p 158
[2] Ibid   [3] Ibid , p 159
[4] Werner, *Uber die Auspragung von Tongestalten*
[5] Werner, *Untersuchungen uber Empfindung und Empfinden*, I, p 160

breath A certain rhythm of respiration, which a moment ago I voluntarily maintained, now becomes my very being, and sleep, until now aimed at as a significance, suddenly becomes a situation In the same way I give ear, or look, in the expectation of a sensation, and suddenly the sensible takes possession of my ear or my gaze, and I surrender a part of my body, even my whole body, to this particular manner of vibrating and filling space known as blue or red Just as the sacrament not only symbolizes, in sensible species, an operation of Grace, but is also the real presence of God, which it causes to occupy a fragment of space and communicates to those who eat of the consecrated bread, provided that they are inwardly prepared, in the same way the sensible has not only a motor and vital significance, but is nothing other than a certain way of being in the world suggested to us from some point in space, and seized and acted upon by our body, provided that it is capable of doing so, so that sensation is literally a form of communion.

Taking this view, it becomes possible to attach to the notion of 'significance' a value which intellectualism withholds from it. My sensation and my perception, according to this theory, are capable of being specified and hence of existing for me only by being the sensation or perception of something—for instance, the sensation of blue or red, or the perception of the table or the chair. Now blue and red are not those incommunicable experiences which are mine when I coincide with them, nor are the table and the chair those short-lived appearances which are dependent on my gaze. The object is made determinate as an identifiable being only through a whole open series of possible experiences, and exists only for a subject who carries out this identification Being is exclusively for someone who is able to step back from it and thus stand wholly outside being In this way the mind becomes the subject of perception and the notion of 'significance' becomes inconceivable If seeing or hearing involved extricating oneself from the impression in order to lay siege to it in thought, ceasing, that is, to be in order to know, then it would be ridiculous to say that I see with my eyes or hear with my ears, for my eyes and ears are themselves entities in the world and as such are quite incapable of maintaining on the hither side of it that area of subjectivity from which it is seen or heard Even by making them instruments of my perception I cannot ensure that my eyes and ears retain any cognitive power, for the notion of perception is ambiguous they are instruments of bodily excitation only, and not of perception itself There is no middle term between *in itself* and *for itself*, and since my senses, being several, are not myself, they can be only objects. I say that my eyes see, that my hand touches, that my foot is aching, but these naïve expressions do not put into words my true

212

experience. Already they provide me with an interpretation of that experience which detaches it from its original subject. Because I know that the light strikes my eyes, that contact is made by the skin, that my shoe hurts my foot, I distribute through my body perceptions which really belong to my soul, and put perception into the thing perceived. But that is merely the spatial and temporal furrow left by the acts of consciousness. If I consider them from the inside, I find one single, unlocalized knowledge, one single indivisible soul, and there is no such difference between thinking and perceiving as there is between seeing and hearing Can we remain within this perspective? If it is true that I do not see with my eyes, how can I ever have been ignorant of this truth? Perhaps I did not know what I was saying, or perhaps I had not thought about it But how could I not have thought about it? How could the scrutiny of my mind, how could the working of my own thought be concealed from me, since by definition my thought is for itself? If reflection is to justify itself as reflection, that is to say, as progress towards the truth, it must not merely put one view of the world in place of another, it must show us how the naive view of the world is included in and transcended by the sophisticated one Reflection must elucidate the unreflective view which it supersedes, and show the possibility of this latter, in order to comprehend itself as a beginning. To say that it is still myself who conceive myself as situated in a body and furnished with five senses is clearly a purely verbal solution, since I who reflect cannot recognize myself in this embodied *I*, since therefore embodiment remains in the nature of the case an illusion, and since the possibility of this illusion remains incomprehensible We must re-examine the dilemma of *for itself* and *in itself*, which involved putting 'significances' back into the world of objects and freeing subjectivity, as absolute non-being, of any kind of inherence in the body. This is what we are doing when we define sensation as co-existence or communion. The sensation of blue is not the knowledge or positing of a certain identifiable *quale* throughout all the experiences of it which I have, as the geometer's circle is the same in Paris and Tokyo It is in all probability intentional, which means that it does not rest in itself as does a thing, but that it is directed and has significance beyond itself But what it aims at is recognized only blindly, through my body's familiarity with it It is not constituted in the full light of day, it is reconstituted or taken up once more by a knowledge which remains latent, leaving it with its opacity and its thisness. Sensation is intentional because I find that in the sensible a certain rhythm of existence is put forward—abduction or adduction—and that, following up this hint, and stealing into the form of existence which is thus suggested to me, I am brought into relation with an external being, whether it be in order to open

213

myself to it or to shut myself off from it If the qualities radiate around them a certain mode of existence, if they have the power to cast a spell and what we called just now a sacramental value, this is because the sentient subject does not posit them as objects, but enters into a sympathetic relation with them, makes them his own and finds in them his momentary law.

Let us be more explicit The sentient and the sensible do not stand in relation to each other as two mutually external terms, and sensation is not an invasion of the sentient by the sensible It is my gaze which subtends colour, and the movement of my hand which subtends the object's form, or rather my gaze pairs off with colour, and my hand with hardness and softness, and in this transaction between the subject of sensation and the sensible it cannot be held that one acts while the other suffers the action, or that one confers significance on the other Apart from the probing of my eye or my hand, and before my body synchronizes with it, the sensible is nothing but a vague beckoning. 'If a subject tries to experience a specific colour, blue for example, while trying to take up the bodily attitude appropriate to red, an inner conflict results, a sort of spasm which stops as soon as he adopts the bodily attitude corresponding to blue.'[1] Thus a sensible datum which is on the point of being felt sets a kind of muddled problem for my body to solve I must find the attitude which *will* provide it with the means of becoming determinate, of showing up as blue; I must find the reply to a question which is obscurely expressed. And yet I do so only when I am invited by it, my attitude is never sufficient to make me really see blue or really touch a hard surface. The sensible gives back to me what I lent to it, but this is only what I took from it in the first place. As I contemplate the blue of the sky I am not *set over against* it as an acosmic subject; I do not possess it in thought, or spread out towards it some idea of blue such as might reveal the secret of it, I abandon myself to it and plunge into this mystery, it 'thinks itself within me',* I am the sky itself as it is drawn together and unified, and as it begins to exist for itself, my consciousness is saturated with this limitless blue. But, it may be retorted, the sky is not mind and there is surely no sense in saying that it exists for itself. It is indeed true that the geographer's or the astronomer's sky does not exist for itself But of the sky, as it is perceived or sensed, subtended by my gaze which ranges over and resides in it, and providing as it does the theatre of a certain living

[1] Werner, *Untersuchungen uber Empfindung und Empfinden*, I, p 158.

* Cf   'Midi là-haut, Midi sans mouvement
             En soi se pense et convient à soi-même '
                                    Valéry, *Le Cimetiere marin*

(Translator's note)

pulsation adopted by my body, it can be said that it exists for itself, in the sense that it is not made up of mutually exclusive parts, that each part of the whole is 'sensitive' to what happens in all the others; and 'knows them dynamically'.[1] As for the subject of sensation, he need not be a pure nothingness with no terrestrial weight That would be necessary only if, like constituting consciousness, he had to be simultaneously omnipresent, coextensive with being, and in process of thinking universal truth. But the spectacle perceived does not partake of pure being Taken exactly as I see it, it is a moment of my individual history, and since sensation is a reconstitution, it presupposes in me sediments left behind by some previous constitution, so that I am, as a sentient subject, a repository stocked with natural powers at which I am the first to be filled with wonder. I am not, therefore, in Hegel's phrase, 'a hole in being', but a hollow, a fold, which has been made and which can be unmade [2]

We must stress this point How have we managed to escape from the dilemma of the *for itself* and the *in itself*, how can perceptual consciousness be saturated with its object, how can we distinguish sensible consciousness from intellectual consciousness? Because (1) Every perception takes place in an atmosphere of generality and is presented to us anonymously. I cannot say that *I* see the blue of the sky in the sense in which I say that I understand a book or again in which I decide to devote my life to mathematics My perception, even when seen from the inside, expresses a given situation: I can see blue because I am *sensitive* to colours, whereas personal acts create a situation I am a mathematician because I have decided to be one. So, if I wanted to render precisely the perceptual experience, I ought to say that *one* perceives in me, and not that I perceive. Every sensation carries within it the germ of a dream or depersonalization such as we experience in that quasi-stupor to which we are reduced when we really try to live at the level of sensation. It is true that knowledge teaches me that sensation would not occur unless my body were in some way adapted to it, for example, that there would be no specific contact unless I moved my hand But this activity takes place on the periphery of my being I am no more aware of being the true subject of my sensation than of my birth or my death. Neither my birth nor my death can appear to me as experiences of my own, since, if I thought of them thus, I should be assuming myself to be pre-existent to, or outliving, myself, in order to be able to experience them, and I should therefore not be genuinely thinking of my birth or my death.

[1] Koehler, *Die physischen Gestalten*, p 180

[2] We have pointed out elsewhere that consciousness seen from outside cannot be a pure *for itself* (*La Structure du Comportement*, pp 168 and ff) We are beginning to see that the same applies to consciousness seen from the inside

I can, then, apprehend myself only as 'already born' and 'still alive'—
I can apprehend my birth and my death only as prepersonal horizons
I know that people are born and die, but I cannot know my own birth
and death Each sensation, being strictly speaking, the first, last and
only one of its kind, is a birth and a death. The subject who experiences it begins and ends with it, and as he can neither precede nor
survive himself, sensation necessarily appears to itself in a setting of
generality, its origin is anterior to myself, it arises from *sensibility*
which has preceded it and which will outlive it, just as my birth and
death belong to a natality and a mortality which are anonymous. By
means of sensation I am able to grasp, on the fringe of my own
personal life and acts, a life of given consciousness from which these
latter emerge, the life of my eyes, hands and ears, which are so many
natural selves Each time I experience a sensation, I feel that it concerns not my own being, the one for which I am responsible and for
which I make decisions, but another self which has already sided
with the world, which is already open to certain of its aspects and
synchronized with them. Between my sensation and myself there
stands always the thickness of some *primal acquisition* which prevents my experience from being clear of itself I experience the sensation as a modality of a general existence, one already destined for a
physical world and which runs through me without my being the
cause of it.

(2) Sensation can be anonymous only because it is incomplete.
The person who sees and the one who touches is not exactly myself,
because the visible and the tangible worlds are not the world in its
entirety When I see an object, I always feel that there is a portion of
being beyond what I see at this moment, not only as regards visible
being, but also as regards what is tangible or audible And not only
sensible being, but a depth of the object that no progressive sensory
deduction will ever exhaust. In a corresponding way, I am not myself
wholly in these operations, they remain marginal. They occur out in
front of me, for the self which sees or the self which hears is in some
way a specialized self, familiar with only one sector of being, and it is
precisely for this reason that eye and hand are able to guess the
movement which will fix the perception, thus displaying that fore-
knowledge which gives them an involuntary appearance

We may summarize these two ideas by saying that any sensation
belongs to a certain *field* To say that I have a visual field is to say
that by reason of my position I have access to and an opening upon
a system of beings, visible beings, that these are at the disposal of my
gaze in virtue of a kind of primordial contract and through a gift of
nature, with no effort made on my part, from which it follows that
vision is prepersonal And it follows at the same time that it is always

limited, that around what I am looking at at a given moment is spread
a horizon of things which are not seen, or which are even invisible
Vision is *a thought subordinated to a certain field*, and this is what is
called a *sense* When I say that I have senses and that they give me
access to the world, I am not the victim of some muddle, I do not
confuse causal thinking and reflection, I merely express this truth
which forces itself upon reflection taken as a whole that I am able,
being connatural with the world, to discover a sense in certain
aspects of being without having myself endowed them with it through
any constituting operation

The distinction between the different senses finds its justification
along with that between the senses and intellection. Intellectualism
does not talk about the senses because for it sensations and senses
appear only when I turn back to the concrete act of knowledge in
order to analyse it. I then distinguish in it a contingent matter and a
necessary form, but matter is an unreal phase and not a separable
element of the total act Therefore there are not the senses, but only
consciousness. For example, intellectualism declines to state the
notorious problem of the contribution of the senses to the experience
of space, because sensible qualities and the senses, as materials of
knowledge, cannot possess space in their own right, for it is the form
of objectivity in general, and in particular the means whereby any
consciousness of quality becomes possible. A sensation would be no
sensation at all if it were not the sensation of something, and 'things'
in the most general sense of the word, for example specific qualities,
stand out from the amorphous mass of impressions only if the latter
is put into perspective and co-ordinated by space. Thus all senses are
spatial if they are to give us access to some form or other of being, if,
that is, they are senses at all. And, by the same necessity, they must
all open on the same space, otherwise the sensory beings with which
they bring us into communication would exist only for the relevant
sense—like ghosts which appear only by night—they would lack fullness of being and we could not be truly conscious of them, that is to
say, posit them as true beings Empiricism could not find facts to refute
this deduction If for example we desire to show that the sense of
touch is not spatial by itself, if we try, in cases of real or psychic
blindness, to discover a pure tactile experience, and to prove that its
articulation owes nothing to space, these experimental proofs presuppose what they are meant to establish. How are we to know in
fact whether blindness and psychic blindness have abstracted from
the patient's experience the merely 'visual data', and whether they
have not also affected the structure of his tactile experience? Empiricism takes the former hypothesis for granted, which fact alone
makes it possible for its assumption to be regarded as crucial, but

217

which equally involves postulating the separation of the senses, which is precisely what has to be proved. To be more precise. if I admit that space belongs primarily to sight and that from sight it is transmitted to touch and the other senses, then since there is in the adult, to all appearances, a tactile perception of space, I must at least concede that the 'pure tactile data' are displaced and overlaid by an experience having its source in sight, and that they become integrated into a total experience in which they are ultimately indiscernible But then what justification is there for distinguishing, within this adult experience, a 'tactile' contribution? Is not the alleged 'purely tactile', which I try to extract by investigating blindness, a highly particularized kind of experience, which has nothing in common with the functioning of touch in its wholeness, and which cannot give any help in the analysis of integrated experience? No conclusions about the spatiality of the senses by the inductive method and by adducing 'facts' (for example, a sense of touch without space in the case of the blind man) can be drawn, for this fact needs to be interpreted, and it will indeed be interpreted as a significant fact which brings to light the distinctive nature of touch, or as an accidental fact showing the peculiar properties of touch when modified by some disorder, according to the notion entertained of the senses in general and of their relations to each other within total consciousness The problem belongs to the domain of reflection and not to that of experiment as the empiricist understands it, which is also as scientists understand it when they dream of an absolute objectivity. There is therefore reason for holding *a priori* that all the senses are spatial, and the question which is the one which presents us with space must be considered unintelligible if we reflect on just what a sense is Two sorts of reflection, however, are possible here. One—intellectualist reflection—thematizes the object and consciousness, and, to use a Kantian expression, it 'leads them to the concept'. The object then becomes *what is*, and consequently what is for everybody and for ever (even if only as a fleeting episode, yet of which it will for ever be true to say that it existed at an objective moment of time) Consciousness, thematized by reflection, *is* existence for itself. And, with the help of this idea of consciousness and this other idea of object, it is easily shown that every sensible quality is fully an object only in the context of universal relations, and that there can be sensation only on condition that it exists for a central and unique *I* If we wished to call a halt in the reflective process, and talk, for example, about a partial consciousness or an isolated object, we should then have a consciousness which in some respect did not know itself and which would therefore not be consciousness at all, and an object which would not be accessible from everywhere, and which to this

extent would not be an object. But we may always inquire of intellectualism whence it derives this idea or this essence of consciousness and of the object If the subject is pure for itself, 'the *I think*
must be able to accompany all our representations'. 'If a world must
be capable of being thought', quality must contain it in embryo. But
in the first place by what means do we know that there is any pure
for itself, and where do we learn that the world must be capable of
being thought? The reply will perhaps be that that is the definition
of subject and world and that, short of understanding them in this
way, we no longer know what we are talking about when we speak
of them And indeed, at the level of constituted speech, such is in fact
the significance of world and subject. But from where do the words
themselves derive their sense? Radical reflection is what takes hold
of me as I am in the act of forming and formulating the ideas of subject and object, and brings to light the source of these two ideas; it is
reflection, not only in operation, but conscious of itself in operation
It will perhaps be replied that analytical reflection does not merely
grasp subject and object 'as an idea', but that it is an experience, that
by reflecting I put myself back inside that subject without finite limits,
that I was before, and put back the object among the relations which
previously subtended it. Finally that there is no reason to ask whence
I derive these ideas of subject and object, since they are simply the
formulation of those conditions without which nothing would exist
for anybody. But the reflective *I* differs from the unreflective at least
in having been thematized, and what is given is not consciousness or
pure being; it is, as Kant himself profoundly put it, experience, in
other words the communication of a finite subject with an opaque
being from which it emerges but to which it remains committed It
is 'pure and, in a way, still mute experience which it is a question of
bringing to the pure expression of its own significance'.[1] We have the
experience of a world, not understood as a system of relations which
wholly determine each event, but as an open totality the synthesis of
which is inexhaustible We have the experience of an *I* not in the
sense of an absolute subjectivity, but indivisibly demolished and remade by the course of time. The unity of either the subject or the
object is not a real unity, but a presumptive unity on the horizon of
experience. We must rediscover, as anterior to the ideas of subject
and object, the fact of my subjectivity and the nascent object, that
primordial layer at which both things and ideas come into being
As far as consciousness is concerned. I can arrive at a notion of it
only by taking myself back in the first place to that consciousness
which I am I must be particularly careful not to begin by defining
the senses, I must instead resume contact with the sensory life which

[1] Husserl, *Méditations cartesiennes*, p 33

I live from within. We are not obliged to endow the world *a priori*
with those conditions in the absence of which it is unthinkable, for,
in order to be thought of, it must in the first place not be outside
knowledge, it must exist for me, that is, be given, and the transcendental aesthetic would be confused with the transcendental analytic
only if I were a God who posits the world and not a man who finds
himself thrown into it, and who, in every sense of the word, 'is
wrapped up in it' We do not therefore need to follow Kant in his
deduction of one single space. The single space is the indispensable
condition for being able to conceive the plenitude of objectivity, and
it is quite true that if I try to thematize several spaces, they merge
into a unity, each one standing in a certain positional relationship
to the others, and therefore amalgamating with them. But do we
know whether plenary objectivity can be conceived? Whether all
perspectives are compossible? Whether they can all be thematized
together somewhere? Do we know whether tactile and visual experiences can, strictly speaking, be joined without an intersensory
experience? Whether my experience and that of another person can
be linked in a single system of intersubjective experience? There may
well be, either in each sensory experience or in each consciousness,
'phantoms' which no rational approach can account for. The whole
Transcendental Deduction hangs on the affirmation of a complete
system of truth. It is precisely to the sources of this affirmation that
we must revert if we wish to adopt a reflective method. In this connection we may hold with Husserl[1] that Hume went, in intention,
further than anyone in radical reflection, since he genuinely tried
to take us back to those phenomena of which we have experience, on
the hither side of any formation of ideas,—even though he went on
to dissect and emasculate this experience The idea of a single space
and a single time, being grounded upon that of a summation of
being, which is precisely what Kant subjected to criticism in the
Transcendental Dialectic, needs in particular to be bracketed and to
produce its genealogy from the starting point of our affective experience. This new conception of reflection which is the phenomenological conception of it, amounts in other words to giving a new
definition of the *a priori*. Kant has already shown that the *a priori* is
not knowable in advance of experience, that is, outside our horizon
of facticity, and that there can be no question of distinguishing two
elements of knowledge one *a priori* and the other *a posteriori*. In so
far as the *a priori* in his philosophy retains the character of what
must necessarily be, as opposed to what in fact exists and is determinate in human terms, this is only to the extent that he has not
followed out his programme, which was to define our cognitive

[1] *Formale und Transzendentale Logik*, e g p. 226

powers in terms of our factual condition, and which necessarily compelled him to set every conceivable being against the background of this world. From the moment that experience—that is, the opening on to our *de facto* world—is recognized as the beginning of knowledge, there is no longer any way of distinguishing a level of *a priori* truths and one of factual ones, what the world must necessarily be and what it actually is The unity of the senses, which was regarded as an *a priori* truth, is no longer anything but the formal expression of a fundamental contingency· the fact that we are in the world—the diversity of the senses, which was regarded as given *a posteriori*, including the concrete form that it assumes in a human subject, appears as necessary to this world, to the only world which we can think of consequentially, it therefore becomes an *a priori* truth. Every sensation is spatial; we have adopted this thesis, not because the quality as an object cannot be thought otherwise than in space, but because, as the primordial contact with being, as the assumption by the sentient subject of a form of existence to which the sensible points, and as the co-existence of sentient and sensible, it is itself constitutive of a setting for co-existence, in other words, of a space. We say *a priori* that no sensation is atomic, that all sensory experience presupposes a certain field, hence co-existences, from which we conclude, against Lachelier, that the blind man has the experience of a space. But these *a priori* truths amount to nothing other than the making explicit of a fact: the fact of the sensory experience as the assumption of a form of existence. Moreover, this assumption implies also that I can at each moment absorb myself almost wholly into the sense of touch or sight, and even that I can never see or touch without my consciousness becoming thereby in some measure saturated, and losing something of its availability. Thus the unity and the diversity of the senses are truths of the same order. The *a priori* is the fact understood, made explicit, and followed through into all the consequences of its latent logic, the *a posteriori* is the isolated and implicit fact. It would be contradictory to assert that the sense of touch is devoid of spatiality, and it is *a priori* impossible to touch without touching in space, since our experience is the experience of a world. But this insertion of the tactile perspective into a universal being does not represent any necessity external to touch, it comes about spontaneously in the experience of touching itself, in accordance with its own distinctive mode Sensation as it is brought to use by experience is no longer some inert substance or abstract moment, but one of our surfaces of contact with being, a structure of consciousness, and in place of one single space, as the universal condition of all qualities, we have with each one of the latter, a particular manner of being in space and, in a sense, of making space.

221

It is neither contradictory nor impossible that each sense should constitute a small world within the larger one, and it is even in virtue of its peculiarity that it is necessary to the whole and opens upon the whole

To sum up, once distinctions between the *a priori* and the empirical, between form and content, have been done away with, the spaces peculiar to the senses become concrete 'moments' of a comprehensive configuration which is the one and only space, and the power of going to it is inseparable from that of cutting oneself off from it by the sequestration of a sense. When, in the concert hall, I open my eyes, visible space seems to me cramped compared to that other space through which, a moment ago, the music was being unfolded, and even if I keep my eyes open while the piece is being played, I have the impression that the music is not really contained within this circumscribed and unimpressive space. It brings a new dimension stealing through visible space, and in this it surges forward, just as, in victims of hallucinations, the clear space of things perceived is mysteriously duplicated by a 'dark space' in which other presences are possible. Like the perspective of other people making its impact on the world for me, the spatial realm of each sense is an unknowable absolute for the others, and to that extent limits their spatiality These descriptions, which to critical philosophy appear as empirical oddities, leaving *a priori* certainties untouched, assume, as far as we are concerned, philosophical importance, because the unity of space can be discovered only in the interplay of the sensory realms That is what remains true in the celebrated empiricist description of a non-spatial perception. The experience of persons blind from birth and operated upon for cataract has never proved, and could never prove, that for them space begins with sight Yet the patient never ceases to marvel at this visual space to which he has just gained access, and compared to which tactile experience seems to him so poor that he is quite prepared to admit that he has never enjoyed the experience of space before the operation [1] The patient's amazement, and his hesitant attitude in the new visual world into which he is entering, show that the sense of touch is not spatial *as is* sight. 'After the operation,' it is said,[2] 'form as given by

---

[1] One subject declares that the spatial notions *that he thought he entertained* before the operation did not in fact give him a genuine representation of space, and were only a species of 'knowledge gained through the workings of thought' (Von Senden, *Raum- und Gestaltauffassung bei operierten Blindgeborenen vor und nach der Operation*, p 23) The acquisition of sight involves a general reorganization of existence which equally concerns touch The world's centre is displaced, the tactile image is forgotten, recognition through touch is less reliable, the existential current henceforth runs through vision, and what the patient is talking about is this weakened sense of touch   [2] Ibid , p 36

sight is for these patients something quite new which they fail to relate to their tactile experience', 'the patient states that he can see, but does not know what he sees. . . . He never recognizes his hand as such, and talks only about a moving, white patch '[1] To distinguish by sight a circle from a rectangle, he has to run his eyes round the outline of the figure, as he might with his hand,[2] and he always tends to take hold of objects set before his eyes [3] What conclusion is to be drawn from this? that tactile experience is no preparation for the perception of space? But unless it were in some way spatial, would the subject stretch out his hand towards the object shown to him? This gesture presupposes that touch opens on to a setting at least analogous to that of visual data The facts show above all else that sight is nothing unless the subject is more or less used to using his eyes. Patients 'at first see colours in the way that we smell an odour it closes round us, and acts upon us, without however filling a determinate form of a determinate extent' [4] Everything is at first confused and apparently in motion. Discrimination between coloured surfaces and the correct apprehension of movement do not come until later, when the subject has learned 'what it is to see'[5] that is, when he directs and shifts his gaze as a gaze, and no longer as a hand. This proves that each organ of sense explores the object in its own way, that it is the agent of a certain type of synthesis, but, short of reserving the word space, by way of nominal definition, for the visual synthesis, we cannot withhold from the sense of touch spatiality in the sense of a grasp of co-existences. The very fact that the way is paved to true vision through a phase of transition and through a sort of touch effected by the eyes would be incomprehensible unless there were a quasi-spatial tactile field, into which the first visual perceptions may be inserted. Sight would never communicate directly with touch, as it in fact does in the normal adult, if the sense of touch, even when artificially isolated, were not so organized as to make co-existences possible. Far from ruling out the idea of a tactile space, the facts prove on the contrary that there is a space so strictly tactile that its articulations do not and never will stand in a relationship of synonymity with those of visual space Empiricist analyses present, in a confused form, a genuine problem The fact, for example, that touch cannot simultaneously cover more than a small amount of space—that of the body and its instruments—does not affect merely the presentation of tactile space, but also changes its significance For the intelligence—or at least for a certain intelligence which is

---

[1] Von Senden, *Raum- und Gestaltauffassung bei operierten Blindgeborenen vor und nach der Operation*, p 93

[2] Ibid , pp 102–4 [3] Ibid , p 124.

[4] Ibid , p 113. [5] Ibid , p 123.

that of classical physics—simultaneity is the same, whether it occurs between two adjacent points or two remote ones, and in any case it is possible gradually to construct with short-distance simultaneities a long-distance one But for experience, the thickness of time which thus intrudes into the operation affects the result, producing a certain 'blurring' in the simultaneity of the extreme points, and to this extent the breadth of visual perspectives will be a true revelation to the patient whose blindness has been cured by operation, because it pro-vides a demonstration, for the first time, of remote simultaneity *itself*. These patients declare that tactile objects are not genuine spatial totalities, that the apprehension of the object is here a mere 'knowledge of the mutual relation of parts', that the circle and the square are not really perceived by touch, but recognized from certain 'signs'—the presence or absence of 'corners'.[1] We conclude that the tactile field has never the fullness of the visual, that the tactile object is never wholly present in each of its parts as is the case with the visual object, and in short that touching is not seeing It is true that the blind and the normal person talk to each other, and that it is perhaps impossible to find a single word, even in colour vocabulary, to which the blind man does not manage to attach at least a rough meaning One blind boy of twelve gives a very good definition of the dimensions of sight 'Those who can see,' he says, 'are related to me through some unknown sense which completely envelops me from a distance, follows me, goes through me, and, from the time I get up to the time I go to bed, holds me in some way in subjection to it' (mich gewissermassen beherrscht).[2] But such indications remain theoretical and problematic for the blind person. They ask a question to which only sight could provide an answer. And this is why the blind person, having undergone his operation, finds the world different from what he expected,[3] as we always find a man different from what we have heard about him The blind man's world differs from the normal person's not only through the quantity of material at his disposal, but also through the *structure* of the whole. A blind man knows quite precisely through his sense of touch what branches and leaves, or an arm and fingers, are After the operation he marvels that there should be 'such a difference' between a tree and a human body.[4] It is clear that sight has not only added fresh details to his knowledge of the tree. What we are dealing with is a mode of presentation and a type of synthesis which are new and which transfigure the object If we take as an example the structure 'light-illuminated object' we shall find only somewhat vague analogies in the realms of touch This is why a

[1] Von Senden, *Raum- und Gestaltauffassung bei operierten Blindgeborenen vor und nach der Operation*, p. 29
[2] Ibid , p 45.   [3] Ibid   [4] Ibid , pp 50 and ff.

patient operated upon after being blind for eighteen years tries to touch a ray of sunlight.[1] The whole significance of our life—from which theoretical significance is merely extracted—would be different if we were sightless There is a general function of substitution and replacement which enables us to gain access to the abstract significance of experiences which we have not actually had, for example, to speak of what we have not seen. But just as in the organism the renewed functions are never the exact equivalent of the damaged ones, and give only an appearance of total restitution, the intelligence ensures no more than an apparent communication between different experiences, and the synthesis of visual and tactile worlds in the person born blind and operated upon, the constitution of an intersensory world must be effected in the domain of sense itself, the community of significance between the two experiences being inadequate to ensure their union in one single experience. The senses are distinct from each other and distinct from intellection in so far as each one of them brings with it a structure of being which can never be exactly transposed. We can recognize this because we have rejected any formalism of consciousness, and made the body the subject of perception.

And we can recognize it without any threat to the unity of the senses. For the senses communicate with each other. Music is not in visible space, but it besieges, undermines and displaces that space, so that soon these overdressed listeners who take on a judicial air and exchange remarks or smiles, unaware that the floor is trembling beneath their feet, are like a ship's crew buffeted about on the surface of a tempestuous sea. The two spaces are distinguishable only against the background of a common world, and can compete with each other only because they both lay claim to total being. They are united at the very instant in which they clash. If I try to shut myself up in one of my senses and, for instance, project myself wholly into my eyes, and abandon myself to the blue of the sky, soon I am unaware that I am gazing and, just as I strive to make myself sight and nothing but sight, the sky stops being a 'visual perception', to become my world of the moment. Sensory experience is unstable, and alien to natural perception, which we achieve with our whole body all at once, and which opens on a world of inter-acting senses Like that of the sensible quality, the experience of the separate 'senses' is gained only when one assumes a highly particularized attitude, and this cannot be of any assistance to the analysis of direct consciousness. I am sitting in my room, and I look at the sheets of white paper lying about on the table, some in the light shed through the window, others in the shadow. If I do not analyse my perception but content

[1] Von Senden, *Raum- und Gestaltauffassung bei operierten Blindgeborenen vor und nach der Operation*, p. 186

myself with the spectacle as a whole, I shall say that all the sheets of paper look equally white However, some of them are in the shadow of the wall. How is it that they are not less white than the rest? I decide to look more closely. I fix my gaze upon them, which means that I restrict my visual field I may even look at them through a match-box lid, which will separate them from the rest of the field, or through a 'reduction screen' with a window in it Whether I use one of these devices or merely observe with the naked eye, provided that in the latter case I assume the 'analytic attitude',[1] the sheets change their appearance: this is no longer white paper over which a shadow is cast, but a grey or steely blue substance, thick and not definitely localized. If I once more look at the general picture, I notice that the sheets over which a shadow is thrown were at no time identical with the sheets lying in the light, nor yet were they objectively different from them. The whiteness of the shaded paper does not lend itself to precise classification within the black-white range.[2] It appeared as no definite quality, and I have brought out the quality by fixing my eyes on a portion of the visual field: then and then only have I found myself before a certain *quale* which absorbs my gaze Now what actually is fixing one's gaze? From the point of view of the object, it is separating the region under scrutiny from the rest of the field, it is interrupting the total life of the spectacle, which assigned to each visible surface a determinate coloration, taking the light into account; from the subject's point of view, it is substituting for the comprehensive vision, in which our gaze lends itself to the whole spectacle and is permeated by it, an observation, that is, a localized vision which it controls according to its own requirements. The sensible quality, far from being co-extensive with perception, is the peculiar product of an attitude of curiosity or observation It appears when, instead of yielding up the whole of my gaze to the world, I turn towards this gaze itself, and when I ask myself *what precisely it is that I see*; it does not occur in the natural transactions between my sight and the world, it is the reply to a certain kind of questioning on the part of my gaze, the outcome of a second order or critical vision which tries to know itself in its own particularity, of an 'attention to the pure visual',[3] which I exercise either when I am afraid of being mistaken, or when I want to undertake a scientific study of the spectacle presented. This attitude does away with the spectacle properly speaking the colours which I see through the reduction screen or those obtained by the painter when he half-closes his eyes are no longer object-colours—the colour *of the walls* or the colour

[1] Gelb, *Die Farbenkonstanz der Sehdinge*, p 600

[2] Ibid , p 613

[3] *Einstellung auf reine Optik*, Katz quoted by Gelb, op cit , p 600

226

of the paper—but coloured areas having a certain density, and all rather vaguely localized in the same unreal plane.[1] Thus there is a natural attitude of vision in which I make common cause with my gaze and, through it, surrender myself to the spectacle in this case the parts of the field are linked in an organization which makes them recognizable and identifiable. The quality, the separate sensory impact occurs when I break this total structuralization of my vision, when I cease to adhere to my own gaze, and when, instead of living the vision, I question myself about it, I want to try out my possibilities, I break the link between my vision and the world, between myself and my vision, in order to catch and describe it When I have taken up this attitude, at the same time as the world is atomized into sensible qualities, the natural unity of the perceiving subject is broken up, and I reach the stage of being unaware of myself as the subject of a visual field. Now just as, within each sense, we must find the natural unity which it offers, we shall reveal a 'primary layer' of sense experience which precedes its division among the separate senses [2] According as I fix my eyes on an object or allow them to wander, or else wholly submit myself to the event, the same colour appears to me as superficial (*Oberflächenfarbe*)—being in a definite location in space, and extending over an object—or else it becomes an atmospheric colour (*Raumfarbe*) and diffuses itself all round the object Or I may feel it in my eye as a vibration of my gaze; or finally it may pass on to my body a similar manner of being, fully pervading me, so that it is no longer entitled to be called a colour. Similarly there is an objective sound which reverberates outside me in the instrument, an atmospheric sound which is *between* the object and my body, a sound which vibrates in me 'as if I had become the flute or the clock'; and finally a last stage in which the acoustic element disappears and becomes the highly precise experience of a change permeating my whole body.[3] The sensory experience has only a narrow margin at its disposal either the sound and the colour, through their own arrangement, throw an object into relief, such as an ashtray or a violin, and this object speaks directly to all the senses, or else, at the opposite end of experience, the sound and the colour are received into my body, and it becomes difficult to limit my experience to a single sensory department: it spontaneously overflows towards all the rest. The sensory experience, at the third stage just described, is distinguished only by an 'accent' which is indicative rather of the direction of the sound or the colour [4] At this level, the

---

[1] *Einstellung auf reine Optik*, Katz quoted by Gelb, op cit., p 600.
[2] Werner, *Untersuchungen uber Empfindung und Empfinden*, I, p. 155.
[3] Ibid , p. 157
[4] Ibid , p. 162.

ambiguity of experience is such that an audible rhythm causes cinematograph pictures to run together and produces a perception of movement whereas, without auditory support, the same succession of images would be too slow to give rise to stroboscopic movement [1] The sounds modify the consecutive images of the colours · a louder note intensifies them, the interruption of the sound produces a wavering effect in them, and a low note makes blue darker or deeper.[2] The constancy hypothesis,[3] which allows to each stimulus one sensation and one only, is progressively less verifiable as natural perception is approached 'It is in so far as conduct is intellectual and impartial (sachlicher) that the constancy hypothesis becomes acceptable as regards the relation of stimulus to specific sensory response, and that the auditory stimulus, for instance, is limited to its specific sphere, in this case the acoustic one.'[4] The influence of mescalin, by weakening the attitude of impartiality and surrendering the subject to his vitality, should therefore favour forms of synaesthetic experience And indeed, under mescalin, the sound of a flute gives a bluish-green colour, the tick of a metronome, in darkness, is translated as grey patches, the spatial intervals between them corresponding to the intervals of time between the ticks, the size of the patch to the loudness of the tick, and its height to the pitch of the sound.[5] A subject under mescalin finds a piece of iron, strikes the window-sill with it and exclaims 'This is magic'; the trees are growing greener [6] The barking of a dog is found to attract light in an indescribable way, and is re-echoed in the right foot.[7] It is as if one could sometimes see 'the occasional collapse of the barriers established, in the course of evolution, between the senses.[8] Seen in the perspective of the objective world, with its opaque qualities, and the objective body with its separate organs, the phenomenon of synaesthetic experience is paradoxical The attempt is therefore made to explain it independently of the concept of sensation: it is thought necessary, for example, to suppose that the excitations ordinarily restricted to one region of the brain—the optical or auditory zone—become capable of playing a part outside these limits, and that in this way a specific quality is associated with a non-specific one Whether or not this explanation

---

[1] Zietz and Werner, *Die dynamische Struktur der Bewegung*

[2] Werner, op cit , p 163

[3] Cf. above. Introduction, section I

[4] Werner, op cit , p 154

[5] Stein, *Pathologie der Wahrnemung*, p. 422

[6] Mayer-Gross and Stein, *Über einige Abänderungen der Sinnestätigkeit im Meskalinrausch*, p 385

[7] Ibid

[8] Ibid

is supported by arguments drawn from brain physiology,[1] this explanation does not account for synaesthetic experience, which thus becomes one more occasion for questioning the concept of sensation and objective thought. *For the subject does not say only that he has the sensation both of a sound and a colour: it is the sound itself that he sees where colours are formed* [2] This formulation is literally meaningless if vision is defined by the visual *quale*, and the sound by the acoustic *quale*. But it rests with us to word our definition in such a way as to provide it with a meaning, since the sight of sounds and the hearing of colours exist as phenomena. Nor are these even exceptional phenomena. Synaesthetic perception is the rule, and we are unaware of it only because scientific knowledge shifts the centre of gravity of experience, so that we have unlearned how to see, hear, and generally speaking, feel, in order to deduce, from our bodily organization and the world as the physicist conceives it, what we are to see, hear and feel.

Sight, it is said, can bring us only colours or lights, and with them forms which are the outlines of colours, and movements which are the patches of colour changing position. But how shall we place transparency or 'muddy' colours in the scale? In reality, each colour, in its inmost depths, is nothing but the inner structure of the thing overtly revealed The brilliance of góld palpably holds out to us its homogeneous composition, and the dull colour of wood its heterogeneous make-up.[3] The senses intercommunicate by opening on to the structure of the thing. One sees the hardness and brittleness of glass, and when, with a tinkling sound, it breaks, this sound is conveyed by the visible glass.[4] One sees the springiness of steel, the ductility of red-hot steel, the hardness of a plane blade, the softness of shavings. The form of objects is not their geometrical shape: it stands in a certain relation to their specific nature, and appeals to all our other senses as well as sight The form of a fold in linen or cotton shows us the resilience or dryness of the fibre, the coldness or warmth of the material Furthermore, the movement of visible objects is not the mere transference from place to place of coloured patches which,

[1] It is for example possible that under mescalin a modification of the chronaxies might be observable This fact would in no way count as an explanation of synaesthesia in terms of the objective body, if, as we shall show, the juxtaposition of several sensible qualities fails to make clear to us perceptual ambivalence as it is presented to us in synaesthetic experience The change in the chronaxies could not be the cause of synaesthesia, but the objective expression or sign of a more profound and all-embracing event, which has no *seat* in the objective body, but which is relevant to the phenomenal body as a vehicle of being in the world.

[2] Werner, op cit , p 163

[3] Schapp, *Beitrage zur Phanomenologie der Wahrnehmung*, pp. 23 and ff

[4] Ibid , p 11.

229

in the visual field, correspond to those objects. In the jerk of the twig from which a bird has just flown, we read its flexibility or elasticity, and it is thus that a branch of an apple-tree or a birch are immediately distinguishable One sees the weight of a block of cast iron which sinks in the sand, the fluidity of water and the viscosity of syrup.[1] In the same way, I hear the hardness and unevenness of cobbles in the rattle of a carriage, and we speak appropriately of a 'soft', 'dull' or 'sharp' sound Though one may doubt whether the sense of hearing brings us genuine 'things', it is at least certain that it presents us, beyond the sounds in space, with something which 'murmurs', and in this way communicates with the other senses [2] Finally, if, with my eyes closed, I bend a steel bar and a lime branch, I perceive in my hands the most essential texture of the metal and the wood If, then, taken as incomparable qualities, the 'data of the different senses' belong to so many separate worlds, each one in its particular essence being a manner of modulating the thing, they all communicate through their significant core

We must, however, give a clearer account of the nature of sensible significance, otherwise we shall merely slip back into the intellectualist analysis which we rejected earlier. The table which I touch is the same one as the table which I see. But must one go on to say, as has in fact been said the sonata which I hear is the same one as Helen Keller touches, and the man I see is the same one as the blind painter paints?[3] Gradually we should come to find that there was no longer any difference between the perceptual and the intellectual syntheses The unity of the senses would then be of the same order as the unity of the objects of science When I both touch and look at an object, it would be said, the single object is the common ground of these two appearances as Venus is the common ground of the Morning Star and the Evening Star, and so perception would be an incipient science.[4] Now, though perception brings together our sensory experiences into a single world, it does not do so in the way that scientific colligation gathers together objects or phenomena, but in the way that binocular vision grasps one sole object. Let us describe carefully this 'synthesis'. When my gaze is fixed on a remote thing, I have a double image of objects nearby. When I transfer my gaze to the latter, I see the two images converge on what is to be the single object, and merge into it We must not at this point say that the synthesis consists in thinking of them together as images of one

[1] Schapp, *Beitrage zur Phanomenologie der Wahrnehmung*, pp 21 and ff

[2] Ibid , pp 32–3.

[3] Specht, *Zur Phanomenologie und Morphologie der pathologischen Wahrnehmungstauschungen*, p 11

[4] Alain, *81 Chapitres sur l'Esprit et les Passions*, p 38

single object; if we were dealing with a mental act or an apperception, this ought to occur as soon as I notice the identity of the two images, whereas I have to wait much longer for the unity of the object to appear. until the moment when correct focusing does away with them The single object is not a certain way of thinking of the two images, since they cease to be given the moment it appears. Has the 'fusion of images' been effected, then, by some innate device of the nervous system, and do we mean that finally we have, if not on the periphery, at least at the centre, a single excitation mediated by the two eyes? But the mere existence of one visual centre cannot explain the single object, since double vision sometimes occurs, as moreover the mere existence of two retinas cannot explain double vision, since it is not a constant phenomenon.[1] If double vision as well as the single object can be included in normal vision, this is not attributable to the anatomical lay-out of the visual apparatus, but to its function-ing and to the use which the psychosomatic subject makes of it. Shall we then say that double sight occurs *because* our eyes do not converge on the object, and because it throws non-symmetrical images on our two retinas? And that these two images merge into one because fixation brings them back to corresponding points on the two retinas? But are divergence and convergence of the eyes the cause or the effect of double and normal vision? In the case of people born blind and operated on for cataract, it is impossible to say, during the period following the operation, whether it is non-co-ordination of the eyes which hampers vision, or whether it is the confusion in the visual field which favours non-co-ordination—whether they fail to see through failure to focus, or whether they fail to focus through not having anything to see. When I focus on the remote distance and, for example, one of my fingers held near my eyes throws its image on non-symmetrical points on my retinas, the arrangement of images on the retinas cannot be the *cause* of the action of focusing which will put an end to the double vision. For, as has been pointed out,[2] the disappearance of images does not exist in itself My finger forms its image on a certain area of my left retina, and on an area of my right retina which is not symmetrical with the former. But the sym-metrical area of the right retina is also full of visual excitations, the distribution of *stimuli* on the two retinas is 'dissymmetrical' only to a subject who compares the two groupings and identifies them On the

---

[1] 'The convergence of the conductors as it exists does not condition the non-distinction of images in simple binocular vision, since a rivalry between the mon-ocular visions can take place, and the separation of the retinas does not account for their distinction when it occurs, since, normally, when nothing varies in receptor and conductors, this distinction is not made ' R. Déjean, *Etude psychologique de la distance dans la vision*, p 74

[2] Koffka, *Some Problems of Space Perception*, p 179

retinas themselves, considered as objects, there are only two groupings of *stimuli* that cannot be compared. It will perhaps be replied
that, unless the eyes are focused, these two groupings cannot be
superimposed on each other, nor give rise to the vision of anything,
and that in this sense their presence alone creates a state of unbalance But this is admitting what we are trying to show: that the
sight of one single object is not a simple outcome of focusing the eyes,
that it is anticipated in the very act of focusing, or that, as has been
stated, the focusing of the gaze is a 'prospective activity'.[1] For my
gaze to alight on near objects and to focus my eyes on them, it must
experience double vision as an unbalance[2] or as an imperfect vision,
and tend towards the single object as towards the release of tension
and the completion of vision 'It is necessary to "look" in order to
see.'[3] The unity of the object in binocular vision is not, therefore, the
result of some third person process which eventually produces a
single image through the fusion of two monocular images. When we
go from diplopia to normal vision, the single object replaces the two
images, one is clearly not superimposed on the other: it is not of
the same order as they, but is incomparably more substantial. The
two images of diplopia are not amalgamated into one single one in
binocular vision; the unity of the object is intentional. But—and
this is the point we are trying to make—it is not therefore a notional
unity. We pass from double vision to the single object, not through
an inspection of the mind, but when the two eyes cease to function
each on its own account and are used as a single organ by one single
gaze. It is not the epistemological subject who brings about the synthesis, but the body, when it escapes from dispersion, pulls itself
together and tends by all means in its power towards one single goal
of its activity, and when one single intention is formed in it through
the phenomenon of synergy. We withdraw this synthesis from the
objective body only to transfer it to the phenomenal body, the body,
that is, in so far as it projects a certain 'setting' round itself,[4] in so
far as its 'parts' are dynamically acquainted with each other, and its

----

[1] R Déjean, op cit , pp 110-11. The author says 'a prospective activity of the
mind', and on this point it will be seen that we do not follow him.
[2] It is known that Gestalt psychology bases this orientated process on some
physical phenomenon in the 'combination zone'. We have said elsewhere that it
is contradictory to recall the psychologist to the variety of phenomena or structures, and to explain them all in terms of some of their number, in this case
physical forms. The focus as a temporal form is not a physical or physiological
fact for the simple reason that all the forms belong to the phenomenal world
Cf on this point *La Structure du Comportement*, pp 175 and ff , 191 and ff
[3] R Déjean, ibid
[4] In so far as there is an 'Umweltintentionalität', Buytendijk and Plessner,
Die Deutung des mimischen Ausdrucks, p. 81.

receptors are so arranged as to make possible, through their synergy, the perception of the object What is meant by saying that this intentionality is not a thought is that it does not come into being through the transparency of any consciousness, but takes for granted all the latent knowledge of itself that my body possesses. Being supported by the prelogical unity of the body image, the perceptual synthesis no more holds the secret of the object than it does that of one's own body, and this is why the perceived object always presents itself as transcendent, and why the synthesis seems to be effected on the object itself, in the world, and not at that metaphysical point occupied by the thinking subject. Herein lies the distinction between the perceptual synthesis and the intellectual On passing from double to normal vision, I am not simply aware of seeing with my two eyes *the same* object, I am aware of progressing towards the object *itself* and finally enjoying its concrete presence Monocular images float vaguely *in front of* things, having no real place in the world; then suddenly they fall back towards a certain location in the world and are swallowed up in it, as ghosts, at daybreak, repair to the rift in the earth which let them forth. The binocular object, in which the synthesis occurs, absorbs the monocular images, which, in this new light, finally recognize themselves as appearances of that object My set of experiences is presented as a concordant whole, and the synthesis takes place not in so far as they all express a certain invariant, and in the identity of the object, but in that they are all collected together, by the last of their number, in the ipseity of the thing. The ipseity is, of course, never *reached·* each aspect of the thing which falls to our perception is still only an invitation to perceive beyond it, still only a momentary halt in the perceptual process. If the thing itself were reached, it would be from that moment arrayed before us and stripped of its mystery. It would cease to exist as a thing at the very moment when we thought to possess it. What makes the 'reality' of the thing is therefore precisely what snatches it from our grasp. The aseity of the thing, its unchallengeable presence and the perpetual absence into which it withdraws, are two inseparable aspects of transcendence. Intellectualism overlooks both, and if we want to account for the thing as the transcendent terminus of an open series of experiences, we must provide the subject of perception with the unity of the body image, which is itself open and limitless. That is what we learn from the synthesis of binocular vision.

Let us apply it to the problem of the unity of the senses. It cannot be understood in terms of their subsumption under a primary consciousness, but of their never-ending integration into one knowing organism. The intersensory object is to the visual object what the

233

visual object is to the monocular images of double vision,[1] and the senses interact in perception as the two eyes collaborate in vision. The sight of sounds or the hearing of colours come about in the same way as the unity of the gaze through the two eyes: in so far as my body is, not a collection of adjacent organs, but a synergic system, all the functions of which are exercised and linked together in the general action of being in the world, in so far as it is the congealed face of existence. There is a sense in saying that I see sounds or hear colours so long as sight or hearing is not the mere possession of an opaque *quale*, but the experience of a modality of existence, the synchronisation of my body with it, and the problem of forms of synaesthetic experience begins to look like being solved if the experience of quality is that of a certain mode of movement or of a form of conduct. When I say that I see a sound, I mean that I echo the vibration of the sound with my whole sensory being, and particularly with that sector of myself which is susceptible to colours. Movement, understood not as objective movement and transference in space, but as a project towards movement or 'potential movement'[2] forms the basis for the unity of the senses. It is fairly well known that the talking film not only adds a sound accompaniment to the show, but also changes the tenor of the show itself. When I go to see a film 'dubbed' in French, I do not merely notice the discrepancy between word and image, I suddenly have the impression that *something else* is being said over there. The 'dubbed' text, though it fills the auditorium and my ears, has not even an auditory existence for me, and I have ears for nothing but those other soundless words that emanate from the screen When a breakdown of sound all at once cuts off the voice from a character who nevertheless goes on gesticulating on the screen, not only does the meaning of his speech suddenly escape me: the spectacle itself is changed. The face which was so recently alive thickens and freezes, and looks nonplussed, while the interruption of the sound invades the screen as a quasi-stupor. For the spectator, the gestures and words are not subsumed under some ideal significance, the words take up the gesture and the gesture the words, and

---

[1] It is true that the senses should not be put on the same basis, as if they were all equally capable of objectivity and accessible to intentionality Experience does not present them to us as equivalent I think that visual experience is truer than tactile experience, that it garners within itself its own truth and adds to it, because its richer structure offers me modalities of being unsuspected by touch The unity of the senses is achieved transversally, according to their own structure But something like it is found in binocular vision, if it is true that we have a 'directing eye' which brings the other under its control These two facts—the taking over of sensory experiences in general in visual experience, and that of the functions of one eye by the other—prove that the unity of experience is not a formal unity, but a primary organization.

[2] Palagyi, Stein

they inter-communicate through the medium of my body. Like the sensory aspects of my body they are immediately and mutually symbolical, precisely because my body is a ready-made system of equivalents and transpositions from one sense to another. The senses translate each other without any need of an interpreter, and are mutually comprehensible without the intervention of any idea. These remarks enable us to appreciate to the full Herder's words 'Man is a permanent *sensorium commune*, who is affected now from one quarter, now from another '[1] With the notion of the body image we find that not only is the unity of the body described in a new way, but also, through this, the unity of the senses and of the object My body is the seat or rather the very actuality of the phenomenon of expression (*Ausdruck*), and there the visual and auditory experiences, for example, are pregnant one with the other, and their expressive value is the ground of the antepredicative unity of the perceived world, and, through it, of verbal expression (*Darstellung*) and intellectual significance (*Bedeutung*) [2] My body is the fabric into which all objects are woven, and it is, at least in relation to the perceived world, the general instrument of my 'comprehension'.

It is my body which gives significance not only to the natural object, but also to cultural objects like words If a word is shown to a subject for too short a time for him to be able to read it, the word 'warm', for example, induces a kind of experience of warmth which surrounds him with something in the nature of a meaningful halo.[3] The word 'hard'[4] produces a sort of stiffening of the back and neck, and only in a secondary way does it project itself into the visual or auditory field and assume the appearance of a sign or a word Before becoming the symbol of a concept it is first of all an event which grips my body, and this grip circumscribes the area of significance to which it has reference One subject states that on presentation of the world 'damp' (*feucht*), he experiences, in addition to a feeling of dampness and coldness, a whole rearrangement of the body image, as if the inside of the body came to the periphery, and as if the reality of the body, until then concentrated into his arms and legs, were in search of a new balance of its parts The word is then indistinguishable from the attitude which it induces, and it is only when its presence is prolonged that it appears in the guise of an external image, and its meaning as a thought Words have a physiognomy because we adopt towards them, as towards each person, a certain

[1] Quoted by Werner, op cit , p 152
[2] The distinction between *Ausdruck, Darstellung* and *Bedeutung* is made by Cassirer, *Philosophie der symbolischen Formen*, III
[3] Werner, op cit , pp 160 and ff
[4] German 'hart'.

235

form of behaviour which makes its complete appearance the moment each word is given. 'I try to grasp the word *rot* (red) in its living expression, but at first it is no more than peripheral for me, no more than a sign along with the knowledge of its meaning It is not red itself. But suddenly I notice that the word pushes its way through my body I have the feeling, difficult to describe, of a kind of numbed fullness which invades my body, and which at the same time imparts to my mouth cavity a spherical shape And, precisely at that moment, I notice that the word on the paper takes on its expressive value, it comes to meet me in a dark red halo, while the letter *o* intuitively presents me with that spherical cavity which I previously felt in my mouth '[1] What is particularly brought out by the word's behaviour here is its indissoluble identity with something said, heard and seen. 'The word as read is not a geometrical structure in a segment of visual space, it is the presentation of a form of behaviour and of a linguistic act in its dynamic fullness.'[2] Whether it is a question of perceiving words or more generally objects, 'there is a certain bodily attitude, a specific kind of dynamic tension which is necessary to give structure to the image, man, as a dynamic and living totality has to "pattern" himself in order to trace out a figure in his visual field as part of the psychosomatic organism'[3] In short, my body is not only an object among all other objects, a nexus of sensible qualities among others, but an object which is *sensitive to* all the rest, which reverberates to all sounds, vibrates to all colours, and provides words with their primordial significance through the way in which it receives them. It is not a matter of reducing the significance of the word 'warm' to sensations of warmth by empiricist standards. For the warmth which I feel when I read the word 'warm' is not an actual warmth It is simply my body which prepares itself for heat and which, so to speak, roughs out its outline In the same way, when a part of my body is mentioned to me, or when I represent it to myself, I experience in the corresponding part a quasi-sensation of contact which is merely the emergence of that part of my body into the total body image We are not, then reducing the significance of the word,

[1] Werner, *Untersuchung über Empfindung und Empfinden*, II, *Die Rolle der Sprachempfindung im Prozess der Gestaltung ausdrucksmässig erlebter Worter*, p 238
[2] Ibid , p 239 What has been said of the word is even truer of the sentence Before even having read through the sentence, we can say that it is 'journalese' (ibid , pp 251–3) We can understand a phrase or at least give it a certain meaning by going from the whole to the parts Not, as Bergson says, because we evolve a 'hypothesis' on the strength of the first words, but because we have an organ of language which takes on the linguistic shape of what is set before it, as our organs of sense are given a direction by the stimulus and are synchronized with it
[3] Ibid , p 230

or even of the percept, to a collection of 'bodily sensations' but we are saying that the body, in so far as it has 'behaviour patterns', is that strange object which uses its own parts as a general system of symbols for the world, and through which we can consequently 'be at home in' that world, 'understand' it and find significance in it.

All this, it will be said, has doubtless some value as description of appearance But how does that help if, in the end, these descriptions mean nothing that can be conceived, and if on reflection they are dismissed as nonsense? As popularly conceived one's own body is both a constituted and constituting object in relation to other objects. But if we are to know what we are talking about, we must choose and, in the last analysis, assign it to the sphere of the constituted object. I do, in fact, one of two things Either I consider myself as within the world, inserted into it by my body which is beset by casual relations, in which case 'the senses' and 'the body' are material instruments which have no knowledge of anything; the object throws an image on to the retinas, and the retinal image is duplicated in the optical centre by a second image, but all this consists of nothing but *things to see* and *nobody who sees*, so that we are thrown back indefinitely from one bodily stage to another, conjecturing within man a 'little man', and within him a smaller one, without ever reaching sight Or else I try really to understand how sight comes about, in which case I must get away from the constituted, from what is *in itself*, and seize by reflection a being for whom the object can exist Now, for the object to exist in the eyes of the subject, it is not enough for this 'subject' to fix his eyes on it or grasp it as my hand grasps this piece of wood, he must in addition know that he is seizing or watching it, he must know himself seizing or watching, his action must be entirely given to himself, and finally this subject must *be* nothing other than what he is conscious of being, otherwise we should have a seizure or a contemplation of the object for some third party, while the alleged subject, being unaware of himself, would be dispersed through his act and unconscious of anything. For there to be any sight or tactile perception of the object, the senses will always lack that dimension of absence, that unreality through which the subject may be self-knowledge and the object may exist for him. The consciousness of the unified presupposes consciousness of the unifying agent and of his act of unification, consciousness of the object presupposes self-consciousness, or rather they are synonymous In so far, then, as there is consciousness of something, it is because the subject *is* absolutely nothing and the 'sensations', the 'material' of knowledge are not phases or inhabitants of consciousness, they are part of the constituted world Of what avail are our descriptions against these self-evident truths and how could they escape from this dilemma?

Let us return to the perceptual experience. I perceive this table on which I am writing This means, among other things, that my act of perception *occupies me*, and occupies me sufficiently for me to be unable, while I am actually perceiving the table, to perceive myself perceiving it. When I want to do this, I cease, so to speak, to use my gaze in order to plunge into the table, I turn my back towards myself who am perceiving, and then realize that my perception must have gone through certain subjective appearances, and interpreted certain of my own 'sensations'; in short it takes its place in the perspective of my individual history I start from unified experience and from there acquire, in a secondary way, consciousness of a unifying activity when, taking up an analytical attitude, I break up perception into qualities and sensations, and when, in order to recapture on the basis of these the object into which I was in the first place blindly thrown, I am obliged to suppose an act of synthesis which is merely the counterpart of my analysis. My act of perception, in its unsophisticated form, does not itself bring about this synthesis; it takes advantage of work already done, of a general synthesis constituted once and for all, and this is what I mean when I say that I perceive with my body or my senses, since my body and my senses are precisely that familiarity with the world born of habit, that implicit or sedimentary body of knowledge. If my consciousness were at present constituting the world which it perceives, no distance would separate them and there would be no possible discrepancy between them; it would find its way into the world's hidden concatenations, intentionality would carry us to the heart of the object, and simultaneously the percept would lose the thickness conferred by the present, and consciousness would not be lost and become bogged down in it But what we in fact have is consciousness of an inexhaustible object, and we are sucked into it because, between it and us, there is this latent knowledge which our gaze uses—the possibility of its rational development being a mere matter of presumption on our part—and which remains for ever anterior to our perception If, as we have said, every perception has something anonymous in it, this is because it makes use of something which it takes for granted The *person who* perceives is not spread out before himself as a consciousness must be, he has historical density, he takes up a perceptual tradition and is faced with a present In perception we do not think the object and we do not think ourselves thinking it, we are given over to the object and we merge into this body which is better informed than we are about the world, and about the motives we have and the means at our disposal for synthesizing it. That is why we said with Herder that man *is a sensorium commune.* In this primary layer of sense experience which is discovered only provided that we really coincide with the act of perception and break with the critical attitude, I have the living experience of the unity of the subject and the intersensory unity of the thing, and do not conceive them after the fashion of analytical reflection and science But what is the unified without unification, what is this object which is not yet an object for someone? Psychological reflection, which posits my act of perception as an event in my personal history, may well be a second order thing But transcendental reflection, which reveals me as the non-temporal thinker of the object, brings nothing to it which is not already there it restricts itself to the formulation of what gives significance to 'the table' and 'the chair', what underlies their stable structure and makes my experience of objectivity possible In short, what is living the unity of the object or the subject, if it is not making it? Even if it be supposed that this unity makes its appearance with the phenomenon of my body, must I not think of it in my body in order to find it there, and must I not effect the synthesis of this phenomenon in order to have the experience of it? We are not trying to derive the *for itself* from the *in itself*, nor are we returning to some form of empiricism, the body to which we are entrusting the synthesis of the perceived world is not a pure datum, a thing passively received For us the perceptual synthesis is a temporal synthesis, and subjectivity, at the level of perception, is nothing but temporality, and this is what enables us to leave to the subject of perception his opacity and historicity I open my eyes on to my table, and my consciousness is flooded with colours and confused reflections, it is hardly distinguishable from what is offered to it; it spreads out, through its accompanying body, into the spectacle which so far is not a spectacle of anything Suddenly, I start to focus my eyes on the table which is not yet there, I begin to look into the distance while there is as yet no depth, my body centres itself on an object which is still only potential, and so disposes its sensitive surfaces as to make it a present reality. I can thus re-assign to its place in the world the something which was impinging upon me, because I can, by slipping into the future, throw into the immediate past the world's first attack upon my senses, and direct myself towards the determinate object as towards a near future. The act of looking is indivisibly prospective, since the object is the final stage of my process of focusing, and retrospective, since it will present itself as preceding its own appearance, as the 'stimulus', the motive or the prime mover of every process since its beginning The spatial synthesis and the synthesis of the object are based on this unfolding of time In every focusing movement my body unites present, past and future, it secretes time, or rather it becomes that location in nature where, for the first time, events, instead of pushing each other into the realm of being, project round the present a double horizon of

239

past and future and acquire a historical orientation There is here indeed the summoning, but not the experience, of an eternal *natura naturans*. My body takes possession of time; it brings into existence a past and a future for a present, it is not a thing, but creates time instead of submitting to it. But every act of focusing must be renewed, otherwise it falls into unconsciousness The object remains clearly before me provided that I run my eyes over it, free-ranging scope being an essential property of the gaze The hold which it gives us upon a segment of time, the synthesis which it effects are themselves temporal phenomena which pass, and can be recaptured only in a fresh act which is itself temporal The claim to objectivity laid by each perceptual act is remade by its successor, again disappointed and once more made This ever-recurrent failure of perceptual consciousness was foreseeable from the start If I cannot see the object except by distancing it in the past, this is because, like the first attack launched by the object upon my senses, the succeeding perception equally occupies and expunges my consciousness; it is because this perception will in turn pass away, the subject of perception never being an absolute subjectivity, but being destined to become an object for an ulterior *I*. Perception is always in the mode of the impersonal 'One' It is not a personal act enabling me to give a fresh significance to my life The person who, in sensory exploration, gives a past to the present and directs it towards a future, is not myself as an autonomous subject, but myself in so far as I have a body and am able to 'look'. Rather than being a genuine history, perception ratifies and renews in us a 'prehistory'. And that again is of the essence of time: there would be no present, that is to say, no sensible world with its thickness and inexhaustible richness, if perception, in Hegel's words, did not retain a past in the depth of the present, and did not contract that past into that depth It fails at this moment to realize the synthesis of its object, not because it is the passive recipient of it, as empiricists would have it, but because the unity of the object makes its appearance through the medium of time, and because time slips away as fast as it catches up with itself It is true that I find, through time, later experiences interlocking with earlier ones and carrying them further, but nowhere do I enjoy absolute possession of myself by myself, since the hollow void of the future is for ever being refilled with a fresh present There is no related object without relation and without subject, no unity without unification, but every synthesis is both exploded and rebuilt by time which, with one and the same process, calls it into question and confirms it because it produces a new present which retains the past. The duality of *naturata* and *naturans* is therefore converted into a dialectic of constituted and constituting time. If we are to solve the problem which we have set ourselves—that of sensoriality, or finite subjectivity—it will be by thinking about time and showing how it exists only for a subjectivity, since without the latter, the past in itself being no longer and the future in itself being not yet, there would be no time—and how nevertheless this subject is time itself, and how we can say with Hegel that time is the existence of mind, or refer with Husserl to a self-constitution of time.

For the moment, the preceding descriptions and those which are to follow serve to make us familiar with a new type of reflection from which we await the solution of our problems. For intellectualism, reflecting is distancing or objectifying sensation and confronting it with a subject without content capable of ranging over this diversity and for whom the latter can exist. In so far as intellectualism purifies consciousness by delivering it of all opacity, it makes a genuine thing out of the *hylé*, and the apprehension of any concrete contents, the coming together of this thing and the mind, becomes inconceivable If it be objected that the material of knowledge is a result of analysis and should not be treated as a real element, it has to be recognized that in a corresponding way the synthetic unity of apperception is also a theoretical version of experience, that it should not be given any first-hand value and, in short, that the theory of knowledge has to be begun all over again. We agree that the matter and form of knowledge are results of analysis I posit the stuff of knowledge when, breaking away from the primary faith inspired by perception, I adopt a critical attitude towards it and ask 'what I am really seeing' The task of a radical reflection, the kind that aims at self-comprehension, consists, paradoxically enough, in recovering the unreflective experience of the world, and subsequently reassigning to it the verificatory attitude and reflective operations, and displaying reflection as one possibility of my being What have we then at the outset? Not a given manifold with a synthetic apperception which ranges over it and completely penetrates it, but a certain perceptual field against the background of a world Nothing here is thematized. Neither object nor subject is *posited* In the primary field we have not a mosaic of qualities, but a total configuration which distributes functional values according to the demands of the whole, for example, as we have seen, a 'white' paper in the shade is not white in the sense of possessing an objective quality, but it counts as white What is called sensation is only the most rudimentary of perceptions, and, as a modality of existence, it is no more separable than any other perception from a background which is in fact the world Correspondingly each act of perception appears to itself to be picked out from some all-embracing adherence to the world. At the centre of this system lies the ability to suspend vital communication, or at least

241

to limit it, by concentrating our gaze on a part of the spectacle and devoting the whole of the perceptual field to it We must not, as we have seen, suppose that the determinate forms reached through the critical attitude are realized in the primordial experience, or, in consequence, talk about a synthesis which is present, so long as the manifold is as yet undissociated Must we then reject the idea of synthesis and of a stuff of knowledge? Are we to say that perception reveals objects as a light illuminates them in the night, are we to adopt for our own purposes that realism which, according to Malebranche, leads us to imagine the soul issuing through the eyes and exploring objects in the world? That would not rid us of even the idea of synthesis since, in order to perceive a surface, for example, it is not enough to explore it, we must keep in mind the moments of our exploratory journey and relate the points on the surface to each other. But we have seen that primary perception is a non-thetic,* preobjective and pre-conscious experience Let us therefore say *provisionally* that there is a merely possible stuff of knowledge. From every point of the primordial field intentions move outwards, vacant and yet determinate, in realizing these intentions, analysis will arrive at the object of science, at sensation as a private phenomenon, and at the pure subject which posits both These three terminal concepts are no nearer than on the horizon of primordial experience It is in the experience of the thing that the reflective ideal of positing thought will have its basis. Hence reflection does not itself grasp its full significance unless it refers to the unreflective fund of experience which it presupposes, upon which it draws, and which constitutes for it a kind of original past, a past which has never been a present

* I e non-positing (Translator's note)

2

SPACE

WE have just recognized that analysis has no justification for *positing* any stuff of knowledge as an ideally separable 'moment' and that this stuff, when brought into being by an act of reflection, already relates to the world. Reflection does not follow in the reverse direction a path already traced by the constitutive act, and the natural reference of the stuff to the world leads us to a new conception of intentionality, since the classical conception,[1] which treats the experience of the world as a pure act of constituting consciousness, manages to do so only in so far as it defines consciousness as absolute non-being, and correspondingly consigns its contents to a 'hyletic layer' which belongs to opaque being. We must now approach this new intentionality in a more direct way by examining the symmetrical notion of a form of perception, and in particular the notion of space. Kant tried to draw a strict demarcation line between space as the form of external experience and the things given within that experience. There is naturally no question of a relationship of container to content, since this relationship exists only between objects, nor even a relationship of logical inclusion, like the one existing between the individual and the class, since space is anterior to its alleged parts, which are always carved out of it. Space is not the setting (real or logical) in which things are arranged, but the means whereby the positing of things becomes possible. This means that instead of imagining it as a sort of ether in which all things float, or conceiving it abstractly as a characteristic that they have in common, we must think of it as the universal power enabling them to be connected. Therefore, either I do not reflect, but live among things and vaguely regard space at one moment as the setting for things, at another as their common attribute—or else I do reflect: I catch space at its source, and now think

[1] By this we understand either that of a Kantian like P. Lachieze-Rey (*L'Idealisme kantien*), or that of Husserl in the second period of his philosophy (the period of the *Ideen*).

243

the relationships which underlie this word, realizing then that
they live only through the medium of a subject who describes
and sustains them, and pass from spatialized to spatializing space.
In the first case, my body and things, their concrete relationships
expressed in such terms as top and bottom, right and left, near and
far, may appear to me as an irreducibly manifold variety, whereas
in the second case I discover a single and indivisible ability to describe space. In the first case, I am concerned with physical space,
with its regions of varied quality; in the second with geometrical
space having interchangeable dimensions, homogeneous and iso-
tropic, and here I can at least think of a pure change of place which
would leave the moving body unchanged, and consequently a pure
position distinct from the *situation* of the object in its concrete context We know how this distinction is blurred in modern conceptions
of space, even at the level of scientific knowledge Here we want
to confront it, not with the technical instruments which modern
physics has acquired, but with our experience of space, the ultimate
court of appeal, according to Kant himself, of all knowledge connected with space. Is it true that we are faced with the alternative
either of perceiving things in space, or (if we reflect and try to discover the significance of our own experiences) of conceiving space
as the indivisible system governing the acts of unification performed
by a constituting mind? Does not the experience of space provide a
basis for its unity by means of an entirely different kind of synthesis?

Let us consider it before any theoretical elaboration has taken
place. Take, for instance, our experience of 'top' and 'bottom'. We
cannot catch it in the ordinary run of living, because it is then hidden
under its own acquisitions. We must examine some exceptional case
in which it disintegrates and re-forms before our eyes, for example,
in cases of vision without retinal inversion. If a subject is made to
wear glasses which correct the retinal images, the whole landscape at
first appears unreal and upside down; on the second day of the experiment normal perception begins to reassert itself, except that the
subject has the feeling that his own body is upside down.[1] In the
course of a second set of experiments[2] lasting a week, objects at first
appear inverted, but less unreal than the first time On the second
day the landscape is no longer inverted, but the body is felt to
be in an abnormal position. From the third to the seventh day,
the body progressively rights itself, and finally seems to occupy a
normal position, particularly when the subject is active When he is
lying motionless on a couch, the body still presents itself against the

[1] Stratton, *Some preliminary experiments on vision without inversion of the
retinal image*
[2] Stratton, *Vision without inversion of the retinal image*

background of the former space, and, as far as the unseen parts of the body are concerned, right and left preserve their former localization to the end of the experiment. External objects increasingly have a look of 'reality' From the fifth day, actions which were at first liable to be misled by the new mode of vision and had to be corrected in the light of the general visual upheaval, now go infallibly to their objective The new visual appearances which, at the beginning, stood out against a background of previous space, develop round themselves, at first (third day) only through a great effort of will, later (seventh day) with no effort at all, a horizon with a general orientation corresponding to their own. On the seventh day, the placing of sounds is correct so long as the sounding object is seen as well as heard It remains unreliable, and with a double, or even inaccurate, representation, if the source of the sound does not appear in the visual field. At the end of the experiment, when the glasses are removed, objects appear not inverted, it is true, but 'queer', and motor reactions are reversed the subject reaches out his right hand when it should be his left. The psychologist is at first tempted to say[1] that after the glasses have been put on, the visual world is given to the subject exactly as if it had been turned through 180°, and *consequently* is upside down for him. As the illustrations in a book appear upside down to us if someone has played the trick of placing it 'top to bottom' while we were looking away, the mass of sensations which make up the panorama has been turned round, and similarly placed 'top to bottom'. That other mass of sensations which is the world of touch has meanwhile stayed 'the right way', it can no longer coincide with the visual world so that the subject has two irreconcilable representations of his body, one given to him by his tactile sensations and by those 'visual images' which he has managed to retain from the period preceding the experiment; the other, that of his present vision which shows him his body 'head downwards' This conflict of images can end only if one of the two contestants withdraws Finding out how a normal situation is restored amounts then to finding out how the new image of the world and one's own body can cause the other to 'pale',[2] or 'displace' it [3] It is noticeable that the normal situation is the more successfully achieved in proportion as the subject is more active; for example, as early as the second day when he washes his hands [4] It would appear then that it is the experience of movement guided by sight which teaches the subject to harmonize the visual and tactile data: he becomes aware,

---

[1] This is, at least implicitly, Stratton's interpretation
[2] Stratton, *Vision without inversion*, p. 350
[3] *Some preliminary experiments*, p 617
[4] *Vision without inversion*, p 346

for instance, that the movement needed to reach his legs, hitherto a movement 'downwards', makes its appearance in the new visual spectacle as one which was previously 'upwards'. Observations of this kind enable inappropriate gestures to be corrected in the early stages by taking visual data as simply signs to be decoded and by translating them into the language of the former space. Once they have become 'habitual',[1] they set up between the old and the new directions, stable 'associations'[2] which do away with the former in favour of the latter, these being dominant by reason of their visual origin The 'top' of the visual field, where the legs at first appear, having been frequently identified with what is 'down' for the touch, soon the subject has no further need of the mediation of calculated movements to pass from one system to the other; his legs settle down at what he used to call the 'top' of the visual field; not only does he 'see' them there, he also 'feels' them there [3] and eventually 'what had previously been "the top" of the visual field begins to give an impression similar to that which belonged to the "bottom", and *vice versa*' [4] As soon as the tactile body links up with the visual one, that region of the visual field in which the subject's feet appeared stops being described as 'the top'. This designation is transferred to the region in which the head appears, and that containing the feet once more becomes the bottom.

But this interpretation is unintelligible The inversion of the landscape, followed by the return to normal vision, are explained by supposing that the top and bottom are turned topsyturvy and made variable with the apparent direction of head and feet *as given in the image*, that they are, so to speak, marked out in the sensory field by the actual distribution of sensations. But in no case—either at the beginning of the experiment, when the world is 'turned upside down', or at the end when it 'rights itself'—can the orientation of the field be given by these contents of head and feet which appear in it. For these contents would themselves have to have a direction, in order to pass it on to the field 'Inverted' or 'upright', in themselves, obviously have no meaning. The reply will run after putting on the glasses the visual field appears inverted in relation to the tactile and bodily field, or the ordinary visual field, which, by nominal definition, we say are 'upright' But the same question arises concerning these fields which we take as standard their mere presence is not enough to provide any direction whatsoever Among things, two points are enough to establish a direction But we are not

[1] Stratton, *The Spatial Harmony of Touch and Sight*, pp 492-505
[2] Ibid
[3] Stratton, *Some preliminary experiments*, p. 614.
[4] Stratton, *Vision without inversion*, p 350

among things, we have as yet only sensory fields which are not collections of sensations placed before us, sometimes 'head to the top', sometimes 'head downwards', but systems of appearances varyingly orientated during the course of the experiment, even where no change occurs in the grouping of *stimuli* So it is precisely a matter of finding out what happens when these floating appearances are suddenly anchored and take up a position in relation to 'up' and 'down', whether at the beginning of the experiment, when the tactile and bodily field seems 'upright' and the visual field 'inverted', or subsequently when the first turns upside down while the second rights itself, or finally at the conclusion of the experiment when both are more or less 'straight'. One cannot take the world and orientated space as given along with the contents of sense experience or with the body in itself, since experience in fact shows that the same contents can be successively orientated in one direction or another, and that objective relationships as registered on the retina through the position of the physical image do not govern our experience of 'up' and 'down' What we want to know is how an object can appear to us as 'the right way up' or 'inverted', and what these words mean.

The question is applicable not only to an empiricist psychology which treats the perception of space as the reception, within ourselves, of a real space, and the phenomenal orientation of objects as reflecting their orientation in the world It is equally relevant to intellectualist psychology in which the 'upright' and the 'inverted' are relationships dependent upon the fixed points chosen. As the axis of co-ordinates selected, whatever it may be, is as yet situated in space only in relation to another guide-post, and so on, so the task of taking the world's bearings is indefinitely postponed. 'Up' and 'down' lose any specific meaning they might have, unless, by an impossible contradiction, we recognize certain contents as having the power to take up a position in space, which brings back empiricism and its difficulties It is easy to show that there can be a direction only for a subject who describes it, and a constituting mind is eminently able to trace out all directions in space, but has at any moment no direction, and consequently no space, without an actual starting-point, an absolute 'here' which can gradually confer a significance on all spatial determinations Intellectualism as well as empiricism remains anterior to the problem of orientated space, because it cannot even begin to ask the question. In the case of empiricism, the question was how the image of the world which, in itself, is inverted, can right itself for me Intellectualism cannot even concede that the image of the world, after the glasses are put on, *is* inverted. For there is nothing, for a constituting mind, to distinguish the experience before from the experience after putting on the glasses, or even anything to make the visual experience of the 'inverted' body incompatible with the tactile experience of the 'upright' body, since it does not view the spectacle *from anywhere*, and since all the objective relations between the body and its environment are preserved in the new spectacle We can therefore see what the question involves; empiricism would willingly take the actual orientation of my bodily experience as the fixed point we need if we are to understand that there are directions for us,—but both experience and reflection demonstrate that no content is in itself orientated Intellectualism starts from this relativity of up and down, but cannot stand outside it in order to account for an actual perception of space We cannot understand, therefore, the experience of space either in terms of the consideration of contents or of that of some pure unifying activity, we are confronted with that third spatiality towards which we pointed a little while ago, which is neither that of things in space, nor that of spatializing space, and which, on this account, evades the Kantian analysis and is presupposed by it. We need an absolute within the sphere of the relative, a space which does not skate over appearances, which indeed takes root in them and is dependent upon them, yet which is nevertheless not given along with them in any realist way, and can, as Stratton's experiment shows, survive their complete disorganization We have to look for the first-hand experience of space on the hither side of the distinction between form and content.

If we so contrive it that a subject sees the room in which he is, only through a mirror which reflects it at an angle at 45° to the vertical, the subject at first sees the room 'slantwise'. A man walking about in it seems to lean to one side as he goes. A piece of cardboard falling down the door-frame looks to be falling obliquely. The general effect is 'queer' After a few minutes a sudden change occurs· the walls, the man walking about the room, and the line in which the cardboard falls become vertical.[1] This experiment, analogous to Stratton's, has the advantage of throwing into relief an instantaneous redistribution of high and low, without any motor exploration We were already aware that it is meaningless to say that the oblique (or inverted) image brings with it a repositioning of high and low which we come to identify by a motor exploration of the new spectacle But now we see that this exploration is not even necessary, and that consequently bearings are taken by a comprehensive act on the part of the perceiving subject. Let us say that perception before the experiment recognizes a certain *spatial level*, in relation to which the spectacle provided in the experiment first of all appears oblique, and that during the experiment this spectacle induces another level in relation to which the whole of the visual field can once more seem

[1] Wertheimer, *Experimentelle Studien uber das Sehen von Bewegung*, p 258

straight It is as if certain objects (walls, doors and the body of the
man in the room), having been seen aslant in relation to a given level,
then take it upon themselves to provide the cardinal directions,
attracting to themselves the vertical, acting as 'anchoring points',[1]
and causing the previously established horizontal to tilt sideways
We are not falling here into the realistic mistake of using the visual
spectacle as a source of directions in space, since the spectacle experimentally provided is turned (obliquely) for us only in relation to
a certain level, and since, therefore, it does not give us by itself the
new up-and-down axis. It remains to be seen what precisely is this
level which is always ahead of itself, since every constitution of a
level presupposes a different, pre-established level—how the 'anchoring points', working from within a certain space from which they
derive their stability, suggest to us the constitution of a fresh one,
what 'top' and 'bottom' really are, unless they are merely names
applicable to an orientation in itself of the contents of sense experience We hold that the 'spatial level' is not confused with the orientation of one's own body In so far as consciousness of one's own body
indubitably contributes to the constitution of level (a subject tilting
his head on one side holds a stick obliquely, when he is asked to hold
it vertically)[2] it is, in this function, in competition with the other
sectors of experience, and the vertical tends to follow the direction
of the head only if the visual field is empty, and if the 'anchoring
points' are lacking, for example when one is working in the dark.
As a mass of tactile, labyrinthine and kinaesthetic data, the body has
no more definite orientation than the other contents of experience,
and it too receives this orientation from the general level of experience Wertheimer's observation serves to show how the visual
field can impose an orientation which is not that of the body. But
although the body, as a mosaic of given sensations, has no specific
direction, nevertheless, as an agent, it plays an essential part in the
establishment of a level. Variations in muscular tonicity, even with
a full visual field, so modify the apparent vertical that the subject
leans his head on one side in order to place it parallel to this deflected
vertical [3] One might be tempted to say that the vertical is the direction represented by the symmetry axis of our body as a synergic
system. My body can, however, move without drawing along with it
the directions of upward and downward, as when I lie down on the
ground, and Wertheimer's experiment shows that the objective direction of my body can form an appreciable angle with the apparent
vertical of the spectacle. What counts for the orientation of the

[1] Wertheimer, *Experimentelle Studien uber das Sehen von Bewegung*, p 253.
[2] Nagel, quoted by Wertheimer, ibid , p 257
[3] *La Structure du Comportement*, p. 199.

spectacle is not my body as it in fact is, as a thing in objective space, but as a system of possible actions, a virtual body with its phenomenal 'place' defined by its task and situation My body is wherever there is something to be done. As soon as Wertheimer's subject takes his place in the experimental situation prepared for him, the area of his possible actions—such as walking, opening a cupboard, using a table, sitting down—outlines in front of him, even if he has his eyes shut, a possible habitat. At first the mirror image presents him with a room differently canted, which means that the subject is not at home with the utensils it contains, he does not inhabit it, and does not share it with the man he sees walking to and fro. After a few minutes, provided that he does not strengthen his initial anchorage by glancing away from the mirror, the reflected room miraculously calls up a subject capable of living in it. This virtual body ousts the real one to such an extent that the subject no longer has the feeling of being in the world where he actually is, and that instead of his real legs and arms, he feels that he has the legs and arms he would need to walk and act in the reflected room: he inhabits the spectacle The spatial level tilts and takes up its new position. It is, then, a certain possession of the world by my body, a certain gearing of my body to the world Being projected, in the absence of anchoring points, by the attitude of my body alone, as in Nagel's experiments—specified, when the body is inert, through the demands of the spectacle alone, as in Wertheimer's experiment—it normally makes its appearance where my motor intentions and my perceptual field join forces, when my actual body is at one with the virtual body required by the spectacle, and the actual spectacle with the setting which my body throws round it It comes to rest when, between my body as the potentiality for certain movements, as the demand for certain preferential planes, and the spectacle perceived as an invitation to the same movements and the scene of the same actions, a pact is concluded which gives me the enjoyment of space and gives to things their direct power over my body The constitution of a spatial level is simply one means of constituting an integrated world. my body is geared onto the world when my perception presents me with a spectacle as varied and as clearly articulated as possible, and when my motor intentions, as they unfold, receive the responses they expect from the world Thus maximum sharpness of perception and action points clearly to a perceptual *ground*, a basis of my life, a general setting in which my body can co-exist with the world. With the notion of a spatial level, and of the body as the subject of space, we begin to understand the phenomena described by Stratton but left unexplained by him If the 'correction' of the field were the outcome of a set of associations between the new

250

positions and the old, how could the operation convey the general
effect of being systematic, and how could whole sections of the perceptual horizon suddenly fall into line with already 'corrected' objects? If, on the other hand, the new orientation sprang from a process of thought, and consisted of a change of co-ordinates, how could
the auditory or tactile field resist transposition? The constituting
subject would, *per impossibile*, have to be cut off from himself and
able to overlook in one place what he was doing in another [1] In
so far as the transposition is systematic, and yet piece-meal and progressive, it is because I go from one system of positions to the other
without having the key to each, and in the way that a man sings, in
another key, a tune he has heard, though he has no knowledge of
music The possession of a body implies the ability to change levels
and to 'understand' space, just as the possession of a voice implies
the ability to change key The perceptual field corrects itself and at
the conclusion of the experiment I identify it without any concept
because I live in it, because I am borne wholly into the new spectacle
and, so to speak, transfer my centre of gravity into it [2] At the beginning of the experiment, the visual field appears both inverted and
unreal because the subject does not live in it and is not geared to it
In the course of the experiment, we notice an intermediate phase in
which the tactile body seems to be inverted and the landscape upright because, since I already live in the landscape, I see it accordingly as upright, the disturbance brought about by the experiment
being concentrated in my own body, which thus becomes, not a mass
of affective sensations, but the body which is needed to perceive a
given spectacle Everything throws us back on to the organic relations between subject and space, to that gearing of the subject onto
his world which is the origin of space

But one may wish to go further into the analysis Why, it may be
asked, are clear perception and assured action possible only in a
phenomenal space which is orientated? This is obvious only if we
suppose the subject of perception and action faced with a world

[1] Change of direction in acoustic phenomena is extremely difficult to bring
about If we arrange, with the aid of a pseudophone, for sounds coming from the
left to reach the right ear before they strike the left, we get an inversion of the
auditory field comparable to the inversion of the visual field in Stratton s experiment Now even with long practice people do not manage to 'correct' the auditory
field The placing of sounds by hearing alone remains incorrect to the end It is
correct, and the sound seems to come from the object on the left only if the object
is seen at the same time as it is heard. P T Young, *Auditory localization with
acoustical transposition of the ears*

[2] The subject can, in experiments on auditory inversion, produce the illusion of
correct localization when he sees the source of sound, because he inhibits his
auditory phenomena and 'lives in the visual P. T. Young, ibid

where there are already absolute directions, so that he has to adjust the dimensions of his behaviour to those of the world. But we are now placing ourselves inside perception, and we are puzzled to know precisely how it can come by absolute directions, and so we cannot suppose them to be given at the source of our spatial experience. The objection amounts to saying what we have been saying from the start: that the constitution of a level always presupposes another given level, that space always precedes itself But this remark is not a mere admission of defeat It enlightens us concerning the essence of space and the only method which enables us to understand it. It is of the essence of space to be always 'already constituted', and we shall never come to understand it by withdrawing into a worldless perception We must not wonder why being is orientated, why existence is spatial, why, using the expression we used a little while ago, our body is not geared to the world in all its positions, and why its co-existence with the world magnetizes experience and induces a direction in it The question could be asked only if the facts were fortuitous happenings to a subject and an object indifferent to space, whereas perceptual experience shows that they are presupposed in our primordial encounter with being, and that being is synonymous with being situated. For the thinking subject a face seen 'the right way up' and the same face seen 'upside down' are indistinguishable. For the subject of perception the face seen 'upside down' is unrecognizable. If someone is lying on a bed, and I look at him from the head of the bed, the face is for a moment normal It is true that the features are in a way disarranged, and I have some difficulty in realizing that the smile is a smile, but I feel that I could, if I wanted, walk round the bed, and I seem to see through the eyes of a spectator standing at the foot of the bed If the spectacle is protracted, it suddenly changes its appearance the face takes on an utterly unnatural aspect, its expressions become terrifying, and the eyelashes and eyebrows assume an air of materiality such as I have never seen in them. For the first time I really see the inverted face as if this were its 'natural' position in front of me I have a pointed, hairless head with a red, teeth-filled orifice in the forehead and, where the mouth ought to be, two moving orbs edged with glistening hairs and underlined with stiff brushes. It will probably be said that the face seen the 'right way up' is, among all the possible aspects of a face, the one which is most frequently given to me, and that the inverted face startles me because I see it only rarely. But faces are not often presented in a strictly vertical position, the 'upright' face enjoys no statistical preponderance, and the question is why, this being the case, it is given to me more often than any other If it be conceded that my perception makes it a standard and refers to it as to a norm for reasons of symmetry, the

252

question arises why, beyond a certain angle, the 'correction' does not operate We must conclude that my gaze which moves over the face, and in doing so favours certain directions, does not recognize the face unless it comes up against its details in a certain irreversible order, and that the very significance of the object—here the face and its expressions—must be linked to its orientation, as indeed is indicated by the double usage of the French word *sens* * To invert an object is to deprive it of its significance. Its being as an object is, therefore, not a being-for-the-thinking subject, but a being-for-the-gaze which meets it at a certain angle, and otherwise fails to recognize it. This is why each object has its 'top' and its 'bottom' which indicate, for a given level, its 'natural' position, the one which it 'should' occupy To see a face is not to conceive the idea of a certain law of constitution to which the object invariably conforms throughout all its possible orientations, it is to take a certain hold upon it, to be able to follow on its surface a certain perceptual route with its ups and downs, and one just as unrecognizable taken in reverse as the mountain up which I was so recently toiling, and down which I am now striding my way. Generally speaking, our perception would not comprise either outlines, figures, backgrounds or objects, and would consequently not be perception of anything, or indeed exist at all, if the subject of perception were not this gaze which takes a grip upon things only in so far as they have a general direction; and this general direction in space is not a contingent characteristic of the object, it is the means whereby I recognize it and am conscious of it as of an object. It is true that I can be conscious of the same object variously orientated, and, as we have said, I can even recognize an inverted face But it is always provided that mentally we take up position in front of it, and sometimes we even do so physically, as when we tilt our head to look at a photograph held in front of him by a person at our side Thus, since every conceivable being is related either directly or indirectly to the perceived world, and since the perceived world is grasped only in terms of direction, we cannot dissociate being from orientated being, and there is no occasion to 'find a basis for space or to ask what is the level of all levels. The primordial level is on the horizon of all our perceptions, but it is a horizon which cannot in principle ever be reached and thematized in our express perception. Each of the levels in which we successively live makes its appearance when we cast anchor in some 'setting' which is offered to us. This setting itself is spatially particularized only for a previously given level Thus each of the whole succession of our experiences, including the first, passes on an already acquired spatiality The condition of our first perception's being spatial is that it should

* 'sense, significance, direction' (Translator's note)

253

have referred to some orientation which preceded it It must, then, have found us already at work in a world. Yet this cannot be a *certain* world, a *certain* spectacle, since we have put ourselves at the origin of all of them The first spatial level cannot find its anchorage *anywhere*, since this anchorage would need a level anterior to the first level in order to be particularized in space. And since it cannot be orientated 'in itself', my first perception and my first hold upon the world must appear to me as action in accordance with an earlier agreement reached between x and the world in general, my history must be the continuation of a prehistory and must utilize the latter's acquired results My personal existence must be the resumption of a prepersonal tradition There is, therefore, another subject beneath me, for whom a world exists before I am here, and who marks out my place in it. This captive or natural spirit is my body, not that momentary body which is the instrument of my personal choices and which fastens upon this or that world, but the system of anonymous 'functions' which draw every particular focus into a general project Nor does this blind adherence to the world, this prejudice in favour of being, occur only at the beginning of my life It endows every subsequent perception, of space with its meaning, and it is resumed at every instant. Space and perception generally represent, at the core of the subject, the fact of his birth, the perpetual contribution of his bodily being, a communication with the world more ancient than thought. That is why they saturate consciousness and are impenetrable to reflection The instability of levels produces not only the intellectual experience of disorder, but the vital experience of giddiness and nausea,[1] which is the awareness of our contingency, and the horror with which it fills us The positing of a level means losing sight of this contingency, space has its basis in our facticity. It is neither an object, nor an act of unification on the subject's part; it can neither be observed, since it is presupposed in every observation, nor seen to emerge from a constituting operation, since it is of its essence that it be already constituted, for thus it can, by its magic, confer its own spatial particularizations upon the landscape without ever appearing itself.

Traditional ideas of perception are at one in denying that depth is visible Berkeley shows that it could not be given to sight in the absence of any means of recording it, since our retinas receive only

[1] Stratton, *Vision without Inversion*, first day of the experiment Wertheimer talks about a 'visual vertigo' (*Experimentelle Studien*, pp 257–9) We remain physically upright not through the mechanism of the skeleton or even through the nervous regulation of muscular tone, but because we are caught up in a world If this involvement is seriously weakened, the body collapses and becomes once more an object.

a manifestly flat projection of the spectacle If one retorted that after
the criticism of the 'constancy hypothesis' we cannot judge what we
see by what is pictured on our retinas, Berkeley would probably
reply that, whatever may be true of the retinal image, depth cannot
be seen because it is not spread out before our eyes, but appears to
them only in foreshortened form. In analytical reflection, it is for
theoretical reasons that depth is to be judged invisible: even if it
could be registered by our eyes, the sensory impression would present
only a multiplicity in itself, which would have to be ranged over, so
that distance, like all other spatial relations, exists only for a subject
who synthesizes it and embraces it in thought Though diametrically
opposed to each other, the two doctrines presuppose the same repression of our affective experience. In both cases depth is tacitly
equated with *breadth seen from the side*, and this is what makes it
invisible Berkeley's argument, made quite explicit, runs roughly like
this What I call depth is in reality a juxtaposition of points, making
it comparable to breadth. I am simply badly placed to see it. I should
see it if I were in the position of a spectator looking on from the side,
who can take in at a glance the series of objects spread out in front
of me, whereas for me they conceal each other—or see the distance
from my body to the first object, whereas for me this distance is
compressed into a point What makes depth invisible for me is
precisely what makes it visible for the spectator as breadth: the juxtaposition of simultaneous points in one direction which is that of my
gaze The depth which is declared invisible is, therefore, a depth
already identified with breadth and, this being the case, the argument would lack even a semblance of consistency. In the same way,
intellectualism can bring to light, in the experience of depth, a thinking subject who synthesizes that experience, only because it reflects
on the basis of a depth already in existence, on a juxtaposition of
simultaneous points which is not depth as it is presented to me, but
as it is presented to a spectator standing at the side, in short as
breadth [1] By assimilating one to the other from the very outset, the
two philosophies take for granted the result of a constitutive process
the stages of which we must, in fact, trace back. In order to treat
depth as breadth viewed in profile, in order to arrive at a uniform
space, the subject must leave his place, abandon his point of view on
the world, and think himself into a sort of ubiquity. For God, who
is everywhere, breadth is immediately equivalent to depth. Intellectualism and empiricism do not give us any account of the human experience of the world, they tell us what God might think about it

---

[1] The distinction between the depth of things in relation to me, and the distance
between two objects, is made by Pahard, *L'Illusion de Sinnsteden et le problème de
l'implication perceptive*, p 400, and by E. Straus, *Vom Sinn der Sinne*, pp 267–9

And indeed it is the world itself which suggests to us that we substitute one dimension for another and conceive it from no point of
view. All men accept without any speculation the equivalence of
depth and breadth, this equivalence is part and parcel of the self-
evidence of an intersubjective world, which is what makes philosophers as forgetful as anyone else of the originality of depth. But
prior to this we know nothing of the world and of space as objective,
we are trying to describe the *phenomenon* of the world, that is, its
birth for us in that field into which each perception sets us back,
where we are as yet still alone, where other people will appear only at a
later stage, in which knowledge and particularly science have not so
far ironed out and levelled down the individual perspective. It is
through this birth that we are destined to graduate to a world, and
we must therefore describe it More directly than the other dimensions of space, depth forces us to reject the preconceived notion of
the world and rediscover the primordial experience from which it
springs it is, so to speak, the most 'existential' of all dimensions,
because (and here Berkeley's argument is right) it is not impressed
upon the object itself, it quite clearly belongs to the perspective and
not to things Therefore it cannot either be extracted from, or even put
into that perspective by consciousness. It announces a certain indissoluble link between things and myself by which I am placed in
front of them, whereas breadth can, at first sight, be taken as a relationship between things themselves, in which the perceiving subject is not implied By rediscovering the vision of depth, that is to
say, of a depth which is not yet objectified and made up of mutually
external points, we shall once more outrun the traditional alternatives and elucidate the relation between subject and object.

Here is my table, *farther away* is the piano or the wall, or again a
car which is standing in front of me is started and *drives away* What
do these words mean? In order to resuscitate the perceptual experience, let us take as our starting point the superficial account given by a
thought obsessed by the world and the object. These words, it is
maintained, mean that between the table and myself there is an interval, between the car and myself an increasing interval that I cannot
see from where I am, but which reveals itself to me by the apparent
size of the object. It is the apparent size of the table, the piano and
the wall which, relative to their real size, assigns to them their place
in space When the car slowly climbs up towards the horizon, all the
while decreasing in size, I account for this appearance by constructing a displacement in terms of breadth such as I should perceive if I
were observing the scene from an aeroplane, and which, in the last
analysis, is the whole meaning of depth But I have also other signs of
distance to go on As an object approaches me, my eyes, as long as they

256

arc focused on it, converge The distance is the height of a triangle with its base and base angles given to me[1] and, when I say that I am seeing something at a distance, I mean that the height of the triangle is determined by its relations to these given sizes The experience of depth, according to traditional views, consists in interpreting certain given facts—the convergence of the eyes, the apparent size of the image, for example—by placing them in the context of objective relations which explain them. But my ability to go back from the apparent size to its significance is conditioned by my knowledge that there is a world of undistortable objects, that my body is standing in front of this world like a mirror and that, like the image in the mirror, the one which is formed on the body screen is exactly proportionate to the interval which separates it from the object My ability to understand convergence as a sign of distance is conditioned by my visualizing my gaze as the blind man's two sticks, which run more sharply together in proportion as the object is brought nearer,[2] in other words, by my inclusion of my eyes, body and the external world into one and the same objective space. The 'signs' which, *ex hypothesi*, ought to acquaint us with the experience of space can, therefore, convey the idea of space only if they are already involved in it, and if it is already known Since perception is initiation into the world, and since, as has been said with insight, 'there is nothing anterior to it which is mind',[3] we cannot put into it objective relationships which are not yet constituted at its level. That is why the Cartesians spoke of a 'natural geometry'. The significance of apparent size and convergence, that is distance, cannot yet be set forth and thematized Apparent size and convergence themselves cannot be given as elements in a system of objective relationships 'Natural geometry' or 'natural judgement' are myths in the Platonic sense, intended to represent the envelopment or 'implication' of a significance in signs, neither signs nor significance being yet posited and explicitly contained in thought, and this is what we must elucidate by returning to perceptual experience. We must describe apparent size and convergence, not as scientific knowledge sees them, but as we grasp them from within Gestalt pyschologists[4] have observed that they are not explicitly known in perception itself—I am not expressly aware of the convergence of my eyes or of apparent size when I perceive at a distance, they do not confront me as perceived facts do—and that they nevertheless enter into the perception of distance, as the stereoscope

[1] Malebranche, *Recherche de la vérité*, Book I, Chap IX   [2] Ibid
[3] Pahard, *L'Illusion de Sinnsteden et le problème de l'implication perceptive*, p. 383.
[4] Koffka, *Some problems of space perception*. Guillaume, *Traité de Psychologie*, Chap IX

and illusions of perspective amply prove. Psychologists conclude from this that they are not signs, but conditions or causes of depth. We observe that organization in depth appears when a certain size of retinal image or a certain degree of convergence is objectively produced in the body; this is a law comparable to the laws of physics, and it has only to be recorded without more ado. But here the psychologist is evading his task when he recognizes that apparent size and convergence are not present in perception itself as objective facts, he is requiring us to return to the pure description of phenomena prior to the objective world, and giving us a glimpse of 'lived' depth, independently of any kind of geometry And then he interrupts the description in order to put himself back in the world and derive organization in depth from a chain of observed facts. Can one thus limit description and, once having recognized the phenomenal order as an original order, re-assign the production of phenomenal depth to some cerebral alchemy only the result of which is recorded by experience? We must choose between the behaviourist course of refusing all meaning to the word 'experience', and trying to build up perception as a product of the world and of science, or else we must concede that experience, too, gives us access to being, in which case it cannot be treated as a by-product of being. Either experience is nothing or it must be total.

Let us try to envisage what an organization in depth produced by cerebral physiology might be. For any given apparent size and convergence, there would appear somewhere in the brain a functional structure homologous with the organization in depth But this is in any case only a given depth, a factual depth, and we still have to become aware of it To experience a structure is not to receive it into oneself passively, it is to live it, to take it up, assume it and discover its immanent significance Thus an experience can never bear the relation to certain factual conditions that it would bear to its cause[1] and, even if consciousness of distance is produced for a certain value of convergence and a certain size of retinal image, it can depend on these factors only in so far as they figure in it Since we have no *express* experience of it, we must conclude that we have a non-thetic* experience of it Convergence and apparent size are neither signs nor causes of depth they are present in the experience of depth in the way that a *motive*, even when it is not articulate and separately posited, is present in a decision. What do we understand by a motive,

[1] In other words an act of consciousness can have no *cause*. But we prefer not to introduce the concept of consciousness, which Gestalt psychology might challenge and which we for our part do not unreservedly accept We shall stick to the unexceptionable notion of experience

* I e not explicitly posited (Translator's note)

258

and what do we mean when we say, for example, that a journey is
motivated? We mean thereby that it has its origin in certain given
facts, not in so far as these facts by themselves have the physical
power to bring it about, but in that they provide reasons for undertaking it The motive is an antecedent which acts only through its
significance, and it must be added that it is the decision which
affirms the validity of this significance and gives it its force and
efficacy Motive and decision are two elements of a situation: the
former is the situation as a fact, the second the situation undertaken
Thus a death motivates my journey *because* it is a situation in which
my presence is required, whether to console a bereaved family or to
'pay one's last respects' to the deceased, and, by deciding to make the
journey, I validate this motive which puts itself forward, and I take
up the situation. The relation between motivating factor and motivated act is thus reciprocal Now a similar relationship exists between
the experience of convergence, or of apparent size, and that of depth.
They do not act miraculously as 'causes' in producing the appearance
of organization in depth, they tacitly motivate it in so far as they
already contain it in their significance, and in so far as they are both
already a certain way of looking at a distance We have already seen
that the convergence of the eyes is not the cause of depth, and that
it itself presupposes an orientation towards the object placed at a
distance. Let us now concentrate on the notion of apparent size If
we look for a long time at an illuminated object which will leave
behind it a following image, and if we focus subsequently on screens
placed at varying distances, the after-image is thrown upon them
with a diameter greater in proportion as the screen is farther away.[1]
The enlarged moon on the horizon has long been explained by the
large number of objects interposed which emphasize the distance and
consequently increase the apparent diameter. It follows that the
phenomenon of 'apparent size' and the phenomenon of distance are
two phases* of a comprehensive organization of the field, that the
first stands to the second neither in the relation of sign to meaning,
nor in that of cause to effect, but that, like the motivating factor to
the motivated act, they communicate through their significance.
Apparent size as experienced, instead of being the sign or indication
of a depth invisible in itself, is nothing other than a way of expressing
our vision of depth. Gestalt psychology has indeed contributed to
showing that the apparent size of a retreating object does not vary
proportionately to the retinal image, and that the apparent shape of
a disc turning round one of its diameters does not vary as one would

[1] Quercy, *Etudes sur l'hallucination*, II, *La clinique*, pp. 154 and ff

* '*moments*' (Translator's note)

expect according to the geometrical perspective The object moving away grows smaller, and the object approaching grows larger, less quickly for my perception than the physical image on my retina. That is why the train coming towards us, at the cinema, increases in size much more than it would in reality It is also why a hill which seemed high becomes insignificant in a photograph. And finally it is why a disc placed obliquely to our face resists geometrical perspective, as Cézanne and other painters have shown by depicting a soup plate seen from the side with the inside still visible It has been rightly said that, if perspective distortions were expressly given to us, we should not have to learn perspective But Gestalt psychologists talk as if the distortion of the oblique plate were a compromise between the shape of the plate seen from above and the geometrical perspective, and as if the apparent size of the retreating object were a compromise between its apparent size when within reach and the much smaller one which geometrical perspective would attribute to it. They talk, in fact, as if constancy of shape or size were a real constancy, as if there were, besides the physical image of the object on the retina, a 'mental image' of the same object which remained relatively constant while the first varied In reality, the 'mental image' of this ash-tray is neither larger nor smaller than the physical image of the same object on my retina: there is no mental image that can be compared, as if it were a thing, with the physical image, no mental image which has a determinate size relative to the physical and which stands like a screen between me and the thing My perception does not bear upon a content of consciousness it bears upon the ash-tray itself The apparent size of the perceived ash-tray is not a measurable size When I am asked what diameter I see it as having, I cannot reply to the question as long as I keep both eyes open. Spontaneously, I shut one eye, I take a measuring instrument, a pencil held at arm's length, for example, and I mark on the pencil the size reached by the ash-tray In doing this, I must avoid merely saying that I have reduced the perceived perspective to the geometrical, that I have altered the proportions of the spectacle, and that I have contracted the object if it is at a distance or that I have expanded it if it is near at hand—I must rather say that by breaking up the perceptual field and isolating the ash-tray, by positing it for itself, I have caused size to appear where hitherto it had no place The constancy of apparent size in a retreating object is not the actual permanence of some mental image of the object capable of resisting the distortions of perspective as a firm object resists pressure The constancy of circular shape in a plate is not the resistance of the circle to the flattening of perspective, and this is why the painter who can represent it only by a real outline on a real canvas surprises the viewer, although he is trying to render perspective as experienced. When I look at a road which sweeps before me towards the horizon, I must not say either that the sides of the road are given to me as convergent or that they are given to me as parallel· they are *parallel in depth* The perspective appearance is not posited, but neither is the parallelism. *I am engrossed in the road itself*, and I cling to it through its virtual distortion, and depth is this intention itself which posits neither the perspective projection of the road, nor the 'real' road And yet is not a man *smaller* at two hundred yards than at five yards away? He becomes so if I isolate him from the perceived context and measure his apparent size Otherwise he is neither smaller nor indeed equal in size: he is anterior to equality and inequality; he is *the same man seen from farther away* One can only say that the man two hundred yards away is a much less distinguishable figure, that he presents fewer and less identifiable points on which my eyes can fasten, that he is less strictly geared to my powers of exploration. Again one can say that he less completely occupies my visual field, provided that one remembers that the visual field itself is not a measurable area. To say that an object takes up only a small part of my visual field is to say in effect that it does not offer a sufficiently rich configuration to absorb completely my power of clear vision. My visual field has no definite capacity, and it can contain more or fewer things according as I see 'at a distance' or 'near'. Apparent size is, therefore, not definable independently of distance, it is implied by distance and it also implies distance Convergence, apparent size and distance are read off from each other, naturally symbolize or signify each other, are the abstract elements of a situation and are, within it, mutually synonymous, not because the subject of perception posits objective relations between them, but on the contrary because he does not posit them separately and therefore has no need to unify them expressly. Taking the various 'apparent sizes' of the retreating object, it is not necessary to link them in a synthesis if none of them has been specifically posited. We 'have' the retreating object, we never cease to 'hold' it and to have a grip on it, and the increasing distance is not, as breadth appears to be, an augmenting externality it expresses merely that the thing is beginning to slip away from the grip of our gaze and is less closely allied to it Distance is what distinguishes this loose and approximate grip from the complete grip which is proximity We shall define it then as we defined 'straight' and 'oblique' above· in terms of the situation of the object in relation to our power of grasping it.

It is principally illusions relating to depth which have made us accustomed to considering it as a construction of the understanding We can produce them by imposing upon the eyes a certain degree of convergence, as at the stereoscope, or by setting before the subject a perspective drawing Since in this case I imagine that I see depth when there is none, is this not because misleading signs have given rise to a hypothesis, and because generally the alleged vision of distance is always an interpretation of signs? But the postulate is clear; we suppose that it is not possible to see what is not there, we therefore define vision in terms of sensory impression, missing the original relationship of motivation and replacing it by one of significance We have seen that the disparity between the retinal images, which stimulates convergence, does not exist in itself, there is disparity only for a subject who tries to fuse monocular phenomena similar in structure and who tends towards synergy. The unity of binocular vision, and with it the depth without which it cannot come about is, therefore, there from the very moment at which the monocular images are presented as 'disparate'. When I look in the stereoscope, a totality presents itself in which already the possible order takes shape and the situation is foreshadowed. My motor response takes up this situation Cézanne said that the painter in the face of his 'motif' is about 'to join the aimless hands of nature'.[1] The act of focusing at the stereoscope is equally a response to the question put by the data, and this response is contained in the question It is the field itself which is moving towards the most perfect possible symmetry, and depth is merely a stage * in arriving at a perceptual faith in one single thing. The perspective drawing is not first of all perceived as a drawing on a plane surface, and then organized in depth. The lines which sweep towards the horizon are not first given as oblique, and then thought of as horizontal The whole of the drawing strives towards its equilibrium by delving in depth. The poplar on the road which is drawn smaller than a man, succeeds in becoming really and truly a tree only by retreating towards the horizon. It is the drawing itself which tends towards depth as a stone falls downwards If symmetry, plenitude and determinacy can be achieved in several ways, the organization will not be stable, as can be seen in ambiguous drawings

Thus Fig 1 below can be seen either as a cube seen from below with the face ABCD in the foreground, or as a cube seen from above with the face EFGH in the foreground, or as a mosaic pattern of ten triangles and a square. Fig 2 on the other hand will almost inevitably be seen as a cube, because that is the only organization which gives it perfect symmetry [2] Depth is born beneath my gaze because the latter tries to see *something* But what is this perceptual genius at work in

[1] J Gasquet, *Cézanne*, p 81
[2] Koffka, *Some problems of space perception*, pp 164 and ff
* 'moment' (Translator's note)

our visual field, tending always towards the most determinate form? Are we not now going back to realism? Let us take an example. Organization in depth is destroyed if I add to the ambiguous drawing not simply any lines (Fig. 3 stubbornly remains a cube) but lines which disunite the elements of one and the same plane and join up those of different planes (Fig. 1).[1] What do we mean when we say that these lines themselves bring about the destruction of depth? Are we not talking the language of associationism? We do not mean that the line EH (Fig. 1), acting as a cause, disorganizes the cube into which it is introduced, but that it induces a general grasp which is not the grasp in depth. It is understood that the line EH itself possesses

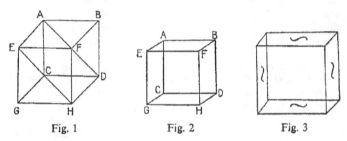

Fig. 1   Fig. 2   Fig. 3

an individuality only if I grasp it in that light, if I run over it and trace it out myself. But this grasp and this delineation are not arbitrary. They are indicated or recommended by phenomena. The demand here is not an overriding one, simply because it is a question of an ambiguous figure, but, in a normal visual field, the segregation of planes and outlines is irresistible; for example, when I walk along an avenue, I cannot bring myself to see the spaces between the trees as things and the trees themselves as a background. It is certainly I who have the experience of the landscape, but in this experience I am conscious of taking up a factual situation, of bringing together a significance dispersed among phenomena, and of saying what they of their own accord mean. Even in cases where the organization is ambiguous and where I can vary it, I do not directly succeed in doing so: one of the faces of the cube moves into the foreground only if I first look at it and if my gaze makes it its starting point from which to follow the oblique lines to the second face, which shows up as an indeterminate background. If I see Fig. 1 as a mosaic pattern, it is on condition that I first of all concentrate my gaze on the centre, and then distribute it equally and simultaneously over the whole figure. As Bergson waits for the lump of sugar to dissolve, I sometimes have to wait for the

---

[1] Koffka, *Some problems of space perception*, pp. 164 and ff.

organization to come about All the more is it the case that in normal perception the significance of what is perceived appears to me as built into it and not constituted by me, and the gaze as a sort of knowledge machine, which takes things as they need to be taken in order to become a spectacle, or which divides them up in accordance with their natural articulations It is true that the straight line EH counts as straight only if I run my eye along it, but it is not a matter of a mental inspection, but of an inspection by the gaze, which means that my act is not primary or constituting, but called forth or motivated Every focus is always a focus on something which presents itself as to be focused upon When I focus upon the face ABCD of the cube, that does not only mean that I bring it to the state of being clearly visible, but also that I make it count as a figure and as nearer to me than the other face, in a word I organize the cube, and the gaze is that perceptual genius underlying the thinking subject which can give to things the precise reply that they are awaiting in order to exist before us.

What, then, to sum up, *is* seeing a cube? It is, say empiricists, associating, with the actual aspect of the drawing presented, a set of other appearances, those which it would present at closer quarters, from the side, from various angles. But, when I see a cube, I do not find any of these images in myself, they are the small change of a perception of depth which makes them possible, but which does not result from them What, then, is thus single act whereby I grasp the possibility of all these appearances? It is, according to intellectualism, the thought of the cube as a solid made up of six equal faces and twelve equal lines at right angles to each other—and depth is nothing but the co-existence of the faces and the equal lines But here again we are being given as a definition of depth what is no more than a consequence of it. The six faces and twelve equal lines are not the whole significance of depth, and yet this definition has no meaning without depth The six faces and twelve lines can both co-exist and remain equal for me only if they are arranged in depth The act which corrects the appearances, giving to the acute or obtuse angles the value of right angles, to the distorted sides the value of a square, is not the idea of the geometrical relations of equality, and the geometrical mode of being to which they belong—it is the investing of the object by my gaze which penetrates and animates it, and shows up immediately the lateral faces as 'squares seen askew', to the extent that we do not even see them in their diamond-shaped, perspective aspect. This being simultaneously present in experiences which are nevertheless mutually exclusive, this implication of one in the other, this contraction into one perceptual act of a whole possible process, constitute the originality of depth It is the dimension in which things or elements of things envelop each other, whereas breadth and height are the dimensions in which they are juxtaposed.

One cannot, therefore, speak of a synthesis of depth, since a synthesis presupposes, or at least, like the Kantian synthesis, posits discrete terms, and since depth does not posit the multiplicity of perspective appearances to be made explicit by analysis, but sees that multiplicity only against the background of the stable thing. This quasi-synthesis is elucidated if we understand it as temporal When I say that I see an object at a distance, I mean that I already hold it, or that I still hold it, it is in the future or in the past as well as being in space.[1] It will perhaps be said that it is there only for me in itself the lamp which I perceive exists at the same time as I do, that distance is between simultaneous objects, and that this simultaneity is contained in the very meaning of perception No doubt. But co-existence, which in fact defines space, is not alien to time, but is the fact of two phenomena belonging to the same temporal wave. As for the relationship of the perceived object to my perception, it does not unite them in space and outside time: they are *contemporary* The 'order of co-existents' is inseparable from the 'order of sequences', or rather time is not only the consciousness of a sequence. Perception provides me with a 'field of presence'[2] in the broad sense, extending in two dimensions. the here-there dimension and the past-present-future dimension. The second elucidates the first. I 'hold', I 'have' the distant object without any explicit positing of the spatial perspective (apparent size and shape) as I still 'have in hand'[3] the immediate past without any distortion and without any interposed 'recollection'. If we want to talk about synthesis, it will be, as Husserl says, a 'transitional synthesis', which does not link disparate perspectives, but brings about the 'passage' from one to the other Psychology has involved itself in endless difficulties by trying to base memory on the possession of certain contents or recollections, the present traces (in the body or the unconscious) of the abolished past, for from these traces we can never come to understand the recognition of the past as past In the same way we shall never come to understand the perception of distance if we start from contents presented, so to speak, all equidistant, a flat projection of the world, as recollections are a projection of the past in the present And just as memory can be understood only as a direct possession of the past with no interposed contents, so the perception of distance can be understood only as a *being in the distance* which links up with being where it appears.

---

[1] The idea of depth as a spatio-temporal dimension is indicated by Straus *Vom Sinn der Sinne*, pp 302 and 306

[2] Husserl, *Präsenzfeld* It is defined in *Zeitbewusstsein*, pp. 32–5

[3] Ibid

Memory is built out of the progressive and continuous passing of one instant into another, and the interlocking of each one, with its whole horizon, in the thickness of its successor. The same continuous transition implies the object as it is out there, with, in short, its 'real' size as I should see it if I were beside it, in the perception that I have of it from here Just as there is no possibility of engaging in any discussion of the 'conservation of recollections', but only of a certain way of seeing time which brings out the past as an inalienable dimension of consciousness, there is no problem of distance, distance being immediately visible provided that we can find the living present in which it is constituted.

As we pointed out at the beginning, we have to rediscover beneath depth as a relation between things or even between planes, which is objectified depth detached from experience and transformed into breadth, a primordial depth, which confers upon the other its significance, and which is the thickness of a medium devoid of any thing. At those times when we allow ourselves simply to be in the world without actively assuming it, or in cases of illness favouring this passive attitude, different planes are no longer distinguishable, and colours are no longer condensed into superficial colours, but are diffused round about objects and become atmospheric colours For example, the patient who writes on a sheet of paper has to penetrate a certain thickness of whiteness with his pen before reaching the paper. This voluminosity varies with the colour in question, and is, as it were, the expression of its qualitative essence [1] There is, then, a depth which does not yet operate between objects, which, *a fortiori*, does not yet assess the distance between them, and which is simply the opening of perception upon some ghost thing as yet scarcely qualified Even in normal perception depth is not initially applicable to things. Just as top and bottom, right and left are not given to the subject with the perceived contents, and are at each moment constituted with a spatial level in relation to which things arrange themselves—in the same way depth and size come to things in virtue of their being situated in relation to a level of distances and sizes,[2] which defines the far and the near, the great and the small, before any object arises to provide us with a standard for comparison When we say that an object is huge or tiny, nearby or far away, it is often without any comparison, even implicit, with any other object, or even with the size and objective position of our own body, but merely in relation to a certain 'scope' of our gestures, a certain 'hold' of the phenomenal body on its surroundings If we refused to recognize this

[1] Gelb and Goldstein, *Über den Wegfall der Wahrnehmung von Oberflächenfarben*

[2] Wertheimer, *Experimentelle Studien*, Anhang, pp 259-61

rootedness of sizes and distances, we should be sent from one 'standard' object to another and fail ever to understand how sizes or distances can exist for us The pathological experience of micropsy or macropsy, altering as it does the apparent size of all the objects in the field, leaves no standard in relation to which objects can appear either larger or smaller than usual, and is to be understood only by reference to a pre-objective standard of distances and sizes Thus depth cannot be understood as belonging to the thought of an acosmic subject, but as a possibility of a subject involved in the world

This analysis of depth links up with the one which we have tried to make of height and breadth If, in this section, we first of all set depth over against the other dimensions, this was merely because they appear, at first sight, to be concerned with the relationships of things among themselves, whereas depth immediately reveals the link between the subject and space But we saw above that in reality the vertical and horizontal too are ultimately to be defined as the best hold our body can take upon the world. Breadth and height, as relations between objects, are derivative, and, viewed in their primary significance, they too are 'existential' dimensions. We cannot be content to say with Lagneau and Alain that height and breadth *presuppose* depth because a spectacle on a single plane supposes the equidistance of all its parts from the plane of my face thus analysis concerns only breadth, height and depth already objectified, and not the experience which opens these dimensions to us. The vertical and the horizontal, the near and the far are abstract designations for one single form of being in a situation, and they presuppose the same setting face to face of subject and world

Movement is a displacement or change of position, even if it cannot be defined as such As we initially encountered an idea of position which defines it in terms of relationships in objective space, so there is an objective conception of movement which defines it in terms of relations within the world, taking the experience of the world for granted. And just as we had to trace back the origin of the positing of space to the pre-objective situation or locality of the subject fastening himself on to his environment, so we shall have to rediscover, beneath the objective idea of movement, a pre-objective experience from which it borrows its significance, and in which movement, still linked to the person perceiving it, is a variation of the subject's hold on his world When we try to think of movement, and arrive at a philosophy of movement, we immediately place ourselves in a critical or verificatory attitude, we ask ourselves what precisely is given to us in movement, we make ready to reject appearances in

order to reach the truth concerning movement, and we remain unaware that it is precisely this attitude which reduces the phenomenon
and must prevent us from coming to grips with it, because it introduces, with the notion of truth in itself, assumptions liable to conceal
from me the genesis of movement for me. Suppose that I throw a
stone It hurtles across the garden. For a moment it becomes an indistinct meteor-like object, and then a stone again when it falls to the
ground some distance away If I want to think 'clearly' about the
phenomenon, it has to be decomposed. The stone itself, I shall say,
is in reality not modified by movement. It is the same stone that I
held in my hand, and that I now find again on the ground at the end
of its flight, and therefore it is the same stone that moved through the
air Movement is merely an accidental attribute of the moving body,
and it is not, so to speak, seen in the stone It can be only a change in
the relations between the stone and its surroundings. We can speak
of movement only so long as it is the same stone which persists
through the different relations with those surroundings. If, on the
other hand, I suppose that the stone is abolished on arriving at point
P, and that another identical stone arises out of nothingness at point
P' which is as close as we like to make it to the first, we no longer have
one single movement, but two There is, then, no movement without
a moving body which bears it uninterruptedly from start to finish
Since it is in no way inherent in the moving body, and consists wholly
in its relations with its surroundings, movement cannot dispense with
an external landmark, and indeed there is no way of attributing it
strictly to the 'body in motion' rather than to the landmark. Once
the distinction has been established between the body in motion and
movement, there is no movement without a moving body, no movement without an objective landmark, and no absolute movement.
Nevertheless this idea of movement is in fact a negation of movement to distinguish strictly between movement and the moving
object is to say that strictly speaking the 'moving body' *does not move*
If the stone-in-motion is not in some way different from the stone at
rest, it *is* never in motion (nor for that matter at rest) As soon as we
bring in the idea of a moving body which remains the same throughout its motion, Zeno's arguments become valid once more. It is, then,
useless to object that we must not regard motion as a series of discontinuous positions successively occupied in a series of discontinuous instants, and that space and time are not made up from a
collection of discrete elements For even if we consider two ultimate
instants and two ultimate points, the difference between them in each
case being smaller than any given quantity, and their differentiation
being at an incipient stage, the idea of a moving body identical
throughout the phases of motion excludes, as a mere appearance, the

phenomenon of 'shift', and implies the idea of a spatial and temporal position always identifiable in itself, even if it is not so for us, and therefore that of a stone which always is and never changes. Even if we invent a mathematical instrument which allows account to be taken of an indefinite multiplicity of positions and instants, it is impossible to conceive in one and the same moving body the very act of transition which always occurs between two instants and two positions, in whatever proximity to each other we choose them So that, in thinking clearly about movement, I do not understand how it can ever begin for me, and be given to me as a phenomenon.

And yet I walk, I have the experience of movement in spite of the demands and dilemmas of clear thought, which means, in defiance of all reason, that I perceive movements without any identical moving object, without any external landmark and without any relativity. If we present to a subject alternately two lines of light A and B, the subject sees a continuous movement from A to B, then from B to A, then again from A to B and so on, even though no intermediate position or indeed the extreme positions be given for themselves; we have one single line ceaselessly moving

Fig 1

back and forth. It is, however, possible to bring out distinctly the extreme positions by quickening up or slowing down the speed of presentation. The stroboscopic movement then tends to be broken up: the line appears first of all held in position A, then suddenly frees itself and jumps to position B. If we go on accelerating or slowing down the rhythm, the stroboscopic movement comes to an end and we are left with two simultaneous lines or two successive ones.[1] The perception of positions, therefore, varies inversely as that of movement It is even possible to show that movement is never the successive occupation, by a moving body, of every position between two extremes. If, for the stroboscopic movement, we use white or coloured figures on a black background, the space through which the movement extends is at no time illuminated or coloured by it If, between the extreme positions A and B, we interpose a short rod C, the rod is at no time completed by the passing movement (Fig 1) We have not a 'passage of the line', but a pure 'passage'. If we work with a tachistoscope, the subject often perceives a movement without being able to say what it is that moves When it is a question of real movements, the situation is no different if I watch workmen unloading a lorry and throwing bricks from one to another, I see the man's arm in its initial and then in its final position, yet, although I do not see it in any intermediate position, I have a vivid perception of its movement.

[1] Wertheimer, *Experimentelle Studien*, pp 212-14

If I quickly move a pencil across a sheet of paper on which I have
marked a point, at no instant am I conscious of the pencil's being over
the point, I see none of the intermediate positions and yet I am aware
of movement Conversely, if I slow down the movement and succeed
in not losing sight of the pencil, at that very moment the impression
of motion disappears [1] The movement disappears at the very moment
when it conforms most closely with the definition which objective
thought gives of it. Thus one can obtain phenomena in which the moving object appears only as caught up in movement. For such an object
moving is not passing successively through an indefinite series of
positions, it is given only as beginning, pursuing or completing its
movement Consequently, even in cases where the moving object is
visible, movement does not bear to it the relation of an extrinsic
entity, a relation between it and the outside, and we shall be able to
have movement without any fixed mark Indeed, if we project the
consecutive image of a movement on to a homogeneous field containing no object and having no outline, the movement takes possession
of the whole space, and what is shifting is the whole visual field, as
in the Haunted House at the fair If we project on to the screen the
post-image of a spiral revolving round its centre, in the absence of any
fixed framework, space itself vibrates and dilates from the centre to
the periphery [2] Finally, since motion is no longer a system of relations
external to the object in motion, nothing now prevents us from recognizing absolute movements, such as perception actually presents to
us constantly.

But to this description the objection can always be raised that it is
meaningless. The psychologist rejects the rational analysis of motion,
and when it is pointed out to him that all movement, in order to be
movement, must be movement of something, he replies that 'that has
no basis in psychological description'.[3] But if what the psychologist
describes is a movement, it must be related to some one identical
thing which moves If I place my watch on the table of my room, and
it suddenly disappears only to reappear a few seconds later on the
table in the next room, I do not say that there has been motion;[4]
there is motion only if the intermediate positions have been actually
occupied by the watch. Even though the psychologist may show that
stroboscopic motion is produced without any intermediate *stimulus*
between the extreme positions, and even that the luminous line A does
not travel through the space which separates it from B, that no light
is perceived between A and B during stroboscopic motion, and, in

[1] Wertheimer, *Experimentelle Studien*, pp 221–33
[2] Ibid , pp 254–5.   [3] Ibid , p 245
[4] Linke, *Phänomenologie und Experiment in der Frage der Bewegungsauffassung*,
p 653

fact, that I do not see the pencil or the workman's arm between the two extreme positions, the fact remains that in some way or other the moving body must have been present at each point of the journey for movement to be apparent, and though it is not perceptibly present in all these places, it is thought of as there What is true of movement is true of change when I say that the fakir changes an egg into a hand-kerchief, or that the magician changes himself into a bird on the roof of his palace[1] I do not mean merely that an object or a being has dis-appeared and been immediately replaced by another. There must be some internal relationship between what is abolished and what comes into being; both must be two manifestations or two appearances, or two stages of one and the same something which is presented succes-sively in two forms.[2] In the same way the arrival of movement at a point must be one with its departure from the 'adjacent' point, and this takes place only if there is an object in motion which simul-taneously leaves one place and occupies another 'A something which is apprehended as a circle would cease to count for us as a circle the moment "roundness" or the identity of all the diameters, which is essential to the circle, ceased to be present in it Whether the circle be perceived or visualized, is a matter of indifference; a common specificness needs to be present which forces us in either case to characterize as a circle the thing presented to us, and to distinguish it from any other phenomenon '[3] Similarly when we speak of a sensa-tion of movement, or of a consciousness *sui generis* of movement, or, like the Gestalt psychologists, of a global movement, a phenomenon ϕ in which no moving object and no particular position of a moving object is given, this is merely verbiage unless we say how 'what is given in this sensation or this phenomenon, or what is grasped through them, is immediately conveyed (*dokumentiert*) as move-ment'[4] Perception of movement can be perception *of movement* and recognition of it as such, only if it is apprehension of it with its signi-ficance as movement, and with all the instants which constitute it, and in particular with the identity of the object in motion Move-ment, the psychologist replies, is 'one of those "psychic phenomena" which, like given sense contents such as colour and form, are related to the object, appearing as objective and not subjective, but which, unlike other mental data, are not of a static but of a dynamic nature For example, the characteristic and specific "passing effect" is the flesh and blood of movement which cannot be composed from ordi-nary visual contents'[5] Indeed it is not possible to build motion out

[1] Linke, *Phänomenologie und Experiment in der Frage der Bewegungsauffassung*, pp 656–7
[2] Ibid   [3] Ibid , p 660   [4] Ibid , p 661
[5] Wertheimer, op cit., p. 227

of static perceptions. But we are not concerned with this, and there is no question of trying to reduce movement to a state of rest The object at rest also needs identification. It cannot be said to be at rest if it is constantly annihilated and recreated, and if it does not survive through its different instantaneous presentations The identity to which we refer is, therefore, anterior to the distinction between movement and rest Motion is nothing without a body in motion which describes and provides it with unity Here the metaphor of the dynamic phenomenon leads the psychologist astray· it seems to us that a force itself ensures its unity, but this is because we always suppose that someone is there to identify it in the development of its effects 'Dynamic phenomena' take their unity from me who live through them, and who effect their synthesis Thus we pass from an idea of movement which is destructive of it to an experience of movement which tries to provide it with a basis, but also from this experience to an idea without which, strictly speaking, the experience is meaningless

We cannot, then, regard either the psychologist or the logician as vindicated, or rather both must be considered vindicated and we must find a means of recognizing thesis and antithesis as both true. The logician is right when he demands some constitution of the 'dynamic phenomenon' itself, and a description of movement in terms of the moving object which we follow through its course—but he is wrong when he presents the identity of the object in motion as an express identity, and this he is forced to recognize himself The psychologist, on the other hand, when describing phenomena as faithfully as possible, is led in spite of himself to put a moving body into movement, but he recovers the advantage through the concrete way in which he conceives this body In the discussion which we have just followed, and which serves to illustrate the everlasting debate between psychology and logic, what, in the last resort, does Wertheimer mean? He means that the perception of movement is not secondary to the perception of the moving object, that we have not a perception of the latter here, then there, followed by an identification linking these positions in a succession,[1] that their diversity is not subsumed under any transcendent unity, and that in short the identity of the object in motion flows directly from 'experience'.[2] In other words, when the psychologist speaks of movement as a phenomenon which embraces

---

[1] The identity of the moving object, says Wertheimer, is not the fruit of a conjecture 'Here and there this *must* be the same object' (p 187)

[2] It is true that Wertheimer does not say in so many words that the perception of motion embraces this immediate identity He says so only implicitly, when he accuses an intellectualist conception, which relates movement to a judgement, of giving us an identity which 'fliesst nicht direkt aus dem Erlebnis' (p 187)

starting point A and arrival point B (AB), he does not mean that there is no subject of movement, but that in no case is the subject of movement an object A initially given as present and static in its place in so far as there is movement, the moving object is caught up in that movement. The psychologist would no doubt allow that there is, in every movement, if not an object in motion, at least a mobile entity, provided that this mobile entity is not confused with any of the static figures which can be extracted by halting the movement at any point on its course And here he has the advantage over the logician For, through not having gone back to the experience of movement independently of any preconceived notion about the world, the logician is talking only about movement in itself, and expressing the problem of movement in terms of being, which makes it insoluble in the last resort If we take, he says, different appearances (*Erscheinungen*) of movement at different points on its course, they will be appearances of one and the same movement only if they are appearances of one and the same object in motion, of one and the same *Erscheinende*, of one and the same something which presents itself (*darstellt*) through them all. But the moving object needs to be posited as a being apart only if its appearances at different points have themselves been brought into being as discrete perspectives The logician knows, on principle, only positing* consciousness, and it is this postulate, this supposition of a wholly determinate world, of pure being, which bedevils his conception of multiplicity and consequently of synthesis. The moving object or rather, as we have called it, the mobile entity, is not identical *beneath* the phases of movement, it is identical *in* them It is not because I find the same stone on the ground that I believe in its identity throughout its movement It is, on the contrary, because I perceived it as identical during that movement—with an implicit identity which remains to be described—that I go to pick it up and recover it. We shall not find in the stone-in-movement everything that we know in other ways about the stone If what I perceive is a circle, says the logician, all its diameters *are* equal But, on this basis, we should equally have to put into the perceived circle all the properties which the geometer has been able and will be able to discover in it. Now it is the circle as a thing in the world which possesses in advance and in itself all the properties which analysis is destined to discover in it. The circular trunks of trees had already, before Euclid, the properties that Euclid discovered in them But in the circle as a phenomenon, as it appeared to the Greeks before Euclid, the square of the tangent was not equal to the product of the whole chord and its exterior portion. the square and the product did not appear in the phenomenon, nor necessarily did the equal radii The

* 'thetic' (Translator's note).

273

moving object, as object of an indefinite series of explicit and concordant perceptions, his properties, the mobile entity has only a style. What is impossible is that the perceived circle should have unequal diameters or that movement should exist without any mobile entity. But for all that, the perceived circle does not have equal diameters because it has no diameter at all: it is conveyed to me, and is recognizable and distinguishable from any other figure by its circular physiognomy, and not by any of the 'properties' which positing* thought may subsequently discover in it. Similarly movement does not necessarily pre-suppose a moving object, that is, an object defined in terms of a collection of determinate properties; it is sufficient that it should include 'something that moves', or at the most 'something coloured' or 'luminous' without any actual colour or light. The logician excludes this middle term: the radii of the circle must be either equal or unequal, motion must either have or not have a moving body. But he can do so only by taking the circle as a thing or by taking movement in itself. Now we have seen that this amounts to making motion impossible. The logician would have nothing to conceive, not even an appearance of movement, if there were not a movement anterior to the objective world which is the source of all our assertions about movement, if there were not phenomena anterior to being which one can recognize, identify, and talk about, in a word which have a significance, even though they are not yet thematized [1] It is to this phenomenal layer that the psychologist leads us back. We do not say that it is irrational or anti-logical. This would be so only of the positing of a movement without an object in motion. Only the explicit denial of the moving object would be contrary to the principle of the excluded middle. We need to say merely that the phenomenal layer is literally prelogical and will always remain so. Our image of

* 'thetic' (Translator's note)

[1] Linke eventually concedes (op. cit., pp. 664-5) that the subject of movement can be indeterminate (as when we see, in stroboscopic presentation, a triangle moving towards a circle and being transformed into it), that the object in motion has no need to be posited by an act of explicit perception, that it is merely a 'co-target' or 'co-apprehension' in the perception of movement, that it is seen only as the backs of objects or the space behind me are seen, and that finally the identity of the moving object, like the unity of the thing perceived, is apprehended through a categorial perception (Husserl) in which the category is operative without being conceived for itself. But the notion of categorial perception once more calls the whole of the preceding analysis into question. For it amounts to introducing non-thetic consciousness into the perception of movement, that is, as we have shown, it amounts to rejecting not only the *a priori* as essential necessity, but also the Kantian notion of synthesis. Linke's work belongs to, and is typical of, the second period of Husserlian phenomenology, which marks a transition from the eidetic method or logicism of the earlier stage to the existentialism of the last period.

the world can be made up only in part of actual being, and we must find a place in it for the phenomenal realm which surrounds being on all sides. We are not asking the logician to take into consideration experiences which, in the light of reason, are nonsensical or contradictory, we merely want to push back the boundaries of what makes sense for us, and reset the narrow zone of thematic significance within that of non-thematic significance which embraces it The thematization of movement ends with the identical object in motion and with the relativity of movement, which means that it destroys movement If we want to take the phenomenon of movement seriously, we shall need to conceive a world which is not made up only of things, but which has in it also pure transitions. The something in transit which we have recognized as necessary to the constitution of a change is to be defined only in terms of the particular manner of its 'passing'. For example, the bird which flies across my garden is, during the time that it is moving, merely a greyish power of flight and, generally speaking, we shall see that things are defined primarily in terms of their 'behaviour' and not in terms of their static 'properties' It is not I who recognize, in each of the points and instants passed through, the same bird defined by explicit characteristics, it is the bird in flight which constitutes the unity of its movement, which changes its place, it is this flurry of plumage still here, which is already there in a kind of ubiquity, like the comet with its tail. Pre-objective being, the non-thematized mobile entity sets merely the problem of implied space and time which we have already discussed We said that the parts of space seen as breadth, height or depth, are not juxtaposed, but that they co-exist because they are all drawn into the hold that our body takes upon the world This relation was already elucidated when we showed that it is temporal before being spatial Things co-exist in space because they are *present* to the same perceiving subject and enveloped in one and the same temporal wave But the unity and individuality of each temporal wave is possible only if it is wedged in between the preceding and the following one, and if the same temporal pulsation which produces it still retains its predecessor and anticipates its successor It is objective time which is made up of successive moments The lived present holds a past and a future within its thickness The phenomenon of movement merely displays spatial and temporal implications in a more striking way We know of movement and a moving entity without being in any way aware of objective positions, as we know of an object at a distance and of its true size without any interpretation, and as we know every moment the place of an event in the thickness of our past without any express recollection Motion is a modulation of an already familiar setting, and once more it leads us back to our central problem, which is how

275

this setting, which acts as a background to every act of consciousness, comes to be constituted.[1]

The positing of an identical mobile object led to the relativity of movement Now that we have reintroduced movement into the object

[1] This problem cannot be posed without already outrunning realism and, for example, the celebrated descriptions of Bergson Bergson's alternative to the multiplicity of things externally juxtaposed is the 'multiplicity of fusion and interpenetration' of consciousness He proceeds by way of dilution, speaking of consciousness as if it were a liquid in which instants and positions dissolve In it he looks for an element in which their dispersal is really abolished The indivisible action of my arm as I move it gives me that movement which I cannot find in external space, because my movement, when put back into my internal life, rediscovers there the unity of inextension The lived-through which Bergson sets over against the thought-about is for him an experience, an immediate 'datum'. But this is to seek a solution in ambiguity Space, motion and time cannot be elucidated by discovering an 'inner' layer of experience in which their multiplicity is erased and *really* abolished For if this happens, neither space, nor movement, nor time remains. The consciousness of my gesture, if it is truly a state of undivided consciousness, is no longer consciousness of movement at all, but an incommunicable quality which can tell us nothing about movement As Kant said, external experience is necessary to internal experience, which is indeed incommunicable, but incommunicable because meaningless If, in virtue of the principle of continuity, the past still belongs to the present and the present already to the past, there is no longer any past or present If consciousness snowballs upon itself, it is, like the snowball and everything else, wholly in the present If the phases of movement gradually merge into one another, nothing is anywhere in motion The unity of time, space and movement cannot come about through any coalescence, and cannot be understood either by any real operation If consciousness is multiplicity, who is to gather together this multiplicity in order to experience it as such, and if consciousness is fusion, how shall it come to know the multiplicity of the moments which it fuses together? Against Bergson's realism, the Kantian idea of synthesis is seen to be valid, and consciousness as an agent of this synthesis cannot be confused with any thing at all, even a fluid one What is for us primary and immediate, is a flux which does spread outwards like a liquid, but which, in an active sense, bears *itself* along, which it cannot do without knowing that it does so, and without drawing itself together in the same act whereby it bears itself along—it is that 'time which does not pass' of which Kant somewhere speaks For us, then, the unity of movement is not a real unity But neither is multiplicity real, and what we object to in the idea of synthesis in Kant, as in certain Kantian texts of Husserl, is precisely that it presupposes, at least theoretically, a real multiplicity which consciousness has to surmount What for us is primary consciousness is not a transcendental Ego freely positing before itself a multiplicity in itself, and constituting it throughout from start to finish, it is an *I* which dominates diversity only *with the help* of time, and for whom freedom itself is a destiny, so that I am never conscious of being the absolute creator of time, of composing the movement through which I live, I have the impression that it is the mobile entity itself which changes its position, and which effects the passage from one instant or one position to another This relative and prepersonal *I* who provides the basis for the phenomenon of movement and in general the phenomenon of the real, clearly demands some elucidation Let us say for the moment that we prefer, to the notion of synthesis, that of synopsis, which does not yet point to an explicit positing of diversity

in motion, this is to be interpreted in one sense only it is in the moving object that it begins, and from there spreads into the field I cannot force myself to see the stone as motionless, and the garden and myself as in motion Motion is not a hypothesis, the probability of which is measured as in physical theory by the number of facts which it co-ordinates. That would give only possible movement, whereas movement is a fact The stone is not conceived, but seen, in motion. For the hypothesis: 'It is the stone which is moving' would have no distinctive meaning, and would be indistinguishable from the hypothesis 'It is the garden which is moving', if motion both in fact and for reflection amounted to a mere change of relationships It therefore inhabits the stone And yet are we to recognize the psychologist's realism as fully justified? Are we going to put motion into the stone as a quality? It does not presuppose any relationship to an expressly perceived object, and remains possible in a perfectly homogeneous field The fact remains that every object in motion is given in a field Just as we need a mobile entity in movement, we need a basis for movement. It has been wrongly asserted that the edges of the visual field always furnish an objectively stable point.[1] Once again, the edge of the visual field is not a real line. Our visual field is not neatly cut out of our objective world, and is not a fragment with sharp edges like the landscape framed by the window We see as far as our hold on things extends, far beyond the zone of clear vision, and even behind us When we reach the limits of the visual field, we do not pass from vision to non-vision: the gramophone playing in the next room, and not expressly seen by me, still counts in my visual field Conversely, what we see is always in certain respects not seen: there must be hidden sides of things, and things 'behind us', if there is to be a 'front' of things, and things 'in front of' us, in short, perception. The limits of the visual field are a necessary stage in the organization of the world, and not an objective outline But it is nevertheless true that an object crosses our visual field, and changes its place in it, and that movement has no meaning outside this relationship. According as we give to a certain part of the field the value of figure or background, it appears to us to be moving or at rest. If we are on a ship sailing along the coast, it is true, as Leibnitz said, that we can watch the coast flowing by in front of us, or take it as a fixed point and feel the boat in motion. Do we then concede the logician his case? Not at all, for to say that motion is a structural phenomenon is not to say that it is 'relative' The very peculiar relationship which constitutes movement does not exist *between objects*, and is one which the psychologist, far from overlooking it, describes better than the logician It is the coast which slips by if we keep our eyes

[1] Wertheimer, op cit, pp 255-6

277

fixed on the rail, and the boat which glides along if we look at the coast Of two points of light seen in the dark, one static and the other moving, it is the one which one is looking at which appears to be in motion [1] The cloud floats over the steeple and the river flows under the bridge, if it is the cloud and the river that we are looking at. The steeple falls across the sky and the bridge slides over a static river if we are looking at the steeple or the bridge

What makes part of the field count as an object in motion, and another as the background, is the way in which we establish our relations with them by the act of looking. The stone flies through the air. What do these words mean, other than that our gaze, lodged and anchored in the garden, is attracted by the stone and, so to speak, drags at its anchors? The relation between the moving object and its background passes through our body How is this bodily mediation to be conceived? How does it come about that the relations of objects to it can differentiate them as in motion or at rest? Is not our body an object, and does it not itself need to be determinate in relation to rest and movement? It is often said that when we move our eyes, objects remain static for us because we take account of the shift of the eyes and that, finding it exactly proportionate to the change of appearances, we conclude in favour of the immobility of objects. In fact, if we are not conscious of any movement of the eye, as in the case of a passive shift of the gaze, the object seems to move If, in paresis of the oculo-motor muscles, we have the illusion of a movement of the eye, without any apparent change in the relation of objects to the eye, we think we see a movement of the object It seems at first as if, the relation of the object to our eye, as it is imprinted on the retina, being given to consciousness, the state of rest or degree of movement of objects is arrived at by a process of subtraction, in which we take into account the shift or immobility of our eye. In fact, this analysis is entirely artificial, and such as to conceal from us the real relationship between our body and the spectacle When I transfer my gaze from one object to another, I am unaware of my eye as an object, as a globe set in an orbit, of its movement or state of rest in objective space, or of what these throw upon the retina. The figures for the alleged calculation are not given to me The immobility of the thing is not inferred from the act of looking, it is strictly simultaneous with it, and the two phenomena envelop each other what we have is not two terms of an algebraic expression, but two 'moments' in an organization which embraces them both My eye for

---

[1] The laws governing the phenomenon would seem, then, to need more precise statement what is certain is that there are laws, and that the perception of movement, even when it is ambiguous, is not arbitrary and depends on the static point Cf Duncker, *Über induzierte Bewegung*

me is a certain power of making contact with things, and not a screen
on which they are projected. The relation of my eye to the object is
not given to me in the form of a geometrical projection of the object
in the eye, but as it were a hold taken by my eye upon the object, indistinct in marginal vision, but closer and more definite when I focus
upon the object What I lack when my eye moves passively, is not the
objective representation of its shift in the orbit, which in any case is
not given to me, but the exact gearing of my gaze to objects, without
which they are incapable of fixity, or indeed of genuine movement
for when I press on my eyeball, I do not perceive a true movement,
the things themselves are not moving, but only a thin film on their
surface In short, in cases of oculo-motor paresis, I do not explain the
constancy of the retinal image in terms of movement on the part of
the object, but I experience that the grip of my gaze on the object
does not relax, my gaze carries it and displaces it along with itself.
Thus my eye is never in the perception of an object If we can ever
speak of movement without an object in motion, it is pre-eminently
in the case of our own body The movement of my eye towards the
thing upon which it is about to focus is not the displacement of an
object in relation to another object, but progress towards reality. My
eye is in motion or at rest in relation to a thing which it is approaching or from which it is receding. In so far as the body provides the
perception of movement with the ground or basis which it needs in
order to become established, it is as a power of perception, rooted in
a certain domain and geared to a world Rest and movement appear
between an object which, in itself, is not determinate in relation to
either, and my body of which, as an object, the same is true when my
body anchors itself in certain objects Like top and bottom, motion is
a phenomenon of levels, every movement presupposing a certain
anchorage which is variable. So much can validly be said when we
talk obscurely about the relativity of movement. Now what precisely
is the anchorage and how does it constitute a background at rest? It
is not an explicit perception. The points of anchorage, when we focus
on them, are not objects The steeple begins to move only when I
leave the sky in the margin of vision It is essential to the alleged fixed
points underlying motion that they should not be posited in present
knowledge and that they should always be 'already there' They do
not present themselves directly to perception, they circumvent it and
encompass it by a preconscious process, the results of which strike us
as ready made. Cases of ambiguous perception in which we can at
will choose our anchorage are those in which our perception is artificially cut off from its context and its past, in which we do not perceive with our whole being, in which we play a game with our body
and with that generality which enables it at any time to break with

any historical commitment and to function on its own account. But although we can break with a human world, we cannot help focusing our eyes—which means that as long as we live we remain committed, if not in a human setting, at least in a physical one—and for any given focus of the gaze, perception is not arbitrary. Still less is it arbitrary when the life of the body is integrated to our concrete existence. I can at will see my own train or the train next to it in motion whether on the one hand I do nothing or on the other consider the illusions of motion. But 'when I am playing at cards in my compartment, I see the neighbouring train move off, even if it is really mine which is starting, when I look at the other train and try to pick out someone, then it is my own train which is set in motion'.[1] The compartment which we happen to occupy is 'at rest', its walls are 'vertical' and the landscape slips by before our eyes, and on a hill the firs seen through the window appear to us to slope. If we stand at the window, we return to the great world beyond our small one, the firs straighten themselves and remain stationary, and the train leans with the slope and speeds through the countryside. The relativity of motion reduces itself to the power which we have of changing our domain within the great world. Once involved in a setting, we see motion appear before us as an absolute. Provided that we take into account, not only acts of explicit knowledge, *cogitationes*, but also that more occult act, always in the past, by which we gave ourselves a world, provided that we recognize a non-thetic* consciousness, we can allow what the psychologist calls absolute movement without falling into the difficulties of realism, and understand the phenomenon of movement without allowing our logic to destroy it.

We have so far considered, as do traditional philosophy and psychology, only the *perception of space*, that is, the knowledge that a disinterested subject might acquire of the spatial relationships between objects and their geometrical characteristics. And yet, even in analysing this abstract function, which is far from covering the whole of our experience, we have been led to bring out, as the condition of spatiality, the establishment of the subject in a setting, and finally his inherence in a world. In other words, we have been forced to recognize that spatial perception is a structural phenomenon and is comprehensible only within a perceptual field which contributes in its entirety to motivating the spatial perception by suggesting to the subject a possible anchorage. The traditional problem of the perception of space and perception generally must be

[1] Koffka, *Perception*, p. 578

* I.e., non-positing (Translator's note)

reintegrated into a vaster problem. To ask how one can, in an explicit act, determine spatial relationships and objects with their 'properties', is to ask a second order question, to give as primary an act which appears only against the background of an already familiar world, to admit that one has not yet become conscious of the experience of the world. In the natural attitude, I do not have *perceptions*, I do not posit this object as beside that one, along with their objective relationships, I have a flow of experiences which imply and explain each other both simultaneously and successively Paris for me is not an object of many facets, a collection of perceptions, nor is it the law governing all these perceptions Just as a person gives evidence of the same emotional essence in his gestures with his hands, in his way of walking and in the sound of his voice, each express perception occurring in my journey through Paris—the cafés, people's faces, the poplars along the quays, the bends of the Seine—stands out against the city's whole being, and merely confirms that there is a certain style or a certain significance which Paris possesses And when I arrived there for the first time, the first roads that I saw as I left the station were, like the first words spoken by a stranger, simply manifestations of a still ambiguous essence, but one already unlike any other. Just as we do not see the eyes of a familiar face, but simply its look and its expression, so we perceive hardly any object There is present a latent significance, diffused throughout the landscape or the city, which we find in something specific and self-evident which we feel no need to define Only the ambiguous perceptions emerge as explicit acts perceptions, that is, to which we ourselves give a significance through the attitude which we take up, or which answer questions which we put to ourselves They cannot be of any use in the analysis of the perceptual field, since they are extracted from it at the very outset, since they presuppose it and since we come by them by making use of precisely those set groupings with which we have become familiar in dealing with the world.

An initial perception independent of any background is inconceivable. Every perception presupposes, on the perceiving subject's part, a certain past, and the abstract function of perception, as a coming together of objects, implies some more occult act by which we elaborate our environment. Under mescalin it happens that approaching objects appear to grow smaller. A limb or other part of the body, the hand, mouth or tongue seems enormous, and the rest of the body is felt as a mere appendage to it.[1] The walls of the room are 150 yards apart, and beyond the walls is merely an empty vastness The stretched-out hand is as high as the wall, and external space and

[1] Mayer-Gross and Stein, *Über einige Abänderungen der Sinnestätigkeit im Meskalinrausch*, p. 375

281

bodily space are divorced from each other to the extent that the subject has the impression of eating 'from one dimension to the other' [1] Sometimes motion is no longer seen, and people seem to be transported magically from one place to another.[2] The subject is alone and forlorn in empty space, 'he complains that all he can see clearly is the space between things, and that this space is empty. Objects are in a way still there, but not as one would expect. . . '[3] Men are like puppets and their movements are performed in a dreamlike slow-motion The leaves on the trees lose their armature and organization every point on the leaf has the same value as every other [4] One schizophrenic says 'A bird is twittering in the garden I can hear the bird and I know that it is twittering, but that it is a bird and that it is twittering, the two things seem so remote from each other .   There is a gulf between them, as if the bird and the twittering had nothing to do with each other.'[5] Another schizophrenic can no longer manage to 'understand' the clock, that is, in the first place the movement of the hands from one position to another, and especially the connection of this movement with the drive of the mechanism, the 'working' of the clock [6] These disturbances do not affect perception as know-ledge of the world the oversized parts of the body, the too small objects near at hand are not posited as such, for the patient the walls of the room are not far from each other as are the two ends of a football field for a normal person The subject is well aware that his food and his own body reside in the same space, since he takes food with his hand Space is 'empty', and yet all the objects of per-ception are there. The disturbance does not affect the information which may be derived from perception, but discloses beneath 'per-ception' a deeper life of consciousness Even where there is failure to perceive, as with regard to movement, the perceptual deficiency ap-pears as no more than an extreme case of a more general disturbance of the process of relating phenomena to each other There is a bird and there is twittering, but the bird no longer twitters There is a movement of the clock hands, and a spring, but the clock no longer 'goes'. In the same way certain parts of the body are enlarged out of all proportion, and adjacent objects made too small because the whole picture no longer forms a system Now, if the world is atom-ized or dislocated, this is because one's own body has ceased to be a

---

[1] Mayer-Gross and Stein, *Über einige Abänderungen der Sinnestätigkeit im Meskalinrausch*, p 377

[2] Ibid , p 381

[3] Fischer, *Zeitstruktur und Schizophrenie*, p 572

[4] Mayer-Gross and Stein, op cit , p 380

[5] Fischer, op cit , pp 558-9.

[6] Fischer, *Raum-Zeitstruktur und Denkstörung in der Schizophrenie*, pp 217 and ff

knowing body, and has ceased to draw together all objects in its one grip, and this debasement of the body into an organism must itself be attributed to the collapse of time, which no longer rises towards a future but falls back on itself 'Once I was a man, with a soul and a living body (*Leib*) and now I am no more than a being (*Wesen*) .
Now there remains merely the organism (*Korper*) and the soul is dead . . I hear and see, but no longer know anything, and living is now a problem for me .. I now live on in eternity . The branches sway on the trees, other people come and go in the room, but for me time no longer passes . . . Thinking has changed, and there is no longer any style. . . What is the future? It can no longer be reached. . . . Everything is in suspense . . . Everything is monotonous, morning, noon, evening, past, present and future Everything is constantly beginning all over again '[1] The perception of space is not a particular class of 'states of consciousness' or acts Its modalities are always an expression of the total life of the subject, the energy with which he tends towards a future through his body and his world.[2]

We thus find ourselves led to a broadening of our investigation Once the experience of spatiality is related to our implantation in the world, there will always be a primary spatiality for each modality of this implantation When, for example, the world of clear and articulate objects is abolished, our perceptual being, cut off from its world, evolves a spatiality without things. This is what happens in the night. Night is not an object before me; it enwraps me and infiltrates through all my senses, stifling my recollections and almost destroying my personal identity. I am no longer withdrawn into my perceptual look-out from which I watch the outlines of objects moving by at a distance Night has no outlines, it is itself in contact with me and its unity is the mystical unity of the *mana* Even shouts or a distant light people it only vaguely, and then it comes to life in its entirety, it is pure depth without foreground or background, without surfaces and without any distance separating it from me [3] All space for the reflecting mind is sustained by thinking which relates its parts to each other, but in this case the thinking starts from nowhere On the contrary, it is from the heart of nocturnal space that I become united with it. The distress felt by neuropaths in the night is caused by the fact that it brings home to us our contingency, the uncaused and tireless impulse which drives us to seek an anchorage and to surmount ourselves in things, without any guarantee that we shall always

[1] Fischer, *Zeitstruktur und Schizophrenie*, p 560
[2] 'The schizophrenic symptom is never anything but a path towards the schizophrenic person' Kronfeld, quoted by Fischer, *Zur Klinik und Psychologie des Raumlebens*, p 61
[3] Minkowski, *Le Temps vecu*, p 394

find them But there is a still more striking experience of unreality
than night provides I can at night retain the general setting of the
daytime, as when I grope about in my flat, and in any case night is
included in the general framework of nature, and there is something
reassuring and earthly even in pitch black space During sleep, on the
other hand, I hold the world present to me only in order to keep it at
a distance, and I revert to the subjective sources of my existence The
phantasms of dreams reveal still more effectively that general spatiality within which clear space and observable objects are embedded
Let us consider, for example, the themes of rising and falling so frequently met in dreams, as indeed in mythology and poetry It is well
known that the appearance of these themes in dreams can be related
to concomitant respiratory states or sexual drives, and it is a first
step to recognize the vital and sexual significance of up and down
But these explanations do not get us very far, for dreamed-of elevation or falling are not to be found in visible space, as are the waking
perceptions associated with desire and the movement of breathing.
We must understand why at a given moment the dreamer lends himself wholly to the physical facts of respiration and desire, and thus
fills them with a general and symbolic significance to the extent of
seeing them appear in the dream simply as an image—for example,
the image of a great bird hovering, which, hit by a shot, falls and is
reduced to a small heap of charred paper. We must understand how
respiratory or sexual events, which have a place in objective space,
are drawn away from it in the dream state, and settle in a different
theatre But we shall not succeed in doing so unless we endow the
body, even in the waking state, with an emblematic value. Between
our emotions, desires and bodily attitudes, there is not only a contingent connection or even an analogical relationship if I say that in
disappointment I am downcast, it is not only because it is accompanied by gestures expressing prostration in virtue of the laws governing nervous mechanisms, or because I discover between the objects
of my desire and my desire itself the same relationship as exists between an object placed high above me and my gesture towards it
The movement upwards as a direction in physical space, and that of
desire towards its objective are mutually symbolical, because they
both express the same essential structure of our being, being situated
in relation to an environment, of which we have already stated that
this structure alone gives significance to the directions up and down
in the physical world When we speak of an elevated or a low morality, we are not extending to the mental a relationship the full significance of which is to be found only in the physical world, we are
making use of 'a direction of significance which, so to speak, runs
through the various regional spheres and receives a particular signifi-

cance (spatial, auditory, spiritual, mental, etc) in each one'.[1] The phantasms of dreaming, of mythology, the favourite images of each man or indeed poetic imagery, are not linked to their meaning by a relation of sign to significance, like the one existing between a telephone number and the name of the subscriber; they really contain their meaning, which is not a notional meaning, but a direction of our existence. When I dream that I am flying or falling, the whole significance of the dream is contained in the flight or the fall, as long as I do not reduce them to their physical appearance in the waking world, and so long as I take them with all their existential implications. The bird which hovers, falls and becomes a handful of ash, does not hover and fall in physical space; it rises and falls with the existential tide running through it, or again it is the pulse of my existence, its systole and diastole. The level of this tide at each moment conditions a space peopled with phantasms, just as, in waking life, our dealings with the world which is offered to us condition a space peopled with realities. There is a determining of up and down, and in general of place, which precedes 'perception' Life and sexuality haunt their world and their space. Primitive peoples, in so far as they live in a world of myth, do not overstep this existential space, and this is why for them dreams count just as much as perceptions There is a mythical space in which directions and positions are determined by the residence in it of great affective entities For primitive man, knowing the whereabouts of the tribal encampment does not consist in locating it in relation to some object serving as a landmark for it is the landmark of all landmarks—it is to tend towards it as towards the natural abode of a certain peace or a certain joyfulness, just as, for me, to know where my hand is is to link up with that agile power which is for the moment dormant, but which I can take up and rediscover as my own. For the augur, right and left are the sources of the lawful and the forbidden, just as for me my right hand and my left are respectively the incarnations of my skill and my awkwardness In dreaming as in myth we learn *where* the phenomenon is to be found, by feeling that towards which our desire goes out, what our hearts dreads, on what our life depends Even in waking life things are no different. I arrive in a village for my holidays, happy to leave my work and my everyday surroundings. I settle in the village, and it becomes the centre of my life. The low level of the river, gathering in the maize crop or nutting are events for me But if a friend comes to see me bringing news from Paris, or if the press and radio tell me that war threatens, I feel an exile in the village, shut off from real life, pushed far away from everything. Our body and our perception always summon us to take as the centre of the world that environment

[1] L Binswanger, *Traum und Existenz*, p 674.

with which they present us But this environment is not necessarily that of our own life I can 'be somewhere else' while staying
here, and if I am kept far away from what I love, I feel out of touch
with real life. The Bovary mentality and certain forms of home-sick-
ness are examples of life which has become decentred. The maniac,
on the other hand, is centred wherever he is: 'his mental space is
broad and luminous, and his thought, sensitive to all objects which
present themselves, flies from one to the other and is caught up in
their movement' [1] Besides the physical and geometrical distance
which stands between myself and all things, a 'lived' distance binds
me to things which count and exist for me, and links them to each
other. This distance measures the 'scope' of my life at every moment [2]
Sometimes between myself and the events there is a certain amount of
play (*Spielraum*), which ensures that my freedom is preserved while
the events do not cease to concern me Sometimes, on the other
hand, the lived distance is both too small and too great: the majority
of the events cease to count for me, while the nearest ones obsess me.
They enshroud me like night and rob me of my individuality and
freedom I can literally no longer breathe, I am possessed.[3] At the
same time events conglomerate among themselves One patient feels
icy blasts of wind, a smell of chestnuts and the coolness of rain Perhaps, he says, 'at that very moment a person undergoing suggestions,
as I was, was walking in the rain past a roast chestnut stall' [4] A
schizophrenic, who is under the care of both Minkowski and a village
priest, thinks that they have met to discuss him.[5] An old schizophrenic woman thinks that someone who is very like someone else has
known her [6] The shrinkage of lived space, which leaves no margin to
the patient, leaves no room for chance Like space, causality, before
being a relation between objects, is based on my relation to things.
The 'short-circuits'[7] of delirious causality, no less than the long
causal chains of methodical thought, express ways of existing [8] 'the

---

[1] Binswanger, *Über Ideenflucht*, pp 78 and ff

[2] Minkowski, *Les Notions de distance vécue et d'ampleur de la vie et leur application en psychopathologie* Cf *Le Temps vécu*, Chap VII

[3] 'In the street, a kind of murmur *completely envelops him*, similarly he feels
deprived of his freedom as if there were always people present *round about him*,
at the café there seems to be something nebulous *around him* and he feels to be
trembling, and when the voices are particularly frequent and numerous, the
atmosphere *round him* is saturated with a kind of fire, and this produces a sort of
oppression inside the heart and lungs and something in the nature of a mist round
about his head ' Minkowski, *Le Problème des Hallucinations et le problème de
l'Espace*, p 69.

[4] Ibid   [5] *Le Temps vécu*, p. 376
[6] Ibid , p 379   [7] Ibid , p 381

[8] That is why one can say with Scheler (*Idealismus-Realismus*, p 298) that
Newton's space translates the 'emptiness of the heart'

experience of space is interwoven . . . with all the other modes of experience and all the other psychic data.'[1] Clear space, that impartial space in which all objects are equally important and enjoy the same right to existence, is not only surrounded, but also thoroughly permeated by another spatiality thrown into relief by morbid deviations from the normal A schizophrenic patient, in the mountains, stops before a landscape After a short time he feels a threat hanging over him There arises within him a special interest in everything surrounding him, as if a question were being put to him from outside to which he could find no answer. Suddenly the landscape is snatched away from him by some alien force It is as if a second sky, black and boundless, were penetrating the blue sky of evening. This new sky is empty, 'subtle, invisible and terrifying' Sometimes it moves in the autumn landscape and at other times the landscape too moves Meanwhile, says the patient, 'a question is being constantly put to me, it is, as it were, an order either to rest or die, or else to push on further'[2] This second space which cuts across visible space is the one which is ceaselessly composed by our own way of projecting the world, and the schizophrenic's trouble consists simply in the fact that the permanent project becomes dissociated from the objective world as the latter is presented to perception, and withdraws, so to speak, within itself. The schizophrenic no longer inhabits the common property world, but a private world, and no longer gets as far as geographical space he dwells in 'the landscape space',[3] and the landscape itself, once cut off from the common property world, is considerably impoverished. Hence the schizophrenic questioning. everything is amazing, absurd or unreal, because the impulse of existence towards things has lost its energy, because it appears to itself in all its contingency and because the world can no longer be taken for granted In so far as the natural space talked about by traditional psychology is by contrast reassuring and self-evident, this is because existence rushes towards it, and being absorbed in it, is unaware of itself.

The description of human space could be developed indefinitely.[4]

[1] Fischer, *Zur Klinik und Psychologie des Raumerlebens*, p 70.
[2] Fischer, *Raum-Zeitstruktur und Denkstorung in der Schizophrenie*, p 253.
[3] E. Straus, *Vom Sinn der Sinne*, p 290
[4] One might show, for example, that aesthetic perception too opens up a new spatiality, that the picture as a work of art is not in the space which it inhabits as a physical thing and as a coloured canvas That the dance evolves in an aimless and unorientated space that it is a suspension of our history, that in the dance the subject and his world are no longer in opposition, no longer stand out one against the background of the other, that in consequence the parts of the body are no longer thrown into relief as in natural experience· the trunk is no longer the ground from which movements arise and to which they sink back once performed, it now governs the dance and the movements of the limbs are its auxiliaries.

It is clear what fault objective thought will always find with it. have these descriptions any philosophical value? That is to say do they teach us anything concerning the structure itself of consciousness, or do they present us merely with contents of human experience? Are the spaces belonging to dreams, myths and schizophrenia genuine spaces, can they exist and be thought of by themselves, or do they not rather presuppose, as the condition of their possibility, geometrical space and with it the pure constituting consciousness which deploys it? The left, the area associated in the primitive mind with misfortune and ill omen—or in my own body the side associated with awkwardness—becomes specifically a direction only if I am first of all capable of conceiving its relation to the right, and it is this relation which ultimately gives a spatial significance to the terms between which it stands. It is not, so to speak, with his anguish or his joy that primitive man 'aims at' a certain space, as it is not with my pain that I know where my injured foot is: anguish, joy and pain experienced are related to a locality in objective space in which their empirical conditions are to be found But for this agile consciousness, free in relation to all contents and deploying them in space, those contents would never be anywhere at all. If we think about the mythical experience of space, and if we ask what it means, we shall necessarily find that it rests on the consciousness of a single objective space, for a space not objective and not unique would not be a space: is it not of the essence of space to be the absolute 'outside', correlative to, but also the negation of, subjectivity, and is it not of its essence to embrace every being that one can imagine, since anything that one might want to posit outside it would by that very fact be in relation to it, and therefore in it? The dreamer dreams, and that is why his respiratory movements and sexual drives are not taken, for what they are, why they break away from the moorings which tie them up with the world and float before him in the form of dreams But what precisely does he in fact see? Are we to believe his account of it? If he is to know what he sees and to understand his dream himself, he will have to awaken. Immediately sexuality will repair to its genital retreat, anxiety and its attendant phantasms will become once more what they have always been some respiratory obstruction at a point in the chest The murky space which invades the schizophrenic's world cannot substantiate its claim to be a space without being related to clear space. If the patient maintains that there is a second space round about him, we must ask him but *where* is it? In his efforts to locate this phantom, he will conjure it away as a phantom. And since, as he himself admits, objects are uninterruptedly present, he always retains, with clear space, the means of exorcising these spectres and returning to the everyday world The phantoms are fragments drawn

288

from the clear world and borrow from it such standing as they are capable of enjoying In the same way, when we try to base geometrical space, along with its relationships within the world, on the primary spatiality of existence, it will be objected that thought knows only itself or things, that a spatiality of the subject is inconceivable, and that consequently the case we are putting is strictly meaningless It is true, we shall reply, that it has no thematic or explicit meaning, and that it dissolves under objective thought But it *has* a nonthematic or implicit meaning, and this is not a *lesser meaning*, for objective thought itself draws on the non-reflective, and presents itself as an explicit expression of non-reflective consciousness, so that radical reflection cannot consist in thematizing as parallel entities the world, or space, and the non-temporal subject which thinks of them, but must go further back and seize this thematizing act itself with the horizons of implication which give it its significance If reflection consists in seeking the first-hand, or that by which the rest can exist and be thought about, it cannot confine itself within objective thought, but must think about those thematizing acts which posit objective thought, and must restore their context. In other words, objective thought rejects the alleged phenomena of dreams, myths and of existence generally, because it finds that it cannot think clearly about them, and that they mean nothing that can be thematized It rejects the fact or the real in the name of the possible and the self-evident But it fails to see that the self-evident itself is founded on a fact Analytical reflection believes that it knows what the dreamer or the schizophrenic experience better than the dreamer or the schizophrenic himself What is more, the philosopher believes that, in reflection, he has a better knowledge of what he perceives than he has in perception itself And it is under these circumstances alone that he is able to reject human spaces as confused appearances of the one true, objective space. But by doubting the testimony of other people about themselves, or of one's own perception about itself, he deprives himself of the right to declare absolutely true what he apprehends as self-evident, even if, in this self-evidence, he is conscious of having a pre-eminent understanding of the dreamer, the madman or perception We cannot have it both ways. either the person who experiences something knows at the time what he is experiencing, in which case the madman, the dreamer or the subject of perception must be taken at their word, and we merely need to confirm that their language in fact expresses what they are experiencing Or else the person with the experience is no judge of what he experiences, and in that case the test of self-evidence may be an illusion In order to divest the experience of dreams, myths or perception of all positive value, and in order to reintegrate these various spaces to geometrical space,

289

we must to all intents and purposes deny that people ever dream, or that they ever go mad, or ever really and truly perceive anything As long as we allow the existence of dreams, insanity or perception, at least as so many forms of absence of reflection—and how can we not do so if we want to leave some value to the testimony of consciousness, without which no truth is possible?—we have no right to level all experiences down to a single world, all modalities of existence down to a single consciousness In order to do so, we should need a higher court of appeal to which to submit perceptual and phantasmal consciousness, a self more intimate with myself than the self which thinks up my dream or my perception when I confine myself to dreaming, or perceiving, which possesses the true substance of my dream and my perception when I have only the appearance of it. But the distinction itself between the appearance and the reality is made neither in the world of the myth, nor in the diseased or infantile one The myth holds the essence *within* the appearance; the mythical phenomenon is not a representation, but a genuine presence The daemon of rain is present in each drop which falls after the incantation, as the soul is present in each part of the body Every 'apparition' (*Erscheinung*) is in this case an incarnation,[1] and each entity is defined not so much in terms of 'properties' as of physiognomic characteristics So much is validly meant when we talk about infantile and primitive animism not that the child and primitive man perceive objects which they try, as Comte says, to explain by intentions or forms of consciousness—consciousness, like the object, belongs to positing thought—but because things are taken for the incarnation of what they express, and because their human significance is compressed into them and presents itself literally as what they mean A shadow passing or the creaking of branches have each a meaning; everywhere there are warnings with no one who issues them [2] Since mythical consciousness has not yet arrived at the notion of a thing or of objective truth, how can it undertake a critical examination of that which it thinks it experiences, where can it find a fixed point at which to stop and become aware of itself as pure consciousness, and perceive, beyond its phantasms, the real world? A schizophrenic feels that a brush placed near his window is coming nearer to him and entering his head, and yet he never ceases to be aware that the brush is over there [3] If he looks towards the window, he still perceives it The brush, as an identifiable term in an explicit perception, is not in the patient's head as a material mass But the patient's head is for him not that object which everyone can see, and which he himself

[1] Cassirer, *Philosophie der Symbolischen Formen*, T III, p 80
[2] Ibid , p 82
[3] L Binswanger, *Das Raumproblem in der Psychopathologie*, p 630.

sees in a mirror it is the listening and observing post which he feels at the top of his body, that power of joining up with all objects through sight and hearing In the same way, the brush which presents itself to the senses is merely an envelope or a phantom The true brush, the stiff, prickly entity which is incarnated in these appearances, is concentrated in the gaze, it has moved from the window, leaving there only its lifeless shell. No appeal to explicit perception can arouse the patient from this dream, since he has no quarrel with explicit perception, and holds only that it proves nothing against what he experiences 'Can't you hear my voices?' a patient asks the doctor; and she comes resignedly to the conclusion 'I am the only one who hears them then.'[1] What protects the sane man against delirium or hallucination, is not his critical powers, but the structure of his space· objects remain before him, keeping their distance and, as Malebranche said speaking of Adam, touching him only with respect What brings about both hallucinations and myths is a shrinkage in the space directly experienced, a rooting of things in our body, the overwhelming proximity of the object, the oneness of man and the world, which is, not indeed abolished, but repressed by everyday perception or by objective thought, and which philosophical consciousness rediscovers It is true that if I reflect on the consciousness of positions and directions in myths, dreams and in perception, if I posit and establish them in accordance with the methods of objective thinking, I bring to light in them once more the relationships of geometrical space The conclusion from this is not that they were there already, but on the contrary that genuine reflection is not of this kind. In order to realize what is the meaning of mythical or schizophrenic space, we have no means other than that of resuscitating in ourselves, in our present perception, the relationship of the subject and his world which analytical reflection does away with We must recognize as anterior to 'sense-giving acts' (*Bedeutungsgebende Akten*) of theoretical and positing thought, 'expressive experiences' (*Ausdruckserlebnisse*), as anterior to the sign significance (*Zeichen-Sinn*), the expressive significance (*Ausdrucks-Sinn*), and finally as anterior to any subsuming of content under form, the symbolical 'pregnancy'[2] of form in content.

Does this mean that psychologism is vindicated? Since there are as many spaces as there are distinct spatial experiences, and since we do not allow ourselves to anticipate, in infantile, diseased or primitive experience, the forms of adult, normal and civilized experience, are we not imprisoning each type of subjectivity, and ultimately each

[1] Minkowski, *Le Probleme des hallucinations et le probleme de l'espace*, p. 64

[2] Cassirer, op cit , p. 80

consciousness, in its own private life? Have we not substituted for
the rationalist *cogito* which discovers a universal constituting consciousness in myself, the psychologist's *cogito*, which remains incommunicable within the experience of its life? Are we not defining subjectivity as the identity of each person with that experience? Is it not
the case that inquiry into the nature of space and, generally speaking,
into nascent experience, prior to their objectification, and the decision
to scrutinize experience itself for its significance, in short phenomenology, ends with the negation of being and significance? Are not mere
appearance and opinion being brought back under the name of the
phenomenon? Is not the origin of precise knowledge being identified
with a decision as unwarrantable as the one which shuts up the madman in his madness, and is not the last word of this wisdom to lead
us back to the anguish of idle and solitary subjectivity? These are
doubts which need to be dispelled Mythical or dream-like consciousness, insanity and perception are not, in so far as they are different,
hermetically sealed within themselves; they are not small islands of
experience cut off from each other, and from which there is no
escape. We have refused to make geometrical space immanent in
mythical space, and generally, to subordinate all experience to an
absolute consciousness of this experience, a consciousness which
would assign to it its place in the general scheme of truth, because
unity of experience thus understood makes its variety incomprehensible But mythical consciousness does indeed open on to a horizon
of possible objectifications Primitive man lives his myths against a
sufficiently articulate perceptual background for the activities of daily
life, fishing, hunting and dealings with civilized people, to be possible
The myth itself, however diffuse, has an identifiable significance for
primitive man, simply because it does form a world, that is, a whole
in which each element has meaningful relations with the rest. It is
true that mythical consciousness is not a consciousness of any thing.
That is to say that subjectively it is a flux, that it does not become
static and thus does not know itself. Objectively, it does not posit
before itself terms definable as a certain number of properties, which
can be isolated from one another and which are in fact interlinked.
But it is not borne away by each of its pulsations, otherwise it would
not be conscious of anything at all. It does not stand back from its
noemata, but on the other hand, if it passed away with each one of
them, and if it did not tentatively suggest objectification, it would not
crystallize itself in myths We have tried to rescue mythical consciousness from those premature rationalizations which, as with Comte,
for example, make the myth incomprehensible, because they look to
it for an explanation of the world and an anticipation of science,
whereas it is a projection of existence and an expression of the human

292

condition. But understanding myth is not believing in it, and if all myths are true, it is in so far as they can be set in a phenomenology of mind which shows their function in arriving at awareness, and which ultimately bases their own significance on the significance they have for the philosopher

In the same way, though it is indeed from the dreamer that I was last night that I require an account of the dream, the dreamer himself offers no account, and the person who does so is awake Bereft of the waking state, dreams would be no more than instantaneous modulations, and so would not even exist for us During the dream itself, we do not leave the world behind the dream space is segregated from the space of clear thinking, but it uses all the latter's articulations, the world obsesses us even during sleep, and it is about the world that we dream Similarly it is round about the world that insanity gravitates Leaving aside those morbid, dream-like or delirious states which endeavour to build a private domain out of fragments of the macrocosm, we can say that the most advanced states of melancholia, in which the patient settles in the realm of death and, so to speak, takes up his abode there, still make use of the structures of being in the world, and borrow from it an element of being indispensable to its own denial This link between subjectivity and objectivity, which already exists in mythical or childlike consciousness, and which still survives in sleep or insanity, is to be found, *a fortiori*, in normal experience I never wholly live in varieties of human space, but am always ultimately rooted in a natural and non-human space As I walk across the Place de la Concorde, and think of myself as totally caught up in the city of Paris, I can rest my eyes on one stone of the Tuileries wall, the Square disappears and there is then nothing but this stone entirely without history· I can, furthermore, allow my gaze to be absorbed by this yellowish, gritty surface, and then there is no longer even a stone there, but merely the play of light upon an indefinite substance. My total perception is not compounded of such analytical perceptions, but it is always capable of dissolving into them, and my body, which through my habits ensures my insertion into the human world, does so only by projecting me in the first place into a natural world which can always be discerned underlying the other, as the canvas underlies the picture and makes it appear unsubstantial. Even if there is perception of what is desired through desire, loved through love, hated through hate, it always forms round a sensible nucleus, however small, and it is in the sensible that its verification and its fullness are found We have said that space is existential; we might just as well have said that existence is spatial, that is, that through an inner necessity it opens on to an 'outside', so that one can speak of a mental space and a 'world of meanings and objects of thought which are constituted in terms of those meanings'.[1] Human spaces present themselves as built on the basis of natural space, and 'non-objectifying acts', to speak the language of Husserl, as based on 'objectifying acts'.[2] The novelty of phenomenology does not lie in denying the unity of experience, but in finding a different basis for it than does classical rationalism. For objectifying acts are not representations. Natural and primordial space is not geometrical space, nor, correspondingly, is the unity of experience guaranteed by any universal thinker arraying its contents before me and ensuring that I possess complete knowledge of, and exercise complete power over it. It is merely foreshadowed by the horizons of possible objectification, and it frees me from every particular setting only because it ties me to the world of nature or the *in-itself*, which includes all of them. We must contrive to understand how, at a stroke, existence projects round itself worlds which hide objectivity from me, at the same time fastening upon it as the aim of the teleology of consciousness, by picking out these 'worlds' against the background of one single natural world.

If myths, dreams and illusion are to be possible, the apparent and the real must remain ambiguous in the subject as in the object. It has often been said that consciousness, by definition, admits of no separation of appearance and reality, and by this we are to understand that, in our knowledge of ourselves, appearance is reality: if I think I see or feel, I indubitably see or feel, whatever may be true of the external object. Here reality appears in its entirety, real being and appearance are one, and there is no reality other than the appearance. If this is true, there is no possibility that illusion and perception should have the same appearance, that my illusions should be perceptions with no object or my perceptions true hallucinations. The truth of perception and the falsity of illusion must be implanted in them in the shape of some intrinsic characteristic, for otherwise the testimony of the other senses, of later experience, or of other people, which would remain the only possible criterion, would then become unreliable, and we should never be aware of a perception or an illusion as such. If the whole being of my perception and the whole being of my illusion lies in the way they appear, then the truth which defines one and the falsity which defines the other must be equally apparent. There will be between them, therefore, a structural difference. True perception will simply be *a* true perception. Illusion will be no perception at all, and certainty will have to extend from the vision or sensation as conceived to perception as constitutive of an object. The transparency of consciousness implies the immanence and absolute certainty of the

---

[1] L. Binswanger, *Das Raumproblem in der Psychopathologie*, p. 617.
[2] *Logische Untersuchungen*, T. II, Vth *Unters.*, pp. 387 and ff.

object. Yet it is of the nature of illusion not to present itself as such, and it is necessary that I should be able, if not to perceive an unreal object, at least to lose sight of its unreality; it is necessary that there should be at least unawareness of failure to perceive, that the illusion should not be what it seems to be, and that for once the reality of an act of consciousness should be beyond its appearance

Are we then to separate appearance and reality within the subject? The difficulty is that once the break is made, it is irreparable· the clearest appearance can henceforth be misleading, and this time it is the phenomenon of truth which becomes impossible. We are not faced with a choice between a philosophy of immanence or a rationalism which accounts only for perception and truth, and a philosophy of transcendence or absurdity which accounts only for illusion and error. We know that there are errors only because we possess truth, in the name of which we correct errors and recognize them as errors. In the same way the express recognition of a truth is much more than the mere existence within us of an unchallengeable idea, an immediate faith in what is presented. it presupposes questioning, doubt, a break with the immediate, and is the correction of any possible error Any rationalism admits of at least one absurdity, that of having to be formulated as a thesis. Any philosophy of the absurd recognizes some meaning at least in the affirmation of absurdity. I can remain in the realm of the absurd only if I suspend all affirmation, if, like Montaigne or the schizophrenic, I confine myself within an interrogation which I must not even formulate for by formulating it I should ask a question which, like any determinate question, would entail a reply. If, in short, I face truth not with its negation, but with a state of non-truth or ambiguity, the actual opacity of my existence. In the same way, I can remain within the sphere of absolute self-evidence only if I refuse to make any affirmation, or to take anything for granted, if, as Husserl has it, I stand in wonder before the world,[1] and ceasing to be in league with it, I bring to light the flow of motivations which bear me along in it, making my life wholly aware of itself, and explicit. When I try to pass from this interrogative state to an affirmation, and *a fortiori* when I try to express myself, I crystallize an indefinite collection of motives within an act of consciousness, I revert to the implicit, that is, to the equivocal and to the world's free play.[2] My absolute contact with myself, the identity of being and appearance cannot be posited, but only lived as anterior to any affirmation. In both cases, therefore, we have the same silence and the same void. The experience of absurdity and that of absolute self-evidence are

[1] Fink, *Die phanomenologische Philosophie Husserls in der gegenwartigen Kritik*, p 350
[2] The problem of expression is referred to by Fink, op cit , p 382

mutually implicatory, and even indistinguishable The world appears absurd, only if a demand for absolute consciousness ceaselessly dissociates from each other the meanings with which it swarms, and conversely this demand is motivated by the conflict between those meanings Absolute self-evidence and the absurd are equivalent, not merely as philosophical affirmations, but also as experiences Rationalism and scepticism draw their sustenance from an actual life of consciousness which they both hypocritically take for granted, without which they can be neither conceived nor even experienced, and in which it is impossible to say that *everything has a significance*, or that *everything is nonsense*, but only that *there is significance*. As Pascal says, doctrines have only to be pressed a little to abound with contradictions, and yet they give a first impression of clarity, and have an initial significance. A truth seen against a background of absurdity, and an absurdity which the teleology of consciousness presumes to be able to convert into truth, such is the primary phenomenon To say that, in consciousness, appearance and reality are one, or that they are separate, is to rule out consciousness of anything whatsoever, even as appearance. Now—such is the true *cogito*—there is consciousness of something, something shows itself, there is such a thing as a phenomenon Consciousness is neither the positing of oneself, nor ignorance of oneself, it is *not concealed* from itself, which means that there is nothing in it which does not in some way announce itself to it, although it does not need to know this explicitly In consciousness, appearance is not being, but the phenomenon. This new *cogito*, because it is anterior to revealed truth and error, makes both possible. The lived is certainly lived by me, nor am I ignorant of the feelings which I repress, and in this sense there is no unconscious. But I can experience more things than I represent to myself, and my being is not reducible to what expressly appears to me concerning myself That which is merely lived is ambivalent, there are feelings in me which I do not name, and also spurious states of well-being to which I am not fully given over. The difference between illusion and perception is intrinsic, and the truth of perception can be read off only from perception itself If, on a sunken path, I think I can see, some distance away, a broad, flat stone on the ground, which is in reality a patch of sunlight, I cannot say that I ever see the flat stone in the sense in which I am to see, as I draw nearer, the patch of sunlight. The flat stone, like all things at a distance, appears only in a field of confused structure in which connections are not yet clearly articulated In this sense, the illusion, like the image, is not observable, which means that my body has no grip on it, and that I cannot unfold it before me by any exploratory action And yet, I am capable of omitting this distinction and of falling into illusion It is untrue

296

that, if I confine myself to what I really see, I am never mistaken and
that sensation at least leaves no room for doubt Every sensation is
already pregnant with a meaning, inserted into a configuration which
is either obscure or clear, and there is no sense-datum which remains
unchanged when I pass from the illusory stone to the real patch of
sunlight. The infallibility of sensation entails that of perception, and
would rule out illusion. I see the illusory stone in the sense that my
whole perceptual and motor field endows the bright spot with the
significance 'stone on the path'. And already I prepare to feel under
my foot this smooth, firm surface. The fact is that correct and illusory
vision are not distinguishable in the way that adequate and inadequate thought are: as thought, that is, which is respectively consummate and lacunary I say that I perceive correctly when my body has
a precise hold on the spectacle, but that does not mean that my hold
is ever all-embracing, it would be so only if I had succeeded in reducing to a state of articulate perception all the inner and outer horizons
of the object, which is in the nature of things impossible. In experiencing a perceived truth, I assume that the concordance so far experienced would hold for a more detailed observation, I place my confidence in the world Perceiving is pinning one's faith, at a stroke, in
a whole future of experiences, and doing so in a present which never
strictly guarantees the future, it is placing one's belief in a world It
is this opening upon a world which makes possible perceptual truth
and the actual effecting of a *Wahr-Nehmung*, thus enabling us to
'cross out' the previous illusion and regard it as null and void Seeing,
some distance away in the margin of my visual field, a large moving
shadow, I look in that direction and the phantasm shrinks and takes
up its due place; it was simply a fly near my eye *I was conscious of
seeing a shadow and now I am conscious of having seen nothing more
than a fly*. My adherence to the world enables me to allow for the
variations in the *cogito*, to favour one *cogito* at the expense of another
and to catch up with the truth of my thinking beyond its appearances.
In the very moment of illusion this possibility of correction was presented to me, because illusion too makes use of this belief in the world
and is dependent upon it while contracting into a solid appearance,
and because in this way, always being open upon a horizon of possible verifications, it does not cut me off from truth But, for the same
reason, I am not immune from error, since the world which I seek to
achieve through each appearance, and which endows that appearance,
rightly or wrongly, with the weight of truth, never necessarily requires
this particular appearance There is the absolute certainty of the
world in general, but not of any one thing in particular Consciousness is removed from being, and from its own being, and at the same
time united with them, by the thickness of the world The true *cogito*

297

is not the intimate communing of thought with the thought of that thought. they meet only on passing through the world The consciousness of the world is not *based* on self-consciousness they are strictly contemporary There is a world for me because I am not unaware of myself, and I am not concealed from myself because I have a world This pre-conscious possession of the world remains to be analysed in the pre-reflective *cogito*

3

THE THING AND THE
NATURAL WORLD

A THING has 'characteristics' or 'properties' which are stable, even if they do not entirely serve to define it, and we propose to approach the phenomenon of reality by studying perceptual constants A thing has in the first place *its* size and *its* shape throughout variations of perspective which are merely apparent We do not attribute these appearances to the object itself, but regard them as an accidental feature of our relations with it, and not as being of it What do we mean by this, and on what basis do we judge that form or size are the form and size *of the object*?

What is presented to us in the case of each object, the psychologist will assert, are sizes and shapes which always vary with the perspective, and it is conventional to regard as true the size which the object has when within reach or the shape which it assumes when it is in a plane parallel to the frontal elevation These are no truer than any other, but since this distance and this aspect are both typical, and evolved with the help of our body, which is an ever-present guide for this purpose, we can always recognize them, and so they themselves provide us with a standard for fixing and distinguishing between fleeting appearances, for constructing objectivity, in short. The square viewed obliquely, as something roughly diamond-shaped, is distinguished from a real diamond shape only if we keep the orientation in mind, if, for example, we settle on the frontal aspect as the crucial appearance, and relate any given appearance to what it would become in this context But this psychological reconstitution of objective size or shape takes for granted what has to be explained, namely a gamut of *determinate* sizes and shapes from which it is sufficient to select one as the real size or shape We have already stated that in respect of one and the same retreating or revolving object I do not have a set of 'mental images' which progressively diminish in

299

size, or become more and more distorted, and between which I make a conventional choice. In so far as I account for my perception in these terms, to that extent I am already introducing the world with its objective shapes and sizes The question is not only how one size or shape, among all apparent sizes or shapes, is regarded as a constant, it is a much more searching one It is a matter of understanding how a determinate shape or size—true or even apparent—can come to light before me, become crystallized in the flux of my experience and, in short, be given to me Or, more concisely still, how can there be objectivity?

There would seem, at least at first glance, to be a way of evading the question, namely by conceding that it is in fact never the case that size and shape are perceived as attributes of a single object, and that they are simply names for the relations between the parts of the phenomenal field. In this case the constancy of the real size or shape which is maintained through the varying perspectives is merely the constancy in the relations between the phenomenon and the conditions accompanying its presentation. For example, the true size of my fountain-pen is not, as it were, a quality inherent in any of my perceptions of the pen; it is not given or noted in a perception, like red, warmth or sweetness. The fact that it remains constant is not explained by my remembering any former experience in which I observed it. It is the constant, or the law governing the variations of the visual appearance in relation to the apparent distance. Reality is not a crucial appearance underlying the rest, it is the framework of relations with which all appearances tally. If I hold my pen near my eyes so that it shuts out almost the whole scene before me, its real size remains small, because the pen which hides everything is also a pen *seen at close quarters*, and because this condition, which is always conveyed to me in my perception, reduces the appearance once more to modest proportions The square which is presented to me obliquely remains a square, not because this apparent diamond shape brings to mind the familiar form of the square seen directly in front of me, but because the diamond-shaped appearance in an oblique presentation is immediately identical to the square appearance in a frontal presentation, because, along with each of these configurations, I am given that orientation of the object which makes it possible, and because these shapes are presented in a context of relations which, *a priori*, equate the various perspective presentations with each other The cube with its sides distorted by perspective nevertheless remains a cube, not because I imagine the successive aspects of the six faces if I turned the cube round in my hand, but because the perspective distortions are not raw data, any more than is the perfectly symmetrical shape which faces me. Each element of the cube, if we unfold from it all the perceived significance, acquaints us with the present point of view taken of it by the observer. A merely apparent shape or size is one with as yet no place in the tightly knit system formed by phenomena and my body together. As soon as it finds its place in that system, it finds its truth, and perspective distortion is no longer passively endured, but understood The appearance is misleading and in the literal sense an appearance only when it is indeterminate The question how there come to be true shapes or sizes, or objective or real ones, amounts to asking how there are, for us, determinate shapes And there are determinate shapes like 'a square' or 'a diamond shape', or any actual spatial configuration, because our body as a point of view upon things, and things as abstract elements of one single world, form a system in which each moment is immediately expressive of every other A certain way of directing my gaze in relation to the object signifies a certain appearance of the object and of neighbouring objects In all its appearances the object retains invariable characteristics, remains itself invariable and is an object because all the possible values in relation to size and shape which it can assume are bound up in advance in the formula of its relations with the context. What we are affirming in the specific being of the object, is in reality a *facies totius universi* which remains unchanged, and in it is grounded the equivalence of all its appearances and the identity of its being In following out the logic of objective size and shape, we should, with Kant, see that it refers to the positing of a world as a rigorously interrelated system, that we are never enclosed within appearance, and that, in short, the object alone is able fully *to appear*.

Thus we place ourselves directly within the object, we overlook the psychologist's problems, but have we really left them behind? When it is said that the true size or shape are no more than the constant law according to which the appearance, the distance and the orientation vary, it is assumed that they can be treated as variables or measurable sizes, and therefore that they are already determinate, when what we are concerned with is precisely how they become so Kant is right in saying that perception is, by its nature, polarized towards the object. But what is incomprehensible in his account is appearance as appearance Since the perspective views of the object are directly and immediately set into the objective system of the world, the subject thinks rather than perceives his perception and its truth. Perceptual consciousness does not give us perception as a body of organized knowledge, or the size and shape of the object as laws, the numerical specifications of science retrace the outline of a constitution of the world which is already realized before shape and size come into being Like the scientist, Kant takes the results of this pre-scientific experience for granted, and is enabled to ignore them only because he makes use of them. When I contemplate before me the furniture in my room, the table with its shape and size is for me not a law or rule governing the parade of phenomena, and an invariable relationship it is because I perceive the table with its definite shape and size that I presume, for every change of distance or orientation, a corresponding change of shape and size, and not the reverse Far from its being the case that the thing is reducible to constant relationships, it is in the self-evidence of the thing that this constancy of relationships has its basis For science and objective thought, an apparently small object seen a hundred yards away is indistinguishable from the same object seen ten yards away at a greater angle, and the object is nothing but the constant product of the distance multiplied by the apparent size. But for me the perceiver, the object a hundred yards away is not real and present in the sense in which it is at ten yards, and I identify the object in all its positions, at all distances, in all appearances, in so far as all the perspectives converge towards the perception which I obtain at a certain distance and with a certain typical orientation. This privileged perception ensures the unity of the perceptual process and draws into it all other appearances For each object, as for each picture in an art gallery, there is an optimum distance from which it requires to be seen, a direction viewed from which it vouchsafes most of itself at a shorter or greater distance we have merely a perception blurred through excess or deficiency We therefore tend towards the maximum of visibility, and seek a better focus as with a microscope [1] This is obtained through a certain balance between the inner and outer horizon· a living body, seen at too close quarters, and divorced from any background against which it can stand out, is no longer a living body, but a mass of matter as outlandish as a lunar landscape, as can be appreciated by inspecting a segment of skin through a magnifying glass Again, seen from too great a distance, the body loses its living value, and is seen simply as a puppet or automaton The living body *itself* appears when its microstructure is neither excessively nor insufficiently visible, and this moment equally determines its real size and shape. The distance from me to the object is not a size which increases or decreases, but a tension which fluctuates round a norm. An oblique position of the object in relation to me is not measured by the angle which it forms with the plane of my face, but felt as a lack of balance, as an unequal distribution of its influences upon me The variations in appearance are not so many increases or decreases in size, or real distortions It is simply that sometimes the parts mingle and become confused, at others they link up into a clearly articulated whole, and reveal their wealth of

[1] Schapp, *Beitrage zur Phänomenologie der Wahrnehmung*, pp 59 and ff

detail. There is one culminating point of my perception which simultaneously satisfies these three norms, and towards which the whole perceptual process tends. If I draw the object closer to me or turn it round in my fingers in order 'to see it better', this is because each attitude of my body is for me, immediately, the power of achieving a certain spectacle, and because each spectacle is what it is for me in a certain kinaesthetic situation In other words, because my body is permanently stationed before things in order to perceive them and, conversely, appearances are always enveloped for me in a certain bodily attitude In so far, therefore, as I know the relation of appearances to the kinaesthetic situation, this is not in virtue of any law or in terms of any formula, but to the extent that I have a body, and that through that body I am at grips with the world And just as perceptual attitudes are not known to me singly, but implicitly given as stages in the act which leads to the optimum attitude, correspondingly the correlative perspectives are not posited before me successively, but present themselves only as so many steps towards the thing itself with its size and shape Kant saw clearly that the problem is not how determinate shapes and sizes make their appearance in my experience, since without them there would be no experience, and since any internal experience is possible only against the background of external experience But Kant's conclusion from this was that I am a consciousness which embraces and constitutes the world, and this reflective action caused him to overlook the phenomenon of the body and that of the thing

The fact is that if we want to describe it, we must say that my experience breaks forth into things and transcends itself in them, because it always comes into being within the framework of a certain setting in relation to the world which is the definition of my body. Sizes and shapes merely provide a modality for this comprehensive hold on the world The thing is big if my gaze cannot fully take it in, small if it does so easily, and intermediate sizes are distinguishable according as, when placed at an equal distance from me, they cause a smaller or greater dilation of my eye, or an equal dilation at different distances. The object is circular if, all its sides being equally near to me, it imposes no deviation upon the regular curvature of my gaze, or if those deviations which are imposed are attributable to the oblique presentation, according to the knowledge of the world which is given to me with my body [1] It is, therefore, quite true that any perception of

---

[1] The constancy of forms and sizes in perception is therefore not an intellectual function, but an existential one, which means that it has to be related to the pre-logical act by which the subject takes up his place in the world When a human subject is placed at the centre of a sphere on which discs of equal diameter are fixed, it is noticed that constancy is much more perfect in the horizontal than in

a thing, a shape or a size as real, any perceptual constancy refers back to the positing of a world and of a system of experience in which my body is inescapably linked with phenomena. But the system of experience is not arrayed before me as if I were God, it is lived by me from a certain point of view, I am not the spectator, I am involved, and it is my involvement in a point of view which makes possible both the finiteness of my perception and its opening out upon the complete world as a horizon of every perception. In so far as I know that a tree on the horizon remains what it is for closer perception, and retains its real shape and size, it is simply that this horizon is the horizon of my immediate environment, and that the gradual perceptual possession of the things which it contains is guaranteed to me. In other words, perceptual experiences hang together, are mutually motivating and implicatory, the perception of the world is simply an expansion of my field of presence without any outrunning of the latter's essential structures, and the body remains in it but at no time becomes an object in it. The world is an open and indefinite unity in which I have my place, as Kant shows in the Transcendental Dialectic, but as he seems to forget in the Analytic.

The qualities of the thing, its colour for example, or its hardness or weight, teach us much more about it than its geometrical properties The table is, and remains, brown throughout the varied play of natural or artificial lighting Now what, to begin with, is this real colour, and how have we access to it? We shall be tempted to reply that it is the colour which I most often see as belonging to the table, the one which it assumes in daylight, a short distance away, under 'normal' conditions, which means those which occur most frequently. When the distance is too great or when the light has a colour of its own, as at sunset or under electric lighting, I substitute for the actual colour a remembered one,[1] which predominates because it is imprinted within me by numerous experiences. In this case the constancy of colour is a real constancy But we have here no more than an artificial reconstruction of the phenomenon. For, with regard to perception itself, it cannot be said that the brown of the table presents itself in all kinds of light as the same brown, the same quality actually given by memory. A piece of white paper seen in shadow and recognized for what it is, is not purely and simply white, it 'does not

---

the vertical plane The huge moon on the horizon contrasted with the very small one at the zenith is merely a particular case of the same law For apes, on the other hand, vertical movement in trees is as natural as is horizontal movement on the ground for us, with the result that vertical constancy is faultless Koffka, *Principles of Gestalt Psychology*, pp 94 and ff

[1] *Gedachtnisfarbe* of Hering.

allow itself to be placed satisfactorily in the white-black series'.[1] Given a white wall in the shade and a grey piece of paper in the light, it cannot be said that the wall remains white and the paper grey; the paper makes a greater impact on the eye,[2] it is lighter and clearer, whereas the wall is darker and duller, and what remains beneath the variations of lighting is, so to speak, only the 'substance of the colour'[3] The alleged constancy of colours does not prevent 'an indubitable modification during which we continue to receive in our vision the fundamental quality and, so to speak, that which is substantial in it'[4] This same reason will prevent us from treating the constancy of colours as an ideal constancy attributable to the judgement. For a judgement capable of distinguishing within a given appearance that element which is to be accounted for by the particular lighting must lead ultimately to an identification of the object's own true colour, and we have seen that this does not in fact remain identical. The weakness of both empiricism and intellectualism lies in their refusing to recognize any colours other than those fixed qualities which make their appearance in a reflective attitude, whereas colour in living perception is a way into the thing We must rid ourselves of the illusion, encouraged by physics, that the perceived world is made up of colour qualities As painters have observed, there are few colours in nature The perception of colours is developed late in children, and in any case follows upon the constitution of a world. The Maoris have 3,000 names of colours, not because they perceive a great many, but, on the contrary, because they fail to identify them when they belong to objects structurally different from each other[5] As Scheler puts it, perception goes straight to the thing and by-passes the colour, just as it is able to fasten upon the expression of a gaze without noting the colour of the eyes. We shall not succeed in understanding perception unless we take into account a colour function which may remain even when the qualitative appearance is modified I say that my fountain-pen is black, and I see it as black under the sun's rays But this blackness is less the sensible quality of blackness than a sombre power which radiates from the object, even when it is overlaid with reflected light, and it is visible only in the sense in which moral blackness is visible The real colour persists beneath appearances as the background persists beneath the figure, that is, not as a seen or thought-of quality, but through a non-sensory presence. Physics and also psychology give an arbitrary definition of colour,

---

[1] Gelb, *Die Farbenkonstanz der Sehdinge*, p 613
[2] It is *eindringlicher*.
[3] Stumpf, quoted by Gelb, p. 598.
[4] Gelb, op cit, p 671.
[5] Katz, *Der Aufbau der Farbwelt*, pp 4-5

which in reality fits only one of its modes of appearance and has for long obscured the rest. Hering requires that in the study and comparison of colours we concern ourselves with only the pure colour, leaving aside all external circumstances We must work 'not on the colours which belong to a determinate object, but on a *quale*, whether plane or pervading the whole of space, which subsists for itself with no determinate vehicle' [1] The colours of the spectrum roughly fulfil these conditions But these coloured areas (*Flachenfarben*) are in reality only one of the possible structures of colour, and already the colour of a piece of paper or a surface colour (*Oberflachenfarbe*) no longer obeys the same laws The differential thresholds are lower in the case of surface colours than in coloured areas [2] Coloured areas are indeed located at a distance, though vaguely; they have a spongy appearance, whereas surface colours are dense and hold the gaze upon their surface Coloured areas, moreover, are always parallel to the frontal plane, whereas surface colours may show any orientation Finally coloured areas are always more or less flat, and cannot, without losing their distinctive quality as such, assume a particular form and appear curved or spread out over a surface [3] Yet both these modes of appearance are to be found in psychologists' experiments, where, moreover, they are often confused But there are many others about which psychologists have for long remained silent the colour of transparent bodies, which occupies the three dimensions of space (*Raumfarbe*), gloss (*Glanz*), glow (*Gluhen*), brightness (*Leuchten*) and generally the colour of lighting, which is so far from running into that of the source of light that the painter can represent the former by the distribution of light and shade on objects and omit the latter altogether [4] We are predisposed to believe that we have here different arrangements of a perception of colour which is in itself invariable, different forms conferred upon one and the same sensible material. In fact, we have different colour-functions in which the alleged material disappears completely, since the act of patterning is effected through a change in the sensible properties themselves It is particularly true that the distinction between the lighting and the object's own colour is not the outcome of any intellectual analysis, or the conferment of notional meanings on a sensible material, but a certain organization of colour itself, the arrival at a structure lighting-thing

[1] Quoted by Katz, *Farbwelt*, p 67.

[2] Ackermann, *Farbschwelle und Feldstruktur*

[3] Katz, *Farbwelt*, pp 8–21.

[4] Ibid , 47–8 Lighting is a phenomenal datum as immediate as surface colour The child sees it as a line of force running through the visual field, and that is why the shadow behind objects and corresponding to it is immediately set in a living relation to it the child says that the shadow 'is running away from the light' J Piaget, *La Causalite physique chez l enfant*, Chap VIII, p 21

lighted, which we need to describe in greater detail, if we are to understand the constancy of a thing's 'own' colour [1]

In gaslight a blue paper looks blue And yet if we look at it with the photometer we are surprised to see that it sends the same mixture of rays to the eye as does a brown paper in daylight.[2] A feebly lighted white wall which, with the reservations already stated, appears white to the unhampered vision, appears a bluish-grey if we look at it through the window of a screen which hides the source of light The painter achieves the same result without a screen and manages to see colours as they are determined by the quantity and quality of re-flected light, provided that he isolates them from their surrounding, by half-closing his eyes, for example This changed appearance is in-separable from a change of structure in the colour by the act of inter-posing the screen between our eye and the spectacle, and half-closing our eyes, we free the colours from the objectivity they acquire on the surfaces of bodies and restore to them the simple state of areas of light We no longer see real bodies, such as the wall or the paper, with a determinate colour and having their place in the world, but coloured patches which are all situated on one and the same 'fictional' plane.[3] How precisely does the screen work? We shall understand this better if we observe the same phenomenon under different condi-tions If we look successively through the eye-holes of two large boxes painted respectively black and white on the inside, and one illuminated faintly, the other powerfully, so that the quantity of light received by the eye in each case is the same, and if we contrive that inside the boxes there shall be no shadow or lack of uniformity in the painting, they then become indistinguishable, and in each case we see only an empty space permeated by grey The whole effect is altered if a piece of white paper is placed in the black box, or a piece of black paper in the white one Immediately the former appears as black and strongly illuminated, the latter as white and faintly lit Hence, for the structure lighting-object lighted to be presented, at least two surfaces of different reflecting power are needed [4] If we so arrange it that the beam of an arc lamp falls exactly upon a black disc, and if the latter is

[1] Indeed it has been shown (Gelb and Goldstein, *Psychologische Analysen Hirnpathologischer Falle, Über den Wegfall der Wahrnehmung von Oberflachen-farben*) that constancy of colours may be found in subjects who have lost the power to receive either surface colour or lighting It would appear that constancy is a much more rudimentary phenomenon It is met with in animals with varieties of sensory apparatus simpler than the eye The structure lighting-object lighted is, therefore, a special and highly organized type of constance But it remains necessary for a precise and objective constancy, and for a perception of things. (Gelb, *Die Farbenkonstanz der Sehdinge*, p 677)

[2] The experiment is already reported by Hering, *Grundzuge der Lehre von Licht-sinn*, p 15

[3] Gelb, *Farbenkonstanz*, p. 600   [4] Ibid , p 673

set in motion to eliminate the influence of the roughness which is always present on its surface—the disc appears, like the rest of the room, faintly lighted, and the beam of light is a whitish solid with the disc as its base. If we then place a piece of white paper in front of the disc, 'immediately we see the disc "black", the paper "white", and both under a strong light.' [1] The transformation is so complete that one has the impression of seeing a fresh disc These experiments in which the screen plays no part elucidate those in which it does: the decisive factor in the phenomenon of constancy, which the screen eliminates, and which may operate in free vision, is the articulation of the totality of the field, the wealth and subtlety of its structures. When he looks through the window of a screen, the subject can no longer 'dominate' (*überschauen*) the relationships introduced by lighting, perceive, that is, in visible space, subordinated wholes, each with its own distinctness, standing out one against the background of another [2] When the painter half-closes his eyes, he does away with the field's organization in depth and with it, the precise contrasts of lighting, so that there are no longer any determinate things with their own colours If the experiment with the white paper in the shadow and the grey paper illuminated is repeated, and if the negative after-images of the two perceptions are projected on to a screen, it is observed that the phenomenon of constancy is not preserved, as if constancy and the structure lighting-lighted object could occur only in things and not in the diffuse space of after-images.[3] By admitting that these structures depend on the organization of the field we immediately arrive at an understanding of all the empirical laws governing the phenomenon of constancy.[4] Firstly, that it is proportional to the size of the retinal area on to which the spectacle is thrown, and the more pronounced in proportion as, in the relevant retinal space, a more extensive and more richly articulated fragment of the world is projected. That it is less perfect in peripheral than in central vision, in monocular than in binocular vision, in brief than in prolonged vision; that it is attenuated at a great distance; that it varies with individuals according to the richness of their perceptual world, and finally that it is less perfect in coloured lighting, which cancels out the superficial structure of objects, and brings the reflecting potentialities of different surfaces to a common level, than in colourless lighting which leaves these structural differences intact.[5] The connection between the phenomenon of constancy, the articulation of the field and the phenomenon of lighting can therefore be regarded as an established fact.

[1] Gelb, *Farbenkonstanz*, p 674   [2] Ibid , p 675   [3] Ibid , p 677
[4] These are the laws set out by Katz in *Farbwelt*
[5] Gelb, *Farbenkonstanz*, p 677

308

But this functional relation has so far failed to make clear either the terms which it links, or consequently their concrete connection, and the greatest benefit of the discovery would be lost if we were content merely to establish a correlative variation between the three terms taken in their ordinary sense *In what sense* are we to say that the colour of the object remains constant? *What is* the organization of the spectacle and the *field* in which it is organized? *What* finally is *lighting*? Psychological induction remains blind as long as we fail to draw together in one single phenomenon the three variables which it connotes, and as long as it does not lead us by the hand to some intuition in which the alleged 'causes' or 'conditions' of the phenomenon of constancy shall appear as 'moments' of that phenomenon and in an essential relation to it [1] Let us then consider the phenomena which have just been revealed to us, and try to see how they motivate each other in total perception. Let us look first at that peculiar mode of the appearance of light or of colours which we call lighting. What is peculiar about it? What occurs when a certain patch of light is taken as lighting instead of in its own right? Only after centuries of painting did artists perceive that reflection on the eye without which the eye remains dull and sightless as in the paintings of the early masters [2] The reflection is not seen as such, since it was in fact able to remain unnoticed for so long, and yet it has its function in perception, since its mere absence deprives objects and faces of all life and expression. The reflection is seen only incidentally It is not presented to our perception as an objective, but as an auxiliary or mediating element It is not seen itself, but causes us to see the rest Reflections and lighting in photography are often badly reproduced because they are transformed into things, and if, in a film for example, a person goes into a cellar holding a lamp, we do not see the beam of light as an immaterial entity exploring the darkness and picking out objects, because it becomes solidified and can no longer display to us the object at its far end. Light moving over a wall produces only pools of dazzling brightness which are localized not on the wall, but on the

[1] In fact the psychologist, however positivistic he tries to remain, certainly feels himself that the whole value of inductive research is to lead us to a view of phenomena, and he never quite resists the temptation to hint, at least, at this new coming to awareness Thus P. Guillaume (*Traité de Psychologie*, p 175), when setting forth the laws governing the constancy of colours, writes that the eye 'takes the lighting into account'. Our researches merely, in a sense, amplify this concise statement It means nothing in the context of a strictly positive approach The eye is not the mind, but a material organ How could it ever take anything 'into account'? It can do so only if we introduce the phenomenal body beside the objective one, if we make a knowing-body of it, and if, in short, we substitute for consciousness, as the subject of perception, existence, or being in the world through a body

[2] Schapp, *Beitrage zur Phänomenologie der Wahrnehmung*, p 91

surface of the screen. Lighting and reflection, then, play their part only if they remain in the background as discreet intermediaries, and *lead* our gaze instead of arresting it.[1] But what are we to understand by that? When I am led through a strange apartment towards its owner, there is someone who knows on my behalf, for whom the unfolding of the visual spectacle has a meaning, and who moves towards a goal, and I entrust or lend myself to this knowledge which I do not possess. When some detail in a landscape, which I have been unable to distinguish alone, is pointed out to me, there is someone who has already seen it, who already knows where to stand and where to look in order to see it The lighting directs my gaze and causes me to see the object, so that in a sense it *knows* and *sees* the object If I imagine a theatre with no audience in which the curtain rises upon illuminated scenery, I have the impression that the spectacle *is in itself visible* or ready to be seen, and that the light which probes the back and foreground, accentuating the shadows and permeating the scene through and through, in a way anticipates our vision Conversely our own vision merely takes up on its own account and carries through the encompassing of the scene by those paths traced out for it by the lighting, just as, when we hear a sentence, we are surprised to discover the track of an alien thought We perceive in conformity with the light, as we think in conformity with other people in verbal communication And just as communication presupposes (even while outstripping and enriching it in the case of new and authentic expression) a certain linguistic setting through which a meaning resides in the words, so perception presupposes in us an apparatus capable of responding to the promptings of light in accordance with their sense* (that is, in accordance both with their direction and their significance, which amount to one thing), of concentrating diffuse visibility and completing what is merely foreshadowed in the spectacle This apparatus is the gaze, in other words the natural correlation between appearances and our kinaesthetic unfoldings, something not known through a law, but experienced as the involvement of our body in the typical structures of a world Lighting and the constancy of the thing illuminated, which is its correlative, are directly dependent on our bodily situation. If, in a brightly lit room, we observe a white disc placed in a shady corner, the constancy of the white is imperfect It improves when we approach the shady zone containing the disc It becomes perfect when we actually

---

[1] In order to describe the essential function of lighting, Katz borrows from painters the term *Lichtführung* (*Farbwelt*, pp 379-81)

* The French word 'sens' may be equivalent to either 'direction' or 'meaning' in English (Translator's note)

enter it.[1] The shade does not become really a shade (and correspondingly the disc does not count as white) until it has ceased to be in front of us as something to be seen, but surrounds us, becoming our environment in which we establish ourselves This phenomenon becomes comprehensible only if the spectacle, far from being a collection of objects, a mosaic of qualities arrayed before an acosmic subject, steals round the subject and offers to come to terms with him. The lighting is not on the side of the object, it is what we assume, what we take as the norm, whereas the object lighted stands out before us and confronts us The lighting is neither colour nor, in itself, even light, it is anterior to the distinction between colours and luminosities This is why it always tends to become 'neutral' for us The penumbra in which we are becomes so natural that it is no longer even perceived as penumbra Electric lighting, which appears yellow immediately upon leaving the daylight, soon ceases to have any definite colour for us, and, if some remnant of daylight finds its way into the room it is this 'objectively neutral' light which seems to have a blue tint about it [2] We must not say that, since the yellow electric lighting is perceived as yellow, we take account of it in the appreciation of appearances and thus theoretically discover the actual colour of objects Nor must we say that as the yellow light becomes all-embracing it is seen as daylight, and that in this way the colour of other objects remains really constant We must say that the yellow light, in assuming the function of lighting, tends to become anterior to any colour, tends towards absence of colour, and that correspondingly objects distribute the colours of the spectrum among themselves according to the degree and mode of their resistance to this new atmosphere Every colour as a *quale* is therefore mediated by a colour-function, and becomes determinate in relation to a level which is variable The level is laid down, and with it all the colour values dependent upon it, as soon as we begin to live in the prevailing atmosphere and re-allot to objects the colours of the spectrum in accordance with the requirements of this basic convention. Taking up our abode in a certain setting of colour, with the transposition which it entails, is a bodily operation, and I cannot effect it otherwise than by *entering into* the new atmosphere, because my body is my general power of inhabiting all the environments which the world contains, the key to all those transpositions and equivalences which keep it constant. Thus lighting is merely one element of a complex structure, the others being the organization of the field as our body contrives it and the thing illuminated in its constancy The functional correlations

[1] Gelb, *Farbenkonstanz*, p 633
[2] Koffka, *Principles of Gestalt Psychology*, pp 255 and ff See *La Structure du Comportement*, pp 108 and ff

311

which can be discovered between these three phenomena are merely manifestations of their 'essential co-existence' [1]

This can be brought out more clearly by scrutinizing the two latter. What are we to understand by the organization of the field? We have seen that, if we insert a white paper into the beam of light thrown by an arc lamp, the beam having hitherto been fused with the disc on to which it falls, and perceived as a solid cone—immediately the beam and the disc are dissociated and the lighting takes on the quality of lighting The introduction of the paper into the beam, by forcing us clearly to recognize the 'non-solidity' of the cone of light, alters its significance in relation to the disc supporting it and brings out its quality as lighting. It is as if there were an incompatibility, vividly experienced, between the sight of the illuminated paper and that of a solid cone, and as if the significance of part of the spectacle induced a reassessment of the significance of the whole. In the same way we have seen that in the various parts of the visual field taken separately, the distinctive colour of the object on the one hand and the lighting on the other are indistinguishable, but that, in the visual field taken as a whole and through a kind of reciprocal action in which each part benefits from the configuration of the rest, a general effect of lighting emerges and endows each local colour with its 'true' value. Here again, it is as if the parts of the spectacle, being unable singly to summon up the vision of lighting, made this possible by their union, and also as if, into the colour values spread through the field, some-one read the possibility of a systematic transformation When a painter wants to depict some striking object, he does so less by apply-ing a bright colour to that object than by a suitable distribution of light and shade on surrounding ones.[2] If we manage momentarily to glimpse a hollowed motif as one in relief, a seal for example, we suddenly have the impression of a magic lighting emanating from the interior of the object. This is because the light and shade relationships on the seal are then the opposite of what they should be by reason of the lighting at the time. If we move a lamp round a bust at a constant distance from it, even when the lamp itself is invisible we see the rotation of the source of light in the complex of changing light and colour which is all that is given [3]

There is, then, a 'logic of lighting'[4] or again a 'synthesis of light-ing',[5] a compossibility of the parts of the visual field, which may well be specified in disjunctive propositions, as when the painter tries to justify his work to an art critic, but which is primarily experienced as the consistency of the picture or the reality of the spectacle What is

---

[1] *Wesenskoexistenz*, Gelb, *Farbenkonstanz*, p 671
[2] Katz, *Farbwelt*, p 36   [3] Ibid , pp 379–81
[4] Ibid , p 213   [5] Ibid , p 456

more, there is a total logic of the picture or the spectacle, a felt coherence of the colours, spatial forms and significance of the object. A picture in an art gallery, when seen at an appropriate distance, has its internal lighting which confers upon each patch of colours not only its colour value, but also a certain representative value. Seen at too close quarters it falls under the prevailing lighting of the art gallery, and the colours 'then no longer act in a representative manner, and no longer present us with the image of certain objects, but act as so much daubing on a canvas'.[1] If, on looking at a mountain scene, we adopt a critical attitude and isolate part of the field, then the colour itself changes, and this green, which was meadow green, when taken out of its context, loses its thickness and its colour as well as its representative value.[2] A colour is never merely a colour, but the colour of a certain object, and the blue of a carpet would never be the same blue were it not a woolly blue The colours of the visual field, as we earlier saw, form an ordered system round a dominant which is the lighting taken as a level. We now begin to see a deeper meaning in the organization of a field it is not only colours, but also geometrical forms, all sense-data and the significance of objects which go to form a system. Our perception in its entirety is animated by a logic which assigns to each object its determinate features in virtue of those of the rest, and which 'cancel out' as unreal all stray data; it is entirely sustained by the certainty of the world In this way we finally see the true significance of perceptual constancies. The constancy of colour is only an abstract component of the constancy of things, which in turn is grounded in the primordial constancy of the world as the horizon of all our experiences It is not, then, because I perceive constant colours beneath the variety of lightings that I believe in the existence of things, nor is the thing a collection of constant characteristics It is, on the contrary, in so far as my perception is in itself open upon a world and on things that I discover constant colours.

The phenomenon of constancy is a general one It has been found possible to speak of a constancy of sounds,[3] temperatures, weights,[4] and indeed data which are in the strict sense tactile, a constancy itself mediated by certain structures, certain 'modes of appearance' of phenomena in each of these sensory fields. The perception of weights remains the same whatever the muscles called into play, and whatever their initial position. When an object is lifted with the eyes closed, its weight is no different, whether or not the hand carries an extra weight (and whether this weight exerts pressure on the back of the hand or a

[1] Katz, *Farbwelt*, p 382   [2] Ibid , p 261
[3] Von Hornbostel, *Das Räumliche Hören*
[4] Werner, *Grundfragen der Intensitatspsychologie*, pp 68 and ff. Fischel, *Transformationserscheinungen bei Gewichtshebungen*, pp 342 and ff.

pull on the palm)—whether the hand is free or is fastened in such a way that the fingers work alone—whether one or more fingers perform the task—whether the object be raised with the hand or the head, foot or teeth—and finally whether the object is lifted in the air or in water Thus the tactile impression is 'interpreted' in the light of the nature and number of the parts of the body brought into play, and even of the physical circumstances under which it appears, thus do impressions, in themselves highly variable, such as pressure on the skin of the forehead and on the hand, mediate the same perception of weight It is impossible here to suppose that the interpretation rests on any explicit induction, and that, in the previous experiment, the subject was able to measure the incidence of these different variables on the actual weight of the object He has probably never had occasion to interpret frontal pressure in terms of weight or, in order to find the ordinary scale of weights, to add to the local impression of the fingers the weight of the arm reduced through immersion in water. Even if it be conceded that, through the use of his body, the subject has gradually evolved a scale of weight-equivalences, and learned that a certain impression furnished through the muscles of the fingers is equivalent to another derived from the whole hand, such inductions, since they are applied to parts of the body which have never been used for the lifting of weights, must at all events be made within the framework of a global bodily knowledge which systematically embraces all its parts The constancy of weight is not a real constancy, or the permanence within us of some 'impression of weight', gained through those parts of the body most often used, and reached by association in the remaining cases Is the weight of the object, then, to be regarded as a theoretical invariant, and the perception of weight a judgement by means of which, the impression and the bodily and physical circumstances in which it occurs being in each case brought into relation with each other, we discern by a kind of natural physics a constant relationship between these two variables? But this can be so only in a manner of speaking we do not know our body and the power, weight and scope of our organs as an engineer knows the machine which he has assembled part by part. And when we compare the work of our hand with that of our fingers, it is against the background of a comprehensive potentiality of our limb as hitherto known that they are distinguished or identified, and in the unity of an 'I can' that the operations of different parts of the body appear equivalent Correspondingly the 'impressions' provided by each one of them are not really distinct and related to each other merely by an explicit interpretation, but present themselves immediately as different manifestations of the 'real weight, and the pre-objective unity of the thing is correlative to the pre-objective unity of the body. Thus the weight appears as the identifiable property of a thing against the background of our body as a system of equivalent gestures This analysis of the perception of weight elucidates the whole of tactile perception: the movement of one's own body is to touch what lighting is to vision [1] All tactile perception, while opening itself to an objective 'property', includes a bodily component; the tactile localization of an object, for example, assigns to it its place in relation to the cardinal points of the body image This property which, at first sight, draws an absolute distinction between touch and vision, in fact makes it possible to draw them together. It is true that the visible object is in front of us and not on our eye, but we have seen that in the last resort the visible position, size or shape are determined by the direction, scope and hold which our gaze has upon them. It is true that passive touch (for example touch inside the ear or nose, and generally in all parts of the body ordinarily covered) tells us hardly anything but the state of our own body and almost nothing about the object Even on the most sensitive parts of our tactile surface, pressure without movement produces a scarcely identifiable phenomenon [2] But there is also passive vision, with no gaze specifically directed, as in the case of a dazzling light, which does not unfold an objective space before us, and in which the light ceases to be light and becomes something painful which invades our eye itself. And like the exploratory gaze of true vision, the 'knowing touch'[3] projects us outside our body through movement When one of my hands touches — the other, the hand that moves functions as subject and the other as object.[4] There are tactile phenomena, alleged tactile qualities, like roughness and smoothness, which disappear completely if the exploratory movement is eliminated Movement and time are not only an objective condition of knowing touch, but a phenomenal component of tactile data. They bring about the patterning of tactile phenomena, just as light shows up the configuration of a visible surface.[5] Smoothness is not a collection of similar pressures, but the way in which a surface utilizes the time occupied by our tactile exploration or modulates the movement of our hand The style of these modulations particularizes so many modes of appearance of the tactile phenomenon, which are not reducible to each other and cannot be deduced from an elementary tactile sensation There are 'surface tactile phenomena' (Oberflachentastungen) in which a two-dimensional tactile object is presented to the touch and more or less firmly resists penetration, three-dimensional tactile environments, comparable to areas of colour, for example a flow of air or water which we allow to run over our hand—and there is also tactile

[1] See Katz, *Der Aufbau der Tastwelt*, p 58   [2] Ibid , p 62
[3] Ibid , p 20   [4] Ibid   [5] Ibid , p 58

transparency (*Durchtastete Flachen*). Dampness, oiliness and sticki-
ness belong to a more complex layer of structures [1] On touching a
piece of carved wood, we immediately distinguish the grain of the
wood, which is its natural structure, from the artificial structure
which has been conferred upon it by the wood carver, just as the ear
picks out a note from a set of noises [2] There are here various structures of the exploratory movement, and the corresponding phenomena cannot be treated as a collection of elementary tactile impressions, since the alleged component impressions are not even given to
the subject if I touch a piece of linen material or a brush, between
the bristles of the brush and the threads of the linen, there does not
lie a tactile nothingness, but a tactile space devoid of matter, a tactile
background [3] Not being really dissectable, the complex tactile phenomenon is, for the same reasons, not theoretically so either, and if we
tried to define hardness or softness, roughness or smoothness, sand
or honey as so many laws or rules governing the development of
tactile experience, it would still be necessary to include in the latter
knowledge of the elements which the law co-ordinates The person
who touches and who recognizes the rough and the smooth does not
posit either their elements or the relations between those elements,
nor does he think of them in any thoroughgoing way. It is not consciousness which touches or feels, but the hand, and the hand is, as
Kant says, 'an outer brain of man'.[4] In visual experience, which
pushes objectification further than does tactile experience, we can, at
least at first sight, flatter ourselves that we constitute the world, because it presents us with a spectacle spread out before us at a distance,
and gives us the illusion of being immediately present everywhere and
being situated nowhere Tactile experience, on the other hand, adheres to the surface of our body, we cannot unfold it before us, and it
never quite becomes an object Correspondingly, as the subject of
touch, I cannot flatter myself that I am everywhere and nowhere; I
cannot forget in this case that it is through my body that I go to the
world, and tactile experience occurs 'ahead' of me, and is not centred
in me It is not I who touch, it is my body, when I touch I do not
think of diversity, but my hands rediscover a certain style which is
part of their motor potentiality, and this is what we mean when we
speak of a perceptual field I am able to touch effectively only if the
phenomenon finds an echo within me, if it accords with a certain
nature of my consciousness, and if the organ which goes out to meet
it is synchronized with it The unity and identity of the tactile
phenomenon do not come about through any synthesis of recognition

[1] Cf Katz, *Der Aufbau der Tastwelt*, pp. 24–35
[2] Ibid , pp 38–9   [3] Ibid , p 42
[4] Quoted without reference by Katz, ibid , p. 4.

in the concept, they are founded upon the unity and identity of the body as a synergic totality 'On the day the child uses its hand as a unique instrument of prehension, it becomes equally a unique instrument of touch' [1] Not only do I use my fingers and my whole body as a single organ, but also, thanks to this unity of the body, the tactile perceptions gained through an organ are immediately translated into the language of the rest; for example, the contact of our back or chest with linen or wool remains in the memory in the form of a manual contact,[2] and it may be said in more general terms that we can, in recollection, touch an object with parts of our body which have never actually been in contact with it.[3] Each contact of an object with part of our objective body is, therefore, in reality a contact with the whole of the present or possible phenomenal body. That is how the constancy of a tactile object may come about through its various manifestations. It is a constancy-for-my-body, an invariant of its total behaviour. The body is borne towards tactile experience by all its surfaces and all its organs simultaneously, and carries with it a certain typical structure of the tactile 'world'

We are now in a position to approach the analysis of the thing as an inter-sensory entity. The thing as presented to sight (the moon's pale disc) or to touch (my skull as I can feel it when I touch it), and which stays the same for us through a series of experiences, is neither a *quale* genuinely subsisting, nor the notion or consciousness of such an objective property, but what is discovered or taken up by our gaze or our movement, a question to which these things provide a fully appropriate reply The object which presents itself to the gaze or the touch arouses a certain motor intention which aims not at the movements of one's own body, but at the thing itself from which they are, as it were, suspended And in so far as my hand knows hardness and softness, and my gaze knows the moon's light, it is as a certain way of linking up with the phenomenon and communicating with it. Hardness and softness, roughness and smoothness, moonlight and sunlight, present themselves in our recollection, not pre-eminently as sensory contents, but as certain kinds of symbiosis, certain ways the outside has of invading us and certain ways we have of meeting this invasion, and memory here merely frees the framework of the perception from the place where it originates If the constants of each sense are thus understood, the question of defining the inter-sensory thing into which they unite as a collection of stable attributes or as the notion of this collection, will not arise The sensory 'properties' of a thing together constitute one and the same thing, just as my gaze,

---

[1] Cf. Katz, *Der Aufbau der Tastwelt*, p. 160
[2] Ibid , p. 46.   [3] Ibid , p 51.

my touch and all my other senses are together the powers of one and the same body integrated into one and the same action. The surface which I am about to recognize as the surface of the table, when vaguely looked at, already summons me to focus upon it, and demands those movements of convergence which will endow it with its 'true' aspect Similarly any object presented to one sense calls upon itself the concordant operation of all the others I see a surface colour because I have a visual field, and because the arrangement of the field leads my gaze to that surface—I perceive a thing because I have a field of existence and because each phenomenon, on its appearance, attracts towards that field the whole of my body as a system of perceptual powers I run through appearances and reach the real colour or the real shape when my experience is at its maximum of clarity, in spite of the fact that Berkeley may retort that a fly would see the same object differently or that a stronger microscope would transform it' these different appearances are for me appearances of a certain true spectacle, that in which the perceived configuration, for a sufficient degree of clarity, reaches its maximum richness [1] I have visual objects because I have a visual field in which richness and clarity are in inverse proportion to each other, and because these two demands, either of which taken separately might be carried to infinity, when brought together, produce a certain culmination and optimum balance in the perceptual process In the same way, what I call experience of the thing or of reality—not merely of a reality-for-sight or for-touch, but of an absolute reality—is my full co-existence with the phenomenon, at the moment when it is in every way at its maximum articulation, and the 'data of the different senses' are directed towards this one pole, as my 'aims' as I look through a microscope vacillate about one predominant 'target'. I do not propose to bestow the term 'visual thing' upon a phenomenon which, like areas of colour, presents no maximum visibility through the various experiences which I have of it, or which, like the sky, remote and thin on the horizon, unlocalized and diffuse at the zenith, allows itself to be contaminated by the structures closest to it without setting over against them any configuration of its own. If a phenomenon—for example, a reflection or a light gust of wind—strikes only one of my senses, it is a mere phantom, and it will come near to real existence only if, by some chance, it becomes capable of speaking to my other senses, as does the wind when, for example, it blows strongly and can be seen in the tumult it causes in the surrounding countryside Cézanne declared that a picture contains within itself even the smell of the landscape.[2] He meant that the arrangement of colour on the thing (and in the work of

[1] Schapp, *Beitrage zur Phanomenologie der Wahrnehmung*, pp 59 and ff
[2] J Gasquet, *Cézanne*, p 81

318

art, if it catches the thing in its entirety) signifies by itself all the responses which would be elicited through an examination by the remaining senses, that a thing would not have this colour had it not also this shape, these tactile properties, this resonance, this odour, and that the thing is the absolute fullness which my undivided existence projects before itself. The unity of the thing beyond all its fixed properties is not a substratum, a vacant X, an inherent subject, but that unique accent which is to be found in each one of them, that unique manner of existing of which they are a second order expression. For exar ple, the brittleness, hardness, transparency and crystal ring of a glass all translate a single manner of being If a sick man sees the devil, he sees at the same time his smell, his flames and smoke, because the significant unity 'devil' is precisely that acrid, fire-and-brimstone essence There is a symbolism in the thing which links each sensible quality to the rest. Heat enters experience as a kind of vibration of the thing, with colour on the other hand it is as if the thing is thrust outside itself, and it is *a priori* necessary that an extremely hot object should redden, for it is its excess of vibration which causes it to blaze forth [1] The passing of sensory givens before our eyes or under our hands is, as it were, a language which teaches itself, and in which the meaning is secreted by the very structure of the signs, and this is why it can literally be said that our senses question things and that things reply to them 'The sensible appearance is what reveals (*Kundgibt*), and expresses as such what it is not itself'.[2] We understand the thing as we understand a new kind of behaviour, not, that is, through any intellectual operation of subsumption, but by taking up on our own account the mode of existence which the observable signs adumbrate before us A form of behaviour outlines a certain manner of treating the world. In the same way, in the interaction of things, each one is characterized by a kind of *a priori* to which it remains faithful in all its encounters with the outside world The significance of a thing inhabits that thing as the soul inhabits the body it is not behind appearances. The significance of the ash-tray (at least its total and individual significance, as this is given in perception) is not a certain idea of the ash-tray which co-ordinates its sensory aspects and is accessible to the understanding alone, it

---

[1] This unity of the sensory experiences rests on their integration in a single life of which they thus become the visible witness and emblem The perceived world is not only a system of symbols of each sense in terms of the other senses, but also a set of symbols of human life, as is proved by the 'flames' of passion, the 'light' of the spirit and so many other metaphors and myths H Conrad-Martius, *Realontologie*, p 302.

[2] H Conrad-Martius, ibid , p 196 The same author (*Zur Ontologie und Erscheinungslehre der realen Aussenwelt*) speaks of a *Selbstkundgabe* of the object (p 371).

animates the ash-tray, and is self-evidently embodied in it That is why we say that in perception the thing is given to us 'in person', or 'in the flesh'. Prior to and independently of other people, the thing achieves that miracle of expression. an inner reality which reveals itself externally, a significance which descends into the world and begins its existence there, and which can be fully understood only when the eyes seek it in its own location Thus the thing is correlative to my body and, in more general terms, to my exist ence, of which my body is merely the stabilized structure. It is constituted in the hold which my body takes upon it; it is not first of all a meaning for the understanding, but a structure accessible to inspection by the body, and if we try to describe the real as it appears to us in perceptual experience, we find it overlaid with anthropological predicates.

The relations between things or aspects of things having always our body as their vehicle, the whole of nature is the setting of our own life, or our interlocutor in a sort of dialogue That is why in the last analysis we cannot conceive anything which is not perceived or perceptible As Berkeley says, even an unexplored desert has at least one person to observe it, namely myself when I think of it, that is, when I perceive it in purely mental experience The thing is inseparable from a person perceiving it, and can never be actually *in itself* because its articulations are those of our very existence, and because it stands at the other end of our gaze or at the terminus of a sensory exploration which invests it with humanity To this extent, every perception is a communication or a communion, the taking up or completion by us of some extraneous intention or, on the other hand, the complete expression outside ourselves of our perceptual powers and a coition, so to speak, of our body with things. The fact that this may not have been realized earlier is explained by the fact that any coming to awareness of the perceptual world was hampered by the prejudices arising from objective thinking The function of the latter is to reduce all phenomena which bear witness to the union of subject and world, putting in their place the clear idea of the object as *in itself* and of the subject as pure consciousness It therefore severs the links which unite the thing and the embodied subject, leaving only sensible qualities to make up our world (to the exclusion of the modes of appearance which we have described), and preferably visual qualities, because these give the impression of being autonomous, and because they are less directly linked to our body and present us with an object rather than introducing us into an atmosphere. But in reality all things are concretions of a setting, and any explicit perception of a thing survives in virtue of a previous communication with a certain atmosphere. We are not 'a collection of eyes, ears and organs of touch with their cerebral projections   . Just as all literary works . . are only particular cases of the possible permutations of the sounds which make up language and of their literal signs, so qualities or sensations represent the elements from which the great poetry of our world (*Umwelt*) is made up But just as surely as someone knowing only sounds and letters would have no understanding of literature, and would miss not only its ultimate nature but everything about it, so the world is not given and things are not accessible to those for whom "sensations" are the given '[1] The perceived is not necessarily an object present before me as a piece of knowledge to be acquired, it may be a 'unity of value' which is present to me only practically If a picture has been removed from a living room, we may perceive that a change has taken place without being able to say what. I perceive everything that is part of my environment, and my environment includes 'everything of which the existence or non-existence, the nature or modification counts in practice for me'·[2] the storm which has not yet broken, whose signs I could not even list and which I cannot even forecast, but for which I am 'worked up' and prepared—the periphery of the visual field which the hysterical subject does not expressly grasp, but which nevertheless co-determines his movements and orientation—the respect of other men, or that loyal friendship which I take for granted, but which are none the less there for me, since they leave me morally speaking in mid-air when I am deprived of them [3] Love *is* in the flowers prepared by Félix de Vandenesse for Madame de Mortsauf, just as unmistakeably as in a caress: 'I thought that the colours and the foliage had a harmony and a poetry which emerges into the understanding by delighting the gaze, just as musical phrases awaken countless memories in hearts that love and are loved If colour is organized light, must it not have a meaning, as different combinations of air have theirs   Love has its heraldry and the countess secretly deciphered it. She gave me one of those sharp looks that seem like the cry of a sick man touched on his wound she was both embarrassed and delighted ' The flowers are self-evidently a love bouquet, and yet it is impossible to say what in them signifies love, and that is even the reason why Mme de Mortsauf can accept them without breaking her vows. There is no way of understanding them other than by looking at them, but to the beholder they say what they mean. Their significance is the track of an existence, legible and comprehensible for another existence. Natural perception is not a science, it does not posit the things with which science deals, it does not hold them at arm's length in order to observe them, but lives with them; it is the 'opinion' or the 'primary faith' which binds us to a world as to our native land, and the being of

[1] Scheler, *Der Formalismus in der Ethik und die materiale Wertethik*, pp 149–51.
[2] Ibid., p. 140   [3] Ibid.

what is perceived is the antepredicative being towards which our whole existence is polarized

However, we have not exhausted the meaning of 'the thing' by defining it as the correlative of our body and our life After all, we grasp the unity of our body only in that of the thing, and it is by taking things as our starting point that our hands, eyes and all our sense-organs appear to us as so many interchangeable instruments. The body by itself, the body at rest is merely an obscure mass, and we perceive it as a precise and identifiable being when it moves towards a thing, and in so far as it is intentionally projected outwards, and even then this perception is never more than incidental and marginal to consciousness, the centre of which is occupied with things and the world One cannot, as we have said, conceive any perceived thing without someone to perceive it. But the fact remains that the thing presents itself to the person who perceives it as a thing in itself, and thus poses the problem of a genuine *in-itself-for-us* Ordinarily we do not notice this because our perception, in the context of our everyday concerns, alights on things sufficiently attentively to discover in them their familiar presence, but not sufficiently so to disclose the non-human element which lies hidden in them. But the thing holds itself aloof from us and remains self-sufficient. This will become clear if we suspend our ordinary preoccupations and pay a metaphysical and disinterested attention to it It is then hostile and alien, no longer an interlocutor, but a resolutely silent Other, a Self which evades us no less than does intimacy with an outside consciousness The thing and the world, we have already said, are offered to perceptual communication as is a familiar face with an expression which is immediately understood. But then a face expresses something only through the arrangements of the colours and lights which make it up, the meaning of the gaze being not behind the eyes, but in them, and a touch of colour more or less is all the painter needs in order to transform the facial expression of a portrait In the work of his earlier years, Cézanne tried to paint the expression first and foremost, and that is why he never caught it. He gradually learned that expression is the language of the thing itself and springs from its configuration. His painting is an attempt to recapture the physiognomy of things and faces by the integral reproduction of their sensible configuration This is what nature constantly and effortlessly achieves, and it is why the paintings of Cézanne are 'those of a pre-world in which as yet no men existed'.[1] The thing appeared to us above as the goal of a bodily teleology, the norm of our psycho-physiological setting. But that was merely a psychological definition which does not make the full

[1] F. Novotny, *Das Problem des Menschen Cézanne im Verhaltnis zu seiner Kunst,* p 275

meaning of the thing defined explicit, and which reduces the thing to those experiences in which we encounter it. We now discover the core of reality a thing is a thing because, whatever it imparts to us, is imparted through the very organization of its sensible aspects. The 'real' is that environment in which each moment is not only inseparable from the rest, but in some way synonymous with them, in which the 'aspects' are mutually significatory and absolutely equivalent This is perfect fulness. it is impossible completely to describe the colour of the carpet without saying that it *is* a carpet, made of wool, and without implying in this colour a certain tactile value, a certain weight and a certain resistance to sound The thing is an entity of a kind such that the complete definition of one of its attributes demands that of the subject in its entirety an entity, consequently, the significance of which is indistinguishable from its total appearance. Cézanne again said. 'The outline and the colour are no longer distinct, in proportion as one paints, one outlines, and the more the colour is harmonized, the more definite the outline becomes . . when the colour is at its richest, the form is at its most complete'.[1] With the structure lighting-lighted, background and foreground are possible With the appearance of the thing, there can at last be univocal forms and positions The system of appearances, the pre-spatial fields acquire an anchorage and ultimately become a space But it is not the case that geometrical features alone are merged with colour. The very significance of the thing is built up before our eyes, a significance which no verbal analysis can exhaust, and which merges with the exhibiting of the thing in its self-evidence. Every touch of colour applied by Cézanne must, as E. Bernard says, 'contain the atmosphere, the light, the object, the relief, the character, the outline and the style'.[2] Each fragment of a visible spectacle satisfies an infinite number of conditions, and it is of the nature of the real to compress into each of its instants an infinity of relations. Like the thing, the picture has to be seen and not defined, nevertheless, though it is a small world which reveals itself within the larger one, it cannot lay claim to the same substantiality We feel that it is put together by design, that in it significance precedes existence and clothes itself in only the minimum of matter necessary for its communication. The miracle of the real world, on the other hand, is that in it significance and existence are one, and that we see the latter lodge itself in no uncertain fashion in the former In the realm of imagination, I have no sooner formed the intention of seeing than I already believe that I have seen The imaginary has no depth, and does not respond to our efforts to vary our points of view; it does not lend itself to our

[1] Gasquet, *Cezanne*, p 123.
[2] E Bernard, *La Méthode de Cézanne*, p 298

observation [1] We never have a hold upon it In every perception, on the other hand, it is the material itself which assumes significance and form. If I wait for someone at a door in a poorly lit street, each person who comes out has an indistinct appearance. *Someone* is coming out, and I do not yet know whether I can recognize him as the person I am waiting for The familiar figure will emerge from this nebulous background as the earth does from a ground mist The real is distinguishable from our fictions because in reality the significance encircles and permeates matter Once a picture is torn up, we have in our hands nothing but pieces of daubed canvas But if we break up a stone and then further break up the fragments, the pieces remaining are still pieces of stone. The real lends itself to unending exploration; it is inexhaustible. This is why objects belonging to man, tools, seem to be placed on the world, whereas things are rooted in a background of nature which is alien to man. For our human existence, the thing is much less a pole which attracts than one which repels We do not begin by knowing the perspective aspects of the thing; it is not mediated by our senses, our sensations or our perspectives; we go straight to it, and it is only in a secondary way that we become aware of the limits of our knowledge and of ourselves as knowing Here is a die; let us consider it as it is presented, in the natural attitude, to a subject who has never wondered about perception, and who lives among things. The die is there, lying in the world. When the subject moves round it, there appear, not *signs*, but sides of the die. He does not perceive projections or even profiles of the die, but he sees the die itself at one time from this side, at another from that, and those appearances which are not yet firmly fixed intercommunicate, run into each other, and all radiate from a central *Wurfelhaftigkeit*[2] which is the mystical link between them

A set of reductions makes its appearance from the moment we take the perceiving subject into account. In the first place I notice that this die is for me only. Perhaps after all people nearby do not see it, and this alone deprives it of some element of its reality; it ceases to be *in itself* in order to become the pole of a personal history. Then I observe that the die is, strictly speaking, presented to me only through sight, and immediately I am left with nothing but the outer surface of the whole die; it loses its materiality, empties itself, and is reduced to a visual structure of form, colour, light and shade But the form, colour, light and shade are not in a void, for they still retain a point of support, namely the visual thing. Furthermore the visual thing has still a spatial structure which endows its qualitative properties with a particular value: if I learn that the die is merely an illusory one, its

[1] J. P Sartre, *L'Imaginaire*, p 19
[2] Scheler, *Der Formalismus in der Ethik*, p 52

colour changes straight away, and it no longer has the same manner of modulating space. All the spatial relations to be found in the die and which are capable of being made explicit, for example the distance from its nearer to its farther face, the 'real' size of the angles, the 'real' direction of its sides, are indivisible in its being as a visible die It is by way of a third reduction that we pass from the visual thing to the perspective aspect: I observe that the faces of the die cannot all fall beneath my gaze, and that certain of them undergo distortions Through a final reduction, I arrive ultimately at the sensation which is no longer a property of the thing, or even of the perspective aspect, but a modification of my body.[1] The experience of the thing does not go through all these mediations, and consequently the thing is not presented to a mind which seizes each constituent layer as representative of a higher layer, building it up from start to finish It exists primarily in its self-evidence, and any attempt to define the thing either as a pole of my bodily life, or as a permanent possibility of sensations, or as a synthesis of appearances, puts in place of the thing itself in its primordial being an imperfect reconstruction of the thing with the aid of bits and pieces of subjective provenance. How are we to understand both that the thing is the correlative of my knowing body, and that it rejects that body?

What is given is not the thing on its own, but the experience of the thing, or something transcendent standing in the wake of one's subjectivity, some kind of natural entity of which a glimpse is afforded through a personal history. If one tried, according to the realistic approach, to make perception into some coincidence with the thing, it would no longer be possible to understand what the perceptual event was, how the subject managed to assimilate the thing, how after coinciding with the thing he was able to consign it to his own history, since *ex hypothesi* he would have nothing of it in his possession. In order to perceive things, we need to live them Yet we reject the idealism involved in the synthetic view, because it too distorts our lived-through relationship to things In so far as the perceiving subject synthesizes the percept, he has to dominate and grasp in thought a material of perception, to organize and himself link together, from the inside, all the aspects of the thing, which means that perception ceases to be inherent in an individual subject and a point of view, and that the thing loses its transcendence and opacity. To 'live' a thing is not to coincide with it, nor fully to embrace it in thought Our problem, therefore, becomes clear. The perceiving subject must, without relinquishing his place and his point of view, and in the opacity of sensation, reach out towards things to which he has, in advance, no key, and for which he nevertheless carries within himself

[1] Scheler, *Der Formalismus in der Ethik*, pp. 51–4

325

the project, and open himself to an absolute Other which he is making ready in the depths of his being The thing is not all of a piece, for though the perspective aspects, and the ever-changing flow of appearances, are not explicitly posited, all are at least ready to be perceived and given in non-positing consciousness, to precisely the extent necessary for me to be able to escape from them into the thing. When I perceive a pebble, I am not expressly conscious of knowing it only through my eyes, of enjoying only certain perspective aspects of it, and yet an analysis in these terms, if I undertake it, does not surprise me. Beforehand I knew obscurely that my gaze was the medium and instrument of comprehensive perception, and the pebble appeared to me in the full light of day in opposition to the concentrated darkness of my bodily organs I can imagine possible fissures in the solid mass of the thing if I take it into my head to close one eye or to think of the perspective It is in this way that it is true to say that the thing is the outcome of a flow of subjective appearances. And yet I did not actually constitute it, in the sense that I did not actively and through a process of mental inspection posit the interrelations of the many aspects presented to the senses, and the relations of all of them to my different kinds of sensory apparatus We have expressed this by saying that I perceive with my body The visual thing appears when my gaze, following the indications offered by the spectacle, and drawing together the light and shade spread over it, ultimately settles on the lighted surface as upon that which the light reveals My gaze 'knows' the significance of a certain patch of light in a certain context, it understands the logic of lighting Expressed in more general terms, there is a logic of the world to which my body in its entirety conforms, and through which things of intersensory significance become possible for us In so far as it is capable of synergy, my body knows the significance, for the totality of my experience, of this or that colour added or subtracted, and the occurrence of any such change is immediately picked out from the object's presentation and general significance To have senses, sight for example, is to possess that general apparatus, that cast of possible, visual relations with the help of which we are able to take up any given visual grouping To have a body is to possess a universal setting, a schema of all types of perceptual unfolding and of all those inter-sensory correspondences which lie beyond the segment of the world which we are actually perceiving. A thing is, therefore, not actually *given* in perception, it is internally taken up by us, reconstituted and experienced by us in so far as it is bound up with a world, the basic structures of which we carry with us, and of which it is merely one of many possible concrete forms Although a part of our living experience, it is nevertheless transcendent in relation to our life because the human body, with its habits which weave round it a human environment, has running through it a movement towards the world itself Animal behaviour aims at an animal setting (*Umwelt*) and centres of resistance (*Widerstand*) If we try to subject it to natural stimuli devoid of concrete significance, we produce neuroses.[1] Human behaviour opens upon a world (*Welt*) and upon an object (*Gegenstand*) beyond the tools which it makes for itself, and one may even treat one's own body as an object Human life is defined in terms of this power which it has of denying itself in objective thought, a power which stems from its primordial attachment to the world itself Human life 'understands' not only a certain definite environment, but an infinite number of possible environments, and it understands itself because it is thrown into a natural world

What needs to be elucidated, then, is this primary comprehension of the world. The natural world, we said, is the schema of intersensory relations. We do not, following Kant, understand thereby a system of invariable relations to which every existent thing is subject in so far as it can be known It is not like a crystal cube, all the aspects of which can be conceived in virtue of its geometrical structure, and which even reveals its hidden sides, since it is transparent. The world has its unity, although the mind may not have succeeded in inter-relating its facets and in integrating them into the conception of a flat projection. This unity is comparable with that of an individual whom I recognize because he is recognizable in an unchallengeably self-evident way, before I ever succeed in stating the formula governing his character, because he retains the same style in everything he says and does, even though he may change his place or his opinions A style is a certain manner of dealing with situations, which I identify or understand in an individual or in a writer, by taking over that manner myself in a sort of imitative way, even though I may be quite unable to define it, and in any case a definition, correct though it may be, never provides an exact equivalent, and is never of interest to any but those who have already had the actual experience. I experience the unity of the world as I recognize a style. Yet even so the style of a person, or of a town, does not remain constant for me After ten years of friendship, even independently of any changes brought about by age, I seem to be dealing with a different person, and after ten years of living in a district, it is as if I were in a different one. Yet it is only the *knowledge of things* which varies Though almost unnoticed at first glance, it is transformed by the unfolding of perception. The world remains the same world throughout my life, because it is that permanent being within which I

[1] See *La Structure du Comportement*, pp. 72 and ff.

327

make all corrections to my knowledge, a world which in its unity remains unaffected by those corrections, and the self-evidence of which attracts my activity towards the truth through appearance and error It is marginal to the child's first perception as a presence as yet unrecognized but incontrovertible, which knowledge will subsequently make determinate and complete I may be mistaken, and need to rearrange my certainties, and reject the being to which my illusions give rise, but I do not for a moment doubt that in themselves things have been compatible and compossible. because from the very start I am in communication with one being, and one only, a vast individual from which my own experiences are taken, and which persists on the horizon of my life as the distant roar of a great city provides the background to everything we do in it. It is said that sounds or colours belong to a sensory field, because sounds once perceived can be followed only by other sounds, or by silence, which is not an auditory nothingness, but the absence of sounds, and which, therefore, keeps us in contact with the being of sound. If, during the process of reflection, I cease to hear sounds, and then suddenly become receptive to them again, they appear to me to be already there, and I pick up a thread which I had dropped but which is unbroken. The field is a setting that I possess for a certain type of experiences, and which, once established, cannot be nullified. Our possession of the world is similar to this, except that it is possible to conceive a subject with no auditory field, but impossible to conceive a subject with no world [1] Just as, in the hearing subject, the absence of sounds does not cut off all communication with the world of sounds, so in the case of a subject deaf and blind from birth, the absence of the visual and auditory worlds does not sever all communication with the world in general There is always something confronting him, a being to be deciphered, an *omnitudo realitatis*, and the foundation of this possibility is permanently laid by the first sensory experience, however narrow or imperfect it may be We have no other way of knowing what the world is than by actively accepting this affirmation which is made every instant within us; for any definition of the world would be merely a summary and schematic outline, conveying nothing to us, if we did not already have access to the determinate, if we did not in fact know it by virtue of the mere fact that we are It is upon our experience of the world that all our logical operations concerned with significance must be based, and the world itself, therefore, is not a certain significance common to all our experiences which we discern in them, some idea which breathes life into the matter of knowledge The world does not hold for us a set of outlines

[1] E Stein, *Beiträge zur phänomenologischen Begründung der Psychologie und der Geisteswissenschaften*, pp 10 and ff

which some consciousness within us binds together into a unity It is true that the world presents itself as outlines, in the first place spatially, here I can see only the south side of the street, whereas if I crossed over, I should see the north side, also I see nothing but Paris, and the countryside which I have just left behind me has relapsed into a kind of latent life. When we go further into it, spatial outlines are also temporal elsewhere is always something we have seen or might see, and even if I do perceive it as simultaneous with the present, this is because it is part of the same wave of duration The town to which I am drawing nearer, changes its aspects, as I realize when I turn my eyes away for a moment and then look back at it. But the outlines do not follow each other or stand side by side in front of me. My experience at these different stages is bound up with itself in such a way that I do not get different perspective views linked to each other through the conception of an invariant The perceiving body does not successively occupy different points of view beneath the gaze of some unlocated consciousness which is thinking about them. For it is reflection which objectifies points of view or perspectives, whereas when I perceive, I belong, through my point of view, to the world as a whole, nor am I even aware of the limits of my visual field. The variety of points of view is hinted at only by an imperceptible shift, a certain 'blurred' effect in the appearance. If the successive outlines are really distinguished from each other, as in the case of my driving towards a town and looking at it only intermittently, there is no longer a perception of the town, for I find myself suddenly confronted by another object having no common measure with its predecessor I finally pass the judgement: 'It *is* Chartres', and weld the two appearances together, but I am able to do so because they are both extracted from one and the same perception of the world, which consequently cannot admit of the same discontinuity We can no more construct perception of the thing and of the world from discrete aspects, than we can make up the binocular vision of an object from two monocular images My experiences of the world are integrated into one single world as the double image merges into the one thing, when my finger stops pressing upon my eyeball. I do not have one perspective, then another, and between them a link brought about by the understanding, but each perspective *merges into* the other and, in so far as it is still possible to speak of a synthesis, we are concerned with a 'transitional synthesis'. It is particularly true that my present vision is not restricted to what my visual field actually presents to me, for the next room, the landscape behind that hill and the inside or the back of that object are not recalled or represented My point of view is for me not so much a limitation of my experience as a way I have of infiltrating into the world in its entirety. When I see the horizon, it

329

does not make me *think* of that other landscape which I should see if I were standing on it, nor does that other landscape make me think of a third one and so on, I do not *visualize* anything, all these landscapes are already there in the harmonious sequence and infinite unfolding of their perspectives. When I see the bright green of one of Cézanne's vases, it does not make me *think* of pottery, it presents it to me. The pottery is there, with its thin, smooth outer surface and its porous inside, in the particular way in which the green varies in shade. In the inner and outer horizon of the thing or the landscape, there is a co-presence and co-existence of outlines which is brought into existence through space and time. The natural world is the horizon of all horizons, the style of all possible styles, which guarantees for my experiences a given, not a willed, unity underlying all the disruptions of my personal and historical life. Its counterpart within me is the given, general and pre-personal existence of my sensory functions in which we have discovered the definition of the body.

But how is it possible for me to experience the world as a positively existing individual, since none of the perspective views of it which I enjoy exhausts it, since its horizons are always open, and since moreover no knowledge, even scientific knowledge, provides us with the invariable formula of a *facies totius universi*? How can any thing ever really and truly *present itself* to us, since its synthesis is never a completed process, and since I can always expect to see it break down and fall to the status of a mere illusion? Yet there *is* something and not nothing. There is a determinate reality, at least at a certain degree of relativity. Even if in the last resort I have no absolute knowledge of this stone, and even if my knowledge regarding it takes me step by step along an infinite road and cannot ever be complete, the fact remains that the perceived stone is there, that I recognize it, that I have named it and that we agree on a certain number of statements about it. Thus it seems that we are led to a contradiction. belief in the thing and the world must entail the presumption of a completed synthesis—and yet this completion is made impossible by the very nature of the perspectives which have to be inter-related, since each one of them, by virtue of its horizons, refers to other perspectives, and so on indefinitely. There is, indeed, a contradiction, as long as we operate within being, but the contradiction disappears, or rather is generalized, being linked up with the ultimate conditions of our experience and becoming one with the possibility of living and thinking, if we operate in time, and if we manage to understand time as the measure of being. The synthesis of horizons is essentially a temporal process, which means, not that it is subject to time, nor that it is passive in relation to time, nor that it has to prevail over time, but that it merges with the very movement whereby time passes Through

330

my perceptual field, with its spatial horizons, I am present to my surrounding, I co-exist with all the other landscapes which stretch out beyond it, and all these perspectives together form a single temporal wave, one of the world's instants. Through my perceptual field with its temporal horizons I am present to my present, to all the preceding past and to a future. And, at the same time, this ubiquity is not strictly real, but is clearly only intentional. Although the landscape before my eyes may well herald the features of the one which is hidden behind the hill, it does so only subject to a certain degree of indeterminacy: here there are meadows, over there perhaps woods, and, in any case, beyond the near horizon, I know only that there will be land or sea, beyond that either open sea or frozen sea, beyond that again either earth or sky and, as far as the limits of the earth's atmosphere are concerned, I know only that there is, in the most general terms, something to be perceived, and of those remote regions I possess only the style, in the abstract. In the same way, although each past is progressively enclosed in its entirety in the more recent past which has followed it, in virtue of the interlocking of intentionalities, the past degenerates, and the earliest years of my life are lost in the general existence of my body, of which I now know merely that it was already, at that time, confronted by colours and sounds, and a nature similar to the one which I now see before me. I possess the remote past, as I do the future, therefore, only in principle, and my life is slipping away from me on all sides and is circumscribed by impersonal zones. The contradiction which we find between the reality of the world and its incompleteness is the contradiction between the omnipresence of consciousness and its involvement in a field of presence. But let us look more closely to see whether in fact we have here a contradiction and a dilemma. Though I may say that I am enclosed in my present, since after all we pass, by imperceptible transitions, from the present to the past, from the recent to the remote, and since it is impossible to separate strictly the present from what is merely presented in actuality, the transcendence of remote experiences encroaches upon my present and brings a suspicion of unreality even into those which I believe to be coincident with my present self Though I am here and now, yet I am not here and now In so far, on the other hand, as I consider my intentional relationships with the past and the 'elsewhere' as constitutive of the past and the elsewhere, and in so far as I try to free consciousness from any localization and temporal abode, in so far as I am everywhere where my perception and memory lead me, I cannot live in any time, and thus, along with the uniquely compelling reality which defines my present here and now, vanishes the reality of my former or my possible presents If the synthesis could be genuine and my

331

experience formed a closed system, if the thing and the world could be defined once and for all, if the spatio-temporal horizons could, even theoretically, be made explicit and the world conceived from no point of view, then nothing would exist; I should hover above the world, so that all times and places, far from becoming simultaneously real, would become unreal, because I should live in none of them and would be involved nowhere If I am at all times and everywhere, then I am at no time and nowhere. Thus no choice is offered between the incompleteness of the world and its existence, between the particular involvement and omnipresence of consciousness, between transcendence and immanence, since each of these terms when pronounced singly brings to mind its opposite What needs to be understood is that for the same reason I am present here and now, and present elsewhere and always, and also absent from here and from now, and absent from every place and from every time. This ambiguity is not some imperfection of consciousness or existence, but the definition of them. Time in the widest sense, that is, the order of co-existences as well as that of successions, is a setting to which one can gain access and which one can understand only by occupying a situation in it, and by grasping it in its entirety through the horizons of that situation The world, which is the nucleus of time, subsists only by virtue of that unique action which both separates and brings together the actually presented and the present; and consciousness, which is taken to be the seat of clear thinking, is on the contrary the very abode of ambiguity. Under these circumstances one may say, if one wishes, that nothing exists absolutely, and it would, indeed, be more accurate to say that nothing exists and that everything is 'temporalized'. But temporality is not some half-hearted existence. Objective being is not plenary existence The model is provided for us by these things in front of us which at first glance seem entirely determinate: this stone *is* white, hard and cool, and it seems that the world is crystallized in it, that it has no need of time in order to exist, that it wholly unfolds itself in the instant, and that any additional existence would involve it in a fresh coming into being, so that we are tempted to think that the world, if it is anything at all, can be only a collection of things analogous to this stone, and time a collection of perfect instants Such are the world and time of Descartes, and it is indeed a fact that this conception of being is almost inevitably arrived at, since I have a visual field with circumscribed objects, and a sensible present, and since every 'elsewhere' is given as another here, every past and every future as a present gone by or still to come The perception of one single thing lays for ever the foundation of the ideal of objective or explicit knowledge which classical logic develops But as soon as we concentrate upon these certainties, and as soon as we set

332

astir the intentional life which produces them, we become aware that objective being has its roots in the ambiguities of time I cannot conceive the world as a sum of things, nor time as a sum of instantaneous 'present moments', since each thing can offer itself in its full determinacy only if other things recede into the vagueness of the remote distance, and each present can take on its reality only by excluding the simultaneous presence of earlier and later presents, and since thus a sum of things or of presents makes nonsense Things and instants can link up with each other to form a world only through the medium of that ambiguous being known as a subjectivity, and can become present to each other only from a certain point of view and in intention. Objective time which flows and exists part by part would not be even suspected, were it not enveloped in a historical time which is projected from the living present towards a past and towards a future. The alleged plenitude of the object and of the instant springs forth only in face of the imperfection of the intentional being. A present without a future, or an eternal present, is precisely the definition of death; the living present is torn between a past which it takes up and a future which it projects It is thus of the essence of the thing and of the world to present themselves as 'open', to send us beyond their determinate manifestations, to promise us always 'something else to see' This is what is sometimes expressed by saying that the thing and the world are mysterious They are indeed, when we do not limit ourselves to their objective aspect, but put them back into the setting of subjectivity. They are even an absolute mystery, not amenable to elucidation, and this through no provisional gap in our knowledge, for in that case it would fall back to the status of a mere problem, but because it is not of the order of objective thought in which there are solutions. There is nothing to be seen beyond our horizons, but other landscapes and still other horizons, and nothing inside the thing but other smaller things The ideal of objective thought is both based upon and ruined by temporality. The world, in the full sense of the word, is not an object, for though it has an envelope of objective and determinate attributes, it has also fissures and gaps into which subjectivities slip and lodge themselves, or rather which are those subjectivities themselves We now understand why things, which owe their meaning to it, are not meanings presented to the intelligence, but opaque structures, and why their ultimate significance remains confused. The thing and the world exist only in so far as they are experienced by me or by subjects like me, since they are both the concatenation of our perspectives, yet they transcend all perspectives because this chain is temporal and incomplete. I have the impression that the world itself is a living, self-subsistent entity outside me, just as absent landscapes live on beyond my visual field, and as my past was formerly lived on the earlier side of my present

Hallucination causes the real to disintegrate before our eyes, and puts a quasi-reality in its place, and in both these respects this phenomenon brings us back to the pre-logical bases of our knowledge and confirms what has been said about the thing and the world The all-important point is that the patients, most of the time, discriminate between their hallucinations and their perceptions Schizophrenics who experience tactile hallucinations of pricking or of an 'electric current' jump when they feel an injection of ethyl chloride or a real electric shock 'That time,' they say to the doctor, 'you were the cause of it, because you are going to operate ' Another schizophrenic, who said he could see a man standing in the garden under his window, and pointed to the spot, giving a description of the man's clothes and general bearing, was astonished when someone was actually placed in the garden at the spot in question, wearing the same clothes and in the same posture He looked carefully, and exclaimed 'Yes, there is someone there, but it's somebody else ' He would not admit to there being two men in the garden A patient who has never entertained any doubts whatsoever about the voices which she hears, listens to similar ones played to her on the gramophone, interrupts her work, raises her head without turning round, and sees a white angel appear, as it does every time she hears her voices, but she does not count this experience among the day's 'voices': for this time it is not the same thing, but a 'direct' voice, perhaps the doctor's An old woman afflicted with senile dementia, who complains of finding powder in her bed, is startled to find in reality a thin layer of toilet powder there: 'What is this?' she asks, 'this powder is damp, the other is dry ' The subject who, in delirium tremens, takes the doctor's hand to be a guinea pig, is immediately aware of the fact when a real guinea pig is placed in his other hand.[1] The fact that patients so often say that someone is talking to them by telephone or radio, is to be taken precisely as expressing that the morbid world is artificial, and that it lacks something needed to become a 'reality' The voices are uncouth voices, or else voices 'of people pretending to be uncouth', or it may be a young man imitating an old man's voice, or 'as if a German were trying to talk Yiddish' [2] 'It is as when a person says something to someone, but without getting as far as uttering any sound '[3] Do not such admissions put an end to all argument about hallucination? Since the hallucination is not a sensory content, there seems nothing

[1] Zucker, *Experimentelles uber Sinnestauschungen*, pp 706-64
[2] Minkowski, *Le problème des hallucinations et le problème de l'espace*, p 66
[3] Schröder, *Das Halluzimeren*, p 606

334

for it but to regard it as a judgement, an interpretation or a belief. But although these patients do not believe in their hallucinations in the sense in which one believes in perceived objects, an intellectualist theory of hallucination is equally impossible Alain quotes Montaigne's words on madmen 'who believe they see what they do not really see'.[1] But in fact the insane do not *believe* they *see*, or, when questioned, they correct their statements on this point. A hallucination is not a judgement or a rash belief, for the same reasons which prevent it from being a sensory content: the judgement or the belief could consist only in positing the hallucination as true, and this is precisely what the patients do not do At the level of judgement they distinguish hallucination from perception, and in any case argue against their hallucinations: rats cannot come out of the mouth and go back into the stomach.[2] A doctor who hears voices climbs into a boat and rows towards the open sea to convince himself that no one is really talking to him.[3] When the hallucinatory attack supervenes, the rat and the voices *are still there*.

Why do empiricism and intellectualism fail to understand hallucination, and by what other method is there some chance of succeeding? Empiricism tries to *explain* hallucination in the same way as it does perception through the effect of certain physiological causes, the irritation, for example, of certain nervous centres, sense-data appear as they appear in perception through the action of physical stimuli on those same nerve centres At first sight, there is nothing in common between these physiological hypotheses and the intellectualist conception. In fact there is, as we shall see, this much in common that the two doctrines presuppose the priority of objective thought, and having at their disposal only one mode of being, namely objective being, try to force the phenomenon of hallucination into it In this way they misconceive it, and overlook its own mode of certainty and its immanent significance since, according to the patient himself, hallucination has no place in objective being For empiricism, hallucination is an event in the chain of events running from the stimulus to the state of consciousness. In intellectualism, an effort is made to get rid of hallucination properly speaking, to construct it, and to deduce what it might be from a certain idea of consciousness The *cogito* teaches us that the existence of consciousness is indistinguishable from the consciousness of existing, and that therefore there can be nothing in it of which it is unaware, and that conversely, everything that it knows with certainty it finds in itself; that

[1] *Système des Beaux-Arts*, p 15

[2] Specht, *Zur Phanomenologie und Morphologie der pathologischen Wahrnehmungstauschungen*, p 15

[3] Jaspers, *Über Trugwahrnehmungen*, p 471

consequently the truth or falsity of an experience must not reside in its relation to an external reality, but be capable of being read off from it as intrinsic denominations, without which they could never be recognized. Thus false perceptions are not genuine perceptions at all The victim of hallucinations cannot hear or see in the genuine sense of these words He judges and believes that he sees or hears, but he does not really see or hear This conclusion does not leave even the *cogito* intact, for the question remains how a subject can believe that he hears when actually he does not. If it be replied that this belief is simply assertive, that it is knowledge of the first kind, one of those vague appearances in which one does not believe in the full sense of the word, and which persist only in the absence of critical scrutiny, in short a mere *de facto* state of our knowledge, the question will then be how a consciousness can be in this state of deficiency without being aware of it, or, if it is aware of it, how it can remain in it.[1] The intellectualist *cogito* leaves in front of itself only a pure *cogitatum* which it possesses and constitutes in its entirety It is a hopeless task to try to understand how it can be mistaken about an object which it constitutes. It is therefore the reduction of our experience to so many objects, the primacy of objective thought, which, here as before, causes us to lose sight of the phenomenon of hallucination. Between empiricist explanation and intellectualist reflection there is a fundamental kinship, which is their common ignorance of phenomena Both construct the hallucinatory phenomenon instead of living it Even the novelty and validity in intellectualism—the difference of nature which it sets up between perception and hallucination —is impaired by the priority given to objective thought: if the hallucinated subject objectively *knows* or thinks of his hallucination as being what it is, how is hallucinatory deception possible? All the difficulties arise from the fact that objective thought, the reduction of things as experienced to objects, of subjectivity to the *cogitatio*, leaves no room for the equivocal adherence of the subject to pre-objective phenomena The consequence is therefore clear. We must stop constructing hallucination, or indeed consciousness generally, according to a certain essence or idea of itself which compels us to define it in terms of some sort of absolute equivalence and makes its decreed development inconceivable. We learn to know consciousness as we learn to know anything else. When the victim of hallu-

[1] Hence Alain's hesitation if consciousness always knows itself, it must immediately distinguish the percept from the figment of imagination, and we shall say that the imaginary is not visible. (*Système des Beaux-Arts*, pp 15 and ff) But if there is hallucinatory deception, then the imaginary must be able to be taken for the percept, and we shall say that the judgement entails vision (*Quatre-vingt-un chapitres sur l'esprit et les passions*, p 18)

cinations declares that he sees and hears, we must not believe him,[1] since he also declares the opposite; what we must do is understand him. We must not be satisfied with the opinions of sane consciousness on the subject of hallucinatory consciousness, and regard ourselves as sole judges of the distinctive significance of the hallucination. To which it will doubtless be replied that I have no means of access to hallucination as it is for itself. The person who mentally experiences either the hallucination, or another person, or his own past, never coincides with the hallucination, or with the other person, or with his past as it was. Knowledge can never overstep this limit of facticity This is true, but it must not be used to justify arbitrary constructions. It is true that we should never talk about anything if we were limited to talking about those experiences with which we coincide, since speech is already a separation. Moreover there is no experience without speech, as the purely lived-through has no part in the discursive life of man. The fact, remains, however, that the primary meaning of discourse is to be found in that text of experience which it is trying to communicate. What is being sought is not a fictitious coincidence of myself and others, of my present self with its past, of the doctor with the patient; we cannot take over another person's situation, relive the past in its reality, or illness as it is lived through by the patient. The consciousness of others, the past, or illness, can never be brought down in their existence to what I know of them But neither can my own consciousness, in so far as it exists and is committed, be made to amount simply to what I know of it. If a philosopher produces hallucinations in himself by means of an insulin injection, either he yields to the hallucinatory impulse, in which case the hallucination is a living experience for him and not an object of knowledge, or else he retains something of his reflective power, and it will always be possible to challenge his testimony, which is not that of a deranged person 'committed' to his hallucination There is, then, no privileged self-knowledge, and other people are no more closed systems than I am myself. What is given is not myself as opposed to others, my present as opposed to my past, sane consciousness with its *cogito* as opposed to consciousness afflicted with hallucinations, the former being sole judge of the latter and limited, in relation to it, to its internal conjectures—it is the doctor *with* the patient, myself *with* others, my past *on the horizon of* my present. When I recall my past at the present time I distort it, but I can allow for these very distortions, for they are conveyed to me by the tension created between the extinct past at which I am aiming and my arbitrary interpretations. I misunderstood another person because I see him from my own point of view, but then I hear him

[1] As Alain accuses the psychologists of doing

expostulate, and finally come round to the idea of the other person as a centre of perspectives Within my own situation that of the patient whom I am questioning makes its appearance and, in this bipolar phenomenon I learn to know both myself and others We must put ourselves back in the actual situation in which hallucinations and 'reality' are presented to us, and grasp their concrete differentiation at the time that it operates in communication with the patient. I am sitting before my subject and chatting with him, he is trying to describe to me what he 'sees' and what he 'hears', it is not a question either of taking him at his word, or of reducing his experiences to mine, or coinciding with him, or sticking to my own point of view, but of making explicit my experience, and also his experience as it is conveyed to me in my own, and his hallucinatory belief and my real belief, and to understand one through the other

The fact that I classify the voices and visions of my interlocutor as hallucinations means that I find nothing similar in my visual or auditory world I am therefore aware of apprehending, through hearing and particularly through sight, a system of phenomena which makes up not only a private spectacle, but which is the only possible one for me and even for others, and this is what is called reality. The perceived world is not only *my* world, but the one in which I see the behaviour of other people take shape, for their behaviour equally aims at this world, which is the counterpart not only of my consciousness, but of any consciousness *which I can possibly encounter*. What I see with my eyes exhausts for me the possibilities of vision It is true that I see what I do see only from a certain angle, and I concede that a spectator differently placed sees what I can only conjecture But these other spectacles are implied in mine at this moment, just as the reverse or the underneath side of objects is perceived simultaneously with their visible aspect, or as the next room pre-exists in relation to the perception which I should actually have if I walked into it The experiences of other people or those which await me if I change my position merely develop what is suggested by the horizons of my present experience, and add nothing to it My perception brings into co-existence an indefinite number of perceptual chains which, if followed up, would confirm it in all respects and accord with it. My eyes and my hand know that any actual change of place would produce a sensible response entirely according to my expectation, and I can feel swarming beneath my gaze the countless mass of more detailed perceptions that I anticipate, and upon which I already have a hold I am, therefore, conscious of perceiving a setting which 'tolerates' nothing more than is written or foreshadowed in my perception, and I am in present communication with a consummate

338

fullness [1] The victim of hallucination enjoys no such belief. the hallucinatory phenomenon is no part of the world, that is to say, it is not *accessible*, there is no definite path leading from it to all the remaining experiences of the deluded subject, or to the experience of the sane. 'Can't you hear my voices?' asks the patient, 'then I must be the only one to hear them.' [2] Hallucinations are played out on a stage different from that of the perceived world, and are in a way superimposed 'Do you know,' says one patient, 'while we are talking, someone is saying one thing or another to me. Now where can it all come from?' [3] The fact that the hallucination does not take its place in the stable and intersubjective world means that it lacks the fullness, the inner articulation which makes the real thing reside 'in itself', and act and exist by itself The hallucinatory thing is not, as is the real thing, packed with small perceptions which sustain it in existence. It is an implicit and inarticulate significance Confronted by the real thing, our behaviour feels itself motivated by 'stimuli' which fill out and vindicate its intention Where a phantasm is concerned, the initiative comes from us, and it has no external counterpart [4] The hallucinatory thing is not, like the real thing, a form of being with depth, which compresses within itself a thickness of duration; nor is hallucination, like perception, my concrete hold on time in a living present It glides over time as it does over the surface of the world. The person who speaks to me in my dream has no sooner opened his mouth before his thought is conveyed miraculously to me; I know what the person is saying to me before he says anything at all. The hallucination is not in the world but 'before' it, because the patient's body no longer enjoys its insertion into the system of appearances All hallucination bears initially on one's own body. 'It is as if I heard with my mouth ' 'The person speaking is on my lips,' say patients. [5] In 'feelings of bodily presence' (*leibhaften Bewusstheiten*) patients feel the presence of someone they never see close to them, or behind them, or on them, and they experience that presence as drawing closer or receding One schizophrenic woman constantly has the impression that she is being seen naked from behind. George Sand has a double whom she has never seen, but who sees her the whole time and calls her by her name with her own voice [6] Depersonalization and disturbance of the body image are immediately

---

[1] Minkowski, *Le Problème des hallucinations et le probleme de l'espace*, p. 66.
[2] Ibid, p 64   [3] Ibid., p. 66
[4] That is why Palagyi could assert that perception is a 'direct phantasm', hallucination an 'inverse phantasm'. Schorsch, *Zur Theorie der Halluzinationen*, p 64.
[5] Schroder, *Das Halluzinieren*, p 606
[6] Menninger-Lerchental, *Das Truggebilde der Eigenen Gestalt*, pp 76 and ff.

translated into an external phantasm, because it is one and the same thing for us to perceive our body and to perceive our situation in a certain physical and human setting, for our body is nothing but that very situation in so far as it is realized and actualized In extra-campine * hallucination the patient believes that he sees a man behind him, that he sees simultaneously in all directions round about him, that he can look through a window situated behind his back [1] The illusion of seeing is, therefore, much less the presentation of an illusory object than the spread and, so to speak, running wild of a visual power which has lost any sensory counterpart. There are hallucinations because through the phenomenal body we are in constant relationship with an environment into which that body is projected, and because, when divorced from its actual environment, the body remains able to summon up, by means of its own settings, the pseudo-presence of that environment To that extent, the thing in hallucination is never seen and is never visible One subject, under mescalin, sees the screw of a piece of apparatus as a glass bulb or a protuberance on a rubber balloon. But what precisely does he see? 'I perceive a world covered with swellings . . It is as if my perception suddenly changed key to become perception in intumescence, as one plays a piece of music in C or B flat . Just then, my whole perception was transformed and, for an instant, I perceived a rubber bulb. Does that mean that I saw nothing else? No, but I had the feeling of being transferred to a setting such that I could perceive in no other way. The belief took possession of me that the world is thus . Later another change took place . . Everything seemed at once clammy and scaly, like some of the large serpents I have seen uncoiling themselves at the Berlin Zoo Then I was seized with the fear of being on a small island surrounded by serpents '[2] Hallucination does not present me with protuberances, or scales, or words like ponderous realities gradually revealing their meaning. It does no more than reproduce for me the way in which these realities strike me in my being of feeling and of language When the patient refuses food because it is 'poisoned', we need to realize that for him the word has not the sense that it would have for a chemist [3] the patient does not believe that the food possesses properties which are actually poisonous to the objective body. The poison in this case is an affective entity, a magic presence comparable to that of illness or misfortune The majority of hallucinations are not things with

* I e when the patient believes he perceives outside the sensory field presented to him (Translator's note)

[1] Menninger-Lerchenthal, *Das Tinggebilde der Eigenen Gestalt*, p 147.

[2] Unpublished self-observation of J P Sartre

[3] Straus, *Vom Sinn der Sinne*, p 290.

different facets, but short-lived phenomena, such as pricking sensations, jolts, explosions, draughts, waves of cold or heat, sparks, points of bright light, glowing lights or silhouetted shapes [1] When it is a question of real things, a rat for example, these are represented only by their general style and physiognomy. These disjoined phenomena do not admit of precise causal connections among themselves Their sole mutual relationship is one of co-existence—a co-existence which always has a significance for the patient, since awareness of contingency presupposes definite and distinct causal sequences, and since we are here among the odd remnants of a world in ruins 'A running nose becomes a specific flow, and the fact of dozing in an underground train acquires a strange and unique significance'.[2] Hallucinations are associated with a certain sensory realm only in so far as each sensory field provides the distortion of existence with particular possibilities of expression The schizophrenic's hallucinations are predominantly auditory and tactile, because the world of hearing and touch, in virtue of its natural structure, is better able to stand for an existence which is possessed, jeopardized and de-individualized. The heavy drinker experiences predominantly visual hallucinations because sight provides the disordered processes with a means of calling into being an opponent or a task which have to be faced [3] The victim of hallucination does not see and hear in the normal sense, but makes use of his sensory fields and his natural insertion into a world in order to build up, out of the fragments of this world, an artificial world answering to the total intention of his being.

But though hallucination is not a sensory process, still less is it a judgement. It is not given to the subject as a construction, and has no place in the 'geographical world', in the being, that is, which we know and judge, in the network of facts subject to laws, but in the individual 'landscape'[4] through which the world impinges upon us,

[1] Minkowski, *Le Probleme des hallucinations et le probleme de l'espace*, p 67
[2] Ibid , p. 68.
[3] Straus, op cit , p 288.
[4] Ibid. The patient 'lives within the horizon of his landscape, under the sway of univocal impressions which, lacking any motif or basis, are no longer made to fit into the universal order of the world of things, or into the universal sense-relationships of language. The things to which patients refer by familiar names have ceased to be the same things for them that they are for us What they have retained and made into parts of their landscape are mere broken remnants of our world, and even these do not remain what they were as parts of the whole ' Things for the schizophrenic are frozen and inert, whereas those of delirium are communicative and living to a greater degree than are ours. 'If the illness grows worse, the disintegration of thought and the disappearance of speech reveal the loss of geographical space, and the blunted feelings reveal the impoverishment of the landscape ' (Straus, op cit , p 291)

and by means of which we are in vital communication with it. A woman patient declares that someone looked at her at the market, and that she felt the gaze fall upon her like a blow, but could not say whence it came. She cannot bring herself to say that in common property space there stood a flesh and blood person who turned his eyes towards her—and it is because of this refusal that the arguments that we can bring against her leave her completely unmoved. For her it is not a matter of what happens in the objective world, but of what she encounters, what touches her or strikes her. The food refused by the victim of hallucinations is poisoned only for him, but to this extent it is poisoned irrefutably. The hallucination is not a perception, *but it has the value of reality*, and it alone counts for the victim The world has lost its expressive force,[1] and the hallucinatory system has usurped it Although hallucination is not a perception, there is a hallucinatory deception, and this is what we shall never understand if we take hallucination to be an intellectual operation. However different it is from a perception, hallucination must be able to supplant it, and exist for the patient in a higher degree than his own perceptions. This can be so only so long as hallucination and perception are modalities of one single primordial function, through which we arrange round about us a setting of definite structure, through which we are enabled to place ourselves at one time fairly and squarely in the world, and at another marginally to it. The patient's existence is displaced from its centre, being no longer enacted through dealings with a harsh, resistant and intractable world which has no knowledge of us, but expending its substance in isolation creating a fictitious setting for itself. *But this fiction can have the value of reality only because in the normal subject reality itself suffers through an analogous process.* In so far as he too has sensory fields and a body, the normal person is equally afflicted with this gaping wound through which illusion can make its way in His representation of the world is no less vulnerable. In so far as we believe what we see, we do so without any verification, and the mistake of the traditional theories of perception is to introduce into perception itself intellectual operations and a critical examination of the evidence of the senses, to which we in fact resort only when direct perception founders in ambiguity. In the case of the normal subject private experience, independently of any express verification, links up with itself and with experiences of external origin, so that the landscape opens on to a geographical world and tends towards absolute plenitude The normal person does not find satisfaction in subjectivity,

[1] Hallucination, says Klages, supposes a '*Verminderung des Ausdrucksgehaltes der ausseren Erscheinungswelt*'. Quoted by Schorsch, *Zur Theorie der Halluzinationen*, p. 71.

he runs away from it, he is genuinely concerned with being in the world, and his hold on time is direct and unreflecting, whereas the sufferer from hallucinations simply exploits his being in the world in order to carve a private sector for himself out of the common property world, and constantly runs up against the transcendence of time. Underlying express acts which enable me to posit before myself an object at its distance, standing in a definite relation to other objects, and having specific characteristics which can be observed, underlying perceptions properly understood, there is, then, sustaining them, a deeper function without which perceived objects would lack the distinctive sign of reality, as they do for the schizophrenic, and through which they begin to count or be valid for us It is the momentum which carries us beyond subjectivity, which gives us our place in the world prior to any science and any verification, through a kind of 'faith' or 'primary opinion'[1]—or which may, on the other hand, become bogged down in our private appearances. In this realm of primary opinion, hallucinatory illusion is possible even though hallucination is never perception, and though the true world is always suspected as there by the patient, even as he turns away from it, because we are still in the antepredicative world, and because the connection between appearance and total experience is merely implicit and presumptive, even in the case of true perception. The child attributes his dreams, no less than his perceptions, to the world, he believes that the dream is enacted in his room, at the foot of his bed, the sole difference from perception being that the dream is visible to sleepers alone.[2] The world is still the vague theatre of all experiences. It takes in without discrimination real objects on the one hand and individual and momentary phantasms on the other—because it is an individual which embraces everything and not a collection of objects linked by causal relations To have hallucinations and more generally to imagine, is to exploit this tolerance on the part of the antepredicative world, and our bewildering proximity to the whole of being in syncretic experience.

We succeed, therefore, in accounting for hallucinatory deception only by removing apodeictic certainty from perception and full self-possession from perceptual consciousness The existence of the percept is never necessary, since perception entails a process of making explicit which could be pursued to infinity and which, moreover, could not gain in one direction without losing in another, and without being exposed to the risks of time But it must not be concluded from this that the perceived is only possible or probable, and that it can be brought down, for instance, to a permanent possibility of

[1] *Urdoxa* or *Urglaube*, of Husserl
[2] Piaget, *La Représentation du monde chez l'enfant*, pp 69 and ff

perception. Possibility and probability presuppose the prior experience of error, and correspond to a state of doubt. The percept is and remains, despite all critical education, on the hither side of doubt and demonstration. The sun 'rises' for the scientist in the same way as it does for the uneducated person, and our scientific representations of the solar system remain matters of hearsay, like lunar landscapes, and we never believe in them in the sense in which we believe in the sunrise The sunrise and the percept in general is 'real', and we spontaneously identify them as part of the world. Each perception, though always capable of being 'cancelled' and relegated among illusions, disappears only to give place to another perception which rectifies it. Each thing can, after the event, appear uncertain, but what is at least certain for us is that there are things, that is to say, a world To ask oneself whether the world is real is to fail to understand what one is asking, since the world is not a sum of things which might always be called into question, but the inexhaustible reservoir from which things are drawn. The percept taken in its entirety, with the world horizon *which announces both its possible disjunction and its possible replacement by another perception,* certainly does not mislead us. There could not possibly be error where there is not yet truth, but reality, and not yet necessity, but facticity. Correspondingly, we must refuse to attribute to perceptual consciousness the full possession of itself, and that immanence which would rule out any possible illusion. If hallucinations are to be possible, it is necessary that consciousness should, at some moment, cease to know what it is doing, otherwise it would be conscious of constituting an illusion, and would not stand by it, so there would no longer be any illusion at all. And if, as we have said, the illusory thing and the true thing do not have the same structure, for the patient to assent to the illusion, he must forget or repress the true world, and cease to refer back to it, and retain at least the ability to revert to the primitive confusion of the true and the false. Yet we do not cut consciousness off from itself, which would preclude all progress of knowledge beyond primary opinion, and especially the philosophic examination of primary opinion as the basis of all knowledge All that is required is that the coincidence of myself with myself, as it is achieved in the *cogito,* shall never be a real coincidence, but merely an intentional and presumptive one In fact, between myself who have just thought this, and myself who am thinking that I have thought it, there is interposed already a thickness of duration, so that I may always doubt whether that thought which has already passed was indeed such as I now see it to have been Since, furthermore, I have no other evidence of my past than present testimony and yet do have the idea of a past, I have no reason to set the unreflective, as an unknowable, over

344

against the reflection which I bring to bear on it. But my confidence in reflection amounts in the last resort to my accepting and acting on the fact of temporality, and the fact of the world as the invariable framework of all illusion and all disillusion: I know myself only in so far as I am inherent in time and in the world, that is, I know myself only in my ambiguity.

4

OTHER SELVES AND THE
HUMAN WORLD

I AM thrown into a nature, and that nature appears not only as outside me, in objects devoid of history, but it is also discernible at the centre of subjectivity. Theoretical and practical decisions of personal life may well lay hold, from a distance, upon my past and my future, and bestow upon my past, with all its fortuitous events, a definite significance, by following it up with a future which will be seen after the event as foreshadowed by it, thus introducing historicity into my life. Yet these sequences have always something artificial about them. It is at the present time that I realize that the first twenty-five years of my life were a prolonged childhood, destined to be followed by a painful break leading eventually to independence If I take myself back to those years as I actually lived them and as I carry them within me, my happiness at that time cannot be explained in terms of the sheltered atmosphere of the parental home; the world itself was more beautiful, things were more fascinating, and I can never be sure of reaching a fuller understanding of my past than it had of itself at the time I lived through it, nor of silencing its protest The interpretation which I now give of it is bound up with my confidence in psychoanalysis Tomorrow, with more experience and insight, I shall possibly understand it differently, and consequently reconstruct my past in a different way In any case, I shall go on to interpret my present interpretations in their turn, revealing their latent content and, in order finally to assess their truth-value, I shall need to keep these discoveries in mind My hold on the past and the future is precarious, and my possession of my own time is always postponed until a stage when I may fully understand it, yet this stage can never be reached, since it would be one more moment, bounded by the horizon of its future, and requiring in its turn further developments in order to be understood. My voluntary and rational life, therefore,

346

knows that it merges into another power which stands in the way of its completion, and gives it a permanently tentative look. Natural time is always there The transcendence of the instants of time is both the ground of, and the impediment to, the rationality of my personal history the ground because it opens a totally new future to me in which I shall be able to reflect upon the element of opacity in my present, a source of danger in so far as I shall never manage to seize the present through which I live with apodeictic certainty, and since the lived is thus never entirely comprehensible, what I understand never quite tallies with my living experience, in short, I am never quite at one with myself Such is the lot of a being who is born, that is, who once and for all has been given to himself as something to be understood. Since natural time remains at the centre of my history, I see myself surrounded by it. The fact that my earliest years lie behind me like an unknown land is not attributable to any chance lapse of memory, or any failure to think back adequately. there is nothing to be known in these unexplored lands. For example, in pre-natal existence, nothing was perceived, and therefore there is nothing to recall There was nothing but the raw material and adumbration of a natural self and a natural time This anonymous life is merely the extreme form of that temporal dispersal which constantly threatens the historical present. In order to have some inkling of the nature of that amorphous existence which preceded my own history, and which will bring it to a close, I have only to look within me at that time which pursues its own independent course, and which my personal life utilizes but does not entirely overlay Because I am borne into personal existence by a time which I do not constitute, all my perceptions stand out against a background of nature While I perceive, and even without having any knowledge of the organic conditions of my perception, I am aware of drawing together somewhat absent-minded and dispersed "consciousnesses". sight, hearing and touch, with their fields, which are anterior, and remain alien, to my personal life The natural object is the track left by this generalized existence. And every object will be, in the first place and in some respect, a natural object, made up of colours, tactile and auditory qualities, in so far as it is destined to enter my life.

Just as nature finds its way to the core of my personal life and becomes inextricably linked with it, so behaviour patterns settle into that nature, being deposited in the form of a cultural world. Not only have I a physical world, not only do I live in the midst of earth, air and water, I have around me roads, plantations, villages, streets, churches, implements, a bell, a spoon, a pipe Each of these objects is moulded to the human action which it serves Each one spreads round it an atmosphere of humanity which may be determinate in a low degree, in the case of a few footmarks in the sand, or on the other hand highly determinate, if I go into every room from top to bottom of a house recently evacuated. Now, although it may not be surprising that the sensory and perceptual functions should lay down a natural world in front of themselves, since they are preper-sonal, it may well seem strange that the spontaneous acts through which man has patterned his life should be deposited, like some sedi-ment, outside himself and lead an anonymous existence as things The civilization in which I play my part exists for me in a self-evident way in the implements with which it provides itself If it is a question of an unknown or alien civilization, then several manners of being or of living can find their place in the ruins or the broken instruments which I discover, or in the landscape through which I roam. The cul-tural world is then ambiguous, but it is already present. I have before me a society to be known An Objective Spirit dwells in the remains and the scenery. How is this possible? In the cultural object, I feel the close presence of others beneath a veil of anonymity. *Someone* uses the pipe for smoking, the spoon for eating, the bell for summon-ing, and it is through the perception of a human act and another per-son that the perception of a cultural world could be verified How can an action or a human thought be grasped in the mode of the 'one' since, by its very nature, it is a first person operation, insepar-able from an I? It is easy to reply that the indefinite pronoun is here no more than a vague formula for referring to a multiplicity of I's or even a general I It will be said that I experience a certain cultural environment along with behaviour corresponding to it: faced with the remains of an extinct civilization, I conceive analogically the kind of man who lived in it But the first need is to know how I experience my own cultural world, my own civilization The reply will once more be that I see a certain use made by other men of the implements which surround me, that I interpret their behaviour by analogy with my own, and through my inner experience, which teaches me the significance and intention of perceived gestures. In the last resort, the actions of others are, according to this theory, always understood through my own; the 'one' or the 'we' through the 'I' But this is pre-cisely the question how can the word 'I' be put into the plural, how can a general idea of the I be formed, how can I speak of an I other than my own, how can I know that there are other I's, how can con-sciousness which, by its nature, and as self-knowledge, is in the mode of the I, be grasped in the mode of Thou, and through this, in the world of the 'One'? The very first of all cultural objects, and the one by which all the rest exist, is the body of the other person as the vehicle of a form of behaviour Whether it be a question of vestiges or the body of another person, we need to know how an object in space can become the eloquent relic of an existence; how, conversely, an intention, a thought or a project can detach themselves from the personal subject and become visible outside him in the shape of his body, and in the environment which he builds for himself. The constitution of the other person does not fully elucidate that of society, which is not an existence involving two or even three people, but co-existence involving an indefinite number of consciousnesses Yet the analysis of the perception of others runs up against a difficulty in principle raised by the cultural world, since it is called upon to solve the paradox of a consciousness seen from the outside, of a thought which has its abode in the external world, and which, therefore, is already subjectless and anonymous compared with mine.

What we have said about the body provides the beginning of a solution to this problem. The existence of other people is a difficulty and an outrage for objective thought. If the events of the world are, in Lachelier's words, a network of general properties standing at the point of intersection of functional relations which, in principle, enable the analysis of the former to be carried through, and if the body is indeed a province of the world, if it is that object which the biologist talks about, that conjunction of processes analysed in physiological treatises, that collection of organs shown in the plates of books on anatomy, then my experience can be nothing but the dialogue between bare consciousness and the system of objective correlations which it conceives The body of another, like my own, is not inhabited, but is an object standing before the consciousness which thinks about or constitutes it Other men, and myself, seen as empirical beings, are merely pieces of mechanism worked by springs, but the true subject has no counterpart, for that consciousness which is hidden in so much flesh and blood is the least intelligible of occult qualities My consciousness, being co-extensive with what can exist for me, and corresponding to the whole system of experience, cannot encounter, in that system, another consciousness capable of bringing immediately to light in the world the background, unknown to me, of its own phenomena. There are two modes of being, and two only. being in itself, which is that of objects arrayed in space, and being for itself, which is that of consciousness Now, another person would seem to stand before me as an *in-itself* and yet to exist *for himself*, thus requiring of me, in order to be perceived, a contradictory operation, since I ought both to distinguish him from myself, and therefore place him in the world of objects, and think of him as a consciousness, that is, the sort of being with no outside and no parts, to which I have access merely because that being is myself, and because the thinker and the thought about are amalgamated in him. There is thus no place for other people and a plurality of

349

consciousnesses in objective thought In so far as I constitute the world, I cannot conceive another consciousness, for it too would have to constitute the world and, at least as regards this other view of the world, I should not be the constituting agent Even if I succeeded in thinking of it as constituting the world, it would be I who would be constituting the consciousness as such, and once more I should be the sole constituting agent

But we have in fact learned to shed doubt upon objective thought, and have made contact, on the hither side of scientific representations of the world and the body, with an experience of the body and the world which these scientific approaches do not successfully embrace My body and the world are no longer objects co-ordinated together by the kind of functional relationships that physics establishes The system of experience in which they intercommunicate is not spread out before me and ranged over by a constituting consciousness *I have* the world as an incomplete individual, through the agency of my body as the potentiality of this world, and I have the positing of objects through that of my body, or conversely the positing of my body through that of objects, not in any kind of logical implication, as we determine an unknown size through its objective relations to given sizes, but in a real implication, and because my body is a movement towards the world, and the world my body's point of support. The ideal of objective thought—the system of experience conceived as a cluster of physico-mathematical correlations—is grounded in my perception of the world as an individual concordant with itself, and when science tries to include my body among the relationships obtaining in the objective world, it is because it is trying in its way, to translate the saturation of my phenomenal body on to the primordial world At the same time as the body withdraws from the objective world, and forms between the pure subject and the object a third genus of being, the subject loses its purity and its transparency Objects stand before me and throw on to my retina a certain projection of themselves, and I perceive them. There can no longer be any question of isolating, in my physiological representation of the phenomenon, the retinal images and their cerebral counterpart from the total field, actual and possible, in which they appear The physiological event is merely the abstract schema of the perceptual event[1] Nor can one invoke, under the name of mental images, discontinuous, perspective views corresponding to the successive retinal images, or finally bring in an 'inspection of the mind' which restores the object beyond the distorting perspectives. We must conceive the perspectives and the point of view as our insertion into the world-as-an-individual, and perception, no longer as a con-

[1] *La Structure du Comportement*, p 125

350

stitution of the true object, but as our inherence in things Consciousness reveals in itself, along with the sensory fields and with the
world as the field of all fields, the opacity of a primary past If I experience this inhering of my consciousness in its body and its world,
the perception of other people and the plurality of consciousnesses
no longer present any difficulty. If, for myself who am reflecting on
perception, the perceiving subject appears provided with a primordial setting in relation to the world, drawing in its train that bodily
thing in the absence of which there would be no other things for it,
then why should other bodies which I perceive not be similarly inhabited by consciousnesses? If my consciousness has a body, why
should other bodies not 'have' consciousnesses? Clearly this involves a profound transformation of the notions of body and consciousness. As far as the body is concerned, even the body of another,
we must learn to distinguish it from the objective body as set forth
in works on physiology. This is not the body which is capable of
being inhabited by a consciousness. We must restore to visible bodies
those forms of behaviour which are outlined by them and which
appear on them, but are not really contained in them.[1] How significance and intentionality could come to dwell in molecular edifices
or masses of cells is a thing which can never be made comprehensible,
and here Cartesianism is right. But there is, in any case, no question
of any such absurd undertaking It is simply a question of recognizing that the body, as a chemical structure or an agglomeration of
tissues, is formed, by a process of impoverishment, from a primordial
phenomenon of the body-for-us, the body of human experience or
the perceived body, round which objective thought works, but without being called upon to postulate its completed analysis As for
consciousness, it has to be conceived, no longer as a constituting
consciousness and, as it were, a pure being-for-itself, but as a perceptual consciousness, as the subject of a pattern of behaviour, as
being-in-the-world or existence, for only thus can another appear at
the top of his phenomenal body, and be endowed with a sort of
'locality'. Under these conditions the antinomies of objective thought
vanish Through phenomenological reflection I discover vision, not
as a 'thinking about seeing', to use Descartes' expression, but as a
gaze at grips with a visible world, and that is why for me there can
be another's gaze; that expressive instrument called a face can carry
an existence, as my own existence is carried by my body, that know-
ledge-acquiring apparatus. When I turn towards perception, and
pass from direct perception to thinking about that perception, I re-
enact it, and find at work in my organs of perception a thinking

[1] This task we have tried to perform elsewhere. (*La Structure du Comportement*,
Chaps I and II)

351

older than myself of which those organs are merely the trace In the same way I understand the existence of other people Here again I have only the trace of a consciousness which evades me in its actuality and, when my gaze meets another gaze, I re-enact the alien existence in a sort of reflection. There is nothing here resembling 'reasoning by analogy'. As Scheler so rightly declares, reasoning by analogy presupposes what it is called on to explain The other consciousness can be deduced only if the emotional expressions of others are compared and identified with mine, and precise correlations recognized between my physical behaviour and my 'psychic events'. Now the perception of others is anterior to, and the condition of, such observations, the observations do not constitute the perception. A baby of fifteen months opens its mouth if I playfully take one of its fingers between my teeth and pretend to bite it And yet it·has scarcely looked at its face in a glass, and its teeth are not in any case like mine The fact is that its own mouth and teeth, as it feels them from the inside, are immediately, for it, an apparatus to bite with, and my jaw, as the baby sees it from the outside, is immediately, for it, capable of the same intentions 'Biting' has immediately, for it, an intersubjective significance. It perceives its intentions in its body, and my body with its own, and thereby my intentions in its own body The observed correlations between my physical behaviour and that of others, my intentions and my pantomime, may well provide me with a clue in the methodical attempt to know others and on occasions when direct perception fails, but they do not teach me the existence of other people. Between my consciousness and my body as I experience it, between this phenomenal body of mine and that of another as I see it from the outside, there exists an internal relation which causes the other to appear as the completion of the system The possibility of another person's being self-evident is owed to the fact that I am not transparent for myself, and that my subjectivity draws its body in its wake We said earlier in so far as the other person resides in the world, is visible there, and forms a part of my field, he is never an Ego in the sense in which I am one for myself In order to think of him as a genuine *I*, I ought to think of myself as a mere object for him, which I am prevented from doing by the knowledge which I have of myself. But if another's body is not an object for me, nor mine an object for him, if both are manifestations of behaviour, the positing of the other does not reduce me to the status of an object in his field, nor does my perception of the other reduce him to the status of an object in mine The other person is never quite a personal being, if I myself am totally one, and if I grasp myself as apodeictically self-evident. But if I find in myself, through reflection, along with the perceiving subject, a pre-personal subject given to itself, and if my perceptions are centred outside me as sources of initiative and judgement, if the perceived world remains in a state of neutrality, being neither verified as an object nor recognized as a dream, then it is not the case that everything that appears in the world is arrayed before me, and so the behaviour of other people can have its place there This world may remain undivided between my perception and his, the self which perceives is in no particularly privileged position which rules out a perceived self, both are, not *cogitationes* shut up in their own immanence, but beings which are outrun by their world, and which consequently may well be outrun by each other The affirmation of an alien consciousness standing over against mine would immediately make my experience into a private spectacle, since it would no longer be co-extensive with being The *cogito* of another person strips my own *cogito* of all value, and causes me to lose the assurance which I enjoyed in my solitude of having access to the only being conceivable for me, being, that is, as it is aimed at and constituted by me. But we have learned in individual perception not to conceive our perspective views as independent of each other; we know that they slip into each other and are brought together finally in the thing In the same way we must learn to find the communication between one consciousness and another in one and the same world. In reality, other people are not included in my perspective of the world because this perspective itself has no definite limits, because it slips spontaneously into the other person's, and because both are brought together in the one single world in which we all participate as anonymous subjects of perception.

In so far as I have sensory functions, a visual, auditory and tactile field, I am already in communication with others taken as similar psycho-physical subjects. No sooner has my gaze fallen upon a living body in process of acting than the objects surrounding it immediately take on a fresh layer of significance they are no longer simply what I myself could make of them, they are what this other pattern of behaviour is about to make of them. Round about the perceived body a vortex forms, towards which my world is drawn and, so to speak, sucked in to this extent, it is no longer merely mine, and no longer merely present, it is present to x, to that other manifestation of behaviour which begins to take shape in it. Already the other body has ceased to be a mere fragment of the world, and become the theatre of a certain process of elaboration, and, as it were, a certain 'view' of the world There is taking place over there a certain manipulation of things hitherto my property. Someone is making use of my familiar objects. But who can it be? I say that it is another person, a second self, and this I know in the first place because this living body has the same structure as mine. I experience my own body as the

353

power of adopting certain forms of behaviour and a certain world, and I am given to myself merely as a certain hold upon the world: now, it is precisely my body which perceives the body of another person, and discovers in that other body a miraculous prolongation of my own intentions, a familiar way of dealing with the world Henceforth, as the parts of my body together comprise a system, so my body and the other person's are one whole, two sides of one and the same phenomenon, and the anonymous existence of which my body is the ever-renewed trace henceforth inhabits both bodies simultaneously [1] All of which makes another living being, but not yet another man But this alien life, like mine with which it is in communication, is an open life. It is not entirely accounted for by a certain number of biological or sensory functions. It annexes . ¹ural objects by diverting them from their immediate significance, it makes tools for itself, and projects itself into the environment in the shape of cultural objects. The child finds them around him at birth like meteorites from another planet. He appropriates them and learns to use them as others do, because the body image ensures the immediate correspondence of what he sees done and what he himself does, and because in that way the implement is fixed in his mind as a determinate *manipulandum*, and other people as centres of human action There is one particular cultural object which is destined to play a crucial rôle in the perception of other people language In the experience of dialogue, there is constituted between the other person and myself a common ground, my thought and his are interwoven into a single fabric, my words and those of my interlocutor are called forth by the state of the discussion, and they are inserted into a shared operation of which neither of us is the creator. We have here a dual being, where the other is for me no longer a mere bit of behaviour in my transcendental field, nor I in his, we are collaborators for each other in consummate reciprocity. Our perspectives merge into each other, and we co-exist through a common world. In the present dialogue, I am freed from myself, for the other person's thoughts are certainly his, they are not of my making, though I do grasp them the moment they come into being, or even anticipate them. And indeed, the objection which my interlocutor raises to what I say draws from me thoughts which I had no idea I possessed, so that at the same time that I lend him thoughts, he reciprocates by making me think too It is only retrospectively, when I have withdrawn from the dialogue and am recalling it that I am able to reintegrate it into my life and make of it an episode in my private history,

---

[1] That is why disturbances affecting a subject's body image can be unearthed by requiring him to point out on the doctor's body the part of his own which is being touched.

and that the other recedes into his absence, or, in so far as he remains present for me, is felt as a threat The perception of other
people and the intersubjective world are problematical only for
adults The child lives in a world which he unhesitatingly believes
accessible to all around him He has no awareness of himself or of
others as private subjectivities, nor does he suspect that all of us,
himself included, are limited to one certain point of view of the
world. That is why he subjects neither his thoughts, in which he believes as they present themselves, without attempting to link them to
each other, nor our words, to any sort of criticism. He has no knowledge of points of view. For him men are empty heads turned towards
one single, self-evident world where everything takes place, even
dreams, which are, he thinks, in his room, and even thinking, since it
is not distinct from words Others are for him so many gazes which
inspect things, and have an almost material existence, so much so
that the child wonders how these gazes avoid being broken as they
meet [1] At about twelve years old, says Piaget, the child achieves the
cogito and reaches the truths of rationalism At this stage, it is held,
he discovers himself both as a point of view on the world and also
as called upon to transcend that point of view, and to construct an
objectivity at the level of judgement Piaget brings the child to a
mature outlook as if the thoughts of the adult were self-sufficient and
disposed of all contradictions. But, in reality, it must be the case that
the child's outlook is in some way vindicated against the adult's and
against Piaget, and that the unsophisticated thinking of our earliest
years remains as an indispensable acquisition underlying that of
maturity, if there is to be for the adult one single intersubjective
world My awareness of constructing an objective truth would never
provide me with anything more than an objective truth for me, and
my greatest attempt at impartiality would never enable me to prevail
over my subjectivity (as Descartes so well expresses it by the hypothesis of the malignant demon), if I had not, underlying my judgements, the primordial certainty of being in contact with being itself,
if, before any voluntary *adoption of a position* I were not already
situated in an intersubjective world, and if science too were not upheld by this basic δόξα. With the *cogito* begins that struggle between
consciousnesses, each one of which, as Hegel says, seeks the death of
the other. For the struggle ever to begin, and for each consciousness
to be capable of suspecting the alien presences which it negates,
all must necessarily have some common ground and be mindful of
their peaceful co-existence in the world of childhood
   But is it indeed other people that we arrive at in this way? What
we do in effect is to iron out the I and the Thou in an experience

[1] Piaget, *La Representation du monde chez l'enfant*, p 21

355

shared by a plurality, thus introducing the impersonal into the heart of subjectivity and eliminating the individuality of perspectives. But have we not, in this general confusion, done away with the alter Ego as well as the Ego? We said earlier that they are mutually exclusive. But this is only because they both lay the same claims, and because the alter Ego follows all the variations of the Ego if the perceiving *I* is genuinely an *I*, it cannot perceive a different one, if the perceiving subject is anonymous, the other which it perceives is equally so, so when, within this collective consciousness, we try to bring out the plurality of consciousnesses, we shall find ourselves back with the difficulties which we thought we had left behind I perceive the other person as a piece of behaviour, for example, I perceive the grief or the anger of the other in his conduct, in his face or his hands, without recourse to any 'inner' experience of suffering or anger, and because grief and anger are variations of belonging to the world, undivided between the body and consciousness, and equally applicable to the other person's conduct, visible in his phenomenal body, as in my own conduct as it is presented to me. But then, the behaviour of another person, and even his words, are not that other person The grief and the anger of another have never quite the same significance for him as they have for me. For him these situations are lived through, for me they are displayed. Or in so far as I can, by some friendly gesture, become part of that grief or that anger, they still remain the grief and anger of my friend Paul Paul suffers because he has lost his wife, or is angry because his watch has been stolen, whereas I suffer because Paul is grieved, or I am angry because he is angry, and our situations cannot be superimposed on each other. If, moreover, we undertake some project in common, this common project is not one single project, it does not appear in the selfsame light to both of us, we are not both equally enthusiastic about it, or at any rate not in quite the same way, simply because Paul is Paul and I am myself Although his consciousness and mine, working through our respective situations, may contrive to produce a common situation in which they can communicate, it is nevertheless from the subjectivity of each of us that each one projects this 'one and only' world The difficulties inherent in considering the perception of other people did not all stem from objective thought, nor do they all dissolve with the discovery of behaviour, or rather objective thought and the uniqueness of the *cogito* which flows from it are not fictions, but firmly grounded phenomena of which we shall have to seek the basis The conflict between myself and the other does not begin only when we try to *think ourselves into* the other and does not vanish if we reintegrate thought into non-positing consciousness and unreflective living; it is already there if I try to live another's experiences,

356

for example in the blindness of sacrifice. I enter into a pact with the other person, having resolved to live in an interworld in which I accord as much place to others as to myself But this interworld is still a project of mine, and it would be hypocritical to pretend that I seek the welfare of another *as if it were mine*, since this very attachment to another's interest still has its source in me

In the absence of reciprocity there is no alter Ego, since the world of the one then takes in completely that of the other, so that one feels disinherited in favour of the other. This is what happens in the case of a couple where there is more love felt on one side than on the other: one throws himself, and his whole life, into his love, the other remains free, finding in this love a merely contingent manner of living. The former feels his being and substance flowing away into that freedom which confronts him, whole and unqualified And even if the second partner, through fidelity to his vows or through generosity, tries to reciprocate by reducing himself, or herself, to the status of a mere phenomenon in the other's world, and to see himself through the other's eyes, he can succeed only by an expansion of his own life, so that he denies by necessity the equivalence of himself with the other that he is trying to posit. Co-existence must in all cases be experienced on both sides. If neither of us is a constituting consciousness at the moment when we are about to communicate and discover a common world, the question then is: who communicates, and for whom does this world exist? And if someone does communicate with someone else, if the interworld is not an inconceivable *in-itself* and must exist for both of us, then again communication breaks down, and each of us operates in his own private world like two players playing on two chessboards a hundred miles apart. But here the players can still make known their moves to each other by telephone or correspondence, which means that they are in fact participants in the same world. I, on the other hand, share no common ground with another person, for the positing of the other with his world, and the positing of myself with mine are mutually exclusive. Once the other is posited, once the other's gaze fixed upon me has, by inserting me into his field, stripped me of part of my being, it will readily be understood that I can recover it only by establishing relations with him, by bringing about his clear recognition of me, and that my freedom requires the same freedom for others. But first we need to know how it has been possible for me to posit the other. In so far as I am born into the world, and have a body and a natural world, I can find in that world other patterns of behaviour with which my own interweave, as we have explained above. But also in so far as I am born and my existence is already at work and is aware that it is given to itself, it always remains on the hither side of the

acts in which it tries to become engaged and which are for ever mere
modalities of its own, and particular cases of its insurmountable
generality. It is this ground of given existence that is disclosed by
the *cogito* every assertion, every commitment, and even every negation and doubt takes its place in a field open in advance, and testifies
to a self contiguous with itself before those particular acts in which it
loses contact with itself This self, a witness to any actual communication, and without which the latter would be ignorant of itself, and
would not, therefore, be communication at all, would seem to preclude any solution of the problem of other people There is here a
solipsism rooted in living experience and quite insurmountable. It is
true that I do not feel that I am the constituting agent either of the
natural or of the cultural world: into each perception and into each
judgement I bring either sensory functions or cultural settings which
are not actually mine. Yet although I am outrun on all sides by my
own acts, and submerged in generality, the fact remains that I am
the one by whom they are experienced, and with my first perception
there was launched an insatiable being who appropriates everything
that he meets, to whom nothing can be purely and simply given
because he has inherited his share of the world, and hence carries
within him the project of all possible being, because it has been once
and for all imprinted in his field of experiences The generality of the
body will never make it clear how the indeclinable *I* can estrange itself in favour of another, since this generality is exactly compensated
by the other generality of my inalienable subjectivity. How should I
find *elsewhere*, in my perceptual field, such a presence of self to self?
Are we to say that the existence of the other person is for me a simple
fact? It is in any case a fact *for me*, and it must necessarily be among
my own possibilities, and understood or in some way experienced by
me in order to be valid as a fact

After this failure to set limits to solipsism from the outside, are
we then to try to outrun it inwardly? It is true that I can recognize
only one Ego, but as universal subject I cease to be a finite self, and
become an impartial spectator before whom the other person and
myself, each as an empirical being, are on a footing of equality, without my enjoying any particular privilege Of the consciousness which
I discover by reflection and before which everything is an object, it
cannot be said that it is myself my self is arrayed before me like any
other thing, and my consciousness constitutes it and is not enclosed
within it, so that it can without difficulty constitute other (my)selves.
In God I can be conscious of others as of myself, and love others as
myself But the subjectivity that we have run up against does not
admit of being called God If reflection reveals myself to me as an
infinite subject, we must recognize, at least at the level of appearance,

358

my ignorance of this self which is even more myself than I I knew it, the reply will be, because I perceived both the other and myself, and because this perception is possible only through him But if I did already know it, then all books of philosophy are useless In fact, the truth needs to be revealed It was, therefore, this finite and ignorant self which recognized God in itself, while God, beyond phenomena, thought about himself since the beginning of time. It is through this shadow that unavailing light manages to be shed on at least something, and thus it is ultimately impossible to bring the shadow into the light, I can never *recognize myself* as God without necessarily denying what I am trying in fact to assert. I might love others as myself in God, but even then my love of God would have to come not from me, and would have to be truly, as Spinoza said, the love which God has for himself through me So that finally nowhere would there be love of others or indeed others, but one single self-love linked to itself beyond our own lives, and nowise relevant, indeed inaccessible, to us The act of reflection and love leading to God places the God sought outside the realm of possibility.

We are thus brought back to solipsism, and the problem now appears in all its difficulty I am not God, but merely lay claim to divinity. I escape from every involvement and transcend others in so far as every situation and every other person must be experienced by me in order to exist in my eyes. And yet other people have for me at least an initial significance. As with the gods of polytheism, I have to reckon with other gods, or again, as with Aristotle's God, I polarize a world which I do not create. Consciousnesses present themselves with the absurdity of a multiple solipsism, such is the situation which has to be understood. Since we live through this situation, there must be some way of making it explicit Solitude and communication cannot be the two horns of a dilemma, but two 'moments' of one phenomenon, since in fact other people do exist for me We must say of experience of others what we have said elsewhere about reflection: that its object cannot escape it entirely, since we have a notion of the object only through that experience Reflection must in some way present the unreflected, otherwise we should have nothing to set over against it, and it would not become a problem for us Similarly my experience must in some way present me with other people, since otherwise I should have no occasion to speak of solitude, and could not begin to pronounce other people inaccessible What is given and initially true, is a reflection open to the unreflective, the reflective assumption of the unreflective—and similarly there is given the tension of my experience towards another whose existence on the horizon of my life is beyond doubt, even when my knowledge of him is imperfect. There is more than a vague analogy between the two problems, for in both cases it is a matter of finding out how to steal a march on myself and experience the un-reflective as such. How, then, can I who perceive, and who, *ipso facto*, assert myself as universal subject, perceive another who immediately deprives me of this universality? The central phenomenon, at the root of both my subjectivity and my transcendence towards others, consists in my being given to myself. *I am given*, that is, I find myself already situated and involved in a physical and social world—*I am given to myself*, which means that this situation is never hidden from me, it is never round about me as an alien necessity, and I am never in effect enclosed in it like an object in a box My freedom, the fundamental power which I enjoy of being the subject of all my experiences, is not distinct from my insertion into the world It is a fate for me to be free, to be unable to reduce myself to anything that I experience, to maintain in relation to any factual situation a faculty of withdrawal, and this fate was sealed the moment my transcendental field was thrown open, when I was born as vision and knowledge, when I was thrown into the world Against the social world I can always avail myself of my sensible nature, close my eyes, stop up my ears, live as a stranger in society, treat others, ceremonies and institutions as mere arrangements of colour and light, and strip them of all their human significance. Against the natural world I can always have recourse to the thinking nature and entertain doubts about each perception taken on its own The truth of solipsism is there. Every experience will always appear to me as a particular instance which does not exhaust the generality of my being, and I have always, as Malebranche said, movement left wherewith to go further. But I can fly from being only into being, for example, I escape from society into nature, or from the real world into an imaginary one made of the broken fragments of reality The physical and social world always functions as a stimulus to my reactions, whether these be positive or negative. I call such and such a perception into question only in the name of a truer one capable of correcting it, in so far as I can deny each thing, it is always by asserting that there is something in general, and this is why we say that thought is a thinking nature, an assertion of being over and above the negation of beings. I can evolve a solipsist philosophy but, in doing so, I assume the existence of a community of men endowed with speech, and I address myself to it Even the 'indefinite refusal to be anything at all'[1] assumes something which is refused and in relation to which the subject holds himself apart I must choose between others and myself, it is said But we choose one *against* the other, and thus assert both The other person transforms me into an object and denies me, I

[1] Valéry, *Introduction à la méthode de Léonard de Vinci, Variété*, p. 200.

transform him into an object and deny him, it is asserted In fact the other's gaze transforms me into an object, and mine him, only if both of us withdraw into the core of our thinking nature, if we both make ourselves into an inhuman gaze, if each of us feels his actions to be not taken up and understood, but observed as if they were an insect's This is what happens, for instance, when I fall under the gaze of a stranger. But even then, the objectification of each by the other's gaze is felt as unbearable only because it takes the place of possible communication A dog's gaze directed towards me causes me no embarrassment. The refusal to communicate, however, is still a form of communication Manifold freedom, the thinking nature, the inalienable core, existence without qualification, which in me and in others mark the bounds of sympathy, do call a halt to communication, but do not abolish it If I am dealing with a stranger who has as yet not uttered a word, I may well believe that he is an inhabitant of another world in which my own thoughts and actions are unworthy of a place. But let him utter a word, or even make a gesture of impatience, and already he ceases to transcend me: that, then, is his voice, those are his thoughts and that is the realm that I thought inaccessible. Each existence finally transcends the others only when it remains inactive and rests upon its natural difference Even that universal meditation which cuts the philosopher off from his nation, his friendships, his prejudices, his empirical being, the world in short, and which seems to leave him in complete isolation, is in reality an act, the spoken word, and consequently dialogue Solipsism would be strictly true only of someone who managed to be tacitly aware of his existence without being or doing anything, which is impossible, since existing is being in and of the world. The philosopher cannot fail to draw others with him into his reflective retreat, because in the uncertainty of the world, he has for ever learned to treat them as *associates*, and because all his knowledge is built on this datum of opinion. Transcendental subjectivity is a revealed subjectivity, revealed to itself and to others, and is for that reason an intersubjectivity. As soon as existence collects itself together and commits itself in some line of conduct, it falls beneath perception. Like every other perception, this one asserts more things than it grasps: when I say that I see the ash-tray over there, I suppose as completed an unfolding of experience which could go on *ad infinitum*, and I commit a whole perceptual future Similarly, when I say that I know and like someone, I aim, beyond his qualities, at an inexhaustible core which may one day shatter the image that I have formed of him It is subject to this condition that there are things and 'other people' for us, not as the result of some illusion, but as the result of a violent act which is perception itself

We must therefore rediscover, after the natural world, the social world, not as an object or sum of objects, but as a permanent field or dimension of existence. I may well turn away from it, but not cease to be situated relatively to it. Our relationship to the social is, like our relationship to the world, deeper than any express perception or any judgement. It is as false to place ourselves in society as an object among other objects, as it is to place society within ourselves as an object of thought, and in both cases the mistake lies in treating the social as an object. We must return to the social with which we are in contact by the mere fact of existing, and which we carry about inseparably with us before any objectification. Objective and scientific consciousness of the past and of civilizations would be impossible had I not, through the intermediary of my society, my cultural world and their horizons, at least a possible communication with them, and if the place of the Athenian Republic or the Roman Empire were not somewhere marked out on the borders of my own history, and if they were not there as so many individuals to be known, indeterminate but pre-existing, and if I did not find in my own life the basic structures of history. The social is already there when we come to know or judge it. An individualistic or sociological philosophy is a certain perception of co-existence systematized and made explicit. Prior to the process of becoming aware, the social exists obscurely and as a summons. At the end of *Notre Patrie* Péguy finds once again a buried voice which had never ceased to speak, much as we realize on waking that objects have not, during the night, ceased to be, or that someone has been knocking for some time at our door. Despite cultural, moral, occupational and ideological differences, the Russian peasants of 1917 joined the workers of Petrograd and Moscow in the struggle, because they felt that they shared the same fate, class was experienced in concrete terms before becoming the object of a deliberate volition Primarily the social does not exist as a third person object It is the mistake of the investigator, the 'great man' and the historian to try to treat it as an object. Fabrice would have liked to see the Battle of Waterloo as one sees a landscape, but found nothing but confused episodes. Does the Emperor really see it on his map? It reduces itself in his eyes to a general plan by no means free from gaps, why is this regiment not making headway; why don't the reserves come up? The historian who is not engaged in the battle and who sees it from all angles, who brings together a mass of evidence, and who knows what the result was, thinks he has grasped it in its essential truth But what he gives us is no more than a representation, he does not bring before us the battle itself since the issue was, at the time, contingent, and is no longer so when the historian recounts it, since the deeper causes of defeat and the fortuitous incidents which brought them into play were, in that singular event called Waterloo, equally determining factors, and since the historian assigns to the said singular event its place in the general process of decline of the Empire The true Waterloo resides neither in what Fabrice, nor the Emperor, nor the historian sees, it is not a determinable object, it is what *comes about* on the fringes of all perspectives, and on which they are all erected.[1] The historian and the philosopher are in search of an objective definition of class or nation is the nation based on common language or on conceptions of life; is class based on income statistics or on its place in the process of production? It is well known that none of these criteria enables us to decide whether an individual belongs to a nation or a class. In all revolutions there are members of the privileged class who make common cause with the revolutionaries, and members of the oppressed class who remain faithful to the privileged And every nation has its traitors. This is because the nation and class are neither versions of fate which hold the individual in subjection from the outside nor values which he posits from within. They are modes of co-existence which are a call upon him. Under conditions of calm, the nation and the class are there as stimuli to which I respond only absent-mindedly or confusedly, they are merely latent A revolutionary situation, or one of national danger, transforms those preconscious relationships with class and nation, hitherto merely lived through, into the definite taking of a stand; the tacit commitment becomes explicit. But it appears to itself as anterior to decision.

The problem of the existential modality of the social is here at one with all problems of transcendence Whether we are concerned with my body, the natural world, the past, birth or death, the question is always how I can be open to phenomena which transcend me, and which nevertheless exist only to the extent that I take them up and live them, *how the presence to myself (Urpräsenz) which establishes my own limits and conditions every alien presence is at the same time de-presentation (Entgegenwärtigung)[2] and throws me outside myself* Both

---

[1] It would therefore seem that history should be written in the present tense It is what Jules Romains, for example, did in *Verdun* Naturally, from the fact that objective thought is incapable of retailing down to the last detail a present historical situation, we must not conclude that we should live through our history with our eyes closed, as if it were an individual adventure, reject every attempt to put it into perspective, and throw ourselves into action with no guiding principle Fabrice misses Waterloo, but the reporter is already nearer to the event, for the spirit of adventure leads us astray even more than objective thought There is a way of thinking, in contact with the event, which seeks its concrete structure A revolution which is really moving with the march of history can be thought as well as lived

[2] Husserl, *Die Krisis der europaischen Wissenschaften und die transzendentale Phanomenologie*, III (unpublished)

idealism and realism, the former by making the external world immanent in me, the latter by subjecting me to a causal action, falsify the motivational relations existing between the external and internal worlds, and make this relationship unintelligible. Our individual past, for example, cannot be given to us either on the one hand by the actual survival of states of consciousness or paths traced in the brain, or on the other by a consciousness of the past which constitutes it and immediately arrives at it in either case we should lack any sense of the past, for the past would, strictly speaking, be present If anything of the past is to exist for us, it can be only in an ambiguous presence, anterior to any express evocation, like a field upon which we have an opening It must exist for us even though we may not be thinking of it, and all our recollections must have their substance in and be drawn from this opaque mass Similarly, if the world were to me merely a collection of things, and the thing merely a collection of properties, I should have no certainties, but merely probabilities, no unchallengeable reality, but merely conditional truths If the past and the world exist, they must be theoretically immanent—they can be only what I see behind and around me— and factually transcendent—they exist in my life before appearing as objects of my explicit acts. Similarly, moreover, my birth and death cannot be objects of thought for me. Being established in my life, buttressed by my thinking nature, fastened down in this transcendental field which was opened for me by my first perception, and in which all absence is merely the obverse of a presence, all silence a modality of the being of sound, I enjoy a sort of ubiquity and theoretical eternity, I feel destined to move in a flow of endless life, neither the beginning nor the end of which I can experience in thought, since it is my living self who think of them, and since thus my life always forestalls and survives itself Yet this same thinking nature which produces in me a superabundance of being opens the world to me through a perspective, along with which there comes to me the feeling of my contingency, the dread of being outstripped, so that, although I do not manage to encompass my death in thought, I nevertheless live in an atmosphere of death in general, and there is a kind of essence of death always on the horizon of my thinking In short, just as the instant of my death is a future to which I have not access, so I am necessarily destined never to experience the presence of another person to himself And yet each other person does exist for me as an unchallengeable style or setting of co-existence, and my life has a social atmosphere just as it has a flavour of mortality

We have discovered, with the natural and social worlds, the truly transcendental, which is not the totality of constituting operations whereby a transparent world, free from obscurity and impenetrable solidity, is spread out before an impartial spectator, but that ambiguous life in which the forms of transcendence have their *Ursprung*, and which, through a fundamental contradiction, puts me in communication with them, and on this basis makes knowledge possible.[1] It will perhaps be maintained that a philosophy cannot be centred round a contradiction, and that all our descriptions, since they ultimately defy thought, are quite meaningless The objection would be valid if we were content to lay bare, under the term phenomenon or phenomenal field, a layer of prelogical or magical experiences. For in that case we should have to choose between believing the descriptions and abandoning thought, or knowing what we are talking about and abandoning our descriptions. These descriptions must become an opportunity for defining a variety of comprehension and reflection altogether more radical than objective thought. To phenomenology understood as direct description needs to be added a phenomenology of phenomenology. We must return to the *cogito*, in search of a more fundamental *Logos* than that of objective thought, one which endows the latter with its relative validity, and at the same time assigns to it its place. At the level of being it will never be intelligible that the subject should be both *naturans* and *naturatus*, infinite and finite But if we rediscover time beneath the subject, and if we relate to the paradox of time those of the body, the world, the thing, and other people, we shall understand that beyond these there is nothing to understand.

---

[1] Husserl in his last period concedes that all reflection should in the first place return to the description of the world of living experience (*Lebenswelt*) But he adds that, by means of a second 'reduction', the structures of the world of experience must be reinstated in the transcendental flow of a universal constitution in which all the world's obscurities are elucidated. It is clear, however, that we are faced with a dilemma either the constitution makes the world transparent, in which case it is not obvious why reflection needs to pass through the world of experience, or else it retains something of that world, and never rids it of its opacity Husserl's thought moves increasingly in this second direction, despite many throwbacks to the logicist period—as is seen when he makes a problem of rationality, when he allows significances which are in the last resort 'fluid' (*Erfahrung und Urteil*, p 428), when he bases knowledge on a basic δοξα

PART THREE

Being-for-Itself and Being-in-the-World

THE COGITO

I AM thinking of the Cartesian *cogito*, wanting to finish this work, feeling the coolness of the paper under my hand, and perceiving the trees of the boulevard through the window. My life is constantly thrown headlong into transcendent things, and passes wholly outside me The *cogito* is either this thought which took shape three centuries ago in the mind of Descartes, or the meaning of the books he has left for us, or else an eternal truth which emerges from them, but in any case is a cultural being of which it is true to say that my thought strains towards it rather than that it embraces it, as my body, in a familiar surrounding, finds its orientation and makes its way among objects without my needing to have them expressly in mind. This book, once begun, is not a certain set of ideas, it constitutes for me an open situation, for which I could not possibly provide any complex formula, and in which I struggle blindly on until, miraculously, thoughts and words become organized by themselves. *A fortiori* the sensible forms of being which lie around me, the paper under my hand, the trees before my eyes, do not yield their secret to me, rather is it that my consciousness takes flight from itself and, in them, is unaware of itself. Such is the initial situation that realism tries to account for by asserting an actual transcendence and the existence in itself of the world and ideas

There is, however, no question of justifying realism, and there is an element of final truth in the Cartesian return of things or ideas to the self The very experience of transcendent things is possible only provided that their project is borne, and discovered, within myself. When I say that things are transcendent, this means that I do not possess them, that I do not circumambulate them; they are transcendent to the extent that I am ignorant of what they are, and blindly assert their bare existence Now what meaning can there be in asserting the existence of one knows not what? If there can be any truth at all in this assertion, it is in so far as I catch a glimpse of the nature

369

or essence to which it refers, in so far, for instance, as my vision of
the tree as a mute *ek-stase* into an individual thing already envelops
a certain thought about seeing and a certain thought about the tree
It is, in short, in so far as I do not merely encounter the tree, am not
simply confronted with it, but discover in this existent before me a
certain nature, the notion of which I actively evolve. In so far as I
find things round about me, this cannot be because they are actually
there, for, *ex hypothesi*, I can know nothing of this factual existence
The fact that I am capable of recognizing it is attributable to my
actual contact with the thing, which awakens within me a primordial
knowledge of all things, and to my finite and determinate perceptions'
being partial manifestations of a power of knowing which is co-
extensive with the world and unfolds it in its full extent and depth.
If we imagine a space in itself with which the perceiving subject
contrives to coincide, for example, if I imagine that my hand perceives
the distance between two points as it spans it, how could the angle
formed by my fingers, and indicative of that distance, come to be
judged, unless it were so to speak measured out by the inner operation of some power residing in neither object, a power which, *ipso
facto*, becomes able to know, or rather effect, the relation existing
between them? If it be insisted that the 'sensation in my thumb' and
that in my first finger are at any rate 'signs' of the distance, how could
these sensations come to have in themselves any means of signifying
the relationship between points in space, unless they were already
situated on a path running from one to the other, and unless this
path in its turn were not only traversed by my fingers as they open,
but also 'aimed at' by my thought pursuing its intelligible purpose?
'How could the mind know the significance of a sign which it has
not itself constituted as a sign?'[1] For the picture of knowledge at
which we arrived in describing the subject situated in his world, we
must, it seems, substitute a second, according to which it constructs
or constitutes this world itself, and this one is more authentic than
the first, since the transactions between the subject and the things
round about it are possible only provided that the subject first of all
causes them to exist for itself, actually arranges them round about
itself, and extracts them from its own core The same applies with
greater force in acts of spontaneous thought The Cartesian *cogito*,
which is the theme of my reflection, is always beyond what I bring
to mind at the moment It has a horizon of significance made up of
a great number of thoughts which occurred to me as I was reading
Descartes and which are not now present, along with others which
I feel stirring within me, which I might have, but never have developed But the fact that it is enough to utter these three syllables in

[1] P Lachièze-Rey, *Reflexions sur l'activité spirituelle constituante*, p 134

my presence for me to be immediately directed towards a certain set of ideas, shows that in some way all possible developments and clarifications are at once present to me. 'Whoever tries to limit the spiritual light to what is at present before the mind always runs up against the Socratic problem. "How will you set about looking for that thing, the nature of which is totally unknown to you? Which, among the things you do not know, is the one which you propose to look for? And if by chance you should stumble upon it, how will you know that it is indeed that thing, since you are in ignorance of it?"' (*Meno*, 80D)[1] A thought really transcended by its objects would find them proliferating in its path without ever being able to grasp their relationships to each other, or finding its way through to their truth It is I who reconstitute the historical *cogito*, I who read Descartes' text, I who recognize in it an undying truth, so that finally the Cartesian *cogito* acquires its significance only through my own *cogito*, and I should have no thought of it, had I not within myself all that is needed to invent it. It is I who assign to my thought the objective of resuming the action of the *cogito*, and I who constantly verify my thought's orientation towards this objective, therefore my thought must forestall itself in the pursuit of this aim, and must already have found what it seeks, otherwise it would not seek it We must define thought in terms of that strange power which it possesses of being ahead of itself, of launching itself and being at home everywhere, in a word, in terms of its autonomy. Unless thought itself had put into things what it subsequently finds in them, it would have no hold upon things, would not think of them, and would be an 'illusion of thought'[2] A sensible perception or a piece of reasoning cannot be facts which come about in me and of which I take note. When I consider them after the event, they are dispersed and distributed each to its due place. But all this is merely what is left in the wake of reasoning and perception which, seen contemporaneously, must necessarily, on pain of ceasing to hang together, take in simultaneously everything necessary to their realization, and consequently be present to themselves with no intervening distance, in one indivisible intention All thought of something is at the same time self-consciousness, failing which it could have no object At the root of all our experiences and all our reflections, we find, then, a being which immediately recognizes itself, because it is its knowledge both of itself and of all things, and which knows its own existence, not by observation and as a given fact, nor by inference from any idea of itself, but through direct contact with that existence. Self-consciousness is the very being of mind in action The act whereby I am conscious of something must itself be apprehended at the very moment

[1] P Lachièze-Rey, *l'Idealisme kantien*, pp 17–18   [2] Ibid , p 25

at which it is carried out, otherwise it would collapse Therefore it is inconceivable that it should be triggered off or brought about by anything whatsoever, it must be *causa sui* [1] To revert with Descartes from things to thought about things is to take one of two courses it is either to reduce experience to a collection of psychological events, of which the *I* is merely the overall name or the hypothetical cause, in which case it is not clear how my existence is more certain than that of any thing, since it is no longer immediate, save at a fleeting instant, or else it is to recognize as anterior to events a field and a system of thoughts which is subject neither to time nor to any other limitation, a mode of existence owing nothing to the event and which is existence as consciousness, a spiritual act which grasps at a distance and compresses into itself everything at which it aims, an 'I think' which is, by itself and without any adjunct, an 'I am' [2] 'The Cartesian doctrine of the *cogito* was therefore bound to lead logically to the assertion of the timelessness of mind, and to the acceptance of a consciousness of the eternal *experimur nos aeternos esse* '[3] Accordingly eternity, understood as the power to embrace and anticipate temporal developments in a single intention, becomes the very definition of subjectivity [4]

Before questioning this interpretation of the *cogito* in terms of eternity, let us carefully observe what follows from it, as this will show the need of some rectification If the *cogito* reveals to me a new mode of existence owing nothing to time, and if I discover myself as the universal constituent of all being accessible to me, and as a transcendental field with no hidden corners and no outside, it is not enough to say that my mind, 'when it is a question of the form of all the objects of sense . is the God of Spinoza',[5] for the distinction between form and matter can no longer be given any ultimate value, therefore it is not clear how the mind, reflecting on itself, could in the last analysis find any meaning in the notion of receptivity, or think of itself in any valid way as undergoing modification for if it is the mind itself which thinks of itself as affected, it does *not* think of itself thus, since it affirms its activity afresh simultaneously with appearing to restrict it in so far, on the other hand, as it is the mind which places itself in the world, it is *not* there, and the self-positing — is an illusion It must then be said, with no qualification, that my mind is God How can M Lachièze-Rey, for example, have avoided this consequence? 'If, having suspended thinking, I resume it again,

[1] P Lachièze-Rey, *L'Idéalisme kantien*, p 55

[2] Ibid, p 184   [3] Ibid, pp 17 18

[4] P Lachièze-Rey, *Le Moi, le Monde et Dieu*, p 68

[5] Kant, *Übergang*, Adickes, p 756, quoted by Lachièze-Rey *L'Idéalisme kantien* p 464

I return to life, I reconstitute, in its indivisibility, and by putting myself back at the source whence it flows, the movement which I carry on. . . Thus, whenever he thinks, the subject makes himself his point of support, and takes his place, beyond and behind his various representations, in that unity which, being the principle of all recognition, is not there to be recognized, and he becomes once more the absolute because that is what he eternally is.'[1] But how could there be several absolutes? How in the first place could I ever recognize other (my)selves? If the sole experience of the subject is the one which I gain by coinciding with it, if the mind, by definition, eludes 'the outside spectator' and can be recognized only from within, my *cogito* is necessarily unique, and cannot be 'shared in' by another. Perhaps we can say that it is 'transferable' to others.[2] But then how could such a transfer ever be brought about? What spectacle can ever validly induce me to posit outside myself that mode of existence the whole significance of which demands that it be grasped from within? Unless I learn within myself to recognize the junction of the *for itself* and the *in itself*, none of those mechanisms called other bodies will ever be able to come to life, unless I have an exterior others have no interior. The plurality of consciousness is impossible if I have an absolute consciousness of myself. Behind the absolute of my thought, it is even impossible to conjecture a divine absolute. If it is perfect, the contact of my thought with itself seals me within myself, and prevents me from ever feeling that anything eludes my grasp, there is no opening, no 'aspiration'[3] towards an Other for this self of mine, which constructs the totality of being and its own presence in the world, which is defined in terms of 'self-possession',[4] and which never finds anything outside itself but what it has put there. This hermetically sealed self is no longer a finite self. 'There is . . . a consciousness of the universe only through the previous consciousness of organization in the active sense of the word, and consequently, in the last analysis, only through an inner communion with the very working of godhead '[5] It is ultimately with God that the *cogito* brings me into coincidence. While the intelligible and identifiable structure of my experience, when recognized by me in the *cogito*, draws me out of the event and establishes me in eternity, it frees me simultaneously from all limiting attributes and, in fact, from that fundamental event which is my private existence Hence the same reasoning which necessarily leads from the event to the act, from thoughts to the *I*, equally necessarily leads from the multiplicity

[1] P Lachièze-Rey, *Réflexions sur l'activité spirituelle constituante*, p 145
[2] Id , *L'Idéalisme kantien*, p 477
[3] Ibid., p. 477 *Le Moi, le Monde et Dieu*, p 83.
[4] *L'Idéalisme kantien*, p 472   [5] *Le Moi, le Monde et Dieu*, p. 33

of I's to one sole constituting consciousness, and prevents me from entertaining any vain hope of salvaging the finiteness of the subject by defining it as a 'monad'.[1] The constituting consciousness is necessarily unique and universal. If we try to maintain that what it constitutes in each one of us is merely a microcosm, if we keep, for the *cogito*, the meaning of 'existential experience',[2] and if it reveals to me, not the absolute transparency of thought wholly in possession of itself, but the blind act by which I take up my destiny as a thinking nature and follow it out, then we are introducing another philosophy, which does not take us *out of* time. What is brought home to us here is the need to find a middle course between eternity and the atomistic time of empiricism, in order to resume the interpretation of the *cogito* and of time. We have seen once and for all that our relations with things cannot be eternal ones, nor our consciousness of ourself the mere recording of psychic events. We perceive a world only provided that, before being facts of which we take cognizance, that world and that perception are thoughts of our own. What remains to be understood precisely is the way the world comes to belong to the subject and the subject to himself, which is that *cogitatio* which makes experience possible, our hold on things and on our 'states of consciousness'. We shall see that this does not leave the event and time out of account, but that it is indeed the fundamental mode of the event and *Geschichte*, from which objective and impersonal events are derived forms, and finally that any recourse we have to eternity is necessitated solely by an objective conception of time.

There can therefore be no doubt at all that I think. I am not sure that there is over there an ash-tray or a pipe, but I am sure that I think I see an ash-tray or a pipe. Now is it in fact as easy as is generally thought to dissociate these two assertions and hold, independently of any judgement concerning the thing seen, the evident certainty of my 'thought about seeing'? On the contrary, it is impossible. Perception is precisely that kind of act in which there can be no question of setting the act itself apart from the end to which it is directed. Perception and the perceived necessarily have the same existential modality, since perception is inseparable from the consciousness which it has, or rather is, of reaching the thing itself. Any contention that the perception is indubitable, whereas the thing perceived is not, must be ruled out. If I see an ash-tray, *in the full sense of the word see*, there must be an ash-tray there, and I cannot forego this assertion. To see is to see something. To see red, is to see red actively in existence. Vision can be reduced to the mere presumption of

[1] As does M. Lachièze-Rey, *Le Moi, le Monde et Dieu*, pp. 69–70
[2] Ibid., p. 72

seeing only if it is represented as the contemplation of a shifting and anchorless *quale*. But if, as we have shown above, the very quality itself, in its specific texture, is the suggestion of a certain way of existing put to us, and responded to by us, in so far as we have sensory fields; and if the perception of a colour, endowed with a definite structure (in the way of superficial colour or area of colour), at a place or distance away either definite or vague, presupposes our opening on to a reality or a world, how can we possibly dissociate the certainty of our perceptual existence from that of its external counterpart? It is of the essence of my vision to refer not only to an alleged visible entity, but also to a being actually seen Similarly, if I feel doubts about the presence of the thing, this doubt attaches to vision itself, and if there is no red or blue there, I say that I have not *really seen* these colours, and concede that at no time has there been created that parity between my visual intentions and the visible which constitutes the genuine act of seeing We are therefore faced with a choice either I enjoy no certainty with regard to things themselves, in which case neither can I be certain about my own perception, taken as a mere thought, since, taken even in this way, it involves the assertion of a thing. Or else I grasp my thought with certainty, which involves the simultaneous assumption of the existence towards which it is projected When Descartes tells us that the existence of visible things is doubtful, but that our vision, when considered as a mere thought of seeing is not in doubt, he takes up an untenable position. For thought about seeing can have two meanings. It can in the first place be understood in the restricted sense of alleged vision, or 'the impression of seeing', in which case it offers only the certainty of a possibility or a probability, and the 'thought of seeing' implies that we have had, in certain cases, the experience of genuine or actual vision to which the idea of seeing bears a resemblance and in which the certainty of the thing was, on those occasions, involved. The certainty of a possibility is no more than the possibility of a certainty, the thought of seeing is no more than seeing mentally, and we could not have any such thought unless we had on other occasions really seen Now we may understand 'thought about seeing' as the consciousness we have of our constituting power. Whatever be the case with our empirical perceptions, which may be true or false, these perceptions are possible only if they are inhabited by a mind able to recognize, identify and sustain before us their intentional object But if this constituting power is not a myth, if perception is really the mere extension of an inner dynamic power with which I can coincide, my certainty concerning the transcendental premises of the world must extend to the world itself, and, my vision being in its entirety thought about seeing, then the thing seen is in itself what I think about it, so that transcendental idealism becomes absolute realism It would be contradictory to assert[1] both that the world is constituted by me and that, out of this constitutive operation, I can grasp no more than the outline and the essential structures, I must see the existing world appear at the end of the constituting process, and not only the world as an idea, otherwise I shall have no more than an abstract construction, and not a concrete consciousness, of the world Thus, in whatever sense we take 'thought about seeing', it is certain only so long as actual sight is equally so When Descartes tells us that sensation reduced to itself is always true, and that error creeps in through the transcendent interpretation of it that judgement provides, he makes an unreal distinction it is no less difficult for me to know whether or not I have felt something than it is to know whether there is really something there, for the victim of hysteria feels yet does not know what it is that he feels, as he perceives external objects without being aware of that perception When, on the other hand, I am sure of having felt, the certainty of some external thing is involved in the very way in which the sensation is articulated and unfolded before me: it is a pain *in the leg*, or it is *red*, and this may be an opaque red on one plane, or a reddish three-dimensional atmosphere The 'interpretation' of my sensations which I give must necessarily be motivated, and be so only in terms of the structure of those sensations, so that it can be said with equal validity either that there is no transcendent interpretation and no judgement which does not spring from the very configuration of the phenomena —or that there is no sphere of immanence, no realm in which my consciousness is fully at home and secure against all risk of error. The acts of the *I* are of such a nature that they outstrip themselves leaving no interiority of consciousness Consciousness is transcendence through and through, not transcendence undergone—we have already said that such a transcendence would bring consciousness to a stop—but active transcendence. The consciousness I have of seeing or feeling is no passive noting of some psychic event hermetically sealed upon itself, an event leaving me in doubt about the reality of the thing seen or felt Nor is it the activation of some constituting power superlatively and eternally inclusive of every possible sight or sensation, and linking up with the object without ever having to be drawn away from itself It is the actual effecting of vision I reassure

[1] As Husserl, for example, does when he concedes that any transcendental reduction is at the same time an eidetic one The necessity of proceeding by essences, and the stubborn opacity of existences, cannot be taken for granted as facts, but contribute to determining the significance of the *cogito* and of ultimate subjectivity I am not a constituting thought, and my 'I think' is not an 'I am', unless by thought I can equal the world's concrete richness, and re-absorb facticity into it

myself that I see by seeing this or that, or at least by bringing to life around me a visual surrounding, a visible world which is ultimately vouched for only by the sight of a particular thing. Vision is an action, not, that is, an eternal operation (which is a contradiction in terms) but an operation which fulfils more than it promises, which constantly outruns its premises and is inwardly prepared only by my primordial opening upon a field of transcendence, that is, once again, by an *ek-stase*. Sight is achieved and fulfils itself in the thing seen It is of its essence to take a hold upon itself, and indeed if it did not do so it would not be the sight of anything, but it is none the less of its essence to take a hold upon itself in a kind of ambiguous and obscure way, since it is not in possession of itself and indeed escapes from itself into the thing seen What I discover and recognize through the *cogito* is not psychological immanence, the inherence of all phenomena in 'private states of consciousness', the blind contact of sensation with itself It is not even transcendental immanence, the belonging of all phenomena to a constituting consciousness, the possession of clear thought by itself It is the deep-seated momentum of transcendence which is my very being, the simultaneous contact with my own being and with the world's being.

And yet is not the case of perception a special one? It throws me open to a world, but can do so only by outrunning both me and itself Thus the perceptual 'synthesis' has to be incomplete, it cannot present me with a 'reality' otherwise than by running the risk of error. It is absolutely necessarily the case that the thing, if it is to be a thing, should have sides of itself hidden from me, which is why the distinction between appearance and reality straightway has its place in the perceptual 'synthesis' It would seem, on the other hand, that consciousness comes back into its rights and into full possession of itself, if I consider my awareness of 'psychic facts' For example, love and will are inner operations, they forge their own objects, and it is clear that in doing so they may be sidetracked from reality and, in that sense, mislead us, but it seems impossible that they should mislead us about themselves. From the moment I feel love, joy or sadness, it is the case that I love, that I am joyful or sad, even when the object does not in fact (that is, for others or for myself at other times) have the value that I now attribute to it. Appearance is, within me, reality, and the being of consciousness consists in appearing to itself What is willing, if it is not being conscious of an object as valid (or as valid precisely in so far as it is invalid, in the case of perverse will), and what is loving other than being conscious of an object as lovable? And since the consciousness of an object necessarily involves a knowledge of itself, without which it would escape from itself and fail even to grasp its object, to will and to know that one wills, to

love and know one loves are one and the same act; love is consciousness of loving, will is consciousness of willing. A love or a will unaware of itself would be an unloving love, or an unwilling will, as an
unconscious thought would be an unthinking one. Will or love
would seem to be the same whether their object be artificial or real
and, considered independently of the object to which they actually
refer, they would appear to constitute a sphere of absolute certainty
in which truth cannot elude us. Everything is, then, truth within consciousness There can never be illusion other than with regard to the
external object A feeling, considered in itself, is always true once it is
felt Let us, however, look at the matter more closely

It is, in the first place, quite clear that we are able to discriminate,
within ourselves, between 'true' and 'false' feelings, that everything
felt by us as within ourselves is not *ipso facto* placed on a single footing of existence, or true in the same way, and that there are degrees of
reality within us as there are, outside of us, 'reflections', 'phantoms'
and 'things' Besides true love, there is false or illusory love This last
case must be distinguished from misinterpretations, and those errors
in which I have deceitfully given the name of love to emotions unworthy of it. For in such cases there was never even a semblance of
love, and never for a moment did I believe that my life was committed to that feeling. I conspired with myself to avoid asking the
question in order to avoid receiving the reply which was already
known to me; my 'love'-making was an attempt to do what was expected of me, or merely deception. In mistaken or illusory love, on
the other hand, I was willingly united to the loved one, she was for a
time truly the vehicle of my relationships with the world. When I told
her that I loved her, I was not 'interpreting', for my life was in truth
committed to a form which, like a melody, demanded to be carried
on It is true that, following upon disillusionment (the revelation of
my illusion *about myself*), and when I try to understand what has
happened to me, I shall find beneath this supposed love *something
other* than love the likeness of the 'loved' woman to another, or
boredom, or force of habit, or a community of interests or of con-
victions, and it is just this which will justify me in talking about
illusion I loved only *qualities* (that smile that is so like another smile,
that beauty which asserts itself like a fact, that youthfulness of gesture and behaviour) and not the individual manner of being which
is that person herself. And, correspondingly, I was not myself wholly
in thrall, for areas of my past and future life escaped the invasion,
and I maintained within me corners set aside for other things. In that
case, it will be objected, I was either unaware of this, in which case it
is not a question of illusory love, but of a true love which is dying—
or else I did know, in which case there was never any love at all, even

'mistaken' But neither is the case It cannot be said that this love, while it lasted, was indistinguishable from true love, and that it became 'mistaken love' when I repudiated it Nor can it be said that a mystical crisis at fifteen is without significance, and that it *becomes*, when independently evaluated in later life, an incident of puberty or the first signs of a religious vocation. Even if I reconstruct my whole life on the basis of some incident of puberty, that incident does not lose its contingent character, so that it is my whole life which is 'mistaken'. In the mystical crisis itself as I experienced it, there must be discoverable in it some characteristic which distinguishes vocation from incident. in the first case the mystical attitude insinuates itself into my basic relationship to the world and other people, in the second case, it is within the subject as an impersonal form of behaviour, devoid of inner necessity 'puberty'. In the same way, true love summons all the subject's resources and concerns him in his entire being, whereas mistaken love touches on only one persona 'the man of forty' in the case of late love, 'the traveller' in the case of exotic appeal, 'the widower' if the misguided love is sustained by a memory, 'the child' where the mother is recalled True love ends when I change, or when the object of affection changes, misguided love is revealed as such when I return to my own self The difference is intrinsic But as it concerns the place of feeling in my total being-in-the-world, and as mistaken love is bound up with the person I believe I am at the time I feel it, and also as, in order to discern its mistaken nature I require a knowledge of myself which I can gain only through disillusionment, ambiguity remains, which is why illusion is possible.

Let us return to the example of the hysterical subject It is easy to treat him as a dissembler, but his deception is primarily self-deception, and this instability once more poses the problem we are trying to dispose of: how can the victim of hysteria not feel what he feels, and feel what he does not feel? He does not *feign* pain, sadness or anger, yet his fits of 'pain', 'sadness' or 'rage' are distinguishable from 'real' cases of these afflictions, because he is not wholly given over to them, at his core there is left a zone of tranquillity Illusory or imaginary feelings are genuinely experienced, but experienced, so to speak, on the outer fringes of ourselves.[1] Children and many grown people are under the sway of 'situational values', which conceal from them their actual feelings—they are pleased because they have been given a present, sad because they are at a funeral, gay or sad according to the countryside around them, and, on the hither side of any such emotions, indifferent and neutral 'We experience the feeling itself keenly, but inauthentically It is, as it were, the shadow of an authentic sentiment ' Our natural attitude is not to

[1] Scheler, *Idole der Selbsterkenntis*, pp 63 and ff

experience our own feelings or to adhere to our own pleasures, but to live in accordance with the emotional categories of the environment 'The girl who is loved does not project her emotions like an Isolde or a Juliet, but feels the feelings of these poetic phantoms and infuses them into her own life It is at a later date, perhaps, that a personal and authentic feeling breaks the web of her sentimental phantasies'[1] But until this feeling makes its appearance, the girl has no means of discovering the illusory and literary element in her love It is the truth of her future feelings which is destined to reveal the misguidedness of her present ones, which are genuinely experienced The girl 'loses her reality'[2] in them as does the actor in the part he plays, so that we are faced, not with representations or ideas which give rise to real emotions, but artificial emotions and imaginary sentiments Thus we are not perpetually in possession of ourselves in our whole reality, and we are justified in speaking of an inner perception, of an inward sense, an 'analyser' working from us to ourselves which, ceaselessly, goes some, but not all, the way in providing knowledge of our life and our being What remains on the hither side of inner perception and makes no impression on the inward sense is not an unconscious 'My life', my 'total being' are not dubious constructs, like the 'deep-seated self' of Bergson, but phenomena which are indubitably revealed to reflection It is simply a question of what we *are doing*. I make the discovery that I am in love It may be that none of those facts, which I now recognize as proof of my love, passed unnoticed by me, neither the quickened drive of my present towards my future, nor that emotion which left me speechless, nor my impatience for the arrival of the day we were to meet Nevertheless I had not seen the thing as a whole, or, if I had, I did not realize that it was a matter of so important a feeling, for I now discover that I can no longer conceive my life without this love Going back over the preceding days and months, I am made aware that my thoughts and actions were polarized, I pick out the course of a process of organization, a synthesis *in the making*. Yet it is impossible to pretend that I always knew what I now know, and to see as existing, during the months which have elapsed, a self-knowledge which I have only just come by Quite generally, it is impossible to deny that I have much to learn about myself, as it is to posit ahead of time, in the very heart of me, a knowledge of myself containing in advance all that I am later destined to know of myself, after having read books and had experiences at present unsuspected by me The idea of a form of consciousness which is transparent to itself, its existence being identifiable with its awareness of existing, is not so very different from the notion of the uncon-

[1] Scheler, *Idole der Selbsterkenntis*, pp 89 95
[2] J P Sartre, *L'Imaginaire*, p 243

scious in both cases we have the same retrospective illusion, since there is, introduced into me as an explicit object, everything that I am later to learn concerning myself The love which worked out its dialectic through me, and of which I have just become aware, was not, from the start, a thing hidden in my unconscious, nor was it an object before my consciousness, but the impulse carrying me towards someone, the transmutation of my thoughts and behaviour—I was not unaware of it since it was I who endured the hours of boredom preceding a meeting, and who felt elation when she approached—it was lived, not known, from start to finish The lover is not unlike the dreamer. The 'latent content' and the 'sexual significance' of the dream are undoubtedly present to the dreamer since it is he who dreams his dream. But, precisely because sexuality is the general atmosphere of the dream, these elements are not thematized as sexual, for want of any non-sexual background against which they may stand out. When we ask ourselves whether or not the dreamer is conscious of the sexual content of his dream, we are really asking the wrong question If sexuality, as we have explained above, is indeed one of our ways of entering into a relationship with the world, then whenever our meta-sexual being is overshadowed, as happens in dreams, sexuality is everywhere and nowhere; it is, in the nature of the case, ambiguous and cannot emerge clearly as itself. The fire which figures in the dream is not, for the dreamer, a way of disguising the sexual drive beneath an acceptable symbol, since it is only in the waking state that it appears as a symbol; in the language of dreams, fire is the symbol of the sexual drive because the dreamer, being removed from the physical world and the inflexible context of waking life, uses imagery only in proportion as it has affective value. The sexual significance of the dream is neither unconscious nor 'conscious', because the dream does not 'signify', as does waking life, by relating one order of facts to another, and it is as great a mistake to see sexuality as crystallized in 'unconscious representations' as it is to see lodged in the depths of the dreamer a consciousness which calls it by its true name. Similarly, for the lover whose experience it is, love is nameless; it is not a thing capable of being circumscribed and designated, nor is it the love spoken of in books and newspapers, because it is the way in which he establishes his relations with the world, it is an existential signification The criminal fails to see his crime, and the traitor his betrayal for what they are, not because they exist deeply embedded within him as unconscious representations or tendencies, but because they are so many relatively closed worlds, so many situations If we are in a situation, we are surrounded and cannot be transparent to ourselves, so that our contact with ourselves is necessarily achieved only in the sphere of ambiguity.

But have we not overshot our mark? If illusion is possible in consciousness on some occasions, will it not be possible on all occasions? We said that there are imaginary sentiments to which we are committed sufficiently for them to be experienced, but insufficiently for them to be authentic. But are there any absolute commitments? Is it not of the essence of commitment to leave unimpaired the autonomy of the person who commits himself, in the sense that it is never complete, and does it not therefore follow that we have no longer any means of describing certain feelings as authentic? To define the subject in terms of existence, that is to say, in terms of a process in which he transcends himself, is surely by that very act to condemn him to illusion, since he will never be able to *be* anything Through refraining, in consciousness, from defining reality in terms of appearance, have we not severed the links binding us to ourselves, and reduced consciousness to the status of a mere appearance of some intangible reality? Are we not faced with the dilemma of an absolute consciousness on the one hand and endless doubt on the other? And have we not by our rejection of the first solution, made the *cogito* impossible? This objection brings us to the crucial point. It is true neither that my existence is in full possession of itself, nor that it is entirely estranged from itself, because it is action or doing, and because action is, by definition, the violent transition from what I have to what I aim to have, from what I am to what I intend to be. I can effect the *cogito* and be assured of genuinely willing, loving or believing, provided that in the first place I actually do will, love or believe, and thus fulfil my own existence. If this were not so, an ineradicable doubt would spread over the world, and equally over my own thoughts I should be for ever wondering whether my 'tastes', 'volitions', 'desires' and 'ventures' were really mine, for they would always seem artificial, unreal and unfulfilled But then this doubt, not being an actual doubt, could no longer even manage to confer the absolute certainty of doubting.[1] The only way out, and into 'sincerity', is by forestalling such scruples and taking a blind plunge into 'doing' Hence it is not *because* I think I am that I am certain of my existence, on the contrary the certainty I enjoy concerning my thoughts stems from their genuine existence My love, hatred and will are not certain as mere thoughts about loving, hating and willing, on the contrary the whole certainty of these thoughts is owed to that of the acts of love, hatred or will of which I am quite

---

[1] in which case, that too, that cynical distaste at her own persona, was deliberately put on' And that scorn for the distaste which she was busy contriving, was so much play-acting too' And her doubt about her scorn   it was maddening Once you started being sincere, was there no end to it?" S de Beauvoir, *L'Invitée*, p 232

sure because I *perform* them. All inner perception is inadequate because I am not an object that can be perceived, because I make my reality and find myself only in the act. 'I doubt' there is no way of silencing all doubt concerning this proposition other than by actually doubting, involving oneself in the experience of doubting, and thus bringing this doubt into existence as the certainty of doubting To doubt is always to doubt something, even if one 'doubts everything'. I am certain of doubting precisely because I take this or that thing, or even every thing and my own existence too, as doubtful It is through my relation to 'things' that I know myself; inner perception follows afterwards, and would not be possible had I not already made contact with my doubt in its very object. What has been said of external can equally be said of internal perception: that it involves infinity, that it is a never-ending synthesis which, though always incomplete, is nevertheless self-affirming If I try to verify my perception of the ash-tray, my task will be endless, for this perception takes for granted more than I can know in an explicit way Similarly, if I try to verify the reality of my doubt, I shall again be launched into an infinite regress, for I shall need to call into question my thought about doubting, then the thought about that thought, and so on The certainty derives from the doubt itself as an act, and not from these thoughts, just as the certainty of the thing and of the world precedes any thetic knowledge of their properties It is indeed true, as has been said, that to know is to know that one knows, not because this second order of knowing guarantees knowledge itself, but the reverse. I cannot reconstruct the thing, and yet there *are* perceived things. In the same way I can never coincide with my life which is for ever fleeing from itself, in spite of which there *are* inner perceptions For the same reason I am open to both illusion and truth about myself that is, there are acts in which I collect myself together in order to surpass myself The *cogito* is the recognition of this fundamental fact In the proposition: 'I think, I am', the two assertions are to be equated with each other, otherwise there would be no *cogito* Nevertheless we must be clear about the meaning of this equivalence it is not the 'I am' which is pre-eminently contained in the 'I think,' not my existence which is brought down to the consciousness which I have of it, but conversely the 'I think,' which is re-integrated into the transcending process of the 'I am', and consciousness into existence.

It is true that it seems necessary to concede my absolute coincidence with myself, if not in the case of will and feeling, at least in acts of 'pure thought'. If this were the case, all that we have said would appear to be challenged, so that, far from appearing as a mere manner of existence, thought would truly monopolize us. We must now, therefore, consider the understanding. I think of the triangle, the three-dimensional space to which it is supposed to belong, the extension of one of its sides, and the line that can be drawn through its apex parallel to the opposite side, and I perceive that this line, with the apex, forms three angles the sum of which is equal to the sum of the angles of the triangle, and equal, moreover, to two right angles. I am sure of the result which I regard as proved; which means that my diagrammatic construction is not, as are the strokes arbitrarily added by the child to his drawing, each one of which completely transforms its meaning ('it's a house; no, it's a boat, no, it's a man'), a collection of lines fortuitously drawn by my hand. The process from start to finish has a triangle in view. The genesis of the figure is not only a real genesis, but an intelligible one; I make my construction according to rules, and cause *properties* to make their appearance in the figure—properties which are relations belonging to the essence of the triangle. I do not, like the child, reproduce those suggested by the ill-defined figure which is actually there on the paper I am aware of presenting a proof, because I perceive a necessary link between the collection of data which constitute the hypothesis and the conclusion which I draw from them It is this necessity which ensures that I shall be able to repeat the operation with an indefinite number of empirical figures, and the necessity itself stems from the fact that at each step in my demonstration, and each time I introduced new relationships, I remained conscious of the triangle as a stable structure conditioned, and left intact, by them. This is why we can say, if we want, that the proof consists in bringing the sum of the angles constructed into two different groupings, and seeing that sum alternately as equal to the sum of the angles of the triangle, and equal to two right angles,[1] but it must be added[2] that here we have not merely two successive configurations, the first of which eliminates the second (as is the case with the child sketching dreamily), the first survives for me while the second is in process of establishing itself, the sum of angles which I equate with two right angles *is* the same as I elsewhere equate with the sum of the angles of the triangle, all of which is possible only provided that I go beyond the order of phenomena or appearances and gain access to that of the *eidos* or of being. Truth would seem to be impossible unless one enjoys an absolute self-possession in active thought, failing which it would be unable to unfold in a set of successive operations, and to produce a permanently valid result.

There would be neither thought nor truth *but for* an act whereby I

[1] Wertheimer, *Drei Abhandlungen zur Gestalttheorie die Schluszprozesse im produktiven Denken*
[2] A Gurwitsch, *Quelques aspects et quelques développements de la théorie de la Forme*, p 460

prevail over the temporal dispersal of the phases of thought, and the mere *de facto* existence of my mental events The important thing, however, is fully to understand the nature of this act. The necessity of the proof is not an analytic necessity the construction which enables the conclusion to be reached is not really contained in the essence of the triangle, but merely possible when that essence serves as a starting point. There is no definition of a triangle which includes in advance the properties subsequently to be demonstrated and the intermediate steps leading to that demonstration Extending one side, drawing through the apex a line parallel to the opposite side, introducing the theorem relating to parallels and their secant, these steps are possible only if I consider the triangle itself as it is drawn on the paper, on the blackboard or in the imagination, with its physiognomy, the concrete arrangement of its lines, in short its *Gestalt* Is not precisely this the essence or the idea of a triangle? Let us, at the outset, reject any idea of a formal essence of the triangle. Whatever one's opinion of attempts at formalization, it is in any case quite certain that they lay no claim to provide a logic of invention, and that no logical definition of a triangle could equal in fecundity the vision of the figure, or enable us to reach, through a series of formal operations, conclusions not already established by the aid of intuition This, it will perhaps be objected, touches only on the psychological circumstances of discovery, so that in so far as, after the event, it is possible to establish, between the hypothesis and the conclusion, a link owing nothing to intuition, it is because intuition is not the inevitable mediator of thought and has no place in logic But the fact that formalization is always retrospective proves that it is never otherwise than apparently complete, and that formal thought feeds on intuitive thought It reveals those unformulated axioms on which reason is said to rest, and seems to bring to reason a certain added rigour and to uncover the very foundations of our certainty; but in reality the place in which certainty arises and in which a truth makes its appearance is always intuitive thought, even though, or rather *precisely because*, the principles are tacitly assumed there. There would be no experience of truth, and nothing would quench our 'mental volubility' if we thought *vi formae*, and if formal relations were not first presented to us crystallized in some particular thing We should not even be able to settle on a hypothesis from which to deduce the consequences, if we did not first hold it to be true A hypothesis is what is presumed to be true, so that hypothetical thinking presupposes some experience of *de facto* truth The construction relates, then, to the configuration of the triangle, to the way in which it occupies space, to the relations expressed by the words 'on', 'by', 'apex' and 'extend' Do these relations constitute a

385

kind of material essence of the triangle? If the words 'on', 'through', etc., are to retain any meaning, it is in virtue of my working on a perceptible or imaginary triangle, that is to say, one which is at least potentially situated in my perceptual field, orientated in relation to 'up' and 'down', 'right' and 'left', or again, as we pointed out earlier, implied in my general grip upon the world The construction makes explicit the possibilities of the triangle, considered not in the light of its definition and as a pure idea, but as a configuration and as the pole towards which my movements are directed. The conclusion follows of necessity from the hypothesis because, in the act of constructing, the geometer has already experienced the possibility of the transition Let us try to give a better description of this act We have seen that what occurs is clearly not a purely manual operation, the actual movement of my hand and pen over the paper, for in that case there would be no difference between a construction and any arbitrary set of strokes, and no demonstration would accrue. The construction is a gesture, which means that the actual lines drawn are the outward expression of an intention But then what is this intention? I 'consider' the triangle, which is for me a set of lines with a certain orientation, and if words such as 'angle' or 'direction' have any meaning for me, it is in so far as I place myself at a point, and from it tend towards another point, in so far as the system of spatial positions provides me with a field of possible movements Thus do I grasp the concrete essence of the triangle, which is not a collection of objective 'characteristics', but the formula of an attitude, a certain modality of my hold on the world, a structure, in short. When I construct, I commit the first structure to a second one, the 'parallels and secant' structure. How is that possible? It is because my perception of the triangle was not, so to speak, fixed and dead, for the drawing of the triangle on the paper was merely its outer covering; it was traversed by lines of force, and everywhere in it new directions not traced out yet possible came to light. In so far as the triangle was implicated in my hold on the world, it was bursting with indefinite possibilities of which the construction actually drawn was merely one The construction possesses a demonstrative value because I cause it to emerge from the dynamic formula of the triangle It expresses my power to make apparent the sensible symbols of a certain hold on things, which is my perception of the triangle's structure. It is an act of the productive imagination and not a return to the eternal idea of the triangle Just as the localization of objects in space, according to Kant himself, is not merely a mental operation, but one which utilizes the body's motility,[1] movement conferring sensations at the particular

[1] P Lachièze-Rey, *Utilisation possible du schematisme kantien pour une théorie de la perception* and *Réflexions sur l'activité spirituelle constituante.*

point on its trajectory at which those sensations are produced, so the geometer, who, generally speaking, studies the objective laws of location, knows the relationships with which he is concerned only by describing them, at least potentially, with his body. The subject of geometry is a motor subject. This means in the first place that our body is not an object, nor is its movement a mere change of place in objective space, otherwise the problem would be merely shifted, and the movement of one's own body would shed no light on the problem of the location of things, since it would be itself nothing but a thing. There must be, as Kant conceded, a 'motion which generates space'[1] which is our intentional motion, distinct from 'motion in space', which is that of things and of our passive body. But there is more to be said. if motion is productive of space, we must rule out the possibility that the body's motility is a mere 'instrument'[2] for the constituting consciousness If there is a constituting consciousness, then bodily movement is movement only in so far as that consciousness thinks of it in that light,[3] the constructive power rediscovers in it only what it has put there, and the body is not even an instrument in this respect: it is an object among objects. There is no psychology in a philosophy of constituting consciousness Or at least there can be nothing valid for such a psychology to say, for it can do nothing but apply the results of analytical reflection to each particular content, while nevertheless distorting them, since it deprives them of their transcendental significance The body's motion can play a part in the perception of the world only if it is itself an original intentionality, a manner of relating itself to the distinct object of knowledge. The world around us must be, not a system of objects which we synthesize, but a totality of things, open to us, towards which we project ourselves The 'motion which generates space' does not deploy the trajectory from some metaphysical point with no position in the real world, but from a certain here towards a certain yonder, which are necessarily interchangeable The project towards motion is an act, which means that it traces out the spatio-temporal distance by actually covering it The geometer's thought, in so far as it is necessarily sustained by this act, does not, therefore, coincide with itself it is purely and simply transcendence. In so far as, by adding a construction, I can bring to light the properties of a triangle, and yet find that the figure thus transformed does not cease to be the same figure as I began with, and in so far, moreover, as I am able to effect a synthesis retaining the character of necessity, this is not because my construction

[1] Lachièze-Rey, *Réflexions sur l'activité spirituelle constituante*, p 132
[2] Lachièze-Rey, *Utilisation possible* , p 7
[3] 'It must disclose intrinsically the immanence of a spatial trajectory, which alone can enable it to be thought of as motion'. Lachièze-Rey, ibid , p 6

is upheld by a concept of the triangle in which all its properties are included, or because, starting from perceptual consciousness, I arrive at the *eidos*. it is because I perform the synthesis of the new property by means of my body, which immediately implants me in space, while its autonomous motion enables me, through a series of definite procedures, to arrive once more at an all-inclusive view of space Far from its being the case that geometrical thinking transcends perceptual consciousness, it is from the world of perception that I borrow the notion of essence. I believe that the triangle has always had, and always will have, angles the sum of which equals two right angles, as well as all the other less obvious properties which geometry attributes to it, because I have had the experience of a real triangle, and because, as a physical thing, it necessarily *has* within itself everything that it has ever been able, or ever will be able, to display Unless the perceived thing has for good and ever implanted within us the ideal notion of a being which is what it is, there would be no phenomenon of being, and mathematical thought would appear to us in the light of a creative activity What I call the essence of the triangle is nothing but this presumption of a completed synthesis, in terms of which we have defined the thing

Our body, to the extent that it moves itself about, that is, to the extent that it is inseparable from a view of the world and is that view itself brought into existence, is the condition of possibility, not only of the geometrical synthesis, but of all expressive operations and all acquired views which constitute the cultural world When we say that thought is spontaneous, this does not mean that it coincides with itself; on the contrary it means that it outruns itself, and speech is precisely that act through which it immortalizes itself as truth It is, indeed, obvious that speech cannot be regarded as a mere clothing for thought, or expression as the translation, into an arbitrary system of symb_'s, of a meaning already clear to itself It is said again and again that sounds and phonemes have no meaning in themselves, and that all our consciousness can find in language is what it has put there. But it would follow from this that language can teach us nothing, and that it can at the most arouse in us new combinations of those meanings already possessed by us. But this is just what the experience of language refutes It is true that communication presupposes a system of correspondences such as the dictionary provides, but it goes beyond these, and what gives its meaning to each word is the sentence It is because it has been used in various contexts that the word gradually accumulates a significance which it is impossible to establish absolutely A telling utterance or a good book impose their meaning upon us. Thus they carry it within them in a certain way As for the speaking subject, he too must be enabled to outrun what he thought before, and to find in his own words more than the thought he was putting into them, otherwise we should not see thought, even solitary thought, seeking expression with such perseverance Speech is, therefore, that paradoxical operation through which, by using words of a given sense, and already available meanings, we try to follow up an intention which necessarily outstrips, modifies, and itself, in the last analysis, stabilizes the meanings of the words which translate it. Constituted language plays the same limited rôle in the work of expression as do colours in painting: had we not eyes, or more generally senses, there would be no painting at all for us, yet the picture 'tells' us more than the mere use of our senses can ever do The picture over and above the sense-data, speech over and above linguistic data must, therefore, in themselves possess a signifying virtue, independently of any meaning that exists for itself, in the mind of the spectator or listener 'By using words as the painter uses colours and the musician notes, we are trying to constitute, out of a spectacle or an emotion, or even an abstract idea, a kind of equivalent or *specie* soluble in the mind. Here the expression becomes the principal thing. We mould and animate the reader, we cause him to participate in our creative or poetic action, putting into the hidden mouth of his mind the message of a certain object or of a certain feeling.'[1] In the painter or the speaking subject, picture and utterance respectively do not illustrate a ready-made thought, but make that thought their own. This is why we have been led to distinguish between a secondary speech which renders a thought already acquired, and an originating speech which brings it into existence, in the first place for ourselves, and then for others. Now all words which have become mere signs for a univocal thought have been able to do so only because they have first of all functioned as originating words, and we can still remember with what richness they appeared to be endowed, and how they were like a landscape new to us, while we were engaged in 'acquiring' them, and while they still fulfilled the primordial function of expression. Thus self-possession and coincidence with the self do not serve to define thought, which is, on the contrary, an outcome of expression and always an illusion, in so far as the clarity of what is acquired rests upon the fundamentally obscure operation which has enabled us to immortalize within ourselves a moment of fleeting life We are invited to discern beneath thinking which basks in its acquisitions, and offers merely a brief resting-place in the unending process of expression, another thought which is struggling to establish itself, and succeeds only by bending the resources of constituted language to some fresh usage This operation must be considered as an ultimate fact, since any explanation of it—whether

[1] Claudel, *Réflexions sur le vers français, Positions et propositions*, pp 11-12.

empiricist, reducing new meanings to given ones; or idealist, positing an absolute knowledge immanent in the most primitive forms of knowledge—would amount to a denial of it. Language outruns us, not merely because the use of speech always presupposes a great number of thoughts which are not present in the mind and which are covered by each word, but also for another reason, and a more profound one. namely, that these thoughts themselves, when present, were not at any time 'pure' thoughts either, for already in them there was a surplus of the signified over the signifying, the same effort of thought already thought to equal thinking thought, the same provisional amalgam of both which gives rise to the whole mystery of expression. That which is called an idea is necessarily linked to an act of expression, and owes to it its appearance of autonomy. It is a cultural object, like the church, the street, the pencil or the Ninth Symphony It may be said in reply that the church can be burnt down, the street and pencil destroyed, and that, if all the scores of the Ninth Symphony and all musical instruments were reduced to ashes, it would survive only for a few brief years in the memory of those who had heard it, whereas on the other hand the idea of the triangle and its properties are imperishable. In fact, the idea of the triangle with its properties, and of the quadratic equation, have their historical and geographical area, and if the tradition in which they have been handed down to us, and the cultural instruments which bear them on, were to be destroyed, fresh acts of creative expression would be needed to revive them in the world. What is true, however, is that, once they have made their first appearance, subsequent 'appearances', if successful, add nothing and if unsuccessful, subtract nothing, from the quadratic equation, which remains an inexhaustible possession among us But the same may be said of the Ninth Symphony, which lives on in its intelligible abode, as Proust has said, whether it is played well or badly, or rather which continues its existence in a more occult time than natural time. The time of ideas is not be confused with that in which books appear and disappear, and musical works are printed or lost a book which has always been reprinted one day ceases to be read, a musical work of which there were only a few copies extant is suddenly much sought after. The existence of the idea must not be confused with the empirical existence of the means of expression, for ideas endure or fall into oblivion, and the intelligible sky subtly changes colour We have already drawn a distinction between empirical speech—the word as a phenomenon of sound, the fact that a certain word is uttered at a certain moment by a certain person, which may happen independently of thought—and transcendental or authentic speech, that by which an idea begins to exist But if there had been no mankind with phonatory or articulatory organs, and a respiratory apparatus—or at least with a body and the ability to move himself, there would have been no speech and no ideas. What remains true is that in speech, to a greater extent than in music or painting, thought seems able to detach itself from its material instruments and acquire an eternal value There is a sense in which all triangles which will ever exist through the workings of physical causality will always have angles the sum of which equals two right angles, even if a time comes when men have forgotten their geometry, and there is not a single person left who knows any. But in this case it is because speech is applied to nature, whereas music, and painting, like poetry, create their own object, and as soon as they become sufficiently aware of themselves, deliberately confine themselves within the cultural world. Prosaic, and particularly scientific, utterance is a cultural entity which at the same time lays claim to translate a truth relating to nature in itself. Now we know that this is not the case, for modern criticism of the sciences has clearly shown the constructive element in them. 'Real', i e perceived, triangles, do not necessarily have, for all eternity, angles the sum of which equals two right angles, if it is true that the space in which we live is no less amenable to non-Euclidean than to Euclidean geometry. Thus there is no fundamental difference between the various modes of expression, and no privileged position can be accorded to any of them on the alleged ground that it expresses a truth in itself. Speech is as dumb as music, music as eloquent as speech Expression is everywhere creative, and what is expressed is always inseparable from it. There is no analysis capable of making language crystal clear and arraying it before us as if it were an object. The act of speech is clear only for the person who is actually speaking or listening, it becomes obscure as soon as we try to bring explicitly to light those reasons which have led us to understand thus and not otherwise. We can say of it what we have said of perception, and what Pascal says about opinions in all three cases we have the same miracle of an immediately apprehended clarity, which vanishes as soon as we try to break it down to what we believe to be its component elements. I speak, and I understand myself and am understood quite unambiguously, I take a new grip on my life, and others take a new grip on it too. I may say that 'I have been waiting for a long time', or that someone 'is dead', and I think I know what I am saying. Yet if I question myself on time or the experience of death, which were implied in my words, there is nothing clear in my mind This is because I have tried to speak about speech, to re-enact the act of expression which gave significance to the words 'dead' and 'time', to extend the brief hold on my experience which they ensure for me These second or third order acts of expression, like the rest, have

391

indeed in each case their convincing clarity, without, however, ever enabling me to dispel the fundamental obscurity of what is expressed, or to eliminate the distance separating my thought from itself. Must we conclude from this[1] that, born and developed in obscurity, yet capable of clarity, language is nothing but the obverse of an infinite Thought, and the message of that Thought as communicated to us? This would mean losing contact with the analysis which we have just carried out, and reaching a conclusion in conflict with what has been established as we have gone along. Language transcends us and yet we speak. If we are led to conclude from this that there exists a transcendent thought spelt out by our words, we are supposing that an attempt at expression is brought to completion, after saying that it can never be so, and invoking an absolute thought, when we have just shown that any such thought is beyond our conception. Such is the principle of Pascal's apologetics; but the more it is shown that man is without absolute power, the more any assertion of an absolute is made, not probable, but on the contrary suspect. In fact analysis demonstrates, not that there is behind language a transcendent thought, but that language transcends itself in speech, that speech itself *brings about* that concordance between me and myself, and between myself and others, on which an attempt is being made to base that thought. The phenomenon of language, in the double sense of primary fact and remarkable occurrence, is not explained, but eliminated, if we duplicate it with some transcendent thought, since it consists in this: that an act of thought, once expressed, has the power to outlive itself It is not, as is often held, that the verbal formula serves us as a mnemonic means: merely committed to writing or to memory, it would be useless had we not acquired once and for all the inner power of interpreting it To give expression is not to substitute, for new thought, a system of stable signs to which unchangeable thoughts are linked, it is to ensure, by the use of words already used, that the new intention carries on the heritage of the past, it is at a stroke to incorporate the past into the present, and weld that present to a future, to open a whole temporal cycle in which the 'acquired' thought will remain present as a dimension, without our needing henceforth to summon it up or reproduce it. What is known as the non-temporal in thought is what, having thus carried forward the past and committed the future, is presumptively of all time and is therefore anything but transcendent in relation to time. The non-temporal is the acquired

Time itself presents us with the prime model of this permanent acquisition. If time is the dimension in accordance with which events

[1] As does B Parain, *Recherches sur la nature et les fonctions du langage*, Chap XI

drive each other successively from the scene, it is also that in accordance with which each one of them wins its unchallengeable place. To say that an event *takes place* is to say that it will always be true that it has taken place. Each moment of time, in virtue of its very essence, posits an existence against which the other moments of time are powerless. After the construction is drawn, the geometrical relation is acquired, even if I then forget the details of the proof, the mathematical gesture establishes a tradition. Van Gogh's paintings have their place in me for all time, a step is taken from which I cannot retreat, and, even though I retain no clear recollection of the pictures which I have seen, my whole subsequent aesthetic experience will be that of someone who has become acquainted with the painting of Van Gogh, exactly as a middle class man turned workman always remains, even in his manner of being a workman, a middle-class-man-turned-workman, or as an act confers a certain quality upon us for ever, even though we may afterwards repudiate it and change our beliefs. Existence always carries forward its past, whether it be by accepting or disclaiming it. We are, as Proust declared, perched on a pyramid of past life, and if we do not see this, it is because we are obsessed by objective thought. We believe that our past, for ourselves, is reducible to the express memories which we are able to contemplate. We sever our existence from the past itself, and allow it to pick up only those threads of the past which are present. But how are these threads to be recognized as threads of the past unless we enjoy in some other way a direct opening upon that past? Acquisition must be accepted as an irreducible phenomenon. What we have experienced is, and remains, permanently ours; and in old age a man is still in contact with his youth. Every present as it arises is driven into time like a wedge and stakes its claim to eternity. Eternity is not another order of time, but the atmosphere of time. It is true that a false thought, no less than a true one, possesses this sort of eternity if I am mistaken at this moment, it is for ever true that I am mistaken. It would seem necessary, therefore, that there should be, in true thought, a different fertility, and that it should remain true not only as a past actually lived through, but also as a perpetual present for ever carried forward in time's succession. This, however, does not secure any essential difference between truths of fact and truths of reason. For there is not one of my actions, not one of even my fallacious thoughts, once it is adhered to, which has not been directed towards a value or a truth, and which, in consequence, does not retain its permanent relevance in the subsequent course of my life, not only as an indelible fact, but also as a necessary stage on the road to the more complete truths or values which I have since recognized. My truths have been built out of these errors, and carry them along in their eternity. Conversely, there is not one truth of reason which does not retain its coefficient of facticity: the alleged transparency of Euclidean geometry is one day revealed as operative for a certain period in the history of the human mind, and signifies simply that, for a time, men were able to take a homogeneous three-dimensional space as the 'ground' of their thoughts, and to assume unquestioningly what generalized science will come to consider as a contingent account of space Thus every truth of fact is a truth of reason, and *vice versa*. The relation of reason to fact, or eternity to time, like that of reflection to the unreflective, of thought to language or of thought to perception is this two-way relationship that phenomenology has called *Fundierung*. the founding term, or originator—time, the unreflective, the fact, language, perception—is primary in the sense that the originated is presented as a determinate or explicit form of the originator, which prevents the latter from reabsorbing the former, and yet the originator is not primary in the empiricist sense and the originated is not simply derived from it, since it is through the originated that the originator is made manifest It is for this reason that it is a matter of indifference whether we say that the present foreshadows eternity or that the eternity of truth is merely a sublimation of the present This ambiguity cannot be resolved, but it can be understood as ultimate, if we recapture the intuition of real time which preserves everything, and which is at the core of both proof and expression. 'Reflection on the creative power of the mind,' says Brunschvicg,[1] 'implies, in every certainty of experience, the feeling that, in any determinate truth that one may have managed to demonstrate, there exists a soul of truth which outruns it and frees itself from it, a soul which can detach itself from the particular expression of that truth in order to adumbrate a deeper and more comprehensive expression, although this drive forward in no way impairs the eternity of the true ' What is this eternally true that no one possesses? What is this thing expressed which lies beyond all expression, and, if we have the right to posit it, why is it our constant concern to arrive at a more precise expression? What is this One round which minds and truths are disposed, as if they tended towards it, while it is maintained at the same time that they tend towards no pre-established term? The idea of a transcendent Being had at least the advantage of not stultifying the actions through which, in an ever difficult process of carrying forward, each consciousness and intersubjectivity themselves forge their own unity It is true that, if these actions belong to that most intimate part of ourselves accessible to us, the positing of God contributes nothing to the elucidation of our life We experience, not a genuine eternity and a participation in the One, but concrete acts

[1] *Les Progrès de la Conscience dans la Philosophie occidentale*, p 794

of taking up and carrying forward by which, through time's accidents, we are linked in relationships with ourselves and others. In short, we experience a *participation in the world*, and 'being-in-truth' is indistinguishable from being in the world.

We are now in a position to make up our minds about the question of evidence, and to describe the experience of truth There are truths just as there are perceptions. not that we can ever array before ourselves in their entirety the reasons for any assertion—there are merely motives, we have merely a hold on time and not full possession of it—but because it is of the essence of time to take itself up as it leaves itself behind, and to draw itself together into visible things, into firsthand evidence. All consciousness is, in some measure, perceptual consciousness If it were possible to lay bare and unfold all the presuppositions in what I call my reason or my ideas at each moment, we should always find experiences which have not been made explicit, large-scale contributions from past and present, a whole 'sedimentary history'[1] which is not only relevant to the *genesis* of my thought, but which determines its *significance*. For an absolute evidence, free from any presupposition, to be possible, and for my thought to be able to pierce through to itself, catch itself in action, and arrive at a pure 'assent of the self to the self', it would, to speak the language of the Kantians, have to cease to be an event and become an act through and through. in the language of the Schoolmen, its formal reality would have to be included in its objective reality; in the language of Malebranche, it would have to cease to be 'perception', 'sentiment' or 'contact' with truth, to become pure 'idea' and 'vision' of the truth It would be necessary, in other words, that instead of being myself, I should become purely and simply one who knows myself, and that the world should have ceased to exist around me in order to become purely and simply an object before me. In relation to what we are by reason of our acquisitions and this pre-existent world, we have a power of placing in abeyance, and that suffices to ensure our freedom from determinism I may well close my eyes, and stop up my ears, I shall nevertheless not cease to see, if it is only the blackness before my eyes, or to hear, if only silence, and in the same way I can 'bracket' my opinions or the beliefs I have acquired, but, whatever I think or decide, it is always against the background of what I have previously believed or done. *Habemus ideam veram*, we possess a truth, but this experience of truth would be absolute knowledge only if we could thematize every motive, that is, if we ceased to be in a situation. The actual possession of the true idea does not, therefore, entitle us to predicate an intelligible abode of adequate thought and absolute productivity, it

---

[1] Husserl, *Formale und transzendentale Logik*, p 221.

establishes merely a 'teleology'[1] of consciousness which, from this first instrument, will forge more perfect ones, and these in turn more perfect ones still, and so on endlessly. 'Only through an eidetic intuition can the essence of eidetic intuition be elucidated,' says Husserl.[2] The intuition of some particular essence necessarily precedes, in our experience, the essence of intuition The only way to think of thought is in the first place to think of something, and it is therefore essential to that thought not to take itself as an object. To think of thought is to adopt in relation to it an attitude that we have initially learned in relation to 'things'; it is never to eliminate, but merely to push further back the opacity that thought presents to itself Every halt in the forward movement of consciousness, every focus on the object, every appearance of a 'something' or of an idea presupposes a subject who has suspended self-questioning at least in that particular respect. Which is why, as Descartes maintained, it is true both that certain ideas are presented to me as irresistibly self-evident *de facto*, and that this fact is never valid *de jure*, and that it never does away with the possibility of doubt arising as soon as we are no longer in the presence of the idea. It is no accident that self-evidence itself may be called into question, because *certainty is doubt*, being the carrying forward of a tradition of thought which cannot be condensed into an evident 'truth' without my giving up all attempts to make it explicit It is for the same reasons that a self-evident truth is irresistible in fact, yet always questionable, which amounts to two ways of saying the same thing: namely, that it is irresistible because I take for granted a certain acquisition of experience, a certain field of thought, and precisely for this reason it appears to me as self-evident for a certain thinking nature, the one which I enjoy and perpetuate, but which remains contingent and given to itself The consistency of a thing perceived, of a geometrical relationship or of an idea, is arrived at only provided that I give up trying by every means to make it more explicit, and instead allow myself to come to rest in it. Once launched, and committed to a certain set of thoughts, Euclidean space, for example, or the conditions governing the existence of a certain society, I discover evident truths; but these are not unchallengeable, since perhaps this space or this society are not the only ones possible. It is therefore of the essence of certainty to be established only with reservations; there is an *opinion* which is not a provisional form of knowledge destined to give way later to an absolute form, but on the contrary, both the oldest or most rudimentary, and the most conscious or mature form of knowledge—an opinion which is primary in the double sense of 'original'

[1] This notion recurs frequently in the later writings of Husserl.
[2] *Formale und transzendentale Logik*, p. 220

396

and 'fundamental'. This is what calls up before us *something in general*, to which positing* thought—doubt or demonstration—can subsequently relate in affirmation or denial There is significance, something and not nothing, there is an indefinite train of concordant experiences, to which this ash-tray in its permanence testifies, or the truth which I hit upon yesterday and to which I think I can revert today.

This evidentness of the phenomenon, or again of the 'world', is no less misunderstood when we try to reach being without contact with the phenomenon, that is, when we make being necessary, as when we cut the phenomenon off from being, when we degrade it to the status of mere appearance or possibility The first conception is Spinoza's. Primary opinion is here subordinated to absolute self-evidence, and the notion, 'there is something' which is an amalgam of being and nothingness, to the notion 'Being exists'. One rejects as meaningless any questioning of being it is impossible to ask why there is something rather than nothing, and why this world rather than a different one, since the shape of this world and the very existence of a world are merely consequences of necessary being. The second conception reduces self-evidence to appearance: all my truths are after all self-evident only for me, and for a thought fashioned like mine; they are bound up with my psycho-physiological constitution and the existence of this world. Other forms of thought functioning in accordance with other rules, and other possible worlds, can be conceived as having the same claim to reality as this one. And here the question why there is something rather than nothing seems apposite, and why this particular world has come into being, but the reply is necessarily out of our reach, since we are imprisoned in our psycho-physiological make-up, which is a simple fact like the shape of our face or the number of our teeth. This second conception is not so different from the first as it might appear it implies a tacit reference to an absolute knowledge and an absolute being in relation to which our factual self-evidences, or synthetic truths, are considered inadequate. According to the phenomenological conception, this dogmatism on the one hand and scepticism on the other are both left behind. The laws of our thought and our self-evident truths are certainly facts, but they are not detachable from us, they are implied in any conception that we may form of being and the possible. It is not a question of confining ourselves to phenomena, of imprisoning consciousness in its own states, while retaining the possibility of another being beyond apparent being, nor of treating our thought as one fact among many, but of defining being as that which appears, and consciousness as a universal fact. I think, and this or that thought

* I e. 'thetic' (Translator's note)

397

appears to me as true, I am well aware that it is not unconditionally true, and that the process of making it totally explicit would be an endless task; but the fact remains that at the moment I think, I think something, and that any other truth, in the name of which I might wish to discount this one, must, if it is to be called a truth for me, square with the 'true' thought of which I have experience. If I try to imagine Martians, or angels, or some divine thought outside the realm of my logic, this Martian, angelic or divine thought must figure in my universe without completely disrupting it [1] My thought, my self-evident truth is not one fact among others, but a value-fact which envelops and conditions every other possible one. There is no other world possible in the sense in which mine is, not because mine is necessary as Spinoza thought, but because any 'other world' that I might try to conceive would set limits to this one, would be found on its boundaries, and would consequently merely fuse with it Consciousness, if it is not absolute truth or $\dot{\alpha}$-$\lambda\epsilon\theta\epsilon\iota\alpha$, at least rules out all absolute falsity. Our mistakes, illusions and questions are indeed mistakes, illusions and questions Error is not consciousness of error; it even excludes such consciousness. Our questions do not always admit of answers, and to say with Marx that man poses for himself only problems that he can solve is to revive a theological optimism and postulate the consummation of the world Our errors become truths only once they are recognized, and there remains a difference between their revealed and their latent content of truth, between their alleged and their actual significance. The truth is that neither error nor doubt ever cut us off from the truth, because they are surrounded by a world horizon in which the teleology of consciousness summons us to an effort at resolving them. Finally, the contingency of the world must not be understood as a deficiency in being, a break in the stuff of necessary being, a threat to rationality, nor as a problem to be solved as soon as possible by the discovery of some deeper-laid necessity. That is ontic contingency, contingency within the bounds of the world. Ontological contingency, the contingency of the world itself, being radical, is, on the other hand, what forms the basis once and for all of our ideas of truth The world is that reality of which the necessary and the possible are merely provinces.

To sum up, we are restoring to the *cogito* a temporal thickness If there is not endless doubt, and if 'I think', it is because I plunge on into provisional thoughts and, by deeds, overcome time's discontinuity. Thus vision is brought to rest in a thing seen which both

[1] See *Logische Untersuchungen*, I, p 117 What is sometimes termed Husserl's rationalism is in reality the recognition of subjectivity as an inalienable fact, and of the world to which it is directed as *omnitudo realitatis*

precedes and outlasts it Have we got out of our difficulty? We have admitted that the certainty of vision and that of the thing seen are of a piece Must we conclude from this that, since the thing seen is never absolutely certain, as illusions show, vision also is involved in this uncertainty, or, on the contrary, that, since vision on its own is absolutely certain, so is the thing seen, so that I am never really mistaken? The second solution would amount to reinstating the immanence which we have banished But if we adopted the first, thought would be cut off from itself, there would no longer be anything but 'facts of consciousness' which might be called internal by nominal definition, but which, for me, would be as opaque as things, there would no longer be either inner experience or consciousness, and the experience of the *cogito* would be once more forgotten When we describe consciousness as involved through its body in a space, through its language in a history, through its prejudices in a concrete form of thought, it is not a matter of setting it back in a series of objective events, even though they be 'psychic' events, and in the causal system of the world He who doubts cannot, while doubting, doubt that he doubts. Doubt, even when generalized, is not the abolition of my thought, it is merely a pseudo-nothingness, for I cannot extricate myself from being; my act of doubting itself creates the possibility of certainty and is there for me, it occupies me, I am committed to it, and I cannot pretend to be nothing at the time I execute it Reflection, which moves all things away to a distance, discovers itself as at least given to itself in the sense that it cannot think of itself as eliminated, or stand apart from itself But this does not mean that reflection and thought are elementary facts there to be observed as such. As Montaigne clearly saw, one can call into question thought which is loaded with a sediment of history and weighed down with its own being, one can entertain doubts about doubt itself, considered as a definite modality of thought and as consciousness of a doubtful object, but the formula of radical reflection is not. 'I know nothing'—a formula which it is all too easy to catch in flat contradiction with itself—but: 'What do I know?' Descartes was not unmindful of this He has frequently been credited with having gone beyond sceptical doubt, which is a mere state, and with making doubt into a method, an act, and with having thus provided consciousness with a fixed point and reinstated certainty. But, in fact, Descartes did not suspend doubt in the face of the certainty of doubt itself, as if the act of doubting were sufficient to sweep doubt away by entailing a certainty. He took it further He does not say: 'I doubt, therefore I am', but 'I think, therefore I am', which means that doubt itself is certain, not as actual doubt, but as pure thought about doubting and, since the same might be said in turn about this thought, the only proposition which is absolutely certain and which halts doubt in its tracks because it is implied by that doubt, is: 'I think,' or again, 'something appears to me'. There is no act, no particular experience which exactly fills my consciousness and imprisons my freedom, 'there is no thought which abolishes the power to think and brings it to a conclusion—no definite position of the bolt that finally closes the lock. No, there is no thought which is a resolution born of its own very development and, as it were, the final chord of this permanent dissonance.'[1] No particular thought reaches through to the core of our thought in general, nor is any thought conceivable without another possible thought as a witness to it. And this is no imperfection from which we may imagine consciousness freed. If there must be consciousness, if something must appear to someone, it is necessary that behind all our particular thoughts there should lie a retreat of not-being, a Self. I must avoid equating myself with a series of 'consciousnesses', for each of these, with its load of sedimentary history and sensible implications, must present itself to a perpetual absentee Our situation, then, is as follows· in order to know that we think, it is necessary in the first place that we actually should think. Yet this commitment does not dispel all doubts, for my thoughts do not deprive me of my power to question; a word or an idea, considered as events in my history, have meaning for me only if I take up this meaning from within I know that I think through such and such particular thoughts that I have, and I know that I have these thoughts because I carry them forward, that is, because I know that I think in general. The aim at a transcendent objective and the view of myself aiming at it, the awareness of the connected and of connecting are in a circular relationship. The problem is how I can be the constituting agent of my thought in general, failing which it would not be thought by anybody, would pass unnoticed and would therefore not be thought at all—without ever being that agent of my particular thoughts, since I never see them come into being in the full light of day, but merely know myself through them. The question is how subjectivity can be both dependent yet irremovable

Let us tackle this by taking language as our example. There is a consciousness of myself which makes use of language and is humming with words. I read, let us say, the *Second Meditation*. It has indeed to do with me, but a me in idea, an idea which is, strictly speaking, neither mine nor, for that matter, Descartes', but that of any reflecting man. By following the meaning of the words and the argument, I reach the conclusion that indeed because I think, I am; but this is merely a verbal *cogito*, for I have grasped my thought and my existence only through the medium of language, and the true formula of

[1] Valéry, *Introduction à la méthode de Léonard de Vinci, Variété,* p 194

this *cogito* should be 'One thinks, therefore one is' The wonderful thing about language is that it promotes its own oblivion my eyes follow the lines on the paper, and from the moment I am caught up in their meaning, I lose sight of them. The paper, the letters on it, my eyes and body are there only as the minimum setting of some invisible operation. Expression fades out before what is expressed, and this is why its mediating rôle may pass unnoticed, and why Descartes nowhere mentions it Descartes, and *a fortiori* his reader, begin their meditation in what is already a universe of discourse. This certainty which we enjoy of reaching, beyond expression, a truth separable from it and of which expression is merely the garment and contingent manifestation, has been implanted in us precisely by language. It appears as a mere sign only once it has provided itself with a meaning, and the coming to awareness, if it is to be complete, must rediscover the expressive unity in which both signs and meaning appear in the first place. When a child cannot speak, or cannot yet speak the adult's language, the linguistic ritual which unfolds around him has no hold on him, he is near us in the same way as is a spectator with a poor seat at the theatre; he sees clearly enough that we are laughing and gesticulating, he hears the nasal tune being played, but there is nothing at the end of those gestures or behind those words, nothing *happens* for him. Language takes on a meaning for the child when it *establishes a situation* for him. A story is told in a children's book of the disappointment of a small boy who put on his grandmother's spectacles and took up her book in the expectation of being able himself to find in it the stories which she used to tell him The tale ends with these words 'Well, what a fraud! Where's the story? I can see nothing but black and white.' For the child the 'story' and the thing expressed are not 'ideas' or 'meanings', nor are speaking or reading 'intellectual operations'. The story is a world which there must be some way of magically calling up by putting on spectacles and leaning over a book. The power possessed by language of bringing the thing expressed into existence, of opening up to thought new ways, new dimensions and new landscapes, is, in the last analysis, as obscure for the adult as for the child. In every successful work, the significance carried into the reader's mind exceeds language and thought as already constituted and is magically thrown into relief during the linguistic incantation, just as the story used to emerge from grandmother's book. In so far as we believe that, through thought, we are in direct communication with a universe of truth in which we are at one with others, in so far as Descartes' text seems merely to arouse in us thoughts already formed, and we seem never to learn anything from outside, and finally in so far as a philosopher, in a meditation purporting to be thoroughgoing, never even mentions language as the condition of the *reading* of the *cogito*, and does not more overtly invite us to pass from the idea to the practice of the *cogito*, it is because we take the process of expression for granted, because it figures among our acquisitions The *cogito* at which we arrive by reading Descartes (and even the one which Descartes effects in relation to expression and when, looking back on his past life, he fastens it down, objectifies it and 'characterizes' it as indubitable) is, then, a spoken *cogito*, put into words and understood in words, and for this very reason not attaining its objective, since that part of our existence which is engaged in fixing our life in conceptual forms, and thinking of it as indubitable, is escaping focus and thought. Shall we therefore conclude that language envelops us, and that we are led by it, much as the realist believes he is subject to the determinism of the external world, or as the theologian believes he is led on by Providence? This would be to forget half the truth. For after all, words, 'cogito' and 'sum' for example, may well have an empirical and statistical meaning, for it is the case that they are not directed specifically to my own experience, but form the basis of a general and anonymous thought. Nevertheless, I should find them not so much derivative and inauthentic as meaningless, and I should be unable even to read Descartes' book, were I not, before any speech can begin, in contact with my own life and thought, and if the spoken *cogito* did not encounter within me a tacit *cogito*. This silent *cogito* was the one Descartes sought when writing his *Meditations*. He gave life and direction to all those expressive operations which, by definition, always miss their target since, between Descartes' existence and the knowledge of it which he acquires, they interpose the full thickness of cultural acquisitions. And yet Descartes would not even have tried to put these expressive operations into operation had he not in the first place caught a glimpse of his existence The whole question amounts to gaining a clear understanding of the unspoken *cogito*, to putting into it only what is really there, and not making language into a product of consciousness on the excuse that consciousness is not a product of language.

Neither the word nor the meaning of the word is, in fact *constituted* by consciousness. Let us make this clear. The word is certainly never reducible to one of its embodiments The word 'sleet', for example, is not the set of characters which I have just written on the paper, nor that other set of signs that I once read in a book for the first time, nor again the sound that runs through the air when I pronounce it Those are merely reproductions of the word, in which I recognize it but which do not exhaust it Am I then to say that the word 'sleet' is the unified idea of these manifestations, and that it exists only for my consciousness and through a synthesis of identification? To do so

402

would be to forget what psychology has taught us about language. To speak, as we have seen, is not to call up verbal images and articulate words in accordance with the imagined model. By undertaking a critical examination of the verbal image, and showing that the speaking subject plunges into speech without imagining the words he is about to utter, modern psychology eliminates the word as a representation, or as an object for consciousness, and reveals a motor presence of the word which is not the knowledge of the word The word 'sleet', when it is known to me, is not an object which I recognize through any identificatory synthesis, but a certain use made of my phonatory equipment, a certain modulation of my body as a being in the world. Its generality is not that of the idea, but that of a behavioural style 'understood' by my body in so far as the latter is a behaviour-producing power, in this case a phoneme-producing one. One day I 'caught on' to the word 'sleet', much as one imitates a gesture, not, that is, by analysing it and performing an articulatory or phonetic action corresponding to each part of the word as heard, but by hearing it as a single modulation of the world of sound, and because this acoustic entity presents itself as 'something to pronounce' in virtue of the all-embracing correspondence existing between my perceptual potentialities and my motor ones, which are elements of my indivisible and open existence The word has never been inspected, analysed, known and constituted, but caught and taken up by a power of speech and, in the last analysis, by a motor power given to me along with the first experience I have of my body and its perceptual and practical fields As for the meaning of the word, I learn it as I learn to use a tool, by seeing it used in the context of a certain situation The word's meaning is not compounded of a certain number of physical characteristics belonging to the object; it is first and foremost the aspect taken on by the object in human experience, for example my wonder in the face of these hard, then friable, then melting pellets falling ready-made from the sky Here we have a meeting of the human and the non-human and, as it were, a piece of the world's behaviour, a certain version of its style, and the generality of its meaning as well as that of the vocable is not the generality of the concept, but of the world as typical Thus language presupposes nothing less than a consciousness of language, a silence of consciousness embracing the world of speech in which words first receive a form and meaning. This is why consciousness is never subordinated to any empirical language, why languages can be translated and learned, and finally, why language is not an attribute of external origin, in the sociologist's sense. Behind the spoken *cogito*, the one which is converted into discourse and into essential truth, there lies a tacit *cogito*, myself experienced by myself But this subjectivity, albeit imperious, has upon itself and upon the world only a precarious hold. It does not constitute the world, it divines the world's presence round about it as a field not provided by itself, nor does it constitute the word, but speaks as we sing when we are happy, nor again the meaning of the word, which instantaneously emerges for it in its dealing with the world and other men living in it, being at the intersection of many lines of behaviour, and being, even once 'acquired', as precise and yet as indefinable as the significance of a gesture. The tacit *cogito*, the presence of oneself to oneself, being no less than existence, is anterior to any philosophy, and knows itself only in those extreme situations in which it is under threat. for example, in the dread of death or of another's gaze upon me. What is believed to be thought about thought, as pure feeling of the self, cannot yet be thought and needs to be revealed. The consciousness which conditions language is merely a comprehensive and inarticulate grasp upon the world, like that of the infant at its first breath, or of the man about to drown and who is impelled towards life, and though it is true that all particular knowledge is founded on this primary view, it is true also that the latter waits to be won back, fixed and made explicit by perceptual exploration and by speech. Silent consciousness grasps itself only as a generalized 'I think' in face of a confused world 'to be thought about'. Any particular seizure, even the recovery of this generalized project by philosophy, demands that the subject bring into action powers which are a closed book to him and, in particular, that he should become a speaking subject The tacit *cogito* is a *cogito* only when it has found expression for itself

Such formulations may appear puzzling: if ultimate subjectivity cannot think of itself the moment it exists, how can it ever do so? How can that which does not think take to doing so? And is not subjectivity made to amount to a thing or a force which produces its effects without being capable of knowing it? We do not mean that the primordial *I* completely overlooks itself If it did, it would indeed be a thing, and nothing could cause it subsequently to become consciousness. We have merely withheld from it objective thought, a positing consciousness of the world and of itself. What do we mean by this? Either these words mean nothing at all, or else they mean that we refrain from assuming an explicit consciousness which duplicates and sustains the confused grasp of primary subjectivity upon itself and upon its world. My vision, for example, is certainly 'thinking that I see', if we mean thereby that it is not simply a bodily function like digestion or respiration, a collection of processes so grouped as to have a significance in a larger system, but that it is itself that system and that significance, that anteriority of the future to the present, of the whole to its parts. There is vision only through anticipation and intention, and since no intention could be a true intention if the object towards which it tends were given to it ready made and with no motivation, it is true that all vision assumes in the last resort, at the core of subjectivity, a total project or a logic of the world which empirical perceptions endow with specific form, but to which they cannot give rise. But vision is not thinking that one sees, if we understand thereby that it itself links up with its object, and that it becomes aware of itself as absolutely transparent, and as the originator of its own presence in the visible world. The essential point is clearly to grasp the project towards the world that we are What we have said above about the world's being inseparable from our views of the world should here help us to understand subjectivity conceived as inherence in the world. There is no *hylé*, no sensation which is not in communication with other sensations or the sensations of other people, and *for this very reason* there is no *morphe*, no apprehension or apperception, the office of which is to give significance to a matter that has none, and to ensure the *a priori* unity of my experience, and experience shared with others. Suppose that my friend Paul and I are looking at a landscape. What precisely happens? Must it be said that we have both private sensations, that we know things but cannot communicate them to each other—that, as far as pure, lived-through experience goes, we are each incarcerated in our separate perspectives—that the landscape is not numerically the same for both of us and that it is a question only of a specific identity? When I consider my perception itself, before any objectifying reflection, at no moment am I aware of being shut up within my own sensations. My friend Paul and I point out to each other certain details of the landscape, and Paul's finger, which is pointing out the church tower, is not a finger-for-me that I *think of* as orientated towards a church-tower-for-me, it is Paul's finger which itself shows me the tower that Paul sees, just as, conversely, when I make a movement towards some point in the landscape that I can see, I do not imagine that I am producing in Paul, in virtue of some pre-established harmony, inner visions merely analogous to mine: I believe, on the contrary, that my gestures invade Paul's world and guide his gaze When I think of Paul, I do not think of a flow of private sensations indirectly related to mine through the medium of interposed signs, but of someone who has a living experience of the same world as mine, as well as the same history, and with whom I am in communication through that world and that history Are we to say, then, that what we are concerned with is an ideal unity, that my world is the same as Paul's, just as the quadratic equation spoken of in Tokyo is the same as the one spoken of in Paris, and that in short the ideal nature of the world guarantees its intersubjective value? But ideal unity is not satisfactory either, for it exists no less between Mount Hymettus seen by the ancient Greeks and the same mountain seen by me. Now it is no use my telling myself, as I contemplate those russet mountain sides, that the Greeks saw them too, for I cannot convince myself that they are the same ones On the other hand, Paul and I 'together' see this landscape, we are jointly present in it, it is the same for both of us, not only as an intelligible significance, but as a certain accent of the world's style, down to its very thisness. The unity of the world crumbles and falls asunder under the influence of that temporal and spatial distance which the ideal unity traverses while remaining (in theory) unimpaired It is precisely because the landscape makes its impact upon me and produces feelings in me, because it reaches me in my uniquely individual being, because it is my own view of the landscape, that I enjoy possession of the landscape itself, and the landscape for Paul as well as for me. Both universality and the world lie at the core of individuality and the subject, and this will never be understood as long as the world is made into an ob-ject. It is understood immediately if the world is the *field* of our experience, and if we are nothing but a view of the world, for in that case it is seen that the most intimate vibration of our psycho-physical being already announces the world, the quality being the outline of a thing, and the thing the outline of the world. A world which, as Malebranche puts it, never gets beyond being an 'unfinished work', or which, as Husserl says of the body, is 'never completely constituted', does not require, and even rules out, a constituting subject. There must be, corresponding to this adumbration of being which appears through the concordant aspects of my own experience, or of the experience I share with others—experience which I presume capable of being consummated through indefinite horizons, from the sole fact that my phenomena congeal into a thing, and display, as they occur, a certain consistency of style—there must be, then, corresponding to this open unity of the world, an open and indefinite unity of subjectivity Like the world's unity, that of the *I* is invoked rather than experienced each time I perform an act of perception, each time I reach a self-evident truth, and the universal *I* is the background against which these effulgent forms stand out. it is through one present thought that I achieve the unity of all my thoughts. What remains, on the hither side of my particular thoughts, to constitute the tacit *cogito* and the original project towards the world, and what, ultimately, am I in so far as I can catch a glimpse of myself independently of any particular act? I am a field, an experience. One day, once and for all, something was set in motion which, even during sleep, can no longer cease to see or not to see, to feel or not to feel, to suffer or be happy, to think or rest from thinking, in a word to 'have it out' with the world There then arose, not a new set of sensations or states of consciousness, not even a new monad or a new perspective, since I am not tied to any one perspective but can change my point of view, being under compulsion only in that I must always have one, and can have only one at once—let us say, therefore, that there arose a fresh *possibility of situations* The event of my birth has not passed completely away, it has not fallen into nothingness in the way that an event of the objective world does, for it committed a whole future, not as a cause determines its effect, but as a situation, once created, inevitably leads on to some outcome. There was henceforth a new 'setting', the world received a fresh layer of meaning. In the home into which a child is born, all objects change their significance; they begin to await some as yet indeterminate treatment at his hands; another and different person is there, a new personal history, short or long, has just been initiated, another account has been opened. My first perception, along with the horizons which surrounded it, is an ever-present event, an unforgettable tradition; even as a thinking subject, I still am that first perception, the continuation of that same life inaugurated by it In one sense, there are no more acts of consciousness or distinct *Erlebnisse* in a life than there are separate things in the world. Just as, as we have seen, when I walk round an object, I am not presented with a succession of perspective views which I subsequently co-ordinate thanks to the idea of one single flat projection, there being merely a certain amount of 'shift' in the thing which, in itself, is journeying through time, so I am not myself a succession of 'psychic' acts, nor for that matter a nuclear *I* who bring them together into a synthetic unity, but one single experience inseparable from itself, one single 'living cohesion',[1] one single temporality which is engaged, from birth, in making itself progressively explicit, and in confirming that cohesion in each successive present. It is this advent or again this event of transcendental kind that the *cogito* reveals. The primary truth is indeed 'I think', but only provided that we understand thereby 'I belong to myself'[2] while belonging to the world When we try to go deeper into subjectivity, calling all things into question and suspending all our beliefs, the only form in which a glimpse is vouchsafed to us of that nonhuman ground through which, in the words of Rimbaud, 'we are not of the world', is as the horizon of our particular commitments, and as the potentiality of something in the most general sense, which is the world's phantom. Inside and outside are inseparable. The world is wholly inside and I am wholly outside myself When I perceive

[1] 'Zusammenhang des Lebens,' Heidegger, *Sein und Zeit*, p 388
[2] Heidegger, *Sein und Zeit*, pp 124–5

this table, the perception of the top must not overlook that of the legs, otherwise the object would be thrown out of joint. When I hear a melody, each of its moments must be related to its successor, otherwise there would be no melody. Yet the table is there with its external parts, and succession is of the essence of melody. The act which draws together at the same time takes away and holds at a distance, so that I touch myself only by escaping from myself In one of his celebrated *pensées*, Pascal shows that in one way I understand the world, and in another it understands me. We must add that it is in the *same* way. I understand the world because there are for me things near and far, foregrounds and horizons, and because in this way it forms a picture and acquires significance before me, and this finally is because I am situated in it and it understands me We do not say that the *notion* of the world is inseparable from that of the subject, or that the subject *thinks himself* inseparable from the idea of his body and the idea of the world; for, if it were a matter of no more than a conceived relationship, it would *ipso facto* leave the absolute independence of the subject as thinker intact, and the subject would not be in a situation. If the subject *is* in a situation, even if he is no more than a possibility of situations, this is because he forces his ipseity into reality only by actually being a body, and entering the world through that body In so far as, when I reflect on the essence of subjectivity, I find it bound up with that of the body and that of the world, this is because my existence as subjectivity is merely one with my existence as a body and with the existence of the world, and because the subject that I am, when taken concretely, is inseparable from this body and this world. The ontological world and body which we find at the core of the subject are not the world or body as idea, but on the one hand the world itself contracted into a comprehensive grasp, and on the other the body itself as a knowing-body.

But, it will be asked, if the unity of the world is not based on that of consciousness, and if the world is not the outcome of a constituting effort, how does it come about that appearances accord with each other and group themselves together into things, ideas and truths? And why do our random thoughts, the events of our life and those of collective history, at least at certain times assume common significance and direction, and allow themselves to be subsumed under one idea? Why does my life succeed in drawing itself together in order to project itself in words, intentions and acts? This is the problem of rationality The reader is aware that, on the whole, classical thought tries to explain the concordances in question in terms of a world in itself, or in terms of an absolute mind. Such explanations borrow all the forces of conviction which they can carry from the phenomenon of rationality, and therefore fail to explain that phenomenon, or ever to achieve greater clarity than it possesses. Absolute Thought is no clearer to me than my own finite mind, since it is through the latter that I conceive the former. We are in the world, which means that things take shape, an immense individual asserts itself, each existence is self-comprehensive and comprehensive of the rest. All that has to be done is to recognize these phenomena which are the ground of all our certainties The belief in an absolute mind, or in a world in itself detached from us is no more than a rationalization of this primordial faith

2

TEMPORALITY

Le temps est le *sens* de la vie (*sens*. comme on dit le
sens d'un cours d'eau, le sens d'une phrase, le sens d'une
étoffe, le sens de l'odorat)

CLAUDEL, *Art Poétique.*

Der Sinn des Daseins ist die Zeitlichkeit
HEIDEGGER, *Sein und Zeit*, p 331.

IN so far as, in the preceding pages, we have already met time on our
way to subjectivity, this is primarily because all our experiences,
inasmuch as they are ours, arrange themselves in terms of before and
after, because temporality, in Kantian language, is the form taken by
our inner sense, and because it is the most general characteristic of
'psychic facts'. But in reality, and without prejudging what the analysis of time will disclose, we have already discovered, between time
and subjectivity, a much more intimate relationship. We have just
seen that the subject, who cannot be a series of psychic events, nevertheless cannot be eternal either. It remains for him to be temporal not
by reason of some vagary of the human make-up, but by virtue of an
inner necessity We are called upon to conceive the subject and time
as communicating from within. We can now say of temporality what
we said earlier about sexuality and spatiality, for example existence
can have no external or contingent attribute It cannot be anything—
spatial, sexual, temporal—without being so in its entirety, without
taking up and carrying forward its 'attributes' and making them into
so many dimensions of its being, with the result that an analysis of
any one of them that is at all searching really touches upon subjectivity itself There are no principal and subordinate problems: all
problems are concentric. To analyse time is not to follow out the
consequences of a pre-established conception of subjectivity, it is to
gain access, through time, to its concrete structure If we succeed in
understanding the subject, it will not be in its pure form, but by

410

seeking it at the intersection of its dimensions. We need, therefore, to consider time in itself, and it is by following through its internal dialectic that we shall be led to revise our idea of the subject.

We say that time passes or flows by We speak of the course of time. The water that I see rolling by was made ready a few days ago in the mountains, with the melting of the glacier; it is now in front of me and makes its way towards the sea into which it will finally discharge itself. If time is similar to a river, it flows from the past towards the present and the future The present is the consequence of the past, and the future of the present But this often repeated metaphor is in reality extremely confused. For, *looking at the things themselves*, the melting of the snows and what results from this are not successive events, or rather the very notion of event has no place in the objective world. When I say that the day before yesterday the glacier produced the water which is passing at this moment, I am tacitly assuming the existence of a witness tied to a certain spot in the world, and I am comparing his successive views he was there when the snows melted and followed the water down, or else, from the edge of the river and having waited two days, he sees the pieces of wood that he threw into the water at its source. The 'events' are shapes cut out by a finite observer from the spatio-temporal totality of the objective world But on the other hand, if I consider the world itself, there is simply one indivisible and changeless being in it Change presupposes a certain position which I take up and from which I see things in procession before me there are no events without someone to whom they happen and whose finite perspective is the basis of their individuality Time presupposes a view of time It is, therefore, not like a river, not a flowing substance The fact that the metaphor based on this comparison has persisted from the time of Heraclitus to our own day is explained by our surreptitiously putting into the river a witness of its course We do this already when we say that the stream discharges *itself*, for this amounts to conceiving, where there is merely a thing entirely external to itself, an individuality or interior of the stream which manifests itself outside Now, no sooner have I introduced an observer, whether he follows the river or whether he stands on the bank and observes its flow, than temporal relationships are reversed In the latter case, the volume of water already carried by is not moving towards the future, but sinking into the past; what is to come is on the side of the source, for time does not come from the past. It is not the past that pushes the present, nor the present that pushes the future, into being, the future is not prepared behind the observer, it is a brooding presence moving to meet him, like a storm on the horizon. If the observer sits in a boat and is carried by the current, we may say that he is moving downstream towards his future, but the future lies in the new landscapes which await him at the estuary, and the course of time is no longer the stream itself it is the landscape as it rolls by for the moving observer. Time is, therefore, not a real process, not an actual succession that I am content to record It arises from *my* relation to things. Within things themselves, the future and the past are in a kind of eternal state of pre-existence and survival; the water which will flow by tomorrow *is* at this moment at its source, the water which has just passed *is* now a little further downstream in the valley. What is past or future for me is present in the world. It is often said that, within things themselves, the future is not yet, the past is no longer, while the present, strictly speaking, is infinitesimal, so that time collapses. That is why Leibnitz was able to define the objective world as *mens momentanea*, and why Saint Augustine, in order to constitute time, required, besides the presence of the present, a presence of the past and of the future. But let us be clear about what they mean. If the objective world is incapable of sustaining time, it is not because it is in some way too narrow, and that we need to add to it a bit of past and a bit of future Past and future exist only too unmistakably in the world, they exist in the present, and what being itself lacks in order to be of the temporal order, is the not-being of elsewhere, formerly and tomorrow The objective world is too much of a plenum for there to be time Past and future withdraw of their own accord from being and move over into subjectivity in search, not of some real support, but, on the contrary, of a possibility of not-being which accords with their nature If we separate the objective world from the finite perspectives which open upon it, and posit it in itself, we find everywhere in it only so many instances of 'now' These instances of 'now', moreover, not being present to anybody, have no temporal character and could not occur in sequence The definition of time which is implicit in the comparisons undertaken by common sense, and which might be formulated as 'a succession of instances of *now*'[1] has not even the disadvantage of treating past and future as presents it is inconsistent, since it destroys the very notion of 'now', and that of succession

We should, then, gain nothing by transferring into ourselves the time that belongs to things, if we repeated 'in consciousness' the mistake of defining it as a succession of instances of now. Yet this is what psychologists do when they try to 'explain' consciousness of the past in terms of memories, and consciousness of the future in terms of the projection of these memories ahead of us The refutation of 'physiological theories' of memory, in Bergson for example, is undertaken in the domain of causal explanation, it consists in showing that paths in the brain and other bodily expedients are not adequate

[1] 'Nacheinander der Jetztpunkte,' Heidegger, *Sein und Zeit*, for example p 422

412

causes of the phenomena of memory; that, for example, nothing can be found in the body to account for the order of disappearance of memories in cases of progressive aphasia The discussion conducted on these lines certainly discredits the idea of a bodily storage of the past: the body is no longer a receptacle of engrams, but an organ of mimicry with the function of ensuring the intuitive realization of the 'intentions'[1] of consciousness But these intentions cling on to memories preserved 'in the unconscious', and the presence of the past in consciousness remains a simple factual presence; it has passed unnoticed that our best reason for rejecting the physiological pre-servation of the past is equally a reason for rejecting its 'psychological preservation', and that reason is that no preservation, no physio-logical or psychic 'trace' of the past can make consciousness of the past understandable. This table bears traces of my past life, for I have carved my initials on it and spilt ink on it But these traces in themselves do not refer to the past: they are present; and, in so far as I find in them signs of some 'previous' event, it is because I derive my sense of the past from elsewhere, because I carry this particular significance within myself. If my brain stores up traces of the bodily process which accompanied one of my perceptions, and if the appro-priate nervous influx passes once more through these already fretted channels, my perception will reappear, but it will be a fresh per-ception, weakened and unreal perhaps, but in no case will this per-ception, which is present, be capable of pointing to a past event, un-less I have some other viewpoint on my past enabling me to recognize it as memory, which runs counter to the hypothesis. If we now go on to substitute 'psychic traces' for physiological ones, and if our per-ceptions are preserved in an unconscious, the difficulty will be the same as before a preserved perception is a perception, it continues to exist, it persists in the present, and it does not open behind us that dimension of escape and absence that we call the past. A preserved fragment of the lived-through past can be at the most no more than an occasion for thinking of the past, but it is not the past which is compelling recognition; recognition, when we try to derive it from any content whatever, always precedes itself Reproduction pre-supposes re-cognition, and cannot be understood as such unless I have in the first place a sort of direct contact with the past in its own domain Nor can one, *a fortiori*, construct the future out of contents of consciousness: no actual content can be taken, even equivocally, as evidence concerning the future, since the future has not even been in existence and cannot, like the past, set its mark upon us. The only conceivable way, therefore, of trying to explain the relation of future to present would be by putting it on the same footing as that between

[1] Bergson, *Matière et Mémoire*, p. 137, note 1, p 139

413

present and past When I consider the long procession of my past states, I see that my present is always passing, and I can steal this passage, treat my immediate past as a remote one, and my actual present as past ahead of it is then a vacuum, and this is the future. Looking ahead would seem in reality to be retrospection, and the future a projection of the past. But even if, *per impossibile*, I could construct consciousness of the past with transferred presents, they certainly could not open a future for me. Even if, in fact, we form an idea of the future with the help of what we have seen, the fact remains that, in order to pro-ject it ahead of us, we need in the first place a sense of the future. If prospection is retrospection, it is in any case an anticipatory retrospection, and how could one anticipate if one had no sense of the future? It is said that we guess 'by analogy' that this inimitable present will, like all the others, pass away. But for there to be an analogy between presents that have elapsed and the actual present, the latter must be given not only as present, it must already announce itself as what will soon be past, we must feel the pressure upon it of a future intent on dispossessing it, in short the course of time must be primarily not only the passing of present to past, but also that of the future to the present. If it can be said that all prospection is anticipatory retrospection, it can equally well be said that all retrospection is prospection in reverse I know that I was in Corsica before the war, because I know that the war was on the horizon of my trip there The past and the future cannot be mere concepts abstracted by us from our perceptions and recollections, mere denominations for the actual series of 'psychic facts'. Time is thought of by us before its parts, and temporal relations make possible the events in time Correspondingly, therefore, the subject must not be himself situated in it, in order to be able to be present in intention to the past as to the future. Let us no longer say that time is a 'datum of consciousness', let us be more precise and say that consciousness deploys or constitutes time. Through the ideal nature of time, it ceases to be imprisoned in the present.

But does it enjoy an opening on to a past and a future? It is no longer beset by the present and by 'contents', it travels freely from a past and a future which are not far removed from it, since it constitutes them as past and future, and since they are its immanent objects, to a present which is not near to it, since it is present only in virtue of the relations which consciousness establishes between past, present and future But then has not a consciousness thus freed lost all notion of what future, past and even present can possibly be? Is not the time that it constitutes similar in every detail to the real time the impossibility of which we have demonstrated; is it not a series of instances of 'now', which are presented to nobody, since nobody is

involved in them? Are we not always just as far away from understanding what the future, the past and the present, and the passage
between them, can possibly be? Time as the immanent object of a
consciousness is time brought down to one uniform level, in other
words it is no longer time at all. There can be time only if it is not
completely deployed, only provided that past, present and future do
not all three have their being in the same sense It is of the essence of
time to be in process of self-production, and not to be; never, that is,
to be completely constituted Constituted time, the series of possible
relations in terms of before and after, is not time itself, but the ultimate recording of time, the result of its *passage*, which objective
thinking always presupposes yet never manages to fasten on to. It is
spatial, since its moments co-exist spread out before thought[1], it is a
present, because consciousness is contemporary with all times. It is a
setting distinct from me and unchanging, in which nothing either
elapses or happens. There must be another true time, in which I
learn the nature of flux and transience itself. It is indeed true that I
should be incapable of perceiving any point in time without a before
and an after, and that, in order to be aware of the relationship between the three terms, I must not be absorbed into any one of them:
that time, in short, needs a synthesis. But it is equally true that this
synthesis must always be undertaken afresh, and that any supposition
that it can be anywhere brought to completion involves the negation
of time. It is indeed the dream of philosophers to be able to conceive
an 'eternity of life', lying beyond permanence and change, in which
time's productivity is pre-eminently contained, and yet a thetic consciousness *of* time which stands above it and embraces it merely destroys the phenomenon of time. If we are in fact destined to make
contact with a sort of eternity, it will be at the core of our experience
of time, and not in some non-temporal subject whose function it is to
conceive and posit it. The problem is how to make time explicit as it
comes into being and makes itself evident, having the *notion* of time
at all times underlying it, and being, not an object of our knowledge,
but a dimension of our being

It is in my 'field of presence' in the widest sense—this moment that

---

[1] In order to arrive at authentic time, it is neither necessary nor sufficient to
condemn the spatialization of time as does Bergson It is not necessary, since
time is exclusive of space only if we consider space as objectified in advance, and
ignore that primordial spatiality which we have tried to describe, and which is
the abstract form of our presence in the world It is not sufficient since, even when
the systematic translation of time into spatial terms has been duly stigmatized,
we may still fall very far short of an authentic intuition of time This is what
happened to Bergson. When he says that duration 'snowballs upon itself', and
when he postulates memories in themselves accumulating in the unconscious, he
makes time out of a preserved present, and evolution out of what is evolved

that I spend working, with, behind it, the horizon of the day that has elapsed, and, in front of it, the evening and night—that I make contact with time, and learn to know its course. The remote past has also its temporal order, and its position in time in relation to my present, but it has these in so far as it has been present itself, that it has been 'in its time' traversed by my life, and carried forward to this moment When I call up a remote past, I reopen time, and carry myself back to a moment in which it still had before it a future horizon now closed, and a horizon of the immediate past which is today remote. Everything, therefore, causes me to revert to the field of presence as the primary experience in which time and its dimensions make their appearance unalloyed, with no intervening distance and with absolute self-evidence. It is here that we see a future sliding into the present and on into the past. Nor are these three dimensions given to us through discrete acts: I do not form a mental picture of my day, it weighs upon me with all its weight, it is still there, and though I may not recall any detail of it, I have the impending power to do so, I still 'have it in hand'.[1] In the same way, I do not think of the evening to come and its consequences, and yet it 'is there', like the back of a house of which I can see only the façade, or like the background beneath a figure. Our future is not made up exclusively of guesswork and daydreams. Ahead of what I see and perceive, there is, it is true, nothing more actually visible, but my world is carried forward by lines of intentionality which trace out in advance at least the style of what is to come (although we are always on the watch, perhaps to the day of our death, for the appearance of *something else*) The present itself, in the narrow sense, is not posited. The paper, my fountain-pen, are indeed there for me, but I do not explicitly perceive them. I do not so much perceive objects as reckon with an environment, I seek support in my tools, and am at my task rather than confronting it. Husserl uses the terms protentions and retentions for the intentionalities which anchor me to an environment. They do not run from a central *I*, but from my perceptual field itself, so to speak, which draws along in its wake its own horizon of retentions, and bites into the future with its protentions I do not pass through a series of instances of now, the images of which I preserve and which, placed end to end, make a line. With the arrival of every moment, its predecessor undergoes a change I still have it in hand and it is still there, but already it is sinking away below the level of presents, in order to retain it, I need to reach through a thin layer of time It is still the preceding moment, and I have the power to rejoin it as it was just now; I am not cut off from it, but still it would not

[1] 'Noch im Griff behalte', Husserl, *Vorlesungen zur Phänomenologie des inneren Zeitbewusstseins*, pp 390 and ff

416

belong to the past unless something had altered, unless it were beginning to outline itself against, or project itself upon, my present,
whereas a moment ago it *was* my present. When a third moment
arrives, the second undergoes a new modification; from being a
retention it becomes the retention of a retention, and the layer of
time between it and me thickens. One can, as Husserl does, represent
this phenomenon diagrammatically. In order to make it complete,
the symmetrical perspective of protentions would have to be added.
Time is not a line, but a network of intentionalities.

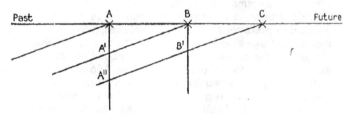

From Husserl (*Zeitbewusstsein*, p. 22). Horizontal line: series of 'present
moments'. Oblique lines: *Abschattungen* of the same 'present moments'
seen from an ulterior 'present moment'. Vertical lines: Successive *Abschattungen* of one and the same 'present moment'.

It will doubtless be maintained that this description and this diagram do not bring us one step nearer to a solution. When we pass
from A to B, and then on to C, A is projected or outlined as A' and
then as A". For A' to be recognized as a retention or *Abschattung* of
A, and A" of A', and even for the transformation of A into A' to be
experienced as such, is there not needed an identifying synthesis linking A, A', A" and all other possible *Abschattungen*, and does this not
amount to making A into an ideal unity as Kant requires? And yet
we know that with this intellectual synthesis there will cease to be any
time at all. A and all previous moments of time will indeed be identifiable by me, and I shall be in a way rescued from time which runs
them into one another and blurs their identity. But at the same time
I shall have lost all sense of before and after which is provided by
this flux, and nothing will any longer serve to distinguish the temporal sequence from spatial multiplicity. Husserl introduced the notion of retention, and held that I still have the immediate past in hand,
precisely for the purpose of conveying that I do not posit the past,
or construct it from an *Abschattung* really distinct from it and by
means of an express act; but that I reach it in its recent, yet already
elapsed, thisness. What is given to me is not in the first place A', A",
or A"', nor do I go back from these 'outlines' to their original A, as
417

one goes back from the sign to its significance. What is given to me is A transparently visible through A', then the two through A", and so on, as I see a pebble through the mass of water which moves over it There are certainly identifying syntheses, but only in the express memory and voluntary recollection of the remote past, that is, in those modes derived from consciousness of the past. For example, I may be uncertain about the date of a memory: I have before me a certain scene, let us suppose, and I do not know to what point of time to assign it, the memory has lost its anchorage, and I may then arrive at an intellectual identification based on the causal order of events, for example, I had this suit made before the armistice, since no more English cloth has been available since then But in this case it is not the past itself that I reach. On the contrary, for when I rediscover the concrete origin of the memory, it is because it falls naturally into a certain current of fear and hope running from Munich to the outbreak of war; it is, therefore, because I recapture time that is lost, because, from the moment in question to my present, the chain of retentions and the overlapping horizons coming one after the other ensure an unbroken continuity. The objective landmarks in relation to which I assign a place to my recollection in the mediatory identification, and the intellectual synthesis generally, have themselves a temporal significance only because gradually, step by step, the synthesis of apprehension links me to my whole actual past There can. therefore, be no question of assimilating the latter to the former The fact that the *Abschattungen* A' and A" appear to me as *Abschattungen* of A, is not to be explained by the fact that they all participate in an ideal unity A, which is their common ground It is because through them I obtain the point A itself, in its unchallengeable individuality, which is for ever established by its passage into the present, and because I see springing from it the *Abschattungen* A', A"   In Husserl's language, beneath the 'intentionality of the act', which is the thetic consciousness of an object, and which, in intellectual memory for example, converts 'this' into an idea, we must recognize an 'operative' intentionality (*fungierende Intentionalitat*)[1] which makes the former possible, and which is what Heidegger terms transcendence. My present outruns itself in the direction of an immediate future and an immediate past and impinges upon them where they actually are, namely in the past and in the future themselves If the past were available to us only in the form of express recollections, we should be continually tempted to recall it in order to verify its existence, and thus resemble the patient mentioned by Scheler, who was constantly turning round in order to reassure

[1] Husserl, *Zeitbewusstsein*, p 430 *Formale und transzendentale Logik*, p 208 See Fink, *Das Problem der Phanomenologie Edmund Husserls*, p 286.

himself that things were really there—whereas in fact we feel it behind us as an incontestable acquisition In order to have a past or a future we do not have to bring together, by means of an intellectual act, a series of *Abschattungen*, for they possess a natural and primordial unity, and what is announced through them is the past or the future itself Such is the paradox of what might be termed, with Husserl, the 'passive synthesis' of time[1]—and of a term which is clearly not a solution, but merely a pointer to the problem.

Light begins to be shed on the problem if we remember that our diagram represents an instantaneous cross-section of time What there really is, is not a past, present and future, not discrete instants A, B and C, nor really distinct *Abschattungen* A', A", B', nor finally a host of retentions on the one hand and protentions on the other. The upsurge of a fresh present does not *cause* a heaping up of the past and a tremor of the future, the fresh present *is* the passage of future to present, and of former present to past, and when time begins to move, it moves throughout its whole length. The 'instants' A, B and C are not successively *in being*, but *differentiate* themselves from each other, and correspondingly A passes into A' and thence into A" In short, the system of retentions collects into itself at each instant what was, an instant earlier, the system of protentions. There is, then, not a multiplicity of linked phenomena, but one single phenomenon of running-off. Time is the one single movement appropriate to itself in all its parts, as a gesture includes all the muscular contractions necessary for its execution. When we pass from B to C, there is, as it were, a bursting, or a disintegration of B into B', of A' into A", and C itself which, while it was on the way, announced its coming by a continuous emission of *Abschattungen*, has no sooner come into existence than it already begins to lose its substance. 'Time is the means offered to all that is destined to be, to come into existence in order that it may no longer be '[2] It is nothing but a general flight out of the Itself, the one law governing these centrifugal movements, or again, as Heidegger says, an *ek-stase* While B becomes C, it becomes also B', and simultaneously A which, while becoming B, had also become A', lapses into A". A, A' and A" on the one hand, and B and B' on the other, are bound together, not by any identifying synthesis, which would fix them at a point in time, but by a transitional synthesis (*Übergangssynthesis*), in so far as they issue one from the other, and each of these projections is merely one aspect of the total bursting forth or dehiscence. Hence time, in our primordial experience of it, is not for us a system of objective positions, through which we pass, but a mobile setting which moves away from us, like the

[1] See, for example, *Formale und Transzendentale Logik*, pp 256–7
[2] Claudel, *Art poétique*, p 57

419

landscape seen through a railway carriage window. Yet we do no really believe that the landscape is moving; the gate-keeper at the level crossing is whisked by, but the hill over there scarcely moves at all, and in the same way, though the opening of my day is already receding, the beginning of my week is a fixed point, an objective time is taking shape on the horizon, and should therefore show up in my immediate past. How is this possible? How is it that the temporal *ek-stase* is not an absolute disintegration in which the individuality of the moments disappears? It is because the disintegration undoes what the passage from future to present had achieved· C is the culmination of a long concentration which has brought it to maturity; as it was being built up, it made its approach known by progressively fewer *Abschattungen*, for it was approaching *bodily*. When it came into the present it brought with it its genesis, of which it was merely the ultimate expression, and the impending presence of what was to come after it. So that, when D comes into being and pushes C into the past, C is not suddenly bereft of its being; its disintegration is forever the inverse or the consequence of its coming to maturity. In short, since in time being and passing are synonymous, by becoming past, the event does not cease to be. The origin of objective time, with its fixed positions lying beneath our gaze, is not to be sought in any eternal synthesis, but in the mutual harmonizing and overlapping of past and future through the present, and in the very passing of time Time maintains what it has caused to be, at the very time it expels it from being, because the new being was announced by its predecessor as destined to be, and because, for the latter, to become present was the same thing as being destined to pass away. 'Temporalization is not a succession (*Nacheinander*) of ecstasies The future is not posterior to the past, or the past anterior to the present. Temporality temporalizes itself as future-which-lapses-into-the-past-by-coming-into-the-present.'[1] Bergson was wrong in *explaining* the unity of time in terms of its continuity, since that amounts to confusing past, present and future on the excuse that we pass from one to the other by imperceptible transitions; in short, it amounts to denying time altogether. But he was right to stick to the continuity of time as an essential phenomenon. It is simply a matter of elucidating this. Instant C and instant D, however near they are together, are not indistinguishable, for if they were there would be no time; what happens is that they run into each other and C becomes D because C has never been anything but the anticipation of D as present, and of its own lapse into the past. This amounts to saying that each present reasserts the presence of the whole past which it supplants, and anticipates that of all that is to come, and that by definition the pre-

[1] Heidegger, *Sein und Zeit*, p 350

sent is not shut up within itself, but transcends itself towards a future and a past. What there is, is not a present, then another present which takes its place in being, and not even a present with its vistas of past and future followed by another present in which those vistas are disrupted, so that one and the same spectator is needed to effect the synthesis of successive perspectives. there is one single time which is self-confirmatory, which can bring nothing into existence unless it has already laid that thing's foundations as present and eventual past, and which establishes itself at a stroke

The past, therefore, *is* not past, nor the future future It exists only when a subjectivity is there to disrupt the plenitude of being in itself, to adumbrate a perspective, and introduce non-being into it A past and a future spring forth when I reach out towards them I am not, for myself, at this very moment, I am also at this morning or at the night which will soon be here, and though my present is, if we wish so to consider it, this instant, it is equally this day, this year or my whole life. There is no need for a synthesis externally binding together the *tempora* into one single time, because each one of the *tempora* was already inclusive, beyond itself, of the whole open series of other *tempora*, being in internal communication with them, and because the 'cohesion of a life'[1] is given with its *ek-stase* The passage of one present to the next is not a thing which I conceive, nor do I see it as an onlooker, I effect it; I am already at the impending present as my gesture is already at its goal, I am myself time, a time which 'abides' and does not 'flow' or 'change', which is what Kant says in various places.[2] This idea of a time which anticipates itself is perceived by common sense in its way. Everyone talks about Time, not as the zoologist talks about the dog or the horse, using these as collective nouns, but using it as a proper noun. Sometimes it is even personified. Everyone thinks that there is here a single, concrete being, wholly present in each of its manifestations, as is a man in each of his spoken words. We say that there is time as we say that there is a fountain: the water changes while the fountain remains because its form is preserved; the form is preserved because each successive wave takes over the functions of its predecessor from being the thrusting wave in relation to the one in front of it, it becomes, in its turn and in relation to another, the wave that is pushed; and this is attributable to the fact that, from the source to the fountain jet, the waves are not separate; there is only one thrust, and a single air-lock in the flow would be enough to break up the jet. Hence the justification for the metaphor of the river, not in so far as the river flows, but in so far as it is one with itself This intuition of time's permanence, however, is

[1] Heidegger, *Sein und Zeit*, p 373
[2] Quoted by Heidegger, *Kant und das Problem der Metaphysik*, pp. 183–4.

jeopardized by the action of common sense, which thematizes or objectifies it, which is the surest way of losing sight of it. There is more truth in mythical personifications of time than in the notion of time considered, in the scientific manner, as a variable of nature in itself, or, in the Kantian manner, as a form ideally separable from its matter There is a temporal style of the world, and time remains the same because the past is a former future and a recent present, the present an impending past and a recent future, the future a present and even a past to come; because, that is, each dimension of time is treated or aimed at *as* something other than itself and because, finally, there is at the core of time a gaze, or, as Heidegger puts it, an *Augen-blick, someone* through whom the word *as* can have a meaning. We are not saying that time is *for* someone, which would once more be a case of arraying it out, and immobilizing it We are saying that time *is* someone, or that temporal dimensions, in so far as they perpetually overlap, bear each other out and ever confine themselves to making explicit what was implied in each, being collectively expressive of that one single explosion or thrust which is subjectivity itself We must understand time as the subject and the subject as time What is perfectly clear, is that this primordial temporality is not a juxtaposition of external events, since it is the power which holds them together while keeping them apart. Ultimate subjectivity is not temporal in the empirical sense of the term: if consciousness of time were made up of successive states of consciousness, there would be needed a new consciousness to be conscious of that succession and so on to infinity We are forced to recognize the existence of 'a consciousness having behind it no consciousness to be conscious of it'[1] which, consequently, is not arrayed out in time, and in which 'being coincides with being for itself'[2] We may say that ultimate consciousness is 'timeless' (*zeitlose*) in the sense that it is not intratemporal.[3] 'In' my present, if I grasp it while it is still living and with all that it implies, there is an *ek-stase* towards the future and towards the past which reveals the dimensions of time not as conflicting, but as inseparable. to be now is to be from always and for ever. Subjectivity is not in time because it takes up or lives through time, and merges with the cohesion of a life

Are we coming back in this way to a kind of eternity? I belong to my past and, through the constant interlocking of retentions, I preserve my oldest experiences, which means not some duplicate or image of them, but the experiences themselves, exactly as they were

---

[1] Husserl, *Zeitbewusstsein*, p 442, 'primares Bewusstsein   das hinter sich kein Bewusstsein mehr hat in dem es bewusst wäre   '
[2] Ibid , p 471 'fällt ja Sein und Innerlich-bewusstsein zusammen '
[3] Ibid , p 464

But the unbroken chain of the fields of presence, by which I am guaranteed access to the past itself, has the essential characteristic of being formed only gradually and one step at a time, each present, in virtue of its very essence as a present, rules out the juxtaposition of other presents and, even in the context of a time long past, I can take in a certain period of my past life only by unfolding it anew according to its own *tempo*. The temporal perspective with its confusion of what is far removed in time, and that sort of 'shrinkage' of the past with oblivion as its ultimate limit, are not accidents of memory, and do not express the debasement into empirical existence of a consciousness of time theoretically all-embracing, but its initial ambiguity: to retain is to hold, but at a distance. Once again, time's 'synthesis' is a transitional synthesis, the action of a life which unfolds, and there is no way of bringing it about other than by living that life, there is no seat of time; time bears itself on and launches itself afresh. Time as an indivisible thrust and transition can alone make possible time as successive multiplicity, and what we place at the origin of intratemporality is a constituting time. When we were engaged above in describing the overlapping of time by itself, we were able to treat the future as a past only by qualifying it as a past to come, and the past as a future only by calling it a future which has occurred; this means that when we came to put all time on the same footing, we had to reassert the originality of each perspective, and derive this quasi-eternity from the event. What does not pass in time is the passing of time itself. Time restarts itself: the rhythmic cycle and constant form of yesterday, today and tomorrow may well create the illusion that we possess it immediately, in its entirety, as the fountain creates in us a feeling of eternity. But the generality of time is no more than one of its secondary attributes and provides only an inauthentic view of it, since we cannot get as far as conceiving a cycle without drawing a distinction, in terms of time, between the point of arrival and the point of departure. The feeling for eternity is a hypocritical one, for eternity feeds on time. The fountain retains its identity only because of the continuous pressure of water. Eternity is the time that belongs to dreaming, and the dream refers back to waking life, from which it borrows all its structures. Of what nature, then, is that waking time in which eternity takes root? It is the field of presence in the wide sense, with its double horizon or primary past and future, and the infinite openness of those fields of presence that have slid by, or are still possible. Time exists for me only because I am situated in it, that is, because I become aware of myself as already committed to it, because the whole of being is not given to me incarnate, and finally because one sector of being is so close to me that it does not even make up a picture before me—I cannot *see* it, just as

I cannot see my face. Time exists for me because I have a present. It is by coming into the present that a moment of time acquires that indestructible individuality, that 'once and for all' quality, which subsequently enables it to make its way through time and produce in us the illusion of eternity. No one of time's dimensions can be deduced from the rest. But the present (in the wide sense, along with its horizons of primary past and future), nevertheless enjoys a privilege because it is the zone in which being and consciousness coincide. When I recall an earlier perception, or when I imagine a visit to my friend Paul who is in Brazil, my aim, it is true, is the past itself in its true place, or Paul himself in the world, and not some interposed mental object. Nevertheless my act of representation, unlike the experiences represented, is actually present to me; the former is perceived, the latter are merely represented. A former experience, a coming experience, in order that they may appear to me, need to be borne into being by a primary consciousness, which in this case is my inner perception of recollection or imagination. We said above that we need to arrive at a consciousness with no other behind it, which grasps its own being, and in which, in short, being and being conscious are one and the same thing. This ultimate consciousness is not an eternal subject perceiving itself in absolute transparency, for any such subject would be utterly incapable of making its descent into time, and would, therefore have nothing in common with our experience: it is the consciousness of the present. In the present and in perception, my being and my consciousness are at one, not that my being is reducible to the knowledge I have of it or that it is clearly set out before me—on the contrary perception is opaque, for it brings into play, beneath what I know, my sensory fields which are my primitive alliance with the world—but because 'to be conscious' is here nothing but 'to-be-at . ' ('être à .'), and because my conciousness of existing merges into the actual gesture of 'ex-sistence'.[1] It is by communicating with the world that we communicate beyond all doubt with ourselves. We hold time in its entirety, and we are present to ourselves because we are present to the world.

That being the case, and since consciousness takes root in being and time by taking up a situation, how are we then to describe it? It must be a comprehensive project, or a view of time and the world which, in order to be apparent to itself, and in order to become explicitly what it is implicitly, that is, consciousness, needs to unfold itself into multiplicity. We must avoid conceiving as real and distinct entities either the indivisible power, or its distinct manifestations; consciousness is neither, it is both; it is the very action of tem-

[1] We borrow this expression from H. Corbin, *Qu'est-ce que la Métaphysique?*, p 14

poralization *—of 'flux', as Husserl has it—a self-anticipatory movement, a flow which never leaves itself. Let us try to give a better
description with the help of an example The novelist or psychologist
who fails to go back to ultimate origins and accepts temporalization
as something ready made, sees consciousness as a multiplicity of
psychic facts among which he tries to establish causal relations For
example,[1] Proust shows how Swann's love for Odette *causes* the
jealousy which, in turn, *modifies* his love, since Swann, always anxi-
ous to win her from any possible rival, has no time really to look at
Odette In reality, Swann's consciousness is not a lifeless setting in
which psychic facts are produced from outside. What we have is not
jealousy aroused by love and exerting its own counter-influence, but
a certain way of loving in which the whole destiny of that love can be
discerned at a glance Swann has a liking for Odette's person, for
that 'spectacle' that she is, for her way of looking, of modulating her
voice, and for the way a smile comes to her lips But what *is* having a
liking for someone? Proust tells us when speaking of another love it
is the feeling of being shut out of the life of the beloved, and of wanting to force one's way in and take complete possession of it. Swann's
love does not cause him to *feel* jealousy. It *is* jealousy already, and
has been from the start. Jealousy does not produce a change in the
quality of love· Swann's feeling of pleasure in looking at Odette bore
its degeneration within itself, since it was the pleasure of being the
only one to do so. The set of psychic facts and causal relationships is
merely an outward manifestation of a certain view that Swann takes
of Odette, a certain way of belonging to another. Swann's jealous love
ought, moreover, to be related to the rest of his behaviour, in which
case it might well appear as itself a manifestation of an even more
general existential structure, which would be Swann's whole per-
sonality. Conversely all consciousness as a comprehensive project is
outlined or made manifest to itself in those acts, experiences and
'psychic facts' in which it is recognized. Here is where temporality
throws light on subjectivity. We shall never manage to understand
how a thinking or constituting subject is able to posit or become
aware of itself in time. If the *I* is indeed the transcendental Ego of
Kant, we shall never understand how it can in any instance merge
with its wake in the inner sense, or how the empirical self still remains
a self. If, however, the subject is identified with temporality, then
self-positing ceases to be a contradiction, because it exactly expresses
the essence of living time. Time is 'the affecting of self by self'.[2] what

* Cf. 'Zeitigung' (Translator's note).

[1] The example is J P. Sartre's in *L'Être et le Néant*, p. 216.

[2] The expression is applied by Kant to the *Gemut*. Heidegger transfers it to
time: 'Die Zeit is ihrem Wesen nach reine Affektion ihrer selbst ' *Kant und das
Problem der Metaphysik*, pp. 180–1.

·exerts the effect is time as a thrust and a passing towards a future; what is affected is time as an unfolded series of presents; the affecting agent and affected recipient are one, because the thrust of time is nothing but the transition from one present to another. This *ek-stase*, this projection of an indivisible power into an outcome which is already present to it, is subjectivity. The primary flow, says Husserl, does not confine itself to being: it must necessarily provide itself with a 'manifestation of itself' (*Selbsterscheinung*), without our needing to place behind it a second flow which is conscious of it It 'constitutes itself as a phenomenon within itself' [1] It is of the essence of time to be not only actual time, or time which flows, but also time which is aware of itself, for the explosion or dehiscence of the present towards a future is the archetype of the *relationship of self to self*, and it traces out an interiority or ipseity.[2] Here a light bursts forth,[3] for here we are no longer concerned with a being which reposes within itself, but with a being the whole essence of which, like that of light, is to *make visible*. It is through temporality that there can be, without contradiction, ipseity, significance and reason. That is seen even in the commonly held notion of time. We mark out the phases or stages of our life, for example, we consider everything that bears a significant relationship to our concerns at the moment as part of our present, thus recognizing implicitly that time and significance are but one thing. Subjectivity is not motionless identity with itself as with time, it is of its essence, in order to be genuine subjectivity, to open itself to an Other and to go forth from itself. We must not envisage the subject as constituting, and the multiplicity of its experiences or *Erlebnisse* as constituted; we must not treat the transcendental Ego as the true subject and the empirical self as its shadow or its wake. If that were their relationship to each other, we could withdraw into the constituting agency, and such reflection would destroy time, which would be left without date or place. The fact that even our purest reflection appears to us as retrospective in time, and that our reflection on the flux is actually inserted into that flux,[4] shows that the most precise consciousness of which we are capable is always, as it were, affected by itself or given to itself, and that the word consciousness has no meaning independently of this duality

Nothing said of the subject is false: it is true that the subject as an absolute presence to itself is something we cannot circumvent, and

[1] Husserl, *Zeitbewusstsein*, p. 436
[2] Heidegger, op cit , p 181 'Als reine Selbstaffektion bildet (die Zeit) ursprünglich die endliche Selbstheit dergestalt dass das Selbst so etwas wie Selbstbewusstsein kann '
[3] Heidegger refers somewhere to the 'Gelichtetheit' of the *Dasein*.
[4] What Husserl, in his unpublished writings, terms *Einstromen*

that nothing could happen to it of which it did not bear within itself the lineaments. It is also true that it provides itself with symbols of itself in both succession and multiplicity, and that these symbols *are* it, since without them it would, like an inarticulate cry, fail to achieve selfconsciousness. It is here that what we provisionally termed the passive synthesis becomes clarified. A passive synthesis is a contradiction in terms if the synthesis is a process of composition, and if the passivity consists in being the recipient of multiplicity instead of its composer. What we meant by passive synthesis was that we make our way into multiplicity, but that we do not synthesize it Now temporalization satisfies by its very nature these two conditions: it is indeed clear that I am not the creator of time any more than of my heart-beats I am not the initiator of the process of temporalization, I did not choose to come into the world, yet once I am born, time flows through me, whatever I do Nevertheless this ceaseless welling up of time is not a simple fact to which I am passively subjected, for I can find a remedy against it in itself, as happens in a decision which binds me or in the act of establishing a concept It withholds me from what I was about to become, and at the same time provides me with the means of grasping myself at a distance and establishing my own reality as myself. What is called passivity is not the acceptance by us of an alien reality, or a causal action exerted upon us from outside it is being encompassed, being in a situation—prior to which we do not exist—which we are perpetually resuming and which is constitutive of us. A spontaneity 'acquired' once and for all, and one which 'perpetuates itself in being in virtue of its being acquired'[1] is precisely time and subjectivity. It is time, since a time without its roots in a present and thence a past would no longer be time, but eternity. Heidegger's historical time, which flows from the future and which, thanks to its resolute decision, *has* its future in advance and rescues itself once and for all from disintegration, is impossible within the context of Heidegger's thought itself: for, if time is an *ek-stase*, if present and past are two results of this *ek-stase*, how could we ever cease completely to see time from the point of view of the present, and how could we completely escape from the inauthentic? It is always in the present that we are centred, and our decision starts from there; they can therefore always be brought into relationship with our past, and are never motiveless, and, though they may open up a cycle in our life which is entirely new, they still have to be subsequently carried forward, and afford only a temporary reprieve from dispersion There can therefore be no question of deriving time from spontaneity. We are not temporal

[1] J P Sartre, *L'Être et le Néant*, p 195 The author mentions this monster only to banish the very idea of it

beings *because* we are spontaneous and because, as consciousnesses, we tear ourselves away from ourselves. On the contrary, time is the foundation and measure of our spontaneity, and the power of out-running and of 'nihilating' ('*néantiser*') which dwells within us and is ourselves, is itself given to us with temporality and life Our birth, or, as Husserl has it in his unpublished writings, our 'generativity', is the basis both of our activity or individuality, and our passivity or generality—that inner weakness which prevents us from ever achiev-ing the density of an absolute individual We are not in some incom-prehensible way an activity joined to a passivity, an automatism surmounted by a will, a perception surmounted by a judgement, but wholly active and wholly passive, because we are the upsurge of time.

We have been concerned[1] with gaining an understanding of the relationships between consciousness and nature, between the inner and the outer. Or again, the problem was to link the idealist per-spective, according to which nothing exists except as an object for consciousness, and the realist perspective, according to which con-sciousnesses are introduced into the stuff of the objective world and of events in themselves. Or finally, we were concerned with finding out how the world and man are accessible to two kinds of investiga-tion, in the first case explanatory and in the second reflective We have already, in another work, set out these traditional problems in another language which strips away all inessentials · the whole ques-tion is ultimately one of understanding what, in ourselves and in the world, is the relation between *significance* and *absence of significance* Is the element of significance which is evident in the world produced and carried forward by the assemblage or convergence of independent facts or, on the other hand, is it merely the expression of an absolute reason? We say that events have a significance when they appear as the achievement or the expression of a single aim There is significance for us when one of our intentions is fulfilled, or conversely when a number of facts or signs lend themselves to our taking them up and grasping them inclusively, or, at all events, when one or more terms exist *as*   representative or expressive of something other than themselves It is characteristic of idealism to grant that all significance is centrifugal, being an *act* of significance or *Sinn-gebung*,[2] and that there are no natural signs. To understand is ultimately always to construct, to constitute, to bring about here and now the synthesis of the object Our analysis of one's own body and of perception has revealed to us a relation to the object,

[1] Cf *La Structure du Comportement*, Introd
[2] The expression is again often used by Husserl, for example *Ideen*, p 107

i e a significance deeper than this. The thing is nothing but a significance, the significance 'thing'. Very well But when I understand a thing, a picture for example, I do not here and now effect its synthesis, I come to it bringing my sensory fields and my perceptual field with me, and in the last resort I bring a schema of all possible being, a universal setting in relation to the world. At the heart of the subject himself we discovered, then, the presence of the world, so that the subject was no longer to be understood as a synthetic activity, but as *ek-stase,* and that every active process of signification or *Sinn-gebung* appeared as derivative and secondary in relation to that pregnancy of meaning within signs which served to define the world. We found beneath the intentionality of acts, or thetic intentionality, another kind which is the condition of the former's possibility: namely an operative intentionality already at work before any positing or any judgement, a 'Logos of the aesthetic world',[1] an 'art hidden in the depths of the human soul', one which, like any art, is known only in its results From this point onwards the distinction made by us elsewhere between structure and signification[2] began to be clarified: what constitutes the difference between the Gestalt of the circle and the signification 'circle', is that the latter is recognized by an understanding which engenders it as the place of points equidistant from a centre, the former by a subject familiar with his world and able to seize it as a modulation of that world, as a circular physiognomy We have no way of knowing what a picture or a thing is other than by looking at them, and their *significance* is revealed only if we look at them from a certain point of view, from a certain distance and in a certain *direction,** in short only if we place, at the service of the spectacle, our collusion with the world. The phrase 'direction of a stream' is meaningless unless I suppose a subject looking from one place towards another. In the world in itself, all directions and all movement are relative, which amounts to saying that there are none at all. There would in fact be no movement, and I should have no notion of it, if, in perception, I did not leave the earth, as my 'ground'[3] of all rest and motion, on the hither side of rest and motion, because I *inhabit* it, and similarly there would be no direction without a being who inhabits the world and who, through the medium of his gaze, marks out the first direction as a basis for

[1] Husserl, *Formale und transzendentale Logik*, p 257 'Aesthetic' is, naturally, taken in the wide sense of 'transcendental aesthetic'
[2] *La Structure du Comportement*, p 302.
[3] 'Boden', Husserl, *Umsturz der kopernikanischen Lehre* (unpublished)

* The argument is here, and in the following sentences, conducted by exploiting different meanings of the French word *sens* (meaning, direction, sense, way, manner) which are not covered by one single word in English (Translator's note)

all others. In the same way; the face or back of a piece of material is intelligible only for a subject who can approach the object from one side or another, so that it is through my upsurge into the world that the material has a face or back Similarly again, the meaning of a sentence is its import or intention, which once more presupposes a departure and arrival point, an aim and a point of view. And finally the sense of sight is a certain preparation for the logic, and for the world, of colours. In all uses of the word *sens*, we find the same fundamental notion of a being orientated or polarized in the direction of what he is not, and thus we are always brought back to a conception of the subject as *ek-stase*, and to a relationship of active transcendence between the subject and the world The world is inseparable from the subject, but from a subject which is nothing but a project of the world, and the subject is inseparable from the world, but from a world which the subject itself projects The subject is a being-in-the-world and the world remains 'subjective'[1] since its texture and articulations are traced out by the subject's movement of transcendence Hence we discovered, with the world as cradle of meanings, direction of all directions (*sens de tous les sens*), and ground of all thinking, how to leave behind the dilemma of realism and idealism, contingency and absolute reason, nonsense and sense The world as we have tried to show it, as standing on the horizon of our life as the primordial unity of all our experiences, and one goal of all our projects, is no longer the visible unfolding of a constituting Thought, not a chance conglomeration of parts, nor, of course, the working of a controlling Thought on an indifferent matter, but the native abode of all rationality.

Our analysis of time has confirmed, initially, this new notion of significance and understanding. Considering it in the same light as any other object, we shall be obliged to say of it what we have said of other objects: that it has meaning for us only because 'we are' it. We can designate something by this word only because we are at the past, present and future It is literally the tenor* of our life, and, like the world, is accessible only to the person who has his place within it, and who follows its direction But the analysis of time has not merely provided an opportunity of reiterating what had been said about the world It throws light on the preceding analysis because it discloses subject and object as two abstract 'moments' of a unique structure which is *presence* It is through time that being is conceived, because it is through the relations of time-subject and

---

[1] Heidegger, *Sein und Zeit*, p 366 'Wenn das "Subjekt" ontologisch als existierendes Dasein begriffen wird, deren Sein in der Zeitlichkeit gründet, dann muss gesagt werden Welt ist "subjektiv" Diese "subjektive" Welt aber is dann als Zeittranszendente "objektiver" als jedes mögliche "Objekt" '

* *sens* (Translator's note)

time-object that we are able to understand those obtaining between subject and world. Let us apply to those problems we began with the idea of subjectivity as temporality. We wondered, for example, how to conceive the relations between the soul and the body, rejecting as hopeless any attempt to tie up the *for-itself* with a certain object *in-itself*, to which it is supposed to stand in a relationship of causal dependence. But if the *for-itself*, the revelation of self to self, is merely the hollow in which time is formed, and if the world '*in itself*' is simply the horizon of my present, then the problem is reduced to the form How is it that a being which is still to come and has passed by, also has a present—which means that the problem is eliminated, since the future, the past and the present are linked together in the movement of temporalization It is as much of my essence to have a body as it is the future's to be the future of a certain present So that neither scientific thematization nor objective thought can discover a single bodily function strictly independent of existential structures,[1] or conversely a single 'spiritual' act which does not rest on a bodily infrastructure. Moreover, it is essential to me not only to have a body, but to have *this* body. It is not only the notion of the body which, through that of the present, is necessarily linked to that of the *for-itself*; the actual existence of my body is indispensable to that of my 'consciousness'. In the last analysis, in so far as I know that the *for-itself* is the culmination of a body, this can be only through the experience of my one body and one *for-itself*, or through the experience of my presence in the world It will be objected that I might have nails, ears or lungs of some other kind which would involve no change in my existence. But then my nails, ears and lungs taken separately have no existence. It is science which has accustomed us to regard the body as a collection of parts, and also the experience of its disintegration at death. But the fact is that a decomposed body is no longer a body. When I restore my ears, nails and lungs to my living body, they no longer appear in the light of contingent details They are not indifferent to the idea that others form of me, contributing as they do to my physiognomy or my general bearing, and it is not impossible that science may tomorrow express in the form of objective correlations precisely how necessary it was that I should have that kind of ears, nails and lungs, and whether, moreover, I was destined to be dexterous or clumsy, placid or highly strung, intelligent or stupid, in short whether I was destined to be myself. In other words, as we have shown elsewhere, the objective body is not the true version of the phenomenal body, that is, the true version of the body that we live by, it is indeed no more than the latter's impoverished image, so that the problem of the relation of soul to body

---

[1] We demonstrated this at length in *La Structure du Comportement*

431

has nothing to do with the objective body, which exists only conceptually, but with the phenomenal body. What is true, however, is that our open and personal existence rests on an initial foundation of acquired and stabilized existence. But it could not be otherwise, if we *are* temporality, since the dialectic of acquisition and future is what constitutes time.

Our replies would be on the same lines to any questions that might be raised concerning the world before man's appearance on it. To our assertion above that there is no world without an Existence that sustains its structure, it might have been retorted that the world nevertheless preceded man, that the earth, to all appearances, is the only inhabited planet, and that philosophical views are thus shown to be incompatible with the most firmly established facts. But in fact, it is only intellectualist, abstract reflection which is incompatible with misconceived 'facts'. For what precisely is meant by saying that the world existed before any human consciousness? An example of what is meant is that the earth originally issued from a primitive nebula from which the combination of conditions necessary to life was absent But every one of these words, like every equation in physics, presupposes *our* pre-scientific experience of the world, and this reference to the world in which we *live* goes to make up the proposition's valid meaning. Nothing will ever bring home to my comprehension what a nebula that no one sees could possibly be Laplace's nebula is not behind us, at our remote beginnings, but in front of us in the cultural world. What, in fact, do we mean when we say that there is no world without a being in the world? Not indeed that the world is constituted by consciousness, but on the contrary that consciousness always finds itself already at work in the world What is true, taking one thing with another, is that there is a nature, which is not that of the sciences, but that which perception presents to me, and that even the light of consciousness is, as Heidegger says, *lumen naturale,* given to itself

At all events, the critic may continue, the world will outlast me, and other men will perceive it when I am no longer here. Now is it not impossible for me to conceive, either after me, or even during my lifetime, other men in the world, if indeed my presence in the world is the condition of the world's possibility? In the perspective of temporalization, light is thrown on the remarks made above about the problem of other selves We said that in the perception of other selves I cover in intention the infinite distance which always stands between my subjectivity and another, I overcome the impossibility of conceiving another for-himself for me, because I witness another behaviour, another presence in the world Now that we have more effectively analysed the notion of presence, linked together presence

432

to oneself and presence in the world, and identified the *cogito* with involvement in the world, we are in a better position to understand how we can find others at the intentional origin of their visible behaviour. It is true that the other person will never exist for us as we exist ourselves, he is always a lesser figure, and we never feel in him as we do in ourselves the thrust of temporalization. But two temporalities are not mutually exclusive as are two consciousnesses, because each one knows itself only by projecting itself into the present where they can interweave. As my living present opens upon a past which I nevertheless am no longer living through, and on a future which I do not yet live, and perhaps never shall, it can also open on to temporalities outside my living experience and acquire a social horizon, with the result that my world is expanded to the dimensions of that collective history which my private existence takes up and carries forward. The solution of all problems of transcendence is to be sought in the thickness of the pre-objective present, in which we find our bodily being, our social being, and the pre-existence of the world, that is, the starting point of 'explanations', in so far as they are legitimate—and at the same time the basis of our freedom.

3

FREEDOM

AGAIN, it is clear that no causal relationship is conceivable between the subject and his body, his world or his society. Only at the cost of losing the basis of all my certainties can I question what is conveyed to me by my presence to myself Now the moment I turn to myself in order to describe myself, I have a glimpse of an anonymous flux,[1] a comprehensive project in which there are so far no 'states of consciousness', nor, *a fortiori*, qualifications of any sort. For myself I am neither 'jealous', nor 'inquisitive', nor 'hunchbacked', nor 'a civil servant'. It is often a matter of surprise that the cripple or the invalid can put up with himself. The reason is that such people are not for themselves deformed or at death's door Until the final coma, the dying man is inhabited by a consciousness, he is all that he sees, and enjoys this much of an outlet Consciousness can never objectify itself into invalid-consciousness or cripple-consciousness, and even if the old man complains of his age or the cripple of his deformity, they can do so only by comparing themselves with others, or seeing themselves through the eyes of others, that is, by taking a statistical and objective view of themselves, so that such complaints are never absolutely genuine when he is back in the heart of his own consciousness, each one of us feels beyond his limitations and thereupon resigns himself to them. They are the price which we automatically pay for being in the world, a formality which we take for granted. Hence we may speak disparagingly of our looks and still not want to change our face for another. No idiosyncrasy can, seemingly, be attached to the insuperable generality of consciousness, nor can any limit be set to this immeasurable power of escape In order to be determined (in the two senses of that word) by an external factor, it is necessary that I should be a thing. Neither my freedom nor my universality can admit of any eclipse. It is inconceivable that I should be free in certain of my actions and determined in others· how

[1] In the sense in which, with Husserl, we have taken this word.

434

should we understand a dormant freedom that gave full scope to determinism? And if it is assumed that it is snuffed out when it is not in action, how could it be rekindled? If *per impossibile* I had once succeeded in *making myself into* a thing, how should I subsequently reconvert myself to consciousness? Once I am free, I am not to be counted among things, and I must then be uninterruptedly free. Once my actions cease to be mine, I shall never recover them, and if I lose my hold on the world, it will never be restored to me. It is equally inconceivable that my liberty should be attenuated, one cannot be to some extent free, and if, as is often said, motives incline me in a certain direction, one of two things happens: either they are strong enough to force me to act, in which case there is no freedom, or else they are not strong enough, and then freedom is complete, and as great in the worst torments as in the peace of one's home We ought, therefore, to reject not only the idea of causality, but also that of motivation.[1] The alleged motive does not burden my decision; on the contrary my decision lends the motive its force Everything that I 'am' in virtue of nature or history—hunchbacked, handsome or Jewish—I never am completely for myself, as we have just explained· and I may well be these things for other people, nevertheless I remain free to posit another person as a consciousness whose views strike through to my very being, or on the other hand merely as an object It is also true that this option is itself a form of constraint: if I am ugly, I have the choice between being an object of disapproval or disapproving of others. I am left free to be a masochist or a sadist, but not free to ignore others But this dilemma, which is given as part of the human lot, is not one for me as pure consciousness. it is still I who makes another to be for me and makes each of us be as human beings Moreover, even if existence as a human being were imposed upon me, the manner alone being left to my choice, and considering this choice itself and ignoring the small number of forms it might take, it would still be a free choice If it is said that my temperament inclines me particularly to either sadism or masochism, it is still merely a manner of speaking, for my temperament exists only for the second order knowledge that I gain about myself when I see myself as others see me, and in so far as I recognize it, confer value upon it, and in that sense, choose it What misleads us on this, is that we often look for freedom in the voluntary deliberation which examines one motive after another and seems to opt for the weightiest or most convincing. In reality the deliberation follows the decision, and it is my secret decision which brings the motives to light, for it would be difficult to conceive what the force of a motive might be in the absence of a decision which it confirms or to which it runs counter When I

[1] See J P. Sartre, *L'Être et le Néant*, pp 508 and ff.

435

have abandoned a project, the motives which I thought held me to it suddenly lose their force and collapse In order to resuscitate them, an effort is required on my part to reopen time and set me back to the moment preceding the making of the decision Even while I am deliberating, already I find it an effort to suspend time's flow, and to keep open a situation which I feel is closed by a decision which is already there and which I am holding off. That is why it so often happens that after giving up a plan I experience a feeling of relief: 'After all, I wasn't all that involved'; the debate was purely a matter of form, and the deliberation a mere parody, for I had decided against from the start.

We often see the weakness of the will brought forward as an argument against freedom. And indeed, although I can will myself to adopt a course of conduct and act the part of a warrior or a seducer, it is not within my power to be a warrior or seducer with ease and in a way that 'comes naturally'; really to *be* one, that is. But neither should we seek freedom in the act of will, which is, in its very meaning, something short of an act We have recourse to an act of will only in order to go against our true decision, and, as it were, for the purpose of proving our powerlessness. If we had really and truly made the conduct of the warrior or the seducer our own, then we should *be* one or the other Even what are called obstacles to freedom are in reality deployed by it An unclimbable rock face, a large or small, vertical or slanting rock, are things which have no meaning for anyone who is not intending to surmount them, for a subject whose projects do not carve out such determinate forms from the uniform mass of the *in itself* and cause an orientated world to arise— a significance in things There is, then, ultimately nothing that can set limits to freedom, except those limits that freedom itself has set in the form of its various initiatives, so that the subject has simply the external world that he gives himself. Since it is the latter who, on coming into being, brings to light significance and value in things, and since no thing can impinge upon it except through acquiring, thanks to it, significance and value, there is no action of things on the subject, but merely a signification (in the active sense), a centrifugal *Sinngebung* The choice would seem to lie between scientism's conception of causality, which is incompatible with the consciousness which we have of ourselves, and the assertion of an absolute freedom divorced from the outside. It is impossible to decide beyond which point things cease to be $\epsilon\phi'\eta\mu\iota\nu$ Either they all lie within our power, or none does

The result, however, of this first reflection on freedom would appear to be to rule it out altogether If indeed it is the case that our freedom is the same in all our actions, and even in our passions, if it

436

is not to be measured in terms of our conduct, and if the slave displays freedom as much by living in fear as by breaking his chains, then it cannot be held that there is such a thing as *free action*, freedom being anterior to all actions In any case it will not be possible to declare 'Here freedom makes its appearance', since free action, in order to be discernible, has to stand out against a background of life from which it is entirely, or almost entirely, absent. We may say in this case that it is everywhere, but equally nowhere. In the name of freedom we reject the idea of acquisition, since freedom has become a primordial acquisition and, as it were, our state of nature. Since we do not have to provide it, it is the gift granted to us of having no gift, it is the nature of consciousness which consists in having no nature, and in no case can it find external expression or a place in our life. The idea of action, therefore, disappears· nothing can pass from us to the world, since we are nothing that can be specified, and since the non-being which constitutes us could not possibly find its way into the world's plenum. There are merely intentions immediately followed by their effects, and we are very near to the Kantian idea of an intention which is tantamount to the act, which Scheler countered with the argument that the cripple who would like to be able to save a drowning man and the good swimmer who actually saves him do not have the same experience of autonomy. The very idea of choice vanishes, for to choose is to choose *something* in which freedom sees, at least for a moment, a symbol of itself There is free choice only if freedom comes into play in its decision, and posits the situation chosen as a situation of freedom. A freedom which has no need to be exercised because it is already acquired could not commit itself in this way· it knows that the following instant will find it, come what may, just as free and just as indeterminate The very notion of freedom demands that our decision should plunge into the future, that something should have been *done* by it, that the subsequent instant should benefit from its predecessor and, though not necessitated, should be at least required by it. If freedom is doing, it is necessary that what it does should not be immediately undone by a new freedom. Each instant, therefore, must not be a closed world, one instant must be able to commit its successors and, a decision once taken and action once begun, I must have something acquired at my disposal, I must benefit from my impetus, I must be inclined to carry on, and there must be a bent or propensity of the mind It was Descartes who held that conservation demands a power as great as does creation; a view which implies a realistic notion of the instant. It is true that the instant is not a philosopher's fiction It is the point at which one project is brought to fruition and another begun[1]—the point at

[1] J P. Sartre, *L'Être et le Néant*, p 544

which my gaze is transferred from one end to another, it is the *Augen-Blick*. But this break in time cannot occur unless each of the two spans is of a piece Consciousness, it is said, is, though not atomized into instants, at least haunted by the spectre of the instant which it is obliged continually to exorcise by a free act. We shall soon see that we have indeed always the power to interrupt, but it implies in any case a power to *begin*, for there would be no severance unless freedom had taken up its abode somewhere and were preparing to move it Unless there are cycles of behaviour, open situations requiring a certain completion and capable of constituting a background to either a confirmatory or transformatory decision, we never experience freedom The choice of intelligible character is excluded, not only because there is no time anterior to time, but because choice presupposes a prior commitment and because the idea of an initial choice involves a contradiction. If freedom is to have *room* * in which to move, if it is to be describable as freedom, there must be something to hold it away from its objectives, it must have a *field*, which means that there must be for it special possibilities, or realities which tend to cling to being As J P Sartre himself observes, dreaming is incompatible with freedom because, in the realm of imagination, we have no sooner taken a certain significance as our goal than we already believe that we have intuitively brought it into being, in short, because there is no obstacle and nothing *to do*.[1] It is established that freedom is not to be confused with those abstract decisions of will at grips with motives or passions, for the classical conception of deliberation is relevant only to a freedom 'in bad faith' which secretly harbours antagonistic motives without being prepared to act on them, and so itself manufactures the alleged proofs of its impotence We can see, beneath these noisy debates and these fruitless efforts to 'construct' ourselves, the tacit decisions whereby we have marked out round ourselves the field of possibility, and it is true that nothing is done as long as we cling to these fixed points, and everything is easy as soon as we have weighed anchor. This is why our freedom is not to be sought in spurious discussion on the conflict between a style of life which we have no wish to reappraise and circumstances suggestive of another the real choice is that of whole character and our manner of being in the world But either this total choice is never uttered, since it is the silent upsurge of our being in the world, in which case it is not clear in what sense it could be said to be ours, since this freedom glides over itself and is the equivalent of a fate—or else our choice of ourselves is truly a

* 'avoir du champ'; in this sentence there is a play on the word 'champ'= field (Translator's note).

[1] J P Sartre, *L'Être et le Neant*, p. 562

choice, a conversion involving our whole existence In this case, however, there is presupposed a previous acquisition which the choice sets out to modify and it founds a new tradition: this leads us to ask whether the perpetual severance in terms of which we initially defined freedom is not simply the negative aspect of our universal commitment to a world, and whether our indifference to each determinate thing does not express merely our involvement in all; whether the ready-made freedom from which we started is not reducible to a power of initiative, which cannot be transformed into *doing* without taking up some proposition of the world, and whether, in short, concrete and actual freedom is not indeed to be found in this exchange It is true that nothing has *significance* and value for anyone but *me* and through anyone but me, but this proposition remains indeterminate and is still indistinguishable from the Kantian idea of a consciousness which 'finds in things only what it has put into them', and from the idealist refutation of realism, as long as we fail to make clear how we understand significance and the self. By defining ourselves as a universal power of *Sinn-Gebung*, we have reverted to the method of the 'thing without which' and to the analytical reflection of the traditional type, which seeks the conditions of possibility without concerning itself with the conditions of reality We must therefore resume the analysis of the *Sinngebung*, and show how it can be both centrifugal and centripetal, since it has been established that there is no freedom without a field

When I say that this rock is unclimbable, it is certain that this attribute, like that of being big or little, straight and oblique, and indeed like all attributes in general, can be conferred upon it only by the project of climbing it, and by a human presence It is, therefore, freedom which brings into being the obstacles to freedom, so that the latter can be set over against it as its bounds However, it is clear that, one and the same project being given, one rock will appear as an obstacle, and another, being more negotiable, as a means My freedom, then, does not so contrive it that this way there is an obstacle, and that way a way through, it arranges for there to be obstacles and ways through in general, it does not draw the particular outline of this world, but merely lays down its general structures. It may be objected that there is no difference; if my freedom conditions the structure of the 'there is', that of the 'here' and the 'there', it is present wherever these structures arise. We cannot distinguish the quality of 'obstacle' from the obstacle itself, and relate one to freedom and the other to the world in itself which, without freedom, would be merely an amorphous and unnameable mass. It is not, therefore, outside myself that I am able to find a limit to my freedom But do I not find it in myself? We must indeed distinguish between my express intentions, for example the plan I now make to climb those mountains, and general intentions which evaluate the potentialities of my environment. Whether or not I have decided to climb them, these mountains appear high to me, because they exceed my body's power to take them in its stride, and, even if I have just read *Micromégas*, I cannot so contrive it that they are small for me. Underlying myself as a thinking subject, who am able to take my place at will on Sirius or on the earth's surface, there is, therefore, as it were a natural self which does not budge from its terrestrial situation and which constantly adumbrates absolute valuations. What is more, my projects as a thinking being are clearly modelled on the latter; if I elect to see things from the point of view of Sirius, it is still to my terrestrial experience that I must have recourse in order to do so; I may say, for example, that the Alps are *molehills*. In so far as I have hands, feet, a body, I sustain around me intentions which are not dependent upon my decisions and which affect my surroundings in a way which I do not choose. These intentions are general in a double sense: firstly in the sense that they constitute a system in which all possible objects are simultaneously included; if the mountain appears high and upright, the tree appears small and sloping, and furthermore in the sense that they are not simply mine, they originate from other than myself, and I am not surprised to find them in all psycho-physical subjects organized as I am. Hence, as Gestalt psychology has shown, there are for me certain shapes which are particularly favoured, as they are for other men, and which are capable of giving rise to a psychological science and rigorous laws. The grouping of dots

.. ..

is always perceived as six pairs of dots with two millimetres between each pair, while one figure is always perceived as a cube, and another as a plane mosaic.[1] It is as if, on the hither side of our judgement and our freedom, someone were assigning such and such a significance to such and such a given grouping. It is indeed true that perceptual structures do not always force themselves upon the observer; there are some which are ambiguous. But these reveal even more effectively the presence within us of spontaneous evaluation: for they are elusive shapes which suggest constantly changing meanings to us. Now a pure consciousness is capable of anything except being ignorant of its intentions, and an absolute freedom cannot choose itself as hesitant, since that amounts to allowing itself to be drawn in several directions, and since, the possibilities being *ex hypothesi* indebted to freedom for all the strength they have, the weight that freedom gives to one is thereby withdrawn from the rest. We *can* break up a shape

[1] See above, p 263.

by looking at it awry, but this too is because freedom uses the gaze along with its spontaneous evaluations. Without the latter, we would not have a world, that is, a collection of things which emerge from a background of formlessness by presenting themselves to our body as 'to be touched', 'to be taken', 'to be climbed over' We should never be aware of adjusting ourselves to things and reaching them where they are, beyond us, but would be conscious only of restricting our thoughts to the immanent objects of our intentions, and we should not be in the world, ourselves implicated in the spectacle and, so to speak, intermingled with things, we should simply enjoy the spectacle of a universe It is, therefore, true that there are no obstacles in themselves, but the self which qualifies them as such is not some acosmic subject, it runs ahead of itself in relation to things in order to confer upon them the form of things There is an autochthonous significance of the world which is constituted in the dealings which our incarnate existence has with it, and which provides the ground of every deliberate *Sinngebung*.

This is true not only of an impersonal and, all in all, abstract function such as 'external perception'. There is something comparable present in all evaluations It has been perceptively remarked that pain and fatigue can never be regarded as causes which 'act' upon my liberty, and that, in so far as I may experience either at any given moment, they do not have their origin outside me, but always have a significance and express my attitude towards the world Pain makes me give way and say what I ought to have kept to myself, fatigue makes me break my journey We all know the moment at which we decide no longer to endure pain or fatigue, and when, simultaneously, they become intolerable in fact. Tiredness does not halt my companion, because he likes the clamminess of his body, the heat of the road and the sun, in short, because he likes to feel himself in the midst of things, to feel their rays converging upon him, to be the cynosure of all this light, and an object of touch for the earth's crust. My own fatigue brings me to a halt because I dislike it, because I have chosen differently my manner of being in the world, because, for instance, I endeavour, not to be in nature, but rather to win the recognition of others I am free in relation to fatigue to precisely the extent that I am free in relation to my being in the world, free to make my way by transforming it.[1] But here once more we must recognize a sort of sedimentation of our life an attitude towards the world, when it has received frequent confirmation, acquires a favoured status for us Yet since freedom does not tolerate any motive in its path, my habitual being in the world is at each moment equally precarious, and the complexes which I have allowed to

[1] J P. Sartre, *L'Être et le Néant,* pp 531 and ff

441

develop over the years always remain equally soothing, and the free act can with no difficulty blow them sky-high. However, having built our life upon an inferiority complex which has been operative for twenty years, it is not *probable* that we shall change. It is clear what a summary rationalism might say in reply to such a hybrid notion there are no degrees of possibility, either the free act is no longer possible, or it is still possible, in which case freedom is complete In short, 'probable' is meaningless It is a notion belonging to statistical thought, which is not thought at all, since it does not concern any particular thing actually existing, any moment of time, any concrete event. 'It is improbable that Paul will give up writing bad books' means nothing, since Paul may well decide to write no more such books The probable is everywhere and nowhere, a reified fiction, with only a psychological existence, it is not an ingredient of the world. And yet we have already met it a little while ago in the perceived *world* The mountain is great or small to the extent that, as a perceived thing, it is to be found in the field of my possible actions, and in relation to a level which is not only that of my individual life, but that of 'any man'. Generality and probability are not fictions, but phenomena, we must therefore find a phenomenological basis for statistical thought. It belongs necessarily to a being which is fixed, situated and surrounded by things in the world 'It is improbable' that I should at this moment destroy an inferiority complex in which I have been content to live for twenty years. That means that I have committed myself to inferiority, that I have made it my abode, that this past, though not a fate, has at least a specific weight and is not a set of events over there, at a distance from me, but the atmosphere of my present. The rationalist's dilemma· either the free act is possible, or it is not—either the event originates in me or is imposed on me from outside, does not apply to our relations with the world and with our past Our freedom does not destroy our situation, but gears itself to it as long as we are alive, our situation is open, which implies both that it calls up specially favoured modes of resolution, and also that it is powerless to bring one into being by itself.

We shall arrive at the same result by considering our relations with history Taking myself in my absolute concreteness, as I am presented to myself in reflection, I find that I am an anonymous and pre-human flux, as yet unqualified as, for instance, 'a working man' or 'middle class' If I subsequently think of myself as a man among men, a bourgeois among bourgeois, this can be, it would seem, no more than a second order view of myself; I am never in my heart of hearts a worker or a bourgeois, but a consciousness which freely evaluates itself as a middle class or proletarian consciousness And indeed, it is never the case that my objective position in the production process is sufficient to awaken class consciousness. There was exploitation long before there were revolutionaries Nor is it always in periods of economic difficulty that the working class movement makes headway. Revolt is, then, not the outcome of objective conditions, but it is rather the decision taken by the worker to will revolution that makes a proletarian of him. The evaluation of the present operates through one's free project for the future From which we might conclude that history by itself has no significance, but only that conferred upon it by our will Yet here again we are slipping into the method of 'the indispensable condition failing which . . .': in opposition to objective thought, which includes the subject in its deterministic system, we set idealist reflection which makes determinism dependent upon the constituting activity of the subject Now, we have already seen that objective thought and analytical reflection are two aspects of the same mistake, two ways of overlooking the phenomena. Objective thought derives class consciousness from the objective condition of the proletariat Idealist reflection reduces the proletarian condition to the awareness of it, which the proletarian arrives at The former traces class-consciousness to the class defined in terms of objective characteristics, the latter on the other hand reduces 'being a workman' to the consciousness of being one. In each case we are in the realm of abstraction, because we remain torn between the *in itself* and the *for itself* If we approach the question afresh with the idea of discovering, not the causes of the act of becoming aware, for there is no cause which can act from outside upon a consciousness—nor the conditions of its possibility, for we need to know the conditions which actually produce it—but class-consciousness itself, if, in short, we apply a genuinely existential method, what do we find? I am not conscious of being working class or middle class simply because, as a matter of fact, I sell my labour or, equally as a matter of fact, because my interests are bound up with capitalism, nor do I become one or the other on the day on which I elect to view history in the light of the class struggle. what happens is that 'I exist as working class' or 'I exist as middle class' in the first place, and it is this mode of dealing with the world and society which provides both the motives for my revolutionary or conservative projects and my explicit judgements of the type 'I am working class' or 'I am middle class', without its being possible to deduce the former from the latter, or *vice versa* What makes me a proletarian is not the economic system or society considered as systems of impersonal forces, but these institutions as I carry them within me and experience them; nor is it an intellectual operation devoid of motive, but my way of being in the world within this institutional framework

443

Let us suppose that I have a certain style of living, being at the mercy of booms and slumps, not being free to do as I like, receiving a weekly wage, having no control over either the conditions or the products of my work, and consequently feeling a stranger in my factory, my nation and my life I have acquired the habit of reckoning with a *fatum*, or appointed order, which I do not respect, but which I have to humour Or suppose that I work as a day-labourer, having no farm of my own, no tools, going from one farm to another hiring myself out at harvest time, in that case I have the feeling that there is some anonymous power hovering over me and making a nomad of me, even though I want to settle into a regular job. Or finally suppose I am the tenant of a farm to which the owner has had no electricity laid on, though the mains are less than two hundred yards away I have, for my family and myself, only one habitable room, although it would be easy to make other rooms available in the house My fellow workers in factory or field, or other farmers, do the same work as I do in comparable conditions, we co-exist in the same situation and feel alike, not in virtue of some comparison, as if each one of us lived primarily within himself, but on the basis of our tasks and gestures These situations do not imply any express evaluation, and if there is a tacit evaluation, it represents the thrust of a freedom devoid of any project against unknown obstacles, one cannot in any case talk about a choice, for in all three cases it is enough that I should be born into the world and that I exist in order to experience my life as full of difficulties and constraints—I do not choose so to experience it But this state of affairs can persist without my becoming class-conscious, understanding that I am of the proletariat and becoming a revolutionary. How then am I to make this change? The worker learns that other workers in a different trade have, after striking, obtained a wage-increase, and notices that subsequently wages have gone up in his own factory. The appointed order with which he was at grips is beginning to take on a clearer shape The day-labourer who has not often seen workers in regular employment, who is not like them and has little love for them, sees the price of manufactured goods and the cost of living going up, and becomes aware that he can no longer earn a livelihood. He may at this point blame town workers, in which case class-consciousness will not make its appearance. If it does, it is not because the day-labourer has decided to become a revolutionary and consequently confers a value upon his actual condition, it is because he has perceived, in a concrete way, that his life is synchronized with the life of the town labourers and that all share a common lot. The small farmer who does not associate himself with the day-labourers, still less with the town labourers, being separated from them by a whole world of customs and value judgements, nevertheless feels that

444

he is on the same side as the journeyman when he pays them an inadequate wage, and he even feels that he has something in common with the town workers when he learns that the farm owner is chairman of the board of directors of several industrial concerns. Social space begins to acquire a magnetic field, and a region of the exploited is seen to appear. At every pressure felt from any quarter of the social horizon, the process of regrouping becomes clearly discernible beyond ideologies and various occupations Class is coming into being, and we say that a situation is revolutionary when the connection objectively existing between the sections of the proletariat (the connection, that is, which an absolute observer would recognize as so existing) is finally experienced in perception as a common obstacle to the existence of each and every one. It is not at all necessary that at any single moment a *representation* of revolution should arise For example, it is doubtful whether the Russian peasants of 1917 expressly envisaged revolution and the transfer of property. Revolution arises day by day from the concatenation of less remote and more remote ends It is not necessary that each member of the proletariat should think of himself as such, in the sense that a Marxist theoretician gives to the word It is sufficient that the journeyman or the farmer should feel that he is on the march towards a certain crossroads, to which the road trodden by the town labourers also leads Both find their journey's end in revolution, which would perhaps have terrified them had it been described and represented to them in advance. One might say at the most that revolution is at the end of the road they have taken and in their projects in the form of 'things must change', which each one experiences concretely in his distinctive difficulties and in the depths of his particular prejudices Neither the appointed order, nor the free act which destroys it, is represented; they are lived through in ambiguity This does not mean that workers and peasants bring about revolution without being aware of it, and that we have here blind, 'elementary forces' cleverly exploited by a few shrewd agitators It is possibly in this light that the prefect of police will view history. But such ways of seeing things do not help him when faced with a genuine revolutionary situation, in which the slogans of the alleged agitators are immediately understood, as if by some pre-established harmony, and meet with concurrence on all sides, because they crystallize what is latent in the life of all productive workers. The revolutionary movement, like the work of the artist, is an intention which itself creates its instruments and its means of expression The revolutionary project is not the result of a deliberate judgement, or the explicit positing of an end It is these things in the case of the propagandist, because the propagandist has been trained by the intellectual, or, in the case of the intellectual, because he regulates his life on the basis of his thoughts But it does not cease to be the abstract decision of a thinker and become a historical reality until it is worked out in the dealings men have with each other, and in the relations of the man to his job. It is, therefore, true that I recognize myself as a worker or a bourgeois on the day I take my stand in relation to a possible revolution, and that this taking of a stand is not the outcome, through some mechanical causality, of my status as workman or bourgeois (which is why all classes have their traitors), but neither is it an unwarranted evaluation, instantaneous and unmotivated; it is prepared by some molecular process, it matures in co-existence before bursting forth into words and being related to objective ends. One is justified in drawing attention to the fact that it is not the greatest poverty which produces the most clearsighted revolutionaries, but one forgets to ask why a return of prosperity frequently brings with it a more radical mood among the masses. It is because the easing of living conditions makes a fresh structure of social space possible: the horizon is not restricted to the most immediate concerns, there is economic play and room for a new project in relation to living. This phenomenon does not, then, go to prove that the worker makes himself into worker and revolutionary *ex nihilo*, but on the contrary that he does so on a certain basis of co-existence. The mistake inherent in the conception under discussion is, in general, that of disregarding all but intellectual projects, instead of considering the existential project, which is the polarization of a life towards a goal which is both determinate and indeterminate, which, to the person concerned, is entirely unrepresented, and which is recognized only on being attained. Intentionality is brought down to the particular cases of the objectifying acts, the proletarian condition is made an object of thought, and no difficulty is experienced in showing, in accordance with idealism's permanent method, that, like every other object of thought, it subsists only before and through the consciousness which constitutes it as an object. Idealism (like objective thought) bypasses true intentionality, which is *at* its object rather than positing it Idealism overlooks the interrogative, the subjunctive, the aspiration, the expectation, the positive indeterminacy of these modes of consciousness, for it is acquainted only with consciousness in the present or future indicative, which is why it fails to account for class For class is a matter neither for observation nor decree, like the appointed order of the capitalistic system, like revolution, before being thought it is lived through as an obsessive presence, as possibility, enigma and myth To make class-consciousness the outcome of a decision and a choice is to say that problems are solved on the day they are posed, that every question already contains the reply that it awaits, it is, in short, to revert to immanence and abandon the attempt to understand history In reality, the intellectual project and the positing of ends are merely the bringing to completion of an existential project It is I who give a direction, significance and future to my life, but that does not mean that these are concepts, they spring from my present and past and in particular from my mode of present and past co-existence Even in the case of the intellectual who turns revolutionary, his decision does not arise *ex nihilo*; it may follow upon a prolonged period of solitude· the intellectual is in search of a doctrine which shall make great demands on him and cure him of his subjectivity, or he may yield to the clear light thrown by a Marxist interpretation of history, in which case he has given knowledge pride of place in his life, and that in itself is understandable only in virtue of his past and his childhood. Even the decision to become a revolutionary without motive, and by an act of pure freedom would express a certain way of being in the natural and social world, which is typically that of the intellectual He 'throws in his lot·with the working class' from the starting point of his situation as an intellectual and from nowhere else (and this is why even fideism, in his case, remains rightly suspect). Now with the worker it is *a fortiori* the case that his decision is elaborated in the course of his life This time it is through no misunderstanding that the horizon of a particular life and revolutionary aims coincide: for the worker revolution is a more immediate possibility, and one closer to his own interests than for the intellectual, since he is at grips with the economic system in his very life For this reason there are, statistically, more workers than middle class people in a revolutionary party Motivation, of course, does not do away with freedom. Working class parties of the most unmistakable kind have had many intellectuals among their leaders, and it is likely that a man such as Lenin identified himself with revolution and eventually transcended the distinction between intellectual and worker But these are the virtues proper to action and commitment, at the outset, I am not an individual beyond class, I am situated in a social environment, and my freedom, though it may have the power to commit me elsewhere, has not the power to transform me instantaneously into what I decide to be Thus to be a bourgeois or a worker is not only to be aware of being one or the other, it is to identify oneself as worker or bourgeois through an implicit or existential project which merges into our way of patterning the world and co-existing with other people My decision draws together a spontaneous meaning of my life which it may confirm or repudiate, but not annul Both idealism and objective thinking fail to pin down the coming into being of class consciousness, the former because it deduces actual existence from consciousness, the latter because it derives consciousness from *de facto* existence, and both because they overlook the relationship of motivation.

It will perhaps be objected, from the idealist side, that I am not, for myself, a particular project, but a pure consciousness, and that the attributes of bourgeois or worker belong to me only to the extent that I place myself among others, and see myself through their eyes, from the outside, as 'another' Here we should have categories of For Others and not For Oneself But if there were two sorts of categories, how could I have the experience of another, that is, of an *alter ego*? This experience presupposes that already my view of myself is half-way to having the quality of a possible 'other', and that in my view of another person is implied his quality as *ego*. It will be replied that the other person is given to me as a fact, and not as a possibility of my own being. What is meant by this? Is it that I should not have the experience of other men if there were none on the earth's surface? The proposition is self-evidently true, but does not solve our problem since, as Kant has already said, we cannot pass from 'All knowledge begins with experience' to 'All knowledge derives from experience' If the other people who empirically exist are to be, for me, other people, I must have a means of recognizing them, and the structures of the For Another must, therefore, already be the dimensions of the For Oneself. Moreover, it is impossible to derive from the For Another all the specifications of which we are speaking. Another person is not necessarily, is not even ever quite an object for me. And, in sympathy for example, I can perceive another person as bare existence and freedom as much or as little as myself. The-other-person-as-object is nothing but an insincere modality of others, just as absolute subjectivity is nothing but an abstract notion of myself I must, therefore, in the most radical reflection, apprehend around my absolute individuality a kind of halo of generality or a kind of atmo-sphere of 'sociality'. This is necessary if subsequently the words 'a bourgeois' and 'a man' are to be able to assume meaning for me. I must apprehend myself immediately as centred in a way outside my-self, and my individual existence must diffuse round itself, so to speak, an existence in quality. The For-Themselves—me for myself and the other for himself—must stand out against a background of For Others—I for the other and the other for me My life must have a significance which I do not constitute; there must strictly speaking be an intersubjectivity; each one of us must be both anonymous in the sense of absolutely individual, and anonymous in the sense of absolutely general. Our being in the world, is the concrete bearer of this double anonymity

Provided that this is so, there can be situations, a direction* of

* 'sens' (Translator's note)

history, and a historical truth three ways of saying the same thing. If indeed I made myself into a worker or a bourgeois by an absolute initiative, and if in general terms nothing ever courted our freedom, history would display no structure, no event would be seen to take shape in it, and anything might emerge from anything else There would be no British Empire as a relatively stable historical form to which a name can be given, and in which certain probable properties are recognizable There would not be, in the history of social progress, revolutionary situations or periods of set-back. A social revolution would be equally possible at any moment, and one might reasonably expect a despot to undergo conversion to anarchism History would never move in any direction, nor would it be possible to say that even over a short period of time events were conspiring to produce any definite outcome. The statesman would always be an adventurer, that is to say, he would turn events to his own advantage by conferring upon them a meaning which they *did not have* Now if it is true that history is powerless to complete anything independently of consciousnesses which assume it and thereby decide its course, and if consequently it can never be detached from us to play the part of an alien force using us for its own ends, then *precisely because it is always history lived through* we cannot withhold from it at least a fragmentary meaning Something is being prepared which will perhaps come to nothing but which may, for the moment, conform to the adumbrations of the present Nothing can so order it that, in the France of 1799, a military power 'above classes' should not appear as a natural product of the ebb of revolution, and that the rôle of military dictator should not here be 'a part that has to be played'. It is Bonaparte's project, known to us through its realization, which causes us to pass such a judgement But before Bonaparte, Dumouriez, Custine and others had envisaged it, and this common tendency has to be accounted for. What is known as the significance of events is not an idea which produces them, or the fortuitous result of their occurring together. It is the concrete project of a future which is elaborated within social coexistence and in the One* before any personal decision is made. At the point of revolutionary history to which class dynamics had carried it by 1799, when neither the Revolution could be carried forward nor the clock put back, the situation was such that, all due reservations as to individual freedom having been made, each individual, through the functional and generalized existence which makes a historical subject of him, tended to fall back upon what had been acquired It would have been a historical mistake at that stage to suggest to them either a resumption of the methods of revolutionary government or a reversion to the social conditions of 1789, not

* In the sense of *das Man*, the impersonal pronoun (Translator's note).

because there is a truth of history independent of our projects and evaluations, which are always free, but because there is an average and statistical significance of these projects Which means that we confer upon history its significance, but not without its putting that significance forward itself. The *Sinngebung* is not merely centrifugal, which is why the subject of history is not the individual. There is an exchange between generalized and individual existence, each receiving and giving something There is a moment at which the significance which was foreshadowed in the One, and which was merely a precarious possibility threatened by the contingency of history, is taken up by an individual. It may well happen that now, having taken command of history, he leads it, for a time at least, far beyond what seemed to comprise its significance, and involves it in a fresh dialectic, as when Bonaparte, from being Consul, made himself Emperor and conqueror. We are not asserting that history from end to end has only one meaning, any more than has an individual life. We mean simply that in any case freedom modifies it only by taking up the meaning which history *was offering* at the moment in question, and by a kind of unobtrusive assimilation. On the strength of this proposal made by the present, the adventurer can be distinguished from the statesman, historical imposture from the truth of an epoch, with the result that our assessment of the past, though never arriving at absolute objectivity, is at the same time never entitled to be arbitrary.

We therefore recognize, around our initiatives and around that strictly individual project which is oneself, a zone of generalized existence and of projects already formed, significances which trail between ourselves and things and which confer upon us the quality of man, bourgeois or worker. Already generality intervenes, already our presence to ourselves is mediated by it and we cease to be pure consciousness, as soon as the natural or social constellation ceases to be an unformulated *this* and crystallizes into a situation, as soon as it has a meaning—in short, as soon as we exist. Every thing appears to us through a medium to which it lends its own fundamental quality; this piece of wood is neither a collection of colours and tactile data, not even their total *Gestalt*, but something from which there emanates a woody essence; these 'sensory givens' modulate a certain theme or illustrate a certain style which is the wood itself, and which creates, round this piece of wood and the perception I have of it, a horizon of significance. The natural world, as we have seen, is nothing other than the place of all possible themes and styles. It is indissolubly an unmatched individual and a significance. Correspondingly, the generality and the individuality of the subject, subjectivity qualified and pure, the anonymity of the One and the anonymity of consciousness are not two conceptions of the subject between which philosophy

450

has to choose, but two stages of a unique structure which is the concrete subject. Let us consider, for example, sense experience I lose
myself in this red which is before me, without in any way qualifying
it, and it seems that this experience brings me into contact with a
pre-human subject. Who perceives this red? It is nobody who can be
named and placed among other perceiving subjects. For, between
this experience of red which I have, and that about which other
people speak to me, no direct comparison will ever be possible. I am
here in my own point of view, and since all experience, in so far as it
derives from impression, is in the same way strictly my own, it seems
that a unique and unduplicated subject enfolds them all Suppose I
formulate a thought, the God of Spinoza, for example, this thought
as it is in my living experience is a certain landscape to which no one
will ever have access, even if, moreover, I manage to enter into a discussion with a friend on the subject of Spinoza's God. However, the
very individuality of these experiences is not quite unadulterated For
the thickness of this red, its thisness, the power it has of reaching me
and saturating me, are attributable to the fact that it requires and
obtains from my gaze a certain vibration, and imply that I am
familiar with a world of colours of which this one is a particular
variation. The concrete colour red, therefore, stands out against a
background of generality, and this is why, even without transferring
myself to another's point of view, I grasp myself in perception as *a*
perceiving subject, and not as unclassifiable consciousness. I feel, all
round my perception of red, all the regions of my being unaffected by
it, and that region set aside for colours, 'vision', through which the
perception finds its way into me. Similarly my thought about the
God of Spinoza is only apparently a strictly unique experience, for it
is the concretion of a certain cultural world, the Spinozist philosophy,
or of a certain philosophic style in which I immediately recognize a
'Spinozist' idea. There is therefore no occasion to ask ourselves why
the thinking subject or consciousness perceives itself as a man, or an
incarnate or historical subject, nor must we treat this apperception as
a second order operation which it somehow performs starting from
its absolute existence· the absolute flow takes shape beneath its own
gaze as 'a consciousness', or a man, or an incarnate subject, because
it is a field of presence—to itself, to others and to the world—and
because this presence throws it into the natural and cultural world
from which it arrives at an understanding of itself. We must not envisage this flux as absolute contact with oneself, as an absolute
density with no internal fault, but on the contrary as a being which is
in pursuit of itself outside If the subject made a constant and at all
times peculiar choice of himself, one might wonder why his experience always ties up with itself and presents him with objects and

definite historical phases, why we have a general notion of time valid through all times, and why finally the experience of each one of us links up with that of others. But it is the question itself which must be questioned: for what is given, is not one fragment of time followed by another, one individual flux, then another, it is the taking up of each subjectivity by itself, and of subjectivities by each other in the generality of a single nature, the cohesion of an intersubjective life and a world The present mediates between the For Oneself and the For Others, between individuality and generality. True reflection presents me to myself not as idle and inaccessible subjectivity, but as identical with my presence in the world and to others, as I am now realizing it I am all that I see, I am an intersubjective field, not despite my body and historical situation, but, on the contrary, by being this body and this situation, and through them, all the rest.

What, then, becomes of the freedom we spoke about at the outset, if this point of view is taken? I can no longer pretend to be a cipher, and to choose myself continually from the starting point of nothing at all. If it is through subjectivity that nothingness appears in the world, it can equally be said that it is through the world that nothingness comes into being I am a general refusal to be anything, accompanied surreptitiously by a continual acceptance of such and such a qualified form of being *For even this general refusal is still one manner of being, and has its place in the world.* It is true that I can at any moment interrupt my projects But what *is* this power? It is the power to begin something else, for we never remain suspended in nothingness. We are always in a plenum, in being, just as a face, even in repose, even in death, is always doomed to express something (there are people whose faces, in death, bear expressions of surprise, or peace, or discretion), and just as silence is still a modality of the world of sound. I may defy all accepted form, and spurn everything, for there is no case in which I am utterly committed. but in this case I do not withdraw into my freedom, I commit myself elsewhere Instead of thinking about my bereavement, I look at my nails, or have lunch, or engage in politics. Far from its being the case that my freedom is always unattended, it is never without an accomplice, and its power of perpetually tearing itself away finds its fulcrum in my universal commitment in the world. My actual freedom is not on the hither side of my being, but before me, in things We must not say that I continually choose myself, on the excuse that I *might* continually refuse what I am. Not to refuse is not the same thing as to choose. We could identify drift and action only by depriving the implicit of all phenomenal value, and at every instant arraying the world before us in perfect transparency, that is, by destroying the world's 'worldliness'. Consciousness holds itself responsible for everything, and takes

452

everything upon itself, but it has nothing of its own and makes its life in the world. We are led to conceive freedom as a choice continually remade as long as we do not bring in the notion of a generalized or natural time. We have seen that there is no natural time, if we understand thereby a time of things without subjectivity There is, however, at least a generalized time, and this is what the common notion of time envisages. It is the perpetual reiteration of the sequence of past, present and future. It is, as it were, a constant disappointment and failure. This is what is expressed by saying that it is continuous· the present which it brings to us is never a present for good, since it is already over when it appears, and the future has, in it, only the appearance of a goal towards which we make our way, since it quickly comes into the present, whereupon we turn towards a fresh future. This time is the time of our bodily functions, which like it, are cyclic, and it is also that of nature with which we co-exist. It offers us only the adumbration and the abstract form of a commitment, since it continually erodes itself and undoes that which it has just done. As long as we place in opposition, with no mediator, the For Itself and the In Itself, and fail to perceive, between ourselves and the world, this natural foreshadowing of a subjectivity, this prepersonal time which rests upon itself, acts are needed to sustain the upsurge of time, and everything becomes equally a matter of choice, the respiratory reflex no less than the moral decision, conservation no less than creation As far as we are concerned, consciousness attributes this power of universal constitution to itself only if it ignores the event which upholds it and is the occasion of its birth. A consciousness for which the world 'can be taken for granted', which finds it 'already constituted' and present even in consciousness itself, does not *absolutely* choose either its being or its manner of being

What then is freedom? To be born is both to be born of the world and to be born into the world. The world is already constituted. but also never completely constituted; in the first case we are acted upon, in the second we are open to an infinite number of possibilities. But this analysis is still abstract, for we exist in both ways *at once* There is, therefore, never determinism and never absolute choice, I am never a thing and never bare consciousness. In fact, even our own pieces of initiative, even the situations which we have chosen, bear us on, once they have been entered upon by virtue of a state rather than an act. The generality of the 'rôle' and of the situation comes to the aid of decision, and in this exchange between the situation and the person who takes it up, it is impossible to determine precisely the 'share contributed by the situation' and the 'share contributed by freedom'. Let us suppose that a man is tortured to make him talk. If he refuses to give the names and addresses which it is desired to extract from him, this does not arise from a solitary and unsupported decision: the man still feels himself to be with his comrades, and, being still involved in the common struggle, he is as it were incapable of talking Or else, for months or years, he has, in his mind, faced this test and staked his whole life upon it. Or finally, he wants to prove, by coming through it, what he has always thought and said about freedom. These motives do not cancel out freedom, but at least ensure that it does not go unbuttressed in being. What withstands pain is not, in short, a bare consciousness, but the prisoner with his comrades or with those he loves and under whose gaze he lives; or else the awareness of his proudly willed solitude, which again is a certain mode of the *Mit-Sein*. And probably the individual in his prison daily reawakens these phantoms, which give back to him the strength he gave to them But conversely, in so far as he has committed himself to this action, formed a bond with his comrades or adopted this morality, it is because the historical situation, the comrades, the world around him seemed to him to expect that conduct from him. The analysis could be pursued endlessly in this way. We choose our world and the world chooses us. What is certain, in any case, is that we can at no time set aside within ourselves a redoubt to which being does not find its way through, without seeing this freedom, immediately and by the very fact of being a living experience, take on the appearance of being and become a motive and a buttress. Taken concretely, freedom is always a meeting of the inner and the outer—even the prehuman and prehistoric freedom with which we began—and it shrinks without ever disappearing altogether in direct proportion to the lessening of the *tolerance* allowed by the bodily and institutional data of our lives. There is, as Husserl says, on the one hand a 'field of freedom' and on the other a 'conditioned freedom';[1] not that freedom is absolute within the limits of this field and non-existent outside it (like the perceptual field, this one has no traceable boundaries), but because I enjoy immediate and remote possibilities. Our commitments sustain our power and there is no freedom without some power. Our freedom, it is said, is either total or non-existent. This dilemma belongs to objective thought and its stable-companion, analytical reflection If indeed we place ourselves within being, it must necessarily be the case that our actions must have their origin outside us, and if we revert to constituting consciousness, they must originate within But we have learnt precisely to recognize the order of phenomena We are involved in the world and with others in an inextricable tangle The idea of situation rules out absolute freedom at the source of our commitments, and equally, indeed, at their terminus No commitment, not even commitment in the Hegelian State, can

[1] Fink, *Vergegenwärtigung und Bild*, p 285

make me leave behind all differences and free me for anything This universality itself, from the mere fact of its being experienced, would stand out as a particularity against the world's background, for existence both generalizes and particularizes everything at which it aims, and cannot ever be finally complete.

The synthesis of *in itself* and *for itself* which brings Hegelian freedom into being has, however, its truth. In a sense, it is the very definition of existence, since it is effected at every moment before our eyes in the phenomenon of presence, only to be quickly re-enacted, since it does not conjure away our finitude By taking up a present, I draw together and transform my past, altering its significance, freeing and detaching myself from it. But I do so only by committing myself somewhere else Psychoanalytical treatment does not bring about its cure by producing direct awareness of the past, but in the first place by binding the subject to his doctor through new existential relationships. It is not a matter of giving scientific assent to the psychoanalytical interpretation, and discovering a notional significance for the past; it is a matter of reliving this or that as significant, and this the patient succeeds in doing only by seeing his past in the perspective of his co-existence with the doctor. The complex is not dissolved by a non-instrumental freedom, but rather displaced by a new pulsation of time with its own supports and motives The same applies in all cases of coming to awareness: they are real only if they are sustained by a new commitment. Now this commitment too is entered into in the sphere of the implicit, and is therefore valid only for a certain temporal cycle. The choice which we make of our life is always based on a certain givenness My freedom can draw life away from its spontaneous course, but only by a series of unobtrusive deflections which necessitate first of all following its course—not by any absolute creation. All explanations of my conduct in terms of my past, my temperament and my environment are therefore true, provided that they be regarded not as separable contributions, but as moments of my total being, the significance of which I am entitled to make explicit in various ways, without its ever being possible to say whether I confer their meaning upon them or receive it from them I am a psychological and historical structure, and have received, with existence, a manner of existing, a style. All my actions and thoughts stand in a relationship to this structure, and even a philosopher's thought is merely a way of making explicit his hold on the world, and what he is The fact remains that I am free, not in spite of, or on the hither side of, these motivations, but by means of them. For this significant life, this certain significance of nature and history which I am, does not limit my access to the world, but on the contrary is my means of entering into communication with it It is by being

455

unrestrictedly and unreservedly what I am at present that I have a chance of moving forward, it is by living my time that I am able to understand other times, by plunging into the present and the world, by taking on deliberately what I am fortuitously, by willing what I will and doing what I do, that I can go further I can miss being free only if I try to bypass my natural and social situation by refusing to take it up, in the first place, instead of assuming it in order to join up with the natural and human world Nothing determines me from outside, not because nothing acts upon me, but, on the contrary, because I am from the start outside myself and open to the world. We are *true* through and through, and have with us, by the mere fact of belonging to the world, and not merely being in the world in the way that things are, all that we need to transcend ourselves. We need have no fear that our choices or actions restrict our liberty, since choice and action alone cut us loose from our anchorage. Just as reflection borrows its wish for absolute sufficiency from the perception which causes a thing to appear, and as in this way idealism tacitly uses that 'primary opinion' which it would like to destroy as opinion, so freedom flounders in the contradictions of commitment, and fails to realize that, without the roots which it thrusts into the world, it would not be freedom at all Shall I make this promise? Shall I risk my life for so little? Shall I give up my liberty in order to save liberty? There is no theoretical reply to these questions. But there are these *things* which stand, irrefutable, there is before you this person whom you love, there are these men whose existence around you is that of slaves, and *your* freedom cannot be willed without leaving behind its singular relevance, and without willing freedom *for all*. Whether it is a question of things or of historical situations, philosophy has no other function than to teach us to see them clearly once more, and it is true to say that it comes into being by destroying itself as separate philosophy. But what is here required is silence, for only the hero lives out his relation to men and the world. 'Your son is caught in the fire; you are the one who will save him. . . . If there is an obstacle, you would be ready to give your shoulder provided only that you can charge down that obstacle Your abode is your act itself. Your act is you. . . . You give yourself in exchange . Your significance shows itself, effulgent. It is your duty, your hatred, your love, your steadfastness, your ingenuity . . . Man is but a network of relationships, and these alone matter to him '[1]

[1] A de Saint-Exupéry, *Pilote de Guerre*, pp 171, 174, 176.

BIBLIOGRAPHY

ACKERMANN, *Farbschwelle und Feldstruktur*, Psychologische Forschung, 1924

ALAIN, *Quatre-vingt-un chapitres sur l'esprit et les passions*, Paris, Bloch, 1917. Reprinted under the title *Eléments de Philosophie*, Paris, Gallimard, 1941.

——*Système des Beaux-Arts*, new (3rd) edition, Paris, Gallimard, 1926

BECKER, *Beitrage zur phänomenologischen Begrundung der Geometrie und ihrer physikalischen Anwendungen*, Jahrbuch fur Philosophie und phanomenologische Forschung, VI, Halle, Niemeyer

BERGSON, *Matiere et Memoire*, Paris, Alcan, 1896

——*L'Energie spirituelle*, Paris, Alcan, 1919.

BERNARD, *La Méthode de Cézanne*, Mercure de France, 1920.

BINSWANGER, *Traum und Existenz*, Neue Schweizer Rundschau, 1930.

——*Uber Ideenflucht*, Schweizer Archiv f. Neurologie u. Psychiatrie, 1931 and 1932.

——*Das Raumproblem in der Psychopathologie*, Ztschr f. d ges. Neurologie und Psychiatrie, 1933.

——*Über Psychotherapie*, Nervenartzt, 1935

VAN BOGAERT, *Sur la Pathologie de l'Image de Soi* (études anatomo-cliniques). Annales medico-psychologiques, Nov and Dec. 1934.

BRUNSCHVICG, *L'Expérience humaine et la causalité physique*, Paris, Alcan, 1922.

——*Le Progrès de la conscience dans la philosophie occidentale*, Paris, Alcan, 1927.

BUYTENDIJK and PLESSNER, *Die Deutung des mimischen Ausdrucks*, Philosophischer Anzeiger, 1925.

CASSIRER, *Philosophie der symbolischen Formen*, III, *Phanomenologie der Erkenntnis*, Berlin, Bruno Cassirer, 1929

CHEVALIER, *L'Habitude*, Paris, Boivin, 1929.

CONRAD-MARTIUS, *Zur Ontologie und Erscheinungslehre der realen Aussenwelt*, Jahrbuch für Philosophie und Phanomenologische Forschung, III.

——*Realontologie*, ibid , VI.

CORBIN, translator of Heidegger, *Qu'est-ce que la métaphysique?* Paris, Gallimard, 1938.

DÉJEAN, *Étude psychologique de la 'distance' dans la vision*, Paris, Presses Universitaires de France, 1926.

DÉJEAN, *Les Conditions objectives de la perception visuelle*, Paris, Presses Universitaires de France

DUNCKER, *Uber induzierte Bewegung*, Psychologische Forschung, 1929

EBBINGHAUS, *Abriss der Psychologie*, 9 Aufl Berlin, Leipzig, 1932

FINK (E), *Vergegenwärtigung und Bild, Beiträge zur Phanomenologie der Unwirklichkeit*, Jahrb f Philo u phan. Forschung, XI

——*Die phanomenologische Philosophie Husserls in der gegenwärtigen Kritik*, Kantstudien, 1933

——*Das Problem der Phanomenologie Edmund Husserls*. Revue internationale de Philosophie, No 2, January 1939

FISCHEL, *Transformationserscheinungen bei Gewichtshebung*, Ztschr f Psychologie, 1926

FISCHER (F), *Zeitstruktur und Schizophrenie*, Ztschr. f. d ges Neurologie und Psychiatrie, 1929

——*Raum-Zeitstruktur und Denkstorung in der Schizophrenie*, ibid , 1930

——*Zur Klinik und Psychologie des Raumerlebens*, Schweizer Archiv fur Neurologie und Psychiatrie, 1932–33.

FREUD, *Introductory Lectures on Psycho-Analysis*, London, Allen and Unwin, 1922.

——*Cinq Psychanalyses*, Paris, Denoel et Steele, 1935

GASQUET, *Cézanne*, Paris, Bernheim Jeune, 1926

GELB and GOLDSTEIN, *Psychologische Analysen hirnpathologischer Falle*, Leipzig, Barth, 1920

——*Über Farbennamenamnesie*, Psychologische Forschung, 1925

——(editors): Benary, *Studien zur Untersuchung der Intelligenz bei einem Fall von Seelenblindheit*, Psychologische Forschung, 1922

——(editors)· Hochheimer, *Analyse eines Seelenblinden von der Sprache aus*, ibid., 1932

——(editors). Steinfeld, *Ein Beitrag zur Analyse der Sexualfunktion*, Zeitschr f. d ges. Neurologie u. Psychiatrie, 1927.

GELB, *Die psychologische Bedeutung pathologischer Storungen der Raumwahrnehmung* Bericht uber den IX. Kongress fur experimentelle˙ Psychologie in Munchen, Jena, Fischer, 1926

——*Die Farbenkonstanz der Sehdinge*, in *Handbuch der normalen und pathologischen Physiologie*, Bethe, XII/1, Berlin, Springer, 1927 and ff

GOLDSTEIN, *Uber die Abhängigkeit der Bewegungen von optischen Vorgangen*, Monatschrift für Psychiatrie und Neurologie, Festschrift Liepmann, 1923

——*Zeigen und Greifen*, Nervenartzt, 1931

——*L'Analyse de l'aphasie et l'essence du langage*, Journal de Psychologie, 1933.

GOLDSTEIN and ROSENTHAL, *Zur Problem der Wirkung der Farben auf den Organismus*, Schweizer Archiv fur Neurologie und Psychiatrie, 1930

GOTTSCHALDT, *Uber den Einfluss der Erfahrung auf die Wahrnehmung von Figuren*, Psychologische Forschung, 1926 and 1929.

GRUNBAUM, *Aphasie und Motorik*, Ztschr f d ges Neurologie und Psychiatrie, 1930

GUILLAUME (P), *L'Objectivité en Psychologie*, Journal de Psychologie, 1932

GUILLAUME, *Psychologie*, Paris, Presses Universitaires de France, new edition, 1943

GURWITSCH (A), Review of *Nachwort zu meinen Ideen* of Husserl, Deutsche Litteraturzeitung, 28th February, 1932

——*Quelques aspects et quelques développements de la psychologie de la Forme*, Journal de Psychologie, 1936.

HEAD, *On disturbances of sensation with especial reference to the pain of visceral disease*, Brain, 1893.

——*Sensory disturbances from cerebral lesion*, Brain, 1911–12

HEIDEGGER, *Sein und Zeit*, Jahrb f Phil u phanomen Forschung, VIII

——*Kant und das Problem der Metaphysik*, Frankfurt a M , Verlag G Schulte Bulmke, 1934.

VON HORNBOSTEL, *Das räumliche Hören*, *Hdbch der normalen und pathologischen Physiologie*, Bethe, XI, Berlin, 1926

HUSSERL, *Logische Untersuchungen*, I, II/1 and II/2, 4th ed Halle, Niemeyer, 1928

——*Ideen zu einer reinen Phanomenologie und phanomenologischen Philosophie*, I, Jahrb f. Phil u Phanomenolog. Forschung, I, 1913.

——*Vorlesungen zur Phanomenologie des inneren Zeitbewusstseins*, ibid., IX, 1928.

——*Nachwort zu meinen 'Ideen'*, ibid , XI, 1930

——*Méditations cartésiennes*, Paris, Colin, 1931

——*Die Krisis der europäischen Wissenschaften und die transzendentale Phanomenologie*, I, Belgrade, Philosophia, 1936.

——*Erfahrung und Urteil, Untersuchungen zur Genealogie der Logik*, L Landgrebe, Prag Academia Verlagsbuchhandlung, 1939

——*Die Frage nach der Ursprung der Geometrie als Intentional-historisches Problem*, Revue Internationale de Philosophie, January 1939.

——*Ideen zu einer reinen Phanomenologie und phanomenologischen Philosophie*, II (unpublished).

——*Umsturz der kopernikanischen Lehre. die Erde als Ur-Arche bewegt sich nicht* (unpublished)

——*Die Krisis der europäischen Wissenschaften und die transzendentale Phanomenologie*, II and III (unpublished)

(The last three works were consulted with the kind permission of Mgr Noel and the Institut Supérieur de Philosophie of Louvain)

JANET, *De l'Angoisse à l'Extase*, II, Paris, Alcan, 1928.

JASPERS, *Zur Analyse der Trugwahrnehmungen*, Ztschr f. d gesamt Neurologie und Psychiatrie, 1911

KANT, *Critique du Jugement*, trans. Gibelin, Paris, Vrin, 1928

KATZ, *Der Aufbau der Tastwelt*, Ztschr f Psychologie, Ergbd 11, Leipzig, 1925

——*Der Aufbau der Farbwelt*, Ztschr f. Psychologie, Ergbd 7, 2nd ed , 1930

KOEHLER, *Uber unbemerkte Empfindungen und Urteilstäuschungen*, Ztschr. f. Psychologie, 1913

——*Die physischen Gestalten im Ruhe und in stationären Zustand*, Erlangen, Brunswick, 1920

KOEHLER, *Gestalt Psychology*, London, G Bell, 1930.

KOFFKA, *The Growth of the Mind*, London, Kegan Paul, Trench, Trubner & Co., New York, Harcourt, Brace & Co., 1925.

——*Mental Development*, in Murchison, *Psychologies of 1925*, Worcester, Massachusetts, Clark University Press, 1928.

——*Some Problems of Space Perception*, in Murchison, *Psychologies of 1930*, ibid., 1930.

——*Perception, an introduction to the Gestalt theory*, Psychological Bulletin, 1922.

——*Psychologie*, in *Lehrbuch der Philosophie*, edited by M Dessoir, Part II, *Die Philosophie in ihren Einzelgebieten*, Berlin, Ullstein, 1925.

——*Principles of Gestalt Psychology*, London, Kegan Paul, Trench, Trubner & Co.; New York, Harcourt Brace & Co , 1935.

KONRAD, *Das Korperschema, eine kritische Studie und der Versuch einer Revision*, Ztschr f d. ges Neurologie und Psychiatrie, 1933.

LACHIÈZE-REY, *L'Idéalisme kantien*, Paris, Alcan, 1932.

——*Réflexions sur l'activité spirituelle constituante*, Recherches Philosophiques, 1933–34.

——*Le Moi, le Monde et Dieu*, Paris, Boivin, 1938.

——*Utilisation possible du schématisme kantien pour une théorie de la perception*, Marseilles, 1938

LAFORGUE, *L'Echec de Baudelaire*, Denoel et Steele, 1931.

LAGNEAU, *Célèbres Leçons*, Nîmes, 1926

LEWIN, *Vorbemerkungen uber die psychische Krafte und Energien und uber die Struktur der Seele*, Psychologische Forschung, 1926

LHERMITTE, LÉVY and KYRIAKO, *Les Perturbations de la Pensée spatiale chez les apraxiques, à propos de deux cas cliniques d'apraxie*, Revue Neurologique, 1925.

LHERMITTE, DE MASSARY and KYRIAKO, *Le Rôle de la pensée spatiale dans l'apraxie*, Revue neurologique, 1928.

LHERMITTE and TRELLES, *Sur l'apraxie pure constructive, les troubles de la pensée spatiale et de la somatognosie dans l'apraxie*, Encéphale, 1933.

LHERMITTE, *L'Image de notre corps*, Nouvelle Revue critique, 1939

LIEPMANN, *Über Storungen des Handelns bei Gehirnkranken*, Berlin, 1905.

LINKE, *Phänomenologie und Experiment in der Frage der Bewegungsauffassung*, Jahrbuch fur Philosophie und phanomenologische Forschung., II.

MARCEL, *Être et Avoir*, Paris, Aubier, 1925.

MAYER-GROSS and STEIN, *Uber einige Abanderungen der Sinnestatigkeit im Meskalinrausch*, Ztschr. f d ges Neurologie und Psychiatrie, 1926

MENNINGER-LERCHENTHAL, *Das Truggebilde der eigenen Gestalt*, Berlin, Karger, 1934

MERLEAU-PONTY, *La Structure du Comportement*, Paris, Presses Universitaires de France, 1942.

MINKOWSKI, *Les Notions de distance vecue et d'ampleur de la vie et leur application en psychopathologie*, Journal de Psychologie, 1930

——*Le Problème des hallucinations et le problème de l'espace*, Évolution psychiatrique, 1932.

BIBLIOGRAPHY

MINKOWSKI, *Le Temps vécu*, Paris, d'Artrey, 1933

NOVOTNY, *Das Problem des Menschen Cézanne im Verhältnis zu seiner Kunst*, Zeitschr f. Aesthetik und allgemeine Kunstwissenschaft, No. 26, 1932

PALIARD, *L'Illusion de Sinnsteden et le problème de l'implication perceptive*, Revue philosophique, 1930

PARAIN, *Recherches sur la nature et les fonctions du langage*, Paris, Gallimard, 1942

PETERS, *Zur Entwicklung der Farbenwahrnehmung*, Fortschritte der Psychologie, 1915.

PIAGET, *La Représentation du monde chez l'enfant*, Paris, Alcan, 1926
——*La Causalité physique chez l'enfant*, Paris, Alcan, 1927

PICK, *Störungen der Orientierung am eigenen Körper*, Psychologische Forschung, 1922

POLITZER, *Critique des fondements de la psychologie*, Paris, Rieder, 1929

PRADINES, *Philosophie de la sensation*, I, Les Belles-Lettres, 1928.

QUERCY, *Études sur l'hallucination*, II, *la Clinique*, Paris, Alcan, 1930

RUBIN, *Die Nichtexistenz der Aufmerkamsamkeit*, Psychologische Forschung, 1925.

SARTRE, *L'Imagination*, Paris, Alcan, 1936
——*Esquisse d'une théorie de l'émotion*, Paris, Hermann, 1939.
——*L'Imaginaire*, Paris, Gallimard, 1940.
——*L'Être et le Néant*, Paris, Gallimard, 1943.

SCHAPP, *Beitrage zur Phänomenologie der Wahrnehmung*, Inaugural Dissertation, Göttingen, Kaestner, 1910, and Erlangen, 1925

SCHELER, *Die Wissenformen und die Gesellschaft*, Leipzig, der Neue Geist 1926
——*Der Formalismus in der Ethik und die materiale Werthethik*, Jahrbuch f Phil und phan. Forschung, I–II, Halle, Niemeyer, 1927
——*Die Idole der Selbsterkenntnis*, in *Vom Umsturz der Werte*, II, Leipzig, Der Neue Geist, 1919.
——*Idealismus-Realismus*, Philosophischer Anzeiger, 1927.
——*Nature et formes de la sympathie*, Paris, Payot, 1928

SCHILDER, *Das Körperschema*, Berlin, Springer, 1923.

SCHRÖDER, *Das Halluzinieren*, Zeitschr. f. d. ges. Neurologie u Psychiatrie, 1926

VON SENDEN, *Raum- und Gestaltauffassung bei operierten Blindgeborenen, vor und nach der Operation*, Leipzig, Barth, 1932

SITTIG, *Über Apraxie, eine klinische Studie*, Berlin, Karger, 1931

SPECHT, *Zur Phänomenologie und Morphologie der pathologischen Wahrnehmungstauschungen*, Ztschr. f. Pathopsychologie, 1912–13.

STEIN (EDITH), *Beitrage zur philosophischen Begrundung der Psychologie und der Geisteswissenschaften*, I, *Psychische Kausalität*, Jahrbuch f. Phil u phan Forschung, V.

STEIN (J.), *Über die Veränderung der Sinnesleistungen und die Entstehung von Trugwahrnehmungen*, in *Pathologie der Wahrnehmung, Handbuch der Geisteskrankheiten*, edited by O Bumke, Bd I, Allgemeiner Teil I, Berlin, Springer, 1928.

STEKEL, *La Femme frigide*, Paris, Gallimard, 1937.

461

BIBLIOGRAPHY

STRATTON, *Some preliminary experiments on vision without inversion of the retinal image*, Psychological Review, 1896

——*Vision without inversion of the retinal image*, ibid , 1897

——*The spatial harmony of touch and sight*, Mind, 1899

STRAUS (E), *Vom Sinn der Sinne*, Berlin, Springer, 1935.

WERNER, *Grundfragen der Intensistatspsychologie*, Ztschr f Psychologie, Ergzbd, 10, 1922.

——*Uber die Ausprägung von Tongestalten*, Ztschr. für Psychologie, 1926.

——*Untersuchungen uber Empfindung und Empfinden*, I and II. *Die Rolle der Sprachempfindung im Prozess der Gestaltung ausdrucksmässig erlebter Worter*, ibid , 1930

WERNER and ZIETZ, *Die dynamische Struktur der Bewegung*, ibid , 1927.

WERTHEIMER, *Experimentelle Studien uber das Sehen von Bewegung*, Ztschr. f Ps 1912

——*Uber das Denken der Naturvolker* and *Die Schlussprozesse im produktiven Denken*, in *Drei Abhandlungen zur Gestalttheorie*, Erlangen, 1925.

VAN WOERKOM, *Sur la notion de l'espace (le sens géometrique)*, Revue neurologique, 1910

WOLFF (W.), *Selbstbeurteilung und Fremdbeurteilung in wissentlichen und unwissentlichen Versuch*, Psychologische Forschung, 1932.

YOUNG (P. T.), *Auditory localization with acoustical transposition of the ears*, Journal of Experimental Psychology, 1928.

ZUCKER, *Experimentelles uber Sinnestäuschungen*, Archiv f. Psychiatrie und Nervenkrankheiten, 1928.

INDEX

CPSIA information can be obtained
at www.ICGtesting.com
Printed in the USA
BVHW092024060222
628185BV00006B/86

9 781376 199789